The New Local Government Series
No. 22

—————

BRITISH DOGMATISM AND
FRENCH PRAGMATISM

The New Local Government Series
Series Editor: Professor Peter G. Richards

BRITISH DOGMATISM AND FRENCH PRAGMATISM

Central–Local Policymaking in the Welfare State

DOUGLAS E. ASHFORD
Cornell University

London
GEORGE ALLEN & UNWIN
Boston   Sydney

George Allen & Unwin (Publishers) Ltd,
40 Museum Street, London WC1A 1LU, UK

George Allen & Unwin (Publishers) Ltd,
Park Lane, Hemel Hempstead, Herts HP2 4TE, UK

Allen & Unwin Inc.,
9 Winchester Terrace, Winchester, Mass 01890, USA

George Allen & Unwin Australia Pty Ltd,
8 Napier Street, North Sydney, NSW 2060, Australia

First published in 1982

British Library Cataloguing in Publication Data

Ashford, Douglas E.
  British dogmatism and French pragmatism.
- (The New local government series; no. 22)
1. Great Britain - Politics and government
I. Title   II. Series
354.4107′2   JF432.G/
ISBN 0-04-352096-0

Library of Congress Cataloging in Publication Data

Ashford, Douglas Elliott.
  British dogmatism and French pragmatism.
(The New local government series; no. 22)
Bibliography: p.
1. Decentralization in government—France.
2. Decentralization in government—Great Britain.
3. Local government—France. 4. Local government—Great Britain.
I. Title.   II. Series: New local government series; no. 22.
JS113.A82   350.007′3   81-10904
ISBN 0-04-352096-0   AACR2

Set in 10 on 10 point Times by Typesetters (Birmingham) Limited
and printed and bound in Great Britain
by William Clowes (Beccles) Limited, Beccles and London

CONTENTS

is subordinated to the two-party structure and the latter
compensates for national party weaknesses.

state and its relation to local government. The ease of dismissing intergovernmental problems in Britain: Kilbrandon and devolution.

PREFACE

There are obvious pitfalls in writing a comparative study that questions the conventional wisdom concerning local politics and policymaking in two countries. Despite the tradition of local autonomy, the immense size and scale of the British local government system may have contributed to its isolation from national policymaking. Despite the centralizing aspirations of French national government, the dispersion of political power in the French communes and the complexity of the administrative system may have given communes more effective influence over national decisions. In the British case, self-reliance may be self-defeating; and in the French case, vulnerability may stimulate more effective use of local political resources. In both cases, I argue that the influence of the local government systems cannot be assessed apart from the national political and administrative structures in which they are imbedded.

These differences cannot be explained without taking into account the relative ease with which Britain established parliamentary rule, and later made the transition to mass democracy. British leaders never needed local allies in the way French leaders did, and one sometimes has the impression that were local government simply to vanish, Westminster and Whitehall would be unimpaired. Democratic political institutions have a more precarious history in France, and the communes are important reservoirs of political strength for the national political system. Local politicians learn how to qualify the power of strong government and administration, and this experience may leave them better equipped to deal with the complexities of the welfare state than does British local government.

Some readers may feel that more attention should have been paid to the socioeconomic setting of the two countries. My hesitation is twofold. First, both the neo-Marxist and neo-liberal writings present extremely abstract proposals about the disaggregation of power in political systems. Local politics and local government are in the curious situation of impeding the free operation of the liberal's marketplace while also reminding Marxists that political culture and traditions are deeply rooted in every polity. Second, the two dominant socioeconomic schools of thought leave very little room for the institutional and constitutional variations found within every political system. As a result, they are both highly apolitical in concept, if not in application. Believing that political structures are separable, and to some extent have independent effects on our lives, my inclination has always been to examine internal political variations before making more sweeping systematic generalizations.

The book is basically an inquiry into how national political and administrative constraints affect the formulation and implementation of local government reform. Were I interested only in the local level, the logic of comparison would suggest that one should select countries with very similar political systems. But my own interest in comparative studies has concentrated more on how systematic constraints operate across political systems. What seemed to be missing in the many studies available was how political constraints operate in the complex policy process of the welfare state. The emphasis, then, is on how national politics and administration structure policymaking in the two countries. My strong suspicion is that were this kind of structural analysis extended to other major problems in the two countries, political constraints would be surprisingly similar across issues.

Comparing policies with the aim of understanding politics involves a rather different approach than the normal procedure used to evaluate a single policy of a particular country. The inquiry begins with a sketch of the continuity and coherence of political institutions over time. The historical materials, while they may be familiar to many experts on either country, are designed to uncover those structural features of central–local relationships in both countries that still influence local politics and policy. A second task is to provide the reader with a basic knowledge of how both national and local institutions interact in the policy process. There has been an enormous amount of specialized research on local government in both countries, much of it ignored by political science, and part of my task has been to provide readers with a variety of interests with this information. I have tried to confine the literature review and technical details to end-of-chapter notes, though I believe they often relate to the full story of the transformation of local government systems in unforeseen ways. If the details also help reveal how the study of public administration and public law might be related to political science, then I shall have achieved part of my aim. In any event, there has not been a general study of two local systems for some years, and an account of the accumulated literature seemed to me to be badly needed, though others might have arranged it differently.

The third issue involved in the study will become apparent on reading the latter portions of the book. Since the last world war all the democratic countries have placed important new burdens on local government, sometimes without realizing it. Local participation and local services somehow did not fit very well with the early versions of the welfare state, but this did not keep government from growing and public benefits from increasing. Over the past decade most democratic countries have begun to see the conflicts and weaknesses of a generation of rapid growth. Local government and local politics, long excluded from 'serious' political science, have now returned to the professional agenda. I believe they never left the agenda of government.

The emergence of the welfare state is in itself an interesting subject, but even more provoking is why the democracies have worked so hard over the past decade to integrate national and local government. The image of local politics in the liberal state, so persuasively advanced by Tocqueville, seems to have disappeared, but we do not know what will take its place. Representative democracy needs local participation and the welfare state requires local decisions. How these two needs will be reconciled is one of the most pressing issues confronting democratic political systems.

In a study that has taken shape over a number of years, it is virtually impossible to do justice to the many persons who intentionally and unintentionally helped toward its completion. Over the past four years I have interviewed numerous British and French officials who will have to remain anonymous. I concentrated on those areas which I think have been less explored in the study of central–local relationships, particularly the budgetary, planning and financial links between levels of government. In particular, I want to thank those in the Ministry of the Interior, the Ministry of Finance (now Budget), the Ministry of Infrastructure (now Environment) in France, and those in the Department of the Environment and the Treasury who have given time, advice and information. Most of these interviews are not cited. Where their confirmation of important points or their contribution is essential to my argument, the interviews are noted without names. Should I sometimes seem hard on the administrative officials of the two countries, it is not because they lack in goodwill or cooperativeness. We are perhaps inclined to despair most of those persons on whom we depend the most.

Special mention should be made of the persons serving on the Guichard and Layfield Commissions. Because their work marks an historic turning point in central–local relations and in intergovernmental relations more generally, I tracked most of the members down quite relentlessly. All of the ministries noted above gave permission for me to use their libraries which were invaluable. I also made ample use of the fine collection of the Institute of Local Government Studies, University of Birmingham, and the local government collections at the University of Rennes and the University of Bordeaux. In each place I can recall unknown librarians who helped me place my fingers on key documents. I am also indebted to the library of the Ecole Nationale d'Administration and the Fondation Nationale des Sciences Politiques. I must also thank my friend from Moroccan days, Louis Fougère, who has always been helpful and who so kindly introduced me to one of the most remarkable living libraries in the world, the Conseil d'Etat, where I met many of his friends.

There have been numerous scholars whose ideas and criticism have helped enormously. For many years I have had a friendly debate with Jim Sharpe who first steered me like so many others toward British local government. In Britain, I had a warm reception from Jeff Stanyer, Howard Machin, Rod Rhodes, Peter Self, George Jones, Ken Newton, John Dearlove, Ken Young and many others. In France, I learned from Jean-Claude Thoenig, Pierre Grémion, Catherine Grémion, Michel Crozier, Yves Mény, Georges Dupuis and Jean-François Médard, to name only a few. They have all helped me test my ideas. If the book does not accurately reflect their thoughts, it is not for lack of their persuasion but my own stubbornness. Two local finance experts have generously commented on the relevant chapters, Yves Fréville and N. P. Hepworth. My Cornell colleague, Steve Kaplan, applied his lucid knowledge of French history to the historical chapter.

Special recognition is due to those who have so unreservedly given time and thought to the book. Jack Hayward read the entire first draft and added the balance at which he excels. His thoughts on institutional inertia have influenced me a great deal. Bruce Wood also read the entire manuscript. His sensitive concern for detail and for British local government generally has, I hope, been captured in this work. Vincent Wright was another stimulating critic of the entire manuscript. His ideas about French administration will hopefully show through this work without too much distortion, and his comments on nineteenth century France are priceless.

I have read a number of theses and much unpublished research that has been invaluable. Happily, the theses of Howard Machin and Catherine Grémion were on their way to press when I began the study, but I must apologize for citing thesis pages instead of the published work which was not then available. In both cases, the theses contain more detail than the final books. I have found Michèle Sellier's thesis extremely useful, and was given unpublished regional studies by Michèle Breuillard. Vincent Wright and Jacques Lagroye let me read the manuscript for their book on local government in France and Britain that they were editing, as did Vincent Wright with his manuscript on French government. I also found the manuscript of Richard Bately and John Edwards on the British urban program helpful and happily coinciding with my thinking, likewise the manuscript on British urban policies of David McKay and Andrew Cox. One can only observe that sharing scholarship has helped to make this book what it is.

I have been extremely fortunate in having a stimulating and cooperative group of colleagues at Cornell. In various ways, Peter Katzenstein, T. J. Pempel, Sid Tarrow, Milt Esman and Woodie Kelley have encouraged me to think more carefully. The comparative policy seminar with Katzenstein and Pempel was a fertile source of ideas and reinforced my belief in what I have always thought universities were for – the collegial testing of new thinking. Ted Lowi's energetic and friendly prodding has always been welcome. Having an agreeable group of Americanists at Cornell has been important in trying to extend the boundaries of knowledge beyond geographical limits. Outside Cornell, Ezra Suleiman and Peter Gourevitch were generous with encouragement and ideas.

Direct support has been forthcoming from many quarters. I have been able to pursue many of my ideas thanks to my work with the Western Societies Program of Cornell's Center for International Studies. I am persuaded more than ever that having modest free-floating resources is essential to having free-floating minds. The Office of Education supported the comparative policy seminar which helped me explore many of the ideas in this study. The Netherlands Institute for Advanced Study provided a Fellowship which enabled me to enjoy a quiet year of writing and reading. Everyone there helped in some way, but Ann Simpson labored especially hard in typing the first draft. My thanks are also due to the University of Manchester where I was Simon Visiting Professor in 1979–80. With their help I was able to add material on the more recent changes – the Bonnet law in France and the Heseltine bill in Britain – which quite happily confirms all my prejudices about the two political systems.

The most treasured help comes from those who are unaware of the gift. In their own ways, my wife, Karen, and youngest son, Matthew, have given this throughout my work on this book.

DOUGLAS E. ASHFORD

Chapter 1

STRATEGIES OF CHANGE: LOCAL REORGANIZATION IN THE WELFARE STATE

A further deep-seated tradition of the British is their spirit of pragmatism and compromise. They look to practice rather than theory, and if something seems to work well enough they tend not to question it. – Royal Commission on the Constitution, 1973

Should the study of urban phenomenon respond to pragmatic exigencies and immediate demands? Planners, programmers, users crave returns. What for? In order to make people happy. In order to arrange their happiness. A curious conception of happiness. – Henri Lefebvre, *La Révolution Urbaine*

For two centuries the reorganization of local government has been one of the most persistent and intractable problems facing modern democracies. Perhaps the most striking aspect of this central–local struggle is the difficulty of getting local government on the political agenda. Federal systems provide more apparent explanations of the difficulty of effecting change because local government systems are generally enshrined in constitutional agreements. Both the United States and the Federal Republic of Germany have struggled with the issue of how to align lower-level government with national objectives and needs.[1] It might appear that finding solutions and making adjustments would be much easier in unitary political systems. But with respect to restructuring local government, unitary systems vary as widely as federal systems. Britain and France – both unitary – are perhaps the two most illuminating examples of the turmoil and conflict generated by undertaking such major structural change.

Whether we are considering the extension of the franchise, the introduction of social welfare, or local government reorganization, structural change has never been easy. These examples all raise fundamental questions concerning individual and collective obligations, the nature of representative government and their relationship to the governmental organization. The complexity and delicacy of the task requires that change should be achieved slowly. Public opinion, local leadership and political parties are not oriented toward refashioning the structure of government. Oddly enough, as government has tried to do more, and as its organization grows, we seem less able to rely on such normal democratic processes as electoral choice and party competition. Structural change is not a 'vote-getter' and few citizens enjoy probing the mysteries of constitutional law or reviewing governmental organization charts. But before we place the blame for inaction too heavily on the citizenry, it should also be noted that few statesmen have found local government particularly exciting. Severe functional or territorial changes dislocate the party organizations and upset channels of patronage. Urging structural change is most often the argument of oppositions, more often than not because they see it as a way of increasing their power. Local government may no longer be the bastion of democratic government that it was thought to be in the nineteenth century, but the growth of the public sector has assured its place in contemporary political systems.

Historically, local reorganization has most often been the *consequence* of political and administrative change rather than the cutting edge of change. This may also explain why local politics and government have not been more popular subjects in the social sciences. Discussing Victorian England, Hennock says 'The problems of the towns in one generation became increasingly the problems of the nation in the next.'[2] Local government systems, and quite possibly other complex structures of modern government, change when the accumulation of grievances, injustices and sheer inefficiencies become unbearable. Some of these inadequacies may stem from local government itself, but others are the reverberations of change at higher levels of government and of secular transformations of society itself. For this reason local government is an indication of the way unconnected and diffuse social and political events eventually coalesce to alter policymaking.

Unquestionably the first-line local defense against change has always been inertia. Putting aside the more polemical arguments about local autonomy, the major historical consistency is the extreme sensitivity of central governments to the possible disruption of lower levels of decisionmaking. Paradoxically, as the nineteenth century liberal state was transformed into the welfare state,[3] the effectiveness of inertia as a defense against central government encroachment has increased rather than declined. Growth of the public sector and public benefits has in fact increased the dependence of contemporary national government on the adjustment and implementation of public policies at lower levels of government. The adoption of more ambitious national objectives has thus increased central government interest in local government, because cooperation and monitoring is essential at lower levels. Simultaneously, new local burdens provided leverage on national government. If the emergence of the welfare state has done nothing else to restructure political systems, it has made localities more important in the policy process.

In nineteenth century Britain the autonomy of local government was a genuine issue. The central government's activities could be fairly readily divided between 'national' and 'local'. An important dogma that took root in British Victorian politics was that some services of the state are 'universal and onerous', and therefore should be provided by the national government, while others are 'local and individual', and therefore should be provided by the locality.[4] Before the end of the nineteenth century it was clear that this seemingly handy distinction was of little use except to justify loading more services and more expenditures on to local government. The Local Government Act of 1888, the rather tardy beginning of relatively democratic local government in Britain, was in many ways more concerned with projecting the dogma of town versus country into the twentieth century than with strengthening local democracy. In fact it became increasingly clear during the nineteenth century that poor relief, assigned to the parishes in 1601 and radically reorganized in 1834, was really a national burden. Furthermore, after the Education Act of 1870, local educational expenditure mounted rapidly from a small percentage of local costs to nearly half the local budgets by 1900. In short, poverty and education were no longer 'local' but, rather, *national* problems. Responsibility for these national problems made British local government more essential to national government, though, as we shall see, in return for assuming heavy responsibilities, the localities extracted remarkably few political or financial concessions from the center.

For many reasons British preoccupation with drawing firm lines between national and local concerns never had an equivalent impact in France. The 'one and indivisible Republic' had a formidable philosophical rationale[5] and a more complex organization to integrate local interests with the center. In fact it is misleading even to speak of 'local government' in France, where localities are encompassed by the *collectivités locales* and are really part of the state. Formally the local collectivities include the communes and the departments, but regional authorities and many intergovernmental agencies also link national government to local needs and influence. The local structure is enmeshed in a system of administrative law that encompasses nearly every sector of French public life and has usually figured in the many French constitutions. Unlike the old British counties and boroughs, the French communes and departments never took on enormous responsibilities, though their financial significance in the total systems of government is comparable. Even so, the local government system was a central issue in the Revolutionary debates and a major concern of Napoleon. The relaxation of some central controls in the Restoration France of 1830 was a major political issue, and the gradual intermingling of central and local influence during the Second Empire was the prelude to the establishment of the Third Republic.

Historical and constitutional circumstances made the communes 'small republics'. The communes and even the departmental councils have a national legitimacy which the British local councils never had. As we shall see in Chapters 4 and 5, this claim is still used with remarkable effectiveness to give mayors access to national policy-making as well as to defend their communes against Paris. The curious result is that French local politicians never relied as much as British local politicians on inertia or territorial jurisdiction in order to influence national policy. Political confrontation has always been part of the rhetoric of French local government.

While administrative subordination is more explicit and (at least in formal terms) more arbitrary for French communes than for British councils, defining national and local interests in major decisions recognizes mutual dependence. As we shall see, this left the French local government system better equipped to deal with the problems of the welfare state. French mayors are not busily guarding jurisdictions, but attacking and infiltrating national government. Because national administration reaches down to the departmental level, this is easier to do in France than in Britain. In short one of the paradoxes of the French unified administrative system is that it more clearly defines ways to influence national policy than the divided administrative system in Britain. It is normal for a French mayor to engage in policy-making at many levels of government. Their ability to do this is enhanced by rivalries within the administration and by their ability to hold several elected offices at once, the *cumul des mandats*.

Both these avenues of influence are closed to British councils. Whitehall is remote and cloaked in official secrecy. Several means of consultation are used, but only at the discretion of the center and usually in confidence. Though a few British council leaders have become important regional political bosses, the national party and the discipline of Parliament diminishes their status and their access to the center. While one may dislike the *complicité* and intense local politics of the French communes, these same energies help France adjust to new needs at many levels of government. They also make local politics lively. This is partially demonstrated by the higher turnout in France, with about two-thirds of the voters participating in French local elections, while in Britain only roughly one-third of the electorate vote in local elections.

CENTRAL–LOCAL RELATIONS IN THE WELFARE STATE

A central argument of this study is that the British emphasis on political and administrative tidiness means sacrifices in policymaking flexibility and effectiveness. While this was much less clear a century ago, the modern welfare state puts a premium on ability to adjust policies in midstream, to redefine spatial units around new goals, and to adjust the size of local units to new functions. At all levels of government one needs flexibility and mutual adjustment. The important issue for this book is how local government systems may or may not respond to the complexities of the welfare state and its activities. The policy perspective presented here helps to identify the unforeseen consequences of decisions at one level of government on another, and reveals the growing interdependence of what were once thought to be isolated decisions. Comparison is one way of revealing such unintended effects.

Britain seems to have carried much nineteenth century baggage into the twentieth century. The insistence that levels of government be kept distinct, persistence of the town-versus-country debate, and the outmoded system of local finance, are all rooted in Victorian (and earlier) dogmas about the proper conduct of government. The persistence of these ideas in the era of the welfare state places severe restrictions on what can be done with local government. Thus despite the huge expenditure of British local government, in some ways it seems politically weak. The hope that territorial, functional, political and economic boundaries in a modern welfare state can be permanently fixed (much less coincide) is a romantic ideal deeply rooted in British history and culture. A local system that cannot readily adapt to or influence change suffers severe limitations.

Comparisons with France are instructive: French communes evade the territorial, functional, political and economic rigidities imposed on British local government. This may seem paradoxical because we often think of France as having an arbitrary and top-heavy administrative system. Although French politics may be less 'progressive' than the British, it would be incorrect to suggest that the French Left has been excluded from policymaking because it has not achieved national power. Indeed, the local government system is a major vehicle which gives French Socialists and Communists an influence over local and national decisions that is denied to a political opposition in the British system. Further, the French local system is more attuned to problem solving *because* it is more intimately linked to higher levels of political and administrative decisionmaking.

There is a growing body of evidence to show that the French national officials need local support and do not always get their way.[6] Consequently in pursuing national objectives the French administrator often seeks close alliance with local politicians, and must make compromises with local political forces. As will be argued in more detail in Chapters 4 and 5, France has devised numerous options to solve central–local differences. The simple fact that national objectives are often translated into a variety of programs, similar to American practice, should lead us to question whether the central government can influence the future as easily as many critics of French government suggest. Britain seems less equipped to devise policy alternatives and there is considerable evidence that neither Westminster nor Whitehall see this as their main task. When central–local conflict occurs there is usually a confrontation. The outcome most often neither achieves national objectives nor enhances local initiative.

The Tortoise and the Hare: Gradual and Global Local Reform

Britain's effort to globally reorganize local government systems looks at first like an amazing display of political and administrative ingenuity. But on closer examination the Local Government Act of 1972 seems a less remarkable feat of intergovernmental innovation. Admittedly, designing and implementing the Act was a major achievement of the thousands of national and local officials who participated. But one must question whether it was comprehensive. Many features of the British local system remain the same, and in a few instances old problems seem to have been aggravated by the 1972 Act. As we shall see in more detail in Chapter 3, the reorganization hoped to draw a territorial map that would improve local services and decisionmaking. Thus, territory was to be subordinated to function, almost the reverse of the French strategy of change. This view of the role of local government is deeply rooted in British history and can easily be traced to early Victorian England (see Chapter 2).

During the reorganization great stress was put on increasing the local government efficiency. But costs continued to soar under adverse economic conditions, and the localities did little to arrest the growth of expenditure until the national government imposed severe spending restrictions in 1974 and 1975. In the midst of the transition from the old to the new system, a major proposal was hurriedly assembled to reorganize the internal decisionmaking structure of the local councils and to develop more long-range planning. Nevertheless organization still varies widely from one local authority to another. There are also signs that the old local committee system, so preoccupied with detail and short-term considerations, is gradually reappearing. While the Royal Commission on Local Government of 1969 emphasized the need to get new people into local government, recent surveys of council membership show that the elderly male and the politically active middle class[7] still tend to be in charge of local government. There was some hope that the British local system might indirectly acquire some of the national political importance of the French communes by making local elections a reliable and intelligible expression of popular sentiments, but last minute political compromises make it more difficult to draw meaning from the local elections now than before 1972.

The Royal Commission had a sound knowledge of what was wrong: institutionalized separation of country and town; the increasingly unworkable division of responsibilities within counties and their second-tier units and between counties and boroughs; the small size of many local authorities; poor relations between local government and the public as well as ambiguities in relations with national government. The Act redistributed functions among the levels of local government and made massive changes in the local government map. But many of the same complaints the Commission acknowledged persist today. Perhaps local government is so complex that it is impossible to deal with all aspects simultaneously. No one thought Britain had devised a perfect local government system in 1972, though not many expected it to be back on the political agenda only three years after the implementation of the Act in 1974.[8]

The reorganization dealt mainly with questions of local areas and function. There had been severe disparities in the populations served by the local authorities. The administrative county of Lancashire, for example, had a hundred times the population of the smallest county, Radnor. Among the boroughs, Birmingham had thirty times the population of Canterbury. Local councils had no clear organizational guidelines, and the new Act established principles for the size of the councils. Aldermen were abolished. Since the Municipal Corporations Act of 1835 — a limited reform touching about 180 towns and cities — borough councils had been one-fourth aldermen, indirectly elected for six years by the councillors. The Act concentrated more on catching up with the past than carving out the future, and the major Victorian anomalies and inequities were removed.

The Royal Commission appointed by the Labour Party in 1966 hoped to eradicate the historical division of town and country by creating unitary authorities. This proved to be physically impossible, and several large two-tier metropolitan areas had to be formed. As we shall see in Chapter 3, this provided the wedge by which the Conservatives, who finally passed the Act in 1972, could overturn Labour's proposals. The new urban authorities, the metropolitan counties, became two-tier units, thus offending the old boroughs that were downgraded to districts. In the non-metropolitan counties, there was greater concentration of powers in the first tier at the expense of their second tier.

A primary focus of this study is how national policies affecting local government are made. The 1972 Act in Britain left the focal point of local reform at the center. Neither the principle of *ultra vires* nor the centralization of policymaking were modified. Under the *ultra vires* principle,[9] the local authorities have no powers beyond those given in parliamentary statutes. The importance of this principle can be exaggerated because local government has many ways to circumvent this restriction, but it reflects the British assumption that local government is an instrument of national policy. The centralization of policymaking in Britain is further enhanced by the vertical links between central departments of Whitehall and their functional counterparts at the local level. Compared to France, the notion that the state benefits from the 'flow of strength from local politics into national politics'[10] is weakly articulated.

While we often think of the French political system as more centralized than the British, in practice the policy process in France disperses more power to lower levels of government than in Britain. Admittedly local political power is more divided in a local government system of over 36,000 communes, but French mayors have successfully resisted every effort to reorganize what is now clearly an archaic and inefficient system. Two strong national leaders, de Gaulle and Pompidou, were defeated in their best efforts to impose reforms in 1964, 1968 and 1971 (see Chapter 3). The political linkage of communes to the center is much more intricate than in Britain, and political parties rely more heavily on their local power bases than do British parties (see Chapter 4). While the French administrative system may merit much criticism, both national and local administrators rely heavily on the support from the mayors. In addition, the communes have direct access to the center through the *cumul des mandats*, a system of accumulating elected office at many levels of government, and through their influence in the Senate, sometimes called 'le grand conseil des communes de France'.

Debbasch has called administrative law 'the refuge of social contradictions',[11] but it also creates policy options and provides an arena for central–local conflict. Unable to concentrate central power sufficiently to force structural change on local government, French public law helps reconcile local needs with national objectives. There are, first, the purely administrative areas, usually called *circonscriptions*, which are usually confined to a single purpose. Next, between the departments and the communes there are *arrondissements* which provide a way of aligning parliamentary and other electoral areas with the local government system. Perhaps the most interesting device to link national and local policies is the *établissement public*.[12] Created in 1901 to facilitate the formation of public schools, the *établissement public* is now used for public and semipublic agencies ranging from the Comédie Française to Orly Airport, most secondary schools, port authorities, the *villes nouvelles* (new towns), the *communautés urbaines* (local development agencies) and the regional authorities. (These are roughly analogous to special districts and authorities in the United States.) All these organizational options are used to form compromises between national and local interests.

The French debate about decentralization has always been lively. The *ancien régime* had a developed, if somewhat chaotic, structure for the administration of France. Tocqueville may be generous in considering it Europe's most highly developed administrative system in the eighteenth century,[13] but certainly even then it was a more developed network than Britain had. During the Revolution, the relationship of the communes to the Republic occupied much of the debates, and constructing the prefectoral system was a major concern of Napoleon. In the 1860s there was a major debate about decentralization.[14] Local politicians were firmly ensconced at the center in the Third and Fourth Republics. Not until the Fifth Republic did local reorganization become unavoidable, and for the past two decades the subject has been a major preoccupation of French government.

France devised a *multiple* attack on the problems, which in itself casts doubt on the assumption about unrestrained central power in the French state. If national politicians and the elite administrative corps were so powerful, would they not have simply undertaken a comprehensive reform similar to Britain's? There is considerable evidence that a direct assault was preferred by the Fifth Republic, at least in its early years, but it was not possible. France's own ponderous bureaucracy and the mutual dependence between levels of government prevented the government from embarking on Britain's course. Nevertheless in a world of complex policy choices the French system may have distinct advantages.

Two factors make central–local relations a more critical issue in France. First, the one thing that the reformers of late seventeenth and eighteenth century England did not have to worry about was local government (see Chapter 2). But in France, local government is a constitutional problem, raises sensitivities about the legitimacy of the state itself, and contributes to violent arguments over the influence of the bureaucracy. But the bureaucracy helped provide continuity, as well as the essential services, while the French struggled until the turn of this century with the establishment of republican government. Second, the excessively large and influential administration that France inherited provided a focal point for policy debates that Britain lacked. A unified heavy-handed administration like that in France not only makes politicians sensitive to their rights, but also produces more awareness of policy problems. A secluded and disjointed administration like Britain's may be equally powerful, but less sensitive to the diverse problems of local government. Moreover, as will be argued later, a unified administration may be more appropriate to policymaking in the welfare state than is the disjointed British system.

In contrast to France, British consideration of local problems has historically been forced on a reluctant central government. The Municipal Corporations Act of 1835 was a detested sequel to the long overdue parliamentary reform of 1832, and was to some extent required by the gross abuses of local funds and elections by the aristocratic elite that also dominated Parliament. A half-century later, the Local Government Act of 1888 was an historical accident caused by the defection of Joseph Chamberlain to the Conservative Party. The British worried about local inefficiency throughout the mid-Victorian era, but did little about it. The Local Government Act of 1929 was another Conservative attempt to retrench a system that was nearly bankrupted by the 1920s depression, and that was also threatened by the rising Labour Party.

Curiously, the British have never really debated *why* a country should have local government. In contrast, the issue has always been present in the annals of French history. Central–local relations have been a constant concern in France. While France has seen few dramatic changes comparable to the British Local Government Act of 1972, a constant accumulation of policy decisions has occurred. In most instances such modifications have involved both national and local actors. French constitutional, institutional and administrative conditions make it virtually impossible to insulate the center from local government. Though perhaps an overstatement, it may be said that French national government could not survive without communes, but British national government could easily find a substitute for local councils.

ORGANIZATIONAL DIFFERENCES: NETWORKS VERSUS HIERARCHIES

This study proceeds on two levels: (1) it treats political and administrative limitations on the local government system as a whole in each country, and (2) it examines how specific decisions are influenced by these constraints within each system. Whether the more detailed consideration of policies contributes to our understanding of politics, as has been argued by Lowi and others,[15] is not the major concern of this inquiry, although the influence of policy on politics is part of the overall design.

France has probably brought more expertise to bear on local problems than Britain because the *grands corps* themselves are organized around specific skills and compete for local support (see Chapter 5). The British higher civil service not only resists acquiring the planning and technical expertise of the French administrator, but its members probably could not perform most of the tasks of local government.[16] Although it is not uniformly the case, the British central official differs from the French administrator because many of the latter (especially those in the *grands corps* associated with communes) begin their careers by serving in the departmental and regional agencies of local government. Given how little first-hand experience most Whitehall administrators have with British local government, it is all the more surprising that they have been able to exercise so much control over the reorganization and other policies that directly affect the local councils.

As will be argued, the central bureaucratic influence over local government strategy and policy multiplies as the welfare state develops, but lower-level decisions also take on increased importance as society tries to provide more services and benefits to its citizens. Nearly every microlevel study of France describes the network linking communes to policymaking at lower levels of government.[17] Central–local relations in France thrive on cutting across the political and administrative hierarchies. Compared to Britain the effect is the more surprising because French communes and departments are not significant in the total system, employing only about 400,000 persons, and those most often in less important positions. By contrast, British local governments employ nearly three million persons, including the skilled planners, accountants, educational and health officials – yet these massive responsibilities do not seem to create the mutual dependence that is common in France.

The microstudies of British local councils find local administrators still confined to their functional roles, and there are signs that tasks requiring coordination among functions are difficult to perform. There are many reasons for this fragmentation of administrative power. Britain places more emphasis on the political neutrality of civil servants than does France. Despite the effort to introduce more sophisticated forms of local budgeting and financial planning, inward looking local council committees remain influential in Britain. The local officials themselves are organized in strong trade unions whose jurisdictional and professional self-interests diminish the collective strength that they might exercise in policymaking, both locally and nationally. Each central government department has developed its own habits of communication and control with its local counterparts, and regards inroads by other departments with suspicion. In guarding their local preserves, the central administration's top civil servants are often backed by ministers who wish to advance their careers and establish their prestige, both within their department and in Parliament.

Britain has avoided creating a dominant national ministry like the French Ministry of the Interior that might become a national spokesman for local interests (see Chapter 2). Instead, from one generation to the next, responsibility for local government matters has been passed around in Whitehall, depending on the current central government priorities. In 1871 the Local Government Board emerged from the early Victorian confusion of local boards, inspectors and commissioners. When health became a central concern, local policy gravitated toward the Ministry of Health whose influence was later severely challenged by the Ministry of Education when it acquired a major interest in local government. Lacking a single national ministry responsible for local problems, local government depended on Private Bills (non-partisan legislation) to meet their immediate needs. Finally, in 1951 the Ministry of Housing and Local Government was established, primarily to fulfil housing promises the Conservatives had made on their return to power. The Department of the Environment was not created until 1969, bringing local government, housing and transportation (until 1976) into one agency. The department still faces stiff resistance when its views clash with educational policies of the Department of Education and Science, as well as opposition from the Department of Health and Social Security when it infringes on local social services.[18]

The French communes and departments have always had a strong central defender, the powerful Ministry of the Interior, although this has not always been an unqualified advantage. Other important ministries, in particular the Ministry of Finance and the National Economy,[19] also have their representatives at lower levels of government, but the Ministry of the Interior clearly predominates. It performs the regulatory and law-and-order functions like those of Britain's Home Office, but also has a direct stake in the entire territorial organization and reviews all local decisions. It provides a home for the important elite civil servant groups, the *corps préfectoral*, and throughout the past three republics has been a favorite post for ambitious politicians. Its closest rival is the Ministry of Infrastructure (*Équipement*)[20] which also has its spearhead elite group, the *ponts et chaussées*, which provides planning and engineering services for cities and towns.

The more important point in comparing France and Britain is the fact that the design and organization of French government seriously concerns the highest and most talented officials.[21] There are numerous works on the organization of French government, ranging from the most abstract of cybernetic theory to specific critiques of governmental organization, some of which influenced the Fifth Republic. The complex organization of France has enabled lower-level decisionmakers to obtain what Thoenig calls 'democracy of access'.[22] All these works give the territorial organization of the state a prominent role. In short, the French central government puts organizations to work at all levels, while British central government concentrates on subordinating local organizations to central departments.

Contrary to the legalistic formality of the system, the coordination and integration of policy objectives in France is in reality highly informal, depending on the skill, patience and ingenuity of politicians and administrators at many levels of government. Thus policy formation and implementation in France bears a greater resemblance to the intricacies of federal systems than it does to the British system. An example is the *tutelle* or tutelage relationship between the central administrative system and the communes and departments, a relationship that has been evolving, especially over the past decade.[23] It was originally considered purely as administrative supervision, to ensure that lower-level decisions kept within the confines of the laws, decrees and regulations of central government. But the formal administrative definition proved inadequate to cope with the rapid urbanization and industrialization of the country, particularly under the Fifth Republic. Many of the reforms described in Chapter 5 were in fact an admission by the center that the system of central–local relations worked poorly. Responding to pressures to rebuild cities, expand industry and develop major national infrastructure, the notion of a technical *tutelle* evolved. The most recent transformation has been toward a financial *tutelle*.

In France financial links to the center had to be reorganized in the 1960s because of the huge infrastructure expenditures of cities and towns. The changes were a further confession that the national administrative system was inadequate. In a more adventurous response than anything seen in Britain, there was an effort to involve other financial agencies, most notably the Caisse des Dépôts et Consignations (CDC) and its array of affiliated public banks. The growing influence of public lending agencies, while consistent with French conservative economic policy, is also a departure from previous practice. The use of the financial institutions and the transformation of the *tutelle* are more significant organizational innovations than anything yet undertaken by Whitehall (see Chapter 7). In contrast, British central government has refused to revise the fiscal and financial foundations of the local government system.

Britain has worked much harder than France to make sure that organizational and institutional boundaries are observed. This tendency is deeply rooted in British government and can be traced at least from early Victorian England, when the pattern of government growth began placing substantial new responsibilities on local government.[24] Victorian England had over twenty different types of local authorities, for such things as poor relief, turnpikes, prisons, police and education. Until the beginning of local government reform in 1888, the British approach was to juggle responsibilities among functionally defined local boards and commissions and, if local rivalries could be overcome, leave integration to chance. Even now, J. D. Stewart, one of the strongest advocates of organizational change within the local councils, described the British local authority as 'a collection of essentially separate services brought together more by historical accident or for administrative convenience than for anything they have in common'.[25] In short, concern with organizational complexity seems almost an afterthought in British policymaking, while it is a precondition of French policymaking. Obviously both approaches can be overdone and both have imposed costs on local government and local democracy.

The service orientation of British local government is deeply ingrained,[26] and meant that territorial flexibility was not a seriously considered policy instrument. Internal organization to increase local government efficiency was stressed in the background reports and by the Commission that led to the 1972 reorganization,[27] but the proposals on how to achieve efficiency were late in appearing.[28] Some cities and counties took the lead (Basildon, Coventry, Liverpool and Cheshire), but the weak horizontal links between local governments made it difficult to adapt this experience to other authorities (see Chapter 5). The strong central initiatives needed to launch local change suggest how the British system is more centralized than the French. In performing the task of modern government, the French system may respond more readily to local initiative than the British. In any event, the alleged evils of the French administration appear less oppressive when compared with the difficulties of organizational change and functional integration in Britain.

REFORMING LOCAL GOVERNMENT: REACTING TO CIRCUMSTANCES VERSUS SEIZING OPPORTUNITIES

Change viewed through the policy process is very different than examining local affairs in isolation. The apparent British success in bringing about a comprehensive reorganization was possible only because institutions outside the local system, that is, the House of Commons and Cabinet, agreed on structural change. Localities disliked change, but could be compelled to reorganize. In France the intransigence of the communes and departments to central demands for change was circumvented, compromised and sometimes even refashioned national efforts to redefine local objectives. Localities disliked change, but had to be incorporated in the process of change itself.

Although France urbanized more slowly than Britain, by the early 1950s nearly twenty-four million persons, or 56 percent of the French population, lived in cities and towns of over 50,000 persons. By 1968 the urban population had increased to nearly thirty-five million persons or 70 percent of the population.[29] Social and economic dislocations multiplied because much of this increase was rural-to-urban migration, which rapidly increased the adult population of French cities and towns. The pace of the change can be seen in the multiplication of cities over 30,000: from 159 in 1965 to 221 in 1977. Second only to Japan, since 1945 France had the highest rate of urban growth of any country in the world.

Britain industrialized earlier than France and by the end of the nineteenth century 80 percent of the population was classified as urban.[30] Over the present century the growth of cities has tapered off, presenting the country with a different set of urban problems: the decay of inner cities and the need for redevelopment of declining industrial areas. Because the British center relies so heavily on localities to provide services and benefits, local spending increased rapidly. In 1890 local government spending in England and Wales was 50 million pounds when the center was spending 130 million pounds. In 1978, British local authorities spent over 22 billion pounds when central government spending was 71 billion pounds.[31] However, central transfers to local government were only 1.6 million pounds in 1875, but by the turn of the century had multiplied seven and a half times, to over 12 million pounds.[32] Although little was done about these local fiscal and financial pressures until 1929, British local government was dependent on national funds from late Victorian times. By 1978 British local government was receiving over 10 billion pounds in operating and capital grants.

In France the changes were less dramatic but equally critical for the cities and towns. In 1890, the communes and departments spent slightly under 7 billion francs when the state budget (excluding local government) was slightly more than 26 billion. In 1973, the local budgets, including Paris, totaled about 68 billion francs when the state budget was 216 billion.[33] The overall result is that both French and British local spending accounts for nearly a third of all public spending. Because the inflationary effects of local spending are probably more difficult to control than nationally stimulated inflation, there are powerful economic and social motivations to keep (or bring) local government systems under control. France has always exercised close financial supervision of local government, and may be better prepared to deal with these problems. In contrast, Britain had no choice in 1974 but to impose the most severe of its spending controls on the local cash limits on about two-thirds of the local budgets.

Comparing the transformation of central–local relations forces one to consider how national institutions influence policymaking across levels of government. The basic structure of local government in Britain was a national compromise between the monarchy and the aristocracy that evolved after the Revolution of 1688. Though there was conflict in Britain between the monarch and the aristocracy throughout the seventeenth century, it never reached the proportions of the French monarch's continual struggles to repress and control provincial and local differences in a less unified France.[34] In the curiously non-partisan political world of the eighteenth century, the British rural aristocracy and gentry were in basic agreement with the ruling elite; institutional conflict over the structure of government was not a major issue. Essentially, the same people ran Parliament and the counties (see Chapter 2). Britain's political stability permitted national leaders to accept the local government system and even to exploit its weaknesses but in France political instability had virtually the opposite effect. Starting with the Revolutionary debates there were institutional alternatives in France.

What was true of politics was also true of administration. Until fairly late in the Victorian period, the British did not have a highly organized central administration and local administration as such did not exist. In contrast, from Napoleon onward French central and local administration were developed and integrated. The evolving role of the prefects during the succession of nineteenth century empires, republics and monarchy is a vivid demonstration of the way in which administration was constantly undergoing change. The communes were both sounding boards for and moderators of national political conflict. National stability and instability were probably the most important factors in shaping central–local relationships in each country. No such key historical role existed for British localities.

The development of the liberal state in the nineteenth century did more to change the central–local politics in France than in Britain. British local and national politics were fiercely competitive,[35] but the two major leaders of the century, Disraeli and Gladstone, had little time for local government. It is not clear why the series of devastating reports on the inefficiency and inadequacy of local government, starting with the Royal Commission on the Poor Law of 1834, and subsequent examinations of the miseries of local health, sanitation and education did not bring about structural change until 1888. Even then many basic local services were not entrusted to local councils, but supervised by inspectors. National suspicion, if not open hostility, toward local government contrasts with the French practice of continual tinkering and intervening in local affairs. In the light of history, British assertions about the autonomy of local government simply do not hold up. Equally, the frequent complaints about local repression and coercion in France, most often by the prefectoral corps, must also be qualified as the center became increasingly immersed in local politics throughout the nineteenth century. Mutual dependence prevailed in the Third and Fourth Republics, a foretaste of the local *complicité* that kept the Fifth Republic from forcing reform on the communes and departments.

Historical comparison clarifies what particular institutions can and cannot do. Understanding the constraints does not guarantee that any society will undertake major structural change, but it provides us with a clearer idea of which structures may change or must be changed if particular goals are to be achieved. The formal and legal description of institutions must be supplemented with the historical continuities of the policy debate. How Britain differs from France in relation to local government policy (and in relation to many other policy problems) can be seen in the relative consistency of the debates, and of the institutional assumptions regularly applied to local government. The dogmatic quality of Britain's institutional response may have advantages, but in effect refused to give local government the priority that France did. In many ways even Britain's 'comprehensive' reform in 1972 avoided important structural change. The politically salient issues are long standing, and remarkably similar to those raised in 1929, 1888 and even 1835.

My preliminary conclusion is that changes in the British local government system have conformed to the requirements for institutional stability at the center. The high priority given to protecting Parliamentary and Cabinet government precluded a debate over centralization. Perhaps the French were never quite so certain that their institutions embodied the essentials of stable government. In any event, French national government has always had difficulty changing *without* itself being changed by the communes, while British government has evolved with little or no concern for the local councils.

CENTRALIZATION: PANACEA OR POLEMIC?

The study of local government has most often been associated with the study of centralizing tendencies in the modern state. But this focus tends to put the relation of the center to the periphery beyond debate as well as research. Until the community power controversy of the 1960s revived interest in local problems,[36] the study of local and municipal politics was isolated from the mainstream of political science. Indeed, one of the few substantial efforts to discuss theories of local government explains why there can be *no* theory of local government.[37] My general perspective is that centralization is a classic problem of the state and of government. Understanding local relationships to larger political patterns is fundamental to understanding power. Considering centralization as simply the uniform subordination to the center is neither inspiring nor surprising. Moreover, it unfortunately tends to foreclose empirical inquiry.

Fesler made the last sustained attack on the centralization concept, concluding that 'no nation's local governments and areas are without archaic features or immune from the trend toward centralization'.[38] The growth of government and the state have renewed interest in this classic controversy. The most frequently cited effect of growth is increased control over citizens, but this is often a polemical objection to the growth of government and a forlorn hope that the state will disappear. Growth of the welfare state has brought an enormous multiplication of decisionmaking bodies at all levels, and often increased reliance on lower-level decisions and policy guidance. Thus, 'bigger' and 'smaller' do not tell us much, because the state is being simultaneously dispersed and concentrated as the public sector is enlarged.

For the French centralization has been a concrete problem and underlay nearly every institutional choice since the Revolution. There have been fierce debates in the National Assembly, the Paris political salons like the Club Jean Moulin, and during elections. French writers set out 'to renovate', 'to manage' or 'to nationalize' the state.[39] While comprehensive restructuring of the local system has been rejected, nearly every policy and program has had to accommodate tensions among levels of government. There are elaborate explanations of the difference between *déconcentration*, meaning the delegation of administrative powers to lower levels, and *décentralisation*, meaning the assignment of functions to lower levels.[40] One pioneering student of French local government wrote that the problem 'is less "centralization" than the maintenance of the status quo due to reciprocal neutralization or tacit complicity between central and local powers'.[41] In Britain one seldom sees similar preoccupation with the organization of the state.

The work of Crozier, Worms, Grémion and Thoenig reveals the intensity of the French centralization debate. Thus Thoenig speaks of the 'antagonism of independent actors', and Grémion describes the dual exchange within the local government system.[42] Similar observations are made by Keselman and Rosenthal in referring to the 'institutional layering' of French central–local relationships.[43] A report, assembled by Peyrefitte to guide Pompidou into 'his next septennat' and the reform of the communes, laments that the communes do not understand the strenuous efforts of Paris to delegate authority; and it notes how mayors so often fail to take advantage of new legislation or take new initiatives.[44] All these findings and interpretations lead to a single conclusion: national and local actors in the French local government system are engaged at all levels of decisionmaking.

Until the surge of Scottish nationalism in the early 1970s, local government policy was rarely a burning national issue in Britain. Councils often complain about specific services and grants, but the working relationship between the councils and Westminster or Whitehall is seldom debated. The causes of central–local confrontation seem to be more than local complacency or national disinterest. Intense local controversies occur, but nearly always arise over the violation of *national* party policy, rather than from generalized resistance to the center or collaboration between councils to extract concessions from the center. The refusal of the Labour-held town, Clay Cross, to increase local rents is only one of the more recent incidents of this kind.[45] Though Clay Cross was initially joined by other Labour-controlled districts, united opposition to the center soon melted away. In fact more serious disruption of central–local relations in Britain has come from the courts than from the local councils. In 1976 the Tameside decision restricted the powers of the Secretary of State for Education in seeking compliance with Labour's comprehensive school policy, causing a furor in London.[46] But it did not produce a coherent response from local governments, nor did anyone expect it to. There is little bargaining over central–local conflicts, but neither is there effective resolution of central–local differences in these exchanges.

By contrast, French officials and mayors would probably work such disagreements out among themselves. Administrative law provides reasonably clear procedures and alternatives to help resolve central–local disputes. But conflict in Britain is focused at the national level, and is used to magnify national party differences. Local government becomes a pawn of national politics, rather than an active participant in policy decisions. Central–local relationships in Britain take two forms, according to Hartley, 'an administrative device for the provision of services in a given area' and 'a system of local independent bodies, each having its own rights and duties'.[47] Neither characterization attaches much importance to the national expression of local preference or needs. The British local councils have no collective identity, and there are many signs that the center is relieved that they do not.

There are still few ways for localities to express collectively their views on national policy. Their ability to act collectively is restricted by the party alignments of local councils (see Chapter 5). Local government associations also divide on national party lines. Conversely, Whitehall's 'detachment' is not particularly effective in getting local compliance when crises do occur. Nor do higher civil servants seem especially effective in the execution of complex policies for the inner city or on race relations. The National Consultative Council on Local Finance was created in 1974 to soften the blow of extraordinary spending controls on local councils, but it provides none of the constitutional or legal protection that localities have in the French local government system.[48] Even when British associations of local authorities are consulted confidentially on major decisions, cabinet government forbids any full-scale airing of alternatives. Moreover, regional government in Britain is also largely an instrument of national industrial policy, and excludes local political intervention. Thus Britain tries to keep intergovernmental relations simple. Local interests appear to be a threat to national policymaking while, by contrast, the formation and nurturing of a central–local network seems to be a French preoccupation, possibly even a precondition of national integration and stability.

A report by the Central Policy Review Staff, a policy analysis unit attached to the Cabinet Office, found three major deficiencies in national decisionmaking for local government: 'central departments, in making and implementing policies, still act for most purposes in isolation from each other, and conduct their relationships with local authorities accordingly'; in giving advice it is 'often not clear how, in particular cases, local authorities are intended or expected to follow it

– or what will happen if they do not do so'; and 'central government finds it very hard to see local authorities "in the round" as corporate entities trying to deal with inter-related problems'.[49] Such deficiencies do not characterize French local government or central–local relations in France.

British national political institutions do not fill the policymaking void between center and periphery, nor are they meant to do so. Except for the heated debates over the reorganization of London in 1963, major local government legislation rarely generates full debate in the Commons[50] (see Chapter 4). Bills affecting local government usually cut across party interests and may create schisms within parties. Thus the benefits of parliamentary stability and adversary politics are not readily transferred to local government. Moreover national parties tend to use local policy for partisan effect and have exploited local confrontation with the center regardless of the policy consequences. The point is not to prejudge the appropriateness of the policy network that any particular country devises to meet historical, institutional and administrative conditions. Nor should governments that concentrate key decisions for the center be thought necessarily undemocratic. Nonetheless, one cannot help concluding that British central–local relations handicap policymaking at both the center and the locality.

In France, the weakness of Parliament enhances the power of the President. But this weakness also means that national politicians must work hard to manipulate and cajole communes into pursuing national objectives. At times the President of France probably may wish he had a House of Commons to insulate him from the relentless pressures of the French local government system. Lammenais' maxim states that France is a country with 'apoplexy at the center, paralysis at the extremities', but, examining the effort needed to align national and local objectives and policies, it seems likely there has been more apoplexy in Paris than paralysis in the provinces. In fact, on major issues Paris often gives way to local demands and preferences.

Absolute measures of centralization are misleading because central control is both relative and diverse. Sometimes Paris gets its way but sometimes not, and the same is true in Britain. One must probe further. To assess whether Britain is more or less centralized than France a number of relationships are set forth schematically in Figure 1.1. Local government interacts with the center along at least four avenues, selected as the most important channels of influence and communication on national and local policymaking. The relative influence of the political and administrative system over policymaking within localities is a major issue in the welfare state. How these two critical links between national and local decisions affect local government in Britain and France are the starting points for the analysis of central–local policymaking in the two countries (see Chapters 4 and 5).

The diagram points to major linkages between levels of government, namely, the hierarchy of the political and administrative systems. These are minimal considerations essential to an assessment of central–local relationships in any political system. The following pages introduce the British and French subnational systems, and include diagrams that portray the key components of these hierarchies in each country. As we shall see in later chapters, the British subnational system tends to isolate the two main hierarchies of the subnational system, while France has many interlocking relationships at the local, departmental and regional levels. There are also more ways that local political actors can cut across the diagram to reach higher levels of administrative decisionmaking and, using the unified administrative structure, more ways that local administrators can reach higher levels of political decisionmaking. Later chapters (6 and 7) deal in more detail with how such cross-cutting influence is actually used in each country.

In a perfectly 'centralized' subnational system, the political and/or the administrative system could independently impose its aims on lower levels of government. Although this has never been the case in democratic governments, the limited objectives of the nineteenth century liberal state simplified intergovernmental exchange (see Chapter 2). The aims of government were of course more modest a century ago, so interdependence was less pronounced. In most democratic systems we would regard policy change wholly under administrative influence as undemocratic even though democracies differ considerably to the extent to which the subnational system is subjected to administrative control. Sweden, for example, appears to rely more heavily on officials than politicians to reorganize and guide local government. France shares this characteristic, but, as we shall see in Chapter 3, there are numerous ways that lower-level politicians and administrators intervene in making and implementing policies. Britain is perhaps the most extreme case where the national political elite remains the major source of policy guidance and their power is further protected by the various ways they are isolated from political and administrative influence at other levels of government.

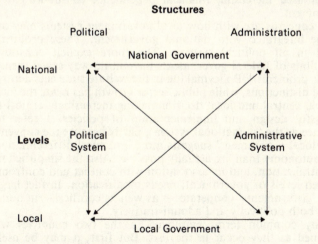

Figure 1.1 *The subnational system*

The rise of the welfare state made simple forms of exchange unworkable. The complications are represented by the cross-cutting arrows of Figure 1.1. Local politicians and administrators have nasty habits of finding new ways to intervene directly at the national level. On the whole, the French have been more prone to do this than the British. The origins of the French network can be easily traced to the nineteenth century and even earlier in French history. As will be argued throughout this study, this gives the French certain advantages in dealing with the complexity and unforeseen effects of policymaking in the welfare state. Many of these structural links can be seen in Figure 1.2. The policymaking activities of government interlock at every level of government and the political and administrative systems are interwoven.

In short, the welfare state has made a simple, hierarchical model of centralization meaningless. Although the British pioneered the welfare state, they continue to behave as though the enormous complication of policymaking in an expanded state, often simply superimposed on central–local relationships, did not exist. Although the French have responded more slowly to demands for a welfare state, they are better prepared to deal with its consequences. All political systems require some form of direction. As central–local relations become more complex, it is to be expected that other forms of control will be devised and indeed there is every reason they should be if government is to be integrated. How this is done will be examined in more detail in Chapters 6 and 7. As political and administrative hierarchies become less effective national government turns toward spending and investment controls to replace the organization controls. As we shall see, Britain has been slow to give localities an effective voice in the use of financial controls although changes have been suggested ever since the Royal Commission on Local Taxation reported in 1901. France developed financial links to communes to bring about change, while Britain used increasing financial dependence to subordinate local government.

My concerns are with how local government systems may or may not be integrated with national government. These problems are found in all political systems. The more explicit constitutional limitations of federal governments have in no way saved them from similar problems.[51] Policymaking in the welfare state cuts across such formal distinctions, while public sector growth has made the interface between central and local decisionmaking increasingly critical to the successful design and implementation of policies. I refer to the interface as the 'subnational system', partly because the conventional term 'local government' suggests more structural differentiation and local autonomy than are actually possible. Also the simplified notion of centralization, and its association with conflict and confrontation between levels of government, needs modification. In fact large and small 'governments' cooperate – as well as conflict – in numerous ways, both politically and administratively.

Many common terms employed in the two countries will be explained as they occur in the text. But first, it may be useful to describe the basic subnational structure of each country as it relates to the national policymaking process. In 1975 France had 36,398 communes distributed among the ninety-five departments. Many of the communes are quite small, for example, the 28,000 smallest communes together account for only one-tenth of the total budgets of the communes.[52] There is an immense diversity in size and needs among the communes. Municipal councils in France vary from nine members for communes under a population of 100 persons, up to forty-nine members for communes over 300,000.[53] This makes a total of about 460,000 municipal councillors in France. While many councillors are inactive, especially in small communes, the huge cumulative total of persons involved in local activities suggests one reason why French local politicians can more successfully challenge the center than British local councillors.

The closer relationship of French local and national politics has also meant that manipulation of local electoral systems is more common than in Britain. But as we shall see in Chapter 5, blatant electoral abuse often backfires. For example, in the hope of handicapping the Left, the Gaullists modified the system in 1964, imposing a 'majority list system' with two ballots on cities over 30,000, and forbidding the reformulation of lists between the first and second ballots. Councillors are elected for six years, and they in turn elect the mayor. At the department level a council (*conseil général*) is directly elected in cantonal areas, with half of the members renewed every three years. Even after the 1975 revision of the cantonal areas, the departmental councils were not representative, but the 3318 departmental councillors of France (the modern notables) have considerable influence. De Gaulle's reorganization efforts were directed against these local influence peddlars, but even such a towering figure could not change the system by a frontal attack.

Prefects are appointed by the Council of Ministers on the recommendation of the Minister of the Interior. They are no longer arbitrary rulers like the early nineteenth century prefectoral corps, but they do remain the *états-majors* of departmental services. They combine political and administrative functions. They are responsible to the state and to the central government for law and order, to the Ministry of the Interior for electoral supervision and the operations of departmental government, and to the communes as their executive agents and advisors. Although the business of a department is beyond the easy manipulation of any single official, the prefects remain pivotal figures in the local government system and have no counterpart in Britain. At the departmental level are also found the representatives of the other major ministries of central government: Finance (*Trésorier Payeur Général* or TPG), Infrastructure (*Directeur Départmental de l'Équipement* or DDE), Agriculture, Education and other services of local government. The 1964 and 1970 reforms (see Chapter 3) were designed to simplify and coordinate services at the departmental level, but the ministerial representatives have maintained direct contact with their ministries.

The national agencies that directly and indirectly influence choices at the local level have no special rationale, nor are they uniformly organized throughout France (see Chapter 5). (The notion that

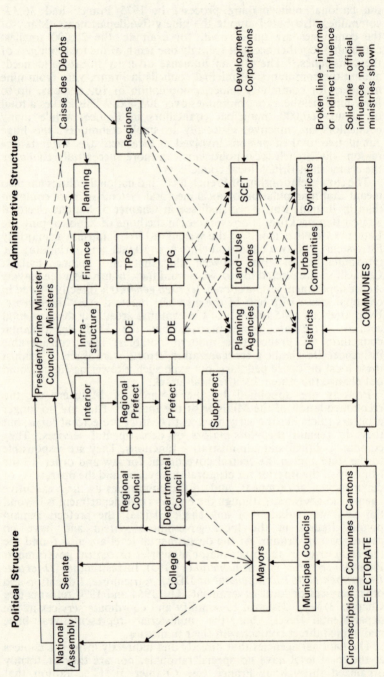

Administrative Structure

Caisse des Dépôts

Development Corporations

Broken line – informal or indirect influence

Solid line – official influence, not all ministries shown

Regions

Planning

Finance

Infra-structure

Interior

TPG

TPG

DDE

DDE

SCET

Land-Use Zones

Planning Agencies

Syndicats

Urban Communities

Districts

President/Prime Minister Council of Ministers

Regional Prefect

Prefect

Subprefect

COMMUNES

Political Structure

National Assembly

Senate

Regional Council

Departmental Council

College

Mayors

Cantons

Communes

Municipal Councils

Circonscriptions | Communes | Cantons

ELECTORATE

Figure 1.2 *The French subnational system*

French logic has simplified French administration should be abandoned.) The many horizontal links shown in Figure 1.2 reveal the complexity of central–local policymaking and policy implementation, and will be given special emphasis in this study. The linkages are effected through a variety of intergovernmental agencies, including planning agencies (*agences d'urbanisme*), semipublic development corporations (*sociétés d'économie mixte*) and the network of financial institutions linked to the Caisse des Dépôts. The ubiquitous device of the *établissement public* has been used to construct at least four types of land-use zones, such as the *zones d'action concertée* or ZAC, each with its own statutes and funding (see Chapter 7). Most of the agencies are designed to overcome the small size of communes and cumbersome administrative procedures in order to respond to the desperate need for urban development.

The mayors have important decisionmaking roles in the political structure, though, of course, these roles vary from mayor to mayor because of the diversity of the communes (see Chapter 5).[54] In addition to their role in the Departmental Councils (about three-fourths of the 3318 departmental councillors are mayors) and Regional Councils (half the regional councillors are mayors or departmental councillors), there is the important national *cumul des mandats* or accumulation of positions. After the 1975 Senate elections, 161 of the 264 Senators were mayors[55] and 247 of the 470 deputies were mayors.[56] The mayors are also part of the electoral college of the indirectly elected Senate. Unlike their British counterparts, they serve in most cases as party leaders in the communes. They also exercise a degree of control over local party policies and politics that far exceeds that of the British local council party leader. Figure 1.2 does not therefore convey the full intricacy of the pattern of visitation, bargaining and mutual adjustment that goes on between mayors and the officials of the administrative structure at the center.

Mayors have substantial political resources when facing the ponderous administration (see the left side of Figure 1.2). Their power has been alluded to already. While the *formal* channels of local government remain under the control of the Ministry of the Interior with its prefects and subprefects, the neat hierarchy is seriously modified by the numerous other policymaking agencies at lower levels of the subnational system (only a few of which are shown). The communes also have a variety of structures from which they may choose in order to extract benefits from the state. As the diagram shows, the new agencies for urban development, land-use planning, etc., combine in a bewildering variety of ways with the various forms of communal grouping. While the prefects are not formally excluded from these arrangements, complexity clearly makes it difficult for the prefects to participate fully and also perform their routine duties for the Ministry and the state. In addition, funds are often provided by semipublic agencies, such as the CDC, which works more closely with networks of the Ministries of Infrastructure and Finance.

The British subnational system (see Figure 1.3) is complex at the base but patterns of interaction are more compartmentalized and are more uniformly observed than those in France. Local services are more directly subordinated to the various central ministries, although over the past decade this relationship has been modified by the introduction of local management committees (see Chapter V). The structure makes organizing around new policy objectives awkward and coordination at intermediate levels is cut off from local councils. Regional and other intergovernmental agencies are the instruments of central departments. A variety of regional bodies is found, some of them co-opting local representatives, but the functionally defined regions do not coincide with local areas and tend to be subordinated to the specific needs of Ministries (see Chapter 5);[57] for example, the Regional Water Authorities, which are under the Department of the Environment (DoE); the Area Health Authorities under the Department of Health and Social Security (DHSS); and the County and Metropolitan police forces under the Home Office. The major departure from this functional pattern is the Scottish Office, separately represented in the Cabinet and having its own territorial organization. The National Economic Development Council (NEDC) is closely related to the Department of Industry, which is also responsible for the regional economic planning councils (abolished in 1979) and for 'assisted areas' (depressed areas designated to receive special employment and industrial assistance). Thus intermediate-level organizations elude local government. In addition, British government avoids the intricate structure of semipublic local agencies found in France.

Both France and Britain incorporate electoral inequities in local elections, although the British set out in 1972 to reduce the complexity of local elections.[58] Because there was no time in 1972 to redraw district boundaries, the central government decided that the metropolitan counties should retain the old three-member districts with one member elected annually, and in the fourth year the county council would be elected. The non-metropolitan counties were allowed to choose whether they preferred the old system of district elections or wished to have all district councils chosen at the same time. The entire Greater London Council (GLC) is elected from the ninety-two parliamentary constituencies every four years (1977, 1981, etc.) so its national implications are fairly clear, and the county councils follow the same cycle.[59] But Scottish regional councils, comparable to English and Welsh counties, are on a different cycle, (1979, 1982, etc.). Delays in national redistricting in 1969 meant that parliamentary electoral boundaries will not coincide with county electoral boundaries until 1984, while districts may remain divided from the county. Thus, although roughly two-thirds of the British electorate goes to the polls each year, it is virtually impossible to extract national significance, and thereby to use local elections as an influence on national policy.

In short, British 'common sense' has not produced an electoral system for local government any simpler than the inequities imposed by French local elections. Not counting Northern Ireland,[60] there are in fact three political subsystems: The Greater London Council (GLC), Scotland, and England and Wales. England and Wales are

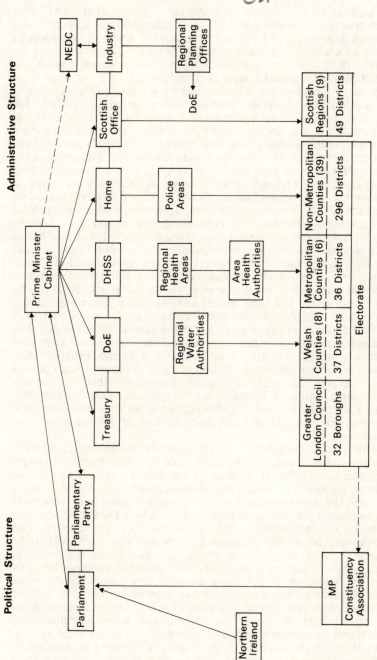

Figure 1.3 *The British subnational system*

divided into two kinds of counties, metropolitan and non-metropolitan. London has thirty-two metropolitan boroughs; the metropolitan counties have thirty-six districts; and non-metropolitan counties not counting Wales have 296 districts.

As will be described in more detail in Chapter 3, policymaking in the British subnational system is complicated by the fact that inter-dependent functions are often differently assigned to the same level. In metropolitan counties, primary and secondary education, for example, rests with the lowest level, the district, but the county has responsibility for locally organized higher education (technical schools, teacher colleges). Districts make the detailed land-use plans, but counties develop the long-term plan for the area. More important, the proliferation of local responsibilities has been accompanied by a proliferation of regional agencies, some of which are portrayed in Figure 1.3. But, unlike France, the regions have different areas and are basically the instrument of central departments which makes local influence less effective. As reorganized, the system does little to diminish central departmental control because each department has its own objectives and maintains an unobstructed channel to the first tier of local government. The powers of both central and the local bureaucracies are further enhanced because the system makes it virtually impossible for Parliament to devise a workable general statement about any local government service.[61] Every statute and order must conform to the peculiar pattern of control that each central department has evolved and often successfully defended. For example, central ministries exercise detailed control over education and housing in ways that would surprise a French official. Their power is further enhanced by the unusually arbitrary fiscal controls (see Chapter 6), and investment limitations that are totally determined within Whitehall (see Chapter 7). Both current and capital spending is closely monitored, but as we shall see below these controls have not been particularly helpful in achieving national objectives.

The French subnational system generates compromises between territorial and functional demands. The British subnational system subordinates territorial choices to functional needs. There is, of course, no reason to assume that this relationship should be the same through the transformations of the democratic state, but it structures opportunities for change in each country. Many French writers have admired the functional 'clarity' of British local government. This would not be readily recognized by many who work within the system.[62] In a state that is providing more goods and services, functionally organized controls facilitate central direction of localized activity. Moreover, if functional controls vary greatly among areas, central guidance becomes even more essential in order to achieve national objectives. British preference for this pattern of control can be traced back to Poor Law reform and helps perpetuate the functional compartmentalization found in the subnational system. Larger territories also make it more difficult for local government to resist such control, particularly if those units are detached from party organization and parliamentary elections.

The aim of this book is to contrast how Britain and France have related the diverse and expanding activities of the subnational system to national policymaking. In so far as there is a defined independent effect running through the analysis, it is the complexity of the welfare state itself, and the mutual dependence that increasingly characterizes central–local relationships. In aggregate spending terms, both countries have roughly similar commitments to the welfare state.[63] Both the political and administrative links between center and locality in Britain resist the mutual adaptation that is commonly found in France. British policies affecting local councils seem to appear in abrupt and often arbitrary ways, and national government, in turn, has problems achieving its policy objectives at the local level. The power of French politicians and administrators to impose their will on communes has probably been overestimated,[64] and on the whole the subnational system is more successfully integrated into the formulation and implementation of national policies.

Of course, France has paid the price of less dramatic and forceful reorganization of the communes, but there has also been enormous change in the social and economic settings of local government. Oddly enough, the British who champion a pragmatic approach to government have made the more erratic changes, the more costly reversals, and find central–local relationships virtually unaltered after a decade of reformist zeal. As we shall see in the next chapter, the historical forces propelling the French state toward compromise and adjustment with the communes run very deep, while the more centralized and arbitrary habits of Westminster are long-standing.

NOTES: CHAPTER 1

1 A useful collection of essays showing how federal systems alter central–local relations is Wallace E. Oates (ed.), *The Political Economy of Fiscal Federalism* (Lexington, Ky: Lexington Books, 1977). One should also examine *Publius* for a wide range of articles on how federal systems influence lower-level government. For the United States, see in particular Martha Derthick, *Between State and Nation: Regional Organization of the United States* (Washington, DC: Brookings Institution, 1974). As will become clear in Chapters 6 and 7, financial and fiscal pressures are probably becoming the major influence in central–local relations in unitary systems. For my more general thoughts on this trend, see my review article, 'Are Britain and France "unitary"?', *Comparative Politics*, vol. 9 (1977), pp. 483–99.

2 E. P. Hennock, 'Finance and politics in urban local government in England, 1835–1900', *The Historical Journal*, vol. 6 (1963), p. 212.

3 For the purposes of this study a precise definition of 'welfare state' is not required. 'A government that spends about a fourth of the gross national product' will be adequate. Until recently the French seldom spoke of the welfare state, but it has a long history in Britain. See Asa Briggs, 'The welfare state in historical perspective', *Archives Européenne de Sociologie*, vol. 2 (1961), pp. 221–58.

4 This view proved especially advantageous to the landowners, who could shift the burden of local taxes to tenants. See the reaffirmation of this in the Royal Commission on Local Taxation, *Report*, Cmd 638 (London: HMSO, 1901), p.12.

5 See Stanley Hoffman, 'An area division of powers in the writings of French political thinkers,' in A. Maas (ed.), *Area and Power* (Glencoe, Ill.: Free Press, 1959), pp. 113–49; Ralph Nelson, 'The federal idea in French political thought', *Publius*, vol. 5 (1975), pp. 7–62; and Patrick Riley, 'Rousseau as a theorist of national and international federalism,' *Publius* vol. 3 (1973), pp. 5–17.

6 Perhaps the seminal essay in reversing the common interpretation of French administration is Vincent Wright, 'Politics and administration under the French

Fifth Republic', *Political Studies*, vol. 22 (1974), pp. 44–65. Much of the evidence collected by the Crozier group, described in Chapters 3 and 6 in particular, could be used to demonstrate the diversity of administrative politics and policy rather than the oppressiveness of the state. A closely related essay that makes a similar argument in comparison to Britain is by Jack Hayward, 'Institutional inertia and political impetus in France and Britain', *European Journal of Political Research*, vol. 4 (1976), pp. 341–59.

7   The Royal Commission on Local Government in England (Redcliffe–Maud Report), *Report*, Cmd 4040 (London: HMSO, 1969), p. 145. The more recent study is the Robinson Report, or Committee of Inquiry into the System of Remuneration of Members of Local Authorities, *Remuneration of Local Councillors* (London: HMSO, 1977), pp. 5–15, where the composition of councils in 1964 and 1975 is compared.

8   A second wave of reform proposals was launched by a consultation paper, *Regional Authorities and Local Government Reform*, London, Labour Party Central Office, 1977. In June 1978 the National Executive Committee of the Party approved the changes, but the party leadership was divided. See further discussion in Chapter 8.

9   William A. Robson, *The Development of Local Government* (London: Allen & Unwin, 1931), p. 195. The preliminary study to the Royal Commission, the *Report* of the Committee on the Management of Local Government (Maud Report) (London: HMSO, 1967), vol. 1, pp. 11–12, recommends abolishing the *ultra vires* principle, but largely on the grounds of its discouragement of local initiative and its inefficient effects. For more details, see J. F. Garner, 'The "ultra vires" doctrine and the local government Bill', *Local Government Studies*, vol. 4 (1973), pp. 17–26; and B. Keith-Lucas, 'Municipal business and *ultra vires*', *Public Administration* (UK), vol. 27 (1949), pp. 87–90.

10 Nevil Johnson, *In Search of the Constitution* (London: Pergamon, 1977), p. 89.

11 Charles Debbasch, 'Le droit administratif face à l'évolution de l'administration française', *International Review of Administrative Sciences*, vol. 39 (1973), pp. 101–7.

12 Conseil d'Etat, *La Reforme des Établissements Publics* (Paris: Documentation Française, 1972). The report was made on the request of the president of the Council of Ministers, Chaban-Delmas, in 1969. As such, it belongs to the series of reforms he initiated that separated him from the more conservative Gaullists and eventually contributed to his fall. The Conseil d'Etat was unable to make a complete list of even those *établissements publics* depending on central government. They list 183 under twelve categories, but these do not include the use of this device for *lycées*, regional development projects and numerous urban development agencies.

13 Alexis de Tocqueville, *The Old Regime and the French Revolution* (trans. by Stuart Gilbert) (New York: Doubleday, 1955), pp. 32–41.

14 Bernard Le Clère and Vincent Wright, *Les Préfets du Second Empire* (Paris: Fondation Nationale de Science Politique, 1973), pp. 396–7, list twenty-one works on decentralization from the late 1860s. See also B. Basdevant-Gaudemet, *La Commission de Décentralisation de 1870* (Paris: Presses Universitaires de France, (PUF hereafter), 1973).

15 Theodore J. Lowi, 'Decisionmaking vs. policy making: toward an antidote for technocracy', *Public Administration Review*, vol. 30 (1970), pp. 314–25; and his 'Four systems of politics, policy and choice', ibid., vol. 32 (1972), pp. 298–310. Also directly relevant is the work of Martin Landau on the necessity for redundancy in complex decision processes. See his 'Federalism, redundancy and system reliability', *Publius*, vol. 3 (1973), pp. 173–96.

16 See, for example, how the Birmingham Public Works Department describes its planning skills in relation to central government in Jerry Webman, *Political Structure and Urban Redevelopment: A Comparative Study of Lyon and Birmingham*, thesis (New Haven: Yale University, 1977), p. 59.

17 The concept of network or *réseau* is used by Thoenig in many of his articles. The most complete account is probably his 'La relation entre le centre et la périphérie en France', *Bulletin de l'Institut International d'Administration Publique*, vol. 36 (1975), pp. 77–123. Pierre Grémion makes his concept of *complicité* the organizing idea of his excellent book, *Le Pouvoir Périphérique: Bureaucrates et Notables dans le Système Politique Français* (Paris: Seuil, 1976). A more concrete study of interlocking mayors and administrators in the north of France is Jeanne Becquart-

Leclerq, *Paradoxes du Pouvoir Local* (Paris: Presses de la Fondation Nationale des Sciences Politiques, 1976). These works will be further described in Chapter 5. See also the section on micro-studies in the Appendix.

18 Cabinet confidentiality means that we know very little of controversies at the highest level of government. Without doubt the best source is Richard Crossman, *The Diaries of a Cabinet Minister*, Vol. 1 (London: New York: Holt, Rinehart and Winston, 1975) which gives details on his experience as Minister of Housing and Local Government, and Vol. 3 (1977) which describes his work as Secretary of State for Social Services.

19 The Ministry of Finance and National Economy was split in the French government formed in 1978. There are now separate Ministries of the Budget and the National Economy. Throughout this study the Ministry will be referred to in its earlier form.

20 There is an excellent study dealing not only with the national infighting involved in the formation of the Ministry of Infrastructure in 1966, but also with its regional and departmental organization. See Jean-Claude Thoenig, *L'Ère des Technocrats: le Cas des Ponts et Chaussées* (Paris: Editions d'Organisation, 1973). In 1978 the Ministry of Infrastructure was also divided, between a Minister of Transport and a Secretary of State for Housing who also heads a new Ministry of the Environment and Quality of Life. Throughout this study the reference will be to the single ministry.

21 An influential administrative organizer within government was Edgar Pisani, who became the first Minister of Infrastructure. See his essay, 'Administration de gestion: administration de mission', *Revue Française de Science Politique*, vol. 6 (1956), pp. 315–30. Throughout the early years of the Fifth Republic there were numerous unofficial groups, such as the Club Jean Moulin, considering how best to modernize the French state. An active participant and influential high civil servant was Francois Bloch-Lainé who outlines some of his experiences in *Profession: Fonctionnaire* (Paris: Seuil, 1977).

22 J.-C. Thoenig, 'Local government institutions and the contemporary evolution of French society', in V. Wright and J. Lagroye (eds), *Local Government in Britain and France* (London: Allen & Unwin, 1979), p. 92.

23 The constitution of the Fifth Republic does not mention the *tutelle*, but Article 72 provides that the communes 'freely administer themselves' under the conditions of 'administrative control'. For a good introduction to this practice, see Brian Chapman, *Introduction to French Local Government* (London: Allen and Unwin, 1953), pp. 124–43. Also Paul Bernard, *Le Grand Tournant des Communes de France* (Paris: Colin, 1969), pp. 225–44. The last major work on the topic was R. Maspétiol and P. Laroque, *La Tutelle Administrative* (Paris: Sirey, 1930). For recent changes see Chapter 7 and Douglas E. Ashford, 'La tutelle financière: new wine in old bottles?', in D. Ashford (ed.), *National Resources and Urban Policy* (Methuen: New York and London, 1980).

24 There are some excellent studies of the development of British services over the nineteenth century, most of them relying heavily on local government. See, for example, Derek Fraser, *The Evolution of the British Welfare State* (London: Macmillan, 1973); Gillian Sutherland (ed.), *Studies in the Growth of Nineteenth-Century Government* (London: Routledge & Kegan Paul, 1972); and Oliver MacDonagh, *Early Victorian Government 1830–1870* (London: Weidenfeld and Nicolson, 1977).

25 J. D. Stewart, *Management in Local Government: A Viewpoint* (London: Knight, 1971), p. 2.

26 See, for example, L. J. Sharpe, 'Theories and values of local government', *Political Studies*, vol. 18 (1970), pp. 153–74. He expresses discomfort with the possibility that the growth of services will become 'incipient syndicalism,' which he hopes can be countered by subjecting professionals to local influences.

27 See the Committee on the Management of Local Government (Maud Report), op. cit., pp. 22–67; and also the dissent of Wheatley, pp. 154–7. In the Royal Commission on Local Government in England (Redcliffe-Maud Report), op. cit., there are strong recommendations on pp. 123–9.

28 In the midst of the reorganization a guidebook was issued for the new internal organization, *The New Local Authorities: Management and Structure* (Bains Report) (London: HMSO, 1972). There was a surge in local government management literature at the time which will be cited in Chapter 5, but good summaries are to be found in Royston Greenwood *et al., In Pursuit of Corporate*

Rationality: Organizational Developments in the Post-Reorganization Period (Birmingham: Institute of Local Government Studies, n.d. [1976]); and R. A. W. Rhodes, 'Ordering urban change: corporate planning in the government of English cities', in V, Wright and J. Lagroye (eds), op. cit., pp. 127–49.

29   See *Les Villes: l'Urbanisation* (Paris: Commissariat Général du Plan, 1970), p. 21. For additional details on urban pressures see I. B. Thompson, *Modern France: A Social and Economic Geography* (London: Butterworth, 1970), pp. 49–51. This provides valuable additional background to urban and demographic change. See also G. Veyret-Verner, 'France', in Roland Jones (ed.), *Essays on World Urbanization* (London: George Philip, 1975), pp. 195–203. This article includes three pages of additional bibliography on French urban development.

30   On the rate of urbanization in Britain see Table 2 of 'Introduction', to Camilla Lambert and David Weir (eds), *Cities in Modern Britain* (London: Fontana, 1975). Also A. G. Champion, 'The United Kingdom,' in Jones, op. cit., pp. 47–66, which has a long bibliography on British urban growth. The classic study of British urbanization with additional information is Peter Hall *et al.*, *The Containment of Urban England* (London: Allen & Unwin, 1973).

31   From Alan T. Peacock and Jack Wiseman, *The Growth of Public Expenditure in the United Kingdom* rev. edn (London: Allen & Unwin, 1967), pp. 153, 164 and 203, and *National Income and Expenditures 1979* (London: HMSO, 1979), including both current and capital expenditure. These trends will be further analyzed in Chapters 6 and 7.

32   *The Economist*, 23 August 1902, p. 1323. The rapid growth of transfers was made by Conservatives and was a way of avoiding local change while also favoring the landowners. See Douglas E. Ashford, 'The financial subordination of local government in Victorian England', in D. Ashford (ed.), *Financing Urban Government in the Welfare State* (London: Croom Helm, 1980).

33   Christine André *et al.*, 'Les dépenses publiques françaises depuis un siècle', *Économie et Statistiques*, no. 43 (March 1973), p. 8. It should be noted that the French state budget does not include social security.

34   See Maurice Bordes, *L'Administration Provinciale et Municipale en France au XVIIe Siècle* (Paris: Société d'Études d'Enseignement Supérieur, 1972), or the useful source book of Roger Mettam (ed.), *Government and Society in Louis XIV's France* (London: Macmillan, 1977). On seventeenth and eighteenth century Britain see J. H. Plumb, *The Growth of Political Stability in England 1675–1725* (Harmondsworth: Penguin, 1969).

35   There are excellent local political histories for Britain and France. For example, see Derek Fraser, *Urban Politics in Victorian England* (London: Leicester University Press, 1976), and Ken Young, *Local Politics and the Rise of Party* (London: Leicester University Press, 1975). On France, Georges Dupeux, *Aspects de l'Histoire Sociale et Politique du Loir-et-Cher, 1848–1914* (Paris: Imprimerie National, 1962). Additional sources can be found in the Appendix.

36   There is no need to recapitulate the controversies over how best to study community power. There is a good overview of this era in contemporary political science by Willis D. Hawley and James H. Svara, *The Study of Community Power: A Bibliographic Survey* (Santa Barbara, Calif.: ABC Clio, 1972).

37   See W. J. M. MacKenzie, *Theories of Local Government* (Greater London Paper) (London: London School of Economics, 1961). A survey of various approaches rather than theories is W. Hardy Wickwar, *The Political Theory of Local Government* (Columbia, SC: University of South Carolina Press, 1970).

38   James W. Fesler, *Area and Administration* (University, Ala.: University of Alabama Press, 1949), p. 153. This is the last sentence in his excellent book. It is, I think, much better than his well-known article, 'Approaches to the understanding of decentralization', *Journal of Politics*, vol. 27 (1965), pp. 536–66, which centers too heavily on the not very useful question of sovereignty. An interesting extension of the centralization debate into the policy literature is Lennart Lundquist, *Means and Goals of Decentralization* (Malmo, Sweden: Studentlitterature, 1972). See also the useful summary of Norman Furniss, 'The practical significance of decentralization', *Journal of Politics*, vol. 36 (1974), pp. 958–82; and Samuel A. Kirkpatrick, 'Multidimensional aspects of local political systems: a conceptual approach to public policy', *Western Political Quarterly*, vol. 23 (1970), pp. 808–28.

39   See Charles Debbasch (ed.), *La Déconcentration pour la Renovation de l'État* (Paris: PUF, 1976); Claude Alphandery (ed.), *Pour Nationaliser l'État* (Paris:

Seuil, 1968); Philippe Galy, *Gérer l'État* (Paris: Berger-Levrault, 1977). Not unrelated to this observation is the fact that French writers almost always capitalize 'state'.

40 Yves Mény, *Centralisation et Décentralisation dans le Débat Politique*, Libraire Générale de Droit et de Jurisprudence, p. 41, places the first usage of the term *déconcentration* in 1852. There is also an extended discussion in George Dawson, *L'Évolution des Structures de l'Administration Locale Déconcentrée en France* (Paris: Libraire Générale de Droit et de Jurisprudence, 1969).

41 Charles Roig, 'Théorie et réalité de la décentralisation', *Revue Française de Science Politique*, vol. 126 (1966), p. 464.

42 Jean-Claude Thoenig, *State Bureaucracies and Local Government in France* (Paris: CNRS, 1975), p. 8, and Pierre Grémion, op. cit., p. 294.

43 Mark Kesselman and Donald Rosenthal, *Local Power and Comparative Politics* (Professional Papers in Comparative Politics) (Beverly Hills, Calif.: Sage Publications, 1974), p. 22. See also their discussion on the necessity of joining policy and politics in local government studies, ibid., pp. 30–3.

44 A. Peyrefitte (ed.), *Décentraliser les Responsibilités. Pourquoi? Comment?* (Paris: La Documentation Française, 1976). This is a report prepared for President Pompidou by the Crozier group. He died before action could be taken, but it remains a valuable guide to thinking in the early 1970s.

45 The government held an inquiry and appointed a Commissioner to run the borough. The issue finally disappeared when Clay Cross vanished in the implementation of reorganization in 1974. An earlier incident in 1921 that took on national significance was the refusal of Poplar, a London borough and a Labour stronghold, to accept surcharges (fines) after rejecting national poor law policy. The mayor and twenty-nine councillors went to prison, but the government finally adjusted the subsidy for the poor. See the full account in Bryan Keith-Lucas and Peter G. Richards, *A History of Local Government in the Twentieth Century* (London: Allen & Unwin, 1978), pp. 65–91.

46 See the account in *New Society* (19 August 1976). Labour had used a circular in 1966 to push for the modernization of secondary schools. The 1970 Conservative government relaxed compliance, and the 1974 Labour government sought new statutory powers. The issue flared again when Manchester County Council used its discretionary funds in 1978 to support the old grammar schools. See *The Times* (London), 11 February 1978. In 1979 the Thatcher government created an entirely new program to save more exclusive schools.

47 Owen A. Hartley, 'The relationship between central and local authorities', *Public Administration* (UK), vol. 49 (1971), p. 439. For an earlier assessment that expresses similar scepticism see Sir Francis Hill, 'The partnership in theory and practice', *Political Quarterly*, vol. 37 (1966), pp. 169–79.

48 The National Council will be described in more detail in Chapter 6. Though clearly a significant institutional innovation in a system that rarely innovates, it is questionable if it is able (or intended) to change the fundamental central–local pattern. In fact the ministers involved made this very clear at its inception. See John A. Taylor, 'A critical analysis of the origins and development of the consultative council on local government finance', 1978, unpublished ms.

49 Central Policy Review Staff, *Relations between Central Government and Local Authorities* (London: HMSO, 1977), pp. 1–2. The report was promptly rejected by most ministers dealing with local government matters. It was discussed in the National Council and nothing more has been done to consider its suggestions.

50 The same was true of the debates on Scottish and Welsh devolution in 1977 and 1978. On the London debate see the excellent case study by Frank Smallwood, *Greater London: The Politics of Metropolitan London* (New York: Bobbs-Merrill, 1965). Labour has a historic attachment to London but was also exploiting the declining fortunes of the Conservative Party in the early 1960s for electoral reasons. When Labour came to power in 1964 nothing was done to reverse the Conservative legislation.

51 See, for example, Samuel H. Beer, 'The modernization of American federalism', *Publius*, vol. 3 (1973), pp. 49–96. This entire issue of *Publius* is given over to problems of federal relationships in the modern state. Policy problems of the federal state appear in another issue, 'Dialogues on decentralization,' *Publius*, vol. 6 (1976). Both nationalist and financial disparities have made the transformation of central–local relations an acute problem in Canada. See Richard Simeon, *Federal-Provincial Diplomacy*, (Toronto: University of Toronto Press, 1972); and

Donald V. Smiley, *Canada in Question: Federalism in the Seventies* (Toronto: McGraw-Hill Ryerson, 1972). For similar views by scholars interested in micro-level studies, see Terry Nichols Clark, 'Community autonomy in the national system: federalism, localism and decentralization', *Social Science Information*, vol. 12 (1972), pp. 101–28; and G. Ross Stephens, 'State centralization and the erosion of local autonomy', *Journal of Politics*, vol. 36 (1974), pp. 44–76.

52 See Victor Convert, 'Les communes françaises à l'aube du VIIe Plan', *Moniteur* (14 February 1975), pp. 15–22.

53 By special law, two large cities, Lyon and Marseilles, have larger municipal councils. The newly formed Paris council has 109 members. See M. Etienne, *Le Statut de Paris* (Paris: Berger-Levrault, 1975). Paris has seen a fierce struggle to provide elected government. It was finally provided by Giscard d'Estaing in 1976, after more than a century of prefectoral rule. Tocqueville said 'Paris is not the state', but it does provide nearly 40 percent of the personal income taxes paid in France. Until Chirac in 1977, the last elected mayor was Bailly in 1870. For an account of the struggle to 'liberate' Paris, see Louis Chevalier, *L'Assassinat de Paris* (Paris: Calmann-Levy, 1977).

54 The diversity of the communes makes their classification a major methodological decision, and the Ministry of the Interior, the Ministry of Finance and the census all use slightly different classifications. A good overall set of categories is provided by Thoenig, op. cit. See also, P. Kukawa *et al., Recherche sur la Structure du Pouvoir Local en Milieu Urbain* (Grenoble: Institut d'Études Politiques, 1969); and Centre de Recherche et de Documentation sur les Collectivités Locales (CEDERCOL), *Rapport sur les Problèmes de Methode Posés par la Construction d'une Typologie des Finances Locales* (Paris: Ministry of the Interior, 1969).

55 Calculated from list of Senator–mayors prepared by the Senate after the 1975 cantonal elections.

56 The actual number varies, of course, with resignations and deaths of deputies. This number follows the May 1977 local elections, and was prepared by the Service des Informations of the National Assembly. Médard arrives at roughly the same proportion for 1970 in 'La recherche du cumul de mandats par les candidats aux élections legislatives sous la Cinquième République', in A. Mabileau (ed.), *Les Facteurs Locaux de la Vie Politique Nationale* (Paris: Pedone (Centre d'Études Politiques sur la Vie Locale, University of Bordeaux), 1972), pp. 139–59.

57 Though I shall return to the provision of services in Chapters 5 and 6, the difference from France is suggested by Robin Hambleton's assessment of area committees and policymaking as 'hopelessly fragmented'. See his 'Policies for areas', *Local Government Studies* (New Series), vol. 3 (1977), p. 23.

58 Additional details can be found in Jackson, op. cit., pp. 97–100; and Richards, op. cit., pp. 64–7.

59 In addition to the variance in how elections are organized, the population in the counties and districts varies a great deal. A GLC councillor, for example, represents about 80,000 people; a metropolitan county councillor anywhere from 100,000 to nearly 200,000; a non-metropolitan county councillor between 50,000 and 100,000. See the averages in *Local Government Trends 1975* (London: CIPFA), pp. 9–11.

60 Northern Ireland is part of the United Kingdom, but not of Great Britain. Though it cannot be fully treated here, the British solution to the Irish question involved a federalist compromise on local government organization. See Anthony H. Birch, *Political Integration and Disintegration in the British Isles* (London: Allen & Unwin, 1977), pp. 28–97, for a succinct analysis.

61 Though now dated, the best work on these relationships remains J. A. G. Griffith, *Central Departments and Local Authorities* (London: Allen & Unwin, 1966).

62 Jean Baret, a critic of the system, speaks of the 'antagonism of functions', in *Le Fin des Politiques* (Paris: Calmann-Levy, 1962), p. 61. The same functional emphasis is made by advocates of change such as Francis de Baecque, 'Pour une politique cohérente de déconcentration', *Revue Française de Science Politique*, vol. 17 (1967), pp. 5–27.

63 Organization for Economic Co-operation and Development, *Public Expenditure Trends* (Paris: OECD, 1978), p. 25. British aggregate figures do not fully reflect social security expenditure.

64 Among the works leading us to reconsider the influence of the central administration over French politics, the most important has been Ezra Suleiman's *Politics, Power and Bureaucracy (Princeton, NJ: Princeton University Press*, 1974).

Chapter 2

BREAKING GROUND: TWO PATHS FROM MONARCHY TO DEMOCRACY

The National Government, in the past three quarters of a century, has successively 'bought' the rights of inspection, audit, supervision, initiative, criticism and control in respect to one local government service after another, and of one kind of local governing body after another, by the grant in aid of local finances, and therefore of the local ratepayers, of annual subventions from the National Exchequer. – Sidney Webb

I wish that the French date their happiness from the institution of the prefects. – Napoleon I

The relationship between central and local authority is a long-standing problem in government. The institutions that evolved with the modern state vary widely, but all of them dealt with the central issue: constructing a new basis of authority, once divine rule had been successfully challenged. Until the twentieth century, this struggle often focused on the relationships between diverse local customs and powers, dating from the Middle Ages, and the new secular authorities at the center. Some of these battles are still being fought today, perhaps more fiercely in France than in Britain, but in both, from the early nineteenth century, local government has been distinct from central government. It has its own institutional character, and has become part of the national policy process as we think of it today.

To a remarkable extent the early development of the state provides the institutional distinctions that policymakers in both Britain and France recognize, and so become the outer limits of change. Indeed, if we are to see local reorganization as a structural problem of deep significance to the modern state, we must first recapture the definitions of 'central' and 'local' as they originated and became institutionalized in earlier centuries.

The essential difference between Britain and France in the conceptualization of central–local relationships is captured by the term *l'État*. Though it translates with deceptive ease, there is no simple English equivalent. The state evolved more slowly in France than in Britain where fundamental authority relationships began to take shape in the Middle Ages and achieved a recognizable, if not entirely workable, form in the Tudor period. Unification came about more slowly and painfully in France. The persistence of religious wars, dynastic rivalries and regional sentiments delayed and complicated the creation of the French *État*. Though the elements of

French government began to be assembled in the sixteenth century,[1] the unified France we think of today was not clearly visible until the age of Napoleon. As we shall see in more detail, the monarchy did little to untangle the complexities of French local politics, and the aristocracy was unable to devise a new relationship between center and locality. In the 1791 Constitution, the Revolution produced the first modern definition of the 'one and indivisible republic' and its relation to local authority, but retained much from the *ancien régime*.[2]

The definition of the state, itself a prerequisite to a definition of local authority, became a national preoccupation in France. French ideas of sovereignty were developed by Bodin, Rousseau and Montesquieu, but a strong local element has always been present in French thinking about the organization of public authority. From the Revolution to the end of the Napoleonic empire, France tried five constitutions. In all of them, and in those that followed, a major concern was how to circumscribe and limit local authority as well as how the state should delegate authority to lower levels of government. That the basic structure remained virtually the same throughout the constitutional debates and the vast works on administrative law is further testimony to the persistence of local influence in the modern French state. The tension between central authority and local political forces has always been greater in France than in Britain. A comparison of local reorganization can have little validity unless such tensions are taken into account, however difficult they may be to quantify.

The fundamental issue of central–local relations was resolved much earlier in Britain. Britain maintained a continuity of local institutions that in France was sharply broken by the Revolution. The Stuart kings tried to increase their power, but steadily lost ground to the aristocracy and gentry. In the evolution of central and local politics in Britain and France, the most dramatic historical contrast is the insignificant role of localities in the major national political struggles of Britain until the nineteenth century. The absence of such a struggle in Britain, as well as the more orderly evolution of the modern state, made the formulation of public law a less pressing issue. The shires dated from Norman times, possibly earlier, and for much of Britain the relation between central and local influence remained basically unchanged until the late nineteenth century. The Protectorate experienced more difficulty in reconciling army factions to government than it did local government,[3] while the revolution of 1688 caused no serious discontinuities at the local level. As J. H. Plumb notes, there was in Britain a 'unanimity of attitude among officeholders' and a 'harmony between offices' that France did not achieve until the nineteenth century.[4]

FRENCH ARISTOCRACY AND LOCAL ADMINISTRATION

The way in which the privileged classes related to the monarch, to the nascent parliamentary institutions and to the provinces is a key element in the transformation of central–local relations in the two societies. Tocqueville epitomized the difference between the British and French nobilities when he observed that in France the aristocracy preserved its privileges but lost power, while in Britain they lost their privileges but gained power. A key difference is that the French nobility at court preserved few institutional or social links to provincial France, whereas the British nobility remained deeply involved with both government and society in the counties.

In France the rudiments of parliamentary power were terminated after 1614, when the monarch decided not to recall the Estates General. As a result, the nobles (the Second Estate) never acquired a corporate forum similar to that provided by the British parliaments. As one French writer noted, 'A nobleman, if he lives at home in the province, lives free but without substance; if he lives at court, he is taken care of, but enslaved.'[5] The nobility was immune from most taxes. The small amounts raised by a *capitation* (head tax) based on social rank were inadequate, and the low income tax or *dixième* introduced in 1710 was difficult to collect. The nobility's interest in court offices became increasingly focused on the pensions and favors attached to them,[6] which in turn made the nobles increasingly dependent on the monarch.

The French aristocracy acquired neither the financial nor the political power that enabled the English nobility to transfer their influence to the development of Parliament. The system of *venalité*, or sale of office, left a divided class that melted away with the Revolution.[7] While the size of the British aristocracy changed very little in the eighteenth century, the French aristocracy grew to as many as 200,000 persons.[8] They held nearly all the offices in the complex array of royal courts, but the manipulations of the kings and the sheer complexity of the courts prevented them from establishing an effective institutional base. Nor did they gain respect in the provinces, where they were exempt from the *taille* or land tax, military service, the quartering of troops, the *gabelle* or salt tax, and the *corvée* or obligatory labor on local projects. Although noble families in some provinces remained powerful and even rich, they did not unite to resist royal absolutism.[9] The Montmorency line in Languedoc, the Condé in Picardy and the Guise in Burgundy, for example, kept their regional identities, but had no role in shaping the new French institutions.

As the monarchy was reinforced throughout the seventeenth and eighteenth centuries, the aristocracy that had a provincial base realized that recalling the Estates General would challenge their local influence, while those at the royal court were helpless.[10] The organization of the monarchy did not provide institutional lines that the nobility might have controlled had they been able to agree on their interests. The sovereign courts of the eighteenth century have been described as 'complexity bordering on utter confusion',[11] with three distinct frameworks for monarchical rule: Gascony, Guyenne, and the southwest of France remained *pays d'élection* and maintained local courts and state offices with some degree of local autonomy; Burgundy, Dauphiné, and northern France, the *pays d'états*, were under the monarchical influence of royal commissioners; and in the rest of France, which had been forcibly brought under the monarchy and was known as the *pays d'imposition*, direct administrative rule was imposed by royal governors or *intendants*.[12]

Moreover, nearly all offices and agents of the monarch existed as judicial bodies, whose complexity was superimposed on the three monarchical structures just noted. On the eve of the Revolution there were forty provincial governors, thirty-three *généralités* or regional administrative areas, initially designated to facilitate tax collection, and thirty-two intendancies.[13] In addition to the overlapping mixture of courts surrounding the king, the *parlements* registered and conveyed royal justice in the major cities. There was of course no territorial consistency to this bewildering array of courts.[14] The most important of the *parlements*, of which there were thirteen at the end of the *ancien régime*, was that of Paris, which was almost continually in conflict with the king.[15] In the more powerful provinces, such as Provence and Brittany, provincial estates continued to meet and were frequently in conflict with the king's intendants. Though Louis XIV recognized the need for legal reform, the need to collect money unfortunately overcame the reorganization efforts of Colbert, his most prominent minister.[16]

Amid the confusing array of administrative institutions set in motion under the Bourbons, the office of intendant was established to facilitate the collection of money for the wars and the court activities essential to monarchical life. In comparison with the royal courts, *parlements*, and military organization, the intendants were a fairly late innovation of the *ancien régime*. Pagès finds *intendants des finances* being appointed in 1554,[17] but they were appointed to supplement the existing financial administration of the monarch and were linked to the reorganization of the *bureaux des finances* in the late sixteenth century. They seem to have taken hold at an early date, however, and by 1577 were in control of these new agencies, though Richelieu saw them as having diverse roles.[18] Like the other members of the royal courts, the early intendants were nobles and personal agents of the king. Early in the seventeenth century they were used more widely to supervise finance, justice and the police.

The intendants began to serve in the provinces as territorially based agents of the king in the late seventeenth century. The movement of the intendants from the *généralité*, in effect a regional office of the court, to the province took place at various times, depending on the ferocity of local resistance to taxation and the strength with which the local nobility claimed its prerogatives. By 1690 intendants were at work in all the provinces, with such strong provincial estates as Brittany and Provence among the last to accept them. There was however no uniform relationship between the provincial intendants and the older territorial organization of the royal courts and agencies. In Normandy, for example, the provincial intendant covered three *généralités*.[19] Only in the *pays d'imposition*, Lorraine, Roussillon, Franche-Comté and Alsace, did they rule without the interference of other royal officers.[20] They were firmly implanted by Colbert, Louis XIV's strongest minister but, not surprisingly, they were seen as a threat by the nobility in other offices and soon developed a reputation for excessive zeal. They were often in conflict with the *parlements* and provincial estates and were driven out of southwest France during the mid-seventeenth century rebellion known as the Fronde.[21]

Like most of the administrators of the *ancien régime*, the intendants had become a very mixed group by the eighteenth century. Though they were originally recruited from the highest court ranks, the *maîtres des requêtes* of the Conseil d'État, their offices were soon being passed from father to son and freely purchased.[22] The relation of the intendants to the local nobility varied greatly from one region to another, as did the strength of provincial estates, provincial governors and *parlements*. Like the prefects of the nineteenth century, the intendants had to form their own alliances and compacts with local political forces, and sometimes became the defenders of local interests. Toward the end of the *ancien régime*, highly successful former intendants such as Turgot played increasingly important national roles in trying to cope with the growing financial crisis of the French state.[23] In the last days of the monarchy, Necker, who followed Turgot in a desperate effort to stabilize the currency, tried to use intendants to create a functional organization of the royal court, but his efforts had no lasting effect.[24] In 1789 the Constituent Assembly abolished the office and France embarked on its first experiment with autonomous local government. This lasted until 1800 when Napoleon appointed the prefects, who were contemporary versions of the intendants.

LOCAL STRENGTH OF BRITISH ARISTOCRACY

The British monarchs were no less eager to control local affairs than the French Bourbons, but discovered early that it was impossible for them to do so. The Tudor monarchs still relied on the skeletal local organization provided by the sheriffs, the lords lieutenant of the counties and the justices of the peace. While the system remained essentially judicial as in France, it never became the basis for the construction of a modern state. Plumb has pointed out that the inability of the Tudors to create a class of royal officials left them unable to control the countryside, contributing to the growth of parliamentary government from the sixteenth century onward and to the close relationship between local government and the House of Commons.[25]

The rapid creation of British peers and noblemen in the early seventeenth century might have gone in the direction of sale and abuse of office as in France, but did not. While the French had no monopoly on *venalité*, the persistence of royal absolutism made it a form of government, destroying potential links between provincial and central aristocracy and eventually undermining the monarchy itself. In contrast, the British House of Commons in 1675 made it illegal for members to accept an office for profit, referring specifically to the Crown.[26] Trevelyan concludes that the revolution of 1688 'effectively checkmated the attempt of the Crown to control the local authorities'.[27]

From very early in Britain's political development, local government was closely linked to parliamentary power. Plumb contends that the local power of the aristocracy was the basis of all political power in the eighteenth century. The beginnings of modern cabinet government date from Walpole's skillful manipulation of local offices through the lords lieutenant of the counties. The Duke of Newcastle, for example, was Lord Lieutenant of three counties, Sussex, Nottingham and Middlesex, for most of his life. This manipulation, however, was not directed, as in France, to the support of absolutism, but to the support of the aristocracy. From these links came the interdependence of county and parliamentary government that determined the direction in which local political authority developed in Britain. Beneath the lords lieutenant were the justices of the peace, who supervised local government over most of Britain until the Local Government Act of 1888. In Plumb's words, 'If the Lord Lieutenancy was the loom upon which the pattern of local patronage was woven, the justices of the peace were its restless shuttles.'[28]

Unable to exploit the opportunities of a royal court as effectively as the French monarchs in their attempts to preserve their authority, the British monarchs might have turned to more direct means of manipulating Parliament itself. But the English Revolution of 1688 deprived them of the right to establish parliamentary boroughs, as most constituencies were then called. The House of Commons was built on aristocratic control of the rudimentary local governments. The early eighteenth century Parliament of 509 members, for example, was based on eighty English counties, twelve Welsh counties, and 218 parliamentary boroughs.[29] This is not to claim that Parliament was in any sense representative. The creation of parliamentary boroughs under the Tudors and Stuarts placed a quarter of the members in southwest England; Cornwall alone had forty-four members.[30] But the 'pocket boroughs' in the hands of aristocrats and their select circles of friends unified local and national elites in support of Parliament.[31]

The dramatic difference between France and Britain in the emergence of local government is, of course, rooted deeply in the constitutional restraints the English aristocracy was able to place on the monarchy from the Magna Carta onward. Beneath this legal struggle, however, is the political role that the British aristocracy fashioned for itself, which included making localities their own preserve. In doing this, new sources of influence and new political opportunities were exploited in ways that never occurred in France. Indeed, the British aristocracy transformed itself into a more influential class than the French nobility, although its claim to privilege rested with much smaller numbers.[32] In addition to the peers, the gentry and freemen also struggled to share in the national and local power that the aristocracy had claimed from the monarch. H. J. Habakkuk has described the gentry as a unique feature of English society, 'distinct from the great territorial aristocracy, on the one hand, and the smaller freeholder and tenant farmer on the other'.[33] The origin of the gentry is a subject of historical debate,[34] but for our purposes it is the emergence of this large, landed class that becomes the crucial link between local and national authority. The gentry were the original 'men of property' who proliferated in minor government offices, above all at the local level. 'Difficult to discipline, secure in their self-importance, [they] became the leaders of political opinion outside London and the great towns.'[35]

The creation of a gentry did not mean that relationships between the aristocracy and its local appendages were tranquil. Walpole was constantly struggling to control the factions in his holdings at Castle Rising, for example, and the county of Essex went to the polls eleven times between 1689 and 1714.[36] Some of the great lords, such as Newcastle and Bedford, kept relatively secure parliamentary footholds among the boroughs and counties, but such maneuvers were expensive, and disputes over the outcomes of elections were bitter. The money spent by the French nobility to purchase offices as sinecures was used in Britain to provide lavish election banquets and to fight disputed parliamentary contests. The landed aristocracy was known to spend nearly ten thousand pounds on an election, and contesting a parliamentary election meant taking witnesses to London and housing and supporting them for weeks, at a cost that often reached several thousand pounds.[37]

The aristocracy, of course, was not unlike the politically powerful of every age in coveting remunerative positions. Among the choicest were those of the Tellers of the Exchequer and the Wardenship of the Cinque Ports, each carrying pensions of thousands of pounds.[38] Admittedly the British aristocracy and gentry were not immune to the indulgences and frivolity found in France. The crucial difference was that the British upper classes accepted responsibility for their national and local governments and, however reluctantly, paid taxes and kept order. Thus, during the years the French nobility was divided by the Revolution and Napoleon, Britain's expanded upper class, strongly entrenched at the local level, was at the pinnacle of its power, where it remained well into the nineteenth century.

The transformation of the ruling elite had important political implications for each country, but in many ways it was the refashioned bureaucracy that became the crucial agent of the modern state. In this respect, Britain and France differ greatly. Thus, the development of the French administrative apparatus, rooted in the *ancien régime*, preceded political change and the rudimentary political parties of the nineteenth century. Whereas in Britain the aristocracy and landed gentry captured control of local administration before the nineteenth century expansion of the state, and their ability to influence the monarchy rested in part on the local services they provided and the local patronage they used to reinforce their control of Parliament.

A different link with local administration developed in Britain, through the office of justice of the peace. Though it stemmed from the judicial prerogatives of the Crown, it became a political office. If the lords lieutenant of the counties were the political bosses, the justices of the peace were the ward heelers. Their transformation into political agents of the aristocracy emerged in the last stages of monarchical absolutism in Britain and became one of the factors that ended Stuart rule. Like Walpole in the eighteenth century, James II had reliable lords lieutenant who helped provide him with a docile Parliament. Royal charters carrying special powers and privileges were used to influence the growing towns and cities, and to create parliamentary boroughs that would support the king. A committee of the Privy Council organized in 1679 to purge the justices of the peace suggests the growing local power of the aristocracy.[39] There was even a trace of the intendant in James II's board of regulators, whose agents were to assess the political situation in the parliamentary boroughs.[40]

Originally there was a justice for each 'hundred', a feudal division of the county. They assembled at the county level in quarter sessions to deal as a group with serious crimes and offenses. Though the justices date from the fourteenth century, the period of their growth corresponds to that of the French intendants. Under the Elizabethan Poor Law of 1601 they became the overseers of public assistance. Under the Tudors, 170 Acts added to their duties. By the seventeenth century they were responsible for keeping the peace; regulating prices, wages, and apprenticeships; maintaining highways and bridges; and enforcing the licensing, game and poor laws. Their task was, in Mingay's words, 'not merely arduous but complex and exacting'.[41] Their numbers understandably grew rapidly in the early sixteenth century, doubling in Kent, Norfolk, Northamptonshire, Somerset and many other counties. The eighteenth century justices of the peace formed the bedrock of parliamentary institutions. Trevelyan describes the House of Commons as the 'national Quarter Sessions at Westminster'.[42] Until the Municipal Corporations Act of 1835 they represented central government at all local levels, and in the counties they continued their functions until the Local Government Act of 1888.

A number of factors contributed to their gradual demise, for instance, the lavish use of parish funds for election bribery and patronage. Though many were lazy and dishonest, this characteristic was hardly unique to Britain's nascent bureaucracy, but the rise of the Whig aristocracy had depended heavily on its manipulation of the justices of the peace.[43] They were considered unreliable and inefficient agents of government by the Benthamites, who became the architects of the new local government system.[44] In any event, the political role of the British justices of the peace in the eighteenth century anticipates the political activity of the French prefects in the nineteenth. Conceivably the justices of the peace and their Quarter Sessions could have become a counterpart to that of French prefects. But by the end of the nineteenth century it was clear that they were unable to fulfil the requirements of an expanding government and were incompatible with strong political parties.

The justices of the peace in Victorian England were confined to a judicial role. Nevertheless, the importance of the justices and of the Quarter Sessions in defining the relationship between central and local authority cannot be overemphasized, because they provided a parliamentary stability that enabled local elites to define central–local relationships. The effects were momentous for the political development of Britain.

Until late in the nineteenth century there were few further territorial subdivisions of parliamentary representation, and the qualifications to hold local office. The core of the argument over local government reorganization in 1888 was whether county government would be preserved for the aristocracy and gentry. The tension between town and country was, and in many respects remains, at the very root of tensions within the British subnational system.[45] If France was locked into the remnants of the intendant's administrative system until the Third Republic, Britain was no less locked into the political framework generated by the justices of the peace until 1888.[46]

PREFECTS AND COMMISSIONERS: THE PARTING OF THE WAYS

In both France and Britain the formation of the modern state was a turbulent process. By the nineteenth century the basic local structures were visible in both countries, but possibly more so in France. In both countries the residue from the period of royal absolutism and divine rule was vital in shaping the relationship between central and local authority. Revolutionary France restored the intendants in the form of the prefects, '*empereurs au petit pied*', as Napoleon dubbed them. The prefects have been described as having 'all the advantages of the ancient absolute agents without any of their inconveniences'.[47] Under the Benthamite impulse Britain developed a system of commissions and boards to deal with local affairs that rivaled in complexity the Bourbon court. Thus, in a strange way Britain's utilitarians introduced into the nineteenth century what France had managed to leave behind. To this day that crucial choice affects the problems of reorganization in both countries.

During most of the nineteenth century, national politics was relatively unimportant for local government in both France and England. The succession of republics, monarchies and empires preceding the French Third Republic responded fairly well to the needs of the bourgeoisie, just as the surge of reform in early nineteenth century Britain left the old and new middle class comfortably in control. In terms of the local political system, the changes were largely administrative. The first steps in forging the links between national and local administration were taken during the Revolution and by Napoleon in France, and in poor law reform and by the Benthamites in Britain.

Though we often think of the French Revolution in connection with other matters, and immense amount of work on the organization of local government was done from 1789 to the end of the Napoleonic Empire. The inadequacy of the French territorial structure had been recognized in the closing days of the *ancien régime*. When Turgot asked the intendant of Limousin to trace the roads in his *généralité*, the embarrassed official confessed that the territorial limits were not known.[48] The provinces were somewhat better defined, but were based on social and ethnic traditions that had little bearing on the needs of modern government. Necker tried to restore provincial assemblies as a counterweight to the *parlements*, but they proved to be even more recalcitrant in the business of administrative reform than the *parlements* themselves.[49] Some maps for a reorganization of France had been drawn but they were not influential because the final decisions of the Revolutionary period, like most policy decisions, were the product of the political forces of the moment. The result was that French departments were first named after their languages, as in Languedoc, or their ancient inhabitants, as in Brittany, Normandy and Burgundy. Even this minor concession to local interests appeared threatening to the Assembly, and the departments finally were given names of wholly geographic origin.[50]

Under the influence of the constitutionalist Abbé Sieyès the Constituent Assembly passed a motion to divide the country into new departments for 'representation and administration'.[51] A revolutionary committee, perhaps the first true board of national planners, was established in 1789 to redraw the map of France. There were three competing proposals. The most elaborate was by Thouret and would have formed eighty departments, each divided into nine communes, which in turn would be divided into four cantons each.[52] In effect, France would be made into a large grid reflecting the notions of equality and uniformity to which the Revolution so fervently aspired. Mirabeau, himself sympathetic to regional interests, wanted a more detailed pattern of 120 departments with no subdivisions. A small sign of the fears that increasingly gripped the revolutionary movement was Thouret's charge that Mirabeau's proposal would cripple the central administrative authority. The plan that appears to have prevailed was devised by du Port. Concessions were made in the debate to Mirabeau's local sympathies – the political organization of the departments was to be relatively decentralized: each department would have a *conseil général* chosen by an electorate of about 500 persons; beneath the department was the district, also with a council; and at the base were communes, which had actually been legalized in 1789, patterned on the old parishes.

But as a result of political dislocation in France the Constitution of 1791 was unevenly enforced, and from the dissolution of the monarchy in late 1792 until the Constitution of 1797 (An III) the relationship between central and local authority was fluid. Territorial tensions were basic elements in the revolutionary conflict. Of the 750 members of the constitutional convention, 390 came from the local administration of the *ancien régime*.[53] The Girondists were, of course, a major faction in the convention, reviving fears of a new Fronde. Nearly 200 of them were from the center and west of France. The constitutional convention is thought to have opted for single member constituencies (*scrutin uninominial*) for election to the new assembly in order to minimize the separatist influence of localities and departments on national decisions.[54] Another radical faction, the *montagnards*, themselves heavily Parisian, were aware of provincial distrust of their growing influence. When the Committee of Public Safety was formed in early 1793, the functions of the local administration were reduced.

In a provincial reaction against the Revolution, bourgeois elements, many heavily Girondist, took control of many departments in the elections of 1792. In the Jura the local councillors invited the deputies to Bourges to form a new convention, and the department of Eure raised 4,000 troops to defend the constitutional monarchy of the early revolutionary period. In all, about sixty departments rebelled, and the department of Meurthe was governed by a revolutionary commission from Paris until the end of the convention. At the height of the Terror, the *conseils généraux* were dissolved and the districts were given the powers of departmental administration. The revolutionary *procureurs* organized purges in the districts, and many of the excesses of the Terror in Paris were reproduced in the municipalities. When departmental government was restored in 1795, the disputes and hatreds generated in this period continued to divide local government.[55] The use of the districts to extend the Terror is one of the major reasons why the intermediate level of local government, the subprefect, continued to be hated in republican France; there were repeated efforts to dissolve the subprefectures even in the Third Republic.

The bourgeois reaction against the Revolution began to take shape in the First Republic. Under the constitution of 1795, government was a cumbersome arrangement of councils to initiate and pass laws, and to elect the Directory or executive. The territory of France was for the first time defined in the constitution and the departments were listed. The resurrection of provincial France and its suspicion of Paris is revealed in the decision to change the name of Paris to the 'department of the Seine', which it retained for precisely 180 years. Beneath the departments were communes and cantons. Under ministerial supervision, the departments were to elect an administration, the franchise being confined to about 500 wealthy citizens. The department also had a *commissaire*, the forerunner of the prefect, appointed by the Directory. He was to attend all meetings of the administration, could modify any of its decisions in the light of national legislation and was directly responsible to the Ministry of the Interior.[56] Though the creation of the prefects was not to come until 1800, it is important to note that the pattern of administrative supremacy was established with the *commissaires*, the successors to the intendants. As they did a century and a half later, the new middle class wanted a stable central government and wrote an elaborate constitution to obtain it, temporarily ignoring the complications of local politics and party factions.

Our vision of modern France is heavily influenced – perhaps excessively – by the First Empire, when the system of the prefect as we think of it today was created.[57] The Constitution of 1799 (An VIII) retained the complicated tiers of legislative bodies, and brought the Senate into existence. The Senate became the stronghold of local interests in later years, though it was certainly not thus designed by its architect, Sieyès, who had a hand in nearly all the constitutions of the revolutionary period. A champion of the bourgeoisie, he knew of the importance of the British middle class to political stability at both national and local levels, and aspired to create a similar stability based on middle-class rule in France.[58] The original Senate was to be the vehicle for local power and serve as the electoral arm of central government. The Senators were nominated for life by the other branches of government. Their failure to regulate Napoleonic excesses is perhaps the first evidence in modern French government that middle class rule without established power at the local level is helpless.[59] In fact, the privileged middle class learned this lesson too late to affect Napoleon. Subsequently the Senate became the stronghold of the local *notables* in the future republics and thus became a key institution in defining the relationship of center to locality in France.

The Constitution of 1799 gave local administration the form we see today. There were initially eighty-eight departments, but their numbers grew to 130 with Napoleon's conquests.[60] Under this constitution the famous law of 1800 (28 pluviose VIII) put an end to the *conseils généraux* and established prefects.[61] The first prefects came from all walks of life: deputies, royalists, ex-ministers and ambassadors, and local notables. Boullé, for example, though imprisoned in 1793 for his regional sympathies, became prefect of Côtes-du-Nord for fourteen years.[62] The initial list was prepared by Napoleon's closest advisors, including Sieyès, but Napoleon himself carefully read and amended the first appointments. The prefects were appointed by the Emperor and only he could remove them. They were graded according to the importance of their posts, and the top prefects were paid nearly as much as Senators, clearly outranking the lower-level national legislators. Napoleon described them in a letter to Fouché as 'small ministers'.[63]

Napoleon was well served by his prefects who, by keeping order in the countryside and collecting taxes and recruiting soldiers, were essential to his conduct of foreign wars. When the prefect of Parma was detained by the army, Napoleon wrote that everything should be arranged to the satisfaction of the prefect.[64] They carried heavy domestic responsibilities, and constructed the local administration that continued in modern France. In the early years of the Empire prefects selected new councils for the *arrondissements* and communes. Initially treated seriously by the prefects, with the growth of the centralized state the councils were forgotten in later years of the Empire.

The prefects prepared detailed reports on political conditions, criminal activities and public reactions to the government. Under the Concordat of 1801 they were responsible for the reorganization of church activity, and with the educational reforms of 1802 the organization of *lycées*. They supervised programs for industrial development, public works and public relief. From 1810 the prefects were given noble titles, part of Napoleon's effort to create his own nobility; and from 1813 the subprefects had titles. Napoleon's control of the prefects anticipated later experience with political purges of their ranks, as regimes and objectives have changed over the years. In fact, Napoleon's treatment of the prefects seems less brutal than many of the purges under republican governments.[65]

Beneath the departmental prefectures were the *arrondissements* with their subprefects. In general their boundaries of 1800 followed those of the districts of 1790, and 402 were established. As Legendre notes, the district had proved its 'political utility' during the Terror.[66] Suppressed during the Directorate, the district reappeared as the *arrondissement*, and became an important link permitting the administrative system to exercise political control in the localities. Many of the original subprefects were young auditors of the Conseil d'Etat, the central executive agency of Napoleon. They had no powers of their own and were purely the agents of the prefect.

The communes, too, were subject to the First Consul's direct authority. In communes of under 5,000 persons, the prefect nominated the mayor, and in the larger ones his suggestions were passed on to Napoleon. There was even a mild effort to consolidate the 44,000 communes, but as in later efforts little was accomplished. In effect the new system, with its domination by the center, reversed the intent of the 1791 Constitution, which had been to create in the communes 'a society of citizens united by their local relationships'. The result, not too surprisingly, was that the French were forced to seek other ways to exercise their political genius through the administrative structure. Their success, as we shall see, has greatly affected the political relationship between locality and center. Instead of being united along local lines, citizens now needed a way to unite against the administrative structure.

Why did the British administrative structure not become the focal point of the political system as it had in France? The Whigs and the Tories had succeeded in working out a congenial relationship between central and local politics in eighteenth century Britain, and the most amazing thing about the politics of local government in the nineteenth century is that the many changes in the responsibilities of counties and boroughs did not disrupt this political relationship. Only in 1888 did new local government legislation alter the legal and political foundations. But despite the inadequacies in the administrative structure, by the turn of the eighteenth century important changes had begun.

The early development of British local administration was remarkably similar to the prefectoral system, and to understand this we must look more closely at the group of reformers operating under the influence of Bentham. Though later ideas moved more dramatically toward a centralized state, he was always concerned that legislative and administrative practice should be organized so as to maximise the transmission of utilitarian principles to government. His *Constitutional Code* has become the subject of a serious historical debate,[67] but it is clear that local authority was to be organized around the needs of the central administration.

Benthamite disciples were to be found throughout early nineteenth century British government. In the rapid reform of the Whig government of 1831 to 1835, the Chancellor of the Exchequer, Brougham, was strongly influenced by utilitarianism; in the nascent administration were advocates like Chadwick and Nassau Senior; in Parliament were men such as Joseph Hume and Hobhouse; and to inform opinion there was the *Westminster Review*. All had the initiative and determination to conduct detailed research into Britain's local government system, and they had dedicated followers such as Place working on political tactics.[68] Whatever the source of their influence, they brought to local government and its activities a tireless energy to which the many Royal Commissions of the early nineteenth century bear testimony.

But the utilitarians in government were by no means uniformly successful. Hume's effort to liberate county government from the local gentry was persistently repulsed, and generated little more enthusiasm among the Whigs than it did among the Tories.[69] Nor were the laws on poor law reform, health and sanitation implemented as the Benthamites would have liked, to some small degree because of the stubborn arrogance of their most forceful administrative exponent, Chadwick.[70] Nevertheless, the Benthamite reforms meant a substantial growth of local government. They superimposed national inspectorates to oversee what was supposed to become a compliant and diligent local civil service. Inspectors multiplied, but not under the circumstances anticipated by the utilitarian reformers. Indeed, by the end of the century, the higher civil service could manipulate local administration more easily than their counterparts in France.

Edwin Chadwick, the 'tactless, impetuous and cocksure'[71] reformer of police, poor laws, sanitation and nearly every other aspect of British government, merits special mention. He is as responsible as any single man for that system of public assistance which was designed to force the 'able-bodied poor' back into productive, self-reliant lives. A relentless utilitarian logic demanded that care for the poor should, therefore, be at a standard below that of the productive worker. The result was the workhouse, the terror of the British working class, later described by the Webbs as 'gaols without guilt'.[72] Public relief was no more humane or generous in France at the time, but the workhouse gave a special imprint to local government in Britain. The reform placed on local governments responsibilities that became unbearable as industrial dislocation grew in severity later in the century. Chadwick, who was virtually devoid of sensitivity to personal and political relationships,[73] constantly advocated more centralization, and was a bitter critic of decentralization. To Chadwick, 'government' meant the scientific application of the new principles of political economy, and local government was to him a 'mischievous fallacy'.[74] But his proposed police reform was rejected out of hand by Lord Russell because it conflicted directly with the whole tradition of local police control.

The cost of poor relief was still borne by the parishes in the late eighteenth century. Under the dislocations of the Napoleonic wars, the forces of industrialization, and the distortions of tariffs on corn [wheat], the cost mounted rapidly.[75] There had been no basic changes in the system of public relief since the Elizabethan Poor Law of 1601. Finally change occurred when the organization recommended by the Royal Commission, appointed by the Whigs in 1832, was enacted after very little political dispute as the Poor Law Amendment Act of 1834.

The Royal Commission's 'brilliant, influential and wildly unhistorical report'[76] became a bestseller. Severely critical of the Speenhamland system, which linked rates (taxes) to the costs of relief, the report argued for more efficient and uniform local administration of relief, with close national inspection. The amendment established a system of national inspection under the Central Board of three national Commissioners who came to be called 'the three wise men of Somerset House'. The parishes were grouped into Poor Law Unions to augment their resources and to provide more efficient administration. The 600 local Boards of Guardians lasted until the Local Government Act of 1929. Their responsibilities, as we shall see below, were later assigned to new agencies that could be more easily aligned with central policy and controlled by a growing national civil service.

The law did not give the Poor Law inspectors or Assistant Commissioners the powers Chadwick thought necessary. Chadwick was also disappointed not to be appointed a Commissioner; and as Secretary to the Board he was constantly at odds with the members, who would not demand compliance from local authorities. (Liverpool, which had a reformed local government of its own making, received a dispensation from the law.[77]) In fact the local Poor Law Guardians were soon taken over by the same local gentry who ruled other local affairs, and in 1847 the chairmanship of the Commission passed back into parliamentary hands.

The second move toward centralized administration began when the Poor Law Commission was instructed in 1838 to investigate the causes of severe epidemics then sweeping the country. The Commissioners were relieved to assign their testy secretary, Chadwick, to the task. In 1842 his *Report on the Sanitary Conditions of the Labouring Population of Great Britain* appeared, no less a sensation than his earlier work on the poor laws and again advocating strong central control. But the centralizing tendencies of reformers had become more widely recognized, and Chadwick's report launched a national debate, while many of the major industrial cities, such as Manchester, Leeds and Liverpool, responded by buying out private water companies and constructing their own sanitation and sewage systems. Parliament emasculated the Public Health Act of 1848, however, and in 1854 re-formed the Poor Law Board. In 1858 the functions of the original General Board of Health were split between the Privy Council and the Home Office. When the Board of Health was reconstituted in 1854, it was, like the Poor Law Commission, subordinate to Parliament. Not until 1872 were local authorities compelled to appoint the Medical Officers who were to be the local operatives of Chadwick's national scheme. By that time administrative relationships between the center and the localities were undergoing important changes, and the final result differed from the centralized agencies envisioned by Chadwick.

Britain thus avoided the development of administrative *grands corps* of the French type, though the impulse was plainly there in the early nineteenth century. The Poor Law and Sanitation inspectors were to be technically competent and administratively armed. But the more conservative local authorities actively resisted central control while the more progressive ones moved ahead without administrative prodding. Centralization did take place, but in a context which had different implications for reorganization a century or more later. Numerous boards were appointed in the nineteenth century, but gradually they came under the framework of central government and departmental supervision. Britain was thus spared prefectoral power, but it developed its own pattern of functionally organized control that in many ways is even less suitable to the requirements of the twentieth century than the prefect.

After the peaceful revolution of 1688, the alliance of the aristocracy and the middle class dominated the House of Commons, the counties and boroughs. 'There was no friction, because the whole machinery of the constitution was now controlled and guided by one and the same class and the same interest.'[78] After the burst of reform by the Whigs and Radicals in the early 1830s, Parliament avoided local conflicts until late in the century.

In France, however, absolutism did not give way as easily. Aided by men like Richelieu, Mazarin and Colbert, the Bourbons constructed a confused hierarchical court system to unify the country. The intendant was the one court official to survive the Revolution in recognizable form. Little else was worth saving. The territorial division of the country was chaotic. The legal system remained a shambles of conflicting courts – despite royalist efforts to reform it – and provided few constructive opportunities for the nobility. The financial and budgetary processes bore no relation to the needs of a modern state.

Was rule by the British lords and aristocrats less abusive? They manipulated the local election lists and flagrantly misdirected local funds to maintain their power in Parliament; they supported poor law reform only after severe agrarian riots and the rapid rise of rates (property taxes); and their national political alliance was to restrict the franchise nearly as long as the successive regimes of nineteenth century France. Their hold on the counties and parliamentary boroughs provided political stability, as we have seen, but it also gave them a grip on public decisions at all levels of government. Until Disraeli and Gladstone, parliamentary government in Britain was the politics of faction, which had important repercussions on the early relation between local and central government. Walpole, the Pitts, Wellington, Melbourne, Peel and Palmerstone had enormous problems extracting decisions from Parliament, surviving in no small part because of the benefits and privileges to be distributed at the local level. The justices of the peace and Quarter Sessions seen from a distance may look benign when we think of the French reign of Terror, but over 200 crimes were punishable by death in early nineteenth century Britain.

We may agree with Pierre Henry's judgement that 'In reality most of the prefectures were purely and simply the model of the ancient intendancies adapted to new necessities.'[79] But we must also acknowledge the changing relationship between administration and politics at the national level. When France went from the turbulence of the Revolution to its Napoleonic adventures, the reorganization of the countryside was left in the hands of the prefects. The prefects had great authority, but it was an authority that depended on working with local leaders and populations. Although the local controls envisaged by the utilitarian reformers were never fully implemented, neither was French revolutionary romanticism possible without the mediation of prefects. Most nineteenth century prefects would understand the caution of Boucheporn, appointed intendant of Paris in

1786, who observed, 'We are not at a time when one might think that in order to approach perfection, the administration should be mysterious and complicated . . .'.[80] But the mysteries and complications of French central–local relationships were products of local demands.

The critical transformation in Britain was at the national level, and arose from efforts to impose administrative order on an established national political system. The Benthamites were influential, but little of their work endured. Under close central supervision inspectorates were the watchword for governmental reform, and when the Municipal Corporations Act of 1835 was passed there were some 200 Improvement Commissioners at work in the provinces, and another hundred in the boroughs.[81] The Royal Commission leading up to the Act had been outspoken, as well it should have been, in its condemnation of British local government: 'the existing municipal corporations of England and Wales neither possess nor deserve the confidence and respect of your Majesty's subjects'.[82] Nevertheless, these commissioners, along with the waves of inspectors for poor relief, prisons, sanitation and even eventually education, never made a lasting impact on administration at either the national or local level. Both national and local political leaders resisted policymaking by experts, a position adhered to until the end of the nineteenth century. As we shall see, they became no less captives of an expanding administration than their French counterparts.

In summary, the justices of the peace and the prefects have a similar history. The crucial difference is that the justices were the product of a relatively stable national system, their role being defined by the mutually supportive political relationship between local and central government that characterized Britain, though ultimately they proved unfit to run a modern state. The political system of the day enabled them to resist the centralizing ambitions of the Benthamites, but the tasks of local government continued to grow. Neither the local nor the national elites could resist the growth of government itself, and in 1888 they accepted reform. In contrast, the prefect's role was designed to meet the needs of the modern state and the prefects retained this administrative capacity because they were politically adept.

In many respects the seventeenth and eighteenth centuries were more important than the nineteenth century in laying the foundations of the subnational political systems, although the French transition from royal absolutism to revolutionary government makes the continuities less evident. Most royalist institutions were abolished, but the crucial office of the intendant was preserved. For France the problem became the organization of authority at the national level. Throughout the bewildering succession of monarchies, republics and empires of the nineteenth century, one institution remains firmly in place: the prefect. From 1789 to 1958 France tried fifteen different constitutions, but the prefects' authority was retained, and they grew in stature.

TESTING THE WATERS: EARLY POLITICAL ADJUSTMENTS

Though Britain recognized the need for local reorganization earlier in the nineteenth century, adjustments came slowly and at the national level were intensely controversial. Concessions to the growing industrial cities were not particularly impressive and, for the most part, were designed to sustain the rural power base of the Whig and Tory aristocracy of the previous century. In short, the nineteenth century was a period when both countries concentrated on building national political and administrative institutions. The changes in local government structure were not substantial, but debate was fierce and almost unending. One can best measure the inertia of the subnational political system by following the detailed and passionate controversies about how to organize local affairs as the modern state expands. Everyone seems to have acknowledged the complex problems of linking national and local policies, but few had the courage or ability to bring about significant change. In France there were various reorganization proposals: the Vivien Report in 1837, the debate following the 1848 Revolution and an intense nationwide debate in the 1860s. With the fall of the Second Empire the controversy became a central issue in the constitutional debates and continued throughout the early years of the Third Republic.

In Britain, important changes were made to the subnational system to preserve some measure of harmony between a growing national franchise and local elections. The transformation of the local government system was to a remarkable series of accommodations with the growing electorate, which Keith-Lucas has admirably set forth.[83] Others might say that the history of local government in nineteenth century Britain is the story of how sewers and standpipes were constructed. Nonetheless, the British debate was no less intense than in France, and marked by the historic confrontation of Chadwick and Toulmin Smith at mid-century. A coincidence of events in 1888 produced a new structure that was to last, with very few major changes, until 1972.

Neither country had a well-defined party structure until the last decades of the nineteenth century. In Britain, the Liberals were internally divided until the leadership of Gladstone, but his determination to resolve the Irish question again threw them into disarray. The Conservative Party, even under Disraeli's leadership, remained a rather uncomfortable collection of landed aristocrats and new financial barons. Perhaps the most surprising aspect of partisan politics, as it evolved over the century, is that it allowed the passage of such a formidable battery of social, economic and administrative legislation. Each party responded to new needs in housing, public health, transportation and many other areas, but neither was particularly eager to upset the relationship between central and local authority. The important changes, as we shall see, were the formation of new ministries to deal with the problems of the modern state, the organization of the civil service and, except for the weak Local Government Board of 1870, the omission of a ministry with responsibility for local-level services and needs. British counties and boroughs did not passively accept the growth of services and duties during the nineteenth century. In fact, many simply refused to comply.

The contrast with France is more marked at the national level. Despite the authority of the prefects, the French provinces of the nineteenth century were still working out their relationships with Paris, and local leaders were beginning to devise ways to subvert the administrative structure. British local leaders were less preoccupied with national politics because the social links between the counties and Westminster remained fundamentally unchanged until the rise of the Labour Party. The acceptable political strategy for change in the twentieth century was fairly well delimited by the end of the nineteenth.

Given France's more turbulent history, one might anticipate difficulties in tracing the way in which institutional limitations on reorganizing the subnational system were shaped. The transformation is less perplexing if one takes into account the constantly simmering debate over centralization itself. The legislation passed in France was no more impressive than in Britain, but the need to resolve tensions between Paris and the provinces was more evident than the relationship between central and local government in Britain. If the British institutional setting for local government seems something of an afterthought, it was the major domestic policy concern of the succession of French political regimes in the nineteenth century.

Nearly all the strong ministers of the nineteenth century, such as Martignac, De Persigny and Guizot, were heavily involved with the Ministry of the Interior, the activities of the prefectoral corps and the mounting demands from republicans that more autonomy be granted to departments and communes. But French instability and British stability had the same effect of working against reform of the subnational system. By 1877, when republican government was relatively secure, little energy was left to refashion local government. Nor did the various radical and liberal factions that dominated the National Assembly and the Senate wish to see their local power bases upset. The rapidly ensuing crises over Dreyfus and the final separation of church and state helped keep local government for the most part untouched. On the other hand this same instability and atmosphere of crisis enabled the *grands corps*, in particular the prefectoral corps, to assert their influence. A relatively weak Parliament and a strong administration became the basic institutional impediments to local reorganization of recent years.

After the Restoration in 1815 France was busy meeting the requirements of the peace treaties. Under the new constitutional monarchy the *émigrés*, a diverse collection of exiles mostly linked to the proliferation of the nobility in pre-Revolutionary days, returned. Most of them found offices in the new regime, many in local government. Communal government had meanwhile been restored under the law of 1789, and prefectoral rule established under the law of 1800. The social and economic differences between the major regimes of France remained substantial,[84] but for the most part the old nobility were able to regain their influence in their traditional strongholds. Even so, the degree of public participation in the monarchy was considerable. In 1817 there were 90,000 electors under a property qualification system known as the *élections censitaires*.[85]

As two distinguished historians of the period have noted,[86] France had more voters than England until the British reform of 1832.

After the Restoration the nobility was a 'nobility without privileges', and like their involvement in other spheres of French life, they were a hundred years too late. But much of their property was restored in 1825, and they played a dominant role in the Chamber of Deputies, holding 176 of 381 seats in 1816, and a majority after the elections of 1821.[87] They were strong in the prefectoral corps and by 1830 held nearly half the prefectoral positions, although in 1815 only one in nine had been from the nobility.[88] By manipulating the electorate the monarch also gained effective control of the communes and mayors. The Ministry of the Interior began to evolve into a key agency, and a Directorate of Departmental and Communal Affairs was established in 1819. Although the renewed prefectoral system came under attack from deputies, opposition to central rule was not as strong as it would become under the Second Empire. Under increasing pressure, Martignac, a leading Restoration minister, proposed changes that gave nobles a more direct voice in selecting mayors and deputies, as a part of his scheme to subdue rural discontent.[89]

From 1830 onward, under the July Monarchy of Louis-Philippe, there were moves toward liberalizing voting and elections in the French local government system. By this time the upper middle class had become a distinct political force. Had the Bonapartists and early republicans continued their cooperation, the future party structure of France, which was to complicate central–local relationships so much, might have developed along very different lines.[90] Nonetheless, the Bonapartist remnants, the Orleanist forces among the nobility and the emergent liberals reached a consensus that brought significant modifications to the national and local government systems. Deputies might run for office at thirty years of age rather than forty, and their term of office was reduced from seven to five years. The voting age was reduced, as was the property qualification.

But Louis-Philippe feared political parties and was paralyzed by the controversy over the future of the throne. Though room was made among the ruling classes for many from the new bourgeoisie, there was little fundamental change in the local government system. Under the Municipal Law of 1831 the electorate for communal councils was extended, the extension being based on occupational categories, but mayors were still selected by the monarch from the commune's nominations. Educational reforms produced a committee at the *arrondissement* level composed of mayors, priests and local notables, which became the crucible for local politics for many years to come. In 1837 there were moves toward liberalizing the departmental councils as well, and they were permitted to have a small administrative office. Their gain was, however, no counterweight to the prefect.

The leading minister of the July Monarchy, Guizot, knew something of British government and had written a book on the subject. Though he remained Minister of the Interior for only a few months, Guizot more than any other single person organized the Ministry in its modern form,[91] and Guizot's administrative changes provided the foundation for prefectoral political influence. The traditional manipulation of prefects to assure political support begins at this time. In 1830 all but three prefects were removed, and during the July Monarchy, 636 of the 764 members of the entire prefectoral corps were replaced.[92] Prefects also extended their influence by sitting in the legislature. There were twenty three in the Chamber of Deputies in 1831, when the practice was discontinued, but many retired prefects continued to be elected. Depriving the prefects of direct access to national politics was a significant change, but both deputy and prefect sought new ways of pursuing their political interests at the national and local levels of government.

Most anecdotes about prefectoral manipulation of local elections in France date from the July Monarchy, abuses that are surely no less outrageous than similar manipulations of local politics by the British local aristocracy of the same period. Chapman describes the subprefect at Plöermel who found that his careful efforts to arrange the electoral list had failed and thus arranged a fire to burn the election records.[93] At this time the prefectoral corps assumed the shape that we associate with it today. The corps' duties were as wide as they had been in the Napoleonic period, and the prefects slowly became advocates of the interests of local governments in their regions and departments, as well as representatives of central authority. Meanwhile the corps underwent a degree of professionalization, the prefects being increasingly recruited from the subprefects, and their influence began to spread to other governmental agencies. Thus, early in the nineteenth century the prefect assumed the pivotal position that still links central and local authority.

RESISTING CHANGE: VICTORIAN PARLIAMENTARY AND MUNICIPAL REFORM

Like the adjustment of the subnational system to the needs of the modern state in France, Britain's adjustment to the needs of the modern state saw changes at both national and local levels of politics.[94] The historically evolved alliance of aristocracy and gentry, described earlier, was badly shaken by the French Revolution. There was, of course, no equity (in terms of property, qualifications or population) to the composition of Parliament before 1832.

Nevertheless in Britain it was the parliamentary elections, not the central administration (as was the case in France), that provided the essential link between national and local authority. Before 1832 parliamentary constituencies heavily favored rural areas, and were easily manipulated by the ruling aristocracy. There were basically two kinds of parliamentary boroughs. In 'nomination' boroughs the dominant landowner simply designated MPs. These boroughs were valuable property, often being sold to other aristocrats or to rising members of the upper class. In the 'closed' boroughs, there was a small electorate determined by a variety of legislation and royal charters, frequently manipulated by both the monarchs and the gentry. In a few, such as Nottingham, Bristol, Norwich and London, enfranchised citizens (the freemen) existed in large numbers. In any event, the overall pattern of abuse and inequity was no less striking than that of France.

The parliamentary boroughs made bribery easy, and corruption often used local rates for bribes in astonishing amounts. In Wycombe a thousand pounds was said to have been paid for a vote. Secure seats in Parliament were often sold to ambitious new aristocrats for fifty to a hundred thousand pounds. 'Rotten' boroughs like Old Sarum, where the lord and gamekeeper appeared in the fields to select a member of parliament, were notorious. But the most serious outrages were at Birmingham, Leeds, Sheffield and Manchester, which had no representation in Parliament.[95] The entire industrial regions of Durham, Nottinghamshire and Lancashire had fewer representatives than rural Cornwall. For the aristocracy, the Reform Bill of 1832 was surely one of the political bargains of modern times – they gave up only the most public abuses among the pocket and rotten boroughs.[96] The ten-pound rate, a tax-based voting qualification, meant that rural political strongholds might be a bit more demanding to manage, but urban and rural voting registers could still be manipulated easily. The reform created 143 new seats, but only sixty-five went to the underrepresented cities and towns, while county representation actually increased, from 95 to 159, in England and Wales. There remained sixty-nine small parliamentary boroughs with a total population of only 390,000.[97] The important effect of the reform, as Redlich and Hirst point out, was to fuel demand in the cities for further reform.

As Trevelyan notes, municipal reform would have been impossible without parliamentary reform.[98] But it may be closer to the truth to see local reform as part of a larger political exchange that enabled the Whigs to sustain their shaky ruling alliance of landowners, merchants and bankers. After the 1832 reform, the Whigs returned to power with a huge majority[99] whereas the Tories were severely divided. Reformist logic demanded that the towns and cities now classified as parliamentary boroughs also have 'democratic government', as it was then defined. The new government appointed a Royal Commission on Municipal Corporations heavily biased toward radical reform. The secretary, Joseph Parkes, was another energetic utilitarian and in close touch with Place.[100]

Like the voluminous reports on sanitation and the poor laws, the report on municipal corporations painted a vivid picture of corruption and incompetence. The justice of the peace at Malmesbury was found to be illiterate. Derby had a school with one pupil. Bath had four independent police forces, one for each quarter of the city. Devonport had 75,000 citizens, of whom 437 voted.[101] There was, of course, more than a touch of partisan politics in this exposé, but the overriding factor was Benthamite fervor for social engineering and efficiency.

In the Upper House the Reform Bill was bitterly opposed by the Tory lords, who refused to follow Peel's lead to offer only minor opposition. The compromises the Tories imposed on the British local government system remained until 1972 and certainly qualify Redlich and Hirst's enthusiasm for the Municipal Corporations Act as a new model of democratic local government.[102] The lords wanted a quarter of the municipal councillors elected for life. The compromise was to elect a quarter of the councillors (the aldermen) for six years by vote of the other popularly elected councillors. The effect was to reduce the level of partisan politics in the councils. The aldermen's patriarchal influence contributed to the British failure to develop strong links between local and national politics. At the local level a body of elders was created, which by its seniority in committees was able to dominate policy-making.

The Whigs wanted the municipalities divided into wards of 6,000 persons, but eventually agreed to larger wards of 12,000, thereby diluting participation at the most basic level of local democracy. The law applied to only 178 of the 285 towns and cities studied in the report. Though the consequences for local finance are difficult to estimate, there was also agreement to drop local regulation of licensing (a potentially important source of local revenue). Possibly the most important political concession made by the Whigs was to exempt London from the Act, thereby helping to preserve Tory rule of the capital until the rise of the Labour Party nearly a century later. Nor were the more direct political effects of the Act much of a victory for democracy. Keith–Lucas has carefully shown that there were in fact fewer voters enfranchised in the new boroughs by the Municipal Corporations Act of 1835 than by the 1832 parliamentary reform.[103]

The Municipal Corporations Act of 1835 (like most local government reorganization) was more a matter of trying to catch up with the past than of preparing for the future. Nevertheless the 1835 Act provided Britain with a local structure that could work within the modern state. In the new boroughs, the justices of the peace were separated from local government. The boroughs were given elected councils (though the franchise was still based on the payment of rates), meetings were to be public, accounts were to be audited and each council was required to have a clerk and a treasurer. In short, this was the beginning of modern local administration. Treasury sanction was required for local loans and property sales, and although it did not seem ominous at the time this became the key to central financial control over the modern local government system. Among the discretionary powers of the boroughs was the possibility of taking over the improvement commissions, dating from the eighteenth century, and using them to enlarge local services. By 1848 only twenty-nine boroughs had done so, suggesting that the new authorities had little interest in voluntarily providing new services,[104] but it is also true that the improvement commissions resisted takeovers.

The Whigs had accomplished their immediate political objectives. In the local elections of early 1836 they swept the country.[105] The elections were a tremendous boost to the party, which took control of most cities and through its rural support even made inroads into the unreformed county governments. Their success caused several lords lieutenant to resign, among them the Duke of Newcastle, who could not tolerate having a dissenter on the county bench.[106] But county government remained firmly in the hands of landed aristocracy and gentry until 1888. In the towns and cities political life soon returned to normal and the Conservatives regained their strength. As in France, the social and economic interests of the ruling oligarchy and the new bourgeoisie were not in fundamental conflict, although there were some areas of friction.

The pace, if not the tempo, of change was much the same in the two countries, and there was a common objective to these early efforts to integrate the local government system and national politics. What the French achieved by making the prefect the political agent of the state, the British accomplished by relying on the local ruling oligarchy. But the internal patterns were different. The relationship of center to locality in France was enmeshed in the administrative structure, where it still remains. In Britain, there was only a rudimentary administrative structure when the efforts at integration began, and reforms were designed to meet the needs of Parliament. These two patterns of policymaking are hardly altered to the present.

LOCAL POLITICS AND REPUBLICAN FRANCE: COMMUNAL SELF-ASSERTION

A striking historical difference between Britain and France is that the French communes, and particularly some of the major regional cities, fought to establish republican rule. While the British local aristocracy and middle class resisted the new responsibilities placed on them by Parliament, the French communes were engaged in more vital political struggle. Even under the most oppressive nineteenth century regimes the communes were able to extract political concessions from Paris, and the prefect began to shape a mediating role between communes and Paris. Unlike Britain, the local political capacities developed over the century provided the foundations of modern democratic government in the Third and Fourth Republics.

The Vivien Report of 1837 set the stage for the mixture of politics and administration that permeates the French subnational system. The system of budgetary controls established in the late 1830s remained essentially unchanged until 1948.[107] One of the crucial debates of Vivien's time was over the property rights to be granted to the communes. If growth of municipal services − like that in Britain later in the century − had been permitted, it would have been difficult to subordinate the commune to the administrative system.[108] The possibility that the local governments might acquire more autonomy arose again in the early months of the 1848 Revolution, and in the most massive sweep of prefects in the century they were all replaced. A proposal that the canton be revived, so that local government might be more closely supervised from the communes, was made in the constitutional commission of the Second Republic by Odilon Barrot, a leading liberal exponent of self-government. In effect, his idea was a renewal of Thouret's notion for a *grande commune*.[109] But the short-lived Republic could not reverse the administrative trends of the century. As in Britain, changes would result from adjustments to the increasingly complex tasks of local government, but not from structural reform. The prefect began to make compromises with modernity, but was no less ingenious than the British local hierarchy in shielding his influence from new demands.

Zeldin has called the Second Empire 'a catalyst in the meeting of democracy and centralisation'.[110] As so often in judging French government, the impact of the Second Empire must be seen as a balance between central repression and republican forces that were still active locally. The results of the reforms of the 1860s are anticipated in the growing network of the prefect, and in the growing complexity of government itself. The repression immediately following the *coup d'état* of 1851 was harsh, with about 26,000 arrests in Paris and another 100,000 in the provinces.

The dual role of the prefects was soon apparent. In the *peur de 1852* that propelled Louis Napoleon to become Emperor, they first cooperated with, and later moderated, the repression. Again in 1858 the prefects efficiently carried out some 600 arrests, but later resisted and even subverted the summary justice of army officials. Nor were the prefects any more secure under a forceful ruler than under the republics. After 1852, twenty-five prefects resigned or were replaced and there were fifty-six changes among departments.[111] In a period of unprecedented construction and industrial development, the prefects formed close attachments to the local notables. The twentieth century system of *cumul des mandats* or multiple elected offices begins to appear, establishing a network of national and local political offices which the prefects could not ignore, and which the more ingenious began to exploit. More than four-fifths of the deputies of the Second Empire held local offices. By the 1860s, the debate on centralization was going full force, and by the late 1860s major concessions were being made to local government.[112]

The parallel between the role imagined for the prefects by Louis Napoleon and de Gaulle is inescapable, though neither was uniformly successful in insulating the prefects from local politics. The overall objective was clear in the 1852 decree on 'decentralization'.[113] Here we find the famous phrase 'one can govern at a distance, but can only administer well nearby', which so neatly summarizes the Jacobin position. This spirit is carried on in the election circular of de Persigny, the Minister of the Interior. 'The public good can only be assured on the condition that the legislative body has a perfect harmony of ideas with the Chief of State.'[114] The official bulletin, *Le Moniteur*, carried the lists of approved local candidates, and the prefects made sure they were elected. The powers of the locally disliked subprefects were increased, and they, too, received careful election instructions. In 1858 a Ministry of Police was briefly revived, entirely staffed by prefects.[115] The Emperor also tried to revive the Napoleonic aristocracy with new uniforms, honors and luxurious headquarters for the prefects. Numerous ex-mayors, Senators and other political favorites were appointed to be subprefects, adding to the opprobrium of that office. But the prefects were not nearly as successful in obtaining important positions as ministerial advisors and Cabinet officials as they have been in recent years.[116] Thus, the main effect of the Second Empire was to politicize the prefectural administration with the introduction of reliable friends and supporters, much like British administration until the late Victorian reforms of the civil service.

The mixture of politics and administration that developed in France under the Second Empire has never been disentangled. In contrast, in Britain keeping the levels of administration distinct helped exclude local politics. This happened in part because the British were placing severe burdens on local government well before there was a professional central civil service. What became an obsession in France, the organization of the state, was almost an accident in Britain, and this has had far-reaching implications for central-local relations.

The French failure to develop a two-party system is, of course, the main reason that national government had such difficulty asserting control over local government policy (and over most other policies as well). French politicians operated within an underlying structure that resembled the triangular division of political interests − Right, Center and Left − found as early as the Convention of 1789. When the parties emerged in the early days of the Third Republic, a similar triangular division appeared, the Right, Center and Left Republicans each having about the same number of seats in the new National Assembly.[117] For a brief period from 1871 to 1877 the trial of strength between the republican and anti-republican forces created something like a two-party situation, but this did not affect the establishment of local institutions in the new republic.[118] The multiple party structure, as well as the importance of local politics at the national level, meant that French local government developed an interest in national policy-making that could, in turn, be reinforced with their potential threat to political stability.

Republicans had been active in the short-lived Second Republic and again entered official discussions in the 1860s. As Louis Napoleon's foreign adventures added to the tax burden he was compelled to liberalize his rule. Though not of major importance, laws were passed in 1866 relaxing administrative controls on the department, and in 1867 on the commune.[119] In 1865 the Nancy Program was published by sixty liberals, the nucleus of the future Radical Party. The title of the program was *Un projet de décentralisation* and its announced objectives were to 'fortify the commune and emancipate the department'.[120] At about the same time a group of liberal journalists and constitutional monarchists in Lyons began publishing a weekly, *La Décentralisation*, and the Congress of Lyons of 1869 again voiced regional sentiments for a relaxation of political constraints. Historic as the tension between national and local authority has been in France, the decade is unrivalled for the intensity of the debate on decentralization.[121]

British Royal Commissions have no exact parallel in France, but from time to time important reports are made on major problems. The Commission on Decentralisation, appointed by Napoleon III in 1870, was a concession to the growing strength of liberal republicans. The chairman, Odilon Barrot, had been briefly prefect of the Seine in the July Monarchy, had been active in the Second Republic and was a leading constitutional monarchist in opposition to Napoleon III.[122] The Commission debates are a useful summary of the issues surrounding local government in France as the Third Republic took shape.[123] Barrot wanted to classify communes as rural or urban, in order to distinguish their functions more clearly and to facilitate the delegation of responsibilities, but was outvoted in the Commission. The idea of electing mayors was discussed at length, and in the final meetings it was approved by a majority of only one vote.

Though the Commission wanted to see the powers of the commune increased, they saw this happening as a result of administrative delegation of authority, and agreed with Barrot that central authority should not be 'disarmed' by diminishing the *tutelle*. The old debate about the regrouping of small communes by canton or by *arrondissement* continued. Barrot had advocated strengthening the canton in the constitutional debates of 1848, but he was overruled by his colleagues who preferred the *arrondissement*. Regionalization was hotly debated but, like the experience of the Fifth Republic, there was no clear outcome. To curb the power of the prefect the notion was advanced of a permanent administrative commission elected by the *conseil général* but, concerned as it was to restrain the prefects, the Commission hesitated over the use of political measures. Giving the departmental councils the right to confer among themselves was hotly debated as a threat to central authority and as a possible vehicle for provincial separatism.[124]

The mobilization of provincial and rural support was crucial in firmly establishing the Third Republic in the 1880s, and this did much to reinforce the communes. Party lines were confused, and remained so until more formal party organizations appeared at the turn of the century, but deputies and Senators had strong local ties, and local interests were clearly communicated in both legislatures. Moreover, the shifting party identities made it easier for local issues to become conspicuous at the national level.[125] On the left a rapidly evolving group of radical republicans, led initially by Gambetta, by the turn of the century was outflanked by the rising Socialist Party. This profusion of parties parallels the experience of the past two decades; all of them took local affairs seriously, but they could not agree on structural reforms. On the right, the monarchists were divided among the legitimists, or Bourbon supporters whose orthodox view of monarchical rule soon eliminated them as contenders for national power; the Orleanites, whose sympathy with provincial France and dispersed government made then more attractive to republicans; and the Bonapartists, whose Jacobin views are carried to the present day by the more militant Gaullists. The center was composed of the constitutional monarchists and conservative republicans of whom Thiers is probably the best example.

LOCALITIES IN VICTORIAN BRITAIN: POLITICAL AND ADMINISTRATIVE SUBORDINATION

With the growth of the modern state the central administration in Britain was no less powerful than that in France but, as we shall see, administrative politics took a different form. After the Whig reforms Britain seemed ready for relief from the rapid pace of change. In the 1840s the struggle over the repeal of the Corn Laws, and the new wave of popular demands by the Chartists, distracted Parliament from local affairs. The General Board of Health, seen as a means of imposing Chadwick's immense sanitation report on local government, was dismantled. The Conservative Party was not enthusiastic for intervention, nor was the Board popular with localities. In 1858 responsibilities were split between the Home Office and the Privy Council. Under the Local Government Act of 1858, in fact much closer to a public health act, the Local Government Act Office was created. For the first time in British history an agency of the central government explicitly claimed an interest in local government.

In the mid-nineteenth century the functional emphasis of British local government took over, and it continues today in the organization and work of local councils. Moreover, the central government began to take an increasing interest in how the services were performed. Toulmin Smith saw increasing central intervention as a constitutional issue of the greatest importance, and it has never been more fiercely examined.[126] He attacked the new health inspectors as an abuse of the Crown's right to appoint inspectors and as an unwarranted growth in political patronage. He argued that Parliament had no right to legislate on local matters, dating the decline of local independence from the 1688 revolution. Like Tocqueville he saw political freedom rooted in local self-government. Using a mixture of Teutonic folklore, early parish history and customary law, Smith tried to show that British parishes had a constitutional foundation that predated parliamentary rule and took precedence over the British constitution.[127] But in a period when 'there was insanity in sanity',[128] Smith's fervent defense of local rule was already too late. Even if the doctrine of parliamentary supremacy were adjusted to his demands, the framework of central supervision of local activities was firmly established and the predominantly functional role of local government defined. There were not to be any small republics in Britain.

Ironically, the Conservative sponsor described the aim of the Local Government Office as 'to decentralize the whole system' of health administration.[129] But in fact the office quickly became a source of arbitrary and coercive intervention in local government that would have delighted a member of the prefectoral corps. As Lambert has so clearly shown, the experience of the new office is an early lesson in the extension of administrative influence over localities with the growth of services. The inspectors involved themselves in the arbitration 'between rival Boards, between companies and Boards, and in internal local affairs'. Lambert neatly summarizes the work of the new office:

> Only eight years after 'the experiment of local government' had begun, the central authority was armed with this clumsy mixture of judicial, administrative, and executive functions, powers the like of which Chadwick had never possessed even in the darkest days of centralization, perhaps the most extreme and certainly the most extraordinary discretionary powers wielded by government in the nineteenth century.[130]

But this venture in strong central control did not continue. Several circumstances intervened, each of which should make us more sensitive to the peculiar nature of administrative politics in Britain. In 1871 the Royal Sanitary Commission reported that the confusion of health districts should be relieved and their powers devolved more directly to local government. New legislation established the Local Government Board in 1871, and the Board inherited nearly all the scattered local government activity accumulating in Whitehall.[131] These activities included the old Local Government Act Office, the Medical Department (inherited from the Privy Council), the Poor Law Boards, the Registry-General's Office and assorted responsibilities for pollution and roads under the Alkali and Metropolitan Water Acts and the Turnpike and Highway Acts. Its strength became its weakness, for it was 'a mosaic with no unifying theme'.[132] In the reorganization of central departments, the Local Government Board was made a 'secondary department'. Its Permanent Secretary was constantly in trouble with the Treasury and at odds with the Board's ministerial link, Sir Charles Dilke. Within the Board there were severe divisions, most notably the isolation of its most talented member, Sir John Simon.[133] Attacked and disliked by the local authorities at the turn of the century, it rapidly fell behind energetic new departments such as Education, under the skilful Permanent Secretary Morant, or was excluded from key decisions by strong ministers, such as Churchill.

There are interesting similarities in the early years of administering the subnational system in Britain and France. What Redlich and Hirst call the 'power of inspectability' was widely used in nineteenth century Britain,[134] but it did not become a major element of the central administrative structure as in France. In both countries one sees the same reluctance to form larger units of local government, though from 1835 the British local boards proliferated for special purposes and operated outside local government. Even this was not done to strengthen government at the local level, but because the current inequities were intolerable and most local government had proved unresponsive. Within the administrative system the French Ministry of the Interior prospered. Although important functions of government were pared off to form new ministries,[135] the Ministry played a key political role. As long as the communal system remained intricate, the prefects were essential in maintaining coherence in local administration. In Britain, an analogue to the Ministry of the Interior never developed. Divided between being 'a healthy Jekyll and a pauper Hyde',[136] the new activities of the state eluded the Local Government Board. Influence passed to the new functional ministries and in 1919 the new Ministry of Health became the focal point for local affairs, while education was supervised from an energetic Ministry of Education, propelled by the Education Act of 1902. 'Local government' did not reappear in the Whitehall lexicon until 1951 when the Ministry of Local Government and Planning was created.

National party organizations were also slow to appear in Britain, though they became much more important than their French counterparts. Even so, the emergence of two well-defined parties in Britain led to substantially different results. The Conservative and National Unionist Party was formed only in 1868, and the Liberal National

Federation in 1877.[137] As we have seen above, the major reforms affecting British local government, except for the futile rebellion of the Tory lords over the Municipal Corporations Act, were bipartisan affairs. This remained the case to a remarkable extent until the reorganization of London government in the early 1960s. As in France, internal crises, most notably the Irish question, distracted politicians from local problems.[138] For the most part, the newly organized Conservatives and Liberals accepted the pattern of local government that their Tory and Whig predecessors had found so comfortable. This harmony was briefly threatened by the party realignment caused by Gladstone's decision to resolve the Irish question and Joseph Chamberlain's subsequent defection to the Conservatives. Indeed, the Local Government Act of 1888 might be considered the only major legislation on local reorganization in Britain that can be directly attributed to political adjustments at the national level.

In his unsuccessful efforts to interest Gladstone in local government reform, Goschen described the system in 1871 as 'a chaos as regards authorities, a chaos as regards rates, and a worse chaos than all as regards areas'.[139] The Reform Acts of 1867 and 1884 made the inconsistency of the franchise in county and national government obvious, though it is not clear that reorganization was simply the product of the recognition of such electoral imbalances. There had been repeated efforts in the previous two decades to extend elected government to the counties.[140] The crucial change was the formation of 'caucus' party government in Birmingham under its flamboyant mayor, Joseph Chamberlain. In 1885, the *Radical Programme* was published as part of his bid for power against Gladstone. For the first time British politics was confronted with the possibility of a struggle for control within a political party, a struggle that was directly linked to urban political organizations.[141] Chamberlain's platform of 'free schools, free church, free land and free labour' was actually not so radical, on close examination. The most progressive proposal of the *Radical Programme* was the expansion of municipal services in order to provide income for cities at the expense of private utilities. But municipal investments were to be carefully monitored by central government, and restricted to essential services by the cautious policies of the Local Government Board.[142]

Had Chamberlain remained President of the Local Government Board, a position he held for a few months in 1886, this conglomerate agency of central government might have had a very different history. His ambition, his talent and his highly successful experience as mayor of Birmingham all suggest that he would not have long remained on the sidelines. As it was, he left the Liberal Party over his disagreement with Gladstone and he made reform of county government a condition of joining the Conservative Party. Chamberlain had already worked out the details of the bill with Dilke, and the Conservative Cabinet 'accepted Chamberlain's terms, not, it would appear, because they believed in the validity of his arguments, but because the political situation drove them to do so'.[143] In fact, as Hamer has pointed out, parliamentary reform could reduce the impact of the urban centers on national government. Birmingham had three MPs at large, but after the Reform Act of 1884 had only one, for the center of the city.[144] Beneath the immediate controversy, there was the new Conservative strategy of capturing the rural vote which stemmed from Disraeli's efforts to redirect the Conservative Party.[145] The Liberals supported the Local Government Act of 1888, mistakenly thinking that they were at last demolishing Tory power in the counties. The Tories were no more enthusiastic than the Liberals, the Conservative leader Lord Salisbury complaining, as many have since, 'I wish there was no such thing as Local Government'.[146] The long overdue law was the product of party realignment at the center, one of the rare instances of major local reorganization resulting from a strong initiative from national parties.

The Local Government Act of 1888 is, nonetheless, a milestone in the reorganization of the subnational system in Britain. The judicial role of the justices of the peace and Quarter Sessions was separated from county government, and the householder vote, introduced in the boroughs in 1832, was extended to the counties. The underlying structure of town and country, however, remained the same. In setting out the boundaries of the new counties, 'the continuity of traditional areas triumphed over any thought that they might be reshaped for the work in hand'.[147] The largest county, Yorkshire, was forty times the size of Rutland. With a population of a little over 21,000, Rutland was governed under the same system as Lancashire's nearly three and a half million persons. The *Economist* seems to have conveyed the feelings of the privileged public in writing 'the more clearly the line is drawn between rural and urban local government the better'.[148] County and borough political differences were further accentuated in defining borough status. The Bill had excluded towns over 150,000 from the counties but the exclusion was reduced to 50,000, further isolating counties from urban political influence.[149] London acquired county council status, but retained the chaotic organization that helped perpetuate almost uninterrupted Conservative rule until 1934. The 1888 Bill also carried provisions for financial reform, but these were at the discretion of the Local Government Board and were never used. The Act also preserved the aldermanic system, thereby imposing on the urban centers the conservative influence of elder statesmen, and helping shield both the county councils and the new borough councils from the full force of political change.[150]

After the 1888 Act the Conservatives maintained their rural strongholds relatively intact, and subsequent elections only slightly diminished their control. But the borough councils were won over by the Liberals, and increasingly by the Labour Party, despite their effective deprivation of a foothold in the counties. This division of local government into politically competitive and politically secure areas helps account for the weak link between national and local politics in Britain.

Parish reform comprised the final changes in the system as it was handed down to the emerging twentieth century welfare state. The Local Government Act of 1894 established rural and urban district councils in counties and attempted to sort out the bewildering array of functions and areas that had accumulated over the nineteenth century.

In the Newcastle Programme of 1891 the Liberals had called for parish reform, an inflammatory proposal that would give more local control to nonconformists. But the local chaos called for some kind of change. For example, Roberts identified 80,000 different local authorities, including separate districts for the 600 boards of guardians, 4,600 local school boards, 290 prisons and 228 asylums under magistrates, and 182 local boards of health.[151] Moreover, after the mid-century wave of social and health legislation, there was little resemblance between administrative and political areas. The Local Government Act of 1894 tried to bring order out of this chaos by establishing 6,880 parish councils beneath the rural districts of county government, hoping to bring the provision of services in county areas to a workable form. But the possibility that the lower tiers of the system might act independently was precluded by the limitations put on parish and district powers.[152] In short, the confusing organization of services was reduced, but there was no way for the subordinate units of county government to take policy initiatives.

THE THIRD AND FOURTH REPUBLICS: MUTUAL DEPENDENCE CONFIRMED

Political dependence between levels of government is shaped by national events, and had opposite effects in Britain and France. Britain's comparatively harmonious relationship between national and local politics tended to make reorganization easier than in France, both a century ago as well as in recent years. But in France, the republicans found a political refuge at the local level[153] and made the commune a counterweight to central authority. For a century or more, the French subnational system has been directly engaged in the national political system, as revealed in the links between the local *notables* and national politicians in both the nineteenth and twentieth centuries.[154] The Third Republic struggle for legitimacy did not leave much time for local government, but the crises gave local politicians a claim on national legitimacy and an influence in policymaking unmatched in Britain. The result was preservation of the complexity and the contradictions of French local government, while in Britain the Conservatives, with considerable support from the Liberals, began to simplify the local government system in the 1880s.

Some of the more radical republican strongholds, such as Lyon, resisted the conservative policies of men like Thiers, but few politicians wanted structural change. In any event, after 1870 the major local-level problem was to restore order and to reconstruct the thirty departments that had been occupied by the Germans. A little later the Dreyfus affair marked the establishment of unchallenged republican rule, most of whose leaders had strong influence in the communes and the departments and from which came their most reliable support during the crisis. These sanctuaries for middle-class rule went relatively unchallenged until the 1920s. By then the lower class was staking out its claim in local government.[155] Britain also had its crises at the turn of the century, but they were not as ideologically divisive as those in France, and their resolution had no impact on the local government system. The Local Government Act of 1888 accommodated the political strategies of both major parties. But Westminster's power over local government was not seriously challenged from below, whereas similar efforts in France have been consistently and successfully challenged by the mayors and departmental councillors. The British Parliament acted on the more glaring inconsistencies and inefficiencies of local government, while French deputies and Senators have consistently resisted encroachments on local power.

Occupied with the turbulence of the Paris Commune in 1871 and the uncertainties of the new regime, French leaders did little to restructure the local government system in the early years of the Third Republic. Among the laws that were extended to restore order was the law on prefectoral administration. Not until 1884 was there sufficient time and the confidence to reconsider the statutes on communal councils and mayors. As in earlier regimes, the prefects were essential in restoring order and resuming the affairs of government. Their involvement with national politicians, notable in the last decade of the Second Empire, continued to increase, and their posts remained as vulnerable to political trends as under more arbitrary regimes. For example, when Gambetta, a radical republican, became Minister of the Interior in late 1870, all but four of the prefects were purged.[156] But national politics eluded their direct influence, and, contrary to republican designs, the national elections of early 1871 returned a strong monarchist majority. Thiers emerged as national leader. He was an adroit conservative republican with no intention of reorganizing local government, though he, too, proceeded with another purge of the prefects when Gambetta resigned. Purges followed again in 1873 when Thiers fell, and in 1877 when the monarchists failed to take control of the Republic.

From the early days of the Third Republic the prefects became more deeply imbedded in a growing network, linking levels of government and reconciling local and national interests. In the 1871 legislature, roughly a third of the deputies and Senators were ex-prefects,[157] who retained some of their local political bases. Thiers consulted them frequently in his shrewdly waged contest with the monarchists, and he read their reports carefully. The law designating Thiers as 'President' of France, which thwarted monarchist designs, was introduced by Rivet, a little-known ex-prefect. French local government thus developed intimate political relationships with central authority, sometimes encouraged by national leaders, and occasionally proving essential to resolve crises. The contrast with Britain could not be sharper.

Under severe pressures, the new French regime renewed the 1790 law regulating the prefectoral system.[158] The revised version of the law on departmental government gave more initiative to the departmental councils, but the legal powers of the prefect and his *tutelle* were essentially unchanged. The intense controversy of the time was over permitting the departmental councils to express 'political views', and formal political links between lower and higher levels of French government were rejected. Article 51 of the new law simply stated that 'All political views are forbidden', an injunction that failed to deter

the departmental councils from playing a key political role in the
Third and subsequent republics. Defining the communes' powers,
however, was a much more difficult task. Thiers had bitterly opposed
the radical republicans under Gambetta, who wanted to install
elected mayors immediately in 1871, and the reform of the communes
had to wait until the power struggle at the center was resolved. In the
meantime Thiers fell from power in 1873, and was replaced by the
more conservative Duke de Broglie who again purged the prefectoral
corps and reinstated the appointment of mayors as practiced in the
Second Empire and indeed throughout most of the century.[159]

An important point of difference between the British and French
subnational systems is the early development of institutional links
between levels of government in France. These can be traced back to
the Farmers General, provincial assemblies and early parliaments. The
design of the upper chambers was rooted in Thouret's notion of an
assembly of 'grand electors', essentially a device to link the local
nobility directly to central government, with the hope of bringing
them under its influence. This tradition continued in the Third
Republic with the organization of the Senate in 1873, a body that
Gambetta called the 'grand commune of France'. There has never
been a similar body in Britain, where the idea of territorial representation, though no less consistent with parliamentary rule than in France,
has never been accepted.[160] While the French republicans at first
resisted reviving a body so closely associated with the old ruling class,
they soon 'infiltrated it and it became one more bastion of the rule of
politicians, for it was a chamber which essentially represented them'.
Fifty years later Caillaux called it 'the assembly of the peasants'.[161]
Despite its conservative views, the Senate became a crucial institutional link between national and local politicians, another illustration
of the French capacity to reconstruct political institutions from
within, and by political means.

The exclusion of territorial politics from British national politics
becomes a crucial element in local government reorganization, while
in France the central influence of the *notables* becomes the major
obstacle to reorganization. The complex network of relationships that
binds local leaders to the administration, the legislature and the
ministers was never duplicated in the British system. To ensure
political stability, Thiers wanted to have a Senate nominated from the
departmental *notables* and elected by universal suffrage. The Duke de
Broglie simply reversed this scheme in 1873, making all Frenchmen
eligible, but confining the senatorial franchise to the local gentry who
sat on the departmental and *arrondissement* councils.[162] The final
solution was an electoral college of local and departmental councillors
who selected 225 Senators, but with each commune being equally
represented. An additional seventy-five Senators were initially chosen
for life by the Chamber of Deputies. With a virtual veto on all legislation, the senatorial system gave immense influence to the conservative
middle class of rural France.[163] Though relieved of the aristocracy, the
French electoral system of the late nineteenth century discriminated in
favor of the new middle class no less than the British system.

As the republican forces gathered strength, the legislature was able to turn to the reorganization of the communal system:[164] mayors were appointed until 1882, after which they were elected by the councils; the law on municipalities was finally agreed in 1884, and remains the basic legislation governing the communes;[165] the communes were subject to the same *tutelle* as the departments, and were forbidden to express political views. Until the 1867 Reform Act, the widening of male suffrage brought the electoral base of French local politics to roughly the level of participation in Britain. In the same year the inequities of the Senate were partially redressed. Greater weight was given to the electoral colleges of more heavily populated communes, and the seventy-five life members were abolished. The way the British Parliament was built on the rural gentry of the eighteenth century parallels the construction of French institutions to accommodate the middle class in the nineteenth century. But the difference in timing makes a great difference in the effect on national policy. The French bourgeoisie's links to the communes and departments was integrated into the political system much later than in Britain, and was closely associated with the struggle for a republican state. British politicians were equally adept in preserving their rural strongholds, but they did not need local influence to resolve national political struggles.

Unlike Britain, the ministry concerned with local affairs and elections became a power center in the modern French state. With the final establishment of republican rule after the elections of 1877, the prefectoral system was again purged and took on a more neutral role in French politics.[166] The prefects remained the eyes and ears of the government while direction of the Ministry of the Interior was constantly changing – there were, for example, seventeen Ministers of the Interior in the first seven years of the Third Republic.[167] The major reorganization of the ministry is credited to Constans, who was intermittently Minister throughout the 1880s. Further changes were made by Waldeck-Rosseau, who implemented the 1884 *loi municipale* and energetically sought out new prefects. The ex-prefects were still active in the elections: twenty-four were elected in 1881 and forty-six in 1885. The prefectoral corps was no more 'depoliticized' in the larger sense of the word than any of the *grands corps*. Its members were courted by many politicians, especially Clemenceau, whose rise to power placed him in charge of the Ministry for several years.[168] On the whole, the prefects were among the most adroit of the elite administrators in maintaining their status and influence, a skill which we shall see was preserved to influence reforms of the past decade.[169]

The prefects were indispensable, but their key role also made them politically vulnerable. With the electoral victories of the radical left in 1902, ninety-eight prefects were reassigned.[170] Another major 'waltz of the prefects' occurred with the victory of the *cartel des gauches* under Herriot in 1924 when some of the more conservative prefects resigned rather than serve under a strongly reformist government. Herriot's government was determined to make structural changes in the system. This was one of the few attempts prior to the Gaullist reorganization to modernize the prefectoral system and lighten the much resented *tutelle* at the subprefect level. In one of the most radical displacements of the century, 106 subprefects and sixty-six

Secretaries-General of departments were removed.[171] A law was passed in 1928 which outlined for the first time qualifications for prefectoral positions, but the political system was never able to make serious inroads into the prestige and power of the prefects. This was in part because of ministerial instability – there were twenty-one Ministers of the Interior under forty-five governments in the twenty-year period after the First World War.[172]

As in Britain in the interwar period, adverse economic conditions and increasing local needs combined to sap local influence. There was a resurgence of administrative power over communes which should not be confused with the more crude, and yet not entirely successful, manipulation of the nineteenth century.[173] The communes were compelled to increase local taxes at an enormous rate, rising from 20 percent of local revenues in 1920 to 50 percent in 1938, but a cautious National Assembly repeatedly refused to reform the local tax structure. Although the techniques of administrative control were devised over these years, political links to the communes remained strong. Powerful ministers such as Poincaré in the Meuse, Augagneur and later Herriot in Lyon, and Clementel in the Puy-de-Dôme moderated the growth of administrative controls in ways that never developed in Britain.

LATE VICTORIAN ENGLAND: PROTECTING PARLIAMENTARY PREROGATIVES

In contrast to the French system, from 1900 onward debate about the relation of administration to local government in Britain was in Whitehall, and perhaps best illustrated by the work of the Haldane Committee.[174] The organizational complications of the modern state were worked out within central government in Britain, while in France the issue was linked to the role of the state itself. Much of the debate was philosophical, but under an administrative system directly involved with local decisions. There is no British parallel to the work of Leroy–Beaulieu, whom Legendre calls the 'official theorist of liberalism applied to administration',[175] or to Hauriou's studies of public law. From the Third Republic onward the development of a modern state takes on a fundamentally different character in France. The direct administrative links to local government policy were never threatened, although it is true that Chardon wanted to dissolve the Ministry of the Interior and, in effect, dismantle the system of public law that is at the very core of French government and administration.

In Britain the Local Government Act of 1888 had extended elected government to the localities on roughly the same terms as then existed for Parliament. But, as Redlich and Hirst note, the vote was not as effectively translated into new forms of power as it was in France. The rural voter remained fairly passive even if '1834 rescued his morale, 1846 gave him bread, 1884 gave him the vote, (and) 1894 gave him a local council'.[176] In the Norfolk county elections of 1898 only six of the fifty-six seats were contested, and across the country fifty-four of the sixty-three incumbent chairmen of county councils were reelected. In the election immediately following the Act, twenty-two of the sixty-one new county borough chairmen had been chairmen of the old Quarter Session courts, and six of the new urban authorities chose ex-lords lieutenant.[177] In the first county council elections only about half the seats were contested, and there is ample evidence that the old pattern of electoral manipulation and corruption did not simply fade away.[178] In the Lancashire county elections of 1907, only two of the 105 seats were contested.[179] Local politics was a serious matter in the larger cities like Manchester, Birmingham, Liverpool and, above all, London but competitive party politics was not widespread in the counties.

The relationship of national politicians to localities also was little changed. Redlich and Hirst note that even in a socialist Bradford, where the borough council was run by the Independent Labour Party from 1891 to 1897, a Member of Parliament 'would never dream' of interfering in local policy.[180] Spared the abuses of the spoils system, and lacking an administrative structure to moderate between local and national policy, the divorce between national and local politics was institutionalized. Changes in national political leadership were not dramatic at this time. The proportion of aristocrats in the Cabinet only dropped from 64 percent in the mid-nineteenth century to 58 percent at the end of the century.[181] Until the rise of the Labour Party the national political agenda excluded structural change, but the problems of internal organization would not disappear.

The substantial social legislation passed in Britain early in this century and the inadequacy of the Poor Law organization during the high unemployment following the First World War generated more pressure for change in Britain than in France. The Education Act of 1902 had increased the educational responsibilities of local government and by the 1920s they were feeling financial strains. The problem was conceived in terms of the delivery of services, the allocation of functions among levels of local government and the achievement of maximum efficiency in the use of local income. The major piece of legislation was the Local Government Act of 1929, but there was an entire battery of new laws which tried to buttress the old system and correct its functional deficiencies.[182] The 1929 Act instituted block grants, largely to aid education. A further move toward efficiency was to abolish road authorities in the rural districts, and to bring the old Poor Law Boards under county and county borough government. There was also concern with inefficient local operation of the hospitals, asylums and poor houses still administered locally. The 1929 Act resulted from long and tortuous negotiations with other central ministries by the Ministry of Health under Neville Chamberlain.[183] The Act did not fully satisfy the Fabians, but socialist leaders grasped the opportunity to increase public assistance at the local level.[184]

Paralleling these adjustments was a simmering quarrel between counties and boroughs which the government chose to avoid. The 1888 Act had created distinctly urban authorities − the county boroughs − and during the passage of the law the boroughs had successfully agitated to increase the proposed number from ten to sixty-one. In the interwar period their number increased to eighty-two, a growth that, by diminishing the tax base of the counties, threatened to undermine their fiscal resources. Urban districts had also multiplied within the counties. In 1921 the counties asked the government to restrict the erosion of their power and influence by forming no more boroughs. The result was the appointment of a Royal Commission on Local Government (the Onslow Commission) which issued three reports after consulting both counties and boroughs.[185] The Local Government Act (County Boroughs and Adjustments) of 1926 was designed to arrest the formation of more urban authorities by requiring both parliamentary authorization and a minimum population of 75,000 persons. With this Act the establishment of boroughs was effectively stalled until applications multiplied after the Second World War, and became part of the pressure which later produced comprehensive reorganization.

As noted earlier, preserving the town versus country distinction was clearly part of the Conservative scheme to protect their rural power base. In France, however, the urban–rural distinction had never taken on similar importance in national politics, partly because France was less urban, and partly because the mayors were from an early date more directly involved in national politics. Part of the Conservative strategy was to bolster the urban and rural districts within the counties as a barrier to the urban encroachment of county boroughs. Many of the changes were contained in the Local Government Act of 1933, which tried to bring order out of the multiplication of services and responsibilities. The 1933 Act, for example, laid down common standards for voting and nomination in the boroughs and counties, an issue not finally settled until the Representation of the People Act of 1948 made the parliamentary and local franchises coterminous.[186] District powers were reinforced to reduce their motives for becoming boroughs. From 1929 to 1938, the consolidation of urban districts (reduced by 159) further strengthened the counties in their battles against boroughs. Less apparent is the way these measures complicated the process of county government and tended to disperse the potential influence of the local government system on the center.

Policymaking grew no less complicated within the French local government system in the interwar period, but these complexities had very different origins and emphases. The unified administrative structure meant then, as now, that problems initially arose as organizational issues, not as conflicts between national parties. The French government was fully aware of the confusion at the local level, but like the British was not eager to reorganize. Starting with a special commission in 1922, there had been twenty-one studies of local organization in France by 1952,[187] though none of them produced important changes. The confusion within government was enormous. The Vendée region, for example, was linked to Parisian ministries by offices located in nine different cities, and the national Ministry of Agriculture had eight separate regional organizations for local services.[188] The politics of this proliferation of governmental activity was, of course, very different from that of Britain. The important difference between the countries is that French administration became imbedded in local politics. Both systems appeared inadequate in the 1920s, but neither made structural changes.

SUBNATIONAL POLITICS AND POLICY BECOME A NATIONAL PROBLEM

In France, perpetuation of the Napoleonic prefect, an absolute necessity in a country torn by war and internal unrest, was not a considered political judgment. In Britain, the Local Government Board, once referred to as the 'rural House of Lords',[189] was an agency formed out of diverse efforts to reorganize local services in Britain, rather than a single effort to build an administrative machine that would dominate local government. The fact that the French prefect became an integral part of the decisionmaking process and the British Local Government Board fell by the wayside demands an historical explanation that goes beyond the framework of this study. Nevertheless, some understanding of the effects of such events on decisionmaking is essential in the comparative analysis of a complex policy problem.

The task of the nineteenth century state was to build national political institutions that could accommodate pressures for political participation. In Britain, the uncertainties about the future of local government were left to ministers and to Whitehall, while in France they became integral to the formation of the Third Republic. The reform of British local government in 1835 and 1888 followed the growth of the national electorate in a very orderly manner. As we have seen, major legislation was in most instances accepted by both parties, but partisan concerns were accommodated within Parliament. The more reactionary Tories thought the 1832 and 1835 reforms spelled the end of constitutional government in Britain; and some very successful efforts were made to curtail the effects of these laws. Local reform in 1888 was grudgingly accepted by the Conservatives in order that the party might benefit from Chamberlain's defection, and as a sacrifice to their intransigent policy on Ireland. The new Act did not upset their hold on county government nor did it threaten the power of a privileged class. The major effect was to impose on Britain an arbitrary division of 'town and county' that still handicaps British local government.

As the welfare state emerged, parliamentary processes were even less satisfactory in adjusting to the complexities of the subnational system, as the experience of the 1972 British reorganization has shown. But in the earlier stages of the modern state, national politics subordinated the local government system to national politics. Liberals and Conservatives, though willing to fight over immediate advantages, united to resist the rise of the Labour party at the local level. When Goschen was discussing county reform with Joseph Chamberlain in 1885, he spoke of change as necessary, 'in view of the prevalence of socialist views'.[190] The Local Government Act of 1929 was written in the full realization that Labour had become a national party and was rapidly capturing the major cities. There were over fifty Labour members in the House of Commons at the turn of the century, and 151 in 1920. The social reforms that added so heavily to the burdens of local government were introduced with a clear awareness of the threat from the Left. But mere political tactics could not stem the rapid growth of services and benefits that constitute the modern welfare state.

The continuity of central–local relationships in France is even more remarkable when we take into account the intense political differences and convulsions at the national level. Partisan politics focused on the survival of the Republic to which both prefects and local politicians contributed. Their collusion softened the arbitrary inclinations of the Second Empire, and their *complicité* supported the Third Republic. Unlike Britain, the French designed a political system that presupposed close links between local and national politics. Despite the excesses of French administrative powers, national leaders needed support from the communes, and local leaders developed their own avenues of intervention in national policymaking. Unlike Britain, French party politics was rooted in the communes and French administration provided a framework for mutual exchange in pursuing national and local interests.

There are many reasons why local reorganization was not high on the political agenda in the nineteenth century. In the early development of the modern state, government did not try to solve economic and social problems. In Britain, for example, government spent only 8 percent of the gross national product in 1890, with local government accounting for roughly one-third of government spending.[191] The French government had a slightly larger role in society, spending about 16 percent of national income in 1890, but the departments and communes accounted for only one-sixth of total public spending.[192]

Thus the state was not yet an instrument of social and economic policy, but many basic institutional choices had already been made. These choices would influence the future distribution of expanded services and benefits among different levels of government and, in turn, would affect the influence of local government on national politics and administration. Local government policy in the nineteenth century was for the most part bipartisan, accomplished by ensuring the appropriate social and political interests were accommodated. But the divergence between France and Britain was already apparent. France integrated local political and administrative institutions with the central government while Britain opted for a local government system that was only indirectly linked to national politics by parliamentary elections. The early growth of services and benefits was parceled out to individual ministries, each of which devised its own relationship to government at the local level.

If national politics appears to have only a marginal effect on local government policy, what would account for the decisions that indeed are taken? To answer this it is necessary to draw on the experience of the nineteenth century. The problems of the modern state require that both countries construct an effective administration. Napoleon endowed France with an administrative system that exceeded the needs of the time, which may account for both the excessive influence of administrators on policy, and the readiness of the various regimes to accept what they found with little change. In 1846, when Chadwick was desperately trying to persuade Whitehall to hire a handful of inspectors, the French Ministry of the Interior had over 200,000 employees, nearly a fourth of all government employees in France.[193] Deputies had begun to infiltrate the administration and the *grands corps* were in place.[194] French training of high-level administrators was far in advance of the British practice of putting one's friends and families to work as secretaries. British central administration was not reorganized until late in the century and was then inspired by colonial, not national, experience.

The relationship of French administration to local government policy and politics was, as we have seen, well established in the nineteenth century. The prefects were sensitive to the political changes of the time, if only because purges could sweep away their careers. To argue that they performed political tasks that might have been better done by party members, at least in the last century, is simply wishful thinking. As the century advanced their political neutrality increased and, by the turn of the century, they became very like the officials we find in contemporary France. None of the major leaders of the period, Thiers, Gambetta, Clemenceau or Herriot, wanted to do away with them. It is true, as Chardon wrote, that the 'principal attribute of the prefect is to represent successively the different fractions of the republican party reaching power',[195] but this is based on a cynical view of the nature of politics itself. Moreover, even in the early days of their development there were limitations to their power.[196] Unless one wishes to take the unrealistic position that administrators do not influence politics, their role at both the national and local levels must be taken into consideration. The possibilities for change in their absence are infinite and, therefore, almost impossible to imagine; the policy problem is much more one of what can be done with them.

NOTES: CHAPTER 2

1   See G. Pagès, 'Essai sur l'évolution des institutions administratives en France', *Revue d'Histoire Moderne*, vol. 1 (1932), pp. 8–57 and 113–37.

2   For an outline of the debate, see J. Godechot, *Les Institutions de la France sous la Révolution et l'Empire*, 2nd edn (Paris: PUF, 1968), pp. 43–90.

3   Antonia Fraser's fascinating *Cromwell: The Lord Protector* (New York: Dell, 1975), though not a constitutional history, makes it vividly clear that the Protector experienced few problems with local government except in the regions where Stuart rebellions took place. See J. S. Morrill, *The Revolt of the Provinces* (New York: Harper & Row, 1976).

4   J. H. Plumb, *The Growth of Political Stability in England, 1675–1725* (Harmondsworth: Penguin, 1969), p. 107.

5   *A. Regnier* (ed.), *Les Grands écrivains de la France*, vol. 1 (Paris, 1856–78), p. 326, quoted in Franklin A. Ford, *Robe and Sword: The Regrouping of French Aristrocracy after Louis XIV* (Cambridge, Mass.: Harvard University Press, 1953), p. vii.

6   Ford estimates the sums being paid nobles in 1708 and 1709 at about three million French pounds, or 12 percent of the monarchy's expenses.

7   The classic study of corruption under the French monarchy is Roland Mousnier, *Les Institutions de la France sous la Monarchie Absolu: 1598–1789* (Paris: PUF, 1974). Modern values should not be projected on this practice, which was common in all the courts of Europe. Recent scholarship indicates that the

weaknesses of the French nobility may have been exaggerated. See, for example, Robert Forster, *The Nobility of Toulouse* (Baltimore, Md: Johns Hopkins University Press, 1960) and Guy Richard, *Noblesse d'Affaires au XVIIIe siècle* (Paris: Colin, 1974). In the years preceding the Revolution the nobles were active in trying to reconstruct French government and finances. See accounts in C. B. A. Behrens, *The Ancien Régime* (London: Thames & Hudson, 1967), pp. 46–84; and R. R. Palmer, *The Age of Democratic Revolution*, Vol. 1 (Princeton, N.J.: Princeton University Press, 1959), pp. 439–65.

8   The numbers attached to the nobility vary. J. McManners, 'France', in A. Goodwin (ed.), *The European Nobility in the Eighteenth Century* (London: Adam and Charles Black, 1967), estimates 190,000. Numbers are not particularly helpful in comparing the roles of the aristocracy in the two countries. In a technical sense, the British nobles are the peers of the realm, and their numbers actually declined in the eighteenth century. Daniel A. Baugh, 'The social basis of stability', in D. Baugh (ed.), *Aristocratic Government and Society in 18th Century England* (New York: New Viewpoints, 1975), p. 9. In contrast, Ford estimates France had roughly 200,000 persons as *nobilité*, op. cit., pp. 29–30. For a reexamination of Ford's findings, see Jean Meyer, *Noblesse et Pouvoirs dans l'Europe de l'Ancien Régime* (Paris: Hachette, 1973).

9   For a brief account, see Menna Prestwich, 'The making of absolute monarchy (1559–1683)', in S. M. Wallace–Hadrill and John McManners (eds), *France: Government and Society* (London: Methuen, 1957), pp. 105–33.

10 See Francois Dumont, 'French kingship and absolute monarchy in the seventeenth century', in R. Hatton (ed.), *Louis XIV and Absolutism* (Columbus, Ohio: Ohio State University Press, 1976), pp. 55–84.

11 Ford, op. cit., p. 35.

12 For details see Maurice Bordes, *L'Administration Provinciale et Municipale en France au XVIIIe Siècle* (Paris: Société d'Education d'Enseignement Supérieur, 1972), pp. 27–35. The classification is roughly derived from the conditions under which the provinces were assembled to create the monarchy. For a local view, see Robert R. Harding, *Anatomy of a Power Elite: The Provincial Governor of Early Modern France* (New Haven, Conn.: Yale University Press, 1978).

13 These numbers are taken from Pierre Henry, *Histoire de Préfets* (Paris: Nouvelles Editions Latines, 1950), p. 11. However, numbers vary with sources. Bordes, op. cit., pp. 131–2, claims there were twenty-six *généralités* and thirty-four *intendants* in 1789. I am omitting here a fourth territorial structure, the Fermier Générale or General Farm, which was basically a system of contracting out the collection of agricultural taxes to important provincial nobles.

14 A description of the royal courts would take many pages, but their proliferation in the course of France's unification and the sinecures they provided for the corrupt nobility were immense. Ford, op. cit., pp. 37–8, finds the *parlements*, nine *chambres des comptes* and four *cours des aides* at work in the early eighteenth century. Their boundaries, responsibilities and prerogatives overlapped, and they spent much of their time fighting each other. See also Bordes, op. cit., Ch. II.

15 See J. H. Shennan, *The Parlement of Paris* (Ithaca, NY: Cornell University Press, 1958) for a full account. A history has been written for nearly all of these bodies. For a list of them, see McManners, op. cit., p. 192.

16 See the essay of D. Dakin, 'The breakdown of the old regime in France', in *Cambridge New Modern History*, Vol. 8 (Cambridge: Cambridge University Press, 1965), pp. 592–617, for a description of the growing financial crisis of the monarch prior to the Revolution. See also J. S. Gromley, 'The decline of absolute monarchy (1683–1774)', in Wallace–Hadrill and McManners (eds), op. cit., pp. 134–60, and Palmer, op. cit., pp. 85–99.

17 Pagès, op. cit., pp. 22–9 and 116.

18 Bordes, op. cit., p. 57. Though relevant details will be discussed in later chapters, French finance in the *ancien régime* was organized around two categories: ordinary expenses, which came within the purview of the royal administration,

and extraordinary expenses, which required, in theory at least, approval of the Estates General. Of course, this approval was never obtained after 1614.

19 Godechot, op. cit., p. 93.
20 Bordes, op. cit., pp. 123–30. See also the account of their activities and correspondence in Roger Mettam, *Government and Society in Louis XIV's France* (London: Macmillan, 1977), pp. 16–31.
21 Pagès, op. cit., p. 119.
22 See J. McManners, op. cit., p. 35. Among Louis XVI's intendants there were fourteen, many very young, who had inherited their positions directly. The definitive work on this period is P. Ardascheff, *Les Intendants sous le Règne de Louis XVI*, 3 vols (Paris: Alcan, 1909).
23 Turgot's efforts are described in Dakin, op. cit., pp. 607–9. Turgot had been a highly successful intendant at Limoges for thirteen years.
24 See J. F. Bosher, 'French administration and public finance in their European setting', in *Cambridge New Modern History*, Vol. 8 (Cambridge: Cambridge University Press, 1965), p. 573.
25 Plumb, op. cit., p. 31.
26 Ibid., pp. 58 and 146. This does not mean that the aristocracy was reluctant to use patronage.
27 Sir Charles Trevelyan, *British History of the Nineteenth Century* (London: Longman, 1937), p. 15.
28 'Robert Walpole's world: the structure of government', in Baugh (ed.), op. cit., p. 123.
29 Josef Redlich and Francis W. Hirst, *Local Government in England*, Vol. 1 (London: Macmillan, 1903), pp. 450–56. After the Act of Union with Scotland in 1706 45 Scottish counties were added. See also Sir Lewis Namier, 'Country gentlemen in Parliament, 1750–84', in his *Crossroads of Power: Essays on England in the Eighteenth Century* (London: Hamish Hamilton, 1962), pp. 30–5.
30 Plumb's *Walpole*, op. cit., p. 132. As Plumb observes, this distribution was not nearly as disproportionate at the time as it became by the nineteenth century.
31 In this regard, it is interesting to note that Burke considered the French effort to create proportionate units of local government in 1790 as a threat to stable government. See Le Comte de Luçay, *La Décentralisation* (Paris: Librairie Guillaume, 1895), pp. 46–7.
32 Baugh (ed.), op. cit., p. 9, notes that the formal nobility of the peerage actually declined in the eighteenth century. In 1700 there were about 775, and in 1755, there were 500.
33 Quoted by Baugh (ed.), op. cit., p. 13, from Habakkuk's essay 'England' in A. Goodwin (ed.), *The European Nobility in the Eighteenth Century* (London: Adam and Charles Black, 1967), pp. 97–115.
34 The dispute is over the ways in which the changing pattern of landownership may or may not have enhanced their growth. See G. E. Mingay, *The Gentry: The Rise and Fall of a Ruling Class* (London: Longman, 1976), pp. 39–79; for additional background see his earlier work, *English Landed Society in the 18th Century* (London: Kegan Paul, 1963).
35 Plumb's *Political Stability*, op. cit., p. 39.
36 Plumb's *Walpole*, op. cit., pp. 133–5 and 138.
37 Plumb's *Walpole*, op. cit., p. 136.
38 Habakkuk, op. cit., p. 102.
39 Plumb's *Political Stability*, op. cit., p. 64.
40 Ibid., pp. 67–8. Plumb notes that during 1688 thirty-five boroughs were put under the direct regulation of these officials. In Buckingham three mayors were removed in succession until the legal costs of fighting the monarch proved impossible.
41 Mingay, 1976, op. cit., p. 126. The information for this paragraph comes from the fascinating description in ibid., pp. 124–34. For additional details, see Esther

Moir, *The Justices of the Peace in England, 1558–1640* (London: Oxford University Press, 1969).

42 Trevelyan, op. cit., p. 22.

43 Plumb's *Political Stability*, op. cit., p. 170, notes that Whigs replaced fifteen justices of the peace in Middlesex to gain control of the county.

44 Some late and ineffective efforts were made to reform the justices of the peace in London and Middlesex, where for the first time they were paid, first from secret service funds and later by an Act of Parliament in 1792.

45 In this regard, the judgment of Trevelyan that the justices of the peace were 'in fact responsible to no one', op. cit., p. 22, needs some qualification. Within the counties this may have been true, but they were inextricably a part of the national political system and played this role very well.

46 There is a large and impressive number of county histories, corresponding to the provincial histories of France. All of them reflect this division. See the Appendix.

47 Pierre Henry, op. cit., p. 18.

48 Pierre Legendre, *Histoire de l'Administration de 1750 à nos Jours* (Paris: PUF, 1968), p. 112.

49 The need to restore the rapidly falling resources of the monarchy was the prevailing reason for considering change. See Pierre Henry, op. cit., p. 114, and Legendre, op. cit., p. 114. The idea of provincial assemblies frightened the nobility even more than paying taxes and outraged *parlements* in Paris and the provinces. Under Calonne they were abandoned.

50 See Godechot, op. cit., pp. 97–102. Maps of the territorial divisions are found for 1790, 1800 and 1812 facing pp. 112, 592 and 688, respectively.

51 Legendre, op. cit., p. 114.

52 The plans are discussed in more detail in ibid., pp. 108–15, and in Godechot, op. cit., pp. 94–6.

53 Godechot, op. cit., p. 273.

54 Ibid., p. 283. For a recent reevaluation of the regional tensions, see Alison Patrick, *Men of the First French Republic: Political Alignments in the National Convention of 1792* (Baltimore, Md: Johns Hopkins University Press, 1972).

55 Ibid., pp. 217–34, from which the examples in this paragraph are taken. Federalist committees were organized at Nimes, Lons-le-Saulnier, Dijon, Toulouse, Nevers, Bordeaux, Lyon and Marseilles. See Godechot's footnote, op. cit., pp. 326–7, for a full list of works on local government in this period.

56 Godechot again provides the essential materials in Godechot, op. cit., pp. 457–76. The provincial studies of this period are listed in a footnote, pp. 469–70.

57 Though extremely useful, Brian Chapman's *The Prefects and Provincial France* (London: Allen & Unwin, 1955) does not give the political and constitutional background needed to understand how the prefect of 1800 relates to the definition of central as well as local authority in France.

58 His major theoretical work has been translated and outlines his ideas. See Emanuel J. Sieyès, *What is the Third Estate?* (trans. by M. Blondel) (London: Pall Mall, 1963).

59 The Senate wanted to appoint Napoleon First Consul for ten years; he resisted suggesting that a plebiscite might be appropriate. See Godechot, op. cit., p. 571. Those who are impatient with the Upper Chamber today might note that among its first acts the Senate deported 130 Jacobins, ibid., p. 570.

60 Godechot, op. cit., pp. 586–92, for additional details. The actual name 'prefect' is the idea of Consul Lebrun and taken from the Roman prefect, Chapman, op. cit., p. 18.

61 See the notes in Godechot, op. cit., pp. 586–7. The major work is R. Regnier, *Les Préfets du Consulat et de l'Empire* (Paris: Nouvelle Revue, 1907). A more recent study, J. Savant, *Les Préfets de Napoleon* (Paris: Hachette, 1958), has been severely criticized. See the notes in Legendre, op. cit., pp. 154–6. An essay that tries to correct these studies, and provides detailed information on their varied

backgrounds is Edward A. Whitcomb, 'Napoleon's prefects', *American Historical Review*, vol. 79 (1974), pp. 1089–118.

62 Godechot, op. cit., p. 588, for this and additional examples.

63 Luçay, op. cit., p. 63.

64 Pierre Henry, op. cit., p. 38. A succinct account of the conduct and organization of government under Napoleon is given by Georges Lefebvre, *Napoleon*, Vol. 1 (trans. by H. F. Stockhold) (New York: Columbia University Press, 1969), pp. 77–94; and Vol. 2 (trans. by J. E. Anderson), pp. 159–204.

65 See the table prepared by Whitcomb, op. cit., p. 111. There were never more than twenty prefects changed at any one time until 1813, and many of those who were moved went on to more important posts. See also Pierre Henry, op. cit., Ch. 3; Chapman, op. cit., pp. 27–31; and Luçay, op. cit.

66 Legendre, op. cit., pp. 133–4.

67 For a summary of the argument see L. J. Hume, 'Jeremy Bentham and the nineteenth-century revolution in government', *The Historical Journal*, vol. 10 (1964), pp. 361–75.

68 See the outline of Place's impatient and exhaustive efforts to supply officials and Members of Parliament with material for local reform, in Bryan Keith-Lucas, *The English Local Government Franchise* (Oxford: Blackwell, 1952), pp. 3–5.

69 See Elie Halévy, *The Triumph of Reform 1830–1841* (London: Benn, 1961), p. 18.

70 See the superb biography by S. E. Finer, *The Life and Times of Sir Edwin Chadwick* (London: Methuen, 1957), for ample demonstration.

71 E. L. Woodward, *The Age of Reform, 1815–1870*, 2nd edn (London: Oxford University Press, 1962), p. 434. His entire chapter I of Book IV is a fine introduction to public policy in this period.

72 Quoted in Bruce, op. cit., p. 108.

73 Typically, Chadwick then became enraged with Lord Russell and launched a bitter attack on him and on mill owners, magistrates and shopkeepers generally. See Finer, op. cit., pp. 176–7.

74 Taken from the portion of Chadwick's *On the Evils of Disunity* (London, 1885), reprinted in H. J. Hanham, *The Nineteenth Century Constitution (1815–1914)* (Cambridge: Cambridge University Press, 1969), p. 383.

75 See the essay by Daniel A. Baugh, 'The cost of poor relief in South-East England, 1790–1834', *The Economic History Review*, vol. 28 (1975), pp. 50–68, for a summary of the conditions of the period and the argument about the effects of the old system. Rates did indeed diminish after the reform. See Fraser, op. cit., p. 46.

76 R. H. Tawney, *Religion and the Rise of Capitalism* (London: Murray, 1926); quoted in Bruce, 'The coming of the Welfare State', p. 95.

77 In Leeds the local council refused to build a new workhouse, though the local one was notorious. See Fraser, op. cit., pp. 48–9. In Leeds, Sheffield and many other towns the cost of relief actually increased and the Act was especially unpopular in the industrial north.

78 Redlich and Hirst, op. cit., p. 54.

79 Pierre Henry, op. cit., p. 32.

80 Bordes, op. cit., p. 157.

81 Woodward, op. cit., p. 442. The Improvement Commissioners actually date from eighteenth-century efforts to improve roads. See K. B. Smellie, *A History of Local Government*, 4th edn (London: Allen & Unwin, 1968), p. 21.

82 Redlich and Hirst, op. cit., p. 116.

83 Bryan Keith-Lucas, op. cit.

84 See the excellent study of social and political life in the provinces by A. Jardin and A.-J. Tudesq, *La France des notables: La vie de la nation 1815–1848* (Paris: Seuil, 1973).

85 Nicholas Richardson, *The French Prefectoral Corps 1814–1830* (Cambridge: Cambridge University Press, 1966), p. 5.

86 Jardin and Tudesq, op. cit., p. 218. For a brief description of the parties and

electorate see their first volume, *La France des Notables: L'Évolution Générale 1815–1848* (Paris: Seuil, 1973), pp. 43–7. In 1832 there were about 650,000 British voters, and about 172,000 French. However the ratio was reversed in the Second Empire when about 6.8 million could vote, and only 5.7 million in Britain. For the French figures see Serge Arné, 'L'esprit de la Vè République: réflexions sur l'exercise du pouvoir', *Revue du Droit Publique et de la Science Politique*, vol. 87 (1971), p. 653.

87   The figures on the early national elections are from Georges Dupeux, *French Society 1789–1970* (London: Methuen, 1976), p. 98.

88   Richardson, op. cit., pp. 8 and 6.

89   Martignac's tactic was to avert local obstruction by providing the commune with sufficient, but carefully defined, powers to preoccupy the localities. See the excerpts from his speech introducing the 1831 reforms in Maurice Bourjol, *La Réforme Municipale* (Paris: Berger-Levrault, 1975), pp. 63–4. For other proposals of Martignac, see ibid., pp. 125, 145, 159, 206, and 254–5. See also Félix Ponteil, *Les Institutions de la France de 1814 à 1870* (Paris: PUF, 1965), p. 33. Two essays by André-Jean Tudesq deal particularly with the July Monarchy, 'Les chefs de cabinet sous la Monarchie de Juillet', in Michel Antoine *et al., Origines et Histoire des Cabinet des Ministres en France* (Geneva: Droz, 1975), pp. 39–53; and 'Les directeurs de ministère sous la Monarchie de Juillet', in Francis de Baecque *et al., Les Directeurs de Ministère en France (XIXe-XXe siècles)* (Geneva: Droz, 1976), pp. 27–37.

90   This intriguing suggestion comes from Frank H. Brabant, *The Beginnings of the Third Republic in France* (London: Macmillan, 1940), pp. 343–54.

91   For a full account of these changes, see Charles H. Pouthas, 'La réorganization du Ministère de l'Interieur et la reconstitution de l'administration préfectorale par Guizot en 1830', *Revue d'Histoire Moderne et Contemporaine*, vol. 9 (1962), pp. 241–63.

92   Pierre Henry, op. cit., p. 125. Following the Restoration the July Monarchy had actually kept thirty-two old prefects in place and many were simply moved to other departments. See ibid., p. 93. The removal of prefects on a change in government, the *coup de balai* or sweeping from office, became a national political sport in France.

93   Chapman, op. cit., p. 34.

94   Our convenient stereotypes often picture France as the country in turmoil and Britain the country of repose. Nothing could be further from the truth. Early nineteenth century Britain was subject to every variety of protest and violence. For background see Pauline Gregg, *A Social and Economic History of Britain 1760–1972*, 7th edn (London: Harrap, 1973), pp. 78–97 and pp. 157–79. For more on the corruption of the parliamentary boroughs, see ibid., pp. 147–57. On the confusion of political forces at the national level, see Michael Brock, *The Great Reform Act* (London: Hutchinson, 1978).

95   For a fascinating account of the early transformation of two major cities, see François Vigier, *Change and Apathy: Liverpool and Manchester during the Industrial Revolution* (Cambridge, Mass.: MIT Press, 1970).

96   A recent political study of the reform bill is David C. Moore, *The Politics of Deference* (Brighton: Harvester Press, 1976). See also Samuel H. Beer, *British Politics in the Collectivist Age* (New York: Knopf, 1965), pp. 3–34.

97   See Redlich and Hirst, op. cit., p. 81. Even under these conditions, the Bill only passed the Commons by one vote, a close scrape for democracy that was to be paralleled in the early days of the Third Republic. Lord Grey had to persuade the king to create new peers if needed, in order to get passage in the Lords. To manipulate local elections, the landowners devised a complex system of limiting registration by merging or 'compounding' rates. See Keith-Lucas, op. cit., pp. 63–8.

98   Trevelyan, op. cit., p. 244.

99   The Whigs had over 500 seats in the reformed House of 658 seats. The Whigs and

their radical allies were in no sense a united party at the time, but the disarray among the Tories was crippling and the party was in eclipse until Peel reassembled it. For a recent account of his work see Norman Gash, *Peel* (London: Longman, 1976).

100 See the account in Keith-Lucas, op. cit., pp. 47–53.

101 The examples are taken from Redlich and Hirst, op. cit., pp. 119–23, which also reprints key sections of the report.

102 See their evaluation of the Act, op. cit., pp. 128–33. Redlich and Hirst are heavily influenced by the legal theory which conditions their magnificent study. Without a doubt it is our richest source of material on the British local government system at the turn of the century, but it is also without any framework relating national and local politics.

103 See Keith-Lucas, op. cit., pp. 59–64, for this early exercise in psephology. The explanation is connected to a complex problem that was part of the compromise with the Lords. It enabled 'freemen' to vote in parliamentary constituencies but did not automatically enfranchise them in boroughs.

104 This point will be elaborated in Chapter 5 dealing with the growth of services and costs. The figure is from Woodward, op. cit., p. 444.

105 See Keith-Lucas, op. cit., pp. 57–8.

106 An account, with Melbourne's consoling letters, is given in E. Halévy, op. cit., pp. 216–17. He also makes the interesting argument, pp. 220–1, that after the police reforms of 1839, Tory rule in the counties was strengthened.

107 Bourjol, op. cit., p. 208. A severe critic of the French system, Bourjol clearly sees that the alliance of republican conservatives and Orleanist aristocracy was united behind the liberal concept of the state. For other sections of the report see his book, op. cit., pp. 63, 198, 223 and pp. 369–70. Also Legendre, op. cit., p. 127.

108 Bourjol, op. cit., pp. 108–14. Without entering into the legal technicalities, the issue was how to preserve the civil nature of the commune without giving them property rights. In effect, *tutelle* provided a scheme whereby the potential economic power of the growing cities could be submitted to central control. The *établissement public* became the central device in later years to circumvent the same problem.

109 Ibid., pp. 314–17. The regional *commissaires* of the Second Republic were also a short-lived move in this direction. See Pierre Henri, op. cit., pp. 153–7. Barrot later wrote a short book on his ideas, *De la centralisation et de ses effets* (Paris: Didier, 1870).

110 Theodore Zeldin, *France 1848–1945*, Vol. 1 (Oxford: Clarendon Press, 1973), p. 521. As he points out, Napoleon III's interest in local government arose from his own *laissez-faire* notions and it is incorrect to consider him a totally unyielding advocate of centralization. See Zeldin's evaluation, op. cit., pp. 521–44; also Jacques Droz, 'Le problème de la décentralisation sous le Second Empire', in *Spiegel der Geschichte, Festgabe für Max Braubach* (Münster: Aschendorff, 1964), pp. 783–94; and Vincent Wright, 'Administration et politique sous le Second Empire', *Procés-verbal de l'Académie des Sciences Morales et Politiques* (May 1973), pp. 287–302.

111 Bernard Le Clère and Vincent Wright, *Les Préfets du Second Empire* (Paris: Fondation Nationale des Sciences Politiques, 1973), p. 36; also Wright, 'Les préfets d'Emile Olliver', *Revue Historique*, no. 487 (July–September 1968), pp. 115–36.

112 The debate went through two stages and reveals how central–local tension in France was of a different quality to that in Britain, which was by now concentrated on electoral and franchise reform. In the early 1860s the excessive privileges of the notables could still be used to argue for more state intervention, a case made by C. B. Dupont-White, *La Centralisation, ses Rapports avec l'Administration* (Paris, 1864), whose ideas are outlined by Zeldin, op. cit., pp. 536–44. Barrot's views will be further discussed below.

113 Large parts of this decree, as well as the decree on elections, can be found in

Gérard Sautel, *Histoire des Institutions Publiques depuis la Révolution Française* (Paris: Dalloz, 1969), pp. 435–8.

114   Quoted in Pierre Henry, op. cit., p. 176.

115   On the repression following the *coup d'état* of 1851 see Howard C. Payne, *The Police State of Louis Napoléon Bonaparte 1851–1860* (Seattle, Wash.: University of Washington Press, 1966). Even at this early stage there were internal administrative conflicts and rivalries that moderated the repression. See Vincent Wright, 'The coup d'état of September 1851: repression and the limits to repression', in R. Price (ed.), *Revolution and Reaction: 1848 and the Second French Republic* (New York: Barnes and Noble, 1976), pp. 303–33; and his 'La loi de sécurité générale de 1858', *Revue d'Histoire Moderne Contemporaire*, vol. 16 (1969), pp. 414–30. Also Howard Machin, 'The prefects and political repression: February 1848 to December 1851', in Price (ed.), op. cit., pp. 280–301.

116   See Vincent Wright, 'Les directeurs et secrétaires généraux des administrations centrales sous le Second Empire', in Francis de Baecque *et al.*, op. cit., pp. 38–78. He finds only three prefects among the 190 Directors. Also Pierre Guiral, 'Les cabinets ministériels sous le Second Empire', in Michel Antoine *et al.*, op. cit., pp. 55–65.

117   See Brabant, op. cit., pp. 63–73, for an account of the 1871 legislative elections.

118   This, of course, does not take into account the territorial polarization created by the Paris commune of 1871. The classic study is Henri Lefebvre, *La proclamation de la Commune* (Paris: Gallimard, 1965).

119   Outlined in Sautel, op. cit., pp. 438–41. Also, Bourjol, op. cit., pp. 125–6.

120   Described by B. Basdevant-Gaudement, *La Commission de décentralisation de 1870* (Paris: PUF, 1973), pp. 28–9. The signatories are listed in Appendix 2, pp. 104–5, and read like a roll of honor for the Third Republic. Included are Jules Ferry, Jules Simon, Odilon Barrot, De Broglie and Prévost-Paradol. Legendre, op. cit., puts the number at sixty, but Basdevant-Gaudement's list is slightly smaller. See also Odette Voilliard, 'Autour de Programme de Nancy (1865)', in C. Gras and G. Livet, op. cit., pp. 287–302.

121   See the list of twenty-one works on decentralization from the period in Le Clère and Wright, op. cit., pp. 396–7. Zeldin, op. cit., p. 538, notes that seventy-seven books on centralization appeared during the Empire.

122   Lest one think that political factions diminished around 1870, it is important to note that Barrot, though regarded as a devoted constitutional monarchist, was sympathetic to the republican cause, was really part of the group that came to be called *les vieux* in the 1871 debates. The *coup d'état* against the emperor became a central theme dividing the new republic. See Brabant, op. cit., pp. 353–8.

123   All the material that follows in this paragraph comes from the study of Basdevant-Gaudement, op. cit., pp. 52–90.

124   Barrot's *De la décentralisation . . .*, was actually written in 1861, but appears in this new edition of 1870 along with his encouraging reply to the authors of the Nancy Program. One cannot avoid noticing how the French turn to local government to champion their liberties in a way that has never happened in Britain. See also, Louis Blanc, *L'État et la Commune* (Paris, 1866); and André Simoit, *Centralisation et Démocratie* (Paris, 1861). As we shall see similar titles abound under the Fifth Republic.

125   For a complete account of the parties see Dorothy Pickles, *The Government and Politics of France*, Vol. 1 (London: Methuen, 1972), pp. 149–235; and Zeldin, op. cit., pp. 383–427.

126   His books are hard to find in the United States. The most relevant is *Local Self-Government and Centralization: The Characteristics of Each; and its Practical Tendencies as Affecting Social, Moral, and Political Welfare and Progress, Including Comprehensive Outlines of the British Constitution* (London: Sweet, 1851). He was not opposed to local government doing more, but to central control itself. The most complete account of his ideas is W. H. Greenleaf, 'Toulmin Smith and the British political tradition', *Public Administration* (UK), vol. 53

(1975), pp. 25–44. There is a brief account in William C. Lubenow, *The Politics of Government Growth: Early Victorian Attitudes Toward State Intervention* (London: Archon, 1971), pp. 88–95.

127 The Germanic legal tradition was carried on by Gneist's interest in British local government, which inspired the Redlich–Hirst study. As had happened half a century earlier, British leaders were frightened by mid-century revolutionary movements in France, but this was not Smith's main concern. Queen Victoria had defended the sanitation proposals before Parliament in 1845.

128 Lubenow, quoting a Birmingham MP in op. cit., p. 72.

129 Royston Lambert, 'Central and local relations in mid-Victorian England: the Local Government Act office, 1858–71', *Victorian Studies*, vol. 6 (1962), p. 122.

130 Ibid., pp. 135, 138–9.

131 For an excellent study of how it was formed and how it failed, see Roy M. MacLeod, *Treasury Control and Social Administration*, Occasional Papers on Social Administration (London: Bell, 1968).

132 Ibid., p. 10. For further evidence on the diversity of the Board's functions, see Milo R. Maltbie, 'The English Local Government Board', *Political Science Quarterly*, vol. 13 (1898), pp. 232–58.

133 The full account can be found in Royston Lambert, *Sir John Simon 1816–1904 and English Social Administration* (London: McGibbon & Kee, 1963), pp. 519–46.

134 Redlich and Hirst, op. cit., Vol. 2, pp. 242–7.

135 For a useful brief account of the changes in the Ministry, see Roger Farcat, 'L'administration centrale du Ministère de l'Intérieur: l'évolution des structures depuis la seconde guerre mondiale', *L'Administration*, no. 94 (December 1976), pp. 24–31. The important early changes were the loss of education in 1828, rural works *(ponts et chaussées)* in 1830 and agriculture in 1833.

136 Smellie, op. cit., p. 74. Though it will be further explored below, we should note here that the local government system was experiencing the first of its many financial crises in the 1870s, which no doubt did little to encourage the growth of the new Local Government Board. The Conservatives did propose the formation of a Ministry of Local Government in 1905, but with an election pending delayed legislation. See MacLeod, op. cit., p. 47.

137 For an analysis of party changes, see Beer, op. cit., pp. 69–125.

138 This does not mean, of course, that there were not fierce political battles in Parliament, as we shall see. For a general history of the period, see David Thomson, *England in the Nineteenth Century* (Harmondsworth: Pelican, 1950).

139 Quoted in Redlich and Hirst, op. cit., Vol. 1, p. 194.

140 Outlined in Keith-Lucas, op. cit., p. 101.

141 For a more complete account of Chamberlain's activity in Birmingham, see M. C. Hurst, *Joseph Chamberlain and West Midland Politics 1886–1895* (London: Dugdale Society, 1962). D. A. Hamer's excellent commentary accompanies a republication of the *Radical Programme* (Brighton (UK): Harvester, 1971).

142 Under the Public Health Act of 1875, which provided directions for the administration of public works loans, careful provisions were made to assure that investments were for permanent ownership. See Redlich and Hirst, op. cit., Vol. 1, p. 390.

143 See Keith-Lucas, op. cit., pp. 109–15.

144 Hamer, op. cit., p. xxxvi.

145 For the nuances of this strategy, see Beer, op. cit., pp. 245–76. For one of its local-level manifestations, see Fraser, *Urban Politics*, op. cit., pp. 133–42, on the alliance of 'beer and church' in Liverpool.

146 Quoted from excellent accounts by J. P. D. Dunbabin, 'The politics of the establishment of county councils', *The Historical Journal*, vol. 6 (1963), pp. 226–52.

147 *The Economist*, vol. 46, 16 June 1888, p. 46. *The Economist*'s account of the initial bill is in vol. 46 (24 March 1888), pp. 371–2. The county boroughs were a

compromise between rural power bases and urban needs.

148   Smellie, op. cit., p. 38. See also Redlich and Hirst, op. cit., Vol. 1, pp. 197–200.

149   The minister in charge of the Bill did not intend to exclude smaller towns from county government but was forced to do so. See Hanham, op. cit., p. 374.

150   The financial aspects of change will be dealt with in Chapter 6. *The Economist* noted in vol. 46 (16 June 1888), p. 755, as others were to do with later reorganizations, that it was 'madness' not to provide income for the counties. There was a long debate about a vehicles tax being assigned to local government, but it was rejected.

151   David Roberts, *Victorian Origins of the Welfare State* (New Haven, Conn.: Yale University Press, 1960), p. 278.

152   See R. K. Ensor, *England: 1870–1914* (London: Oxford University Press, 1936), pp. 213–14; also Redlich and Hirst, op. cit., Vol. 1, p. 211. For additional details on the reception of the Act, see Hugh H. L. Bellot, 'The Local Government Act of 1894', *The Westminster Review*, vol. 141 (1894), pp. 477–89; and for an account of the first elections, Richard Heath, 'The rural revolution', *The Contemporary Review*, vol. 67 (1895), pp. 182–200.

153   Bourjol, op. cit., p. 23, notes that in the local elections of 1871 only 8,000 of the 700,000 municipal councillors were Orleanist, Bonapartist or royalist.

154   Compare the slow but similar rates of change in the departmental councils. Unfortunately there is no comparable study for the Third Republic, but see L. Girard *et al., Les Conseillers Généraux en 1870* (Paris: PUF, 1967), and Marie-Hélène Marchand, *Les Conseillers Généraux en France depuis 1945* (Paris: Colin, 1970).

155   See the description in Zeldin, op. cit., pp. 570–604, on the activity of the deputies and the influence of the Chamber of Deputies. He dates the rise of the petty bourgeoisie as 1925 (p. 620), citing a study of Bordeaux by Jacqueline Herpin, 'Les milieux dirigeants à Bordeaux sous la Troisième République', *Revue Historique de Bordeaux*, vol. 15 (1966), pp. 146–65. For a view of the unfolding debate within one major party, see Serge Bernstein, 'Le parti radical et le problème du centralisme (1870–1939)', in Gras and Livet, op. cit., pp. 225–40. A more gradual change is suggested by Jean Charlot's figures on the social composition of the Chamber of Deputies, 'Les élites politiques en France de la IIIe à Ve République', *Archives Européenne de Sociologie,* vol. 14 (1973), p. 79.

156   On the role of prefects under the emergency government established at the proclamation of the republic, see Vincent Wright, 'Les préfets du gouvernement de défense nationale', *Revue d'Histoire Moderne et Contemporaire, Suppl.*, no. 3 (1975), pp. 16–24. Nearly every famous leader of the Third Republic served at this time.

157   Pierre Henry, op. cit., pp. 212–13.

158   See Sautel, op. cit., pp. 447–50. A good summary of the politics of the period is David Thomson's *Democracy in France*, 2nd edn (London: Oxford University Press, 1952), pp. 73–115.

159   Pierre Henry, op. cit., pp. 222–4. On the de Broglie period see Daniel Halévy, *La République des Ducs* (Paris: Grasset, 1937).

160   Except for the Irish problem, there is virtually no discussion of territorial representation until the 1920s. See J. C. Banks, *Federal Britain?* (London: Harrap, 1971), pp. 142–60. The Royal Commission on the Constitution did propose a way of converting the House of Lords into a deliberative body for regional governments. See Chapter 6.

161   Quotes from Zeldin, op. cit., pp. 591, 592.

162   Bourjol, op. cit., p. 53.

163   Though not directly related to the institutions governing the subnational system, the debate over universal suffrage took place in 1874. Democratic sentiments were not a great deal stronger in France than Britain. As Thomson notes, op. cit., p. 44, the Third Republic was indeed built from the locality to the center. Universal suffrage in the communes was the main argument for extending it to the national level.

164   For an outline of the groupings of republican France, see J. J. Chevallier, *Histoire des Institutions et des Régimes Politiques de la France Moderne (1789–1958)* (Paris: Dalloz, 1967).

165   See Sautel, op. cit., pp. 450–553, for an outline of the law.

166   In 1877 all but two prefects were replaced. See Vincent Wright, 'Les Épurations administratives de 1845 à 1885', in P. Gerbod *et al.*, *Les Épurations administratives: XIXe et XXe siècles* (Geneva: Librairie Droz, 1977), pp. 69–80.

167   Pierre Henry, op. cit., pp. 231–62. There is a thesis published on the ministry, Henri Terson, *Origines et Évolution du Ministère de l'Intérieur* (Montpellier: n.p., 1913), but it provides no political information.

168   Clemenceau enjoyed being Minister of the Interior in 1906. He wanted to nominate a man called Gapais to be prefect for Gap and a mulatto for subprefect of Le Blanc, ibid., pp. 256–61. See also Chapman, op. cit., pp. 50–2.

169   An excellent summary of their diminishing political role over the century is Guy Thuillier and Vincent Wright, 'Notes sur les sources de l'histoire du corps préfetoral (1800–1880)', *Revue Historique*, no. 513 (January–March 1975), pp. 139–54.

170   Pierre Henry, op. cit., p. 252. For general background see Chevallier, op. cit., pp. 554–571. Though it will be outlined in more detail below, it should be noted that it was at this time that the prefects developed a professional association to represent their interests, although a loose association had existed since 1907. Their transformation into a pressure group is perhaps the clearest evidence that they had indeed become part of a modern state and had forgotten the direct political role they had once played in national politics.

171   See Pierre Henry, op. cit., pp. 301–2. It is interesting to note that the traditional resentment of the subprefect surfaced in the late nineteenth century. Goblet abolished sixty-six *arrondissements*, and there was legislation prepared to abolish the post in 1906. See ibid., pp. 242–7.

172   Ibid., p. 285. See also the detailed study of their social background by Jeanne Siwek-Pouydesseau, *Le Corps Préfetoral sous la Troisième et la Quatrième République* (Paris: Colin, 1969).

173   Jean-Claude Thoenig, 'Local subsidies in the French Third Republic: the political marketplace and bureaucratic allocation', in D. Ashford (ed.), *Financing Urban Government in the Welfare State* (London: Croom Helm, 1980).

174   *Report on the Machinery of Government*, Cd 9230 (London: HMSO, 1918).

175   Legendre, op. cit., pp. 77–8. See his excellent summation of the relations of history and administration, ibid., pp. 70–103. Leroy-Beaulieu, as might be guessed, was interested in the British system of government and wrote *L'Administration Locale en France et Angleterre* (Paris: n.d. [1871?]) continuing the Tocqueville tradition.

176   Redlich and Hirst, op. cit., Vol. 2, p. 46.

177   Keith-Lucas, op. cit., pp. 114–15.

178   See J. P. D. Dunbabin, 'IV. Expectations of the new county councils, and their realization', *The Historical Journal*, vol. 8 (1965), pp. 353–79. In the southern counties the hold of the aristocracy and Quarter Session judges was particularly strong, and the inclusion of lower class councillors was viewed by the Conservative Party with some alarm. In Staffordshire the chairman, Lord Harrowby, tried too hard. He mistakenly greeted a porter as a new councillor!

179   J. D. Marshall (ed.), *The History of Lancashire County Council 1889–1974* (London: Martin Robertson, 1977).

180   Redlich and Hirst, op. cit., vol. 1, p. 273.

181   Samuel H. Beer, op. cit., p. 252, based on Laski's analysis, 'The personnel of the English cabinet, 1801–1924', *American Political Science Review*, vol. 22 (1928), pp. 12–31. See also W. L. Guttsman, *The British Political Elite* (London: MacGibbon and Kee, 1963).

182   The other pieces of legislation were the Rating and Evaluation Act of 1925 which ended separate rates for poor relief and districts; and the controversial Audit Acts

of 1927 and 1933 to deal with a major fight with Labour over surcharging councillors for unauthorized expenditures. On the latter, see the full account in B. Keith-Lucas and P. Richards, *A History of Local Government in the Twentieth Century* (London: Allen & Unwin, 1978), pp. 65–91.

183   The most complete account is by Gerald Rhodes, 'Local government finance, 1918–1966', *Local Government Finance* (Layfield Report) (London: HMSO, 1976), App. 6, pp. 102–73.

184   When the 1888 Act had been passed, Lord Salisbury resisted giving the Poor Law Boards to the new county and borough councils because it would be 'rather like leaving the cat in charge of the milk jug'. Quoted in Keith-Lucas and Richards, op. cit., p. 43. The Webbs' reaction confirms his view. See Fabian Tract No. 231 by Sidney Webb, *The Local Government Act, 1929 – How to Make the Best of it* (London: The Fabian Society, 1929).

185   The three reports from the Onslow Commission were: *Constitution and Extension of County Boroughs*, Cmd 2506 (London: HMSO, 1925); *Areas and Functions*, Cmd 3213 (London: HMSO, 1928); *Functions and Constitutions of Local Authorities*, Cmd 3436 (London: HMSO, 1929). Possibly less important, but indicative of the local preoccupations of the period, was a Royal Commission report on London (Ullswater Report), *Local Government of Greater London*, Cmd 1830 (London: HMSO, 1923), which did not produce important changes.

186   The 1933 Act also prevented a person from running for office in more than one ward; limited the number of co-opted members that might serve on council committees; and required disclosure of financial interest by councillors. The most controversial part of the Act was to deny salaries for councillors; a matter which the Labour Party had long considered a barrier to its full participation in local councils. See Keith-Lucas, op. cit., p. 160 and p. 178.

187   See Edouard Bonnefous, *La Reforme Administrative* (Paris: PUF, 1958), pp. 59–105, for a discussion of the proposals.

188   Bonnefous, op. cit., p. 31.

189   J. G. Dodson, President of the Board under Gladstone in 1881, quoted in Keith-Lucas, op. cit., p. 107. Dodson was referring only to counties.

190   Hamer, op. cit., p. xxvii. Chamberlain agreed.

191   Alan T. Peacock and Jack Wiseman, *The Growth of Public Expenditure in the United Kingdom*, 2nd edn (London: Allen & Unwin, 1967), pp. 107–79. It is important to note that over the century the growth of government expenditure on a per capita basis at current prices had barely doubled.

192   Unfortunately, French statistics are usually calculated on the basis of national income rather than gross national product, so the two sets of figures are not directly comparable. These figures are taken from Christine André *et al.*, 'Les dépenses publiques françaises depuis un siècle', *Économie et Statistiques*, no. 43 (March 1973), p. 8.

193   Roberts, op. cit., p. 13. The total Home Office staff was then twenty-nine persons. See also Lubenow, op. cit.

194   In the Second Republic there was an effort to train administrators with republican sympathies, another early sign of the politicization of French administration. See Vincent Wright, 'L'école nationale d'administration de 1848–1849: un échec révélateur', *Revue Historique*, no. 255 (1976), pp. 21–42.

195   Chardon, *Le Pouvoir Administratif* (Paris: Librairie Academique, 1911), p. 39.

196   See the chapter on limitations in Le Clère and Wright, op. cit., pp. 110–31.

Chapter 3

DECISIONS AND NON-DECISIONS:
POLICY IN THE 1960s

It is but a small portion of the public business of a country, which can be well done, or safely attempted, by the central authorities; and even in our own government, the least centralized of Europe, the legislative portion of at least the governing body busies itself far too much with local affairs, employing the supreme power of the State in cutting small knots. – J. S. Mill.

Dignity of the government, authority of the state, necessity to guard one's distance, and to put between the minister and the population all the necessary apparatus to conserve the prestige of office, danger of exposure to manifestations? In what century are we? – Françoise Giroud.

The intricacy of local government policy makes any contemplated change vulnerable to criticism from competing parties. Within the central administration proposals for structural reform easily touch off infighting and old rivalries. Only slightly less obvious are the unforeseen pitfalls of reorganization itself: monetary cost, dislocation of relationships among services at several levels of government and administrative conflict. The resistance of existing local governments to proposals for change is matched only by their ingenuity in deflecting new policies from the intended objectives and using sheer inertia to reject those found most distasteful. The previous chapters contain considerable evidence that the wise politician simply avoids structural change. Sharpe put it succinctly, 'Local government reorganization is loved by no one'.[1]

Employing a policy perspective in analyzing change enables us to assess the different ways in which political systems accumulate the pressure that requires change. The comparative analysis of subnational politics and policy is, as was argued in Chapter 1, necessarily dynamic. Thus neither de Gaulle nor Wilson set out to devise a new local government system, but both found themselves heavily involved in restructuring subnational relationships. The pressures for change were similar: problems of economic growth, social justice and effective governmental decisionmaking constantly spilled over into questions concerning local government. These pressures might be generally characterized as the needs of the welfare state. The expanding role of government eventually altered relationships in the local government system in both countries. Hence aversion to change in itself does not differentiate the two countries.

Decisions to restructure the subnational system gradually accumulated after 1945. The British case is more dramatic because the reforms, culminating in the Local Government Act of 1972 for England and Wales and comparable legislation for Scotland, affected the entire population. Britain was able to undertake a massive territorial reorganization while France was not. Nonetheless, France has made important changes in its subnational system. The organization of districts, *communautés urbaines* or urban communities, and the various types of *syndicats* or unions among communes involve nearly a third of the French population. If the reorganization of Paris is included, then France has devised new structures affecting the lives of roughly half of its citizens.[2] As Chapters 4 and 5 will show, the major differences between the two systems as they now operate lie in how decisions are made, the degree of interdependence in territorial and functional reorganization, and the priorities assigned to reorganization.

The major concern of this chapter is how the subnational system got onto the political agenda. Neither country had a clear vision of what was needed. De Gaulle, as we shall see below, was extremely vague as to what should be done about local government.[3] This is to some extent inherent in the very complexities of the issues, and also is a result of the kind of leadership in democratic systems, which requires elites to be constantly sensitive to political pressures. In the first four years of his rule, 1958 to 1962, de Gaulle left the reorganization questions to his disciple, Debré. After Pompidou became Prime Minister, policies affecting the subnational system were shifted to a team of civil servants. De Gaulle reviewed major decisions only after full debate at higher governmental levels. If the policies that emerged had any overall objective, it was not to tamper with the structure of local government, but to modernize French industry and commerce. Meanwhile, in Britain, Wilson was wrestling with many of the same problems when the Royal Commission on Local Government was appointed. As we shall see, the Commission itself was unforeseen and its recommendations, with substantial changes, were made into law by the Conservatives. In neither country did the leaders or parties have a grand design that guided the reconstruction of local government. The remarkable difference was that Britain was pursuing a vision of local harmony, while France was devising a curious compound of administrative and political adjustments to remedy the inadequacies of the old subnational system.

THE FOURTH REPUBLIC POSTPONES REORGANIZATION

In the constitutional debates on the formation of the Fourth Republic, France relived many of the Third Republic's conflicts. The struggle over a strong or weak executive ended with de Gaulle's dramatic resignation in 1969, leaving relatively little time to thrash out the reorganization of local government. Nevertheless, strong feelings about the territorial organization of the state were always close to the surface, conditioned both by the experience of Vichy and by the appearance of a potentially strong majority on the political left.

But France's opportunity to restructure the subnational system under the Fourth Republic was lost because the different forces favoring change could not agree among themselves. The Communists saw the prefect as the key to repression in the departments and favored abolishing the position. The Socialists had strong ties to departments and regions and wanted a weakened prefectoral system. The liberal catholics in the Mouvement Républicain Populaire (MRP) were prepared to keep prefects, but felt there should be more democratic control exercised at the departmental level.[4] Because of these disagreements some crucial decisions were not made, but left to future laws. Thus Article 86 of the 1946 Constitution simply stated that 'the organization of communes, departments and overseas territories, are fixed by law'. Article 88 did not mention the issue of prefectoral power at all, and laid down only that 'delegates of the government [are] designated by the council of Ministers'.

While the disgrace of Vichy weighed heavily on France, the territorial reforms made under Vichy were influential.[5] The regime appointed eighteen regional prefects with deputies for police and economic affairs. In 1942 Vichy organized departmental committees to arrange mergers between small and underpopulated communes, and in 1943 a similar law was imposed to supervise urban development. With the liberation of France and the establishment of the provisional government, the organization of the subnational system became a pressing issue.

De Gaulle gave sweeping powers to *commissaires régionaux de la République*.[6] He had suspended all prefects before D-Day and the *commissaires* were supposed to take over the functions of Vichy's regional prefects. For two years the *commissaires* were the backbone of regional and local administration, but they were disliked and distrusted by the parties of the left. In 1946 Parliament refused to appropriate funds, and the office was discontinued. Meanwhile, some Vichy prefects had received summary justice at the hands of the liberated populace, and many had retired. The new prefects replacing them were drawn from many parts of French society, and were often closely linked to the Free French movement and de Gaulle. Nearly half the prefects in office in 1947 were *parachutages*, or persons chosen from outside the ranks of the prefectoral corps. Two of the prefects were Communists.

These emergency measures might have become the basis for a structural reform of local government, but change depended on continued cooperation between Communists, Socialists and MRP. Instead the national coalition broke apart with the Soviet Union's decision to forcefully resist the reconstruction of Europe under American auspices. The Communists were a thoroughly disciplined Stalinist party under Thorez, and in 1947 they organized crippling strikes and serious sabotage. In some major industrial areas, such as Metz, where the Communists were particularly strong, there were virtual insurrectionary governments, and there was widespread destruction of factories and mines.

As on so many previous occasions, parties that could barely agree on how to organize the Republic rallied to save it. During 1947 the government shifted to a non-Communist coalition in which the Socialists were prime movers, installing emergency rule in the military regions. When the Socialist leader Blum became President of the Council of Ministers in late 1947, he declared, 'It is necessary to make the authority of the republican state clear and to impose a discipline and a coordination on all public administration'.[7] His rallying speech was supported by the MRP leader Schuman. In early 1948 legislation established eight *inspecteurs généraux de l'administration en mission extraordinaire* (IGAME) throughout the country. These regional military inspectors combined police and military powers and were directly linked to the security apparatus of the French state.

Crisis conditions did not permit a major debate of the future territorial and functional organization of the French state. For the non-Communist Left and the Center, local government policy became essentially 'the defense of acquired positions'. Nevertheless leaders of the Fourth Republic were not oblivious to the cumbersome nature of the local government system. In early 1947, for example, the Radical Party leader Ramadier called for a *déconcentration* of ministerial powers to the departments and communes.[8] Nor did France lack proposals for regional government; there had been thirty-four such proposals under the Third Republic.[9] Moreover, contrary to the stereotype of French government, there were no serious legal barriers to reform. Title X of the constitution of the Fourth Republic made the departmental council the local executive. But one legally feasible reform – the proposed law to extend the council's powers so that the departments might have stronger elected governments – was put aside as too dangerous.[10]

When the IGAMEs were established, the Minister of the Interior took great pains to reassure the prefects that the new office would not infringe on their powers. When changes in IGAME powers were made in 1951, there was strong protest from the Association of the Prefectoral Corps. One deputy spoke of 'the risk to the entire territorial organization', whereupon the Minister of the Interior reassured the Assembly that 'the prefect remains the sole representative of the government in his department', and that 'the department, as for 150 years, is the normal framework of our administrative life'.[11] Another reform, a law proposed in early 1947 to ease the conditions under which communes might form unions for the provision of local services, died in Parliament.

LOCAL GOVERNMENT NOT A LABOUR PRIORITY IN BRITAIN

If policies affecting the subnational system were considered in France only under duress in the immediate postwar period, Britain positively rejected them. Before their massive defeat in 1945, the Conservative-led coalition had set in motion several inquiries relating to local government organization. A 1945 Act created a new Local Government Boundary Commission, and two committees were appointed to review London government: the Reading Committee on boundaries, and the Davies Committee on planning.

In many ways the time seemed opportune for reform. Labour came to power with a huge majority, and had also swept the local elections after the war. The initial Conservative moves toward reorganization suggest that they, too, saw that the gestures of 1929 and 1933 would no longer suffice. Moreover reform had vocal advocates, especially at the London School of Economics.[12] But in addition to the immense amount of work needed to repair war damages, the Labour government had a full slate of social and economic reforms at the national level. Unlike in France, local government in Britain had no single department that might have defended its interests, nor did national government provide ways in which ministers, even if willing, might have defended local government. Labour's major policy affecting local government was the nationalization of health and welfare. This task monopolized the attention of the Ministry of Health, which had retained principal responsibility for local government.[13]

Although Britain did not actually embark on a global reform for another twenty years, the need was already widely recognized. But the inability of the local authority associations to agree on a course of action after the Second World War meant that little could be done at the time. As part of the preparation for postwar reconstruction, discussions with the local authority associations began in 1942, and in 1945 the Coalition government issued a White Paper.[14] The Labour Party position included strengthening two-tier local government, which, of course, would favor their urban voting base. Labour's Minister of Health, Aneurin Bevan, was not known for his patience and tact. Confronted with local association bickering, he was unwilling to make major changes in functional responsibilities. In reply to suggestions from the Association of Municipal Corporations in 1946, he said 'It is not a matter for me. I throw the charge back.' Robson, a major reform spokesman, charged that the minister had 'virtually relinquished his constitutional responsibility as Minister of Health for the general well-being of local government'.[15]

Without a single voice and with no coordinated access to national policymaking, local government became a bystander in the subsequent centrally-organized reforms of education, fire services, health and town planning. A Boundary Commission produced a weak White Paper in 1948 under Sir Malcolm Trustram Eve. After two years of study the Commission concluded that little could be accomplished by altering boundaries unless functions were also adjusted. By 1947 Bevan was encountering stiff resistance from local government over the nationalization of hospitals and other municipal services. Again confronted with the complexities of local reorganization, he brusquely terminated the Commission.[16] The same fate awaited the Committee on London under Lord Reading, which left the long-overdue task of London's reorganization to the Conservatives, a decade later.[17] Although Bevan had some ideas about local reorganization,[18] the Labour Party's national objectives did not then mesh with local policies, and were in fundamental conflict with ideals of increased local autonomy. The early twentieth century concerns with local reform of the Webbs and other Labour intellectuals were forgotten, once the party came to power. There was no discussion of local government at the Annual Conferences for nearly a decade after the war. *The New Fabian Essays*, a collection of writings by Labour leaders, did not include a chapter on local government.[19]

The ill-fated Boundary Commission, however, deserves some discussion. For the first time it recognized that Britain could no longer consider territorial organization apart from functional responsibilities. The Commission was empowered to review all boundaries of boroughs and counties. Its recommendations were to be submitted to the Minister of Health, and were subject to parliamentary review. But it had no power to consider the distribution of functions among different levels of county government, though it could recommend creating a unified local authority in the form of a new county borough. As with every previous inquiry, it was forbidden to alter Middlesex, the county surrounding London, or London itself. Thus the Commission was confined to the terms of the 1888 and 1894 Acts.

Its recommendations foreshadowed the 1972 legislation, and are in some respects superior. The Commission proposed the abolition of the town and country distinction. It would have created two kinds of counties rather than perpetuating the duality of local government, which the 1972 reforms were to invert, but not remove. Counties would in effect have been adjusted to function in two different situations. Large metropolitan areas would have two-tier governments, making policy coordination possible, whereas the rural counties could retain two-tier government to cope with the problems of dispersed population through the use of districts. Unified, single-tier governments could still be used for those towns and cities that did have dispersed metropolitan areas and were not suitable for integration in the older version of the county. Given the terms of reference, the suggestions were ingenious, and included ways of dealing with the difficult boundary problems of Manchester, Liverpool and Lancashire that have plagued every modern reorganization effort.[20] While some single-tier or unified governments for towns might have remained, both large cities and rural areas could have benefited from the flexibility of two-tier government. The report displays a pragmatic view of local government that the British have rarely achieved.

Reform was also neglected at the time because of massive changes in nearly every national policy. These changes, in turn, affected the functions of local government, and until they were completed it was virtually impossible to consider what might appropriately be the role of a reorganized local government. The loss of local functions was, of course, formidable, and was widely protested by champions of local government.[21] The Trunk Roads Act of 1946 doubled the mileage taken away from local control and gave the Minister of Transport power to declare any additional route a trunk road, and therefore under national jurisdiction. The Transport Act of 1947, later reduced in scope by the Conservatives and not applied, gave the British Transport Commission wide powers to take over municipal buses and trams. The Electricity Act of 1947 nationalized the municipal power companies, and the Gas Act of 1948 added 274 municipal gas plants. The National Health Service Act of 1946 transferred all local-authority hospitals to the Ministry of Health, and the National Assistance Act of 1948 eliminated nearly all assistance administered through the local governments. In addition, changes in the inspection and regulation of police and fire services brought them increasingly under central control.

In short, by 1950 for all practical purposes Britain had totally refashioned the functions of its local government system, but had done nothing to make sense of boundaries or deal with territorial imbalances and population disparities. Instead, national decisions increased centralization and simply bypassed local government. The growth of central government characterizes all welfare states, and the expansion of services and benefits envisaged by the Labour government could not have been achieved using the existing local government system. The second reason for the neglect of structural change was the central government's reluctance to deal with the resource problems of local government. The block grant system, introduced in 1929, had been made obsolete by the constant addition of new, specific grants. Even before the war, the amount made available in block grants was less than half the total money transferred to counties and boroughs.[22] Labour was especially interested in this problem because of the unequal resources of local governments; many of the poorer were, of course, the cities controlled by Labour councillors.

The Local Government Act of 1948 introduced resource equalization, providing Treasury funds to redistribute revenues in order to help poor cities and depressed rural areas. The 1929 Act's cumbersome process was replaced by a formula based on the average per capita taxation for the country. Establishing this principle meant that localities had to have standard valuations so local assessment was given to the Board of Inland Revenue. The process of revaluation took until 1956, but with the 1948 Act the Treasury acquired a role similar to that of the French Ministry of Finance. The aim was not to establish a financially independent system of local government, but to make sure, in Bevan's words, that local authorities would not 'determine the size of the spoon with which they will scoop up Exchequer money'.[23] Although not foreseen at the time, the change brought local government more directly under the financial control of central government, while providing it with no new sources of revenue. While the overall implications of resource allocation will be considered in Chapter 6, it is important to note how Labour's quest for uniformity restricted local government.

Stalemate was the immediate reaction to proposals to reshape the subnational political system in both Britain and France. In both countries the complexity of central government was increasing rapidly with the growth of the welfare state. Both retained cumbersome territorial divisions, but France, under open attack from the Communists, clung to the past more stubbornly than Britain. Though only a tentative step toward reform and a highly controversial innovation, the French regional IGAME pointed a clearer way toward reorganization than Britain's ill-fated boundary discussion. Meanwhile local services were growing in both countries, perhaps more visibly in Britain because of the vigorous nationalization policies of Labour. Even so, in 1950 there were some forty regionally organized services in France, of which only eight were coordinated through the departments. Each of these activities depended, in turn, on a different regional organization of the Paris ministries.[24] In short, the growth and complexity of functions in themselves do not explain the politics of local government reorganization, but rather how these functions are linked with the local level. Immediately after the war, these links were not changed in France, while in Britain there were moves toward more central control. But neither government was yet forced to recognize the full dimensions of the policy choice being forced upon them by the growth of the welfare state.

EARLY MOVES IN FRANCE: WHETHER TO DESIGN NEW TERRITORIES

France has never been at a loss for comprehensive proposals to restructure the local government system. Debré, for example, came forth in 1947 with a plan to reduce the number of departments from ninety to forty-seven,[25] but his proposal was essentially administrative consolidation which would have retained the existing structure. Its Jacobin design was apparent both in its reliance on central government and in the hope that larger departments would protect the state against provincial separatism. Like the Gaullist proposals of the 1960s, it was politically unrealistic 'to neglect the notables' conservatism and to ignore departmental chauvinism'.[26] This issue was forcefully brought to public attention by the now famous book by Gravier, *Paris and the French Desert*.[27] While there is no way to gauge how much the book's acclaim affected the French government, it is difficult to imagine such a book being written in Britain or seriously considered by Whitehall. Gravier denounced the historic rivalry between Paris and the provinces, and produced compelling evidence that the growth of Paris absorbed the talent, resources and influence of the entire country. His study was enthusiastically accepted by the regions that felt neglected for cultural, economic or political reasons. Meanwhile a response was being fashioned within government, not because of the potential for separatist movements, but because social and economic pressures forced change.

Shortly after the war, France formed a Planning Commission under Monnet, whose initial task was to rebuild the destroyed and depleted economy.[28] A Ministry of Reconstruction had also been formed, to deal with problems of urban and rural infrastructure. The ideas that dominated French thinking about the subnational system until 1970 germinated at this early stage. These ideas were enforced by a minister, Claudius-Petit, who did not wish to see his reconstruction ministry disappear with its own success, and, in searching for new activities, coined the phrase *aménagement du territoire*.[29] The phrase is another French characterization that defies translation. Prudhomme calls it a 'vague and beautiful' phrase, combining the concepts of planning, design and implementation.[30] Claudius-Petit defined it as activity 'to favor the better distribution of population in relation to natural resources and economic activity'.[31] In any event, the notion captured the imagination of both politicians and administrators – the first requirement of any successful policy proposal. By the mid-1950s, territorial planning had been accepted by most of the leaders of the coalition that governed France in the last years of the Fourth Republic: among them Pflimlin, Pleven, Edgar Faure and Mendès-France. In the predatory world of French administration, the idea also attracted able young administrators like Pisani, and appealed to provincial leaders such as Lajugie from Bordeaux and Phlipponneau from Rennes.[32] Contradicting the stereotype of a methodical administration, the Ministry of Reconstruction assembled what has been called a 'kaleidoscope of institutions' to establish its concept of local-level reform.[33] There were study committees, industrial development boards and regional groups. No special emphasis was placed on the level of government. By the end of 1955 there were five regional and seven departmental groups actively engaged in territorial design and development.

In 1950 a central committee to study territorial development was formed in the Ministry of Reconstruction, and modest financial backing was provided in a special fund, Fonds National d'Aménagement du Territoire (FNAT). The first regions to benefit were among the poorest, such as Languedoc, Corsica, Provence and the lower Rhône Valley. The idea might have remained just another new subsidy to neglected areas were it not for the strong regional leadership that it provoked. In the Gironde a bright young mayor, Chaban-Delmas, seized on the opportunity to rebuild the declining economy of the Bordeaux area.[34] In Brittany the regionalist movement responded under the leadership of Phlipponneau.[35] In the northeast, Pflimlin provided strong leadership both as mayor of Strasbourg and as an influential deputy. Although Mendès-France, the Premier determined to modernize France, had reservations about encouraging separatism, he found the possibility of increasing industrial productivity and economic growth appealing. In 1954, the first *comités d'expansion* were formed under national auspices. By decree *programmes d'action régionale* (PAR) were approved from 1955 onward, and the twenty-two programs that emerged became the basis for the future development of regional government. The complexity that characterizes so many French policy initiatives was multiplied in this case by the formation of local *Sociétés de développement régional* (SDR), to encourage private investment in the regions.

Several aspects of these tentative moves toward restructuring the French subnational system bear further examination. First, the existing administrative links between central and local government were simply bypassed. At the local level, mayors did have a role in the new development committees, but the possibility that departments and communes might operate these new organizations was barely mentioned. In Britain, when the question of new regional government finally appeared on the agenda, local government not only failed to stop it, but was virtually excluded from the discussion. In France, at first the prefects, with the support of most mayors, were also unalterably opposed to regional reform, but they were able to use it for their own ends. Throughout the 1950s the *Bulletin* of the prefectoral corps was filled with protests against regional authorities, but, as we shall see below, they were eventually reconciled to regional government. The important point is that in France the functional requirements of the welfare state overcame the resistance of prefects and mayors by devising new relationships to the local political elites, and by appealing to economic self-interest.

Nevertheless conflict continued, and the early form of regional government in France posed a peculiarly difficult problem. The Planning Commission had priority in allocating industrial funds, which were concentrated in the *Fonds de développement économique et social* (FDES), and initially designed to transfer Marshall Aid to France. Thus the Ministry of Reconstruction was clearly impinging on planning interests. However, the Ministry's 1957 requirement that it approve the *programmes d' action régionale* established its claim to a voice in central decisionmaking as the new programs developed.[36] The administrative conflict continued in the 1960s, when Gaullists revised regional government, and was revived once again in the 1970s. Efforts to establish policies to deal with the subnational system are, of course, never immune to the politics of administration. But the significant contrast with British administrative politics lies in the way these struggles become an integral part of the French policymaking process.

CONSERVATIVE DELAYING ACTION IN BRITAIN

The relocation of Britain's urban population, the reconstruction of the economy and the growth of government activity under the Labour government until 1951, made the subnational system of the time less and less appropriate for policymaking needs. Just as many early adjustments in France can be traced to the last years of the Fourth Republic, so many Labour policies in the 1960s can be traced to the Macmillan government of the late 1950s. When Britain swung back to Conservative rule in 1951, the party had made large advances at the local level. While these increases in local Conservative strength made it less likely that major changes would be made, the Conservatives recognized that the system was not working well.

They had come to power promising a major housing program, and this resulted in the 1957 Housing Act.[37] In 1954 a prominent Conservative leader, Duncan Sandys, had taken over the previously neglected Ministry of Local Government and Planning, renamed the Ministry of Housing and Local Government. The territorial issue again arose, despite the emphasis on housing, in part because of the cities' difficulties in obtaining land from the surrounding rural jurisdictions. In 1955, for example, Ilford, Poole and Luton had petitions before Parliament for county borough status, in order to increase their ability to handle urban problems; but these changes would have left the Conservative counties of Middlesex, Dorset and Bedford impoverished rural hinterlands.[38] Aware of the conflict, Sandys promised a statement from the Conservative government on local reorganization, and a year later agreed to talks with the local government associations to establish the common principles. The result was a series of White Papers treating the various aspects of the problem separately. The attempt to compartmentalize local problems is the major characteristic of local reorganization policy in Britain, and contrasts sharply with the ambitious French designs of the following decade. The first of these papers dealt with areas and functions[39]. Essentially, it reestablished the complex procedures of the 1945 Boundary Commission, but also acknowledged some of the problems that had arisen since the 1929 Act.

Under the Local Government Act of 1958, the new Boundary Commission was to take into account the conurbations or large metropolitan areas that were now sprawling over the British country-side, and was empowered to use the county borough device in order to create unified urban governments. But the procedures were cumbersome and laborious, moving in three stages from the Commission's examination of possible changes, to its recommendations to the Minister, his own inquiry and decision, and eventually to parliamentary approval for each region. In *The Economist*'s view, the proposal 'put the clock back to 1945'.[40]

This view was essentially correct. While the Commission could investigate both boroughs and counties, the subsequent reorganization of districts within counties was left to later negotiations, and to be carried out by the county councils. The county governments were protected by the complex procedures, even though they could still lose territory to newly formed county boroughs. The local authorities themselves could enter litigation to resist the changes, as happened in the Midlands proposals. No central 'principle' for the resolution of tensions between town and country was built into the British system, which proved to be its fatal weakness.[41] The Conservatives, as they had done so successfully for a century or more, provided procedural complications that protected their rural strongholds.

Starting work in 1959, the Commission divided England into nine areas. There were three 'special review areas' for the conurbations and six 'general review areas'. A separate commission was organized for Wales. The Commission was criticized for the enormous amount of time needed to formulate recommendations, but this seems unreasonable given the complexity of the contemplated changes.[42] Reports were made for the East and West Midlands and the southwest, and studies of the other three general review areas were initiated. Important compromises were worked out for the special review areas. The significant change in the 1958 proposal was that reorganization became a national issue and, for the first time, was lifted above the murky world of negotiations among individual local authorities and the rivalries of the local government associations.[43]

However, the Conservatives did not intend to fully support the proposals of the Commission, and were ready to make crippling compromises. This was signaled by the minister's refusal to alter the status of the tiny county of Rutland, following an energetic campaign by the local authority. There was intense campaigning by the local government associations, each seeking to preserve its special interest in the complex British local territorial structure, but partisan interests prevailed.

Although local government had finally appeared on the British political agenda, the divorce between various aspects of reform continued. The Local Government Act of 1958 recognized the growing financial strain on local government, but financial changes were not linked to the territorial studies of the Boundary Commission. Nonetheless, the Act illustrates early thinking on the relation of local fiscal and financial policy to national economic needs, and shows that both Conservatives and Labour recognized that there had to be some redistribution of local finances.[44] The new block grant system had been designed to preserve the independence of the local governments, while permitting the central government to anticipate and influence the level of expenditure more accurately. In 1958 specific grants, provided for eleven services, were merged and by a complex formula a single allocation was made which took into account population density, population, age, etc. A separate system of 'rate deficiency grants' was established to equalize the incomes of local governments, adhering to the Conservative view that equalization should be based on local tax capabilities, not on local needs. It followed that the central government must assess how well local governments meet their fiscal responsibilities. In effect, the law compromised the Labour government's 1948 Act, by which the entire equalization grant had been determined as though the central government were a ratepayer. Instead the central government now subsidized local needs through the block grant, while separately dealing with the equalization problem in the rate deficiency grant.

The dissociation of the components of local government policy in the British system becomes apparent in the debates over financial reform. Territorial reorganization was being carried on separately, while financial reorganization became a national political issue. The Labour party, encouraged by large gains in the local elections in the spring of 1957, bitterly fought the new grant system.[45] Their presumption was that a Conservative government would use the system to influence levels of educational spending, which comprised roughly two-thirds of the new grant. The work of the local educational authorities in the cities controlled by Labour, especially in London, was regarded by Labour as one of its major accomplishments. The change was also bitterly opposed by the educational pressure groups, and the financial procedure was repeatedly challenged by the local government associations.[46] The new Conservative minister for local government, Brooke, was even attacked by his own backbenchers because of the threat of the reform to the 'Baedeker towns', or resort areas, that were likely to be swallowed up in any major change.

In both Britain and France, political leaders realized that new structures were needed. The Macmillan government laid the foundation for regional agencies, to be described later, and tried to establish new principles for a reorganization of local government. Similarly, the expanding economic functions of French regional organizations were evident in the 1950s. In each case, the primary concern was to ensure that changes in the subnational system should do minimal damage to the existing political structure.

REORGANIZING CAPITAL CITIES: ADMINISTRATIVE NEEDS PREVAIL

The reorganization of London and Paris set the pattern for more pervasive metamorphosis of the local government systems. The reorganization of Paris reveals the administrative emphasis that underlies French policymaking.[47] Paris did not have a regional government comparable to the rest of France until 1976. Following the brief incumbency of Bailly in 1790, Paris had no elected mayor until 1977. Jules Ferry was appointed mayor for a few months early in the Third Republic, but the Paris Commune of 1871 soon persuaded politicians of all persuasions that the Paris mobs were not to be trusted. During the Third and Fourth Republics no less than twenty-three proposals were made to reorganize the city. In the final analysis it was economic and social pressure, not political will, that produced reorganization. The first changes were administrative, consistent with French practice, and Paris was made a district in 1961. It was given a specially designed form of regional government in 1964. The inner city remained only one of seven departments which formed the Paris region. The first regional prefect, Delouvrier, shared the Gaullists' modernizing zeal, and most of the steel and glass monstrosities now marring the Paris horizon can be attributed to him.[48]

Finally, in 1976 Paris got a regional government. Parisian politics are no less intense than in the rest of France, but the political infighting is more difficult to follow. Although the Paris prefecture was reorganized in 1968,[49] there was no elected mayor until Giscard d'Estaing decided the anomaly of prefectoral rule of the French capital should end. He appointed the Maspétiol Inquiry, whose recommendations became the basis of the Paris statute of 1975. In effect, the inner city becomes a commune for political purposes, with its own mayor and council, while it remains a department for administrative purposes,[50] one of many instances where the juridical predispositions of French government give way to political necessity. French caution about the unruliness of Parisian politics was soon confirmed in the comic opera of the Gaullist leader, Chirac, fighting a mayoral election against the President's chosen man, d'Ornano. In a way unimaginable under the discipline of separation of British local and national politics, Chirac used his position as mayor to criticize the governing majority, of which he himself was a major figure. The mayor, in turn, soon began to manipulate the arrondissement commissions, half directly elected and half appointed by the mayor, to extend his influence into the subgovernment of Paris.

London's old government, the London County Council, like that of Paris, was designed in 1889, and by the 1960s was wholly inadequate for the needs of a modern city. The Royal Commission on Local Government in London (Herbert Commission) studied the problem for nearly three years,[51] and the resulting Greater London Act of 1963 only survived bitter opposition from the Labour Party because Macmillan invoked the 'guillotine' to foreclose debate. In short, the decision to reorganize London was nearly as controversial and arbitrary as the reorganization of Paris.

Until Labour's historic victory in the London elections of 1934, London government had been almost continually manipulated by conservative forces. Thereafter, the London boroughs played an important role in Labour's rise to power. The ferocious debate of the 1960s was an outgrowth of the importance of these boroughs to

Labour, and Labour reformers were tenacious in protecting the important services they had gradually built over the years as a prelude to national reform.[52] Accordingly reorganization quickly became an ideological issue of great proportions. As *The Economist* noted, 'the one time when English local government springs into life is when some antiquated institution is condemned to die'.[53]

The London reorganization reveals numerous characteristics of central–local policymaking that persist throughout the 1970s. The Herbert Commission was itself exposed to a series of departmental proposals that bore little relationship to each other, and tended to repeat the well-known vested interests of each department. Like later reports, the Herbert Commission championed local self-government, but without giving a very clear idea how a major city might achieve participation in policymaking. In the parliamentary debate, Labour opposition soon became a 'phalanx hardened into a monolithic mass that was unable to offer anything in the way of creative originality as an opposition force'.[54] The educational authorities of inner London waged a national battle to preserve their accomplishments, while the new Greater London Council (GLC) was left almost devoid of planning powers.[55] However therapeutic the intense debate may have been for Labour's parliamentary leaders, their fears were misplaced. Labour returned to power with a huge majority in the first GLC election of 1964, and at the time felt no need to reorganize London further. The full complexity of the problem became clear only a decade later when both Conservatives and Labour found that the lower level of metropolitan boroughs needed more powers.[56]

The reorganizations of Paris and London underline how the policymaking process for the subnational system differs in each country. In France, administrative resistance slowly gave way to unruly party politics. A coalition of local political parties, often reaching across partisan lines, attacked the administrative machinery and infiltrated the decisionmaking process. Where the French used a strategy of gradual administrative conversion followed by political intrigue, the British substituted political polarization and central departmental intervention organized around individual services. In both countries procrastination was due largely to political rivalries and uncertainties at the national level, and in both cases one sees local government policies subordinated to the system's overriding institutional forces. In the British reform of London, the primary concern was to preserve functional compartmentalization of services and to protect central departmental interests. In France, it took the power of the President to penetrate the administrative superstructure. Perhaps there was even less participation in Britain, where the debate, for all its fury, was a 'private and restricted affair . . . fought out against a backdrop of widespread public apathy'.[57] The heated but ineffective debate in the House of Commons must be balanced against the feeble role of the French National Assembly.

CONFRONTING THE ISSUES: DE GAULLE AND WILSON

Many of the difficulties confronting local government, as outlined in

Chapter 1, arise from dilemmas inherent in the search for the ideal combination of territories and functions. To this we must add the growing importance of intermediate levels of government and administration. The changes undertaken by the two governments in the early 1960s reveal essential differences between the two subnational systems. In France, de Gaulle and Debré (the latter replaced by Pompidou in 1962) set in motion an array of reforms affecting all levels of government and administration. The newly constituted Fifth Republic was, of course, organized to provide more presidential power, and to advance Gaullist convictions that France's position in the world required rapid and efficient modernization of French society. In evaluating the reforms of local institutions, it is important to remember that the new government was deeply involved in the war in Algeria. Until 1962 this crisis outweighed all other policy concerns, although many new domestic policies were actually launched in the midst of the Algerian crisis. The crisis also worked to the advantage of the regime. It not only enhanced the President's power, but produced a strong Gaullist party in the National Assembly. At no time during the Fourth Republic had a party obtained over 200 seats, whereas the Gaullists held 200 or more seats through four legislative elections over the next decade.

British national government was no less preoccupied and even weaker. Several Labour leaders, including Richard Crossman, the Minister of Housing and Local Government in Wilson's first Cabinet, were troubled over the declining power of Parliament and the inability of government to control the administration. The capacity of the 1964 Labour government to initiate such controversial matters as local reorganization was limited by their small majority in the House of Commons. Not until the general election of 1966, which provided Labour with a Commons' majority of 110 votes, could substantial changes be made in the organization of central government. The most important of these (for present purposes) was the formation of a superministry, the Department of the Environment (DoE), to include transportation, housing, and local government policy. Like the 1972 reorganization, this change was completed by the Conservatives, even though the consolidation had been planned by Labour.

By the late 1960s neither Britain nor France had a clear design for local government reform. Nevertheless, Britain was prepared to pass the Local Government Act of 1972, delayed by the 1970 general election and the revisions of the new Conservative government. For its part, France had implanted a wide variety of new intergovernmental agencies and programs to relieve congestion and confusion at the local level. In both nations the basic strategy for change was apparent by the time Pompidou replaced de Gaulle in 1969 and Heath replaced Wilson in 1970. In France acceptance of the interdependence of policies among ministries and levels of government proved crucial to reform. When the reformers of the Fifth Republic set out to reshape French local government, their aim was to create an administrative network that could deal effectively with the numerous programs and decisions.[58] Their early experience from 1958 to roughly 1966 qualifies the frequent charges about the 'arbitrary' nature of administration in

France. In fact, the complexities of French organization, society and government probably restrain French administrative action more effectively than the more limited complexity of the British system. The clearest evidence is the course taken by Debré and his team in initiating change. They first had to find a better way of organizing lower-level administration, consider the nascent regional agencies, placate the concerns of the long-standing departments and subdue the anxieties of communes. The French policy process does not allow the British luxury of working with one problem at a time.

The initial steps taken to rebuild the French subnational system were much more prosaic than the issues discussed in the literature of regional reform. For one thing, the national and local administrative areas did not coincide and needed some reconciliation. Moreover, even without the centralizing presumptions of the Gaullists, it was clear that the confusion of local administration needed to be reduced. The external services of the French ministries are organized in *circonscriptions*: these are essentially territorial units defined at the convenience of each agency of government. There are roughly forty external services, and of these about thirty rely on departments for coordination and support.[59] The conflicting accounting systems of the *collectivités locales* and the state also had to be reconciled.[60] Decrees in 1959 set these changes in motion.

De Gaulle's policy toward communal reorganization is rooted in the reforms of 1964, affecting both departments and regions. Five years of intensive negotiation among national administrators and politicians preceded discussion of the archaic communes. The first phase of the decision was planned by Debré himself and the Ministry of the Interior. Debré brought to his cabinet an old colleague, Joxe, to conduct a study of departmental reorganization.[61] His report recommended experiments with a unified prefectoral organization in three departments: Seine-Maritime, where the prefect was an old friend of Debré; Corrèze, a small prefecture where the prefect was known to be favorable; and Vienne, added later because it was agreed a middle-sized department should be included. The departments of Eure and Seine-Maritime were included in order to coordinate the prefectoral experiment with regional experimentation. This addition meant the entire region of Normandy was included in the trial of the new system. Isère was also added because of its strong regional program. The proposals immediately ran into stiff resistance from other ministries, the technical ministers fearing loss of central control, and the Ministry of Finance refusing to give economic powers to the prefect.[62] The central negotiations continued until early 1962, when it was finally agreed that the prefect might have an assistant for economic affairs (*sous-préfet chargé des affaires économiques*). But the powers of the departmental and regional officials of the Ministry of Finance were virtually unchanged, and the *trésoriers-payeurs généraux* (TPG) retained most of their powers to initiate and inspect economic programs. In effect the prefect would become a 'chief of staff', but economic decisions would still require full approval from the Ministry of Finance.[63]

The reorganization of the departments set off a fierce debate within the prefectoral corps itself, which was by no means agreed on its future.[64] It also overlapped with regional reform policy. In comparing these first decisions with what happened in Britain, it is important to note how powerful a team was required at the very highest levels of government to make even minor changes. Though their interests did not always coincide, reform took the combined efforts of the Prime Minister (Debré and later Pompidou), the Director of the Planning Commission (Massé), the Minister of the Interior (Frey, from 1961 to 1967) and the Director of the *Délégation à l'Aménagement du Territoire et à l'Action Régionale* (DATAR, formed in 1963) under Guichard. The reorganization thus involved both politicians and higher civil servants. Closely linked to the Cabinet and a key figure in the negotiations was Joxe, who was first a secretary of state under Debré, and then returned to the Cabinet under Pompidou as a minister without portfolio (*ministère déléguée*) for administrative reform.[65] Policies were shaped through a complex process of negotiation with the interested technical ministries, and finally combat with the Ministry of Finance. Through this procedure the administrative structure became both an actor in hammering out the new policies, and the object of change.

In addition to these departmental reforms, the regional reforms also stemming from the 1964 decrees were worked out. Though the regional agencies mark an important advance in the reorganization of the subnational system, their ability to actually change political and administrative relationships at lower levels of government has probably been exaggerated. Regional policy was even more controversial than departmental reform, and its early formulation was not resolved until 1963 when Pompidou intervened in the struggle between the Ministry of Construction and the Planning Commission. The regions had, of course, been slowly acquiring an administrative life of their own: *régions de programme* in 1956; *conférences interdépartmentales* of prefects and departmental planning committees in 1959; *circonscriptions d'action régionale* in 1960; and finally the *Commissions de Développement économique régionale* (CODER) in 1964.

The Ministry of the Interior was involved because the departmental prefects were resolutely opposed to the notion of regional prefects.[66] The ministry thought that the threatened subordination of departmental prefects to new regional agencies, even if run by regional prefects, would dilute ministerial influence at lower levels of government.[67] But the more intense struggle was between the Ministry of Finance and the Planning Commission allied with DATAR. The deadlock was broken by Pompidou in 1963 when he assigned long-term investment planning and regional development to the influential alliance of national and regional planners. An experienced administrative infighter, Guichard, the first director of DATAR, also made certain that DATAR had sufficient economic powers to be heard in the policymaking process.[68]

The policy effects of the 1964 reforms should not be overestimated, particularly because the dramatic check to regional government in 1969 suggests the weaknesses of central intervention at the regional level. In fact, the regional agencies never had a great deal of political or economic power. The prefects themselves were for the most part opposed to the idea and Frey, when Minister of the Interior, appointed the first regional prefects against their wishes. In at least one region the prefects were unable to agree on where the regional agency should meet, and for a year they moved from one departmental headquarters to another to avoid offending prefectoral sensitivities.[69] At the last moment, the Ministry of Finance successfully intervened to ensure that the regional TPG would retain full powers over all state property and all investments. Two experiments in regional government were launched, the one in Haute-Normandie going fairly well because of links with the Gaullists, but the one in Burgundy, selected because it was a more traditional prefecture, moving very slowly. By 1964 it was too late to involve the new agencies in the Fourth Plan, and in any event the *missions régionales* were not well enough organized to contribute. While the new offices did attract a number of able young prefects from the École Nationale d'Administration (ENA), their modernist views clashed with traditional practices of the older prefects.

The French state intervenes directly at the local level through three devices: the district, the *syndicat intercommunal à vocation multiple* (SIVOM), created by decree in 1959, and the *communautés urbaines* created by law in 1966. The district is based on the urban *agglomération*, a territorial unit formed for administrative purposes and used by the central government for development.[70] Applied once by decree in a large city, Tours, the district device faltered, and has never been forced on a city again. In Nancy one commune refused to cooperate for political reasons, and the district did not coincide with the areas set out for urban planning by the central government. Its most important application was the creation of a Paris district to permit the administration to implement urban projects while evading the usual decision process. Although by 1976 there were 148 districts, including 1259 communes and a population of just over four million people, an evaluation of the urban districts in 1964 concluded that they were not particularly effective.[71] In fact, the district has not been an important unit for policymaking or for regrouping communes, and has been largely abandoned as an instrument of reorganization.

The multiple-purpose syndicates (SIVOM) are simply extensions of the 1890 procedure whereby communes might voluntarily enter a contractual agreement for the provision of services. They are often used by the mayors to avoid pressure from prefects and the central government which might otherwise force more substantial forms of consolidation. Because of their limited objectives, however, the SIVOM have not influenced the underlying territorial and administrative arrangements of the local government system. By 1976 there were 1703 SIVOM, affecting slightly over 19 million residents and involving nearly 17,000 communes. But the old single-purpose *syndicat* remains by far the most acceptable to the communes, and there were over 10,000 of these in 1973. Although the Ministry of the Interior urged its prefects to encourage fusion and contractual cooperation among communes, the results were not impressive.[72]

Constructed to meet the service needs of groups of communes, the SIVOM has not been a particularly controversial administrative device. Nevertheless, there are important disputes over how the prefect may organize a SIVOM. These disputes, in turn, relate to the use of administrative power in the French state. The commune of Cayeux-sur-Mer, for example, did not wish to join a *syndicat* consolidating schools, and took its case to the Conseil d'État.[73] Though the high court ruled only that the prefect could not issue retroactive rules for the *syndicat*, the case reveals the continuing conflict between administrative power and the communes. The issue is whether the SIVOM, as stated by one lawyer, 'constitutes a part of the territorial establishment and does not represent an arbitrary creation of the state', or whether the SIVOM is in fact simply another *établissement publique* and therefore subject to the full exercise of the prefectoral *tutelle*. Because of their diversity,[74] the SIVOM are unlikely to become part of the territorial and political substructure of France, but their operations none the less involve the traditional dispute over the power of the central administration.

The *communautés urbaines* were the third experiment in direct intervention at the local level, and they also proved controversial. Unified metropolitan government had been delayed in France, unlike in Britain, and by the mid-1960s the central government had decided to force a decision. The law of 1966 obliged four cities (Bordeaux, Lille, Lyon and Strasbourg) to regroup with the surrounding communes in order to form a metropolitan government.[75] The overall concept was based on the idea of *métropoles d'équilibre*, advanced by urban planners in the Ministry of Equipment, DATAR and the Planning Commission. But the merger did not apply to four additional cities (Marseille, Toulouse, Nancy and Metz) that were also designated *métropoles d'équilibre*, because of local rivalries or of geographic difficulties. Nantes was also a candidate, but was exempt because the district established for its region was going well. Though the record is not entirely clear, it appears that the government initially wished to impose the new structure by decree, but the compromise on a total of four obligatory urban communities was forced by the Senate. The basic concept originated in the Paira Report, which had deemed the efforts to 1964 ineffective.[76]

The Constitutional Commission held hearings in the various cities, to try to pacify those that had been selected. In Lyon, two communes that were to be merged, one with a Socialist mayor and another with a Communist mayor, bitterly fought the proposal. In the Bordeaux area, seventeen of the twenty-one communes involved voted against the proposal and sent a delegation to the Ministry of the Interior. The law's implementation was assigned to a special commission, which added a note of 'technical and democratic legitimacy' to the proceedings.[77] By 1976 only five additional cities had voluntarily adopted the new scheme. Brest, Cherbourg, Dunkerque, Lille and Le Mans in cooperation with three nearby towns. The total urban communities effort embraced only 251 communes, though they involve slightly more than four million French. Despite the political resistance, however, the *communautés urbaines* remain the primary instrument whereby a unified urban government with elected representatives might be created in France.

Urban communities have financial and planning responsibilities for their areas, for example, relations with the national housing authority (HLM), land zoning and land-use planning, and the planning of public investments, as well as the customary services provided by communes. As the cities' financial situation worsened, the burden of debt and service costs became unmanageable and a Ministry of Finance report in 1972 indicated the growing risk of financial collapse.[78] Also, the political controversies persisted. A recent proposal for an additional urban community for Nantes was defeated after three attempts by the administration.[79] The major apprehension was that the surrounding communes, increasingly electing Socialist and Communist mayors with the growth of working-class suburbs, would form a 'red belt' (*ceinture rouge*) and control the city government. As the consolidated cities dispersed, the communes at the center of the urban community lost control of the community council. After the local elections of 1977, for example, the suburban communes of the Bordeaux area took control of that urban community.[80] None the less, despite the controversy, there seemed to be no acceptable alternative to consolidated urban government in France.

Though the French system can attempt coercion to achieve reorganization, it has rarely been successful. In sharp contrast to the British approach to subnational problems, the aim in France has been to create a decisionmaking structure and incentives for change rather than force through any specific policy. Though only partially successful, the approach in the early Gaullist years addressed long neglected problems of French local government. Mény summed up the developments and the outcome well when he wrote that 'in 1962 the regional push seemed irresistible, the obsolescence of the department unavoidable; ten years later, the department had consolidated its position, the region remained fragile.'[81] The new network for subnational policy was shaped from remnants of old institutions. Despite being coldly technocratic and Jacobin, the elite had to observe the organizational and political complications of lower-level decisionmaking. However much the Gaullist leaders disapproved of dispersed policymaking, the Gaullist reforms, whether they liked it or not, were qualified by the institutional complexities of the decisionmaking process. The striking contrast with the British approach to reform is to be seen in the enormous political complexities of change in France, and the inability of French national political institutions to impose structural change.

WILSONIAN REORGANIZATION STRATEGY

The more stable political environment in Britain has made it easier to make decisions about local government reform, but stability alone is not enough, and may even put local interests at a disadvantage. The Labour government took office in 1964 with only a small majority. Crossman, the new Minister for Housing and Local Government, neither encouraged the old Boundary Commission nor offered radical proposals for reform.[82] The Labour government had inherited two committees of inquiry on local government problems: the Committee on Local Government Management chaired by Sir John Maud, and the Committee on Staffing of Local Government chaired by Sir George Mallaby. These Committees had been formed after laborious negotiations with the local government associations, and relieved the minister of immediate pressures related to local government reorganization. In September 1965, Crossman decided to air the entire problem at the Torquay conference of the Association of Municipal Corporations (now the Association of Metropolitan Authorities or AMA). Crossman dropped his bombshell by saying that 'the whole structure of local government is out of date, . . . our county boroughs and county councils as at present organised are archaic institutions', and by attacking the principles of the 1958 legislation that left town and country divisions intact.[83] For a few months, however, nothing was done until the Boundary Commission's Lancashire recommendations appeared. Their effects on parliamentary constituencies might have cost the hard-pressed Labour government twenty seats in Parliament.[84] With this additional incentive, Wilson and Crossman decided to appoint a Royal Commission, which provided an excuse to delay redistricting of the local wards.

The Royal Commission is a uniquely British means of making policy; it permits leaders to address difficult issues without making a political commitment. There is no equivalent in the French system, where high level administrators would be much more likely to thrash out such choices in inter-ministerial committees, and to consider a public airing of crucial issues as a slight to their own abilities. A central question in the appointment and role of a Royal Commission relates to whether the body is brought together because the government already knows what it wants to do, or does not yet know. In this case, very little seems to have been decided in advance beyond the common acknowledgment that the local government system was unworkable, and that the division of town and country was a barrier to many reforms advocated by the Labour Party. (Local government reform had not figured in the 1964 election manifesto.) Wilson and Crossman gave careful attention to the selection of the chairman, Sir John Maud, who was later made Lord Redcliffe-Maud as a reward for his toils.[85] All but two of the eleven members of the Commission had impressive local government experience, and four had worked on Maud's Committee on Local Government Management.[86] Perhaps the most overtly political aspect was the inclusion of Derek Senior, whose known support for regional cities was almost sure to make unanimous recommendations impossible. It is a tribute to Maud's diplomatic skills, no doubt enhanced by his experience as British High Commissioner to South Africa, that such a high degree of unanimity was achieved. The Redcliffe-Maud report had the distinction of incorporating a dissent from Senior that was longer than the text of the main Commission report.

The Commission had a broad, almost ambiguous, charge: 'to consider the structure of Local Government in England, outside Greater London, in relation to its existing functions; and to make recommendations for authorities and boundaries, and for functions and their division, having regard to the size and character of areas in which these can be most effectively exercised and the need to sustain a viable system of local democracy'. Though not entirely an after-thought, it is noteworthy that Maud was most concerned that the phrase on local democracy be included. The exclusion of Wales and Scotland was also important. The Welsh Boundary Commission's recommendations had recently been rejected, perhaps to reassure the strong Labour supporters in Wales that their system of local government would not be disrupted. Scotland and Northern Ireland were the subjects of separate reports by other bodies.[87] Such differentiation in the treatment of territorial organization would, of course, be un-imaginable in France. It is possible in Britain because Westminster so effectively dominates political relationships between central and local government. None the less, the upshot was that Britain ended with five different local government structures, including London; six if one adds Northern Ireland.

The Commission was handicapped by being limited to the examination of existing services, although its freedom was greater than that of the old boundary commissions, which could do so only for the special review areas. The organizational solutions were constrained because the Commission could not take into account services between local authorities, nor did the terms of reference encourage a critical examination of the way existing services related to central government.[88] In fact, the confusion was compounded because Labour in the late 1960s and the Conservatives in the early 1970s were making important changes in other local government activities, notably in the police, transportation, health and personal social services.[89] The restriction was crippling because it confined the examination to the existing division of powers, thus excluding the interest of localities in industrial development, regional development and a number of related activities of importance to towns and cities. These economic activities are not 'services' in the British sense, a distinction that differentiates French and British subnational policy. In effect, this implicit constraint meant that the Commission accepted the separation of the private and public sectors in British politics, and further accepted the departmental practices within Whitehall that regulate local government activities. In short, they were free to study the local government system 'from below,' but could not criticize it 'from above'.

The most restrictive condition of the Commission's work was the uncertainty about devolution, an issue that was crucial to the future of provincial government, but the Report contained a chapter on pro-vincial government that is remarkably similar to discussions of regional government in France.[90] The main provincial function would be to review regional plans, together with some responsibility for co-ordinating higher educational institutions, but the provinces would have no independent financial resources and would be indirectly elected from the lower-tier authorities. The dispute over the powers and resources of regional government was at the core of Senior's lengthy dissent, and, of course, had reverberations that affected both

Scottish and Welsh nationalism. Though the regional recommendations were quite modest, they nevertheless proved embarrassing to
both the Labour and Conservative governments, and implementation
was postponed. By 1966 Wilson was already thinking of appointing a
Royal Commission on the Constitution, possibly to delay a decision
on this explosive issue. The Constitutional Commission was appointed
in 1969, and in 1973 provided an entirely new set of regional
proposals.[91]

The recommendations of the Redcliffe-Maud report will be
discussed in later chapters, and have been commented on and
criticized widely elsewhere.[92] The suggested structure was a division of
England into sixty-one local government areas, fifty-eight of them
unitary authorities comparable to the old county boroughs, and three
of them two-tier authorities (the metropolitan areas of Birmingham,
Liverpool and Manchester). A number of long overdue changes were
also suggested, such as the abolition of aldermen, simplification of
voting procedures and modernization of local government organization. But national political considerations introduced a number of
changes, despite the carefully documented plans of the commission.
The process unfolded in roughly three stages: (1) consideration of the
proposals by the Wilson government, (2) the general election of 1970,
producing a Conservative government under Heath, and the renewed
examination of the reform proposals, and (3) the parliamentary and
administrative process of formulating and implementing the new law.
At each step one sees important characteristics of British decisionmaking that contrast sharply with the French approach to local
reorganization.

The public debate for which Maud and others had hoped did not
take place, and Senior's monumental dissent, which might have
formed the basis of a real alternative, was barely discussed in
Parliament. Press reports were on the whole favorable, though *New
Society* proved a poor political predictor in suggesting that the report
was another way 'to slide reform through in the country'.[93] In the
event, three years elapsed between the reformulation of the report and
the Local Government Act of 1972. Modifications neatly reversed the
Commission's intentions. While the basic concept of unified
authorities was never questioned, the proposals were bitterly opposed
from many quarters. As might be expected, the County Councils'
Association launched a strong attack; and there was similar outrage
among the many urban and rural district councils that would be
merged in the unified urban governments.

Although the attack resembled French efforts to resist change, the
British system has no way of crystalizing effective local opposition.
Instead, there was a piecemeal struggle by individual local governments to preserve their identities, while Whitehall carried on direct
negotiations with the local government associations on the overall
scope of the new law. In any event, a month after the Royal Commission report was submitted, the new Minister for Housing and
Local Government, Anthony Crosland, formally opened consultation
with local governments, making clear that the Labour government
intended to design legislation. The bipartisan character of local

reorganization policy is apparent in the Labour government's White Paper of 1970,[94] outlining legislation and making remarkable concessions to the protesting counties and districts. First, two additional metropolitan or two-tier counties were accepted, West Riding and South Hampshire, thereby reducing the number of unitary authorities from fifty-eight to fifty-one. Second, education in the two-tier units was moved from the district to the county level, thereby restoring control to the old county governments, and balancing off the greater dispersion of population introduced by the additional two-tier counties. Third, the community participation of the smallest unit, the local council, was eliminated by allocating its advisory role to the district committees. The entire issue of provincial councils was postponed, in view of the recent appointment of the Royal Commission on the Constitution.

The overall aim was to dampen controversy, especially by giving way to strong established interest groups. The increase in two-tier units (metropolitan counties) consoled the old counties and districts, while the elevation of the educational function to the county level provided a palliative for the old county boroughs who did not want to see their educational establishments dismantled.[95] The rejection of a significant role for the local councils, which had been recommended to encourage more participation at the ward and parish levels, no doubt accurately reflected the importance (or lack of it) attached to increased participation by both political and administrative officials at the center. It was apparent during 1969 that the Labour Party would be hard pressed in the next national election. It had done very poorly in the 1968 local elections. Under these electoral pressures, Wilson and Callaghan, then at the Home Office and thus responsible for electoral supervision, decided to postpone the redistribution of parliamentary constituencies. Their reasoning, hotly contested by the Conservatives and challenged in court, was that the revised constituencies should conform to local authority boundaries, and that the country should wait until these boundaries were known in order to avoid making two parliamentary changes.[96]

The political dimensions of the decision were again underscored when Peter Walker, the Conservatives' shadow minister for local government, announced that the party would favor smaller metropolitan counties and possibly the restoration of the two-tier structure throughout the country. The changes that Labour had made brought it under fire from the Association of Municipal Councils, normally sympathetic to Labour but then under Conservative influence due to local election losses. Both parties chose to maximize ambiguities as the national election approached, Crosland hinting that more concessions might be made to local interests and the Conservatives vaguely suggesting 'a sensible reform' in their election manifesto. Clearly the intricacies of local reorganization were such that neither the Labour nor the Conservative parties wished to formulate a decisive choice for the national elections of 1970, nor is it at all clear that they could have done so. The British people, like the parties, went into the election with no consistent idea of the kind of local government structure that might emerge in the new Parliament.

While all agreed in principle that the system needed overhauling, the Conservative victory produced another round of proposals from the local authority associations, followed by renewed consultation between the new minister and the associations. In eight months Walker produced a new White Paper[97] that neatly ditched the commission's original proposals. The concept of unitary authorities was rejected. The number of metropolitan counties was increased to six. A proposed new county, South Hampshire, was merged with Southampton and became a non-metropolitan county. Two other areas with complex boundary problems were added: South Yorkshire and Tyneside. At the same time the size of large metropolitan authorities was shrunk by assigning more districts to non-metropolitan authorities, thereby reducing the population under conurbations from the sixteen million proposed by Maud to just under twelve million.[98]

A further concession to Conservative followers in small towns and suburbs was the restoration of a two-tier structure for the entire system. The non-metropolitan authorities would now have districts, although with fewer powers than districts in the metropolitan authorities, which would retain substantial powers over education, planning and housing. In short, the overall effect was to reduce the scale of the subnational system by multiplying the number of local governments (adding metropolitan counties and districts) and by devolving several crucial local functions in the urban areas to lower levels of government. This also had the 'side benefit' of protecting Conservative voters in suburbia from change. Wherever possible the old county boundaries were restored. Though the broad objectives of the Maud proposals were followed, the Conservative plan came as near as it could to a reversal of the original scheme without simply rejecting reform.

PARTIAL SOLUTIONS AND POLITICAL COMPLEXITY IN FRANCE

The complications of local government came after the growth of government services and benefits that accompanied development of the welfare state, not before. In a wholly rational world, one would expect that government, in responding to these complexities, would design a new territorial structure adequate to the tasks of the welfare state. However, theoreticians' neglect of the institutional constraints that influence decisions has perhaps made this course of action seem more attractive to analysts than to practitioners. There was little discussion about changing French communes until the administrative structure could be modernized. And in Britain the complexities of local government reform were shunted aside by the various boundary commissions until Crossman's impetuous decision in 1965. Britain was capable of directly attacking the local government system, while France was not. This meant, of course, that the British had to explicitly or implicitly make important assumptions about present and future relationships of local and national government, many of which proved to be wrong. In their pragmatic way, the French chose other-wise, although we should acknowledge that their system probably never possessed the capacity to impose a major structural change anyway. In France, as Médard notes, the 'slow death of the communes was preferred to the brutal death'.[99]

When Pompidou became Prime Minister in 1962, as when he became President after 1969, there was a relaxation of pressure for change within the subnational system. Though a dedicated Gaullist he lacked the sense of mission that Debré brought to the task of organization, and he was certainly much more sensitive to the complexities of French local politics. As we have seen above, the major administrative reforms had begun and the critical decisions concerning departments and regions had been made. The decision to make a direct attack on the communal system resulted more from immense pressures from the economic state agencies for modernization than from the Ministry of the Interior, which prospered from its direct responsibility for local affairs.

The Ministry was naturally aware of the variations among the 37,000 communes, but not prepared to press for structural change. Shortly after establishing the SIVOM procedure, for example, a ministerial circular advised prefects not to use the decree procedure to force communes to form syndicats.[100] In both the Fourth and Fifth Republics, policy affecting communes was not based on political imperatives at all, but on the need to encourage investment. The reorganization of the communes was to be left to the pressures of industrial growth and population movement. In relation to the economic goals of the state, it mattered little that in 1968 there were nearly 4000 communes with less than a hundred persons or 24,000 with less than 500 persons. Were it not for a new Minister of the Interior, Fouchet, an unconditional Gaullist with ambitious ideas about restructuring the communes, reorganization might well have remained dormant. But Fouchet undertook what so many prudent officials had avoided – a complete examination of the relation between the state and the *collectivités locales*.

Much of the preliminary research was done under Paira, the Secretary General of the Ministry, whose report on the failures of the *communautés urbaines* appears to have provided a stimulus for a new attack. A commission formed in 1968 never produced a report, but did provide the basic ideas for a communal reorganization.[101] Fouchet's notion was that the canton should be used to consolidate communes in what he called *secteurs intercommunaux*. As in the British approach, the implications for rural and urban areas were quite distinct. In rural areas the aim was simply to merge tiny communes, a problem that, for geographic reasons, was more acute in the mountainous regions of France than elsewhere. A decade later many of the small communes were still fighting the merger plans in the courts, often successfully.[102] In the urban regions, the result would resemble the district, coordinating the political and administrative structures in new areas similar to the rural canton.

Although Fouchet pushed hard for his reform, he was unable to avoid the debate on how merger was to be accomplished; a debate that had no counterpart in Britain. The project was first circulated for official consultation in 1966, provoking what Roussillon considers the first real debate about the communes since 1789.[103] Though never as strong as their British equivalents, the local government associations were consulted. But the French system provides ample opportunity for the more influential local politicians to be heard at the center, and they effectively resisted change. The proposed law was still being discussed when the events of May 1968 forced postponement, and brought about Fouchet's replacement by Marcellin, a provincial leader of the Republican party.

The arbitrary features of the Fouchet project quickly disappeared. He had proposed that communes with fewer than one hundred inhabitants or budgets under 20,000 francs be compelled to merge and that the studies for merger be carried out solely by the prefects. The government took a more conciliatory view in the aftermath of the riots and de Gaulle's resignation. The new President himself took particular pains in his inaugural speech to observe that 'the French remain profoundly attached to their municipal life, and the commune constitutes the foremost living expression of this collective confidence which finds its expression in national unity'.[104] Speaking to the presidents of departmental councils, the new Secretary General of the Ministry of the Interior, Bord, said, 'It is necessary that local liberties not only remain but find a new expression.'[105] Marcellin repeated these assurances before the National Assembly, no doubt aware that local elections were to be held in 1971.

Clearly sobered by the defeat of the 1969 referendum, in the second round of consultations Marcellin made it clear that the prefect would not have arbitrary powers to recommend mergers, and that the law would focus on urban problems; thereby reassuring the mayors of small rural communes that they would not be the primary target of consolidation. For the first time the debate about communes penetrated party policy, and the Communists prepared a counterproject that foreshadowed their proposals of 1972 and 1976.[106] The Association of French Mayors also made counterproposals, suggesting that the departmental councils rather than the prefects should study how mergers were to take place; that the new communal structures take the weaker form of a SIVOM; and that their budgetary powers be confined to the investment plan.[107] In effect, their proposals would have left the entire question in the hands of the local *notables* and deprived the enlarged commune of economic influence. A comparison of the proposed and actual versions of the *loi Marcellin* of 1971 makes clear how many concessions were made.[108] The electoral arrangements were modified to assure the old communes that they would be fully represented. The mayors of displaced communes were allowed to keep their titles, offices and even skeletal staff. The entire strategy of *secteurs intercommunaux*, implying a uniform regrouping throughout France, was simply abandoned. Though the proposal for merger could be initiated either by a referendum or by experts, a formula was added to make certain that small communes could effectively veto a merger.

The most striking contrast with the British reorganization is the complex system of local consultation imposed on the French authorities. While the British could use indirect consultation and

administrative orders, the French had to employ individual consultation with each department and commune. The major change in the
final version of the *loi Marcellin* was the provision that each prefect's
inquiry into desirable mergers must include a *commission d'élus*, to
include the president of the departmental council, four additional
departmental councillors chosen by the council itself and ten mayors
representing all categories of communes. In effect, prefects would
make no proposals without the consent of the communal and departmental councils. A vast survey was then started by the Ministry of the
Interior to draw up a merger plan for each department.[109] The
commissions recommended 1,992 mergers that would reduce the
communes by 3,516, roughly 10 percent. The prefects recommended
3,589 mergers, which would have eliminated 6,186 communes or
about 18 percent of all communes. But by mid-1974 the prefects themselves had failed to notify a third of the communes of their plan, thus
foreclosing further action, and where plans were distributed the
communes could veto action by simply not responding. In these ways,
local politics is given power over territorial reorganization that would
be unimaginable in Britain.

The symbolism is more important than the actual result. As Becet
noted, the citizens were allowed to vote on the territorial organization
of the state for the first time in French history,[110] though they did not
choose to do so in most cases. Substantial progress was made in 1972,
when 1,328 communes were merged into 526 new communes, but
progress rapidly dropped off once the willing cases were completed.
By the end of 1975, 1,957 communes had merged, including fifty-
seven cases where decrees were used.[111] Though the reform ran
aground, it reduced the number of communes by roughly 800, and
took the problem to the grassroots of the French system in a way that
has been rarely attempted by any modern state.

Over 60 percent of the French population recognized that there were
too many communes, but a poll taken shortly after the law was passed
showed nearly 80 percent of the mayors hostile to its implementation.
Despite polemical defenses[112] and a number of serious studies,[113]
communal reform remains low on the political agenda. The Gaullists
have retreated from their aggressive stance, which was an ill-judged
sequel to the ambitious efforts in the early years of the regime to
reorganize the state. On the Left, neither the Socialists nor
Communists have plans to reduce the numbers of communes. The
Ministry of the Interior still supports mergers where they can be
worked out, but rarely imposes mergers by decree.[114] Unlike Britain,
territorial reorganization at the grassroots in France proved
impossible despite the best efforts of the allegedly powerful
administrative machinery.

The Strange Debate of the 1972 Local Government Act

The power of the British Parliament is purchased at a price the French
have never been prepared to pay. In the course of territorial reorganization, Parliament gave the local governments repeated
opportunities to plead their special interests and argue for boundary
changes. From 1969 to 1974 there were at least seven such

opportunities in Britain.[115] The debate transformed the legislative process into an appeal procedure, and concentrated attention on boundary problems at the expense of the requirements of the new local government system. In the course of the debates and committee hearings in the Commons, over 1,800 amendments were made, many of them simply minor boundary changes. Wood estimates that roughly 40 percent of the time spent considering the new law was concerned with boundaries.[116] This is not to imply that all proposed changes were accepted by the Conservatives, but many of the difficult and controversial decisions were simply played out again.

Arrangements for debate and review of the Local Government Act in committee were essentially nonpartisan. While Labour's shadow minister for local affairs, Crosland, put up stiff resistance, he made it clear that Labour would accept the general form of the bill, despite fears that the amendments would make the new law unworkable. To minimize this possibility, care was taken to exclude from the parliamentary committee MPs who were known to bear strong local grievances.[117] Some clearly partisan concessions were made to local forces such as adjustments to the new county of Merseyside that improved the Conservatives' chances of winning local elections, and changes in North Yorkshire that helped protect the parliamentary seat of the MP who was Heath's Parliamentary Secretary.[118] But blatant partisan politics proved the exception rather than the rule.

The Conservative government hoped to adhere to the Labour government's initial schedule and have legislation passed by 1972, so that elections could be held in 1973, with full transfer of powers in 1974. While the Conservative majority in Parliament was not large, and there were many disgruntled MPs on both sides of the House, the main decision embodied in the White Paper was sustained – Britain was to have two-tier local government throughout England and Wales and, as it turned out, Scotland, too. The individual grievances of merged towns and districts only made the government's task easier, for it meant that the more critical debate over the distribution of functions was neglected.

Crippling compromises were made on the functions of the new local governments in order to get the law passed. For example, districts received more control over development plans, in effect creating over 500 local planning authorities in the new local government system where there had been approximately 150 in the old. The entire question of local finance was postponed. In the midst of the re-organization debate, plans were announced for Regional Water Authorities that would take water and sewerage responsibilities from localities. Both the strength of central control and the bewildering complexity of local reform are revealed in the many policies closely related to local government that the Conservatives set about changing. The Housing Finance Act of 1972 reduced local powers over public housing, most importantly their power to set local rents. There was separate legislation affecting health, local social services and transportation. The paradoxical effect was that while Parliament was presumably creating larger and more responsible local authorities, new constraints were being generated in a number of other policy areas.

Accomplishing a major reorganization in two years is no small feat. Implementation took place in two phases: the preparations made prior to the final drafting of the law, and the preparations required by law between 1972 and 1974. In France, as we have seen with the 1964 reforms, the initial concern is with how a new decisionmaking structure will be accommodated within the political and administrative systems. This involves politicians and civil servants at many levels in the decision process, which they use to protect their interests. It also means that few programs are launched until the entire sequence of responsibilities from Paris to the commune is mapped out.

British administrative institutions impose a very different set of constraints, largely because the higher civil service has no field staff of its own to compare with the *services extérieurs* of French central administration. The administrative structure of the British local government system is both organized and supervised by the localities. For reasons to be explored in Chapter 4, this means that the local administrators are insulated against local political interests, while the higher civil service at the center is primarily tuned to ministerial priorities. Unlike their French counterparts, at neither level of government do British administrators have a distinctly political role.

In the implementation of the 1972 law, the separation of the central and local levels of administration posed special problems. On the one hand, the ministries needed to be assured that local services would not be jeopardized, while, on the other hand, the local governments faced the intricate task of moving offices and agencies to the newly determined authorities. Given the British system, there is no way that implementation could be assigned to a single government department. The first phase of the transition was organized by a team within the Department of the Environment, which issued a set of consultative papers on how the various services would be relocated and reorganized.[119] Many of these decisions were made before the statute was passed in order to hold elections in 1973. The addition of districts in the non-metropolitan counties, combined with the merger of the old rural and urban districts, meant that new electoral wards were needed, and this was placed in the hands of the Home Office.[120] In the metropolitan counties, the wards from the old boroughs and districts were more easily transferred to the new system. Another sensitive matter was making sure that local administrators were not upset by the expected reduction of local staff, and providing incentives for early retirement and relocation. A special Local Government Staff Commission worked closely with the local government unions. A Local Government Boundary Commission was established to determine boundaries of the districts within the non-metropolitan counties in the year prior to the full implementation of 1974. The entire process suggests how the weak field administration and isolation of central departments handicaps the British subnational system.

Lacking the administrative flexibility, special arrangements had to be made for functions that overlapped districts and counties. During the debates Walker referred to the proposed 'agency' clause of the new law, which would relieve pressure for more precise definition of functional relationships among the new authorities. These problems were particularly acute for libraries, traffic control and safety, garbage disposal and consumer protection activities. The most serious damage was probably the dislocation of planning services, as the reorganization disrupted relations between counties and old boroughs and districts that had developed good planning services. During 1973 the new authorities were to make agency arrangements, which under the law were to remain in effect at least until 1979. The resulting confusion at the local level generated over 200 petitions for ministerial revision.

The Tortoise and the Hare: National Politics and Local Complexities
The search for a compromise between national and local interests revealed important political differences between Britain and France, and, in turn, produced very different strategies to refashion local government so that it might take a more active role in policymaking. As we have seen, until Crossman's unforeseen decision to undertake global reform the inadequacies and confusion of the British local government system were effectively excluded from the top levels of decisionmaking. British ministers and top officials wrestled with the shortcomings of local councils for nearly twenty years. But the terms of their inquiries, most often redrawing boundaries, were defined by central government, and, in turn, effectively stalemated the counties and boroughs who felt estranged from national government and threatened by structural change.

In contrast, the issues involved in central–local policymaking were never distant from national policymaking in France. Even with a much weaker parliament than Britain, the political interests of communes could not be excluded. If local level change came about much more slowly than in Britain, it was because local leaders were integrated into the decision process itself. Despite the frequent charges of administrative manipulation, it should also be noted that the process of change was retarded by conflicts within the administrative system, but this conflict, too, was not carried on in secrecy, but permeated the entire territorial administration, and often included alliances with local political forces. For all the authority of the Gaullists in their early years in office, compromises were being formed throughout the 1960s, and the frontal attack on the communes from 1968 failed.

In the context of British politics, reform has most often meant putting more powers in the hands of national government, and the structure of national government itself makes it relatively easy to erode local government. The 1945 Labour government had little time for local problems and the 1951 Conservative government also saw local issues as a way of pursuing their own objectives. From a national perspective, what was often regarded as the arbitrary actions of the early Gaullist years was close to the standard policy process in Britain. British national leaders inherited a local government system that effectively neutralized itself in respect to national policymaking. On the whole, local government was regarded as a rather troublesome and hopeless problem which could be put aside with much more ease than in France. In this respect, the politics of policymaking had changed very little since the nineteenth century.

Neither French leaders nor administrators could push local reform onto the political agenda as abruptly as had happened in Britain. The process of reform was a more gradual process, involved more consideration of the intricacies of application and implementation, and ultimately involved dealing with the collective interests of local government. Was the more dramatic effort of Britain more successful? What began as proposals for fifty-eight unitary authorities emerged in the form of thirty-nine counties and 296 districts.[121] The functional requisites of the system which figure so strongly in British reform efforts were seldom debated, and the minimum population of the districts, in any event, was reduced from the 75,000 recommended by the Royal Commission to about 40,000. A third of the new districts (121) were less than the recommended size.

The ironical result was that even with the relative freedom of central policymakers to define the objectives of reform, they were unable to achieve some of their most essential aims. For many years experts had lamented the complex and often ineffective internal organization of local councils which gave local committees much control and made local policies incoherent. But Whitehall lacked the contact with local problems that the French administrative system provides, and the DoE proposals for internal reorganization of British local government appeared almost as an afterthought to the 1972 law.[122] The transition to the new system between 1972 and 1974 was a monumental exercise in governmental reorganization, but it was made at the expense of other compromises, sometimes hastily made improvisations, about elections, organization and services.[123] As we shall see in later chapters, it seems doubtful if national policymakers wanted the working relationship between center and locality that is found in France. Moreover, it seems unlikely that the constitutional and institutional assumptions of strong cabinet government could accommodate such a change.

If change came more slowly in France, it was also impossible for French leaders and administrators to ignore the necessity for structural change. However poorly conceived in Britain, the French could not take refuge in a tidy separation of functional and territorial problems, but had to confront the full complexity of local reform. Thus, if less progress was made, it can also be argued that more profound political change was also made. Indeed, the communes and provinces of France had a critical role in taming the excesses of the Fifth Republic, and by the time of Pompidou's Presidency there were fundamentally important shifts in national politics. British local government has never aspired to such importance, and, as we shall see in Chapter 4, there are reasons to think that ministers and their top advisors are much relieved that they do not. Indeed, it will be argued in the Conclusion that this was perhaps the most important, underlying aim of British local reorganization.

NOTES: CHAPTER 3

1 L. J. Sharpe, *Why Local Democracy?*, Fabian Tract 361, (London: Fabian

Society, 1965), p. 17. He also notes that the 'low status of local government in the eyes of the public' contributes to this aversion (ibid., p. 1). Though this is true in the general sense, political systems vary in transmitting local values to government and, of course, local governments by no means display this disinterestedness once the question is raised.

2   Interview, Ministry of Interior, 15 July 1976. See also *Receuil d'Information Statistique sur l'Urbanisme* (Paris: Ministère de l'Équipement, 1976), pp. 14–15. For annual figures on districts and unions, see *Statistiques et Indicateurs des Régions Françaises*, Série R (Paris: Institut National de la Statistique et des Études Économiques).

3   The ambiguous nature of de Gaulle's thinking on local level problems is outlined by Howard Machin, 'The prefects of the Fifth Republic 1958–1969', thesis, University of London, 1973, pp. 60–73.

4   The MRP was isolated after the breakdown of tripartism among the three progressive parties. None the less, they continued their effort to get the department reorganized. See the list of seven *loi-projects* in Yves Mény, *Centralisation et Décentralisation dans le Débat Politique Français* (Paris: Librarie Générale de Droit et de Jurisprudence, 1974), p. 344.

5   On the continuities between Vichy and postwar France, see Robert O. Paxton, *Vichy France: Old Guard and New Order* (New York: Knopf, 1972). The administrative links are described in Maurice Bourjol, *La Réforme Municipale* (Paris: Berger Levrault, 1975).

6   See Brian Chapman, *The Prefects and Provincial France* (London: Allen & Unwin, 1955), pp. 58–61. For additional background on France at the time see Pierre Doueil, *L'Administration à l'Épreuve de la Guerre (1939–1949)* (Paris: Sirey, 1950); and Charles-Louis Foulon, *Les Pouvoirs en Province à la Libération* (Paris: Presses de la Fondation Nationale des Sciences Politiques, 1975).

7   Quoted in Mény, op. cit., p. 179.

8   Mény, op. cit., p. 177. The Radicals played a crucial central role in the formation of governments in the Fourth Republic, although they had little more than 10 percent of votes cast in national elections.

9   Machin, op. cit., p. 48fn.

10 See the description of the Depeux proposals in Mény, op. cit., pp. 178–9.

11 Mény, op. cit., p. 354.

12 William A. Robson inherited the Webbs' concern with local government and had been a passionate advocate of local democracy since his early work, *The Development of Local Government* (London: Allen & Unwin, 1931). He continued to write extensively on the plight of local government after the war, his case still being argued in *Local Government in Crisis* (London: Allen & Unwin, 1966, rev. edn 1968). Nearly all the postwar leaders in the Labour party had strong connections with local government. Attlee had written a book on local councillors with Robson.

13 Another important change relieving pressure for local reform was the Conservative Education Act of 1944, which established compulsory and free primary education. Thus, a major issue that might have focused Labour on local government matters had already been removed by 1945. The Ministry of Education, of course, continued to have a major interest in local government.

14 On reconstruction proposals see *Future of Local Government*, Labour Party Central Committee on Reconstruction, 1943; the Interim Report of the NALGO Reconstruction Committee, 1943. The White Paper mentioned is *Local Government in England and Wales during the Period of Reconstruction*, Cmd 6579 (London: HMSO, 1945).

15 This exchange is recorded by William A. Robson, 'Labour and local government', *Political Quarterly*, vol. 24 (1953), p. 49.

16 See the discussion in B. Keith-Lucas and P. Richards, *A History of Local Government in the Twentieth Century* (London: Allen & Unwin, 1978), pp. 204–6. Eve later wrote a book on his experience: Sir A. M. Trustram Eve, *The Future of Local Government* (London: Athlone Press, 1951).

17 Herbert Morrison remained a champion of the old system of London government and remained active in the Borough of Lambeth after he became a major Labour minister. There was an old antipathy between Attlee and Morrison, and Morrison's relations with Bevan were also rather stormy.

18 See Michael Foot, *Aneurin Bevan: A Biography*, Vol. 2 (London: Davis-Poynter, 1973), pp. 266–7fn. Bevan appears to have favored small, unitary authorities and

was responsible for the Local Government Act of 1948 which had financial implications and introduced payment for local councillors. See Chapter 6.

19 This gap in party policy at the national level is raised by Robson, op. cit., p. 46. See also Winston Crouch, 'Local government under the British Labour government', *Journal of Politics*, vol. 12 (1950), pp. 232–59.

20 The essentials of the Report are outlined in Smellie, *A History of Local Government* (London: Allen & Unwin, 1968), pp. 115–18; see also the review of the Report by Robson, 'The reform of local government', *Political Quarterly*, vol. 19 (1948), pp. 254–63. Robson was especially critical of the failure to consider resources, though, as we shall see below, the 1972 reforms did little to resolve this problem.

21 A good account can be found in Smellie, op. cit., pp. 88–129. See also Robson, op. cit.; and Peter Self, *Whither Local Government?*, Fabian Tract No. 279 (London: Fabian Society, 1950).

22 See D. N. Chester, *Central and Local Authorities* (London: Macmillan, 1951), p. 195.

23 Quoted in Smellie, op. cit., p. 133. The point here is not that local governments might have generated new taxes which would, as in France, require parliamentary authorization. The important aspect is the immediate dynamic: for by taking such a large responsibility central government no longer had to defend the limited resource base given to localities. The distribution of resources became in effect a non-issue.

24 See E. Bonnefous, *La Réforme administrative 1922–1957* (Paris: PUF, 1958), p. 31.

25 Michel Debré, *La Mort de l'état républicain* (Paris: Gallimard, 1947). He did not pursue this idea in later books.

26 Mény, op. cit., p. 163.

27 J. F. Gravier, *Paris et le désert français* (Paris: Le Portulan, 1947).

28 The relation of the Planning Commission to the national and local government systems will be analyzed in Chapter 6. For a general description see J. Hackett and A. M. Hackett, *Economic Planning in France* (London: Allen & Unwin, 1963); and Stephen S. Cohen, *Modern Capitalist Planning: The French Model* (Berkeley, Calif.: University of California Press, 1969).

29 According to Paul Camous, 'La genèse du projet gouvernemental', in J.-L. Bodiguel *et al.*, *La Réforme Régionale et le Référendum du 27 Avril 1969* (Paris: Cujas, 1970), p. 21. Claudius-Petit outlined his ideas in a ministerial pamphlet, *Pour un Plan d'Aménagement du Territoire* (Paris: Ministry of Reconstruction, 1950).

30 See the explanation Prudhomme provides in his essay, 'Regional economic policy in France, 1962–1972', in N. M. Hansen (ed.), *Public Policy and Regional Economic Development* (Cambridge, Mass.: Ballinger, 1974), p. 34.

31 Quoted in Camous, op. cit., p. 21.

32 On the early organization in Brittany and Phlipponneau's role, see J. E. S. Hayward, 'From functional regionalism to functional representation in France: the Battle of Brittany', *Political Studies*, vol. 17 (1969), pp. 48–75.

33 Mény, op. cit., p. 208.

34 See the excellent account of the combination of private and public interests that Chaban-Delmas assembled to rebuild Bordeaux in Jacques Lagroye, *Chaban-Delmas à Bordeaux* (Paris: Pedone, 1973), esp. pp. 75–102 on the formation of the regional committee, Centre d'Expansion Bordeaux-Sud-Ouest (CEBSO).

35 See M. Phlipponneau, *Le Problème Breton et le Programme d'Action Régionale* (Paris: Colin, 1957).

36 Camous, op. cit., p. 23. There was a third contender on the horizon, but it did not enter directly into the conflict at this time. The Ministry of Public Works was undergoing its own internal power struggle. Under the leadership of the *ponts et chaussées* elite administrative body, this group was the eventual victor in the battle over local-level development. See J.-C. Thoenig, *L'Ère des Technocrates: Le Cas des Ponts et Chaussées* (Paris: Editions d'Organisation, 1973), pp. 62–3.

37 On the housing and rental reforms planned by the Conservatives, see Malcolm Joel Barnett, *The Politics of Legislation: The Rent Act 1957* (London: Weidenfeld & Nicolson, 1969).

38 *The Economist*, no. 174, 5 February 1955, p. 441.

39 *Areas and Functions of Local Authorities in England and Wales*, Cmd 9831 (London: HMSO, 1956). The most complete account of the local government

associations' role in preparing these papers is by Jack Brand, *Local Government Reform in England* (London: Croom Helm, 1974), pp. 88–130.

40 *The Economist,* no. 180, 4 August 1956, pp. 385–6. Sandys announced the agreement in early 1955; see *The Economist,* no. 174, 26 March 1955, pp. 1066–7.

41 See the critical review of the proposal by Peter Self, 'New prospects for local government', *Political Quarterly,* vol. 28 (1957), pp. 20–31. Also Bryan Keith-Lucas, 'Three White Papers on local government', *Political Quarterly,* vol. 28 (1957), pp. 328–38.

42 See Stanyer, in Wiseman (ed.), *Local Government in England, 1958–69* (London: Routledge & Kegan Paul, 1940), pp. 36–41. Also G. W. Jones, 'The Local Government Commission and county borough extensions', *Public Administration* (UK), vol. 41 (1963), pp. 173–87; and his 'County borough expansion: the Local Government Commission's views', *Public Administration,* vol. 42 (1964), pp. 277–90.

43 The Association of Municipal Corporations, which became the Association of Municipal Authorities after reorganization, was founded in 1872 when efforts were made in Parliament to restrict the formation of county boroughs. The County Councils Association dates from the 1888 Act. There were also an Urban District Councils Association, a Rural District Councils Association, a London Boroughs Association and a Parish Councils Association. See Keith-Lucas and Richards, op. cit., pp. 180–98.

44 See *Local Government Finance,* Cmd 209 (London: HMSO, 1957) for the government's proposals. The third Conservative proposal was *Functions of County Councils and County District Councils in England and Wales,* Cmd 161 (London: HMSO, 1957). The standard assessment of local rates, enacted in 1948, came into effect in 1956.

45 See *The Economist,* no. 185, 14 December 1957. With its usual aplomb, *The Economist* noted that the entire project was fruitless because finance had been divorced from reorganization, no. 189 (11 December 1958), pp. 975–6.

46 See the lengthy memoranda of qualification in the *Municipal Review,* vol. 29 (April 1968), pp. 68–71; (June 1968), pp. 104–11; (November 1968), pp. 112–86.

47 Only a sketch of the two reorganizations can be provided here. On the social and economic pressures facing London, see J. H. Westergaard, 'The structure of London', in R. Glass (ed.), *London: Aspects of Change* (London: MacGibbon & Kee, 1964), pp. 91–144. On Paris, André Delion, *Paris: Institutions Sociales et Aménagement du Territoire* (Paris: Documentation Française, 1974); also Daniel Valot, 'La région parisienne, un monstre ingouvernable?', *Vie Publique,* no. 28 (1974), pp. 60–5.

48 Delouvrier was responsible for the destruction of Les Halles, whose replacement paralyzed French government, the construction of the huge office complex, La Défense, and the express commuter railroad system (RER) now nearing completion. On the effects, see the book by a leader of the Parisian protest, Louis Chevalier, *L'Assassinat de Paris* (Paris: Fayard, 1977). On the organization and powers of the Paris prefecture, see Mariette Sineau, 'Le Préfecture de Paris: quel pouvoir?', *Bulletin de l'Institut International de l'Administration Publique,* no. 29 (January–March 1974), pp. 83–99.

49 The important changes were to replace the three, often warring, Secretary Generals with a single executive; to reduce the number of main city agencies from seventeen to ten; and to discontinue separate recruitment of Parisian officials from the graduates of ENA. Even under the 1975 reforms, control of the police and of the 35,000 personnel of the inner city remain outside the mayor's direct control. On the formal organization, see M. Etienne, *Le Statut de Paris* (Paris: Berger-Levrault, 1975); and Patricia and Jean-Michel Lemoyne de Forges, *Aspects Actuels de l'Administration Parisienne* (Paris: PUF, 1972). See also the prognosis of J. F. Simon, 'Paris aura-t-il un vrai maire?', *Le Monde,* 3 December 1975; and 'Un maire pour Paris?', *Vie Publique* (November 1975), pp. 28–36.

50 This is another example of how the French pile governments on top of each other. The source of most administrative power still comes from the district but there is now in addition the commune of Paris, corresponding to the inner city as well as the region. Not unrelated to the reform was the growing scandal about the construction of the *villes nouvelles* around Paris. See Jacques Chirac, 'L'Avenir de Paris et les villes nouvelles de la région parisienne', *Moniteur* (25 January 1975); also Maurice Doublet, 'Pitié pour la région de Paris', *La NEF,* vol. 56 (March–May 1975), pp. 10–32; and the general study, Jacqueline Beaujeu-

Garnier and Jean Bartie, *Paris et la Région Parisienne* (Paris: Berger-Levrault, 1972).

51 See Royal Commission on Local Government in Greater London, *Report*, Cmd 1164 (London: HMSO, 1960). The Conservative White Paper on the Report appeared a year later, *London Government: Government Proposals for Reorganization*, Cmd 1562 (London: HMSO, 1961). See the admirable account by Frank Smallwood, *Greater London: The Politics of Metropolitan Reform* (New York: Bobbs-Merrill, 1965), for details. Other good critiques are Peter Self, 'The Herbert Report and the values of local government', *Political Studies*, vol. 10 (1962), pp. 146–62; and Marjorie McIntosh, 'The Report of the Royal Commission on Local Government in Greater London', *British Journal of Sociology*, vol. 12 (1961), pp. 236–48.

52 The full story is linked to Herbert Morrison's career, which was, in fact, probably handicapped once Labour came to power because of his preoccupation with London politics. See G. W. Jones, 'Political Leadership in local government', *Local Government Studies* (1973), pp. 1–12, and Bernard Donoughue and G. W. Jones, *Herbert Morrison: Portrait of a Politician* (London: Weidenfeld & Nicolson, 1973).

53 'Battle for London', *The Economist* (6 January 1962).

54 Smallwood, op. cit., p. 306. Smallwood notes that the ideological character of the debate had expressive value, but one could also argue that in effect this represents a way to turn the issue into dichotomous form to meet the needs of Parliament. See Chapter 4. On the exclusion of local politics generally from policymaking, see Paul Kantor, 'The ungovernable city: islands of power and political parties in London', *Polity*, vol. 7 (1974), pp. 4–31

55 See Donald L. Foley, *Governing the London Region: Reorganization and Planning in the 1960's* (Berkeley, Calif.: University of California Press, 1974). For more on local planning problems in the British system see Chapters 5 and 7.

56 In 1978 the Conservative GLC asked Sir Frank Marshall to study its problems. On Marshall's report, see *The Times* (London) (8 July 1978). On the general problem, 'London's burning', *The Economist* (1 January 1977).

57 Smallwood, op. cit., p. 306.

58 The best account from a Gaullist perspective is Jacques Aubert, 'L'Administration du territoire', in B. Tricot *et al.*, *De Gaulle et le Service de l'État* (Paris: Plon, 1977), pp. 281–322. De Gaulle was more interested in cultivating the prefectoral corps and reorganizing the police than forcing communal reform.

59 For background see J. Bancal, *Les Circonscriptions Administratives de la France* (Paris: Sirey, 1945). The numbers vary over time as ministries take on new functions. On the progress of the reorganization see Machin, 1973, op. cit., pp. 127–9.

60 See Francis J. Fabre, 'La Réforme de l'apurement administratif des comptes des communes et établissements publics', *Revue Administrative*, vol. 27 (1974), pp. 565–71.

61 The materials for this paragraph come from the excellent thesis of Catherine Grémion, 'Décision ou indécision dans la haute administration française: l'exemple des réformes départementales et régionales de 1964', Paris, Institut D'Études Politiques, 1977, pp. 20–75.

62 Reports by the prefects of the early activities appear in various issues of *Administration*: Seine-Maritime, 15 December 1962; Eure and Vienne, 1 August 1962.

63 The terms of the dispute will be examined more closely in Chapter 5. The Ministry of the Interior wanted the prefect to have more control over investments, to receive notice of all subsidies provided by all ministries and to become the second ordonnateur or director of all development projects in the department.

64 See, for example, Guy de Caumont, 'Reforme des structures départementales', *Revue Administrative*, vol. 13 (1960), pp. 657–61; and G. T. (anon.), 'Sur l'action des préfets dans la vie économique locale', ibid., pp. 126–30.

65 Another key figure in working out compromises and decrees for the implementation was Francis de Baecque, Joxe's cabinet director. His views are presented in 'Pour un politique cohérente de déconcentration', *Revue Française de Science Politique*, vol. 17 (1967), pp. 5–27. The new policies were, of course, conceived throughout as *déconcentration*, not *decentralisation*.

66 See G. Delaunay, 'Le préfet et la crise de la conscience civique française', *Bulletin de l'Association du Corps Préfectoral*, vol. 31 (1957), pp. 137–51; A. Chadeau,

'L'évolution du rôle de préfet de région depuis 1964', *Administration*, no. 68 (1970), pp. 19–32; G. Delaunay, 'La conférence interdépartementale: une institution à devenir', *Administration*, no. 48 (1963), pp. 49–54; and R. Deugnier, 'Réflexions sur les origines et les développements des conférences interdépartementales', *Administration*, no. 48 (1963), pp. 57–61.

67 See C. Grémion, op. cit., pp. 380–99. See also A. Colliard and J.-C. Groshens, 'La sous-prefectorisation des préfets des départements', *Revue du Droit Public*, vol. 81 (1965), pp. 5–30. A side issue of some importance was whether the regional prefect should also sit as departmental prefect in the department where he was located. The Ministry of the Interior won the first round of this struggle, but some independent regional prefects were assigned after 1972. DATAR felt that its aims would be more easily achieved with separate officials. The dispute broke out again when the Ministry of the Interior wanted the new officials to have more control over long-term investments than DATAR and the Planning Commission were willing to allow them. Groschens, ibid., p. 402.

68 These powers were not negligible. DATAR acquired control of the regional improvement fund (FIAT), took over the aménagement functions of the Ministry of Construction, became head of the National Council for Regional Planning (CNAT), a member of the boards allocating the economic development fund (FDES) and the urban development fund (FNAFU). See Grémion, op. cit., pp. 244–8.

69 Most of the material in this paragraph comes from Grémion, op. cit., pp. 260–400. She provided me with the story about the ambulatory regional government. There is so much written about the experiments that extensive citation is not needed. See the full account and lengthy bibliography covering this period in the first three volumes of the DATAR yearbook, *Aménagement du territoire et développement régionale*, for 1967, 1968, 1969, published by the Institut d'Études Politiques, University of Grenoble.

70 The basic book explaining their legal and administrative status is Maurice Bourjol, *Les Districts urbains* (Paris: Berger-Levrault, 1963).

71 *Structures administratives des grandes agglomérations urbaines* (Paira Report) (Paris: Ministry of Interior and DATAR, 1964).

72 See the ministerial circulars in Jean-Claude Venezia, 'Les regroupements de communes: bilan et perspectives', *Revue du Droit Public*, vol. 87 (1971), pp. 1079–84. A more optimistic account is given by René Maurice, 'Bilan de la politique des regroupements de communes', *Administration*, no. 75 (June–July 1972), pp. 133–6. A review of the administrative arrangements is Jean Hourticq, 'Vie des collectivités locales: les zones urbaines et l'administration', *Revue Administrative*, vol. 27 (January–February 1974), pp. 61–7. He also outlines the special forms of *agglomération* used only for the Paris region.

73 Elisabeth Zoller, 'La création des syndicats de communes: une décision des communes ou de l'État?', *Revue du Droit Public*, vol. 92 (1976), pp. 985–94. The official view is given by René Maurice, *Le Syndicat des Communes* (Paris: Collection Vie Publique, Masson, 1976).

74 The diversity is not only of varied functions, but also of distribution within the territorial system. Henry Roussillon, *Les structures territoriales des communes: Réformes et perspectives d'avenir* (Paris: Libraire Générale de Droit et de Jurisprudence, 1972), p. 47fn, notes the great differences in their adoption among departments. In the departments of Lot and Meuse, for example, 80 percent or more of the communes belong to SIVOM, while in the departments of the Creuse and the Loire only 10 percent or less.

75 The information in this paragraph comes from the very good survey of the program by Jean-Francois Médard, 'Les communautés urbaines: renforcement ou déclin de l'autonomie locale?', *Revue du Droit Public*, vol. 84 (1968), pp. 737–800. See also J. Bodiguel, 'Les Communautés urbaines', in *Aménagement du Territoire et Développement Régional*, vol. 2 (1968), pp. 347–79.

76 The report (Paira Report, op. cit.) recommended a new framework midway 'between a *collectivité locale* and an *établissement publique*', p. 40. Four methods of selecting the councils are outlined. Nancy and Metz are delayed because of intense rivalry which then centered over the expansion of the university system, while Toulouse and Marseille are, of course, too far apart and regional rivals in the south. Like the departmental and regional proposals, the idea can be traced to Debré. See his 'A propos de l'administration des grandes agglomérations', *Revue Administrative* (1951), p. 56.

77   Médard, op. cit., p. 764.
78   *Le Monde*, 19 April 1972. See also the analysis of investment and spending in the local government system in later chapters; and Henri Albert 'Une fausse solution: les communautés urbaines', *Revue Politique et Parlementaire*, vol. 75 (1973), pp. 2–5.
79   *Vie Publique*, no. 45 (February 1976), pp. 9–10.
80   In 1977 the National Assembly adopted a procedure for the dissolution of urban communities; see *Le Monde* 4 June 1977, p. 8. Not all the recent crises have been political. Lille, for example, was troubled by debt and fiscal problems; see *Le Monde*, 29 September 1977, p. 12. The various legal difficulties of the urban communities are outlined by Maxime Sauzet, 'Les Institutions départmentales, intercommunales et communales à travers les litiges provoqués par leur conditions actuelles de fonctionnement', *Administration*, no. 59 (1967), pp. 95–110. There are numerous articles summing up the accomplishments of the urban communities: Le Mans, Strasbourg, Lyons, Dunkerque and Lille are reviewed in *Administration*, no. 77 (1972); Bordeaux is reviewed in *Moniteur*, no. 52 (December 1971).
81   Mény, op. cit., p. 217.
82   Crossman had rejected the Boundary Commission's recommendations on Merseyside in 1965, after which one member resigned. He was also at odds with the Commission over the reorganization of Tyneside. When the Commission chairman died he was not replaced and the Commission remained in limbo until formally terminated by Crossman's successor, Anthony Greenwood, in 1967. See the account of the subsequent Tyneside decision in Bruce Wood, *The Process of Local Government Reform (1966–1974)* (London: Allen & Unwin, 1976), pp. 15–20. Also G. W. Jones, 'Mr. Crossman and the reform of local government', *Parliamentary Affairs*, vol. 19 (1966), pp. 77–89.
83   Crossman's own account in *The Diaries of a Cabinet Minister*, Vol. 1 (New York: Holt, Rinehart and Winston, 1976), p. 331, makes the decision sound a bit more spontaneous than was likely for even so impetuous a minister. There is ample evidence in the volume that he found the Tyneside dispute tiresome. His speech appears in the *Municipal Review*, vol. 36 (1965), pp. 655–60.
84   Crossman, op. cit., pp. 439–41. There is a glimpse of the internal politics of the Cabinet when Crossman rounds up three important MPs whose seats might be affected before approaching Wilson. His first reaction to the Lancashire proposals was favorable; ibid., p. 426. There was 'virtually no discussion' in the Cabinet meeting on forming the Royal Commission.
85   On the selection of the Chairman, see Crossman, op. cit., pp. 481, 485, 491 and 494. Though Crossman wanted someone more 'radical' than Maud, it is interesting that on this, as on so many policy matters, Wilson had his way. Maud later made some adjustments in the membership of the Commission to get strong union representation and also someone from the education field.
86   On the make-up of the Commission see Bruce Wood, op. cit., pp. 39–41; and Stanyer, 'The Redcliffe-Maud Royal Commission on Local Government', in Chapman (ed.), op. cit., pp. 111–12. Short biographies of the members are in Chapman (ed.), op. cit., pp. 129–31. Stanyer feels that only the two members without experience were 'neutral', though it is hard to see how anyone could approach so complex a subject without some simplifying judgments. His reservations are more on the technical inadequacies of the research, for which he soundly rebukes the Committee on Local Government Management. See his essay 'The Maud Committee Report', *Social and Economic Administration*, vol. 1 (1967), pp. 3–19.
87   Appointed and reporting in the same years as the English Commission was the Royal Commission on Scottish Local Government under Sir Andrew Wheatley. See *Scotland: Local Government Reform*, Cmd 4150 (London: HMSO, 1969); and *Local Government in Northern Ireland: Report of the Review Body*, Cmd 546 (London: HMSO, 1970). On details of the new system see William Reid, 'Scottish local government reorganisation', *Public Finance and Accountancy*, vol. 1 (1975), pp. 384–9. The regional issue in relation to subnational politics and policy will be further considered below.
88   Chapter III of the *Report*, Cmd 4040 (London: HMSO, 1969) does contain some recommendations on relations to central administration, but these are wholly within the existing administrative structure.
89   An account of concurrent developments is in Wood, op. cit., pp. 47–54. See also

Douglas E. Ashford, 'Reorganizing British local government: a policy problem', *Local Government Studies*, vol. 2 (1976), pp. 1–18. The Ministry of Health was about to impose changes. After a public exchange, the Ministry finally agreed to wait for the Commission's recommendations.

90   See the *Report*, pp. 109–17. There were to be eight regions. Senior's proposal went much farther and is built on thirty-five 'regions' with statutory powers, which are, in turn, organized in five 'provinces'. There would be legally based devolution of powers, a clear transfer of capital spending powers and a political organization that bears a close resemblance to the French departments and regions. See the *Report*, Vol. 2, pp. 134–58.

91   The historical irony is worth noting. The Conservatives appointed the original Maud Committee, leaving the Labour government to deal with its recommendations. In turn, Labour appointed the Constitutional Commission, which then reported to the Heath government. The *Report* of the Royal Committee on the Constitution, Cmd 5460 (London: HMSO, 1973) will be discussed further below.

92   The multiple reasons for criticizing the proposals are in themselves an important indicator of the complexity of subnational policy. See G. Smith (ed.), *Redcliffe-Maud's Brave New England* (London: Charles Knight, 1969); B. Rose (ed.), *England looks at Maud* (London: Justice of the Peace Ltd, 1970); Jane Morton, *The Best Laid Schemes – A Cool Look at Local Government Reform* (London: Knight, 1970); Stephen L. Bristow, 'The criteria for local government reorganisation and local authority autonomy', *Policy and Politics*, vol. 1 (1972), pp. 143–62; William Hampton, 'Political attributes to changes in city council administration', *Local Government Studies* (1972), pp. 23–35; C. J. Davies, 'The reform of local government with special reference to England', *Studies in Comparative Local Government*, vol. 7 (1973), pp. 35–45; R. A. W. Rhodes, 'Local government reform: three questions', *Social and Economic Administration*, vol. 8 (1974), pp. 6–21.

93   Editorial, 'A politic report', *New Society*, 12 June 1969, p. 903. See also 'A careful carve-up', *The Economist*, 14 June 1969, pp. 12 and 19–21; and 'After Redcliffe-Maud: looking beyond self interest', *The Times* (London), 22 August 1969. Academics were, in their individual ways, very critical. See the essays of Michael Steed, Bryan Keith-Lucas and Peter Hall in *New Society*, 19 June 1969.

94   *Reform of Local Government in England*, Ministry of Housing and Local Government, Cmd 4276 (London: HMSO, 1970). See Anthony Crosland, *Socialism Now* (London: Cape, 1974), pp. 173–89, for his speech in the Commons introducing the White Paper. On the changes in the law through this process, see the excellent table of Bruce Wood, op. cit., pp. 191–4.

95   Under different constraints, much the same compromise was made in order to get a new government for London in 1963. The Inner London Education Authority, a highly successful school system, successfully lobbied to preserve its identity. See Frank Smallwood, *Greater London: The Politics of Metropolitan Reform* (New York: Bobbs-Merrill, 1965), pp. 107–16 and 228–36; also Gerald Rhodes (ed.), *The New Government of London: The First Five Years* (London: London School of Economics and Political Science, 1972), pp. 148–212.

96   Wilson, *The Labour Government, 1964–1970* (Harmondsworth: Penguin, 1974), pp. 853–5. What he calls a 'somewhat disagreeable chapter of controversy' was a statutory responsibility under the Redistribution of Seats Act of 1949. He says no more than six or eight seats were at stake, although there had been no changes since 1954, and the suburbs, with their conservative tendencies, had been growing for fifteen years. The psephologists' estimate is that eleven more seats would have gone to the Conservatives had seats been redistributed. See David Butler and Michael Pinto-Duschinsky, *The British General Election of 1970* (London: Macmillan, 1971), pp. 414–15.

97   *Local Government in England: Government Proposals for Reorganisation*, Cmd 4584 (London: HMSO, 1971). At the same time, papers were published on the reform of Wales and Scotland: *Reform of Local Government in Scotland*, Cmd 4583 (London: HMSO, 1971), and *The Reform of Local Government in Wales* (London: Welsh Office, 1971). See also Bruce Wood, 'The Tory plan for local government', *Political Quarterly*, vol. 42 (1971), pp. 316–19, and his book, *The Process of Local Government Reform*, op. cit., pp. 104–10. See also 'The carve up', *New Society*, 18 February 1971, p. 259; and *The Economist*, 7 February 1971, p. 20; and 20 February 1971, pp. 18–21.

98   Most of this transfer took place in the initial modifications of the Wilson

government, and not in the small, but highly controversial, dismemberments by the Conservatives. Wood, op. cit., p. 133, estimates that the Conservative revision took 150,000 persons from the six metropolitan counties.

99 Op. cit., p. 799.

100 See Venezia, op. cit., p. 1081.

101 See Yves Madiot, *Fusions et regroupements de communes* (Paris: Librairie Générale de Droit et de Jurisprudence, 1973), pp. 43–4. The work of the Mondon group later reappears in the report of the Intergroup on Local Finance for the Sixth Plan, which will be considered later in this book.

102 Interviews, Ministry of the Interior, 1976 and 1977. See also *Vie Publique* (March 1974), p. 77 and (September 1977), p. 8; *Le Moniteur*, 17 August 1976, p. 36.

103 Roussillon, op. cit., p. 84. His thesis is the most complete account of how the bill was written and debated.

104 Ibid., p. 175. See also the government statement, *Le Monde*, 18 September 1969, p. 2.

105 Roussillon, op. cit., p. 178.

106 Their plan is outlined in Madiot, op. cit., pp. 200–3; and in Roussillon, op. cit., pp. 160–5. P. Grémion, op. cit., p. 92, notes that parties did not respond to the 1964 reforms.

107 This plan is outlined in Madiot, op. cit., pp. 196–200; and in Roussillon, op. cit., pp. 180–1; the text of the law, pp. 444–6.

108 The parallel texts are given by Venezia, op. cit., pp. 111–28, and Roussillon, op. cit., pp. 441–5 and 451–9. See also the presentation by Marcellin, 'Principaux problèmes concernant l'administration générale du territoire et des collectivités locales', *Départements et Communes* (March 1971), pp. 77–87. A summary of the law and its operation is given by J. Hourticq, 'La loi du 16 juillet 1971 sur les fusions et regroupements des communes', *Revue Administrative*, vol. 24 (1971), pp. 686–91.

109 Interviews, Ministry of the Interior, July 1976 and October 1977. Some details are given in Madiot, op. cit., pp. 170–2. I have also used the *comptes rendus* of the prefects for the merger meetings, by courtesy of the Ministry of the Interior. The discussions will enter more directly into the analysis of local politics in Chapter 4.

110 J.-M Becet, 'Le référendum intercommunal et l'article 8 de la loi du 16 juillet 1971 sur les fusions et regroupements de communes', *Revue Administrative*, vol. 24 (1971), pp. 528–534.

111 Figures supplied by the Direction des Collectivités Locales, Ministry of the Interior, Paris. Annual accounts can also be found in the annual *Statistiques et indicateurs des régions françaises*, Series R (Paris: INSEE) which gives total fusions under all conditions.

112 For example, Paul Lambin, *L'État Contre les Communes* (Paris: Pensée Universelle, 1973); Jean Savigny, *L'État Contre les Communes* (Paris: Seuil, 1971).

113 Madiot, op. cit.; Paul Bernard, *Le Grand Tournant des Communes de France* (Paris: Colin, 1969); and Club Jean Moulin, *Les Citoyens au Pouvoir* (Paris: Seuil, 1968).

114 For recent examples see André Terrazzoni, 'Les fusions et regroupements de communes dans l'arrondissement d'Avranches', *Administration*, no. 90 (1975), pp. 44–52; A. Pinary, 'La naissance d'une nouvelle commune: le grand Saint-Chamond', *Administration*, no. 77 (1972), pp. 100–7; and Jean-Michel Forges, 'Le regroupement communal en Meurthe-et-Moselle', *Revue Administrative de l'Est de la France*, vol. 1 (1971), pp. 33–65.

115 They are responses to the initial Commission Report, the Labour White Paper, the Conservative White Paper, the circular preparatory to drafting the bill, the second debate in the Commons, the committee stage in the Commons, the third debate in the Commons and the Lords debate. The most detailed account of the sequence of changes is found in Wood, op. cit., pp. 128–60. For the committee proceedings, in two hefty volumes, see *Parliamentary Debates*, Commons, Standing Committee D, vols IV and V, Session 1971–72 (London: HMSO, 1972).

116 Wood, op. cit., p. 162.

117 See Wood, op. cit., pp. 139 and 184. Only one seriously aggrieved Conservative was appointed to the Committee. Areas that were intensely resisting change, such as Blackpool, Bournemouth, Glamorgan and Somerset, were not represented, while counties that had been preserved more or less intact, like Kent, Dorset and

Wiltshire, had two representatives apiece. See also *The Economist*, 6 November 1971, p. 29; and ibid., 22 January 1972, p. 26.

118 *The Economist*, 29 January 1972, p. 22. On the way in which cross-pressures within in each party tended to reduce partisan debate, see Brand, op. cit., pp. 131–48.

119 For a full treatment of the transformations see Peter G. Richards, *The Local Government Act of 1972: Problems of Implementation* (London: Allen & Unwin, 1972); and also Joyce Long and Alan Norton, *Setting Up the New Authorities* (London: Charles Knight, 1972). For a glimpse of the local confusion, see Jane Morton, 'Walsall's way ahead', *New Society*, 27 December 1973, pp. 779–80; and Gavin Weightman, 'After the shuffle', *New Society*, 15 August 1974, pp. 418–19. He notes that the reorganization cost Cambridgeshire about half a million pounds, though there have been, to my knowledge, no careful studies of the costs of reorganization.

120 Wood, op. cit., p. 168, notes how the Home Office, thoroughly mauled in the reorganization of London boroughs a few years before, made sure that they had firm control of the new electoral arrangements. Even so, some new councilmen found their wards abolished in the final boundary determinations after the 1973 elections. See Chapter IV.

121 The best summary is the Appendix in Wood, op. cit., pp. 191–4, which traces the elections. See Chapter 4.

122 See Department of the Environment, *The New Local Authorities: Management and Structure* (Bains Report) (London: HMSO, 1972). The entire question will be examined more in Chapter 5. The Bains Report was completed in a hurry when the government realized that they in fact had no organizational guidelines for the new authorities.

123 We have few studies so far that enable us to follow the internal problems of the transition. For a county study, see J. M. Lee and Bruce Wood, *The Scope of Local Initiative: A Study of Cheshire County Council 1961–1974* (London: Martin Robertson, 1974); and for a London borough, see Enid Wistrich, *Local Government Reorganisation: The First Years of Camden* (London: Borough of Camden, 1972).

Chapter 4

THE POLITICAL CONNECTION: CAN NATIONAL POLITICS MAKE LOCAL POLICY?

All governments and Ministers are a bit schizophrenic about their relationship with local authorities. On the one hand, they genuinely believe the ringing phrases they use about how local government should have more power and freedom and that's why we all want local government reform. On the other hand, a Labour government hates it when Tory councils pursue education or housing policies of which it disapproves, and exactly the same is true of a Tory government with Labour councils. – Anthony Crosland.

From the legislative campaign of 1973, one passed to the presidential campaign for 1974, after which one began to prepare for the cantonal campaigns of 1976, themselves followed by the municipal campaign of 1977, which was prolonged by the legislation campaign of 1978. Now there is the campaign for the second ballot and, more distant, the presidential campaign of 1981. If one adds to these the campaigns in the press, the publicity campaigns, and the campaigns against tobacco, one finds that the French are always campaigning, but rarely at rest. – Bernard Chapius.

The reorganization of local government has been high on the national political agendas of France and Britain for a decade or more but for very different reasons. The elaborate subnational system of France was visibly outmoded in the early 1960s, if not much earlier. France placed a high priority on reorganizing the subnational system, but not as high as other national priorities, such as industrial modernization. The Gaullists also had to take into account the determined resistance of the mayors and administrators to territorial changes. Britain opted for a global change, which, as we have seen, proved to be less workable than the legislators and experts had expected. Nonetheless, the striking political difference between Britain and France is that Britain could make massive changes in both the territorial and functional dimensions of local government, while France could not.

Britain is probably the only welfare state that could have produced a global reorganization of the subnational system, although there have been several major consolidations of local government in other democracies.[1] Simply put, the conditions are that the Cabinet retains collective responsibility for policy decisions; that MPs remain subject to the 'whips' or parliamentary discipline and that the legal supremacy of Wesminster remains immune to judicial or administrative checks.[2] Every other democratic system in the world falls short of the constitutional and conventional practices that place full and unlimited policy-making authority in Parliament. The question then becomes not why Britain was able to undertake a massive reorganization, but how appropriate such a concentration of lawmaking power is in making a complex decision; and further, what constraints are necessarily placed on such fundamental legislation in order to preserve parliamentary preeminence.

If the British Parliament and the Cabinet agree that a major reform should be enacted, it is carried out, even if the reform might prove fatal to the government of the day.[3] Given the Presidential and parliamentary limitations on French government, there is much less certainty that government will be able to ensure structural change. De Gaulle's decision to increase presidential power through his own direct election in 1962 was bitterly fought in the National Assembly, the Senate and the Constitutional Council. De Gaulle was able to rely on plebiscitary power only at the crest of his popularity. When he tried the same tactic seven years later he failed, largely because the local politicians opposed Senate reform.[4] The Fifth Republic incorporated a number of measures, such as the *vote bloqué*,[5] joint parliamentary committees (*commissions paritaires*) and ministerial control of parliamentary business, but these parliamentary tactics in themselves were not sufficient to produce local government reorganization. In this sense, the French system is subject to political control, if we mean by this the influence of nationally and locally elected leaders over structural change of the system. Despite the arbitrary controls built into the Fifth Republic, structural change was not easy and when badly handled it proved disastrous.

Although the British system is generally regarded as permitting freer policy debates than the French, the capacity of the executive to manipulate and even to intimidate elected representatives is quite similar. There is no shortage of evidence of the inability of the House of Commons to compete with the Cabinet and departmental ministers.[6] The various writs, orders in council and delegated legislation of the British system enhance executive power in the ways that *loi-cadres* (framework laws), *ordonnances* and *décrets* strengthen the French cabinet and higher administration. Nor is it more difficult to uncover outrage over the arbitrary use of executive power in Britain than in France. De Gaulle's barely concealed disdain for political parties and his abrupt treatment of disciples have possibly left bitter memories. But his powers do not appear so great when measured against the complex policy decision of local reform.

At the height of his power de Gaulle could force through major structural changes, as he did with the 1959 *ordonnance* reorganizing the central government. But by the mid-1960s party politics and coalition government had again become the rule, making massive structural change of the system virtually impossible. Except for the feebly implemented *loi Marcellin*, the French decided not to act. The French system is dependent on electoral and partisan forces in ways that elude British politics.

A second prerequisite for passing legislation, with far-reaching constitutional and institutional implications, is a strong majority in Parliament. In recent years parliamentary majorities in Britain and France have not differed substantially. Basic reforms require large majorities which both countries' governments have enjoyed. When the Wilson government began the local reform process, it had a majority of over a hundred votes in the House of Commons, the largest majority of any British government since the Labour landslide of 1945. Of course, Macmillan had enjoyed similar voting power in Westminster after the 1959 election. But as in France, such strong parliamentary majorities do not necessarily make structural change easy. Macmillan, for example, placed severe strains on Tory MPs representing the London suburbs when he reorganized the metropolis in 1963. The 1972 reorganization also cut across party lines and jeopardized party discipline in Parliament.

In France, the parliamentary honeymoon did not last very long, though, as President, de Gaulle and later Pompidou could probably have assembled a majority to pass major local government legislation. But the multiparty system, and the realignments throughout the 1960s, made parliamentary calculations difficult. After 1962 de Gaulle was forced to form a coalition, and in 1965 he was forced into the embarrassing situation of a hero appearing in a second round in the presidential elections.[7] But the Gaullists and their allies had a majority after the 1967 elections (245 of 487 seats) and an even greater one after the 1968 elections (358 of 485 seats) when the Left badly miscalculated the effects of the May riots.[8] Even President Giscard d'Estaing inherited a sizeable majority (278 of 490 seats) in the National Assembly, but by the early 1970s local reorganization had been dropped from the political agenda.

The more disciplined British parties have been internally divided over local reform, while the less disciplined French parties have been forced to protect their local political resources. Even though the British Parliament can exercise constitutional authority in ways that the French National Assembly cannot, forging agreement on local government policy is divisive in both settings. The most persuasive evidence of this is that in both legislatures the ruling elite has not lacked votes over the past decade, nor has either government been reluctant to use its respective forms of parliamentary coercion to force through other unpopular legislation. Parliamentary discipline has had to be tempered with a sense of political advantage which, as we have seen in Chapter 3, puts local reorganization low on the list of priorities. More recent British trends toward minority and coalition government have made local issues even more divisive.[9]

On the other hand, popular support for the French regime has been comparable to that accorded British government. In the presidential elections of both 1965 and 1974 a majority of the French citizens who voted supported the winning candidate, and the percentage of voters supporting the majority group governing France has not been much less than the support given the two major British parties.[10] These conditions suggest that the chances for major legislation on local reform are not governed simply by political feasibility at the national level, where capacity to pass legislation is similar despite the institutional differences of the two systems. If legislative authority alone does not appear sufficient, then it may be that the central–local political relationships will actually determine whether global local reform is possible.

The political implications of massive local reorganization may be more readily recognized in France than in Britain. Unless a state can effectively neutralize territorial politics – a task which Britain has more effectively accomplished than any other modern country – reorganization touches the most sensitive nerves of political life. Thus, French policy on local reorganization is more deeply rooted in the workings of the party system than is Britain's. As we shall see, French party organization is weaker than the British, and deputies are more dependent on their local strongholds than are MPs. These issues were paramount in the minds of all political leaders as the Fifth Republic returned to normality after the Algerian revolution. Indeed, a number of French leaders thought the new regime was only a transitory phenomenon. Mollet, the Socialist leader, still spoke of the 'Gaullist parenthesis' in 1967,[11] expecting that the patterns of the Fourth Republic would soon reassert themselves. More realistic political strategists, including both de Gaulle and Mitterrand, saw that a local power base was essential to the exercise of influence, and each in his own way set out to acquire one.

De Gaulle found an electoral solution to central–local politics in the Third Republic, though he hoped to regulate communes in the manner of Napoleon III. In doing so, he inadvertently restored much of the prestige and influence of local politics in France.[12] The direct impact of local politics on the electoral system, the party structures and representative politics explain why the locality remains politically crucial to French policymaking. For the moment, it will suffice to note that local reorganization in France is intimately linked to the acquisition of legitimacy by the state and its political leaders. In Britain, local government policy is more nearly a simple assertion of a legitimacy that has been firmly concentrated in Whitehall and Westminster for over a century.

The ability of a government to put local reform on the political agenda is regulated partly by parliamentary and partly by party limitations. A third limitation, and possibly the most important from the perspective of local government policy, is the effectiveness of the executive in directly influencing the agenda. The direct relationship between local and national political power in France produces an effect which seems paradoxical when compared to the British case. The penetration of French political leadership at all levels of government, and the administration as well, means that putting reorganization on the agenda in France is a task for the parties rather than for the Cabinet and President. The Jacobin state of de Gaulle has been frequently castigated,[13] but the fact remains that he was unable to have his own way. The modest steps toward reorganization under Pompidou and Chaban-Delmas after 1969, most notably the regional reform of 1972, were viewed with considerable suspicion by the right wing of the Gaullist party. The effort to build Chaban's *nouvelle société* eventually produced the intrigues that brought his collapse, and the conservatives asserted their strength by making a 'safe' Gaullist, Messmer, Prime Minister.[14] Local reform legislation in 1978 and 1979 placed severe strains on the delicate structure of President d'Estaing's coalition.

There is no comparable link between party politics and policy-making in Britain. There are, of course, elements of partisan advantage in the calculation of grants and the provisions of specific programs, which will be described further in Chapters 6 and 7, but the reorganization of the subnational system in 1972 was quite unrelated to major party objectives. Crossman was intensely aware of the implications of possible boundary changes in 1969, but local-level partisan interests had relatively little direct involvement in the reorganization itself. The Labour Party was, of course, interested in strengthening its urban base and reducing Conservative voting strength in the suburbs, but the decision to reorganize was a distinctly national one. It did not presuppose careful involvement of and consultation with local political elites, the essential prelude to even the more modest reforms made in France. The British decision to reorganize was essentially an executive decision influenced by national political calculations of fairly short-term importance. The French leaders had a similar capacity to place the communes on the political agenda, but hesitated because the political repercussions were difficult to assess, and, above all, because the party structure was rapidly changing as Mitterrand and Marchais began to cooperate. The local elections of 1977 dramatically revealed the interdependence of national and local politics. The French leaders quietly scuttled the most recent effort to reform, the Guichard Report of 1976, once the mayors began to protest the new threat, however mild, to the local government system of 1789.[15]

In neither country do the formal powers of the political executive assure that complex policies will be adopted without party support. There has been a good deal of speculation about the growing power of the British Prime Minister.[16] But his/her effective powers are limited by factions within parties and the size of the majority in the House of Commons. In France, the Fourth Republic's dilemma of rapid cabinet turnover has declined.[17] There are also signs that ministerial instability has increased in Britain. While there is no doubt that the presidential republic of de Gaulle enhanced executive powers, the French President must also avoid the appearance of instability and indecision. Both Pompidou and Giscard d'Estaing took pains to assert presidential precedence, and the French Cabinet is now most often chaired by the President.[18] The net effect, then, seems to be that the two executive arrangements, though vastly different in constitutional terms, are rather similar in their operation. The critical difference is that leaders can mobilize party and parliamentary support in Britain while avoiding the pitfalls of local politics. Policymaking powers in local affairs can thus exclude local politics, while in France policy-making is almost impossible without accommodating the multiple roles of the French politician.

Structural reform of the subnational system in France is barred not so much by parliamentary weaknesses as by political relationships *across* levels of government. Neither French nor British local elites showed strong predispositions favoring reform, much less the populace at large. The difference was that both locally and nationally elected representatives in France were able to make themselves heard. Despite the extraordinary power often attributed to the Gaullist regime, proposals to change the communal system were blocked and have shown few signs of being revived. French elected officials enter the policymaking process directly at many levels of government, and possess a formidable array of devices to maximize their influence at the higher levels. British local elections, though they often disclose national trends, are not institutionally linked to higher-level policy-making, nor do British local leaders possess the armory of weapons to combat central government that exists in France. Studies of British local politics suggest that they would not use them even if they existed.

In brief, the French system cannot function without local politics, while the British system would be hard pressed to accommodate any partisan intervention from lower levels of government. The reasons for this are complex, involving the electoral system, the interlocking of representative institutions and the organization of political parties across levels of government. Before these political components of the central–local political relationship are examined in more detail, it will be helpful to trace the historical roots of local politics in the two countries. Over the past century both countries have shown great political vitality at the local level. The historical material also suggests that if France is ever to remodel the subnational system, change must come from the grassroots.

LOCAL POLITICAL TRADITIONS: DO THE GRASSROOTS HAVE BLOSSOMS?

As pressures for local reorganization grew over the past two decades, each country devised its own strategy for change. These strategies observe the political and historical constraints that had accumulated over the years and through the major transformations of the political system. Without recapitulating the historical development of the two subnational systems, this section will outline the relationship of national and local politics in Britain and France. In neither country were the growing needs of cities and towns quickly recognized by national government, nor were the local parties and elites eager to make major adjustments in tested procedures and established habits. From a policy perspective, it is not so much resistance to change that is surprising, but how central–local relations within each system found characteristic ways of adapting local reform to the political system.

At the national level, the growth of democracy was no less turbulent in Britain than in France. British local politics successfully, if some-what unevenly, adjusted to the growth of the franchise and the changing relationship between central and local government. Long before the appearance of the welfare state, British localities were taking their lead from the center, and they were never called upon to defend democracy in the way that the 1848 Revolution and the 1871 crises of central authority propelled French local politicians into

national affairs. British counties were never in the vanguard of democratic politics. Neither counties nor boroughs could claim that they
had played a central role in establishing popular government or in
averting disasters. Political tranquillity made the direct support of the
local politicians less crucial in Britain, while political uncertainty
made the loyalty of the local elites and local party cliques essential to
French government. From this historical difference stems the
underlying dependence of the French Republic on local government,
and out of it grew the institutional forms that enable local politicians
to this day to intervene directly in national politics and policy.
Underlying the efficacy of local politics, as Williams has noted,[19] is a
popular confidence in local leaders that national leaders have never
acquired.

In no small degree, skepticism about national representation was
well founded in the minds of Frenchmen. From the very beginnings of
the commune, manipulation of the electoral laws had been acceptable.
Napoleon was only the first strong national leader of France who
wanted to insulate the center from local influence. An indirect
franchise was introduced in 1795, and under the Restoration the
income qualification for voting was even more restrictive than the
British property qualification[20] – in the elections of 1849 only fifty-
eight of the 833 voters of Montpelier voted.[21] Electoral manipulation
went on to become a highly developed art under the Second Empire.
Moreover, the national electoral law tended to reinforce the local
identification of the national level by making the *arrondissement* the
deputy's constituency. As the crises of the Third Republic unfolded,
starting with the rescue of the republic from the monarchists, and
going on to Boulanger,[22] the Dreyfus affair, the dreadful costs of the
First World War, and the threat of fascism in the 1930s, it always
seemed to be the local *patron* who mobilized at the grassroots to
protect France from chaos.

Spared the turbulence of French politics, the growth of the
franchise at both levels of government was a much more orderly
process in Britain, as Keith-Lucas has so carefully documented.[23] The
Select Vestries Act of 1831 proposed that every man and woman
should have a parish vote, and even a secret ballot if five voters so
requested. But this early enlightenment was not shared at the national
level, and only thirteen parishes made such a bold step toward local
democracy. The Municipal Corporations Act of 1835 was severely
amended to ensure that the 'right' people remained in local office, and
the law itself applied to only 178 boroughs. Until the Local
Government Act of 1888 the British upper class displayed all the
ingenuity of the French prefect in making sure that local elections
reflected national interests. The most notorious distortion was 'compounding', or the manipulation of the rate-based local franchise.[24]
The complex ways of electing the numerous local boards as services
grew played into the hands of the local gentry who had the time and
interest to manipulate the system. The general pattern throughout the
nineteenth century was to extend the local franchise with the steady
growth of the national electorate. The British local politician never
acquired a direct claim on national legitimacy like his French counter-

part; but neither did he accumulate the grievances and suspicions with regard to the central government that prevailed in the French communes. British towns and cities did not need to build a vigilant defense of democratic government, which explains in part why local politicians so complacently accepted a secondary role in national politics.

The stability of British parliamentary government may have even retarded the growth of parties at the local level, in comparison to France. Tudesq finds early signs of local party politics in 1849 during the elections leading to the Second Empire. As he illustrates, the pattern of French central–local relations was set from an early time with the insistence of voters in Bordeaux and Haut-Rhin that they should send to Paris representatives of their own choosing.[25] Unlike in Britain, local elections were a way of acting out national political conflicts. Indivisible the French Republic may be, but the elections of 1849 were only one of many occasions when national issues were projected on to local politics, as seen in Bordeaux in the contest between monarchist and republican candidates.[26] The 'red peril' did not begin with the Communists winning the communes around Paris in the Fifth Republic, but with fears that radical peasants of Var, Cher, Dordogne and Lot-et-Garonne would threaten bourgeois stability as it had developed since Napoleon. The pattern of urban–rural tensions changed very little for nearly a century, as illustrated so well by the electoral geography of Siegfried and Goguel.[27] Conservative strength was consolidated in the west, north and northeast with the Republicans dominating the *massif central*, the Rhone valley and Provence.[28] In a way, local politics became a safety valve for the shortcomings of the national political system. National differences in British politics were certainly reflected in the rough-and-tumble local politics of nineteenth century Britain, but Westminster never looked to the towns and counties for solutions to national problems.

The French communes learned that favors and advantages were to be obtained by courting Paris. Sometimes the efforts bordered on the ridiculous, such as the intervention of the deputy from Dijon demanding that the railroad to Strasbourg be built through his town.[29] As Goguel writes, 'local influences absorbed more and more of political life', and the centrifugal force was stemmed by the 'revolutionary role of Paris which became a kind of compensation, a way of nationalizing politics . . .'.[30] Although the prefects were active during elections, they helped make compromises with local elites, and linked national and local electoral politics in a way that rarely occurred in Britain. There were ample rewards of prestige and influence in British local politics in the nineteenth century, of course, but they were locked into a complex system of local boards and councils. Contrary to the impression of Redlich and Hirst,[31] patronage was common, but it was both provided and distributed at the local level. In this way, British local politics did not need the French pattern of *complicité* between administration and politics in order to extract rewards; but at the same time local politicians lost direct access to national benefits.

The development of party politics in the last half of the nineteenth century had direct impact on local government in the two countries, and underscores why French local politicians so carefully nurtured their influence through the last three republics. On the other hand, the very active local politicians of Britain did not collectively influence parties, nor directly enter into policymaking at the center. The rise of national parties in Britain did not radically change the eighteenth century foundations of British politics, where 'the constitution was . . . controlled and guided by one and the same class in one and the same interest'.[32] In 1880, after nearly fifty years of electoral reform and expansion of the franchise, only 110 of the 487 seats in Parliament were contested.[33] If anything, political life was less secure at the local level, particularly in the boroughs, than in Westminster. As Fraser points out,[34] the new social and political forces in British society arose in the new towns and cities. The new national party organizations of the late nineteenth century were not all that strong and then, as now, were not an important conduit for central–local political exchange. There was no opportunity for local politics to weigh heavily at the national level until the Labour Party emerged in 1918 in full strength.[35] By then the British party system was in disarray, and the Labour leaders themselves uncertain about their best strategy to achieve national power. That they did not revive Chamberlain's notion of urban caucus politics, built around either urban interests or the working class, is one of the more curious accidents of British history, if not a noteworthy tribute to the lure of upper-class politics.

But even without the incentive of national payoffs for strong local organizations, party politics thrived in British cities and towns from the late eighteenth century. Sir Francis Hill provides a vivid picture of Whigs and Tories battling for local offices and prestige in the town of Lincoln. National issues were up for discussion, and strongly influenced the thinking of local leaders. Sibthorp, the Tory leader of Lincoln, opposed Catholic emancipation, the Reform Bill of 1832, the Municipal Reform Bill of 1835, the new Poor Laws and the 1851 Exhibition.[36] In Leeds there was an intense party struggle throughout much of the nineteenth century even though the Tories never threatened Whig control. The mayor himself argued in 1836 that parties 'were useful in exciting a spirit of competition and vigilance and had the effect of bringing a greater degree of energy into the service of the public'.[37] In Liverpool the 'very wealthy rival elites of merchants and gentlemen'[38] fought for control of the municipal council for most of the century, even though the Conservatives more skilfully manipulated votes. Though the city enjoyed good government, the sights of its local politicians were most often set on national elections, a Liberal leader in 1862 noting that now was the chance to 'return two members for Liverpool and dumbfound Lord Derby'.[39] Radical Leicester, the 'citadel of King and country', was taken over by the Whigs after parliamentary and municipal reform legislation and remained in their control for the rest of the century.[40]

Although the rising Labour Party made forays into the fundamentally Conservative territory of county government, mostly around London and in the north,[41] it was not until 1945 that Labour widely contested county elections. Even so, one should not assume that partisan interests did not influence county government, which Lee has so thoroughly demonstrated for Cheshire. As he points out, in Cheshire the low level of contested seats resulted from mutual understanding between the Liberal and Conservative leaders.[42] The entrenched social elite tended to prevail in the counties while new leadership arose more quickly in the cities. As Hill notes, county government was controlled until 1888 through the Quarter Sessions and by a 'class [that] could not be precisely defined [though] there was little doubt who was within it, the rest of the world [being] outside'.[43] There was certainly a great deal of consultation about elections in the paternal government of British counties, but national parties made few inroads in rural Britain. As late as 1901, only 433 of the 3349 seats on county councils were contested.[44] The impact at the national level was made through the indirect link of parliamentary elections. The counties were the preserve of upper-class politics and even after the Local Government Act of 1888 the organization of the British local government system protected the rural haunts of the gentry from party politics.

In Fraser's conclusion to his study of Victorian urban politics, he raises the intriguing point that interest in municipal politics in Britain appears to have declined when the functions and power of local government were increasing.[45] The local activities of Victorian Britain had real incentives, namely, the variety of favors and sinecures that nineteenth century local government offered. With the growth of central government these posts were gradually abolished or came under more careful supervision. From 1850 the office of church-warden was no longer political; by 1870 surveyors (engineers) and improvement commissions had been absorbed into town councils under national legislation; after 1870 school boards were mandatory and in 1902 school standards came under surveillance; and in 1929 the Poor Law guardians finally disappeared. Nineteenth century local politics was above all patronage politics at the local, and often at the national, level. City governments were more prone to 'throw the rascals out' and bring in their own party officials, often to the dismay of city clerks and the central government inspectors. The whole game of central–local politics was changing. The policy role of municipal councils diminished as centrally designed services grew, and the nationalization of party politics left the towns little but the MP through which to express their needs and preferences.

Unlike in Britain, the French provinces and communes have never been disarmed in their apparently perpetual combat with Paris. After the Third Republic had become secure in 1877, the republican notables took control of the Senate in 1879, and the Republicans, like the Gaullists in the Fifth Republic, began to install themselves in local offices. The new liberal state in France did not go to the extremes of the Second Empire in manipulating local politics, but Goguel reminds us that even in the 1880s direct political pressure on departments and communes could be fierce. The people of Gers and the Hautes-Pyrénées, where Conservatives and Bonapartists still clung to office, were told 'If you vote against the Republic you will have no right to favors of the government and administration . . . if you send them [the enemies of the Republic] to the *conseil général* you will be open to having no more subsidies for your schools, for your town halls, for your vicarage, for your sick vineyards, for your storm-damaged wheat'.[46] They were bluntly told that a rail connection in the department would not be built. The struggle was not this intense throughout France, but nationally arranged patronage was widespread and on a scale that would no doubt have shocked nineteenth century British mayors and parliamentarians. Political loyalty to the republican parties brought high rewards. In staunchly radical and anticlerical Auxerre, the mayor went on with Gambetta's blessing to become Minister of Interior. The town's deputy defended the republic for thirteen years, eventually to become Gambetta's Minister of Instruction.[47] Under these circumstances, the pattern of reciprocal favors and rewards was established from the first days of democratic politics in France.

The pattern of mutual dependence between levels of government thrived in the Third Republic, particularly after the stabilization of the party system around the turn of the century. In the legislative elections of 1902 the party system assumed what would be its basic structure until the Fifth Republic; Conservatives and Nationalists on the Right; Radicals and Radical Socialists making up the Center; and Socialists and later Communists on the Left. At the national level the result was that policymaking in the Assembly was tempered by the demands of the local cliques and factions of these parties. At the local level, party leaders became adept in overlooking party differences in order to keep office. Duverger eloquently deplores the consequence: the center (*marais*) was able to exercise an influence disproportionate to its numbers, a tradition that was similarly exploited by Jean-Jacques Servan Schreiber and Giscard d'Estaing in the Fifth Republic.[48]

In France national politics tended to reproduce local politics on a large scale. As in Britain, the industrial cities were an important stronghold for the Left. Even after the disastrous effects of the split in the Socialist International, the Socialist Party clung to office in Lille, Strasbourg, Brest and Grenoble.[49] But whereas national party organizations and parliamentary politics could define local political conflict in Britain, the relationship was reversed in France. Unless parties could resolve their local differences, they were deprived of a national platform. Grenoble is a good example.[50] In 1930 the growing Communist Party refused to cooperate with the Socialists. In 1936 the Socialists came back to power under Blum's Popular Front. The Left was again divided after the war, and in 1959 Grenoble was one of the few major cities controlled by the Gaullists. Finally, in 1965, the Left was able to unite under a dynamic mayor, Dubedout, and the city's progressive image in French politics was restored. In this way, national political uncertainties increase local influence, and, in turn, strong local leaders can propel themselves onto the national scene. The similarity of national and local election results also reflects the primacy of local politics, and is a clearer measure of national trends than British local elections.[51]

The fact that many political practices have their roots in earlier French republics does not mean, of course, that the significance of these practices remains the same. In the Third and Fourth Republics no party could risk advocating major local reorganization, and the political system was founded on the delicate modulation of national and local politics. Even the practice of *parachutage* (nominating national figures for local office and constituencies), which became so controversial as the Gaullists courted local politicians in the 1960s, also has historical roots. No less a figure than the constitutional expert Benjamin Constant was parachuted into a constituency in Alsace in the early nineteenth century. Mendès-France sought local office in the Eure in 1932 and, like some of the Gaullists thirty years later,[52] succeeded in penetrating the local power structure of Grenoble only after three years of laborious cultivation of the local citizens. The direct link between levels of government presupposes relative ease in moving between national and local politics. What the Gaullists did in the 1960s was done with comparable aplomb by Socialists and Communists in the 1970s.

NATIONAL AND LOCAL ELECTORAL POLITICS: DO THEY MIX?

The access of French local politicians to national decisionmaking is enhanced by electoral procedures, while in Britain the elections tend to isolate elected representatives at each level of government. The British work much harder than the French to devise and operate an electoral system at both levels of government that is democratic in the sense of 'one man one vote'. But democratic principles may not affect policy-making in the welfare state, especially in such complex and remote decisions as reorganization. Indeed, representative government may be unable to make the detailed and finely adjusted decisions that increasingly characterize government in the welfare state. Throughout the history of France, electoral systems have been freely altered and manipulated for partisan reasons. But few can disagree with the aim of British electoral practice, which works quite well in a stable party system, and is consistent with the abstract values of democratic politics. The British cling to the notion that preferences and needs expressed in elections should determine results and objectives which the relative stability of the political system has enabled them to preserve. For the French, electoral systems are a political device to bolster the precarious legitimacy of the successive republics, and to make sure that locally elected representatives have influence at higher levels of government.

While it is no doubt correct and desirable that popular preferences define general policy objectives,[53] party structures and parliamentary conduct probably have more influence over results. Shifting party alignments and electoral alliances at both levels of government force the French to take a more pragmatic view of elections. The weakness of Parliament justifies electoral manipulation which, in turn, gives loyal mayors and notables direct access to decisions about local benefits and projects. In contrast, these incentives are more removed from political actors at both levels of government in the British system. MPs and local councillors alike usually conform to parliamentary discipline and accept the anonymity of party discipline. The pragmatic view of the French and more idealistic one of the British both have unintended consequences in the policymaking process at both levels of government.

In relation to central–local influence over policymaking, the causal effects of elections may be reversed in the two countries. In Britain, the single-member constituencies and plurality count help preserve the stability, and therefore the power, of Parliament over local affairs. In France, the importance of local electoral alliances in national elections and locally-rooted power of most national politicians makes national elections a more localized event. In a word, British elections tend to protect central policymaking powers, while French elections tend to perpetuate the influence of local political forces. In the absence of local elections, national politics in France would be handicapped and national parties would be set adrift. On the other hand, in Britain there is every reason to think that the functioning of the House of Commons and parliamentary government would be barely affected were local elections discontinued.

The treatment of national elections in this section is not meant to repudiate representative democracy, but simply to acknowledge that representation has different meanings for policy formation in different systems. In France, local elections, and to some extent national elections as well, compensate for other political weaknesses: the splintered parties, the divided leaders and the weak Assembly. Paradoxically, this provides the communes with access to the policy process that is denied British councillors. Being able to influence policies may be a better test of democracy than knowing that one's vote counts exactly the same as the next person's, and this ability to influence events appears to stimulate a high level of participation in French local elections and politics. The multiple political roles (*cumul des mandats*) of French politicians make them more sensitive to national policy affecting the localities than does life at Westminster for the MPs. At both levels of government British electoral practice has an opposite objective, which is to maximize the political strength of the center by excluding local actors.

People are on the whole uncomfortable with complex policy decisions, partly because they lack knowledge and interest, and partly because the word 'local' has different meanings for individuals and for governments.[54] As Dearlove puts it 'electors are ignorant of quite basic facts of local political life and vote, not on the basis of local issues, policies, and candidates, but on the basis of a strong orientation to national candidates'.[55] Whatever the individual psychology may be, the citizens of France and Britain have made it clear that they would not reorganize local government of their own accord. A recent survey of French mayors has sampling problems, but showed 60 percent against global reform.[56] In a survey of the British electorate for the Royal Commission on Local Government, 65 percent of the respondents thought that the local authority areas should stay the same and an unhappy few (7 percent) wanted them smaller.[57] An earlier survey of local government electors for the Committee on the Management of Local Government showed that 90 percent of the people living in boroughs, and 75 percent of those in counties, thought their councils ran things very or fairly well.[58] Local government is not a glamorous activity in either country, so these responses are not too surprising. But they do address the primary concern of this study. If government waited for citizens to support local-level structural reform we might still be living in eighteenth century parishes.

From a policymaking perspective it makes more sense to view national representation and its associated procedures as a way of protecting the center from local interference, if one has a fairly stable party structure as in Britain. But where parties are weak and divided as in France, elections enable local politicians to infiltrate the decisionmaking process. Thus, the policymaking link between the national elections and the formulation of local government policy is reversed in the two countries. British electoral laws, party organization and party leadership work to minimize local political influence and indeed make sweeping legislation possible. French electoral laws, party organization and leadership help preserve local influence in national decisionmaking.

The House of Commons made a clearly unpopular decision in 1972, which may be the reason that both major parties were prepared to share responsibility for it. The single-member constituency, the deposit required for parliamentary candidates, and the pitfalls of the nomination process distort the representativeness of British national elections. But the decision to reorganize was made possible because representation is subordinate to the needs of the party system and of Cabinet government. The British are not disturbed that three times in this century (1929, 1951, and 1974) governments were formed by parties with a minority of the popular vote. The Scottish National Party got 128,000 votes and no seats in 1966, and with over 300,000 votes in 1970 could win only one parliamentary seat. Though it probably made no difference to the reorganization, parliamentary constituencies were distributed very poorly in 1970 because Labour delayed redistricting.[59]

The electoral penalties of being a minority party in Britain are severe and help exclude localized politics from the House of Commons. Despite the great emphasis placed on redistribution of seats and electoral procedures in British politics, it should also be noted that the system itself is hardly less biased than the French electoral system. The average constituency has 64,000 voters, but in 1974 the sizes varied from 26,000 to over 96,000 voters.[60] Malapportionment creates more inequities in British than in American national elections.[61] From a local perspective, the technical problems and the haste of the 1972 reorganization meant that local election constituencies for the most part still do not coincide with parliamentary constituencies, which becomes another hurdle in equating national election results with local elections, and makes it difficult, even if local leaders wished to so, to bring local problems to bear more directly on MPs.

Thus, even if national elections served as a guideline to local reform, the biases of British elections would affect policies. Because the relation of the communes to the state in France is within the specified lawmaking responsibilities of the Assembly (Art. 34), there can be no major reform without permission of Parliament. The resistance to reorganization in France is due to many forces, but the fact that the Assembly does appear to represent French opinion on this issue may justify a closer look at the national electoral arrangements. De Gaulle hoped the 1958 Constitution would reduce the number of parties, extract parliamentary discipline from the deputies and, as far as possible, eliminate the Left. Although the archaic territorial structure left little option, another hurdle was placed in the way of the direct communication of local feelings to Parliament by the departure from the *arrondissements* in drawing constituency boundaries. The new electoral law provided single-member constituencies with a second ballot to encourage two-party contests. In nearly all the legislative elections since then, 80 percent or more of the contests not decided on the first ballot have become two-party duels.[62] But the intricate alliances now needed within the party structure help bring parties of the Left closer together.[63]

Although de Gaulle revived the electoral system of the Third Republic, he also conducted the most complete overhaul of the constituencies since 1927. Even so, there were immense disparities among constituencies by 1967, when the smallest had about 23,000 voters and the largest had nearly 116,000.[64] By 1974 the disparities had become even greater, with one constituency containing 120,000 voters and four fewer than 32,000 voters. While political inequality is not the most desirable way to stimulate voters and parties to intervene in policymaking, these disparities help keep local government policy on the national agenda. The handicap that the Socialists and Communists encounter makes local office more important to them, and reinforces the determination of more progressive communes to resist reorganization. Despite, and possibly because of, the unfairness of national elections, the ultimate effect has been that national and local politicians have a common interest in defending the communes.

The multiparty structure means, of course, that national election contests vary greatly from one constituency to another. Nonetheless, the interesting contrast with Britain is that French legislative contests have also been a test of local forces and a way of thrashing out local issues. While the nationalization of French politics may eventually concentrate elections at both levels more exclusively on national policy interests, this did not happen in the 1970s. An illustration is the legislative election in the Normandy city of Evreux.[65] Andrews found the forces of earlier republics much in evidence and parties behaving much as before. A notable of the Republican Independents, de Broglie, faced Socialist, Communist and Radical opponents. Each candidate depended on his local organization, and national party headquarters had little influence on the conduct of the election or the selection of candidates. In the first round, the government's candidate who had run in every contest since 1951 slipped back to the lowest plurality he had had since 1958. But the Left could not muster the votes in the second round to defeat him, even though the Socialist, who polled fewer votes than his Communist competitor, stepped down. Whether one should consider national elections of this kind truly 'national' is difficult to decide, but it shows how locally-defined conflict immerses deputies.

There are a number of other ways in which national and local policy might be joined in the electoral process. In theory, both countries take pains to see that national representatives are not subject to local control.[66] The Constitution of the Fifth Republic forbids deputies to receive instructions from their constituency (Art. 27), though they nearly all campaign on the election manifesto of their party. British constitutional custom also says that MPs should not be bound by constituency demands, and parties in fact take care to show that their parliamentary members are immune from demands from both national and local party organizations.[67] The nomination process itself is another way that local constraints could be placed on a national representative. In Britain, the local constituency party selects candidates, often from a list kept by the party's central offices. These choices are subject to central review, but are seldom reversed.[68] But the MP who uses a local constituency against the party and breaks party discipline as did Taverne at Lincoln, sacrifices influence in the House of Commons. The MP is in a position to help his constituency to be heard in Whitehall, but rarely in the House of Commons, when there are special requests and problems.[69] Even the controversy over periodic reviews of Labour MPs by constituency party organizations was seen as a constitutional and national party crisis, not as a way of more directly introducing local government interests into Parliament.[70]

In designing the Fifth Republic, de Gaulle saw that insulating the center from local political forces was essential to his Jacobin concept of the state. A key element in the presidential republic was to require the ministers to resign their seats in the Assembly or Senate (Art. 23), though a minister is not required to give up unsalaried elected office, such as mayor or departmental councillor. Like many constitutional and legalistic devices designed to isolate the executive from the legislature, this practice had a reverse effect. In typically French fashion another set of rules was found to cancel out rules that offend. To further insulate the new Republic from the shocks of an excessive number of by-elections, deputies were given *suppléants* or substitutes to replace them in case of death or appointment to a ministerial position.

What has actually happened is quite the opposite. Those elevated to ministerial position can protect their local constituency seat by arranging to have the substitute resign when they leave the Cabinet.[71] Though the practice does not involve large numbers of representatives, it suggests the importance of holding local office as well as the preference of many communes for a representative who is well placed in national government. The futility of this device and others intended to insulate Paris against local influence, was noted by Chenot: '. . . the deputy-minister has remained, in general, the man of his constituency, attentive to the gestures of the shadow who replaces him, present every week in his fief, and consolidating his local power by his post as mayor general councillor'.[72] Ministers rarely detach themselves from their local constituencies, and most appoint a member of their staff to handle constituency matters even though they have temporarily vacated their elected office.

Except for the Communist Party, national party discipline and organization is weak, but both the Socialist and Communist Parties have strong departmental-level federations. Though the Left screens candidates, and the Communists rarely adapt their national program to local interests, it is important that candidates for national office have local endorsement. Although many critics of French politics have condemned the procedure which permits national figures to acquire local offices, the effect has been to embroil leaders in local problems. The Gaullists have no doubt been the worst offenders, but they were also the most determined defenders of the *cumul des mandats* when their opponent, Giscard, set out to reform local government in 1979. The *parachutage* of national leaders into localities has probably been as successful and as important for the Left as for the Right,[73] and accumulation of offices works in both directions. In the 1977 local elections in Bourges, for example, a Communist, who had steadily accumulated the offices of assistant mayor of a nearby town, departmental councillor and deputy, became mayor because the Gaullists and Republican Independents could not agree on a candidate.

The main differences are that the Right has had more opportunities and a longer period to enjoy the benefits of high office. For the Center and Right, relations between national and local parties are more complex, but governing parties are no less dependent on local wishes and the promise of local benefits. The governing parties are themselves handicapped in pressing for national policies that offend the local cliques and factions of their supporters.[74] From the 1965 local elections onward, the Gaullists aggressively sought local office and so were co-opted into the very system their leaders had once rejected.[75] Though more distinguished than most deputy-mayors, Chaban-Delmas is typical. Starting as deputy from Bordeaux in 1946 and mayor of that city in 1947, he eventually accumulated the offices of president of the regional council, the urban community and the departmental council, as well as presiding over numerous developmental agencies for his city and region.[76] The Left protests the descent of national figures into local elections and the Right resents the political opportunities that the Left accumulates at the local level. Each side prefers the form of political mobility that serves it best, but both tactics help preserve the intimate connection between local and national politics.

There is no legal barrier to MPs holding local office, but the rigors of parliamentary life are generally given as the reason why it is not a common practice.[77] In fact, this is a rather weak explanation as most MPs are very conscientious about holding regular 'surgeries' in their constituencies where voters are invited to discuss individual problems. For a number of reasons the strength of local constituency associations is declining, and as this happens the possibility increases that MPs may need to consider some of the more direct political practices of French politicians.[78] Nonetheless, the tortured debate in the House of Commons over elections for the European Assembly and devolution illustrates how uncomfortable holding multiple office would appear to be under the British constitution.[79] In France, virtually the opposite is the case: ambitious politicians from both the local and national levels eagerly seek additional mandates.

Analyzing French local politics a decade ago, Kesselman noted that the Fourth Republic persists at the local level.[80] In the Third Republic, two-thirds of the deputies were also mayors (*députés-maires*); and in the Fourth and Fifth Republics the proportion stayed almost the same.[81] In their study of the French deputy, Cayrol and his colleagues conclude that 'a local political career appears nearly obligatory' for Socialist and Radical deputies, over 90 percent of whom are municipal or departmental councillors before becoming deputies.[82] They found only two Socialist deputies who did not previously hold local office, which also helps explain the Gaullist attack on local election procedures. Roughly two-thirds of center and conservative (Republican Independent) deputies hold local office, while slightly more than half of both the Gaullist and Communist deputies are local-level councillors before achieving national office. Nearly half of all deputies begin their careers with local office, compared with slightly over a third in Britain.[83]

In the early years of the Fifth Republic, the Gaullists hoped to remain above this local free-for-all and were in any event not well equipped for it. The transformation of party politics changed their views, and 172 of the 248 Gaullist deputies fought in the 1971 local elections. In the local elections of 1977, 249 of the 473 metropolitan deputies were mayors.[84] In fact, the accumulation of offices goes well beyond electoral politics and reaches into all kinds of policymaking bodies. For example, the Socialist mayor of Dunkerque in 1974 was also a deputy, president of the *communauté urbaine*, president of two public housing societies, of a chain of cooperative stores and of the national public housing agency (HLM).[85] The accumulation of offices, then, is not only a way of linking national and local politics, but a widely used device to assure that resources and benefits are distributed to favor one's local power base.

While it is true, as Peyrefitte argued in his 1974 report, that there are no other countries with accumulated electoral offices, French critics tend to underestimate how the *cumul des mandats* works to strengthen parties and to enhance local influence. In fact, the accumulation of offices reached higher levels in the Fifth Republic than ever before, and was no doubt a check on centralizing tendencies. In 1978, 79 percent of the deputies and 93 percent of the Senators held one or more additional elected offices. Despite the criticism of the *cumul des mandats* from the Left, Socialists and Communists accumulate office more frequently (83 and 82 percent, respectively) than do Gaullists and Republicans (77 and 75 percent, respectively).[86] Thus, all parties have a vested interest. The most serious policymaking effect may be that accumulation is heavily concentrated in provincial and rural France. The Léotard report found four-fifths of the accumulated offices in rural France. The department of Corrèze, for example, has as many multiple-office holders as Paris.[87] Although everyone agrees that the *cumul des mandats* can be abusive, none of the parties is eager to see it abolished, not even the President himself whose centrist party was built from remnants of provincial parties. After the disastrous local elections of 1977 and on the eve of the threatening legislative elections of 1978, it was not surprising that the Guichard Commission only asked for a debate on the future of the *cumul des mandats*.[88]

The political sensitivity of the *cumul des mandats* was underscored in 1979 when the President asked Barre, the Prime Minister, to personally conduct consultations on limiting the accumulation of offices. The replies tell us a good deal about the intricacies of French party politics. Although part of the ruling coalition, the Gaullists opposed limitations, fearing that they might be used 'personally'.[89] By this they meant that the Gaullist leader, Chirac, might find his position jeopardized as deputy of Corrèze, president of a regional council and mayor of Paris. The latter position provides a platform for his battles with the President. The Giscardians, following the approved course of action, suggested that one might have two offices in addition to deputy or Senator so long as they were not 'functionally incompatible', a thinly veiled thrust at Chirac. The Socialists felt that no one should hold offices involving conflict of interest. The Communists reasserted their objective of instituting direct elections by proportional representation.

The British do not collect offices in the central–local hierarchy because it is not a pathway to power. There have, nonetheless, been important cases of strong regional leaders. For example, the chairman of the Association of Municipal Authorities in 1978, Jack Smart, was president of the Labour Party organization in his district, his constituency and his region, and sat on the local government committee of the party's National Executive Committee and on the party's industrial construction subcommittee.[90] Is this less accumulated influence than, say, the mayor of Marseille has? Probably not, but it is used in even less visible ways than the power exercised by the French mayors.

The appearance of a dual mandate at the local level in Britain also raises an interesting question about the constitutional and practical limitations of British politics. In the reorganized local government system, Stewart found a growing number of councillors sitting on both district and metropolitan councils.[91] There is little indication thus far that this is a deliberate attempt to maximize their national influence. It seems rather a reaction against the downgrading of some old county boroughs to districts in the reorganization itself. In a system with many fewer local representatives than in France, dual office may represent an even greater concentration of policymaking powers, and, of course, also limits participation in decisionmaking contrary to the aims of the Royal Commission.

In fact, the reorganized British local government system drastically reduced locally elected representation. The councillors for England and Wales were reduced by a third (from 34,080 to 22,400) and for Scotland were reduced by more than half (from 3,450 to 1,550).[92] Compared to the French system, which has over 400,000 locally-elected councillors, the concentration of decisionmaking power in Britain is extreme. In the light of this change, it is even more remarkable that local party leaders do not seek more direct ways to exercise influence over national decisions. As we shall see in Chapter 5, local councils have so many responsibilities under the British system that they are forced to concentrate their efforts at the local level in order to do their job. The heavy administrative requirements placed on local councils also deter local politicians from seeking higher office, and further protect MPs from direct local pressure.

The clearest indication of the influence that local politicians exercise over the center in France is the history of the Senate, the closest French institutional parallel to the British House of Lords. The important difference is that Britain disarmed the Lords in 1911 to assure the integrity of the national electoral process. But the Senate became the *conservateur de la République*,[93] while the Lords made the error of directly confronting democratic government. The Senate is perhaps the best example of the compromise between territorial politics and political representation that France requires, and explains in turn why global reform of the subnational system has proved impossible. When de Gaulle first aired his proposals for a presidential republic at Bayeux in 1946, Senatorial reform was a key element. The reasons for his change of mind in 1958 are not entirely clear, but the Algerian crisis made him dependent on the grassroots support of the Senators. Marichy suggests that a Senate with powers comparable to the Assembly provided him with a way to play off one legislature against the other, and thereby weaken local influence on Paris.[94] Perhaps the scheme that de Gaulle revealed in his 1966 speech at Lille was already afoot, and the Senate was preserved in order to provide functional representation once the indirect election process could be revised.

In any event, nothing portrays French electoral ingenuity more clearly than senatorial elections. These elections are organized on departments, using an electoral college of deputies, departmental and municipal councillors, and their delegates. In large communes (over 9,000 persons) and for communes of the Paris region, all local councillors are senatorial electors. In small communes, electors (most often the mayors) are chosen from the councillors, depending on the council's size. Thus, each of the 295 Senators for metropolitan France (316 including colonies) is elected by about 100,000 electors.[95] In a gesture to electoral fairness, in the nine most populated departments the electoral college votes by proportional representation.

But if de Gaulle had expected a compliant tool to use against the Assembly and to dampen party politics, he was sadly mistaken. The 1959 senatorial elections returned his most bitter critics, men like Mitterrand, Defferre, and Lecanuet, in what Williams has called 'the revenge of the Fourth Republic'.[96] The Senate again became a bastion of the Republic manned by local politicians. Two-thirds of the Senators were mayors and four-fifths were departmental councillors, another dimension of the *cumul des mondats*. When de Gaulle forced the plebiscite on presidential rule in 1962, the President of the Senate denounced him and took the issue to the Constitutional Council. The dispute poisoned relations between the Senate and the President, and did much to entrench opposition to any local government reform that might threaten senatorial power.[97] The *loi Marcellin*, for example, was carefully phrased to leave the Senate's electoral college untouched.

Under the indirect electoral system, the Socialists and Communists have fewer senatorial seats than their popular support would provide. Though both parties favor the election of all Senators by proportional representation, neither wants to abolish the 'grand council of the communes', nor to change the electoral college.[98] In the 1977 Senate elections, the Socialists increased their representation by ten seats, and the Communists by three. With only 125 seats belonging to the Left in 1977, the Left does feel excluded but adds to its strength through the gradual process of winning commune elections.[99] If the Senate's prestige has grown rather than declined over the past decade, it is in no small part due to a plucky centrist, Alain Poher, who found himself elevated to the presidency of the Senate in 1968.[100] He was reelected president of the Association of French Mayors in 1977, 1978 and 1979, and clearly delights in the important role he played in defeating the 1969 referendum. Relying on their local strongholds, the Senators restrain the national executive, an exercise of localized influence that would be unimaginable in Britain.

LOCAL POLITICS AND NATIONAL POLICYMAKING: DO THEY CONNECT?

Local influence is transmitted to the center in many additional ways. The fact that most governments, including those of Britain and France, insulate the center against excessive and controversial demands from lower-level governments is not too surprising, and perhaps essential to the orderly conduct of business at the national level, but British politics more successfully subordinates local politics to the center than does France. The French contrast is instructive because it appears that the 'over-institutionalization' of local politics, stressed by Kesselman, gives French local politicians more direct leverage on national policies. The French local government system tends to compound national political conflict and tensions rather than reflect them, as is the British case.

One of the ways to protect the center against too much local political influence is to make local election procedures and results unintelligible within the context of national politics. Aside from requiring that all local elections take place on the same day, the Local Government Act of 1972 does not do much to facilitate the direct impact of local elections at higher levels of government. The county and most non-metropolitan district councils are elected entirely every four years, but in the metropolitan counties district elections are divided in thirds on the off-years of county elections.[101] To placate the boroughs that were demoted to second-tier status and to facilitate prompt local elections, the metropolitan districts kept the three-member wards of the old borough system, where one councillor is chosen each year. The significant step toward more direct democratic expression was to abolish aldermen, whose long term of office pre-served party control as opinion changed.[102]

The net effect is that about two-thirds of the British electorate can participate in local elections of one kind or another every year. This level of electoral intensity is paralleled in France, not surprisingly, by having a national election of some kind nearly every year.[103] Though participation is not the main object of this study, it is relevant that the French local elections attract almost twice as many voters to the polls as the British, and to this extent are indeed a more reliable indicator of popular opinion.[104] Despite all the efforts to reform local elections in Britain a city council is most often elected by a minority. In the 1976 elections, the single-member ward system and the delays in redistricting meant that in Bristol 52,000 Conservative voters elected thirty-four councillors, while 45,000 Labour voters elected forty-seven councillors.[105] Though there is pressure from the Liberal Party to introduce proportional representation in local elections, it seems unlikely that this will be done.[106] In France there has also been some discussion of returning to the proportional system used in the French Fourth Republic.[107] The President's proposals to reform local government in 1978 included proportional representation for communes of more than 30,000 persons. Unlike in Britain, however, local-level electoral reform is primarily a strategy of national parties to maximize their strength through the network which links communes and departments to the central government, spurred on by the dramatic gains of the Left in the 1971 and 1977 local elections.

French leaders, except for the Communists, cannot rely on disciplined parties to regulate local elections and to reflect national priorities. Were French local politicians as easily controlled as their British counterparts, the policy influence of the local elites would very likely be reduced. Although there are limits to local alliances and exchanges, limits most often imposed by the Communist Party, the local parties directly enter into a tumultuous bargaining process to form local lists of many different kinds. The Gaullists have had the most difficult time, and indeed have worked hard to find the electoral system that would maximize their chances. In 1959 they adopted a majority list system with two ballots, except for two cities over 120,000; continued the 'amiable anarchy' of *panachage* which allowed candidates' names to be rearranged on the lists; and encouraged alliances between the two ballots. The Gaullists themselves entered into alliances with Socialists in the east of France, even entering a Socialist alliance in Belfort against another Gaullist faction.[108] The result was that 45 percent of the towns and cities over 30,000 elected mayors from the Left, and Communist strength in Paris grew.

The election law of 1964 was reportedly designed specifically to force the Communists from local office, and somewhat less urgently hopefully to eliminate Defferre from the approaching Presidential race by defeating him in Marseille.[109] The majority list system was extended to all cities over 30,000, eliminating proportional representation in the large cities where, at that time, it was helping the Left more than the Right. Even more effective was blocking the list so that the voter could not introduce names from other lists, forbidding fusion of lists between ballots, and placing a minimum requirement of 10 percent of the votes in the first ballot to eliminate splinter groups. But Gaullist manipulation did not prevent a shift to the Left in 1965, and in cities over 30,000, the number of Communist mayors increased from twenty-five to thirty-four.

Compressing the results of French local elections is an almost impossible task. The overall effect that relates most directly to policy-making is the pressure on the Left to unite. As we shall see below, the links of the Socialists to the local notables made this as delicate a task for them as it was for the Gaullists, who were virtually without a grassroots organization. To contrast the effects of national and local elections, in Figure 4.1 national results have been given as percentages of deputies and the local results as percentages of cities over 30,000 held by the major groupings of parties. Although this probably under-estimates conservative tendencies at the grassroots, it conveys how local elections in France are connected to the struggle for national power. The Fifth Republic never saw a government formed by a single party, and from 1968 to 1973 the Gaullists needed at least one other party to form a coalition government. The opposition was protected by and grew in strength around local elections. In national elections the parties of the Right and Center could generate enough fear of the Left to intimidate voters, while the Left and more progressive Center parties survived because of their grassroots strength. Were it not for the 1968 riots which left both the Communists and Socialists in dis-array and again triggered fears of chaos, the resurgence of the Left, so apparent in the 1971 and 1977 local elections, might have come sooner. The system that de Gaulle hoped would destroy the opposition, above all the Communists, actually helped to preserve them.[110]

British local elections are often regarded, like by-elections, as a weathervane for national trends,[111] but they do not bear directly on local government policy. As Figure 4.2 shows, local political effects are rather feebly communicated to higher levels. Labour managed to carry on with a large parliamentary majority throughout the late 1960s when it encountered nothing but disaster in local elections. A major reason why the 'nationalization' of local elections in Britain has not produced more localized demands is that national party policy prevails, as applicable, in local elections.[112] In French local elections local issues and needs predominate because national parties cannot as effectively define the parameters of party competition and, except for the Communists, are often unable to cope with the complexities of local electoral alliances. Thus, the nationalization of local elections in the two countries tends to occur in opposite ways: in Britain from the top downward, and in France from the grassroots upward.

Watching local elections is no less popular among British than French political leaders, but the increasingly large swings in the local vote make it difficult to interpret national implications, and, in turn, to formulate national policies to attract local voters to the two major parties.[113] Of course, neither major party sees this as a central aim of national party policy. If national parties were pressed to more directly reflect the local interests of their supporters, major adjustments would

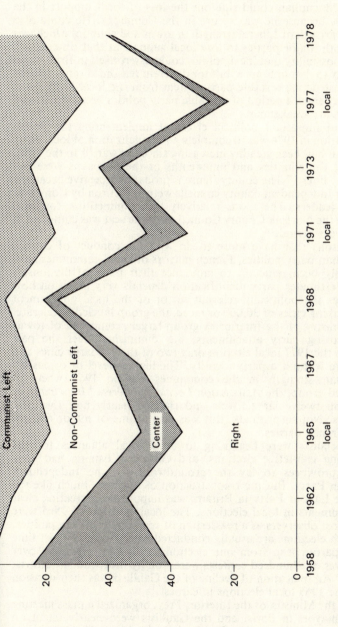

Figure 4.1 Party strength in French national and local elections 1958–1978[3]

1   For purposes of comparing national and local strength, the parties are made into four groups. The Communist Left includes the PCF and any fringe parties of the extreme Left; the non-Communist Left includes the SFIO of the 1960s and subsequently the PS, plus any parties aligned with them; the Center includes a number of small parties unaligned with either the Left or the Right; and the majority includes the Gaullists, Republicans and other minor parties aligned with them.

2   The strength of parties in local elections is based on the number of cities over 30,000. See *Le Monde*, 23 March 1965, 23 March 1971 and 22 March 1977. The number of cities naturally increases with time, being made up of 158 in 1965, 192 in 1971 and 220 in 1977.

3   The figures for national legislative elections are based on the total popular vote for the National Assembly.

be needed in both parliamentary and party practices. But even a waning parliamentary majority is not particularly vulnerable to local elections. Macmillan could ride out the loss of local support in the early 1960s because he was secure in the Commons. He could also ignore the growth of Liberal strength in towns and counties which was causing both major parties to lose local support at that time. Thus, there is a possibility that local politics could assert itself in Britain in a similar way to that in France, but for different reasons. France may be slowly constructing a stable party system from the local level, while Britain may enter a period of unstable party politics because national alignments are weakening.

The most important political effect of implementing the British reorganization in 1974 was to complete a nationalization of local party politics that had been steadily increasing since the war.[114] In the 1930s about half the counties and nine-tenths of the boroughs were run along party lines.[115] The county figure is probably deceptive because a number of Independent county councils were in fact run by Conservative local leaders. There was relatively little competition for local office. On the Norfolk County Council only one seat was contested in a twenty-year period.[116]

For reasons that have more to do with the conduct of council business than party politics, French mayors of small communes have traditionally been reluctant to announce their party affiliations.[117] How one estimates party identification depends very much on how one defines the politically relevant sector of the local government system. Taking cities of 30,000 or more, the group labeled 'moderate' by the Ministry of the Interior, a group largely composed of towns without strong party attachments, has diminished over the past decade. In the 1977 local election only two of the 220 large cities and towns were without a party identity. The highest level of ostensibly non-partisan strength in the communes was in 1965 when an unaffiliated group, the *Association Locale et Intéréts Municipaux* or ALIM won twelve large towns and claimed nearly half the local councillors. Not surprisingly, this was also a time of major realignment of French parties.

The Socialists were beginning to build local alliances for the approaching legislative elections, and Giscard d'Estaing had gone into the provinces to lay the groundwork for the Independent Republican Party. But the reconstruction of the Left, much like the rise of the Labour Party in Britain, was important in creating clear party alignments in local elections. The local elections of 1965 were seen by most observers as a reassertion of centrism in French politics. But French elections are usually conducted within a fairly short time span, as parties leap from one election to the next. In cities over 30,000, over one hundred contests were won by Independent, centrist mayors.[118] An indication of decline of the Gaullists was their decision to fight the 1965 local elections in earnest.

In 1965 the Minister of the Interior, Frey, organized a mass meeting of 6,000 mayors in Paris, and the Gaullists were clearly intent on building grassroots strength. The Socialist leader, Defferre, with an eye to presidential elections at the end of 1965, was also busily trying

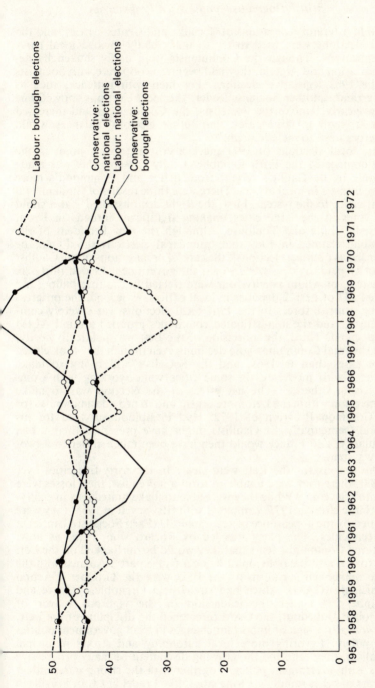

Figure 4.2 *Percentages voting Labour and Conservative in borough elections and national elections 1957–1972*

Note: The percentages voting in national elections are from Craig, op. cit., p. 33. The only compilation of local turnout by local authority is made by the Conservative Central Office who kindly provided their statistics. Their tables are only made for the county boroughs and unfortunately have not been continued after reorganization. The included population is just under ten million persons or about a third of the national electorate. *See Registrar General's Statistical Review*, part II (London: HMSO, 1972), p. 106.

to build a 'grand federation' of Socialist and Center parties, and the local elections were used to try to unify badly divided local party organizations. Though the Communists were badly shaken by de-Stalinization and Algeria, they had begun to cooperate with Socialists in the 1962 legislative elections. For men with patience, such as Mitterrand, another Socialist leader, the local elections showed one thing clearly. Unlike the Socialists, the Communists had increased their strength in large cities; and future electoral alliances would therefore need to include them.[119]

The local elections of 1971 mark a crucial turning point in the development of the Fifth Republic. Oddly enough, this was made possible by de Gaulle's retreat from office and Pompidou's more active interest in local affairs. There were three results of fundamental significance to the system. First, the Right demonstrated that it could win votes in the large cities, making significant inroads in Lyon, Marseille, Lille and Toulouse. Although the new President of the Republic claimed in 1969 that 'municipal elections should not be regarded as political elections', the careful preparations of the Gaullist majority paid dividends.[120] In fact, the government fielded thirty-six ministers, of whom twenty-four were elected in the first ballot, and placed 157 of its 172 deputies in local offices.[121] Second, the progress of the centrist forces in the 1965 local elections was severely compromised, and the non-affiliated communes grouped around ALIM disappeared. Third, the indecision of the Left was politically costly, with the total Communist vote declining even though they took eleven more cities than in 1965, and the Socialists still trying to make alliances with moderates in some cities while working with Communists in others.[122] The net effect of the election was to make cooperation within the Left more urgent and to provide an impulse for the Common Program of 1972. Had Pompidou survived for his second 'septennat', the Gaullists might have preserved their urban popularity, and France would then have been much closer to a two-party system.

The lessons for the Left were clear. In the forty-five cities over 30,000 where they were unable to form a united list, their losses were the most severe.[123] While they were able to make united lists in eighty-four large cities in 1971, compared with fifty-seven in 1965, they were plagued by the appearance of separate PSU (Parti Socialiste Unifié) in thirteen cities. The party was led by Rocard who, then, as now, triggered Communist fears that they would be outflanked on the Left and forced into the oblivion of being a fringe party. Aligned with the more outspoken socialism of the PSU were the Groupes d'Action Municipale (GAM), which had strength in Grenoble, Valence and Chambéry.[124] Under the leadership of the vigorous mayor of Grenoble, Dubedout, the GAM threatened the discipline of the Left, but were also a sign of important changes in local government politics and policy. Favoring more local autonomy and strong municipal socialism, they reflected the growing discontent of many progressive cities with government policy. Together with the strong independent mayors of other rapidly growing cities, like Pradel in Lyon, Fréville in Rennes and (in local government matters) Defferre in Marseille,[125] the elections revealed the growing plight of the large cities. The question was whether the Left would be able to pull their diverse forces together for the legislative elections of 1973, and, as it transpired, the presidential elections of 1974.

The 1971 elections show that the complex alliance pattern of French local politics could approximate the orderliness of British local elections. A study of the interdependence of legislative and municipal elections in France has traced the gradual evolution of French politics into dual electoral contests. Of ninety-two cities that had three-cornered contests in 1965, forty-nine were two-way contests in 1971, and of ninety-three cities with two-way contests in 1965 only nineteen had relapsed into three-cornered contests by 1971.[126] Measured by the number of lists, competition in the 1965 and 1971 elections was roughly the same.[127] Seen against the backdrop of national politics, however, the pictures are very different. But the progress of the Left in large cities could be lost, and never translated into national power, if internal schisms were not healed. The first step was taken only three months after the election at the Epinay Congress of the Socialist Party when it was agreed that cooperation with the Communists must be vigorously pursued. In the 1973 legislative elections the Left approximately doubled its strength in the National Assembly. Under these pressures, Chirac replaced Marcellin at the Ministry of the Interior and Gaullists once again tried to develop grassroots strength.

By 1977 the bipolarization of French politics was complete, but the realigned party structure had yet to be superimposed on national institutions. Mitterrand had come within 200,000 votes of defeating Giscard d'Estaing for the presidency in 1974.[128] In persistent hopes of sustaining his centrist strategy, the new President had driven a wedge between the Gaullists and the Republicans. The culmination was Chirac's resignation from the government in 1976. With the Right in disarray, there had never been a more opportune moment for the Left. Guichard, in the traditional play on fears of the Left in government, pronounced that the Left only wanted the state,[129] while failing to note that his own plans for local reform had been quietly shelved because they made unacceptable demands on the communes. The Socialists stuck to their agreement with the Communists, although the two leaders, Mitterrand and Marchais, never appeared together during the campaign. The Socialists agreed to withdraw from alliances with the Center. They disciplined local federations who refused to end centrist alliances,[130] and the two parties presented united lists in over 90 percent of towns and cities over 30,000.[131]

Late in 1976 the President himself publicly entered the local election campaign, and sent a letter to all mayors on the government's program to improve the communes. In a meeting of 800 mayors in Paris, the Mouvement National des Elus Locaux, the local organization of the Right, issued its *Manifeste Communal* and received the blessing of the Prime Minister.[132] Election manifestos also came from the Socialists, the Communists and the Gaullists.[133] Party realignment brought local and national issues into focus and made the 1977 local elections, and to a considerable extent the legislative elections of 1978, a proving ground for national policy on local government. Two-thirds of the large towns and cities were won by the Union de la Gauche, seventy-two with Communist mayors and eighty-one with Socialist mayors. The parties associated with the government lost a total of fifty-four large towns and none was left without a political identification.

The electoral divisions of the Left in the 1960s now plagued the Right. Party schisms on the Right in Brest, Toulon and Bourges made the progress of the Left spectacular. The Left toppled such 'ornaments of provincial conservatism'[134] as Beauvais, Rheims and Chartres. They won traditional historic strongholds of the Right such as Angers and penetrated Catholic cities like Rennes where the Left had never been strong. Overshadowing the entire campaign was the unexpected decision of Chirac to run against the President's personal choice for mayor of Paris, d'Ornano, a minister in the government. Sitting in the mayor's office in Paris a few hours after the election, Chirac needled the Republicans (and the President) by admitting that the local elections were 'a failure in the nation as a whole, regardless of what success there was here and there'.[135]

In the euphoria of the local elections, the possibility that the more fragile alliances of the Left might weaken once decisions had to be made went unnoticed.[136] In a few months the Union de la Gauche was embarrassed when the Socialists in a small commune near Dijon locked the Communist members out of the town hall. There were a number of festering disputes in and around Evreux, where the Socialist councillors failed to vote with the Communists. In the historic Socialist strongholds of Lille and Marseille the mayors continued to treat their Communist assistant mayors heavy-handedly, and Mauroy, the mayor of Lille, had bitter fights with the Communists in the regional council. The Left had acquired sufficient confidence to overcome local fears of communism, but it was still uncertain whether they *could* rule France.[137] Despite these tribulations, each party reassured the other, and the public at large, that the growing acrimony, revealed in the 1978 legislative elections, would not be allowed to disrupt the communes or threaten the Left's municipal alliances.[138]

The overall strength of the major parties and groupings is given in Table 4.1. The percentage of councillors can be misleading, because large communes do not have proportionally larger councils. Even so, the table suggests the local strength of the parties and the amount of patronage that each might acquire through local government. The table also shows the strong local roots of the Socialist Party, whose strength among councillors has never been equaled by any other party. The Socialists and Communists have more than doubled their control of large cities and towns over the past decade. Whether they can fashion a more modern local government system for France remains to be seen, but it is clear that national reforms are not likely to work without their help.

The relative simplicity of the British party system compared to the French might lead to the mistaken conclusion that local-level politics in Britain are therefore more coherent and orderly. In fact, the best efforts to classify the political character of local councils in Britain produce nearly as much variation as the French communes. The important difference is that national politicians in France are dependent on the local base, and are through the administrative machinery

Table 4.1   *Percentages of Local Councillors by Party in French Cities over 30,000 in 1965, 1971 and 1977.*

	Councillors[a] (%)			Large Towns[b] (#)		
	1965	1971	1977	1965	1971	1977
Communist	4	4	5	34	45	72
Socialist	9	9	10	32	40	81
Non-Communist Left	13	21	23	14	29	23
Radical Opposition	5	4	2	6	4	2
Opposition Subtotal	31	38	40	86	118	159
Gaullist	9	10	7	25	30	15
Republican	4	6	9	8	12	13
Minor Parties	6[c]	2[d]	6[e]	13[c]	12[d]	68[e]
Other Pro-Government	6[f]	12	7	13[f]		9
Pro-Government Subtotal	25	30	29	59	54	45
Local and Diverse	43[g]	30	31	12[g]	17	16

[a]*Le Monde*, 24 March 1971, and 23 March 1977.
[b]*Le Monde*, same issues and 23 March 1965. (Paris not included. Totals are 158 in 1965, 192 in 1971 and 220 in 1977.)
[c]MRP
[d]CDP
[e]CDS
[f]CNI
[g]ALIM

more closely linked to local affairs. But even with respect to electoral politics, the changing fortunes of Labour and Conservative councils do not have the direct national impact that the past three local elections have provoked in French politics. All studies on British local politics stress the diversity within councils. Bulpitt's important early work shows the variety of forms that party control can take, and concludes that 'the national parties regard their role in local government as secondary to their activities at Westminster'.[139] A decade ago, Sharpe noted that 'there remains a reluctance to accept *national* parties'.[140] Though this tendency has been largely overcome with reorganization, the political link between levels of government remains ambiguous and in some ways more ambiguous than France.

Unlike the French, British electors and councillors express ambivalence about party politics in local government. Although the voters have very high levels of confidence in democracy at both levels of government,[141] most local councils are now run by party caucuses and local councils vote on party lines. But with a remarkable consistency in all types of local government, in 1967 nearly half the councillors felt that the introduction of party politics would not make it more likely that better persons would be elected to local government. Three-fourths felt that attachment to parties did not affect the council's work, but that parties did help in getting elected. Again, across all types of local government, councillors thought that approximately 60 percent of the public was not interested in their work.[142] In addition to confirming the common knowledge that local government is a tedious and thankless task, the results suggest that in Britain the relation of parties to local government may be enmeshed in a self-confirming dilemma: councillors distrust the public and the public feels remote from local decisions.[143]

As at the national level, local elections reproduce the national two-party systems in local government, but at a price in the policymaking process. A French mayor needs to have his party alignments, and even the distribution of patronage, clear before elections. Like Parliament, a British council assumes that partisan policies can be satisfactorily defined by national party differences.[144] An important indirect effect

Table 4.2   *Percentages of Local Councillors by Party in British Local Councils in 1978*[a]

	Indep.	Cons.	Lab.	Others	Total
England					
Metropolitan Counties (6)	2	359	213	27	601
Metropolitan Districts (36)	28	1,151	1,127	211	2,517
Non-metropolitan Counties (39)	210	2,370	435	115	3,127
Non-metropolitan Districts (296)	2,091	6,904	2,784	1,820	13,599
Wales					
Non-metropolitan Counties (8)	176	140	190	72	578
Non-metropolitan Districts (37)	396	207	454	457	1,514
GLC					
Inner London (12 boroughs)	4	237	453	9	703
Outer London (20 boroughs)	3	723	429	50	1,205
Scotland					
Regions (9)	81	135	171	45	432
Island Councils (3)	74	—	—	25	99
TOTAL	3,065	12,226	6,256	2,831	24,365

[a]Table compiled from *The Municipal Yearbook: 1979*, London, 1979, pp. 644, 734, 794, 1,311 and 1,326. These results are compiled by a questionnaire of the publisher, and councillors, like French mayors, tend to avoid party labels. Hence, the column of 'independent' councillors, which also includes 'non-party' from the *Yearbook*, is considerably overstated. On the whole, Conservative councillors are more reluctant to accept party labels. The Liberals constitute roughly a third of the 'other' category. County, London and Scottish elections are for 1978; the latest district elections included are for 1977.

of the subordination of British local parties is that councils as such have little influence in shaping national proposals affecting local government. For the more controversial issues, councillors usually take their cue from national party headquarters.[145] The curious result is that in Britain national party policies are imposed by local elections, while in France local elections help define national party policy.

Of course, the strength of the majority party varies. Jones identified five types of party control in local councils: non-party, one-party with a monopoly of the council, one-party dominant, two-party competitive and multiparty.[146] The policy implications are no less confusing than those of the highly articulated French local government system. Party strengths on the British councils in 1974 are given in Table 4.2. The diverse results show that any expectation that strong parties would necessarily facilitate agreement on local government policy is mistaken. More than a fourth of the local councils in England have no party majority.[147] As might be expected, Labour more easily dominates the metropolitan counties and most of the metropolitan districts. Conservatives have to be content with their enduring influence in the non-metropolitan counties, and their ability to rally votes in London.

Another analysis of the nationalization of British local politics has produced very similar results, showing that in 1973 nearly two-thirds of councils in England and Wales were under party control, with an additional 12 percent moving toward party government.[148] Again, those councils of uncertain party identification were found almost entirely among the districts. These results cannot be attributed to lack of competition for local office. Like the French parties, British parties take local elections very seriously. In the 1973 elections only 12 percent of the candidates were unopposed, and two-thirds of these were in the districts.[149]

As in national elections, very small swings in local elections can radically change the pattern of party control. The district elections of 1976, for example, brought a strong shift to the Conservatives.[150] The Tories took control of Birmingham, and Labour was severely strained to keep control of major cities such as Manchester, Coventry and Bristol. Labour even lost Swansea which they had held for forty years. After the 1977 county elections, nearly 90 percent of the British population was locally under Tory rule, including London.[151] Labour held only 879 of 4,391 seats in county councils. One might think that the sensitivity of the local electoral system would enhance local council strength in bargaining with central government. As we shall see, after the Conservative victory of 1979 Tory control of local government was more nearly an embarrassment for the Thatcher government. Were success in national elections more dependent on mobilizing local electoral strength, as it is in France, the national party consequences of local elections would be much greater.

Twenty-five years ago, McKenzie argued that the main function of the local party was to act as electoral agent for the national party.[152] Despite all the changes in the British local government system, this remains the most important political function of local government, the very heavy responsibilities placed on British counties and cities notwithstanding. In a study of 120 ward officers from both parties, two-thirds agreed that their main function was to return MPs to Westminster.[153] There were signs of dissatisfaction, especially among Labour party organizers, with relations between the national and local parties, but the vast majority still thought that differences could be ironed out through existing arrangements. More than 85 percent saw their work as keeping the local party organization alive, and the control of local government as one of the best ways of doing this when the opposing party controls Parliament. The party regulars in France are the mayors and deputies, and they, too, would be likely to take the same position. The difference between the two systems is that the French mayors, unhappy as they are with administrative constraints, acquire more political access to the higher levels of decisions for providing these services.

The reluctance of local government in Britain to influence higher-level decisions is a function of its well-defined electoral role, a role that is, in turn, imbedded in the party structure. In Sheffield, the constituency association was reluctant to approach the MP because 'they did not wish their vote on a *policy* issue to be interpreted as an attack upon the right of the MP to form his own opinion'.[154] While the six MPs from Sheffield had frequent individual contact with their constituents, they expressed caution about being involved in council matters apart from helping with contacts, and on one occasion were rather bluntly told not to interfere. In Newcastle-under-Lyme, relations between the Labour group on the borough council and the Labour constituency association were delicate.[155] In Wolverhampton, the council and the constituency association worked more closely and national policy was passed down to the Labour councillors, but there is little evidence of the MPs intervening in local affairs.[156] The Cheshire county council made use of its MPs during the boundary disputes with Manchester, but oddly enough the contacts were handled by the county clerk and not by the party leaders.[157] National representatives do not figure in Birmingham politics, in part because internal disputes are so fierce that any outsider is likely to be badly burned. On occasions when Birmingham did turn to its MPs for help, results were not forthcoming.[158]

Even with consolidation of the British local government system, local councillors have no intermediate level of government which might effectively transmit their demands to the center. As we shall see in Chapter 5, there are numerous functional links, but national government has discouraged any form of territorial politics that might challenge parliamentary supremacy.

French politicians have learned to use local institutions to influence policy, and the departmental council is part of the network leading to Paris. As Longpierre states, 'if the powers of the prefect to forbid are great, they are practically nil to accomplish'.[159] With the prefects, the departmental councils were among the first local bodies to be approved by the Third Republic in 1871, and they have remained virtually unchanged since then. Half of the 1,801 departmental councillors are elected every three years by direct election in the cantons. Like the communal councillors, they are forbidden to express political views; and also like the communes the departmental councils have become an integral part of the political linkage between local and national politics.

Next to the Communists, the departmental notables were the main political target of the Gaullists, but twenty years of determined effort has not eliminated their influence. Local notables, entrenched in the cantons and departments, resisted Gaullist penetration of local elections and were seen as the bulwark of an archaic system, obstructing the modernization of the French economy. To a party that wanted to propel new industrial and commercial leaders into local office, the departmental councillor, the departmental 'family father',[160] was an anachronism of the worst kind. In fact the Gaullists gave way, making fatal concessions to them in regrouping communes and failing to displace them through regional reform in 1969. Peyrefitte is, of course, correct in his report on local reorganization when he says they represent 'neither the population, the soil [territory] nor the basic administrative division' of France.[161] Until minor reforms in 1975, for example, the department of Haute-Garonne, a city of 500,000, elected four councillors, while the remaining 200,000 persons in the department elected thirty-five. Though the changes in local politics of the past few years have begun to alter the composition of the departmental councillors, they are the closest thing to a 'political class' in France, controlling their own membership, arranging local political compromises, and coming from similar backgrounds. An important family in the Basse Pyrénées has represented one canton in the departmental council since the July Monarchy, and one departmental councillor from Nièvre remained in office for over 50 years.[162]

Rather like the Senate, the departmental councils have been gradually modernized in spite of themselves. While nearly 70 percent of the contests were decided on the first ballot in 1961, only half were in 1973, and in that year half the councillors were elected for the first time.[163] Also like the Senate, the influence of the departmental councils comes from the *cumul des mandats*, not from its legal powers. Of all those elected between 1945 and 1964, 85 percent held other elected office and 12 percent held three or more offices. More than three-fourths were mayors.[164] As the political complexion of communes changed in recent years, so did the departmental councils. In 1976, 56 percent of the votes went to the Union de la Gauche with the parties of the Right getting only about 10 percent each.[165] Thus the councils provided a way for candidates of the Left to convert their local victories into departmental influence, and to penetrate a system that took every opportunity to exclude them at every level of government. As Longpierre concludes, 'If other forms of local administration are found, it is desirable that they should be no less human than those which exist.'[166]

The twenty years needed for the Gaullists to understand the nature of local politics in France also brought a reversal of their policies. One of the most interesting aspects of the Guichard report is the newly discovered importance of the department and, with it, praise for the much maligned local notables on the departmental councils. In an about-face from the Peyrefitte recommendations, *Vivre Ensemble* promises new powers for the department and an enhanced role for the councillors. They are to have a permanent administrative commission to enable them to regularly follow the work of the prefect who is to be downgraded.[167] Care is taken to note that the inequities of the cantonal elections are not to be immediately disturbed, but it is suggested that the new communal agencies should also probably be represented. The departmental councils, with similarly enhanced powers, also survive in the Socialist proposal for local reorganization.

The influence of local political forces on French policymaking was amply demonstrated in 1978 and 1979 as Giscard and Barre fashioned new laws on communal responsibilities and local taxation. The reforms were launched by a special Cabinet meeting in the summer of 1978 at the President's retreat, and involved coordinated efforts of the entire Cabinet. Under presidential instructions, Barre conducted a series of meetings over the fall of 1978 to mobilize support and to sound out the reactions of party leaders.[168] The parties, in turn, organized meetings of mayors and local party activists. Often both national and local leaders were divided among themselves and, contrary to the procedure in Britain, political support could not be won simply by imposing party discipline.[169] To add to the confusion, the Gaullists in the governing coalition had strong reservations about tax reform (see Chapter 6), and on several occasions abstained in Senate votes.[170] Elaborate reports from both the National Assembly and the Senate introduced numerous amendments to placate both national and local politicians.[171] However, the pressures of national politics, and most important the approaching presidential elections of 1981, meant that the laws were eventually passed, but only after a laborious and extended period of public debate and local consultation.

In contrast, in Britain the Thatcher government announced major changes in central–local relationships in late 1979 with virtually no consultation. Only a crowded parliamentary agenda delayed their quick conversion into law.[172] Although the Conservative approach owed much to the determined style of the new government, and also to the flamboyant style of the Secretary of State for the Environment, Heseltine, it was not essentially different from the abrupt redefinition of the problem of Labour in 1965. Unlike the French, the Conservative government was not particularly alarmed that the Conservative-controlled local associations were opposed to the changes, nor did outspoken doubts among Conservative backbenchers in the House of Commons noticeably deter these plans. That the local government associations were themselves Tory-controlled made little difference, and in the final analysis even the more urban-based Association of Municipal Authorities (AMA) voted to support severe educational and social service spending cuts.[173] As we shall see in Chapter 5, the compartmentalized administration made it easier to impose these cuts even though the national government itself had little idea of the consequences. After five years of tedious preparation and two years of laborious political negotiation, the French leaders must have looked with envy at the concentrated powers of Westminster.

LOCAL POLITICS AND THE COMMUNITY IN THE WELFARE STATE

Institutional continuity in France is demonstrated by the extent to which the French have rearranged political and administrative roles throughout the past two centuries. Grémion's *complicité* is surely not Bourbon *venalité*, but it nevertheless preserves the idea that local favors are bestowed by state officials. Theonig's 'honeycomb' of political and administrative officials is the contemporary manifestation of an historic ingenuity which has enabled the French to establish new goals within old institutions. Outmoded as the communal and departmental structure may seem, political adaptations have enabled them to introduce new policies and to adjust to enormous changes in the society without massive reorganization.

Until 1888 British counties had quasi-judicial local government run by justices of the peace. The formation of a strong, centralized national civil service elite probably prevented the growing inspection corps from becoming mediators between national and local government. The effort to insulate the functions of government from local political influence was already well advanced when Chadwick became the first President of the Association of Sanitary Inspectors in 1875.[174] By the turn of the century the Local Government Board had been relegated to a secondary policymaking role and was 'forced by circumstance and repressive Treasury control to oppose the innovation of fresh policy and the acquisition of new duties'.[175] While the French Ministry of the Interior was becoming the road to power in the Third Republic, British local leaders had no major spokesman in Whitehall, nor did they appear to want one.

An increasingly important question is whether the demands for more direct representation at the local level will somehow disrupt the historical and institutional stability of central–local policymaking. Like most modern democracies, both France and Britain have experienced increasing activity by groups speaking for consumers, environmentalists, the poor and the community.[176] These new demands raise a perplexing problem for both local government systems. If one starts from the assumption (which this study finds misleading) that local government is in some sense the first stage in formulating popular demands on higher levels of government, then neither local government system is working very well. If one begins with a more realistic picture of local government as a component of the political system as a whole, then new demands become merely further problems to be accommodated by both central and local government. From either perspective, community demands question the representative role of local government, and indirectly the efficacy of national government. It should come as no surprise that neither France nor Britain have leapt at the offered invitations to refashion their local government systems.

The British local government system, which one might think the more politically responsive, is for several reasons more vulnerable to community protest. The extension of national party discipline to the local level has meant that the reverberations of spontaneous dissent are criticisms of national leadership, while heavily burdened and circumscribed local governments are less able to divert their energies in new directions. Political schisms are much more a way of life in France, and pave the way for local dissent. Despite the heavy administrative hand on the communes, the mayors and their colleagues have more ways of absorbing protest, and the more localized functions of communes provide them with concrete ways to respond to new demands. The multiparty system and coalition politics provide more opportunities to involve diverse local groups. The ecologists provide the best example. In the 1974 presidential election, all candidates were asked to respond to a '*Charte de la Nature*' and the loosely-grouped ecology faction polled over 300,000 votes for their own candidates.[177] In the local elections of 1977, *listes vertes* appeared in over a hundred cities, and the ecologists gained 10 percent of the votes in Paris.[178] The ecologists may be overestimated as a national force; but, in a system that has long depended on coalition government, even Chirac was soon welcoming ecologists at city hall receptions.[179]

Perhaps the best illustration of the way that the French local government system can accommodate disruptive forces at lower levels of government is the experience of the Groupes d'Action Municipale (GAM). They first came into prominence running as a '*liste de gauche*' in the 1965 Grenoble elections.[180] The movement probably reached its peak in 1971, when it ran over a hundred lists in local elections, won control of four municipal councils, and was represented in half a dozen more.[181] Though of no distinct political coloration, the GAMs have been most clearly identified with the more radical side of the Socialist Party and therefore have been violently condemned by the Communist Party.[182] Like most spontaneous movements, the GAMs went through a crisis over whether to become a legitimate political participant or to remain an independent force trying to influence public policy. Their 1972 Congress opted for the latter path, and the GAMs became an advocate of independent urban management (*autogestion*). Like the ecologists, the GAMs were able to prosper under the aggressive urbanization policies of the early 1970s when, for example, the mayor of the Paris suburb Boulogne-Billiancourt wanted to sell a fifty-acre municipal park to build a luxury hotel. But as Sellier concludes, new groups have great difficulty in avoiding the web of French local politics, nor is it easy for such groups to ignore the national influence they might have. The GAMs helped create an awareness of what rapid urbanization was doing in France, and they were able to demonstrate alternative policies by taking control of several cities. Such possibilities are virtually excluded in British local politics.

Both the ecologists and the GAMs demonstrate the relative ease with which French politics assimilates new political groups. If they tend to become middle-class organizations, it is at least partly because they are generated within middle-class society. Nonetheless, new groups have easier access to power than their British counterparts.

The comparison is instructive in several respects, because Britain once had relatively strong parishes underpinning county government. French parishes diminished steadily after the Revolution, although neighborhood associations (*unions de quartier*) were not uncommon after the turn of the century.[183] In contrast, the overarticulated commune system offers possibilities for small-scale community activities. In Britain, community groups must compete with large local governments with heavy responsibilities for national policies. Toulmin Smith may have lost his debate with Chadwick in the 1850s, but recent events have vindicated his concerns.[184]

The British experience with community and neighborhood associations is a reminder that in designing the future we are often reconstructing the past. The Royal Commission on Local Government recommended that 'local councils' be organized, to revive the old parish council as a community spokesman.[185] Oddly enough, the Commission did not think that there would be the same need for community representation in the urban areas even though these were the areas undergoing the most drastic consolidation, and the places where alienation from local government is most pronounced.[186] Of the roughly 10,000 rural parishes that once thrived in rural England, active ones were found concentrated in the south of England and some northern areas, most notably Durham County and West Yorkshire. Both the Commission and the Labour White Paper on their report excluded groups of this kind from any close link with local services. The Conservatives seemed no more enthusiastic when they designed the 1972 Local Government Act, but parish councils were rescued from oblivion and the possibility of non-statutory (powerless) neighborhood councils was offered.

At the same time as the reorganization proposals were being launched, British citizens were becoming less and less content with the condition of inner cities. Although Wilson once characterized community groups as 'looking for a snark',[187] there were about fifty autonomous neighborhood associations by the early 1970s, the most active being in Liverpool, Stockport, Sheffield and the London Borough of Lambeth. The desire to protect local councils against the intrusion of such groups surfaced when all the local government associations resisted the first community development grants under the Heath government.[188]

When Labour returned to power in 1974 with an election promise to help build neighborhood councils, the forgotten element of local government reform received new impetus. Soon afterward a DoE consultative paper was circulated, asking for suggestions for the formation of statutory neighbourhood councils.[189] Although a few local councils now provide subsidies for neighborhood councils, relationships are ambiguous and sometimes delicate. Local authorities appear reluctant to devolve responsibility to associations of this kind, while the voluntary groups are themselves often wary of dependence on their local governments.[190] While the work done by local voluntary groups fits within the objectives of the new inner city programs, elected councillors are cautious.[191] Launched nearly a decade ago, the neighborhood councils remain in the political limbo of non-statutory agencies.

In relation to the policymaking role of central and local government, the issue is how, if at all, voluntary groups can enter into the decision process.[192] As in France, special interest groups in Britain can also effectively intervene in local decisions, often at the expense of the community.[193] But the renewed sense of community places more strain on a large-scale and functionally compartmentalized local government system. Although Britain made participatory planning a statutory requirement somewhat earlier than France, often with mixed results,[194] neither government has rushed to embrace street-corner policymakers. But French communes are not only free to make room for them, but also elevate them to local office.

The pitfalls in the path of increased popular control over local policymaking are many. British central government has already decided what the local government should do, so that community groups cannot change decisions already taken at higher levels of government.[195] Community groups are most successful when they work within the functional structure of British local government.[196] The issue has been particularly difficult for the Labour Party, because it believes more strongly than the Conservatives in planning, and because Labour has generally favored more forceful imposition of centrally designed redistributive policies. Had the party had its way, local government in Britain would be even further removed from the people than it is now. There is an unmistakable irony in the Labour Party efforts in 1978 to create smaller units of local government in order to advance its inner city program, and to restore powers to the Labour-controlled districts within predominantly Conservative county organizations. But even these changes are conceived as a redistribution of functions rather than making local government decisions more subject to local demands. New community groups in Britain appear likely to be allowed only those privileges which the center approves, perhaps because 'Britons feel they will get more for their money out of national levels of control than if local authorities had control of services'.[197]

In relating the community to the local government system, Britain has historically decided to nationalize first and to provide a local role later. Many services not attached to local government have had the same experience. For example, Community Health Councils were added nearly twenty years after nationalizing health. A careful study of the Councils finds them 'a Gothic Folly to the Palladian Mansion'.[198] Both political parties helped fashion this cosmetic addition to the National Health Service. The Labour Green Paper recommended that they have no statutory powers and no budget. The Conservative decision spoke of 'a dangerous confusion between management on the one hand and the community's reaction to management on the other'. Restoring the appearance of local control over services once they have been institutionally isolated from local government makes little sense.

British local government is not designed to formulate demands and to aggregate preferences. As Dearlove notes, 'activity is largely geared to servicing and *maintaining* established policies and as such they are involved in the taking of routine decisions and these do not necessitate the use of ethical decisional premises'.[199] Paradoxically, the growth of the welfare state has reduced the possibilities for community intervention in both Britain and France, but probably more so in Britain. British local government cannot use the French alternative of using administration against itself and of actively resisting policies that undermine the prestige of local government.

CAN NATIONAL POLITICS MAKE STRUCTURAL CHANGE?

Can the policymaking process of the welfare state change political and institutional structures? Experience with local government reorganization is one test of this proposition, though there are many other policy areas of similar interdependence and complexity. First, one must ask whether the local governments of the two countries have displayed the vitality and interest needed to influence national policy. The history of British and French local politics shows that national political competition and national policy have been lively local issues in both countries from the late nineteenth century to the present, but the important difference between the two countries is that national and local political leaders are linked to national policymaking in very different ways. The basic pattern of the political relationship, in fact, predates the welfare state.

In the Third Republic the communes both stabilized and made a claim on the republican state, a claim which many national leaders encouraged. The issues dividing France were not simply reflected in local politics; they were reproduced at the local level. Historical circumstances gave British local government a smaller part in establishing political stability, and there was, in turn, much less need to integrate local and national political forces. At the turn of the century British cities and towns became a pathway to Parliament for the rising Labour Party, but the party's goal was to seize national power, not to revolutionize local government. For a still weak party, redrawing town boundaries to include Conservative countryside was no more advisable in 1900 than redrawing cities to include Conservative suburbs was in 1970. Labour intelligentsia, like Joseph Chamberlain and the Liberals, hoped municipal socialism would conquer, but the lure of Parliament was greater. After the Second World War, the Labour Party nationalized most of the public utilities owned by cities, and key local services. British local government has never been given an important voice in structural change, and the events of the 1970s only confirm this tradition.

A closely related question is whether either government had at any time the capability to enact sweeping reform. The response to this question has many elements. In looking at the parliamentary procedures of the two systems, it is clear that each executive has its own way of forcing unpopular decisions on Parliament. The British Parliament depends more heavily on party discipline than the French National Assembly, but in neither country does Parliament design legislation or determine the parliamentary agenda. We have already seen in Chapter 3 the extent to which Wilson and Heath treated reform as a non-partisan issue, and the extent to which the House of

Commons' debate avoided many basic issues of central–local relations. The law was proposed when Labour was at the peak of its power, and the later Conservative government, committed to making government efficient, could not deny the underlying rationale of reorganization. The Gaullists also made their most serious attempt to bring about global reorganization when at the peak of their legislative power. The 1968 legislative elections put them in a position to pass major legislation, but the political process overtook them. Despite the *dirigisme* of the Gaullists, the *loi Marcellin* presupposed prolonged consultation with the communes, and party politics had intervened by the time this consultation finished. The education of the Gaullists is reflected in both the Peyrefitte and Guichard Reports, which used administrative concessions as an incentive for local reform.

Closer to the heart of national policymaking is whether the representative process can achieve structural reform. In this respect the two systems are, for all the party differences, very similar. There are serious electoral inequities in both countries. From a policy perspective, the most interesting effect of the French electoral system is the way in which elections give more influence to local elites, and thereby enhance their chances of influencing national policies which affect the communes. British national elections are kept carefully insulated against such confusion by the party system itself and by the national party organizations. Ironically, de Gaulle hoped to achieve something similar in reorganizing local elections in 1964, but the effect was almost the opposite of the desired result. Forced into a two-party posture by the electoral laws, French parties found local alliances and local solidarity more, rather than less, important. National politicians were compelled to pay even closer attention to their grassroots. The Right wanted a local power base and the Left wanted national office so that the issue of local reform was joined.

Thus, in France electoral and party politics make local reform an issue, while in Britain these forces tend to muffle it. In both countries national representatives have about the same degree of security – nearly four-fifths of the seats in the House of Commons and the National Assembly are safe. Most national representatives prefer not to raise controversial and complex issues such as local reform. In both countries the nomination process is subject to local control, though national parties, especially in France where parties have weaker national executives, are immersed in quarrels and party factions. But none of these aspects of representation would suggest that local government policy should be necessarily propelled onto the national agenda. Indeed, polling and survey data show that were the political system truly representative national government would not even consider local reorganization. Resistance to communal reorganization in France was possible because of deputies' dependence on local political alignments and the *cumuls des mandats*. Resistance was impossible in Britain because MPs are not integrated in the local government system.[200] Policymaking in France is not insulated from territorial politics.

If the national political system lacks the will to change the subnational system, change through local politics is an alternative. In

France, the variation in local representation is immense because of party realignment and population shifts over the past decade or two. Party discipline, if not the abstract principles of representation, is to some extent restored by the list system in local elections. The variation in electoral wards in British counties and districts is also very great.[201] In both systems the national and local constituencies no longer coincide. What makes the difference, and, in turn, has direct effect on local government policy is that French parties fight for control of communes in order to gain national power. In the rapid sequence of elections in France, the local elections became the battlefield for the Left and Right. From this encounter have emerged proposals for local reform. In Britain, the prevailing pattern of 'top-down' policymaking leaves much less scope for local politics. Local elections mark important turning points in the fortunes of the Labour and Conservative parties, but strong parliamentary majorities often survive local trends, and attention is riveted on the constituency association rather than the local council. MPs are sensitive to requests from councils, but their political survival and their commitments do not lead them into local matters.

National parties in Britain work to win a majority in Parliament, not to forge a compromise among parties and to transmit local demands to central government. Political contact with localities is left to the party organization. Both major parties hold annual conferences on local government and MPs with a special interest in local government often speak there or in regional conferences. When the Labour Party considered changes in the system in 1977, a number of regional conferences were held and were instrumental in the decision not to press for modifications of the 1972 law.[202] Local government councillors had just recovered from the dislocations of the last reorganization, and it was apparent to all that further expensive changes would not be popular, but the decision was made on grounds of national politics.

Although roughly 30 percent of Conservative and 40 percent of Labour MPs have local government experience, they rarely cross party lines to support local government, nor would the parliamentary system encourage them to do so. An increasing number of MPs with local government experience are being elected from areas where they have held local office.[203] While these representatives are a source of local government expertise in Parliament, they are effectively subordinated to ministerial and Cabinet rule.

French national politicians are divided in their loyalties and in their dependence on national and local government. The reforms proposed by the President in 1978 only emerged after two laborious years of compromise between ministerial designs and political necessities. In contrast, Shore, the Labour Secretary of State of the DoE, was able to pursue his plan to rescue the Labour-controlled districts subordinated to Tory-controlled county councils regardless of the policy consequences. The plight of the larger cities trapped within the consolidated British local government system can be traced directly to Labour's confidence in 1969 that larger local governments would help achieve their national policy aims, though, of course, this was not acknowledged. Shore's plans for 'organic change' certainly compares with the most cynically conceived French proposal to cater to local partisan interests.[204] Some of the most dedicated supporters of Labour's efforts to modernize the local government system were driven to oppose his proposals.[205] More important, in contrast to France, his ideas to further complicate British local government were only put aside because Labour lost the 1979 election.

The pattern of central–local relationships changed very little with the incoming Thatcher government in 1979. Although many welcomed the well dramatized efforts of the new Secretary of State for the Environment, Heseltine, to simplify the enormously complex regulations surrounding local government,[206] his decisions were no less arbitrary than those of his predecessor. As we shall see in Chapter 6, spending controls were imposed with very little choice left to the local councils, and the entire grant system was replaced with little consultation. While Giscard was beating off crippling amendments to his plans in the Senate, Heseltine could rely on a safe majority in the House of Commons. Economic conditions may have justified the new restrictions, but an even more economic-minded France had to battle with locally-oriented politicians for two years just to fashion new laws.

As was reflected in the party platforms for the 1978 legislative elections and the 1977 local elections, the French mayor is directly involved in national parties. Both the Socialist and Communist Parties held post-election meetings in 1977 to celebrate their victories, and to launch local organizations for the 1978 elections.[207] The communes were viewed as the mobilizers of votes and a key to strong local party organization. The Communists marshaled their 28,000 elected officials in the fall of 1977 and organized their own local government association, the Association Nationale des Élus Communistes et Républicains.[208] The Communists are probably the only party that could survive in France without local strongholds, but accumulation of local office has been essential to reconstructing its image in French politics. Chirac's *Rassemblement pour la République* also assembled its 5,000 mayors, and the Socialists organized a large meeting of delegates of locally-elected officials.[209] With a more loosely organized party and a more diverse following, the groups aligned with the President formed a federation with various local political clubs of the Center and Right.[210] All the parties use local leaders on a massive scale to organize elections and this in turn gives the communes opportunities to inject their demands directly into national politics. Party competition thus put local reform on the national agenda. In contrast to Britain, the reorganization of the French communes is a grassroots phenomenon, the product of a decade of agitation by unhappy mayors from across the political spectrum.

One would not expect a state 'carved in granite'[211] to change as effortlessly as one relying on deference. Nonetheless, the weakness of the French Parliament and parties may, in this instance, become a strength. In any country national leadership and legislatures have great difficulty dealing with structural problems. One can hardly claim that the Local Government Act of 1972 was created in the House of Commons. The people and their representatives seem in accord in regarding major institutional reform as too threatening and too complex. The impulse for change in both countries originated with administrative inadequacies and administrative needs rather than with popular demand. The implications of this perplexing problem for the welfare state, and more broadly for both national and local democracy, will be considered in the Conclusion. The French parties may not keep their promises, and the British may have second thoughts about sweeping change, but the administrative structure is the bedrock of the subnational system in every welfare state. Administrative politics is the essential link between levels of government, and its relation to local government will be examined next.

NOTES: CHAPTER 4

1 Between 1950 and 1974 Sweden managed to reduce over 3000 local authorities to 277, a reduction proportionately rather greater than that in Britain. However, this appears to have been because of the peculiar administrative capabilities of the Swedish system rather than because of any greater political capacity. See Tom Anton, 'Policymaking and political culture in Sweden', *Scandinavian Political Studies*, vol. 4 (1969), pp. 88–102.

2 There are interesting signs that local forces are to some extent undermining these conditions, particularly when internal differences in the parties lead local constituency associations to impose discipline on MPs, often against the wishes of the Cabinet and the procedures of the national party. See, for example, the case of Northampton North constituency, *The Times* (London), 15 December 1977. Likewise, the intervention of the courts in several key Cabinet decisions has stimulated a discussion of indirect judicial review in Britain, most notably over the Tameside and the Post Office decisions. See *The Economist*, 29 January 1977.

3 This is obviously not intended to imply that the Cabinet and Parliament can act capriciously, and there is, of course, abundant evidence that both British prime ministers and French presidents follow their electoral support very carefully. The point is simply that the *potential* power of the British system is unlimited by law. It is significant that every issue that casts a shadow over this supremacy leads to an intricate debate and often procrastination, as in the cases of Scottish devolution, the demand for a list of basic individual rights and modification of the very strict rules of confidentiality and secrecy.

4 An excellent account of the 1969 referendum is J. E. S. Hayward, 'Presidential suicide by plebiscite: de Gaulle's exit, April 1969', *Parliamentary Affairs*, vol. 22 (1969), pp. 280–311. See also William G. Andrews, 'The politics of regionalization in France', in M. Heisler (ed.), *Politics in Europe* (New York: David McKay, 1974), pp. 293–322; F. Bon, 'Le référendum d'avril 1969: suicide politique ou nécessité stratégique?', *Revue Française de Science Politique*, vol. 20 (1970), pp. 205–23; and the volume by J.-L. Bodiguel *et al.*, *La Réforme Régionale et le Référendum du 27 Avril 1969* (Paris: Editions Cujas, 1970).

5 On the use of the *vote bloqué*, similar to the guillotine in British parliamentary practice, see Pierre Avril, 'Le vote bloqué (1959–1970)', *Revue du Droit Public et de la Science Politique*, vol. 87 (1971), pp. 469–503. In fact, it was not unusual for laws to be passed in several days, and the organization of the budget debates over the fall left little more than a day for debating each section. The results of the new constitution are somewhat ironical, for there is evidence that Debré hoped to emulate the orderly and presumably careful consideration given to legislation in the British Parliament.

6 For more details on efforts to strengthen the House of Commons' legislative power, see A. H. Hansen and Bernard Crick (eds), *The Commons in Transition* (London: Fontana, 1970); and S. A. Walkland and Michael Ryle (eds), *The Commons in the 70's* (London: Fontana, 1977).

7 The French election studies are in many ways more pertinent to the formulation of local government policy because trends in French politics and parties are deeply imbedded in local political rivalries. This will be outlined below in more detail. Except as noted, the elections here referred to are legislative. For 1962 see F.

Goguel (ed.), *Le Référendum d'Octobre et les Élections de Novembre 1962* (Paris: Colin, 1965); on the presidential election of 1965 the collective volume of the Fondation Nationale des Sciences Politiques, *L'Élection Présidentielle des 5 et 19 Décembre 1965* (Paris: Colin, 1970).

8 A similar collective volume of the Fondation Nationale covers the 1967 election: Roland Cayrol (ed.), *Les Élections Législatives de Mars 1967* (Paris: Colin, 1971). Events outstripped the formidable capacity of French scholars to conduct electoral studies in 1968, but see F. Goguel, 'Les élections législatives des 23 et 30 juin 1968', *Revue Française de Science Politique*, vol. 18 (1968), pp. 837–58.

9 On the growth of minority parties, David Butler and Anne Sloman, *British Political Facts, 1900–1975*, 4th edn (London: Macmillan, 1975), p. 151. It should not be forgotten that the attribution of stability to British parliamentary politics has important historical exceptions. Parliament functioned for nearly a generation with a vocal and disruptive Irish Nationalist minority party, and party lines were vague throughout the 1920s rise of Labour.

10 For the comparative figures for France, see Frederic Bon, *Les Élections en France: histoire et sociologie* (Paris: Editions du Seuil, 1978), pp. 198–210. Popular support for the majority in legislative elections has varied from 37 percent to 46 percent in recent years. On the question of political trust, see René Lenoir, 'Société et liberté', *Le Monde*, 21 October 1977; and John Ambler, 'Trust in political and nonpolitical authorities in France', *Comparative Politics*, vol. 8 (1975), pp. 31–57.

11 Frank L. Wilson, *The French Democratic Left 1963–1969: Toward a Modern Party System* (Stanford, Calif.: Stanford University Press, 1971), p. 36. For additional background on the Socialists in the Fourth Republic and in the early years of de Gaulle's regime, see Harvey G. Simmons, *French Socialists in Search of a Role 1956–1967* (Ithaca, N.Y.: Cornell University Press, 1970).

12 Indirectly contributing to the importance of local leaders was the almost complete renewal of deputies. After the 1958 legislative elections there were only 131 deputies from the last election of the Fourth Republic. In the 1962 legislative elections there were 225 new deputies. Again, it should be noted that however haughty the General might have been, his new Republic brought in a whole new generation of political leaders to replace the rather tired politicians of the Fourth Republic.

13 Most notably by Debbasch, *L'Administration au Pouvoir* (Paris: Calmann-Lévy, 1969). The anti-Gaullist argument, like the party itself in recent years, has turned to how it builds its local strength and parliamentary strongholds. The more recent argument is summarized in Pierre Birnbaum, *Les Sommets de l'État* (Paris: Seuil, 1977).

14 On the transition to a more relaxed, but no less strongly presidential, system under Pompidou, see Gilles Martinet, *Le Système Pompidou* (Paris: Seuil, 1973); and Michèle Cotta, *La Ve République* (Paris: Flammarion, 1974), where there are good accounts of Chirac's intrigues against Chaban. See also Daniel Amson, 'Chaban-Delmas révoqué ou l'apparente continué de la "république des Cadets"', *Revue Politique et Parlementaire*, vol. 75 (1973), pp. 28–43; and André Homont, 'La démission de Jacques Chaban-Delmas en juillet 1972', *Revue de Droit Public et de la Science Politique*, vol. 85 (1973), pp. 1479–530.

15 The presidential election of 1974 does not relate as clearly to local government policy because of the changes described in this paragraph. The new President effectively stopped the pressure for regional reform in 1975 and never gave strong support to the Guichard Commission. See *Le Monde*, 26 November 1975, in particular Raymond Barillon, 'Un décentralisateur jacobin'. On Giscard d'Estaing's rise to power, see Michel Bassi and André Campana, *Le Grand Tournoi: Naissance de la VIe République* (Paris: Grasset, 1974); also R. de Lacharrière, 'Gaullisme Mark II', *Government and Opposition*, vol. 8 (1973), pp. 280–9.

16 It is no coincidence that the concern about excessive executive power appeared at roughly the same time in the two countries. Both had gone through a decade of rapid development and both had strong and politically shrewd leaders. The case for Britain is made by A. H. Brown, 'Prime Ministerial power', in M. Dogan and R. Rose (eds), *European Politics: A Reader* (Boston: Little Brown, 1971), pp. 459–81. A more balanced assessment is G. W. Jones, 'The Prime Minister's power', *Parliamentary Affairs*, vol. 18 (1965), pp. 167–85. A good general introduction to the changing character of the Cabinet is Valentine Herman and James E. Alt (eds), *Cabinet Studies: A Reader* (London: Macmillan, 1975).

17 There have been several careful studies of ministerial changes in the Fifth Republic. See Pascale Antoni and Jean-Dominique Antoni, *Les Ministres de la Ve République* (Paris: PUF, 1976), which describes the roughly 150 ministers serving between 1959 and 1974.

18 See Daniel Amson, 'La démission des ministres sous la IVe et la Ve République', *Revue de Droit Public et de la Science Politique*, vol. 91 (1975), pp. 1653–91.

19 Williams, *Crisis and Compromise: Politics in the Fourth Republic* (London: Longman, 1964), p. 332. Lest this preference for local government be too freely interpreted, it should be noted that the basic structure of the Fifth Republic was accepted by the mid-1960s and few Frenchmen wanted to return to the *république des députes*, the unrestrained parliamentary politics of the Fourth Republic. See 'Images politiques des Français', *Projet*, vol. 74 (1971), pp. 637–44.

20 On the early growth of the electorate see Serge Arné, 'L'Esprit de la Ve République: Réflexions sur l'exercice du pouvoir', *Revue de Droit Publique et de la Science Politique*, vol. 87 (1971), p. 653. At the Restoration barely more than 100,000 Frenchmen were enfranchised; in the July Monarchy 172,000; rising to 245,000 in 1845. For the brief existence of the Second Republic there were nearly ten million voters, reduced to about seven million in 1850. The interesting contrast with Britain is, of course, that France acquired a large electorate before Britain, even if there were considerable misgivings about its role. On the growth of the electorate see Peter Campbell, *French Electoral Systems and Elections 1789–1957* (London: Faber, 1958).

21 Bernard Le Clère and Vincent Wright, *Les Préfets du Second Empire* (Paris: Fondation Nationale des Sciences Politiques, 1973), p. 69.

22 Boulanger attempted an even greater outrage against election procedures. In exile, he ran as deputy from a number of constituencies in hopes of restoring his power. This is now forbidden. Jacques Médecin, founder of the Nice political dynasty, did the same in local elections in the 1920s.

23 On the Select Vestries Act see Bryan Keith-Lucas, *The English Local Government Franchise* (Oxford: Blackwell, 1952), pp. 31–5.

24 Ibid., pp. 72–4. Also Derek Fraser, *Urban Politics in Victorian England* (London: Leicester University Press, 1976), pp. 85 and 157. The national electorate grew steadily throughout the nineteenth century with the various reform and representation acts. In 1832 about 650 thousand people could vote; in 1867 about 2.5 million and in 1884 there was near universal male suffrage with 5.7 million voters. On the growth of the electorate see Sir Ivor Jennings, *Party Politics: Appeal to the People*, Vol. 1 (Cambridge: Cambridge University Press, 1960).

25 A.-J. Tudesq, 'Les Influences locales dans la vie politique française sous la Monarchie Censitaire', in A. Mabileau (ed.), *Les Facteurs Locaux de la Vie Politique Nationale* (Paris: Pédone, 1972), pp. 343–6.

26 J.-C. Drouin, 'Les élections du 13 mai 1849 à Bordeaux', ibid., pp. 361–74.

27 André Siegfried was the founder of the electoral geography in France, a tradition carried on by Francois Goguel. Their work will be discussed further below, but showed remarkable consistencies in French voting since the Third Republic. For evaluations, see R. Arambourou, 'Réflexions sur la géographie électorale', *Revue Française de Science Politique*, vol. 2 (1952), pp. 521–48.

28 See Howard Machin, 'The prefects and political repression: February 1848 to December 1851', in R. Price (ed.), *Revolution and Reaction: 1848 and the Second French Republic* (London: Croom Helm, 1975), pp. 280–302.

29 Tudesq, op. cit., p. 351.

30 For the quote, see Goguel in Mabileau, op. cit., p. 331. An election study from the Restoration begins to show how administrators were being made into intermediaries. See Sherman Kent, *The Election of 1827 in France* (Cambridge, Mass.: Harvard University Press, 1975).

31 Josef Redlich and Francis W. Hirst, *Local Government in England*, Vol. 1 (London: Macmillan, 1903), p. 276, states that 'A municipal spoils system in England is almost unthinkable.' Their admiration for British government, and possibly the paucity of local government research at the time, seems to have carried them away. See the examples cited in Chapter 2 and also below. My interpretation will, I hope, not be taken as a defense of corruption, but only as an observation that the effect of corruption, like so much else in central–local relations, varies with the level of government which has control of this important political resource.

32　Redlich and Hirst, op. cit., Vol. 1, p. 54. The authors of this classic history tend to share British suspicions that national politics is a thing apart from local politics and that on the whole it is desirable for local leaders not to be directly involved in national policy and politics.

33　Peter J. G. Pulzer, *Political Presentation and Elections in Britain*, rev. edn (London: Allen & Unwin, 1972), pp. 62–3. In fact, competition measured by contested seats declined, for 210 of 487 seats were contested in 1868, and 174 of 401 seats in 1835.

34　Fraser, op. cit., p. 281.

35　In the 1919 local elections Labour's local strength soared to 938 seats, including control of twelve metropolitan boroughs, three Welsh counties and Bradford. By 1939 they controlled the London County Council, and 198 localities. See G. D. H. Cole, *A History of the Labour Party from 1914* (London: Routledge & Kegan Paul, 1948), pp. 445–58.

36　Sir Francis Hill, *Victorian Lincoln* (Cambridge: Cambridge University Press, 1974), p. 30. As in most towns, the Municipal Reform Act of 1835 did not change local government very much. When the Whigs were swept into power in the protest of the 1820s and wanted to introduce change, the county clerk thought they 'hankered after affairs over which it (the council) had no legitimate control', ibid., p. 39. Things were very different in the nearby Lincolnshire town of Grimsby, where the government was dominated by the local industrial leader, Lord Yarborough. He also continued to manipulate the parliamentary seat despite reform.

37　Fraser, op. cit., pp. 125–6 and 131. This historical study of British city politics is invaluable, and one can only hope that similar studies will be forthcoming on French urban politics in the nineteenth century. See, in particular, Fraser's chart, ibid., pp. 311–16, listing national and local changes for most of the century.

38　Fraser, op. cit., p. 141. Liverpool was an 'unreformed' city, that is, it did not come under the Municipal Reform Act of 1835. Over the century a number of unreformed cities, among them Birmingham and Manchester, applied for charters so they might establish more orderly governments.

39　Ibid., p. 137.

40　See A. Temple Patterson, *Radical Leicester* (Leicester: University College Press, 1954).

41　The first municipal government won by a socialist majority was Bradford, which the Independent Labour Party ruled from 1891 to 1897.

42　J. M. Lee, *Social Leaders and Public Persons: A Study of County Government in Cheshire since 1888* (London: Oxford University Press, 1963), p. 61.

43　Hill, op. cit., p. 63.

44　For additional details on the workings of local elections in the nineteenth century, see H. J. Hanham, *Elections and Party Management* (London: Longman, 1959), pp. 387–96. The contrast with France, so well documented in Weber, op. cit., merits special notice. The urban–rural cleavage in French society was more contained within regions and provinces, where the departmental notables and prefects could moderate conflicts. Britain elevated social change to the national level through the local organization itself, thereby depriving local leaders of the opportunity to become the effective moderators between national and local interests.

45　Fraser, op. cit., p. 284. He gives examples of diminishing control. It is not all that clear, of course, that interest actually did decline in levels of voting.

46　Goguel, in Mabileau (ed.), op. cit., pp. 335–6. One canton that did return a bonapartist three times running had its returns annulled each time by the prefect.

47　Charles Bettelheim and Suzanne Frère, *Auxerre en 1950: Étude de Structure Sociale et Urbaine* (Paris: Colin, 1950), pp. 14–15. See also Georges Rougeron, *Les Consultations Politiques dans le Département de l'Allier: le Personnel Politique Bourbonnais, (1789–1965)* (Paris: Pottier, 1964).

48　Maurice Duverger, *La Démocratie sans le Peuple* (Paris: Editions du Seuil, 1967).

49　Jean Lacouture, *Léon Blum* (Paris: Seuil, 1977), p. 182.

50　The historical information in this paragraph comes from P. Barral, *Le Département de l'Isère sous la Troisième République 1870–1940* (Paris: Colin, 1962). For additional election studies see the Appendix.

51　This point is elaborated by Jean-Williams Lapierre, 'Note introductive sur l'étude des campagnes électorales', in Mabileau (ed.), op. cit., pp. 181–2.

52　See how Chirac cultivated the Corrèze in Jean-Marie Denquin, *Le Renversement de la Majorité Électorale dans le Département de la Corrèze 1958–1973* (Paris: PUF, 1976).

53 The clearest statement is by V. O. Key and Milton Cummings, Jr., *The Responsible Electorate: Rationality in Presidential Voting 1936–1960* (New York: Random House, 1968). My argument is not that elections should not reflect popular opinion, but only that they have other functions, too, and these must also be determined within the political system. Put differently, would results be different were electoral systems in these countries radically changed?

54 Grassroots influence will be further discussed in Chapter 8. I know of no similar studies in France, but on localism in Britain see Ken Young, 'Values in the policy process', *Policy and Politics*, vol. 5 (1977), pp. 1–22. There are a number of local studies showing the confined identification of citizens with their locality. For example, see William Hampton, *Democracy and Community: A Study of Politics in Sheffield* (London: Oxford University Press, 1970), pp. 98–121.

55 John Dearlove, *The Politics of Policy in Local Government* (Cambridge: Cambridge University Press, 1973), p. 44. In the national election study by David Butler and Donald Stokes, *Political Change in Britain* (London: Macmillan, 1969), pp. 38–9, four of five voters said that no local issues concerned them, and 90 percent voted the same way in both national and local elections. Party identification among French voters has been a more elusive and controversial topic. See Philip E. Converse and Georges Dupeux, 'Politicization of the electorate in France and the United States', *Public Opinion Quarterly*, vol. 26 (1962), pp. 1–23, where it appears about half the voters claim party allegiance, and David R. Cameron, 'Stability and change in the patterns of French partisanship', *Public Opinion Quarterly*, vol. 36 (1972), pp. 19–30.

56 Results from the controversial Bécam questionnaire reported in *Le Dossier des Maires: La Réponse des Maires de France Recueille par la Commission des Communes de France* (Aubert Report) (Paris: Ministry of the Interior, 1978), p. 151. These results are divided: 7559 communes for reform and 21,904 against. One mayor wrote the Commission, 'A global reform has no chance of seeing day in a country that is reformist in words and conservative in temperament. It risks, moreover, being prepared and implemented by good minds that are totally ignorant of local life', ibid., p. 147. Because the questionnaire was administered just before the 1978 legislative elections, it was considered with some justification to be a political maneuver. See *Le Monde*, 26 October 1977 and 17 December 1977.

57 Royal Commission on Local Government in England, *Community Attitudes Survey*, Research Study No. 9 (London: HMSO, 1969), p. 128. The confusion is revealed in the reasons given for these views. Both those wanting and those opposing larger areas gave the improvement of facilities as their most important reasons, ibid., p. 131. The report also devotes a whole chapter to knowledge of and attitudes toward local government services.

58 Mary Horton, *The Local Government Elector*, Report of the Committee on the Management of Local Government, Vol. 3 (London: HMSO, 1967), p. 63. Her study is the most complete account of attitudes toward and perceptions of British local government.

59 The reason that Labour postponed redistribution was that the emigration from the inner cities to suburbs was going to cost it seats in Parliament. The shift was in some cases very dramatic. Pulzer, op. cit., p. 34, notes two inner city constituencies in Manchester and Birmingham that had declined from about 55,000 in 1953 to just over 18,000 voters in 1969. There is some evidence that boundary disparities cancel each other out, though for reasons different than in France. See P. J. Taylor and Graham Gudgin 'A fresh look at the Parliamentary Boundary Commission', *Parliamentary Affairs*, vol. 28 (1975), pp. 405–15.

60 For more details see R. W. Johnson, *Political, Electoral and Spatial Systems* (Oxford: Oxford University Press, 1979).

61 P. J. Taylor and R. J. Johnson, *Geography of Elections* (Harmondsworth: Penguin, 1979), p. 350. Consistent with the emphasis on national electoral competition, national leaders have sometimes been prepared to inflict delays in redistricting that are certainly the equal of French electoral manipulation. See David H. McKay and Samuel C. Patterson, 'Population inequality and the distribution of seats in the House of Commons', *Comparative Politics*, vol. 4 (1971), p. 66.

62 Raymond Barrillon, 'La réforme électorale renforcera la bipolarisation', *Le*

Monde, 10 April 1976. Jean Charlot, *Quand le Gauche peut Gagner* (Paris: Moreau, 1973), argues that the distribution of disparities and the effect of the second ballot tends to cancel out these inequalities.

63 See Jacques Lagroye and Guy Lord, 'Trois fédérations des partis politiques: esquisse de typologie', *Revue Française de Science Politique*, vol. 24 (1974), pp. 559–95, for a study of the readiness of local parties to enter alliances. The responses are remarkably similar across the ideological spectrum.

64 See Marie-Thérèse and Alain Lancelot, *Atlas des Circonscriptions Électorales en France Depuis 1875* (Paris: Colin, 1970), pp. 71–8. On the more recent periods, see Jean Bancal, 'Représentativité parlementaire et découpage électoral', *Revue Politique et Parlementaire*, vol. 76 (1974), pp. 22–45; and Byron Criddle, 'Distorted representation in France', *Parliamentary Affairs*, vol. 28 (1975), pp. 154–79. The Communists' case is given by Alain Vivien, 'Une démocratie inégalitaire', *Le Monde*, 30 August 1977. The average size of a constituency is about 75,000 voters.

65 William G. Andrews, 'Presidentialism and parliamentary electoral politics in France: a case study of Evreux, 1962 and 1973', *Political Studies*, vol. 21 (1973), pp. 311–20.

66 Though it cannot be fully explored here, there is intriguing evidence that except for the Communists the deputies actually see themselves as relatively unrestrained in making decisions. See Roland Cayrol *et al.*, 'Les Députés français et le système politique', *Revue Française de Science Politique*, vol. 25 (1975), pp. 72–105.

67 The problem is a more delicate one for the Labour Party, whose annual conference has been known to vote against parliamentary policy. However, this has not been a threat to local government policy because Labour's concerns are mostly with national economic policy and welfare, and these concerns touch the localities only indirectly. For more details, see Richard Rose, *The Problem of Party Government* (London: Macmillan, 1974), pp. 133–66.

68 Neither party appears to overrule constituency nominations very often, but many factors could account for this. See Michael Rush, *The Selection of Parliamentary Candidates* (London: Newson, 1969). On the nomination process, see Rose, op. cit., pp. 248–73.

69 On the attitude of MPs toward local requests, see Lionel H. Cohen, 'Local government complaints: the MP's viewpoint', *Public Administration* (UK), vol. 51 (1973), pp. 175–84. MPs, like the councillors, place great stress on local contacts, but their comments on contacts with councillors are skeptical, if not unflattering. See Anthony Barker and Michael Rush, *The Member of Parliament and His Information* (London: Allen & Unwin (PEP Study), 1970), pp. 209–15.

70 The 1977 Conference had passed a motion that all Labour MPs should be reviewed (or resign) after forty-two months in office. A conference study group was appointed from the Parliamentary Labour Party, the National Executive and the unions. In the 1978 Conference automatic reselection was rejected on the advice of the National Executive Committee. After Labour's defeat in the 1979 elections, the Annual Conference rejected the Prime Minister's advice, and passed a motion to compel MPs to undergo reselection at least once during the life of each Parliament. Though this measure was spearheaded by local constituency organizations, it was not linked to discontent about local government but intended to make the MP more responsive to local political demands.

71 For additional details on how the substitute system works, see J. P. Charnay, *Le Suffrage politique en France* (Paris and the Hague: Mouton, 1965), pp. 382–4. This is probably the most complete work on French electoral laws.

72 Bernard Chenot, *Être Ministre* (Paris: Plon, 1967), p. 13; quoted in Suleiman, *Politics, Power and Bureaucracy in France* (Princeton, NJ: Princeton University Press, 1974), p. 363. In contrast, the minister–MP in Britain has to rely more heavily on the party agent in the constituency, though he is rarely defeated in elections subsequent to becoming a minister. Within the British context, the growth in the number of ministers and their inability to intervene only further separates local and national politics. See Rose, op. cit., p. 367.

73 On local party rules see F. G. Dreyfus, 'Les instances locales des forces politiques nationales', in Mabileau, op. cit., pp. 51–66. In the 1977 local elections, for example, the Socialists had many people they wished to place ready for the legislative elections of 1978. There ensued an intricate bargaining process between various party federations and the party executive, who finally agreed that, where there was no local agreement, the party would select a candidate. See *Le Monde*,

18 September 1976. See also Charnay, op. cit., pp. 476–80.
74 A good example is the failure to implement the *loi Royer*, described in Birnbaum, op. cit., pp. 126–34. The modernizers in the government wanted more large shopping centers to improve commerce, but the implementation was eventually and reluctantly handed over to departmental committees where the small merchants could arrest its application. Opposition came heavily from Gaullist and Republican deputies. Both Pompidou and Giscard d'Estaing were forced to compromise.
75 See the perceptive column of Jacques Fauvet, 'Variations électorales', *Le Monde*, 2 March 1965, where he outlines how the Gaullists and the Communists have arrived at the same view of local elections, namely, that each sees them as part of a search for power. In fact *parachutage* worked very poorly for the Gaullists in 1965. See Machin, 'Prefects of the Fifth Republic', thesis, University of London, 1973, p. 270.
76 His rise to power is described by Jacques Lagroye, *Chaban-Delmas à Bordeaux* (Paris: Pedone, 1973).
77 Herbert Morrison was perhaps the most important exception. On his local attachment to local office, see his *How London Is Ruled* (London: Peoples University Press, 1949), pp. 189–90, where he notes that with severe local losses in the early 1950s the Labour Party began to consider ways of recovering their local strength. There are cases of MPs with multiple offices. For example, one of the Stoke-on-Trent MPs in 1977 was also on the district and county councils. Even so, these instances appear subordinated to national party requirements, rather than an assertion of local influence over national decisions.
78 Because the Conservatives have a better constituency organization than the Labour Party, pressure may be greater on the latter. See Tom Forester, 'Labour's local parties', *New Society*, 25 September 1975. On financial problems see *The Times* (London), 5 August 1976, for the Conservatives, and the *Guardian*, 5 September 1977, for Labour.
79 See *The Economist*, 10 December 1977, and Vernon Bogdanor, 'Why the word "devolution" hides the real power for Scotland', *The Times* (London), 6 January 1978. The Labour Party faction from Scotland that opposed the bill actually included many local councillors. The Royal Commission of the Constitution, *Report*, vol. 1, Cmnd 4040 (London: HMSO, 1969), pp. 246–7, accepts the double mandate, but adjusts regional representation. In fact, a British representative could rival his or her French counterpart with five elected offices: parish, district, county, national and European.
80 Kesselman, *The Ambiguous Consensus* (New York: Knopf, 1967), p. 135.
81 See Mattei Dogan, 'Political ascent in a class society: French deputies 1870–1958', in D. Marvick, *Decision-Makers* (Glencoe, Ill.: Free Press, 1961), pp. 79–80; and J.-F. Médard, La Recherche du cumul des mandats par les candidats aux elections législatives sous la Ve République', in Mabileau, op. cit., pp. 139–59. On the early Fifth Republic, see Williams, *French Parliament* (London: Allen & Unwin, 1968), pp. 34–5.
82 Roland Cayrol *et al.*, *Le Député Français* (Paris: Colin, 1973), pp. 115–16.
83 Colin Mellors, 'Local government in Parliament – 20 years later', *Public Administration* (UK), vol. 52 (1974), p. 223. See also Bryan Keith-Lucas, 'Local government in Parliament', *Public Administration* (UK), vol. 33 (1955), pp. 207–10; and T. Regan, 'Councillors rarely enter Parliament', *New Society*, 21 March 1968. See also Anthony Sutcliffe, 'The British Member of Parliament and local issues', *The Parliamentarian*, vol. 51 (1970), pp. 87–95.
84 *Le Monde*, 11 March 1971. 157 were elected; *Le Monde*, 25 March 1971. A discussion of local political contests and elections will be found in the next section of this chapter. Also *Le Monde*, 25 March 1977. Of the twenty-nine deputies who were defeated in the local election landslide to the Left, sixteen were Gaullists and five were Republican Independents.
85 Manuel Castells and Francis Godard, *Monopoville: L'Entreprise, l'etat et l'urbain* (Paris: Mouton, 1974), p. 301.
86 The most complete report was done by a Gaullist deputy for the unsuccessful consultations by Barre as part of Giscard's overall reform effort of 1978–9. See François Léotard, 'Fault-il limiter le cumul des mandats?', *Revue Politique et Parlémentaire*, vol. 81, no. 883, November–December 1979, pp. 18–33.
87 Léotard, op. cit., p. 27.
88 *Vivre Ensemble*, Vol. 1 (Paris: Documentation Française, 1976), pp. 137–9. For

current figures, see *Vivre Ensemble*, Vol. 2, p. 16. The accumulation of paid positions is differentiated from accumulating elected offices and called *cumul des fonctions*. The 1979 law on communal reform provided ways of limiting (and significantly sharing) stipends from elected office. See Chapter 6.

89   *Le Monde*, 3 July 1979. New rules governing the *cumul des mandats* are hoped for under a new law on elections and political parties. There was no agreement by the end of 1979.

90   *Municipal Review*, no. 570 (June 1977), p. 79.

91   John D. Stewart, 'The politics of local reorganization', in K. Jones (ed.), *The Yearbook of Social Policy in Britain: 1973* (London: Routledge and Kegan Paul, 1974), p. 25.

92   *Local Government Trends 1973* (London: CIPFA), p. 25.

93   The phrase originated with Jules Ferry, a staunch defender of the republic. Less background is needed for the Lords, though the upper House remains a source of ideas and criticism in the British lawmaking process. Their debate on the 1972 law was in many ways more serious than that in the Commons.

94   Jean Pierre Marichy, *La Deuxième Chambre dans la Vie Politique Française Depuis 1875* (Paris: Librairie Générale de Droit et de Jurisprudence, 1969), pp. 189–96. It might be noted that Mendès-France also had ideas about modernizing the Senate or the Council of the Republic in the Fourth Republic. In any event, the elitist concept of functional representation was not confined to de Gaulle.

95   The elections are staggered, one-third of the departments electing Senators every three years. The electoral law of 1976 added thirty-three seats but did not change boundaries. Just over half the seats are now filled by proportional representation. See *Le Monde*, 3 September 1977.

96   Williams, op. cit., pp. 30–1.

97   With typical presidential petulance, de Gaulle forbade ministers to speak in the Senate, and Senators were excluded from presidential receptions. The most complete account of the conflict is Jacques Georgel, *Le Sénat dans l'adversité (1962–66)* (Paris: Cujas, 1968).

98   See, for example, the Communist weekly *La France Nouvelle*, no. 1662, 19 September 1977, p. 15. Despite the break in the Common Front, both parties worked together in the 1977 Senate elections. Of course, there was nothing to be gained in disputes because the electors had already been chosen and both parties were minorities. See *La Monde*, 27 September 1977. The shift toward a younger, more progressive Senate was noticed in 1971. See A. and M. C. Delcamp, 'Les élections Sénatoriales du 26 septembre 1971', *France-Forum*, no. 114–115 (1972), pp. 29–35.

99   The full results are in *Le Monde*, 7 October 1977. Because only a third of the Senators are elected every three years the swing toward the Left is delayed. Nonetheless, Senators closely followed reorganization proposals. See, for example, Alain Guichard, 'Le sort des collectivités locales préoccupe les Senateurs', *Le Monde*, 23 May 1975.

100   His prominence, and possibly his enthusiasm for politics, grew in his careful handling of the interregnum between the presidencies of de Gaulle and Pompidou in 1969. He decided to run against Pompidou and received 42 percent of the votes in the second ballot, an amazing number for an unknown politician in any system. In 1974 he threw his support to Giscard d'Estaing. On recent events see *Le Point*, 15 August 1977. On his earlier career, Dominique Pado, *Les 50 Jours d'Alain Poher* (Paris: Denoël, 1969).

101   For a more detailed account, see Jackson, op. cit., Ch. 4. Nothing is said here about the franchise, for it is identical to the national franchise. As a further concession to demoted boroughs, non-metropolitan districts could choose which type of election they wished, and about forty-four opted for election in thirds. In 1969 the property-based vote for local elections was abolished and the vote extended to eighteen-year-olds. All this was done by national legislation. France lowered the voting age in 1974.

102   In the local elections of 1972, Labour would have won eight more cities had there been no aldermanic vote. See *The Economist*, 13 May 1972. Of course, with the three-year election cycle, the popular meaning of the election is obscured.

103   See the outline of the new election cycles in *The Economist*, 15 May 1976. Since 1974 the local elections would barely be comprehensive without the ingenious efforts of *The Economist*'s local election psephologist, Michael Steed, of Manchester University. According to Pierre Viansson-Ponté, 'Première ou

dernière chance?', in *Le Monde*, 1 May 1978, the French national electorate has been called to the polls twenty-one times since May 1958. There have been fifteen purely national votes, including legislative and presidential elections and referenda. See Chapter 4. There is also the array of localized elections for various government services and for enterprises. See, for example, Pierre Laroque, 'Problèmes posés par les élections sociales', *Revue Française de Science Politique*, vol. 3 (1953), pp. 222–45.

104 About 85 percent of the French electorate votes in presidential elections and 80 percent in legislative and local elections. In the local elections of 1965, 70 percent of the eligible voted in communes over 30,000 and in 1971, 66 percent. For smaller communes, the figures were a remarkable 82 percent in 1965 and 81 percent in 1971. If participation as measured by turnout indicates the strength of local democracy, the French system should not be changed. Since the war British national elections have drawn from 73 to 84 percent of the eligible voters, but only about 35 percent of the eligible voters turned out for local elections. See Douglas E. Ashford, 'Parties and participation in British local government and some American parallels', *Urban Affairs Quarterly*, vol. 11 (1975), p. 69. Voting declined in the 1970s.

105 *The Economist*, 15 May 1976. For an account of the internal workings of a local council with splintered parties, see Andrew Blowers, 'Checks and balances – the politics of minority government', *Public Administration* (UK), vol. 55 (Autumn 1977), pp. 305–16.

106 In adversity, parties predictably ask for fairer elections. The Liberals were hard-pressed in local elections once they joined the coalition with Labour, but have always been interested in proportional representation. See Bryan Keith-Lucas, 'Has the time come for electoral reform?', *Municipal Review*, no. 559 (1976), p. 100, and his pamphlet *Local Elections – Let's Get Them in Proportion* (London: National Committee for Electoral Reform, 1977).

107 J. Chaban-Delmas, 'La réforme de la loi électorale municipale', *Le Monde*, 6 February 1975. Debré's proposal for a family vote in 1978 was a stroke of unadulterated Gaullism.

108 *Le Monde*, 11 March 1959.

109 See the description of the election in Phillip Williams, 'Party presidency and parish pump in France', *Parliamentary Affairs*, vol. 18 (1965), pp. 257–65. Rather than be forced into a coalition with the French-Algerian rebel Right, which to de Gaulle was even more obnoxious than the Left, the UDR withdrew.

110 The exact point when the Gaullists' ability to govern was challenged is difficult to pinpoint, but it is clear that the 1968 riots came after difficulties were already apparent. In 1963 the Gaullists gave way to the miners' demands in coalfield strikes. In 1965, de Gaulle was forced to run on the second ballot. There was a revolt from the floor during the 1967 party congress at Lille and the President's popularity was falling. See Jean Charlot, *Le Phénomène gaulliste* (Paris: Fayard, 1970).

111 The national party leaders can easily misread trends from local elections, as Wilson is generally thought to have done in 1969 when planning the 1970 general election. On the other hand, Macmillan seems to have acted very wisely in the early 1960s by holding off national elections until his party started improving its local performance. See 'Beware the entrails of May', *The Economist*, 20 April 1974. How much effect can be attributed to each level of elections is a very complex technical question and virtually impossible to disentangle in the French electoral system. For Britain, see Geoffrey Green, 'National, city and ward components of local voting', *Policy and Politics*, vol. 1 (1972), pp. 45–54. He concludes that only 6 percent of the variance in election results can be attributed to city factors. See also Jeffrey Stanyer, 'Local support for national political parties: a theoretical analysis', *Political Studies*, vol. 3 (1970), pp. 395–9.

112 The tendency for local elections to be run on national issues emerges from most of the local election studies. See, for example, Ian Budge, 'Attitudes toward local governments: a survey in a Glasgow constituency', *Political Studies*, vol. 13 (1956), pp. 383–97; J. D. Bartholomew and F. Bealey, 'The local election in Newcastle-under-Lyme, May 1958', *British Journal of Sociology*, vol. 13 (1962), pp. 273–85, 350–68. Further ideas about the sociology of elections may be found in John A. Garrard, 'The history of local political power – some suggestions for analysis', *Political Studies*, vol. 25 (1977), pp. 252–69.

113 For more analysis of the swings, see Peter Fletcher, 'An explanation of variations

in "turnout" in local elections', *Political Studies*, vol. 17 (1969), pp. 495–502; and B. Pimlott, 'Does local party organization matter?', *British Journal of Political Science*, vol. 2 (1972), pp. 381–3.

114   For the figures from 1949 to 1967 see Ashford, op. cit., in *Urban Affairs Quarterly*, pp. 64–5. The nationalization effects of reorganization were widely acknowledged. See *The Economist*, 21 April 1973; and Michael Steed, 'Politics: more balance?', *New Society*, 19 June 1969, pp. 951–2, and 'The new style of local politics', *New Society*, 15 April 1972, pp. 11–13.

115   A useful synthesis of the changes is provided by John Gyford, *Local Politics in Britain* (London: Croom Helm, 1976). See also Keith-Lucas and Richards, op. cit., pp. 211–45.

116   R. W. Johnson, 'The nationalization of English rural politics: Norfolk South West 1945–1970', *Parliamentary Affairs*, vol. 26 (1973), p. 15. In the 1973 non-metropolitan county elections, three (Gwynedd, Powys and Cornwall) were classified as non-political; *The Economist*, 21 April 1973. In the 1977 elections there were four (the above plus Dyfed); *The Economist*, 14 May 1977.

117   This is a major conclusion of the Kesselman study, op. cit. The policy relevance of *apolitisme* of French mayors will be further examined in Chapter 5, but it has much to do with their administrative role within the communes. See Jeanne Becquart-Leclerc, *Paradoxes du Pouvoir Local* (Paris: PUF, 1976), esp. pp. 71–104 on the effects of the single list. On rural communes, see Sidney Tarrow, *Partisanship and Political Exchange in French and Italian Politics: A Contribution to the Typology of Party Systems* (Beverly Hills, Calif.: Sage Professional Papers in Comparative Political Sociology, 1974).

118   Chapsal and Lancelot, *La Vie Politique en France Depuis 1940* (Paris: PUF, 1975), p. 554. The revival of centrist politics was the theme of Duverger's book in 1967; it was also the major conclusion drawn by F. Goguel, 'Les Élections municipales des 14 et 21 mars 1965', *Revue Française de Science Politique*, vol. 15 (1965), pp. 911–17. It is followed by short articles on the local contests in Marseille, Grenoble and The Seine. See Wilson, op. cit., pp. 117–29. The duplicity that had handicapped the growth of the Socialist Party was continued by its most determined elder statesman. Mollet was quite prepared to enter into a coalition with the Radicals and the MRP to win the Arras local election, but two months later he helped destroy the idea of federation by opposing their inclusion; ibid., p. 174.

119   The Socialists were still a remarkably rural party in 1965. Of their 40,000 municipal councillors, only 1806 were seated in towns with populations over 9,000; Wilson, op. cit., p. 178. The Socialists lost because they did not make good alliances. See Jacques Fauvet, 'Mythe et politique', *Le Monde*, 16 March 1965. But they did cooperate with the Communists in Paris.

120   See the perceptive analysis of the Gaullists' changing tactics by Tanguy Kenec'hdu, *Le Monde*, 2 March 1971; Hayward and Wright, op. cit., p. 299; and G. Badel, 'Les partis politiques et les élections municipales', *Revue Politique et Parlementaire*, vol. 72 (1970), pp. 66–80. The UDR ran lists in twenty-five cities over 30,000 where they had none in 1965. See the analysis by Frédéric Bon and Jean Ranger, 'Bilan des élections municipales de mars 1971 dans les villes de plus de 30,000 habitants', *Revue Française de Science Politique*, vol. 22 (1972), pp. 213–37; and also Alain Lancelot, 'Les élections municipales (14 et 21 mars 1971)', *Projet*, no. 56 (1971), pp. 645–55.

121   *Le Monde*, 11 March 1971 and 25 March 1971.

122   The success of the alliances of the Right and Left are compared in a collective article, 'Les Stratégies du PCF et de l'UNR dans les villes de plus de 30,000 habitants', *Revue Française de Science Politique*, vol. 72 (1972), pp. 283–93, edited by Georges Lavau. See also E. Seror, 'Le prémier tour des élections municipales: stratégie des alliances et comportements électoraux', *Revue Française de Sociologie*, vol. 12 (1971), pp. 113–34.

123   Bon and Ranger, op. cit., pp. 224–7.

124   See Jean-Pierre Bernard *et al.*, 'Les groupes d'action municipale dans le système politique local: Grenoble, Valence, Chambery', *Revue Française de Science Politique*, vol. 22 (1972), pp. 296–318.

125   On the continued acrimony between Socialists and Communists in Marseille, see Colette Ysmal, 'L'élection de M. Gaston Defferre à Marseille', *Revue Française de Science Politique*, vol. 22 (1972), pp. 319–47. As it had done in 1965 in Lyon, the UDR dispatched the Minister of Youth and Sports to try to unseat Defferre.

Because local sports clubs are so popular in France this minister has special appeal, though the tactic did not work in either case. As in Toulouse, the Communists were the victims of a three-cornered contest. See R. Boules, 'Toulouse: une lutte complexe pour l'union des forces démocratiques', *Cahiers du Communisme*, vol. 47 (1971), pp. 16–22.

126 Elisabeth Dupoirier and Gérard Grunberg, 'Vote municipal et vote législatif. Évolution de 1965 à 1971 dans les villes de plus de 30,000 habitants', *Revue Française de Science Politique*, vol. 22 (1972), p. 241.

127 In 1965 there were 3.3 lists per city of over 30,000; in 1971 there were 3.5. Calculated from figures in *Le Monde*, 14–15 March 1971.

128 See Marc Wolf, 'L'élection presidentielle de mars 1974: la redistribution des électeurs de droit', *Revue Française de Science Politique*, vol. 25 (1975), pp. 259–90.

129 *Le Monde*, 26 February 1977.

130 The mayors of Marseilles and Lille won with centrist support and in Orléans, Annecy and Nantes, Socialists still participated in municipal councils with centrists. The Nantes federation resigned rather than change the alliance. See Jack Hayward and Vincent Wright, 'Governing from the centre: the 1977 French local elections', op. cit., p. 451, and *Le Monde*, 18 September 1976. See also Jean-Luc Parodi, 'Après les élections municipales: la fin de la transition?', *Revue Politique et Parlementaire*, no. 867 (1977), pp. 3–15; Alain Lancelot, 'Le rouge et le vert, les élections municipales des 13 et 20 mars 1977', *Projet*, no. 116 (1977), pp. 703–18; Jean Charlot, 'La politisation des municipales', *Projet*, no. 112 (1977), pp. 135–40; and Elisabeth Dupoirer and Gerard Grunberg, 'Qui governe la France? Les élections municipales dans les villes de plus de 9000 habitants', *Revue Française de Science Politique*, vol. 28 (1978), pp. 27–54.

131 In 1965 there were united lists with Communists in sixty of 159 large cities; in 1971 in 124 of 193; and in 1977 in 204 of 221.

132 The President's letter is reproduced in *L'Élu local* (February 1977), p. 9, and the Manifesto in ibid., pp. 17–18. A more complete account of the Right's program is given by their local election organizer, Antoine Rufenacht, 'Agir pour nous communes', ibid. See also *Vie Publique*, no. 37 (May 1975), on early preparations.

133 Local reform has always been a delicate matter for the Socialists, who published a small book by a group of their experts, *Citoyen dans sa Commune* (Paris: Flammarion, 1977). The Communist proposals can be found in *Communes et Départements d'Aujourd'hui*, 3e and 4e quarters (1976), pp. 2–3 and 2–8, respectively. The Socialist Party organizer for local elections was Charles Hernu, mayor of Villeurbanne and a long-time supporter of Mitterrand in party struggles. The Communist local election campaign was headed by Marcel Rosette, a member of the party's Central Committee. Though the break in the Common Front did not occur until the fall of 1977, it is interesting that neither the Communist nor Socialist local government journals published the winners from the other party.

134 Hayward and Wright, op. cit., p. 443.

135 *New York Times*, 22 March 1977. The entire issue of the *Revue Française de Science Politique*, vol. 27 (1977), is devoted to the Paris local election.

136 An exception was the editor of *Vie Publique*. See his editorial, 'Le virus politique', ibid. (October 1977), p. 5. See also the column of Thierry Pfister, 'Les fruits de cactus', *Le Monde*, 23 April 1977.

137 The Dijon case is described in *Le Monde*, 31 May 1977, along with other divisive differences. The lockout was at Bischheim; *Le Monde*, 23 April 1977. The Lille problems are discussed in *Le Monde*, 22 September 1977, and those of Marseilles, 11 October 1977. The Communists also walked out in Saint-Malo; *Le Monde*, 5 July 1977.

138 See *Le Monde*, 11 October 1977 and 27 January 1978.

139 J. G. Bulpitt, *Party Politics in English Local Government* (London: Longman, 1967), p. 107.

140 L. J. Sharpe, 'In defense of local politics', in L. J. Sharpe (ed.), *Voting in Cities; the 1964 Borough Elections* (London: Macmillan, 1967), p. 11. (His italics.)

141 Horton, op. cit., pp. 68, 69. The complaints were quite evenly distributed with no overwhelming single reason. On the whole, they are consistent with the differences observed by Gabriel Almond and Sidney Verba, *The Civic Culture* (Boston: Little Brown, 1963), pp. 64–78, when they measured confidence in and efficacy of national and local government in Britain.

142 Louis Moss and Stanley R. Parker, *The Local Government Councillor*, Vol. 2, Committee on the Management of Local Government (London: HMSO, 1967), pp. 204, 211 and 234. In elaborating their response and at a consistent level across different types of local government, about 60 percent felt that the major reason against parties was the imposition of doctrinaire policies. On local councillors' feelings that partisan politics does not help much in reaching most decisions, see Ian Budge, 'Attitudes toward local governments: a survey in a Glasgow constituency', *Political Studies*, vol. 13 (1965), pp. 386–99.

143 In contrast, a French poll showed that 51 percent of the public thought their elected representatives well occupied and wanted to be involved with commune affairs. SOFRES poll, reported in *La Lettre du Maire*, no. 35 (2 January 1976), p. 3.

144 Prior to reorganization, a major point of dispute and one that materially affected party control was the election of aldermen. Some councils agreed to split them according to the councillors' party strength while more militant councils went on a winner-take-all principle. In 1949 Labour kept control of the London County Council by packing the aldermanic seats. For this and other examples, see Jackson, op. cit., pp. 108–12.

145 The local Labour Party group has imposed a 'whip' or party discipline on local councillors ever since the Standing Orders of the party were devised in 1918. The Conservatives have been more reluctant to use parliamentary discipline in councils, but in recent years have also imposed a whip. See *The Economist*, 14 May 1977, on the use of the whip to eliminate Independents in elections in Conservative areas.

146 G. W. Jones, 'Varieties of Local Politics', *Local Government Studies* (new series), vol. 1 (1975), pp. 17–32. Bulpitt's version appeared as 'Party systems in local government', *Political Studies*, vol. 11 (1963), pp. 11–35.

147 For more on the underlying conditions leading to non-partisanship in British districts see W. P. Grant, 'Non-partisanship in British local politics', *Policy and Politics*, vol. 1 (1973), pp. 241–55. For more on how the electoral process relates to partisanship see Jeffrey Stanyer, 'Electors, candidates and councillors: some technical problems in the study of political recruitment processes of local government', *Policy and Politics*, vol. 6 (1977), pp. 71–92.

148 R. A. W. Rhodes, 'The changing political-management system of local government', paper presented at ECPR Workshop, 1975. See also his *Local Government Trends, 1974* (London: CIPFA, 1975), pp. 21–2, for increases in party control.

149 *Registrar General's Report, 1973*, p. 110. See also Peter Fletcher, 'The results examined', in Sharpe (ed.), op. cit., pp. 290–328. Fletcher also provides an analysis of how proportional representation would affect local councils. Rather like the complexities of the French electoral system, the changes in counties and cities very nearly balance each other out. Electoral reform of local elections is not high on the political agenda, but has been carefully reviewed by W. P. Grant, 'Electoral reform and local government', in S. Finer (ed.), *Adversary Politics and Electoral Reform* (London: Anthony Wigram, 1975), pp. 343–59.

150 *The Economist*, 15 May 1976, with tables.

151 *The Economist*, 15 May 1977; and for a remarkably accurate forecast, ibid., 10 April 1977. Close electoral interdependence is indicated by the fact that the swing in the previous by-elections for parliament was almost exactly that of the county elections.

152 R. T. McKenzie, *British Political Parties* (London: Macmillan, 1954), p. 647.

153 M. Parkinson, 'Center-local relations in British parties: a local view', *Political Studies*, vol. 19 (1971), pp. 440–6. In view of the deep division within the Labour Party over constituency control of MPs in 1977, these activist tendencies are prophetic.

154 Hampton, op. cit., p. 86. (His italics.)

155 Frank Bealey *et al.*, *Constituency Politics: A Study of Newcastle-under-Lyme* (London: Faber & Faber, 1965), pp. 350–9.

156 G. W. Jones, *Borough Politics: A Study of Wolverhampton Borough Council 1888–1964* (London: Macmillan, 1969).

157 Lee *et al.*, op. cit., pp. 78–82. Their success should be compared with the futility of appeals to MPs in Bristol. See Roger Clements, 'Political leadership in Bristol and Avon', *Local Government Studies* (new series), vol. 2 (1976), pp. 39–52.

158 See Anthony Sutcliffe and Roger Smith, *Birmingham 1939–1970*, Vol. III

(London: Oxford University Press, 1974), pp. 67–75; also Kenneth Newton, *Second City Politics: Democratic Processes and Decision-Making in Birmingham* (London: Oxford University Press, 1976).

159 Michel Longpierre, *Les Conseillers Généraux dans le Système Administratif Français* (Paris: Cujas, 1971), p. 103. This is the most complete account of how the councils work. See also his essay, 'Permanence des conseilleurs généraux et rénouveau des traditions administratives départmentales', *Aménagement du Territoire et Développement Régional* (Grenoble: Institut des Études Politiques), vol. 3, (1970), pp. 3–32.

160 From an interview in Longpierre, op. cit., p. 31. The importance of the notable in policymaking will be further explored in Chapter 5, but see Grémion, *Pouvoir périphérique* (Paris: Seuil, 1976), pp. 221–75.

161 Peyrefitte (ed.), *Décentraliser les responsabilités*, op. cit., p. xiii. The relaxation of this pressure was denoted by Peyrefitte's omission from the new Cabinet in 1974. The example of Haute-Garonne is given in his report. Longpierre, op. cit., pp. 44–5, gives the example of the department of Isère, where it takes over 28,000 votes to be elected as a councillor from Grenoble and 548 votes in a nearby rural canton. Urban departmental councillors are, of course, often unknown to the electors and do not have as crucial a role as their rural counterparts. See also Marie-Hélène Marchand, *Les Conseillers Généraux en France Depuis 1945* (Paris: Colin, 1970), for more electoral demography.

162 Machin, 'Prefects of the Fifth Republic', op. cit., p. 264.

163 Alain Lancelot, 'La reproduction des législatives dans le puzzle cantonal', *Projet*, vol. 76 (1973), p. 1223.

164 Longpierre, op. cit., pp. 57, 193. Slightly less than 10 percent are deputies, and about the same number are Senators. Each council also elects three representatives to the regional council.

165 See *Le Monde*, 9 and 16 March 1976. Also Alain Lancelot, 'Elections cantonales: les roses de mars', *Projet*, vol. 76 (1976), pp. 713–23. On the 1970 results see Alain Lancelot, 'Les élections cantonales et l'implantation du gaullisme', *Projet*, vol. 74 (1970), pp. 593–6.

166 Longpierre, op. cit., p. 174.

167 Guichard Report, op. cit., pp. 256–60.

168 On preliminary consultations within the government see *Le Monde*, 2 August 1978. The consultations with the Socialists and MRG are reported in *Le Monde*, 14 October 1978; and with the Gaullists, *Le Monde*, 24 October 1978. The Communists refused to participate, and considered Socialist acceptance further display of disloyalty to the Common Front.

169 In the national meeting of the Socialist local government group, the Fédération Nationale des élus socialistes et républicains (FNFSR), was itself divided between regional and departmental schemes. See *Le Monde*, 10 October 1978.

170 Over this period Chirac unleashed a particularly outspoken attack on the President, and the Gaullists abstained from several key votes on local reform in the Senate. See *Le Monde*, 17 November 1978 and 16 June 1979.

171 The Senate report on the expansion of communal responsibilities, the de Tinguy Report, appeared in four volumes. See Annexe au procès-verbal de la séance du 3 mai 1979, *Journal Officiel (Sénat), Rapport*, 1978–79 session, no. 307. The National Assembly prepared a report on reform of direct taxation (the Voisin Report), *Rapport, Journal Officiel*, annexe du 9 mai 1979, 1978–79 session, no. 1043; and the Boileau Report on communal personnel.

172 Indicative of how parliamentary prerogatives supercede lawmaking, there was a heated, if inconsequential, dispute between the Labour Opposition and the government when it was proposed that the reforms might conveniently be discussed first in the House of Lords. Under Labour pressure the government reversed its decision. See *Guardian*, 7 December 1979.

173 See *The Times* (London), 10 December 1979 and 19 December 1979.

174 S. Finer, *Life and Times of Sir Edwin Chadwick* (London: Methuen, 1957), p. 510.

175 R. M. McLeod, *Treasury Control and Social Administration* (London: Bell, 1968), p. 8.

176 The entire literature on urban and community protest is clearly beyond the limits of this study, and little will be said here of what are called 'advocacy' groups, that is, special interest groups based on specific community problems and direct protest, such as squatters. A cross-section of these views in Britain is Peter Hain

(ed.), *Community Politics* (London: Calder, 1976). For France there has been a large number of studies, many coming from the Centre de Sociologie Urbaine and reflecting criticisms by the Left. See J. O. Retel, *Vie Communale et Occulation du Politique* (Paris: CSU, 1974); J. O. Retel, *Organisation Communale et Groupements de Localités dans Deux Agglomérations Françaises* (Paris: CSU, 1974); and Annie Riou, *Propriété Foncière et du Processus d'Urbanisation* (Paris: CSU, 1973).

177   All candidates made environmental statements. See *L'Ecologie: enjeu Politique* (Paris: *Le Monde* Dossiers et Documents, March 1978), pp. 78–83.

178   In some cities of the Paris region they received over 25 percent of the vote. See Hayward and Wright, 'Governing from the centre: the 1977 French local elections', *Government and Opposition*, vol. 12 (Autumn 1977), op. cit., pp. 448–50; and A. Lancelot, 'Le rouge et le vert': les élections municipales des 13 et 30 mars 1977', *Projet*, no. 116 (June 1977), pp. 703–18, pp. 705–6. As these authors point out, the ideology of the ecologists shows wide variations in different parts of the country.

179   The politically sensitive Pompidou appointed a Cabinet-level environmental delegate in 1972; elevated to a minister in 1973. Giscard d'Estaing sees more help for his centrist formation in these movements, and in 1974 a Ministry of Quality of Life was created. Not unrelated to internal ministerial jockeying for power, environment was added to the Ministry of Infrastructure after the 1978 legislative elections. Environmental officials have been added to many of the regional governments.

180   In Grenoble they were allied with the Socialist mayor, Dubedout, after 1971, and this remains their most important local base. See Albert Rousseau and Roger Beaunez, *L'Experience de Grenoble* (Paris: Editions Ouvrières, 1971); and J. P. Bernard *et al.*, 'Les groupes d'action municipale dans le système politique local: Grenoble, Valence, Chambéry', *Revue Française de Science Politique*, vol. 22 (1972), pp. 296–318. For the general argument favoring more voluntary action, see François D'Arcy, 'Vers un urbanisme volontaire', *Aménagement du territoire et développement régional* (Grenoble: Institut des Études Politiques), vol. 3 (1969), pp. 33–62.

181   The background of the members suggests that the movement became an offshoot of the Catholic Left. In the most careful study available, Michèle Sellier, 'Les groupes d'action municipale', thesis, Paris I, 1975, it appears that 61 percent of the members identify themselves as Christian. They also represented the reaction against the excessive technocratic tendencies of the time and included many young technicians affiliated with the Socialist and Unified Socialist Parties. She summarizes the work in 'Les groupes d'action municipale', *Sociologie du Travail*, vol. 18 (1976), pp. 41–58.

182   On the PCF denunciation, see Jean Girard, 'Action politique et pédagogie', *Les Cahiers du Communisme* (1972), pp. 47–59. Some of the force of the movement was drained off by the rise of CERES, a strong advocate of *autogestion* and also passionately rejected by the Communists. For the CERES view, see 'La gauche et les problèmes municipaux', *Les Cahiers du CERES* (July 1970). Sellier, op. cit., also found that 67 percent of the GAM members were members of the CFDT, another *autogestion* advocate.

183   See Catherine Pouyet, 'Les comités de quartier', *Aménagement du Territoire et Developpement Régional* (Grenoble: Institute of Political Studies), vol. 2 (1969), pp. 595–634.

184   In 1977 the government began an official review of parishes. See DoE circular 121/77, *Local Government Act 1972: Parish Reviews* (London: HMSO, 12 December 1977).

185   Royal Commission on Local Government, op. cit., Vol. I, Ch. IX, pp. 95–108; and Vol. III, App. 8, 'Parish councils', pp. 165–96. A much stronger role was given to local councils in Derek Senior's dissent, Vol. II, pp. 126–33. For a general account, see William Hampton and Jeffrey J. Chapman, 'Towards neighbourhood councils – I', *Political Quarterly*, vol. 42 (1971), pp. 247–54; and on their active neighborhood project in Sheffield, 'Part II', ibid., pp. 414–22. See the perceptive critique of the Commission's proposals by Roland Newman, 'The relevance of "community" in local government reorganisation', *Local Government Studies*, no. 6 (1973), pp. 59–68.

186   This is another illustration of how irrelevant public opinion can be to the designs of government. *The Community Attitudes Survey: England*, Research Studies 9,

Royal Commission on Local Government in England (London: HMSO, 1969), pp. 11–82, provided ample evidence that people's 'home areas' are indeed very small, about a quarter mile from their home. In rural areas, 85 percent still thought of the parish, not the relatively small rural districts, as their home.

187 Quoted by Paul Harrison, 'The neighbourhood council', *New Society*, 12 April 1973, pp. 73–5. The ambiguities of the trend toward new forms of participation even confused one of Labour's most open-minded leaders, Crosland. He advised leaving the word 'participation' out of the 1974 election manifesto. See Geraint Parry, 'The revolt against "normal politics": a comment on Mr. Grimond's paper', *Government and Opposition*, vol. 7 (1972), pp. 145–51; and Anthony Barker, " 'Communities" and "normal politics": a further comment', ibid., pp. 153–65. See also the similar comments by J. G. Bulpitt, 'Participation and local government: territorial democracy', in B. Anderson *et al., Participation in Politics* (Manchester: Manchester University Press, 1972), pp. 281–302.

188 The neighborhood associations should not be confused with the Community Development Projects launched by the Conservative minister, Sir Keith Joseph, and discussed in Chapter 5. For a report on the Islington experiment see Sean Baine, *Community Action and Local Government*, Occasional Papers on Social Administration no. 59 (London: Bell, 1975). The Community Development Councils were part of the urban programme begun by the Home Office in 1968, and later allied with the inner city proposals. See Robert Holman and Lynda Hamilton, 'The British urban programme', *Policy and Politics*, vol. 2 (1973), pp. 97–112; David McKay and Andrew Cox, 'Confusion and reality in public policy: the case of the British urban programme', *Political Studies*, vol. 24 (1978), pp. 491–506.

189 Department of the Environment, *Neighbourhood Councils in England*, Consultation Paper (London: HMSO, July 1974). It should be noted that the local reorganization proposals for Wales and Scotland made much clearer recommendations about community councils.

190 When in doubt governments do more research. Contracts were made with the Association of Neighbourhood Councils, formed in 1970, to do some pilot studies, and with INLOGOV to carry out a survey. The early results have appeared. See Jennifer Talbot and Stephen Humble, 'Neighbourhood councils defined', *Local Government Studies* (1977), vol. 3, no. 3 (new series), pp. 37–50; and their report, *Neighbourhood Councils in England* (Birmingham: INLOGOV, November 1977). A summary appears in the *Municipal Review* (March 1977).

191 P. F. Cousins, 'Voluntary organizations and local government in three South London boroughs', *Public Administration* (UK), vol. 50 (1976), pp. 63–81. On resistance even in a progressive London borough, see Cockburn, *The Local State* (London: Pluto, 1977), pp. 132–57.

192 See Anthony Rowe in *The Times* (London), 11 August 1976, on how some centrally run programs have actually undercut voluntary groups, and how they are the first to be cut in budget reductions. For more general studies of participation at the local level, see Dilys M. Hill, *Democratic Theory and Local Government* (London: Allen & Unwin, 1974); Roy Darke and Ray Walker, *Local Government and the Public* (London: Leonard Hill, 1977); and Paul E. Peterson and Paul Kantor, 'Political parties and citizen participation in English city politics', *Comparative Politics*, vol. 9 (1977), pp. 197–218.

193 The most careful study is Howard Scarrow's 'Policy pressures by British local government', *Comparative Politics*, vol. 4 (1971), pp. 1–28. Also his reflections in 'Participation through decentralization: the case of Britain', in J. Hallowell (ed.), *Prospects for Constitutional Democracy: Essays in Honor of R. Taylor Cole* (Durham, N.C.: Duke University Press, 1967), pp. 134–45. See also Dearlove, op. cit., pp. 155–204; and Kenneth Newton, *Second City Politics* (Oxford: Clarendon Press, 1976), pp. 165–93.

194 Participatory planning received its impetus from the Skeffington Report, *People and Planning: Report of the Committee on Public Participation in Planning* (London: HMSO and DoE, 1969), appearing at the same time as local reorganization initiatives. In some towns there has been genuine participation, but on the whole the experiment proved a failure. See Carol Vieba and Les Bridges, 'Reaction to planning', *New Society*, December 1975; Peter Levin, 'Participation: the planners vs the public?', *New Society*, 24 June 1971; Patrick T. Whitehead, 'Citizen participation in structure-planning: A review article', *Town Planning Review*, vol. 47 (1976), pp. 349–58; John Ferris, *Participation in Urban Planning:*

The Barnsbury Case, Occasional Papers on Social Administration No. 48 (London: Bell, 1972); Michael Fagence, *Citizen Participation and Planning* (Oxford: Pergamon, 1977). See also *Municipal Review* (November 1977), p. 256, and Alan P. Brier, 'The decision process in local government: a case study of fluoridation in Hull', *Public Administration* (UK), vol. 48 (1970), pp. 153–68, for accounts of participation gone wrong.

195   A great deal of effort can produce disappointingly meager results. One neighbourhood council project succeeded in raising turnout in a Notting Hill area to 28 percent, which the observers, Hampton and Chapman, op. cit., p. 253, fn14, are pleased to see is 10 percent more than in local elections. The point here is not that the improvement is negligible, but that one must ask why parties are complacent.

196   See L. J. Sharpe, 'Smaller can be beautiful', *Municipal Review* (July 1978), pp. 77–8. These views represent a considerable change from Sharpe's earlier stress on the functional nature of local government. His more recent thinking is elaborated in '"Reforming" the grass roots', in David Butler and A. H. Halsey (eds), *Politics and Policy* (London: Macmillan, 1978).

197   George E. Berkeley, 'Community control in Britain: going, going . . .', *National Civic Review* (May 1973), pp. 248–53.

198   The information in this paragraph comes from Rudolf Klein and Janet Lewis, *The Politics of Consumer Representation: A Study of Community Health Councils* (London: Centre for Studies in Social Policy, 1976), pp. 13–15.

199   Dearlove, op. cit., p. 225, his emphases. The difficult part of this argument is, of course, that value judgments can bite both ways. The Labour government passed legislation in 1976 to make sure that local education authorities could not support private education (the 'independent sector'), but cries of outrage followed when one county council, Greater Manchester, decided to use its unrestricted income to subsidize private schools. Because they are not educational authorities, the metropolitan counties are free to use their money as they wish for education. See *The Times* (London), 11 February 1978.

200   Robert E. Jennings, 'Political perspectives on local government reorganization', *Local Government Studies* (new series), vol. 1 (1975), pp. 21–37. See also in Newton, op. cit., pp. 259–62, how the 'rent rebels' in the Birmingham City Council were disciplined by the National Executive Committee of the Labour Party for rebelling against local procedures.

201   For details, see *Local Government Trends 1973* (London: CIPFA, 1974), p. 20. The ratio electorate/council member in counties varied from 1,417 to 19,031.

202   Interview, Local Government Officer, Labour Party Central Office, November 1977. The details of the proposals to make functional changes will be further analyzed in Chapter 6.

203   Mellors, op. cit., pp. 225–7, notes that 40 percent of the Labour MPs and 15 percent of the Conservative MPs formerly held local office within their constituencies. As he notes, the percentages are difficult to interpret because local government background is stronger among MPs of a party when its majority is large, and we may be witnessing a cyclical phenomenon when times are hard for their party.

204   *Organic Change in Local Government*, Cmnd 7457 (London: HMSO, January 1979). The proposals could, of course, be made with little risk of coming before Parliament because of the approaching elections, while assuring Labour-held districts of the party's good intentions.

205   J. D. Stewart *et al.*, *Organic Change: A Report on Constitutional Management and Financial Problems* (Birmingham: Institute of Local Government Studies, November 1978).

206   *Central Government Controls over Local Authorities*, Cmnd 7634 (London: HMSO, September 1979). The order removed about 300 detailed controls on local government. See also the immense list prepared by the local government associations, *Review of Central Controls over Local Authorities* (London: Association of County Councils, February 1979).

207   The Socialists met at Dreux; see *Le Monde*, 21 April 1977, and *Communes de France*, no. 158 (May 1977). The Communists met at Nanterre; see *Communes d'Aujourd'hui*, no. 3 (1977).

208   *Le Monde*, 11 October 1977.

209   *Le Monde*, 11–12 September 1977.

210   Described in the MNEL journal, *L'Élu local*, no. 76 (November 1977). The other

groups are the Amicale Internationale des Élus Municipales et des Collectivités Locales, the Centre d'Information des Communes Rurales, and the Association des Jeunes Élus Locaux.
211 Georges Dupuis, 'La "chance d'un fruit mûr"', *Le Monde*, 22–23 January 1978.

Chapter 5

THE ADMINISTRATIVE CONNECTION: HOW ADMINISTRATORS MAKE POLICY

All England is afraid of being put under a central board in London . . . . The parochial soil in on fire – provincial patriotism is big with indignation at the prospect of a central despotism. But the cry is too hasty; the alarm and indignation are premature. The Administration is still local. – *The Times*, 15 June 1847.

There are no 'natural frontiers' between the State and the localities. There are only the frontiers traced by history – and they change. If there is a domain where it is difficult to invoke natural rights, it is the domain of administrative organization. It results from successive and never permanent compromises between habits and aspirations. – *Vivre Ensemble*.

The growth of the welfare state has obviously increased the burden of government, and much of this burden has fallen on local government. Although the consequently increased influence of national administrators over public policy has provoked alarm,[1] there are few signs that either politicians or the general populace have any intention of reversing this trend. The aim of this chapter is not to take issue with what appears to be an irreversible development, but to describe how it has affected the formulation and implementation of local government policy in the two countries, and, more specifically, how it relates to the British decision to undertake global reform and the French decision to follow more of an incrementalist path. The changes within each system are probably more influenced by the administrative structure than by political relationships. Despite this, those who lament the demise of the liberal state may find some consolation in observing the extent to which bureaucracies remain rooted in the earlier practice. In the area of local government policy, at least, there is little evidence that administration itself selected desirable outcomes and a great deal of evidence that in both systems the administration worked very hard to achieve the goals, however ill-conceived or vague, that were provided by political leadership.

Chapter 4 concluded that both national governments have roughly similar capabilities to reflect public preferences, to engage in lawmaking, and to moderate partisan demands at the center. The main difference between the two is that local politics has not been isolated from national issues in France, while the nationalization of local politics from the 'top down' in Britain has resulted in local elections being increasingly fought around national policy issues. While local politicians in Britain seem less able to assert local interests, French local politicians have worked to make local grievances and needs more visible at the national level. In recent years, the structural changes advocated by French mayors have become central features of national party platforms and the basis for local election alliances. There are many features of the French political system that make this more direct relationship between local and national politics possible, and these are matched by features in the administrative system which also encourage closer links between national and local decisions.

Just as the central–local political relationships are a multi-dimensional problem, so also are the administrative connections between national and local government. Though many French experts would not agree, there is a remarkable similarity between the administrative complexities linking communes to national policymaking and the complexities of political relationships. To some extent the explanation is structural. The French administrative system depends on its territorial organization in ways that have never developed in Britain. The French tradition of administrative law and the unified administrative system itself means that bureaucracy is more visible to both local politicians and citizens. Alarm over administrative control and manipulation has a long history in France, while it is a relatively recent phenomenon in Britain. As we shall see, the bifurcated administrative system of Britain may have actually disarmed British local government, while the potential, if not the actual, power of French administration keeps local mayors and elected officials at all levels of government militantly aware of possible abuses and arbitrary decisions.

The curious result may be that where local government policies are involved, the upper levels of administrative policymaking in France are more constrained than is the British higher civil service. In the formulation of local government policies, the national-level organization is itself important. As we have seen, the historical development of the British welfare state tended to exclude the formation of a strong ministry, comparable to the French Ministry of the Interior, that could integrate at the national level both political and administrative demands on national government. In Britain, local interests are spread among the Home Office (elections and law and order), the Department of Education, the Department of Health and Social Security, and the Department of the Environment, to name only the most important. Within departments, the main objective of ministers and civil servants is to protect their departmental budgets and to pursue legislation to enhance the department's influence in Whitehall. The coordinating devices that exist are not well suited to handle complex local problems, nor are they primarily designed for this purpose.

There are also interesting ways in France, by which elite administrators are limited by their own organization, which do not exist in Britain. Despised as they may be, several of the *grands corps* have a vital interest in preserving their relationship to the communes. Unlike Britain, their local services become part of their defense at the national level. If they extract exorbitant fees from communes for their services, they also provide a direct link to local problems and needs that barely exists for the British higher civil service. As we shall see, the major struggle within the French administrative system over the past two decades has been how the *grands corps* would share the influence to be gained from the increased responsibilities of local government. The territorial administrative system needs its local political allies and the *complicité* of local politics is rooted in the administrative system itself. Although steps have been taken since 1970 to relieve local dependence on the *grands corps*, most important the law on the development of local responsibilities of 1980, the French administrative system interlocks with the political system at all levels of government, and, of course, at the level of the department has an integrative device in the prefect that assures that territorial demands will be focused in ways that British local councils find virtually impossible to achieve.

The functional emphasis of the British local government system combines with strong Cabinet government and ministerial responsibility to produce a pattern of national control over local administration that is no less complex, but which is also almost unintelligible. Each department fashions its own rules and regulations, and ultimately is only limited in imposing these practices on local government by the strength of the government's majority. When repulsed or checked by law, British ministers need only to write a new law to increase their discretionary powers and to establish new local controls. In the area of public housing, for example, there is almost no action that cannot be supervised by Whitehall. The fact that we know relatively little about administrative bargaining and policymaking between levels of government is due to the fact that each local government service has its own particular tradition of interaction with Whitehall counterparts, who, in turn, are shrouded by the confidentiality of government itself. More damaging perhaps have been the difficulties of fashioning policies on more complex issues such as inner city development and racial integration because there are few incentives to generate lateral integration at either the national or local levels. In France, the intricacies of administrative politics and *complicité* itself provide an integrative stimulus that has been difficult to generate in the British local government system.

The paradoxical result is that, despite the complaints about arbitrary administration in France, the administrative system, at least in relation to local government problems, neither insulates national administrators from local demands nor imposes such highly varying demands for local services on communes as does the British system. Though French communes need more local civil servants, which have been promised in reforms since 1974, they are also free of the burden of a huge local administration which consumes so much time and energy of British local politicians and which introduces immense complexities into the organization and control of local business. French communes develop administrative capacities to suit their needs and in proportion to their own political will to be free of national interference.

Large cities like Marseille, Lyon, Rennes and Bordeaux have local administrative organizations that compare to the huge organizations of large British cities. Smaller cities and towns are more dependent on national officials, and the small rural communes are virtually totally dependent on national officials within the territorial administrative system. A major question to be raised in this chapter is whether there may not be distinct advantages to allowing administrative linkages to be formed as local situations and needs require rather than imposing high administrative costs on localities according to nationally designed policy requirements as is done in Britain. In this respect, the administrative connections between national and local government appear more rigid and more burdensome in Britain than in France.

The strange result is that French mayors evade many of the heavy functional responsibilities placed on British local councils while also penetrating the administrative system more successfully. In fact, the spending burdens of the two systems are roughly comparable (see Chapter 6), but French mayors, enhanced by the political influence over higher-level decisions described in the previous chapter, become policymaking entrepreneurs and are essentially brokers between nationally defined policies and local capabilities. They are officially involved in several major policy areas, such as public housing and welfare assistance, where they in fact have only minor roles. They are able to influence some policies affecting industrial development and employment that remain almost the exclusive preserve of national departments in Britain. As the activities of government have expanded with the growth of the welfare state, French mayors have acquired a key role in reconstructing France while, for historical reasons, British local councils, despite their critical importance to the activities of government, have been more effectively subordinated to administrative demands generated in Whitehall, and over which they frequently have little control.

A VIEW FROM THE TOP: ADMINISTRATIVE STRUCTURES IN BRITAIN AND FRANCE

There are a number of structural features of French administration that make the interdependence of national and local decisions different from the British system. The differences within each system are probably more important in understanding the policymaking process than those between the two governments. The crucial internal difference is that the French system is ostensibly a unified civil service with field agencies, while Britain has separate administrative services at each level of government. For the most part, French local administration is in the hands of the *service extérieurs*, the field services of the central ministries. Excluding the military but including teachers, there are approximately 1.6 million civil servants in France, and only 32,000 of these are assigned to the central administration.[2] There are few locally-employed civil servants, about 529,000 in 1977, who are less skilled than their national counterparts.[3] The relationship is significantly different in Britain. The British central government employs roughly 700,000 civil servants, while local government is the biggest single employer in the country, having over 1.7 million employees in 1977.[4]

Viewing the administrative process as a whole, the relation of central policymaking to lower levels of government is reversed. British central government must work very hard to find out what is happening at the local level, while French central government is infiltrated by administrative demands from the local level. There are, of course, few incentives for British higher civil servants to complicate the lives of their ministers with excessive detail, but the bifurcated system also means that national policies are often made with only rudimentary knowledge of local conditions. For example, when the Secretary of State of the DoE set out in 1979 to impose severe cuts on local government, it appeared that Whitehall had no detailed figures on local manpower that would permit him to estimate their effects. Many of the more technical tasks of local government such as land-use planning could not even be performed by the higher civil service. Thus, the potential abuse of French administrative powers must be weighed against the less apparent irony that British higher civil servants can exercise as stiff controls as they do without having the understanding and experience in local administration that is common to French administration.

The total figures provide only a rough indication of the major administrative problems of each country, but they also reflect historical conditions surrounding the development of local administration in the two welfare states. The historical roots in France begin with the transformation of the Ministry of the Interior in the nineteenth century. Until about 1830 the Ministry supervised nearly all local services, including education, welfare, agriculture and commerce.[5] As more specialized ministries were formed during the century, the Ministry survived, not unlike the Home Office in Britain, as the agency concerned with law and order. The difference is that the Home Office never had local links to these additional services, nor did it seek them as more specialized agencies developed in the late nineteenth century.[6] As the role of government expanded, each ministry devised its own relationships with local government. At the national level in Britain the growing service ministries had no obligation to work through intermediary bodies like the prefecture. The functional relationships between Whitehall and local government were direct and, for the most part, compartmentalized. In France, the prefect remained the departmental representative of the state, if not an effective coordinator of services.[7] The 1964 reforms, outlined in Chapter 3, were designed to enlarge the prefects' integrative role, not to make basic changes in the functions of communes and departments.

As the activities of the state expanded, there were organizational tensions built into the French subnational system. The prefect, oddly enough, resisted enlarging his authority as the *état-major* at the departmental level, contrary to the self-aggrandisement often attributed to the prefect and other elite administrators. In Britain, the new requirements of government not only enlarged the tasks of local government, but provided few coordinating and integrative devices at the local level. Consistent with the British pattern of insulating the higher civil service against local complications and demands, policy integration was made a new objective of the local government during the reorganization; but no clear links to central policymaking were formulated.

Central–local policymaking relationships have necessarily been refashioned in both countries, and in neither country is there much evidence that the central administration had predatory designs on the local government system. Large central agencies naturally wanted to keep direct control of their interests at the local level, which is precisely why the system of local governance was failing in both countries. However, excessive administrative powers in France provided some local advantages because the rudiments of an integrative mechanism existed in the department and the region. The problem was more to persuade administrators to overcome their parochial traditions.[8] Similar weaknesses were noted in Britain. The Royal Commission and a number of studies since then have underscored the inability of local government to make its needs known to the center.[9] But no ministry rose to the occasion, and Britain only began to organize a more coherent linkage to lower-level government when the fiscal unmanageability of the system became unmistakable. In a word, Britain has had modern organizational needs forced upon it, while France reveled in organizational complexity.

Considering the administrative relationships within the subnational system as a network of mutually-dependent actors pursuing overlapping goals provides a much clearer notion of how policies are made, and avoids the tendency of centralization theory to reduce complex problems to irreconcilable conflict between actors or levels of government. But the long history of administrative separation between national and local needs in Britain has more often than not produced confrontation where the French would produce compromises. The structure itself in Britain makes it difficult to fashion administrative compromises and, in turn, to adjust new policies to highly varying local conditions and preferences. Perhaps the undiluted advocacy of local autonomy or of national priorities creates a much too simple image of central–local administrative problems. There are, of course, numerous illustrations of French and British administrators dictating the minutiae of policy to their subordinates, but the obvious faults and inefficiencies do not tell us much about the policy process.

In France, the relationship of central policies to local conditions cannot be excluded from the local government system. Though never fully accepted by the Gaullists, the best example is probably the effort to reconcile the administration to new planning needs or *planification concertée*.[10] In the early 1970s major efforts were made to cut through the complications of the traditional administration, to establish policy objectives within organizations not smothered by routine administrative controls, and to enable such organizations to draw more freely on talent and resources outside government. Unlike Britain, the first stage of reform was to see how new administrative capacities could be developed. From 1969 to 1972 the Prime Minister, Chaban-Delmas, made these ideas part of his *nouvelle société*.[11] Such reforms as the *globalisation des investissements*, the regionalization of the Plan and the revision of land-use and planning policy were to involve communes with new national policies,[12] not to exclude them. Of course, the Gaullist disciples of the 1960s wanted the administration to work for the state as they imagined it. But by 1970 the traditional *étatiste* view had proved ineffective, and their objective had become both more simple and more complex: to convert the administration into a policymaking instrument. The struggle between advanced and traditional concepts puts the notion of legalistic and arbitrary administration in an accurate perspective. The administrators, like politicians, were not about to demolish their privileges, but this hardly distinguishes France from other countries.

More to the point, in the early 1970s a massive effort was made by the top administrative and political leaders to disperse administrative power. The complexity of the administrative system itself meant that national administrative reform was virtually synonymous with reforming the territorial administration. Contrary to the view of French administration as all-powerful, the aim was to do away with traditional practice and, as often happens in French reforms, simply to bypass administrative hurdles that seemed to block the modernization of French local government and ultimately France itself. These efforts so rankled the traditional Gaullists that Chaban-Delmas was eventually discredited and removed from office. But the task of administrative modernization was nonetheless renewed by the President, Giscard d'Estaing, after 1974 and the 1980 law on local responsibilities finally emerged as the most acceptable compromise between national and local government. In contrast, few British national leaders would ever stake their reputations on such complex reforms, nor is there any reason why they need be concerned with the intricacies of local administration.

British concern with administrative reform was no less lively, but was never conceived as a problem of integrating national and local government. The important role of the British local civil service, reinforced by twenty or more professional associations and unions that defend the civil servants' interests, has meant that central and local administration are almost always discussed as separate entities. Since the Fulton Report[13] national administration has been considered a special problem, which, of course, it is in many respects. The unintended effect of this concentration on national administration has been to leave local government to its own devices.[14] The most frequently supplied justification is 'ministerial responsibility', that is, the now outworn and unworkable principle that ministers are responsible for all decisions in their departments. The principle is closely attached to the constitutional customs that enshrine Cabinet government and parliamentary supremacy.

As we have seen in other instances, these principles are sorely strained as government proliferates and, in turn, as decisionmaking is necessarily dispersed through larger, more diverse agencies of government. The remarkable thing is that Britain has been able to preserve these constitutional constraints while local government has been growing so rapidly. The Royal Commission devoted three pages to the relations between central and local government, and basically argued that local government should be less subject to central control and should improve its capacity to confront Whitehall with a united voice.[15] But a decade later British local councils are no more able to moderate ministerial demands. The paradox of British central–local administrative relationships is that the more localities are asked to do, the easier it becomes to slip back into time-worn organizational formulas, which are for the most part designed to relieve national administrators of the consequences of their own decisions.

The administrative relationship between levels of government in Britain makes the avoidance of conflict *more* essential than in France. Only the strong professional ties that develop between the local officials of specific services and their national counterparts save British local government from becoming unmanageable. The unfortunate effect – to a large extent unavoidable where local government fills such a key role in policy implementation – is that policies are in fact executed in diverse ways while national government is hard-pressed to find out what has been accomplished. The cost is twofold because the functionally compartmentalized controls not only fail to produce uniform results, but also make local administrative procedures and practices less intelligible to local councillors. Despite the pleas for more managerial skill and more careful definition of local objectives contained in such proposals as the Seebohm and Bains reports,[16] the policymaking links between national and local administration are difficult to change and almost impossible to subject to the global reconsideration that has taken place in France.

An important unintended effect of the intricacies of French administration has been that little national reform can be accomplished without considering the territorial administration or at least working out ways to circumvent archaic practices. Compared to Britain, national policymakers cannot avoid the complexities of implementation and the great variations among conditions within the communes. The unified civil service is not without its problems, but the tensions and interests of French administration have also made it easier to devise new solutions and to establish new aims. This is not to presume that French innovations such as the mixture of private and public agencies is necessarily desirable, but only that reform presupposes working out organizational and administrative problems. Whether one approves the entrepreneurial character of local reforms in the early 1970s is another question. But as with the reorganization of departments and regions in 1964, the changes of the 1970s involved a fundamental reassessment of the role of administration in the welfare state that would be almost impossible to launch within the British administrative system.

The British administrative system is both vertically and horizontally compartmentalized. This is a function not only of strong ministerial control and the desire of a well-established national administrative elite to retain its power, but also of the burden placed on local government and its own organization. The French local administrative system is best thought of as a network where mayors, local leaders and administrators from all levels of government engage in decision-making.[17] The process requires an accumulation of strength from a variety of sources and contacts in order to pursue desired policy objectives. In this respect the French administrative system utilizes mutual dependence, which would threaten British policymaking. Even the most accomplished French technocrats cannot avoid the bargaining process that goes on both between levels of government and within the central government.[18]

Although this study is not primarily concerned with the more formal administrative aims of control and efficiency, it should be noted that it is by no means obvious that the ostensibly autonomous structure of British local government better achieves these objectives than the more intricate French system. There are no difficulties in finding illustrations of inefficiency in either subnational system. In order to hold additional classes in a small communal primary school in the Jura, fifty pounds of documents were prepared with 766 signatures at a cost of over 200,000 francs.[19] But when a British local authority constructs a primary school, it is told the minimum specifications for cloakrooms, bathrooms, lunchrooms, ventilation, heating, lighting and a host of additional requirements.[20] In a period of rapidly rising building costs, the freedom to spend more if one so chooses is a dubious tribute to pay to local initiative.

The British have on the whole been suspicious of grandly abstract theories of administration that thrive in France,[21] but they have also been unable to redefine the aims of administration in a vastly expanded state. Paradoxically, it is the intricacy of central–local administration that forces the French to rethink this relationship while the carefully drawn and institutionalized boundary that differentiates national and local administration makes the task less attractive in Britain. As we shall see, the curious result over the past decade has been the unilateral, and generally ineffective, demand by Whitehall that local councils quickly generate more rational forms of local organization and management – reforms that Whitehall itself would have difficulty achieving. In searching for the best of both worlds, the British may not have developed administrative incentives to be either efficient or effective.

ADMINISTRATIVE INFLUENCE: RELATING NATIONAL AND LOCAL POLICY OBJECTIVES

The relation of central administration to local government is a function of both the organization of the higher civil services and the way that they enter the local policymaking process. Stimulated by the Fulton Report, there has been an immense amount of research into the organization and effectiveness of the British higher civil service, which unilaterally excludes local administration.[22] The higher civil service in France is often equated with the elite bodies or *grands corps* which dominate its activities. The lively concern with the role of the state in France has resulted in an enormous number of attacks, eulogies and analyses of the French higher civil service. Given governments of roughly the same magnitude, it is not surprising that the top civil services are about the same size. In 1974 there were about 3,000 members of the most prestigious *grands corps* working within ministries, and probably nearly 2,000 detached for service with nationalized industries, banks, public corporations and other state enterprises.[23] Taking the higher grades in the British civil service there were about 2,600 civil servants at policymaking levels (Permanent Secretary to Senior Principal) and nearly another 4,500 Principals or younger members likely to advance to top levels of the civil service in 1978.[24] The different structures of the two governments notwithstanding, the central decisionmakers are also of similar social backgrounds. Both groups are unmistakably part of the social and political elite of the two societies.

The size of ministries can be a very misleading indicator of influence in decisionmaking, but provides clues to central priorities in the two countries. The ministries most involved in local government policy in Britain are the Home Office and the Departments of the Environment, Transport and Education and Science. In 1973 they employed nearly 80,000 persons or about 10 percent of the civil service.[25] Taking similar ministries from France (Culture and Environment, Infrastructure, Interior and Transportation) one arrives at 321,000 persons or 17 percent of all government employees.[26] Perhaps more pertinent to judging how central decisionmakers affect local government would be a comparison of the sizes of the ministries most directly responsible for local needs. In 1978 the Department of the Environment had nearly 13,000 civil servants and the Ministry of Infrastructure (Environment and Quality of Life after 1978) in 1976 had 76,000.

National differences are revealed in the central law and order agencies, the Home Office and the Ministry of the Interior. The fundamentally different structures of central policy machinery are clear, with the former having almost 32,000 civil servants in 1978, and the latter 133,000 in 1976. We shall examine the influence of the financial ministries over local government policy more carefully, and discover that their relative strengths are also revealing.[27] Both are influential ministries, but the interesting figure is that the two agencies most closely connected with local finance, the Treasury and the top French directorates of the ministries of the budget and of the economy and finance, each have about 1,000 members. The struggle between the large central service ministries and the finance ministries goes on in both countries.

Though the size of the service ministries is not the sole determinant of their influence in decisionmaking, central governments must be sensitive, as the ministers are, to the scope of the services each provides. One fundamental difference between the two countries is that Britain's large service ministries have relatively little incentive to coordinate their activities in relation to local government, while there are a variety of pressures at the top levels of the French civil service that help integrate policies which affect lower levels of government. A British ministry may have several politically appointed ministers, especially the large service ministries like the Department of the Environment, but the boundaries between the elite administrative class and the politicians are carefully patrolled. The Permanent Secretary, the top civil servant in the ministry, is the conduit for all administrative decisions rising to and descending from the political decisionmakers. Ministers have a voice in selecting their top administrative officials, but do not select their own team.

Permanent Secretaries often outlast ministers, are powerful figures in their own right, and often interpret the timing and content of political decisions being passed down to lower levels of the government. A new minister, in particular, is almost totally dependent on his top civil servants for advice and for interpretation of the law affecting his ministry.[28] The overall effect is that national-level policymaking is geared to ministerial needs and sheltered from outside influences. Like most important clients of national government, local government is often consulted, but effective power is concentrated in a small circle within Whitehall and, in turn, cloaked in secrecy. Compared to France, local government has less chance of influencing policy priorities and less chance of amending policy aims that are established. Thus, much like the political leaders, the top civil servants have neither reason nor cause to be particularly concerned with local-level priorities or needs. Although the growth of government has made ministerial responsibility an empty principle, every effort is made to keep 'political' matters strictly separate from 'administrative'. Major policy papers are usually not even passed on from one government to the next.[29] The organization of both central and local services insulates British civil servants from politics. The continuity provided by the French administration is neither desired nor possible. One important result is that British civil servants are less occupied with the consequences of national policies for lower-level bodies, and especially for local government.

A minister relies upon the higher civil service for policy advice, and there are very few mechanisms by which local government or anyone else can review this advice or even learn what it is.[30] The minister is traditionally viewed as the advocate of his department, though of course there are interministerial committees and an elaborate network of advisory groups. His ability is judged by how much money he brings to his ministry and on his success in getting his department's legislation on the parliamentary agenda. Attention is thus focused on organizing government to fit the constraints and timetable of Parliament and Cabinet, and on sustaining the constitutional and institutional procedures of one-party government. The result is that even the consolidation of local policymaking powers under the 1972 Act did not basically alter the pattern of national policymaking.

Nearly every major policy document and inquiry concerning central–local administration confirms the undisputed primacy enjoyed by national policymakers. Ministers and civil servants are not even required to respond to major inquiries on public works, and, as we shall see, may take months and even years to respond to land-use plans. The most important spending controls such as the Rate Support Grant and the forecasts of the Public Expenditure Committee (see Chapter 6) are formulated with only indirect and confidential consultation with local government and even then are almost impossible to modify through local action. Neither ministers nor top civil servants are embarrassed when national policies impose conflicting demands. For example, while the Treasury was trying to limit spending in the early 1970s, the Department of Education was urging local authorities to build nursery schools. Under the Thatcher government, a few years later, aid for nursery schools was being withdrawn with little concern for the costs to, much less the preferences of, local government. A number of recent inquiries into central–local relations in Britain confirm this view. The major planning document is the report of the Public Expenditure Survey Committee (PESC), which is basically a Treasury projection of public spending. There is no local government involvement in the division of resources between central and local needs, although the projection itself becomes the guide for subsequent local government grants and programs.

The Layfield Committee concluded that there 'appears to have been in the past no accepted means of framing and expressing government policy about spending by local authorities'.[31] Indeed, so far as the Committee could discover, 'there are no arrangements for drawing together the expenditure plans of local authorities as a whole'.[32] This, in effect, leaves local government at the mercy of a macroeconomic estimate whose disaggregation into specific services is turned over to the appropriate ministries. The Treasury feels no obligation, nor does it have the manpower, to coordinate departmental decisions about local services. With economic adversity an exercise that was supposed to improve policymaking actually became a major source of uncertainty for local government, concentrating their attention on the subsidy (Rate Support Grant) negotiations rather than on the best use of grants or on the more effective organization of services. As the Central Policy Review Staff (CPRS) study points out, local governments may ignore departmental advice 'at their own risk', but they have 'no friend in court' at Whitehall. With no ministry able, and apparently none willing, to take overall responsibility for local needs and preferences, the functional control by department can be both arbitrary and disruptive. The local governments are without recourse when inconsistencies appear, while at the same time being subject to more and more stringent standards of accountability.

The central administrative machinery of France has a very different relationship to local government. At the apex of the national ministries there are ministerial cabinets which are both larger and more politicized than the comparatively small staff of British ministers. The French minister has more opportunity to launch reforms and to independently assess policy options. As in Britain, the influence of top administrators over the formulation and implementation of policy is the center of a heated dispute.[33] As Suleiman observed 'the central administration in France is by no means a rationally or coherently organized entity, the proverbial French penchant for rationality notwithstanding'.[34] The traditional notion that French administrators effortlessly get their way is nowhere more completely contradicted than in the policymaking process surrounding local government.

Many factors contribute to the comparatively greater care given to policies affecting lower levels of government, by no means all of which can be attributed simply to the overarticulated and generally unmanageable local government system itself. But the complexity of central–local administration as well as rivalries at the apex of the system force French government to devise multiple strategies to accomplish national objectives, and the territorial administration cannot be excluded from national decisions as automatically happens in British central–local administration. There has been a variety of tactics in France: strengthening the prefect, consolidating local investment programs, creating a multitude of new developmental agencies, trying to superimpose regional coordination on local government, to name a few. Nearly every major policy decision involving the service ministries is vulnerable to lower-level criticism from both the field administration and local politicians working through the administration. Recommendations that do not take the complexities of local government into account are seldom persuasive, and often prove unworkable.

There are at least two important illustrations of how central administration is compelled to consider the local implications of national policies. From the early years of the Gaullist regime, planning was not only being given high priority but was directly related to communes and departments. Britain's short-lived experiment with national planning in 1966 never developed links to local government, nor are the regional planning bodies closely linked to local government. When the Thatcher government abolished the regional councils of the National Economic Development Organisation in 1979, there was not even a murmur of protest from local government. The planning needs of French government reflect different priorities.

When the Commissariat Général du Plan was attached to the Prime Minister's office in 1962, the Délégation à l'Aménagement du Territoire et à l'Action Régionale (DATAR) was formed the following year specifically to integrate planning at lower levels of government. Since then it has most often been directly linked to the Cabinet by a minister of state. The British Cabinet has never given recognition to the vital interest of local government in planning nor are there any reasons why it should, but in France regional concerns have been represented at the national level almost continuously since 1963 by a minister of state who oversees DATAR and coordinates regional programs throughout the administration. The relation of local government to the French Plan has evolved, but each Plan was made after extended consultation with local government and administration. Like administrative politics generally in France, the 'consultation process is torn by centrifugal forces which tend to reverse roles and to disintegrate the totality'.[35] Planning the future without involving the array of agencies concerned with local problems would be unimaginable in France, but is relatively commonplace in Britain.

A second complication of French administration that brings policymaking closer to local government is the competition among the *grands corps*. The British higher civil service is not without internal tensions, but the civil servant is basically aligned behind his minister. The French higher civil servant, of course, also irons out disputes among ministries, but the process is complicated by the competition of the elite bodies within the higher civil service. The Ministry of Infra-structure, for example, is considered the preserve of the *ponts et chaussées*, and engaged in the continuing struggle with the outmoded *génie rural* of the Ministry of Agriculture. The Ministry of the Economy and Finance is, of course, dominated by the *inspecteurs de finances*, but this dominance is complicated by the general-purpose administrators or *administrateurs civils* from the classes of the Ecole Nationale d'Administration. The *corps préfectoral* has an obvious hold on the Ministry of the Interior, and often uses its pervasive influence to protect prefectoral powers.

The overall effect is to create tensions within the administration and to some extent to reproduce these conflicts at lower levels of local government. The paradox is, of course, that though often charged with arbitrary and high-handed administration, the most important check on administrative fiat in France is built into the structure itself. Every new local program initiates another round in the competition for local clients and support. The competitive relationship among the *grands corps* keeps them alert to their future and how that future is affected by new policies. The various field services of the administration often amplify competition among the *grands corps*, and, in turn, help make them sensitive to local demands.[36]

The global reorganization of British local government appears even more ambitious when one considers how poorly equipped central government is to assess the probable impact of its decisions on local government. The role of the higher civil service is defined and con-strained by the rules of anonymity and ministerial loyalty. The effect is that national administration escapes both the political and admini-strative constraints that operate in France. The local controls exercised by British central government focus on national fiscal or financial policy, thereby falling within the secluded province of the Treasury. Specific controls are devised by ministries to suit their individual needs,[37] and there are no general principles that localities can use to define their relationship to central decisionmakers. While it is true, as Chester has pointed out,[38] that as statutory authorities the British local governments have a direct connection to Parliament, in the normal legislative process their legal status provides them with no special consideration or bargaining power. On the contrary, departments have a relatively free hand in deciding how they will draw the guidelines, standards and orders, and Parliament has little time to review the host of delegated powers given ministers.

The statutory controls exercised by the central departments over the local authorities are formidable and complex. What Dame Evelyn Sharp called 'the forest of local government law' affects every decision made at lower levels.[39] Her observation that a minister has no responsibility for 'what authorities do or how they do it; [that] he has no general right of supervision over them, nor any right of inspection' is a rather elliptical way of saying that it takes years to master the intricate array of statutory controls for each local service. There are, for example, 203 laws affecting how local governments may use open space, not including the additional battery of legislation affecting planning and land use.[40] In comparison, the French Code de

Communes seems a model of simplicity.

Many British legal controls affect the internal organization of councils no less directly than the elaborate administrative network of the French local government system. Although the 1972 Act eliminated most of the central departmental approvals required for many local appointments, chief officials for education, fire, weights and measures, and social services must still be centrally approved.[41] There is scant consolation in Griffith's view that control is concentrated at 'key points'.[42] Local governments have no direct voice in deciding what such key points should be nor have they any general right to appeal these decisions. Each department decides its own priorities and determines how its objectives can be best achieved at the local level. Compared to France, the British system of central–local administrative relations obscures and complicates local government business, and places ultimate, if ill-defined, power with the minister and his chief advisors.

Because neither the structure nor the process of central–local administration need meet any general standards, each central department uses the controls and policy instruments it prefers.[43] The most common device is the circular, which can convey anything from an urgent and inflexible necessity to simple exhortation. Most of these come from the Department of the Environment (DoE), which issued 127 circulars in 1975. During the enthusiasm for local reorganization in 1971 the government prepared a list of 1,254 statutory controls that it planned to remove, and a study group was assembled in the DoE. Though a few legal restrictions were removed over the next few years, the effort to make some sense of the entire system died a quiet death in Whitehall until revived by the local government associations in 1978. When the Conservative Secretary of State for the Environment, Heseltine, finally removed 300 detailed controls in 1979, his reasons had more to do with Tory determination to dismantle government than with any coherent plan to restructure central–local relations.[44]

There is a virtually unclassifiable array of memoranda, notes and letters passing between levels of government, the mysteries of which increase the local council's dependence on its administrative officers. As the CPRS study notes, '"central government" is . . . an abstraction which conceals reality. Central government is, in fact, a federation of separate departments with their own ministers and their own policies'. Griffith's optimistic view that mutual understanding emerges for each service does not serve well in a period of financial crisis, nor does it curb erratic ministers. The CPRS found 'a surprising degree of mutual misunderstanding on the part of both central and local government'.[45] Perhaps the most onerous task is the vast increase in planning responsibilities that have descended on local government since reorganization, including plans for transportation, health, manpower and housing as well as structure and development plans for land use. What happens to these proposals in Whitehall is only vaguely communicated to lower levels of government.[46]

The most frustrating characteristic of the British administrative controls over local government is that they can be neither attacked nor defended. There is considerable evidence that the system does not help in achieving the goals of either central or local government. The Department of Education, for example, encouraged comprehensive education by ministerial advice in 1965, and then turned to legislation five years later. This was prevented by the change of government in 1970, further complicated by a court decision rejecting ministerial directives in 1976, and finally discontinued by the Tories in 1979. By 1979, of course, there were only a dozen or so local governments that had not modernized their school system, but Conservative determination to preserve private secondary education promised to keep the issue alive by devising an 'assisted places scheme' that would subsidize brighter pupils attending independent schools. Again, the immediate issue is not who may be right or wrong, but that decisions affecting both national and local responsibilities are so abruptly changed and erratically formulated.

Other examples of central–local confusion which places enormous administrative demands on local government are land-use and financial planning. During the reorganization there was great concern that local governments should reorganize internally to improve their planning capabilities. Elaborate consultation papers on financial planning were circulated by the DoE, and ninety-nine groups made detailed responses.[47] But in the final analysis no single structure for local planning could be found and each group, as we shall see in more detail below, was left to its own devices. Whether a standard local organization is in fact desirable is doubtful, nor was it the aim of most reform advocates. But in relation to administrative linkages the point is that the vitally important function of internal decisionmaking could not be raised in the highly compartmentalized British administrative system without strong central support. Once raised, the inability of administrators at the two levels of government to collaborate meant that the results were much less than hoped for, and did little to enhance local influence over departmental decisions within Whitehall. What was initially conceived as a major objective of global reorganization simply dwindled away in the void between national and local administration. Whitehall could not provide the leadership and local councils could not provide the determination to create new administrative capacities that might have given British local government a more effective voice in administrative decisions at higher levels of government.

Both national and local leaders have recognized the growing inability of central government to deal coherently with local problems.[48] In 1972, Stewart wrote that the 'Department of the Environment is not capable in its present form of dealing with urban problems, it is only capable of dealing with physical planning problems because it has cut itself off by the structure of government from the social and deeper problems'.[49] The economic crisis of 1973 made the weaknesses of central–local communication obvious. The subsequent economic crises of the late 1970s showed time and time again how the unstructured relationship left national government with nothing but crude and indiscriminate spending controls, while localities were unprepared, and in some cases unwilling, to formulate their policies and needs to meet new conditions. Tempers flared in early 1974 when the Prime Minister struck out at what he called 'the gross irresponsibility' of local government, and the Minister of Local Government and Housing announced that 'the party's over'. Late in 1974 the DoE began monitoring local government employment and any increase over existing numbers was forbidden. In mid-1975 the government notified local authorities that wage settlements with local employees that exceeded national standards would be deducted from the grant.[50] In fact, there is only one matter which forces officials at both levels to examine the overall structure of local government policy, and that is the subsidy to local budgets. Stunned and outraged, local government under both the Callaghan and Thatcher governments labored under arbitrary cuts in subsidies. At both the national and local levels, the major services fought their individual battles to survive. A decade of reform had not provided a workable organizational network between levels of government.

As happened so often in the past, it was national, rather than local, government that took the initiative to moderate local distress. The Consultative Council on Local Government Finance was announced by the Chancellor of the Exchequer in early 1975. Chaired by the Secretary of State for the Environment, the Council includes the ministers from the major service departments, representatives of the Treasury, local government associations and a small number of elected local government leaders. With a membership of about fifty persons, its quarterly meetings are the sole official forum for discussing central–local issues collectively. Detailed preparations, as well as preliminary talks, occur in the subgroups organized around major problems: the grant, capital investment, statistics, manpower.[51] Although the Council was created because ministers realized they often gave inconsistent advice to local authorities, it has no powers to amend national directives from the functional departments, nor does the Treasury or the DoE have to take its advice.[52] Lacking the network to influential local leaders and the localized administrative network of France, the Council remains an instrument of national policymaking rather than a collective force to bargain with Whitehall.

Another important concession was to admit the local government associations to the early discussions of the Public Expenditure Survey in 1976. Such a request had been made four years previously and some information had been forthcoming. But the PESC exercise has no direct input from local government, and the Treasury works with estimates independently prepared by the national departments for each local service. There remain important issues to be resolved over how the Treasury calculates spending needs, the inability to convert local accounts into national accounting form, and the failure of PESC to provide clear guidelines about how total local spending might relate to services. As the DoE testified before the Layfield Committee, 'There is no organized system of consultation and planning stretching across from local to central government.' In a revealing addition, they note that this 'merely reflects central government's own organization and procedures'.[53] Enmeshed in an administrative structure that provides little opportunity for close communication and that effectively excludes conflict, the central administration has begun to recognize its dependence on local government. Compared with the elaborate network interlocking central and local administration in France, it is, nonetheless, a rudimentary structure. The fragility of these arrangements was fully exposed in 1979 when the Secretary of State of the DoE announced with virtually no discussion that the entire grant system would be abolished, to be replaced with a subsidy based on criteria of national government's own choosing and coupled to equally arbitrary measures to limit local tax powers.

Unable to compartmentalize national and local level administration, the formulation and execution of French policy emerges from protracted bargaining and mutual adjustment. Even the strong governments of de Gaulle were unable to cut through this network, and from Pompidou's presidency in 1970 its influence grew to proportions comparable to the Third and Fourth Republics. But France, unlike Britain, has always been fascinated with the structure of the state. In the late 1960s there were a number of serious studies and telling attacks on the weaknesses of French administration,[54] but, unlike similar dissatisfaction with the civil service in Britain in the 1960s, French analyses necessarily fastened on the central–local administrative and political network. The paradoxical, and by no means unintentional, purpose was to use local influence *against* a cumbersome national administrative system. The bifurcated British administrative system rules out such a subtle strategy, and it is indicative of the grip of national administration that two decades of reform and reorganization at the national level have done little to check Whitehall's influence, and virtually nothing to create a more elaborate system of communication and bargaining between national and local government. There are, of course, no reasons why a powerful central administration should immerse itself in local problems if national objectives can be imposed so effortlessly. The spirit of change in the new French regime was conveyed in Pompidou's speech before the Cour des Comptes. 'Our system of control has developed progressively and without doubt exaggerates the opinions, permits, formalities and previous authorizations needed for decisions. This method certainly has the advantage of foreseeing errors and abuses, but at the price of grave inconvenience . . . This situation should be redressed . . . .'[55]

There were some signs that compromise began under de Gaulle. The *loi foncière* of 1967, which was considered an advance in local land-use planning, gave communes the right to engage private planners. When the central administration failed to produce the decrees putting the reform into effect, the large cities, particularly those under Socialist mayors, found other legal loopholes, in order to engage their own urban planners and engineering contractors.[56] Though not always perceived as such at the grassroots, the urban communities in 1969 were a step toward increased local influence over administrative decisions. But the flood of reforms came with Pompidou and Chaban-Delmas. In late 1970 a hundred or more detailed and antiquated controls on the communes were removed. More important, a law in November 1970 envisaged a clearer division of responsibilities for local investment, and established a method of placing public investment in four categories: state, regional, departmental and communal.[57] Modifications to the *loi foncière* in 1970 expanded the idea of contractual relationships between lower-level government and the center, the most important device being the Zones d'Aménagement Concerté (ZAC).[58]

The theme running through all these changes was the necessity to form new local organizations that did not rely directly on the state. In Britain, interlocking organizations of this type have often been regarded with suspicion by both national and local government. Both British practice and preference more sharply differentiate private and public interests so that the French objective to introduce more private management and private investment in new organizations to link local and national aims was not pursued. In Britain in the early 1970s there was great stress on *internal* reorganization of local authorities, but relatively little concern with the instruments by which hopefully stronger localities would then bring their new capacities to bear on national decisions. The structural design was in its essentials unchanged.

Even in an organizationally more complex France the force behind many of these changes diminished because the hard-line Gaullists saw these measures as threats to the hegemony of the state.[59] Indeed, their hostility toward these reforms is perhaps the best proof that a major policy departure had been undertaken. They were equally suspicious under Giscard d'Estaing when central controls were further diminished by the *loi Galley* of 1974 on land use, the housing reforms of Barre in 1975 and the law of 1980 on the development of local responsibilities. While these efforts to disperse the power of the central administration are obviously controversial, especially the 'privatisation' of public power, these new policies suggest that our stereotype of the French administrator may need revision.

Another important link in central–local administration is the planning process. There is a large literature on the Commissariat Générale du Plan (CGP) and extensive speculation about myth and reality in the French planning process. From a policy perspective, the critical change was that the Gaullists, motivated by their determination to rebuild France, took state intervention seriously and worked to integrate local level administration with central planning machinery. As happened with other Gaullists efforts to manipulate the communes, the outcome was a curious blend of local demands and national objectives. By the time that the Gaullists settled into power the Fourth Plan (1962–65) was nearing completion, and planning remained a creature of the Ministry of Finance. De Gaulle inherited the modest regional organization from the 1950s, a regionalism which the plan had recognized by creating *tranches opératoires*, but like the larger plan itself the regional targets were not closely linked to the ministries and the planners had no access to local government.[60] The regional and local objectives of the plans were loosely framed and, much as they remain in Britain, concentrated on boosting depressed regions, mostly by encouraging industrial development.

The Fifth Plan (1966–70) was the first well-developed effort to transform a plan into regional components. The regional reforms of

1964 had created consultative bodies which were able to react to proposals, if not yet actually able to participate.[61] The plan's regional investment goals were still spelled out in general terms, but organized over the plan period in *tranches régionales*. The weaknesses that appeared during the implementation of the Fifth Plan inspired many of the reforms of the early 1970s. The regional investment proposals were not sufficiently detailed, and rarely translated into economic terms that would permit their evaluation and integration in the central planning process.

Although planning established a beachhead in the Ministry of Finance with the foundation of the Forecasting Directorate in 1965, the financial shortcomings of the regional and local proposals were easy targets for the ministry. Like the British Treasury, the Ministry of Finance resisted external control over its economic powers. But unlike Treasury decisions on local finance, the organizational conflicts were reproduced at most levels of government, and have been carefully documented by the Crozier group.[62] In brief, the enthusiastic planners in Paris were sadly disappointed. Industry had the managerial staff and the close communication to respond to planning incentives, but government seemed lethargic. The unintended effects were not only to blunt Gaullist designs to use regional planning to control communes and departments, but also to give the despised local notables yet another instrument to plague national government.

By 1970 both the energetic modernizers of France and their critics on the Left were upset, but the experience of the previous two plans clarified the necessity for institutional change. Ironically, the administrative system was despised by both groups. The reformers were impatient with administrative infighting, while the Left felt that the plan was only another instrument of a corrupt and arbitrary state. Had the administrative system been as successful as industry in accomplishing the plan's objectives, these complaints would have been more credible. By the Sixth Plan (1971–75), regional plans were more developed and the regional organizations could discuss the future with real programs before them.[63] The preparations of the 1960s began to pay off. Under the 1967 *loi foncière*, regions, departments and large towns were required to produce investment plans with financial and economic documentation. The CGP organized 'intergroups' to try to link its recommendations more closely to both the Ministry of Finance and the service ministries. Another step toward interministerial cooperation was the regional formulation of the budget, itself a major concession by the Budget Directorate which previously had regularly opposed any limitations on its annual cycle of approval and control.[64] An even greater obstacle has been the regional and departmental representatives of the Ministry of Finance, the *trésoriers payeurs généraux*, whose approval is required for local investment credits. Nonetheless, after a decade, the combined efforts of the planners, DATAR, and their allies in the Ministries of the Interior and Infrastructure, managed to move investment planning, if not its control, out of the Ministry of Finance.

Not all the contractual schemes worked well, but the contracts could be adapted to a variety of local problems and overcame the difficulties of linking central administration to the cities and towns. In contrast to the British tendency to rely on direct controls organized around specific services, France built a new network of influence which enveloped the subnational system and relied on the incentive of investments. Unlike Britain, the strategy unfolded over several years of mutual adjustment, rather than being pronounced by Parliament and ministers. The first stage was to organize contractual investments for the urban communities and the new towns (*villes nouvelles*), later adding contractual arrangements for middle-sized towns (*villes moyennes*), then for small towns and eventually rural areas (*contrats du pays*).[65] The lower levels of the administration were buttressed and reorganized as the contractual devices were extended. The overlapping problems of land use, housing and industrial development were interlocked rather than functionally isolated from each other. The British administrative system does not have a similar organizational capacity to build on the interdependence of local decisions, and neither national nor local decisionmakers are disposed to use their influence in this way.

The intransigence of both British and French national administrators on the subjects of reform and democratization is clear, but the French have displayed an ability to organize government around problems rather than around functions. When Pompidou demanded in 1970 that the regions should not become 'screens' between the state and the localities, new administrative devices were found and indeed were then already being generated in the diverse and interlocking investment plans and local contracts. Giscard took a more cautious view of national and regional planning, partly because of his disapproval of more autocratic Gaullist planners when he was Minister of Finance in 1965 and partly because economic growth was a less compelling and attractive goal by 1974.[66] In any event the ties between DATAR and the CGP were broken by moving DATAR to the Ministry of Infrastructure, and later to the Interior.[67] With the economic dislocation and energy crisis of 1973, planning itself was downgraded and the contractual process, especially with the proliferation of small programs, was more overtly politicized. By the Seventh Plan, the regional projects were confined largely to assistance for depressed regions such as Languedoc-Roussillon and the Pyrénées. Thus, what many regard as a more ponderous administrative system had, over a period of ten years, shaped new policy aims and adjusted to new national objectives in ways that elude British central–local administration.[68]

If the transformation of central–local relationships means an ability to remold administrative procedures and reallocate administrative resources, the French administrative system, however reluctant and defensive it might have been, seems to have come closer to transforming itself over the past decade than the British system. Administrative change in the British system has been largely confined to the local level. To a considerable extent, the adaptability of French administration is derived from local pressures and infiltration. Paris must keep in touch with its field administration, central departments must take account of the calculations of their own and other ministries' field services, and the frontiers of the administrative system are guarded by ambitious junior members of the various *grands corps*. Although the departmental planning units may have become 'bureaus for studies whose conclusions are obligatory for neither industrialist or ministers',[69] the efforts to remodel French government over the past two decades elicited responses from administrators at all levels of government.[70] The hierarchical bifurcation of the British administrative system makes the territorial networks and mutual adjustment unnecessary. Just as Parliament does not wish to be disturbed by direct political intervention of local politicians, so also the higher civil service avoids much of the tiresome process of local bargaining that is commonplace in France. In Britain national-level politics and administration are mutually reinforcing to exclude local influence on national policies, and, in turn, local government often appears to obstruct national objectives.

AGGREGATING LOCAL DECISIONS: NETWORKS FOR WHAT?

As the state takes on more responsibilities, intermediate levels of government to monitor, guide and evaluate localized activities become increasingly necessary. In every welfare state the territorial substructure of national agencies has multiplied, and the reconciliation of these organizations with the politics and administration of local government is a major structural problem.[71] History provided France with one peculiar advantage, the prefecture, but after two centuries of development this institution also has limitations as a policymaking structure. For both political and administrative reasons, no similar intermediate-level decisionmaking bodies had been widely accepted in Britain. Thus, while France rearranges and recombines territorial units in order to meet new national objectives, the situation has been almost the reverse in Britain. Matching functions to territory is a major problem within any subnational system, but has become a constant source of confusion and controversy in British local government. The reasons are partly political, and they extend the unfortunate dichotomy of town and country which was described in Chapter 2. If anything, the design of new policymaking units has aggravated local government's problems as national policies continually erect and dismantle new territorial organizations that are often incompatible with the territorial jurisdiction of local government. As new intermediate-level agencies are formed, they become the tools of central departments; links to local government are, at best, tenuous.

The uncertainties surrounding British intergovernmental relations are a product of the compartmentalized functional control exercised from the center, and with the high priority on keeping Parliament and the Cabinet in name, if not in practice, as the supreme policymaking bodies of the entire system. The global reorganization accepted this tradition, but the growth of public services, many of them directly loaded onto local government, directly conflicted with the simplifying assumptions of central–local relationships. In the course of the reorganization itself, the new territorial design created severe redundancies and inefficiencies in the provision of local services.

Many of the old boroughs that were demoted to districts resented their loss of functions to the new counties. The result was that in the initial stages of reorganization a special plan for 'agency arrangements' was needed,[72] and in 1978 Labour unsuccessfully tried to make changes to strengthen some districts.

Agency arrangements had been incorporated into the 1972 Act and gave the DoE sweeping powers to arrange and to adjudicate requests to share services. Wood notes that the 'aspirations of departmental officers were pipe-dreams' and during 1973 the Department received over 200 requests for modifications of the functional responsibilities mandated by a law which had not even gone into effect.[73] The arrangements for highway construction, garbage disposal, libraries and planning facilities posed particularly difficult problems. Those who think French administrators have excessive powers should note that there was no appeal from DoE decisions. Nevertheless, in only a few cases are appeals from districts to the central administration successful.[74] Although the DoE's arbitrary power to accept and reject collaborative proposals among local councils was to be terminated in 1974, the intricacy of local services necessitated extending this power.

The confusion between the spatial jurisdiction of services and the political demarcation of local government is a classic problem. Following the Local Government Act of 1972, a number of regional bodies were organized to coordinate regional health, transport and water services. Local government had only a minor voice in their design and in several instances strong objections were ignored. Finding appropriate decisionmaking bodies has been most difficult where policies overlap and do not readily fit the functional organization of local governments; as in consumer services, pollution control and, more recently, inner city programs.[75] A recent survey of progress in solving area and functional needs concludes that 'policies for areas have been hopelessly fragmented'.[76] Because demands change from year to year, and the scope of existing services is altered for numerous reasons, the intermediate links are of crucial importance. British officials were not unaware of these problems, but the strong claims of central departments meant that intergovernmental problems did not figure strongly in the new legislation. The intermediate links were left to each major service under central supervision.

The problem of reconciling local services with central administration was raised over a decade ago by the Committee on the Management of Local Government and is rooted in the shortcomings of local government committees. Although central government reviews the Standing Orders, or council procedures, for local government, there is no general statutory control over internal organization beyond checks on appointment and conditions of service for the directors of some local services.[77] As major new services have been added to local government since the turn of the century, the laws sometimes required a local committee of elected councillors to oversee the service concerned and to make budgetary recommendations to the council. But the law 'does not define the relationships between members and officers, between officers and committees or the council, or between one officer and another: the official structure is left to custom and to the conditions of service of officers'.[78] Much like Parliament, the local councils are individually responsible for their own organization and procedures. The result was that under the old structure councillors often spent over fifty hours a month in committee meetings, and held an average of nearly six committee memberships, over eight in the top-tier authorities for counties and boroughs.[77] The time-consuming and detailed demands made on committees meant that older members and often the indirectly-elected aldermen tended to dominate committee business. These pressures also meant that committees had to rely heavily on the local administrative official for each service. A number of Town Clerks frankly admitted 'that, in the main, policy springs from the official side'.[80]

The surveys of the inner workings of the British councils left little doubt that the country was getting the worst of both worlds. Local democracy and efficiency was handicapped by the long tenure and proprietary inclinations of committee chairmen. Like French mayors, many chairmen had run their committees for over fifteen years. Officials were sometimes frank in expressing their distaste for having to submit written requests to their committee chairmen for erasers and pens. The task of the chief local government executive, in most instances the Chief Clerk, varied unpredictably throughout local administration. In some cases, notably Coventry, Bedford, Newcastle-upon-Tyne and Camden in London, the councils had begun to introduce more efficient, coherent methods.[81] The Maud Committee praised these steps toward modern management, and recommended that all councils should adopt some form of 'management board'. The Committee also felt that the membership and number of committees should be reduced, that the Clerk should be transformed into a chief executive with enlarged planning and financial responsibilities, and that the departmental structure of the local governments should be simplified. The plea for further delegation of local government business to administrative officials was repeated by the Royal Commission.[82] The aim, as Richards says, was 'to transform each local government unit into a minor model of our system of national government'.[83] That this strategy might simply reproduce the problems of national government at the local level does not seem to have been considered. Nor was concern voiced over whether the relationship between politicians and administrators in Whitehall was either appropriate or even workable for local government.

The appearance of the Bains Report[84] in the midst of the reorganization testifies to the growing internal problems of local government, and to the peculiar relationship worked out in the British subnational system. The parliamentary debate concentrated on territorial problems, and dealt much less with local services. At the national level, Whitehall officials were themselves confined to their departments and unfamiliar with organizing local government. Both Whitehall and Westminster wanted to improve the organization of local government, but neither had very clear ideas about how to achieve this goal. Virtually reversing the French sequence of reorganization, there was relatively little thinking about why local government had become so inefficient or why a few local authorities had taken the initiative in introducing more sophisticated executives and policy committees. In 1974 a survey showed that the policy committee had been widely accepted and the number of committees had been reduced, but that the number of members remained much the same as before.[85] New internal structures appeared to be grafted onto old habits.

The Bains Committee wanted a unified 'policy and resources committee' involving both managerial methods and financial planning. It provided several models, but the assumption was that local committees would cease individual bargaining for services in the Whitehall fashion and would jointly adjust needs and resources in the policy committee. In fact, the service committees survived more or less unchanged as the functionally defined guardians of specific services. Advanced forms of corporate management often did not penetrate the top levels of decisionmaking.[86] A 1975 survey of the less ambitious proposals for improved planning showed that nearly a third elected to keep the finance committee separate from the general policy committee, which, of course, insures that comprehensive planning will be stubbornly resisted. As the report noted, the past lives on in many ways.

The term 'corporate planning' as used in Britain does not mean giving local government to the systems analysts, but simply working on a more unified policy process and overcoming the departmental compartmentalization that exists locally as well as nationally. The 1975 survey concluded that although nearly all the reorganized authorities had a policy committee, 'most local authorities have preferred to adapt the traditional kind of departmental structure, i.e. one based upon the profession, than to construct elaborate directorates'.[87] While most reorganized governments did have a management team, it seldom reached beyond the heads of services. Spending cuts in 1974 and 1975 focused attention on the annual budget cycle and intensified rivalries for funds. Lacking the stimulus to adapt to administrative conditions that is found in France, the British councils revived their old habits of simply confronting national government.

There is some reason to think that budgetary reform within local councils has even reinforced old habits of decisionmaking rather than providing long-term perspectives and innovation.[88] One minister complained in 1975 that local government had 'too many chiefs too few Indians', but of course no one ever volunteers to become an Indian.[89] A recent study concludes 'there will be a gradual development of diversity, or rather that the diversity which is real in local government, if it is allowed by central government to develop by itself, will become apparent again'.[90] In practice, the result often proved even worse than the predicted decline into the old committee system. In 1976 the Birmingham City Council simply threw out the whole corporate management scheme, and in other councils the consolidated committee system and modernized management did not appear to protect councillors against their officials' expertise.[91]

The hope of achieving organizational homogeneity is only one of the more obviously idealistic aims of the British reorganization. Having placed emphasis on boundary changes, the central government had in fact diminished its bargaining power over how to organize the new authorities. With no direct administrative links, and virtually no exchange of personnel between levels of government, there was no way to encourage localities to accept common procedures. Even if this had been achieved, it would have had little effect on national departments who guard their prerogatives no less assiduously than local officers and committee chairmen. Though the situation is almost the reverse in France, the effect is similar. The administrative system imposes common rules and procedures on all local governments, but in practice there are immense variations to accommodate differences in the size, importance and political composition of communes. Both governments must, therefore, adjust to the diversity of local government, but the British do so through inadvertence and the French by intent. French mayors and prefects never define their roles according to administrative formalities, but their common interests are partially defined by the administrative system itself.

Of the many alterations in French administration under the Fifth Republic, the reforms of the prefectoral corps are most directly related to the aggregation of local needs and preferences. Like the other *grands corps*, they are not without their own organizational defenses. Since 1907 there has been an association of the prefectoral corps, enlarged and extended after the Second World War to include most senior employees of the Ministry of the Interior.[92] The restoration of their powers owes a good deal to Vichy, when they once again became the 'sole representatives of the state' and were widely used for other state functions.[93] They publish their own journal, and until 1964 organized their own internal grading system and recruited their own members. As they work more closely with the shifting political forces in the country, they have been more politically sensitive than the other *grands corps*. The organization of a special institute to train higher civil servants in 1945, the École Nationale d'Administration, was a potential threat to the prefectoral corps, but its organizational defenses proved strong.[94] Prefects have also been attractive candidates for ministerial Cabinets, and for high ministerial posts outside the Ministry of the Interior, where knowledge of the territorial structure is important.[95] In many ways the prefects were potentially the most vulnerable of the *grands corps* as France modernized, but in fact, as so often in the past, they have successfully weathered internal politics and change.

In contrast, Britain prefers an ostensibly autonomous local government system where strong local executive leadership might meet national needs. The ambitiousness of British plans for internal reorganization is suggested by seeing how an even stronger French administrative system was forced to make compromises as the tasks of local government grew over the past two decades. By the Fifth Republic the duties of the prefect were already proving to be too demanding for one person. In the Department of the Isère, for example, there were 114 committees through which local notables and officials consult on departmental decisions.[96] A study of the Department of Drome revealed sixty-eight consultative bodies for the prefect, although many of them rarely met.[97] In comparison with Britain, which is seeking to elicit participation and consultation at the local level, France seems inundated with consultative bodies.[98] In effect the prefect becomes both mediator and integrator at the departmental level. He or she is often responsible for the smooth operation of twenty or more local offices of Parisian ministries, and thousands of employees.[99] The organizational contrast in the two countries should not be missed. In Britain, central government hoped that local authorities would devise some version of a stronger executive, while in France, the central government set out to relieve an overburdened prefect of the detailed and time-consuming activities that kept him from becoming an effective executive.

Most prefectures involve four basic divisions: general administration (police, traffic, communications); finance (state, departmental and communal budgets, treasury officials); social assistance (public health, child care, services for elderly, ambulances); and engineering or urban services (land-use, construction, urban plans). The main divisions are responsible to ministries and to the prefect. The 1964 reforms tried to strengthen prefectoral control, but the service officials, often linked to their *grands corps*, were difficult to handle. The most important are the Directors of Infrastructure (DDE), who organized and consolidated departmental engineering and planning in the mid-1960s and who wield the influence of the prestigious *grands corps* of *ponts et chaussées*. The trend toward increased financial and investment planning in the 1970s created new tensions between the TPG and the prefect at both regional and departmental levels. Financial officials are linked to the entire system of banking and credit through the *grands corps* of the *inspecteurs de finance*. Situations of this kind mean that prefectoral relationships with the external services of major ministries involve delicate diplomacy. Their ambivalence is apparent in all the studies of prefectures. For example, Worms found that about a third of the prefects have confidence in their service chiefs while something over a third expressed reserve or indifference. They perceive their own roles with the same ambivalence. Roughly a third felt that regulatory control was working, while another third saw the need for collaboration.[100] Although the prefect is alleged to have over 2,000 legal powers, this multiple role as representative of the state, executive of the department and advisor of communes makes reorganization of the prefectoral system an exercise no less delicate than introducing chief executives in Britain.[101]

Like the British chief executive, the prefect must live with numerous cross-pressures and conflicting demands as well as a heavy workload. The most important difference between the two offices is that the political sensitivities of the prefect must, if anything, be more highly developed. In recent years, the 'waltz of the prefects' has increased in tempo, though it is perhaps now a little less bruising than under earlier Republics. After the 1962 elections about three-fourths of the prefects in those departments where Gaullist candidates had lost were changed.[102] Another reshuffle took place in 1967 when Fouchet, the

Minister of the Interior, relocated forty-eight departmental prefects.[103] Following the disastrous 1977 local elections, Barre is reported to have reassigned twenty-three prefectures, and another sixteen were moved after the 1978 legislative elections.[104] As Passeron has pointed out, such changes create serious discontinuities in local government, even though some changes are made to deal with particular problems and not all are political victims. Even so, in nearly every year since 1971 there have been about thirty new appointments in a system that includes only 120 top executive positions. The prefects have always lived under the dual threat of political manipulation from above and of capture by the mayors from below. But the movement of prefects can also be seen as a way to make key local-level officials sensitive to national policy, a more difficult problem for Britain which must rely on each central department to communicate with its professional counterparts within each local authority.

Unlike the other *grands corps*, the prefectoral corps has always been a mixture of political and administrative appointments. Although the corps itself resisted the formality of a statutory definition, it was agreed in 1964 that four-fifths of prefects would be recruited from the subprefects,[105] and that additional appointments to the corps would be made only to fill vacancies in the local government system, not for honorific or general administrative purposes. The rather complex system of grading seniority according to the importance of the department was abandoned, and a special effort was made to ease removal (*congé spécial*). Purely political appointments have become relatively rare, although the intermixture of political and administrative roles at the national level means that persons with distinctly political careers can be retired as prefects.[106] Despite assurances, the prefects responded slowly to the challenge of the 1964 reorganization and the discussion about the role of prefects continued into the 1970s.[107] National policymakers often saw the prefects as an obstacle to change and, further, as a weak link in implementing more advanced planning and development techniques. Nonetheless, progress was made in the 1960s to simplify departmental administration. The number of advisory committees was drastically reduced, information procedures were modernized and the prefect acquired the right to be consulted on any changes of the chiefs-of-staff of the various external services. In 1969, 140 procedures were simplified and shortly thereafter the Ministry of the Interior specified thousands of decisions that would be left at the prefectoral level.[108]

Contrary to the nineteenth century notion of the overbearing prefect, the expanded local tasks of the welfare state combine with administrative jealousies to make his job one of the most demanding administrative jobs in France.[109] In 1964 the Ministry of Finance fiercely resisted proposals to enlarge the prefect's economic role by giving him a voice in the use of state property and financial management. An attempt to give prefects the power to endorse the budgets of local Chambers of Commerce in 1968 was soon neutralized by the Ministry of Industry. The construction of primary schools is now totally decentralized, but the construction funds still are approved on a school-by-school basis by the Ministry of Education. Similar projects in agriculture, sports and health were assigned to prefects for approval, only to be rapidly recovered by the central ministry, which claimed the right to review budgets and investments. But the evidence of French internecine administrative warfare has its analogue in the British local government system. For example, the Department of Education carefully regulates book fines for local libraries. The more difficult question is how the conflicts and tensions within the administrative system relate to the formulation and implementation of national policy.

The formal unity of French administration is checked as each ministry, its external services and its local clients search for opportunities and advantages. The classic illustration is the deadly struggle between the *ponts et chaussées corps* of the Ministry of Infrastructure and the *génie rural*, the elite corps linked to the Ministry of Agriculture. The *ponts et chaussées* hoped to pursue their goals as communes modernized, while the *génie rural* relied more heavily on rural alliances with notables and officials.[110] The historic struggle focused on appointing Directors for the expanding DDE and on control of the departmental Groupe d'Étude et de Programmation (GEP) which would oversee urban development. In seventy-two of ninety-five departments the *ponts et chaussées* officials prevailed, and by 1971 most GEP directors were also from the same corps. When the Ministry of Infrastructure was again reshaped following the 1978 legislative elections, in order to organize a new Ministry of the Environment, the conflict over policy objectives revived. In contrast, the reorganization of the DoE in Britain has had almost no visible effects on local-level policy, and the departments brought under its umbrella continued to operate much as before.

The reallocation of tasks and reformulation of objectives creates new administrative networks, and, of course, renews administrative tensions. Viewed from within the French system, this may appear as just another form of administrative obstruction and inefficiency. Viewed comparatively, it may be that the French have an administrative system, at least for central–local relationships, that is more sensitive to policy change than the service-based British model. Prefects, departmental service chiefs and mayors recognize their mutual dependence, and in doing so collectively react to national programs and aims.[111] Although the administrative relationships between national and local government are even more specialized in Britain, developing incentives to adapt to new conditions and to formulate new procedures has proved more difficult. The reason may be that Whitehall hoped that local administration would modernize without the incentives and tensions that accompany the process of mutual concessions and bargaining which Paris builds into central–local administration.

British local government is more resistant to changing administration to meet new needs because there are comparatively few avenues through which to work out hierarchical and functional conflicts. The central government could only propose an improved local system – the corporate management scheme – which the localities then amended as each saw fit. While local autonomy has renewed the organizational diversity that complicates intergovernmental relations, this may prove a Pyrrhic victory, because each central department also remains free to maintain its own form of control and influence. The possibility that local decisionmaking might be ineffective or inefficient because central demands are either so erratic or ambiguous is seldom discussed. The net effect is that national policymakers have difficulty anticipating how new policies will be received and implemented and localities have difficulty responding collectively to what may be perceived as the shortcomings of national directives and programs.

THE VIEW FROM THE BOTTOM: DO LOCAL DECISIONS AFFECT THE CENTER?

For many years inertia was the major weapon of local government against the inroads and demands of national government. When localities were financially self-sufficient and when services were provided according to the vagaries of the marketplace, the center had much less bargaining power over local policy. The center was likewise much less dependent on how towns and rural areas did or did not implement national policy goals and how they conformed to the needs of the national economy. The protests by local mayors and councils over the past two decades can be looked upon as a sign of major re-structuring of central–local relationships in nearly all welfare states. Local government is being asked to depart from its sometimes petulant and usually passive posture of the prewar era, but national governments themselves have ambivalent responses to and uncertain strategies for the necessity for closer integration of decisions between levels of government.

The efforts of the British to introduce more refined policymaking procedures at the local level have yet to develop effective links to national policy; so that, in many respects, local choices are more con-tained than are those of French mayors and councils. In a way, Britain tried to preserve nineteenth century national constraints while building twentieth century urban government. Again we find that the alleged formality of the French system paradoxically proves an advantage. The supervisory powers of the prefect and the *tutelle* provide an unmistakable, if not always workable, focus for the inte-gration of local and national decisions. The transformation of the *tutelle* from its old administrative emphasis to the tasks of planning and finance has not always pleased the localities, but the mutual interests of national and local government are now more explicitly defined than they were in the days of arbitrary supervision.

Both countries have undertaken a number of reforms to bolster the local decisionmakers.[112] Perhaps the most controversial of these was to pay local councillors and mayors. If elected members are asked to take on more executive functions and if councils are to be more repre-sentative, then compensation is needed. The charitable tradition has died slowly in Britain and the political system had always fiercely proclaimed that elected representatives should have no pecuniary interest in their decisions.[113] Since the Local Government Act of 1948 councillors could apply for a small allowance to cover expenses and loss of income. The Committee on the Management of Local Government made it clear that there was not 'an inexhaustible supply of leisured gentlemen ready to undertake council work',[114] and recommended that members of the new 'management boards' have part-time salaries. The 1972 Act still tried to hedge the issue by providing attendance allowances, but based them on equal rights to compensation and eliminated the laborious procedures for specific allowances. The Labour Party, however, has long felt that its members are disadvantaged in participating in local government, and the issue was reopened in 1976. The Robinson Committee recommended that all councillors should be paid £1,000 a year. Additional payments could be made at local discretion for special duties, depending on size of the local authority, and the earnings allowances were to be continued but simplified.[115]

As happened on many previous occasions, Labour was again cast as the villain because the Callaghan government could not afford the cost, estimated at £30 million, to adequately compensate local councillors. All the efforts to reorganize internally seemed to have brought little relief to hard-pressed councillors who were found to be working seventy-nine hours a month on the average in 1974, compared with fifty-six hours a month in 1964. Nor had the re-organization significantly changed the social composition of local councils. Women were still underrepresented; the middle-aged and middle class predominated; and the retired continued to carry the burden. Though circumstances differ greatly among councils, the Victorian attitude of charitable good works still seemed to permeate local government service, and, in turn, no doubt reinforced resistance to more modern methods of planning local business.

Compensation for French mayors is complicated by the great variation in the size and importance of the communes. The government has been no less reluctant than the British government to compensate mayors. The conditions of their service, their legal responsibilities and their compensation is part of the Code de Communes, which provides allowances for lost earnings and expenses connected with their duties. Finding a solution is easier in France because payment could be attached to a similar system worked out for deputies, which the Socialist Party favors. The Socialists proposed a law to give mayors of cities over 150,000 the same treatment as deputies and to give full-time pay to mayors in towns over 20,000 persons. Until 1980 the earnings allowance, adjusted to the population of the commune, ranged from 676 francs a month for the smallest communes to over 9,000 francs for the mayors of Lyon, Marseille and Paris.[116] Employers are also obliged by law to give elected officials leave in order to fulfill their duties, but there have been complaints that these obligations are not properly observed.

Being more important political figures than British mayors, the French mayors are better able to extract compensation from Paris. The Prime Minister himself promised more support in the Blois Program and his 1978 election statement, and the 1979 law on developing communal responsibilities consolidated and extended compensation, including pension rights and social security benefits.

Ever sensitive to the political advantages of the *cumul des mandats*, it was also agreed that a Senator or deputy, who receives more generous allowances and pay, might assign half his compensation to an assistant on the municipal council. This concession will, of course, be of value to local party organizations and help perpetuate the links between national and local politics. Mayors of cities of over 30,000 persons (229 cities in 1975) will be fully paid, and in cities over 100,000 (39 cities in 1975) assistant mayors will also be paid.

The complexity of French bargaining over compensating local politicians contrasts with the persistence of centrally-designed and centrally-organized reform in Britain. The creation of a relatively weak local ombudsman or Commissioner for Local Administration is another example. Like his parliamentary counterpart, the local ombudsman cannot initiate investigations nor are local councils bound by his decisions. In 1969, Wilson proposed machinery to investigate complaints about local administration, and Labour's White Paper on reorganization outlined how a review body could be established outside the central machinery of government. The Conservatives also favored a local ombudsman, but placed more stress on efficiency. Just before Labour returned to office in 1974, the Conservatives established a Commission for Local Administration, composed of three ombudsmen for England and one each for Wales and Northern Ireland. Although the Commission receives several thousand complaints each year, only a few result in full investigations and enforcement is left to public opinion.[117] A recent evaluation reports that the Commission is not swamped with frivolous complaints, as was anticipated, but that there is a tendency for middle-class citizens to use the service more than the less privileged.[118] Under the French system, protection against maladministration is a standard feature of administrative law and every citizen has the right to appeal his or her treatment to the local Administrative Tribunal and ultimately to the Council of State.

The local government systems of most advanced states have tried to strengthen locally-elected officials in part because the influence of the local administration increases as the burden of local government grows. Unless ways can be found to retain active and effective local councils not only local democracy but also effective local influence over public policy diminishes. The growing importance of local decisions has produced another threat to effective government. A rash of corruption has swept over both the British and the French systems in the past five years. The Poulson affair in Britain and the Aranda affair[119] in France are examples of the ways that cynicism and abuse can undermine local administration and, in turn, justify new and stronger central control and supervision. A recent scandal in Wales produced thirty convictions, including the vice-chairman of a county planning committee.[120] Under these pressures the Heath government, no doubt aware of the harm that such exposure might do, appointed the long-serving Lord Redcliffe-Maud to head an inquiry on local government conduct. The inquiry documented the small (in absolute terms) number of infractions and recommended that there be a public register of local councillors' financial interests.[121] It also gave advice that Whitehall has not yet observed in its own conduct, namely, that 'the aim should be to keep the total quantity of confidential business as small as possible'.

Not to be outdone by the Conservatives, Wilson, on returning to office in 1974, appointed a Royal Commission on Standards of Conduct in Public Life. Without waiting for new recommendations, the Prime Minister had a draft code of local conduct circulated to local authorities and their associations in 1974, and a year later it was confirmed by a DoE circular.[122] One year later the Royal Commission recommended that legislation on corrupt practices affecting both councillors and administrators be consolidated, that internal review procedures involve the minority party in the council, and that national parties more promptly and severely discipline local councillors charged with a criminal offense.[123] Many of these situations are, of course, already covered in the codes and laws affecting French local government and administration. Like Britain, France has also turned to more open administration to restore public confidence, and to provide a public check on official abuse. Many towns and cities, particularly those under Socialist and Communist mayors, have more active public information programs than in the past.

In relation to local decisions, the visibility of French departmental administration and the controversial use of the *tutelle* had a parallel in the office of the Clerk. Although we lack studies of how administrative influence is used within British local councils, it was the Clerk who ensured that councillors were informed, placated and organized, and who ultimately tried to coordinate services.[124] The introduction of the policy committee has not produced uniform structures within councils, nor has it provided an effective link between policymaking at local and national levels of government. How councillors express their views varies greatly with the political composition of the councils.[125] Within the councils interservice rivalries persist, and are not mediated at intermediate levels of government as in France.

In councils where Labour or the Tories have ruled by caucus for many years, the policy committee and chief executive may concentrate policymaking powers even more.[126] In Humberside, for example, the local Labour Party rigidly followed the Model Standing Orders provided by the national party headquarters and took all chairmanships for itself.[127] In a non-partisan local authority the effect may be to estrange councillors even further from decisionmaking, while preserving many of the defects of overly detailed local control that plagued the old system.[128] For Britain even more than France, the vast majority of local decisions are inescapably non-partisan and effective organization is crucially important in the provision of basic services.[129] In some respects the chief executive and the policy committee produce the worst of both worlds, both accentuating arbitrary political control where councils are dominated by a single party, and providing less opportunity for councillors to enter into decisionmaking under mixed political control. It is no doubt for these reasons that most local authorities established larger policy committees than recommended by Bains, and tended to preserve the independence of service-based committees.

The advocates of the policy committee did not see it as reducing local control of policy, but quite the reverse. Stewart, one of the most enthusiastic advocates of advanced planning, writes that improved management 'should be to assist the political process not to assist a retreat from politics'.[130] What its advocates could not do was to alter relationships with central government. An unending flow of requests placed more complex responsibilities on local government, while presuming that localities would develop their own abilities to coordinate and plan interdependent services.[131] In fact, the central departments had almost nothing to say on the Bains Report, nor were they helpful in suggesting how local services might be reorganized.[132] Central government was left with a variety of local decisionmaking processes even less susceptible to overall direction than the old system, and the vertical compartmentalization of policymaking was reinforced. The reformers were very explicit that 'local government has yet to govern',[133] because of its concentration on single services, but they could do nothing to overcome a functional compartmentalization at the national level which is endowed with all the force of Cabinet and ministerial power. The reorganization of the policymaking machinery of local government has become a lost opportunity,[134] not only because localities naturally adapted it to their own needs and preferences, but because national administration had neither the incentive nor the capacity to encourage change and to utilize the more sophisticated proposals for which reformers hoped. Unlike France, the rewards and success of national administration are not dependent on improved performance at the local level.

The British local government system, not too surprisingly, duplicates the politics of Westminster and the policymaking of Whitehall. Internal reorganization would be easier if local administration were more relevant to national objectives and guidelines. The expanded role of local government presupposes a continual process of reshaping and redirecting policies. If the interdependent organization of central and local services is not asserted, control tends to gravitate toward the officials that can exercise an overall, if somewhat indiscriminate, control at both levels of government, namely, the Treasury and the local finance officer. Unlike in France, the administrative system precludes comprehensive evaluation or comprehensive reform. A curious effect has been that local councillors may even resent national efforts to change local administration which may sometimes undo local initiatives, and may introduce more political uncertainties in a system that already has difficulty exercising overall guidance. In a lively exchange in the *Municipal Review*, a backbencher on the Newcastle District Council protested the arbitrary control of information and agendas in the modernized local council. Though the replies were mixed, councillors often felt excessively dependent on chief officers and found service committees, if not entangled in detail, deprived of information.[135]

Both territorial and functional constraints on the British subnational system discourage local administrative innovation. This British deficiency is present in excess in the French subnational system. The term 'network' (*réseau*) has been applied to decisionmaking in the communes because it describes the interlocking relationship of administration which generates endless possibilities for local collaboration.[136] The large cities are virtually autonomous in relation to the prefect and the administration carry on their business directly with Paris.[137] The intermediate-sized cities and larger towns work more closely with the prefect, but their relationship is one of mutual dependence and often one of *complicité* against Paris and its unreasonable demands. In the village or town, the mayor remains the *patron* so vividly portrayed by Wylie, and survives in small communes which have neither the resources nor the staff to meet the needs of modern government.[138] The local government system, contrary to the stereotype of French administration, adjusts to local conditions and bends the legal and formal requirements. The network introduces a self-adjusting mechanism in central–local administration which is unwelcome in the British subnational system.

Essentially, the French administrative system provides a wide variety of opportunities and incentives for the local government system. If most are based on national objectives, the local government system is left to engage itself. Although the policy of contractualization and economic planning analogue, *concertation*, have roots in administrative reform proposals from the 1960s, these ideas were not elaborated for local government until the 1970s, most clearly by the steps taken by Pompidou and Chaban-Delmas in the early 1970s to free communes from detailed administrative supervision. The aim essentially was to find new ways to disperse risks and conflict in the local government system. As Ledruc describes the new efforts, by no means welcomed by the more hard-line Jacobins of the Gaullist party, *concertation* 'translates (problems and difficulties) into tolerated and tolerable conflicts and provides ways of arriving at compromises'.[139] In many ways, the intricacy of the *réseau* linking administrators and mayors is ideally suited for such a strategy, but it is also ideally suited to exploit the incentives and funds that accompany it.

The network demonstrates the inability of French administration to unilaterally impose its will on communes. Grémion calls this 'the weakness of formal prohibitions of the state'.[140] Compared to Britain, the locally-elected officials are not pitted against local administrators, but are part of a political and administrative hierarchy reaching the top levels of decisionmaking. Senators and deputies, departmental officials and higher civil servants, mayors and technicians influence the administrative system. The critical exchange is not confined to local politicians interacting laterally with local administrators, but works through a complex system of bargaining and mutual dependence extending from the locality to ministries in Paris. Achieving local objectives and preserving local interests depends on alliances in the network. 'The capacity for effective intervention by the more important intermediaries depends on their aptitude to extract a local consensus in relation to the center.'[141] The prefect and the department have a special place in avoiding direct confrontation. 'The first virtue of the department is to be invisible, not to have itself talked about, to appear always as an outmoded structure and to benefit however from a strong republican legitimacy.'[142]

The network is also adaptable to local conditions and needs. Mayors are valued for their skill in manipulating diverse political resources, and are consulted on a wide variety of plans for local government, including the national plan, the local investment plan (*plan de modernisation et d'équipement* or PME), the territorial development plan (*plan d'aménagement rural* or PAR), as well as through the variety of semipublic corporations that may be established either solely in his commune or with other communes. The mayors' sphere of influence is not limited by service needs or administrative formalities, nor are they burdened with the heavy managerial responsibilities held by party leaders in British local councils. The result is that the mayor is able, as Becquart-Leclercq has outlined,[143] to manipulate social, political and organizational contacts in order to extend his or her influence over a wide range of official decisions at many levels of government.

Unlike the British local council party leader, the French mayor does not try to reproduce parliamentary order and party discipline in the commune. The local electoral system presupposes that he assemble a team rather than extend one-party government to local politics. Once in office the council in most cases unites to penetrate the administration.[144] There is little evidence that mayors feel discrimination on party lines in the local distribution of benefits, though towns with major national figures as mayors are able to extract more benefits from the state.[145] Whereas in Britain, the non-partisan behavior of local councils is elicited by the sheer burden of routine tasks, in France moderating party differences becomes a prerequisite to successfully penetrating the administration. The phenomenon of *apolitisme* has been most thoroughly explored by Kesselman and appears in the crucial brokerage role of mayors.[146] As described by Becquart-Leclercq, 'the power of the mayor depends largely on the favors he can obtain: jobs at city hall, recommendation for employment, getting a scholarship, improving a road, a ditch, advancing a file on retirement or construction, advice and services which combine to form a platform for the power [*assiette du pouvoir*] of the mayor in the commune, the power of intervention'.[147]

Through the network, relations between administrators and elected officials are governed more by policy decisions than by law or party politics. This is not to say that the powers of the prefect to review communal budgets, annul communal elections, dissolve communes and correct communal files are not important, but all these actions come under administrative law and can be reviewed in the courts. Nor does it appear that prefectoral power is regularly used in partisan ways. No less a figure than the leading Gaullist, Debré, found his commune of Amboise placed under direct prefectoral supervision in 1979 once the budget deficit exceeded approved limits. Neither the mayor nor the prefect benefit from prolonged legal disputes, although there have been some intensely fought decisions.[148]

There has also been a substantial effort to train local administrators so that they may compete more successfully with the national administrators.[149] An increasing reliance on private consulting firms was a further important step toward increasing local choice of technical assistance and freeing communes of domination by the national officials at lower levels of government.[150] Thus, the communes had two major concerns in the strengthening of local personnel powers under the 1980 law on communal responsibilities: to be freed of obligatory fees paid national civil servants in the preparation of local projects and loan applications, and to extend their rights to hire their own personnel. On the first issue, the law went no further than to guarantee that administrative fees could not be made a condition of acquiring permission for public works and to promise that a special committee (Comité d'allègement des procédures et des prescriptions techniques) would devise standard charges for technical services – an issue of special concern to smaller communes.

The law contains an entire section (Title IV) on communal personnel, which is a complex issue because of the variation in size of the communes and, of course, because local jobs enhance mayors' influence. Under the 1972 decree only communes with 150 or more employees could hire personnel without ministerial approval but permission to hire will now be given by a national commission (*Commission nationale paritaire*) which includes mayors as advisors. With understandable concern that mayors would overextend even these minor concessions, recruitment will be supervised by the departments and qualifications will be judged by a national training center in Paris (Centre de formation des personnels communaux). Communal employees will not be classified on the same standards as national civil servants, but the upper echelons (about 20,000 of the 539,000 local employees) are assured the same pay and benefits as national civil servants.

AREA VERSUS FUNCTION: HOW TO ENJOY TENSION

A major unforeseen problem of the welfare state has been the continuing conflict between allocating power by area and function. In the years immediately following the Second World War improved services and benefits were for the most part distributed, organized and financed from the center. The consequent national problems of coordination, evaluation and direction have only come to the fore in the past decade or so. The result has been that we have now passed through a decade of unparalleled reorganization, experimentation and prodding involving local government. Given the reluctance of both local and national politicians to take the lead in this process, change has been for the most part controlled, if not actually designed, by national administrators. But civil servants are rarely eager to change tested procedures and structure, nor was the bureaucracy a unified and coherent force.

In both local government systems, local partisan politics was unable to resist administrative requirements and central control. In the 1960s the numerous independent mayors of large cities were the bulwark of resistance to Gaullist reforms and in the 1970s even the mayors of the French Left proposed few radical changes. Though the political context differs, local politicians in Britain also find partisan attitudes of diminishing importance in most local council business. Corina finds that 'far from the parties giving a political aspect to the decision-making they frequently helped to eliminate political dialogue by inhibiting discussion in order to expedite the decision-making and by organizing a context to produce a working consensus'.[151] Much like national policymaking, the more complex local administration becomes, the more difficult it is for local politicians to change it.

The weakness of central–local political linkages in Britain, as compared to the French network, meant that national parties could embark on major changes that not only failed to respond to the administrative problems experienced at the local level, but that promised to make the administrative tasks of local government even more unwieldy. Labour was upset to see its urban strongholds functionally subordinated in the non-metropolitan counties, and the 1974 Election Manifesto, seldom a formidable constraint on the parliamentary party, stated that local authorities would be consulted about future regional arrangements for health, planning and water. The left wing of the party hoped to use the regional debate to increase the powers of the regional economic planning councils and to use these powers indirectly to restore control of local services to the cities and towns that had been downgraded to districts and that often found themselves working under Conservative county councils.[152] Labour's dilemma was that the new system of local government provided neither territorial nor functional flexibility. The administration links between national and local government had neither the authority nor the capacity to initiate the kind of self-adjusting process found in France. Tampering with areas was out of the question, while functions remained vertically compartmentalized under central departmental supervision. Neither major dimension of the local government system was open to change.

Early in 1977 the Labour Secretary of State for the Environment, Peter Shore, admitted that widespread changes were ruled out because 'if a mistake is made, the effects of that are felt across the country as a whole, and not confined to particular areas. Because the system is a uniform one, it restricts the opportunity for experimentation . . . and further, the uniform approach fails fully to allow for the proper expression of the regional and local diversities which add such richness to our cultural and political life'.[153] He did not explain why this enlightened view of diversity within local government was not more fully considered in 1970, but he did suggest that 'organic' change was now possible. The reorganization divorced many of the earlier larger, Labour-controlled boroughs from education and social services decisions in their counties.[154] Although Callaghan hoped to postpone the devolution debate, and the issue of stronger regional government within England, the local government group within the Labour Party favored modifications to help restore powers to oppressed Labour strongholds.[155] After local election losses in 1977, it appeared that Shore was hoping to restore lost powers to nine major cities of England, seven of which were under Conservative county councils. The Association of County Councils and the major service ministries opposed change.[156] In many ways, Shore was reliving Crossman's experience in 1966 when he had proposed reorganization. Without instruments for gradual change, there was no alternative to statutory reorganization. Shore's experience summarizes the dilemma of adapting the British local government system to changing needs and objectives.

Despite the resistance throughout 1978 from the DES and the DHSS, Shore succeeded in getting the Labour Party National Executive Committee to endorse his plan. The major immediate change would be to restore control of education to the nine deprived large cities, but changes in the health services were to be delayed until the Royal Commission on the National Health Service completed its work. Social services, traffic control, libraries, and consumer protection would also be reassigned to those enhanced non-metropolitan districts that so desired.[157] The plan would, as one critic pointed out, decimate counties with a single major city, such as Avon, where Bristol contains nearly half the county's population.[158] The longer-term intent of the plan, which kept alive the possibility of elected regional councils combined with further enhanced district powers, was to eliminate the counties as effective units of government and to resurrect the strong unitary authorities proposed by the Royal Commission in 1969.

Shore's plans for 'organic change' died when Labour lost the election, but they reveal how easily national politicians can intervene in issues of immense complexity at the local level with little regard for the consequences. Perhaps even more lamentable, the structural division of national and local administration means that even if a minister were prepared to take local advice, it would be most difficult to assemble advice in usable form and within narrowly conceived partisan objectives. As a distinguished local official wrote, 'The chief problem now is that, when power is seen to be up for grabs, sensible joint working arrangements and experiments between counties and the larger districts become difficult or impossible.'[159]

In fact, Shore's proposal would have introduced a fourth division of functional relationships by creating two different allocations of responsibilities in non-metropolitan counties (plus the GLC, metropolitan counties and Scotland). Britain had somehow managed to construct a pattern of central–local administration that is no less intricate than the diversity of the French system, but has not, and is not given, the capacity to solve administrative conflicts. One of the tireless advocates of local reform, Stewart, also condemned the proposals and pleaded for 'gradual adaptation of a structure to meet varying and changing needs'.[160] As we shall see in Chapter 7, the Tory Secretary of State, for quite different reasons, was no less reticent in using the concentrated powers of Parliament to reach his goals.

While Britain was reliving old problems in the 1970s, the French political debate on central–local relationships gradually produced a new consensus about changing the local government system. Unlike Britain, national leaders had a stake in this debate, and a somewhat complex series of laboriously constructed agreements became law. Without admitting that the prefect would become solely an executive of the department council, the parties of the Right and the Left favored lightening the *tutelle* by confining administrative approval to *a posteriori* controls.[161] These reforms were supported by both the Communist and Socialist Parties, though they would go further and have the departmental and regional councils elected by proportional representation. The Republican Party was specific about a number of administrative changes: the subprefect to be downgraded to a technical advisor; mayors and their assistants in towns over 30,000 to be fully compensated for full-time work; a law to protect local councillors and employees; and measures to 'bridge' local and national administration.

As we have seen, neither local nor national party organizations in Britain are instrumental in fashioning local reform policies. In France, the reforms of the late 1970s were the product of gradually accumulated political compromises involving both national and local party leaders. The Socialists spoke of the need to 'preserve and reinforce the multiplicity of cells at the base of democracy',[162] but like most parties were cautious about imposing cooperative and intercommunal arrangements. The Communists appeared more hesitant to endorse the proliferation of intercommunal agencies, and opposed 'supra-communal' agencies such as districts, urban communities and the new cities program.[163] The Gaullists and the Republicans were no less fervent in their defense of the commune as the bastion of French democracy, but the Republicans wanted more local democracy by introducing a communal referendum on major decisions and an annual public accounting of the budget. Though the Left would probably prefer that the region have stronger planning powers, its evolution into an intermediate-level planning body was accepted. All the parties supported efforts to train and upgrade the quality of local personnel.

The Guichard Report built on the emerging consensus about restructuring the administrative system. The objective was to improve the capacity of the communes to bargain with the administration by removing the necessity for previous approval of communal plans and projects. The *tutelle* would be 'banished'. The prefect would remain the departmental executive, but the departmental council was to be strengthened by a permanent departmental commission of councillors, which would, in turn, have specialized commissions to deal with major communal functions.[164] The proposed changes were consistent with the proposals of the parties: devising ways to allocate effective decisionmaking to lower levels of government and giving the communes more leverage over the departments. The policies of contractualization and *concertation* in the early 1970s had begun to devolve powers onto the departmental level, and the issue now became how to extend deconcentration to the elaborate communal structure. The changes were designed to respond to the expressed needs of mayors. The Bécam questionnaire showed that mayors feel more oppressed by the departmental services than by the prefect.[165] Of course, as Bourjol pointed out, change still depended on whether the state would tolerate unavoidable dislocations as policy implementation shifted to the new structure.[166]

As we have seen, in Britain national politicians rarely take a keen interest in local reform, but in France developing communal responsibilities became a key objective of Giscard's majority. But in virtually the reverse sequence of British reorganization, national compromises were made after local preferences were expressed and local agreement emerged. Strengthening the communes is, of course, consistent with Giscard's hopes to build a coalition of centrist parties, and his reform proposals were given wide publicity in the 1978 legislative elections. But in deference to his Gaullist supporters, more controversial issues, such as the *cumul des mandats*, were put aside. The Guichard Report rather ambiguously recommended that the 'local debate should not be confused with the national debate'.[167] Local reform was a major element in the Prime Minister's Blois Program. Following the victory of the Gaullists and Republicans in the 1978 elections, the President and the Prime Minister launched a major national debate on local reform.[168] Significantly, the issue was first raised in the Senate, where the Minister of the Interior outlined a threefold legislative plan affecting local elections, resources, personnel and councillors.[169]

Possibly the most dramatic contrast with the British approach to local reform is how French policymaking requires that gradual change be made on many problems, rather than seeking massive, and hopefully final, resolution of one issue at a time. From 1978 the Directorate of Local Government in the Ministry of the Interior became a task force for the coordination of the multiple reform strategy, and for the continued negotiation of delicate issues as the new legislation slowly moved through the Senate and National Assembly. The first law to be accepted in 1979 provided a global operating subsidy (*dotation globale de fonctionnement* or DGF), and was in many ways an expression of good faith by the government to help the next two, and more controversial, measures. The law on reform of direct local taxation and on a global investment subsidy (*dotation globale d'équipement* or DGE) was carried over into the 1979–80 parliamentary session. (On the details of the DGF and DGE, see Chapters 6 and 7.) The third measure – the law on communal responsibilities – became an omnibus measure, including mild provisions to encourage communal mergers, improved conditions of service for communal employees, more compensation and benefits for mayors, and further heightening of tutelary powers over communes.

Although the communes were disappointed in not acquiring more responsibility for local services, the diversity of needs and resources in the more articulated French system makes complete decentralization almost impossible. The mayors' own resistance to consolidation makes the British model inapplicable, and the more conservative economic policies of France no doubt make French policymakers reluctant to transfer functions which, as in Britain, the national government will necessarily be required to support. Both the Senate and National Assembly reports on the Omnibus Bill made it clear that, like local governments the world over, the communes would welcome more executive powers if the costs of new tasks were not also transferred.[170] Even so, France does not insist on the sharp demarcation of national and local functions found in Britain. The law could also take advantage of the more flexible territorial structure to construct intergovernmental groupings, some linked to departments and others to communal syndicates, to enlarge local controls over welfare, education, urbanization and police services.

MINIMIZING INTERGOVERNMENTAL CONFLICT: GOVERNING THE WELFARE STATE

Administrative power has grown because many of the policies of the welfare state have multiplied intergovernmental agencies, and because this trend confuses territorial and functional jurisdictions. Local councils and local-level administrators have a Hobson's choice. If they succumb to new demands placed on them through such agencies, they lose control of their own activity. If they refuse to cooperate with such agencies, they are almost certain to lose access and influence at higher levels of government. In both Britain and France, and very likely in most of the modern democracies, centralization advances by default. Although often resented, the closer relationship of French mayors to national administration gives them more national influence than does the large administrative burden for which the British local government system takes sole responsibility.

The devolution debate in Britain is only a more recent example of a long-standing habit of British national government to insulate itself against regional and local threats to parliamentary and cabinet powers. Although the Royal Commission on the Constitution, to be discussed in this section, made some intriguing suggestions on how territorial and functional problems might be adjusted to local needs, none of these was acceptable. Labour's White Papers on devolution and the subsequent legislation, while beyond the scope of this study in some respects, are full of precautions to see that the conduct of local affairs remains unchanged; perhaps even more important, to make sure that exclusive controls will remain unchallenged.

Much as in the case of central–local conflicts surrounding communal reform, French administration embodies regional tensions that can be traced back to the Revolution and earlier. Bloody as it was, Britain (or more properly England) had overcome regionalized resistance to national government before modern democratic government began to emerge in the late eighteenth century. The contrasting historical developments are of profound significance for subsequent attitudes and policies toward regional agencies and administration. In the nineteenth century, the Irish question again paralyzed Parliament and parties, and eventually led to another civil war, which reinforced British suspicions of intergovernmental organizations, and very likely British determination that parliamentary supremacy should be immune to the legal and political compromises of regional government. Oddly enough, the quasi-federal arrangements made for Northern Ireland have always seemed a constitutional aberration well remote from government in Britain itself.

But the emergence of the welfare state brought with it a multiplication of governmental agencies at intermediate levels of government.[171] Some of these, like British assisted areas and French regional planning, can be traced to the 1930s, but essentially the explosion of *ad hoc* boards, public corporations, regional organizations, and the rest came after the war. British local government was never consulted about most of these changes. Indeed, one of the unintended effects of relatively weak regionalism in Britain was to preserve differences within the local government system that have plagued every reform effort since 1888. Had the country faced the difficult regional problems of France, there might likely have been more concern with developing regional administration, and the Conservatives could not have indulged themselves so easily in the 'town versus country' dichotomy that dominated the 1888, 1929 and 1972 Acts.

The local government associations simply reproduced this dichotomy at the national level. The slow-moving postwar boundary commissions could be tolerated by national government in part because there were no other territorial and political forces demanding devolution. The two major parties found other disagreements to keep national politics alive, and they were not plagued by the regional differences in party organization and alignments found in France. By default more than design, regional policies on employment, industrial growth and income simply accrued to Whitehall. Local government was, as we have seen, heavily burdened and politically isolated. In the rapid nationalization of services and industries after 1945, localities were rarely consulted; nor is there any reason to suppose that they would have presented their own options if asked.

The proliferating intergovernmental agencies in France had a much more difficult time evading local politicians. After their initial suspicion in the early Gaullist years, the prefects, once the conduit for central authority, found it in their interests to buttress territorial influence. However poorly conceived and executed, the regional development of Brittany and the south of France depended on the field agencies of the departments, and defusing regional nationalism was no less crucial to de Gaulle's policies of *grandeur* than to industrial modernization. For the Gaullists, as for Giscard, regional development was a way of taking the political struggle into the enemy camp, especially in the Communist strongholds of southwest France and the Socialist strongholds of the north. In fact, the Socialist mayors and regional council presidents of Marseille and Lille have organized highly effective regional agencies which, in turn, use regional problems to extract resources from Paris. The game can, of course, be played by all levels of government including the President himself.[172] Giscard's dramatic visit to the southwest took him into Socialist strongholds where he proposed an ambitious development plan in 1979 involving 15 billion francs and embracing three regions. The Socialist deputy-council presidents, of course, quickly protested that his efforts were deceptive and inadequate.

For these reasons, intermediate-level organizations in France, even those spawned by the state, are embroiled in the central–local network. Only the Communist Party still argues for strong regional government, but even its aims are moderated by the departmental and communal compromises needed to win elections and to strengthen Communist mayors.[173] The complexity of central–local administration is also advanced by elite administrators, as we have seen in the multiplication of the *sociétés d'économie mixte*. The regional governments of France are stronger than anything yet attempted in Britain, but they are also infiltrated by departmental and local councillors, and compromised by the necessities of local administration.

If the communes create complexity by their numbers and size, Whitehall creates complexity simply by establishing directly dependent, but uncoordinated, subordinate regimes. Within the subnational system there are in fact four different regional arrangements: the essentially federalized government of Northern Ireland, the special cabinet status devised for the Scottish Office, the symbolic recognition of a Welsh subnational identity since the establishment of the Welsh Office in 1964, and England. Without describing all these arrangements in detail, an interesting point worth noting is that although they are ostensibly different regimes, their diversity has never impeded the growth of services and benefits. Except in the case of the Stormont Assembly before its demise in 1974, there is little evidence that these territorial administrative devices have influenced national policy, and virtually none that they serve as a channel from local government to Whitehall and Westminster. Were it not that the center has managed to do pretty much what it wished, one might suppose that Britain had indeed taken a leaf from the French book. The best measure of the power concentrated in London is the distance that the British government can travel toward regional government without making compromises with local government.[174]

The persistent regional tensions of France seem to have produced a compromise, while the centuries of plundering wars pacified Scotland, Wales and Ireland, and left them subordinate to Westminster. One can attribute the extremes to which the British have gone in order to preserve their territorial unity to some cultural quirk; or to an almost fanatical compulsion to preserve parliamentary rule uncompromised by territorial politics. Of the many ironies in this tragic tale, not the least is the continued refusal of Parliament and cabinet to risk failure in Northern Ireland.[175] The point is not that solutions to ethnic or religious regional conflicts are easy to find, but that compared to France the administrative simplifications that maximize the power of Whitehall to impose its will also minimize possibilities of using regional assistance and programs to build compromises with regional forces. Because the intermediate-level agencies of government are fashioned as instruments of central departments they are automatically excluded from the intricate process of bargaining and compromise to save political ends that has been used relatively successfully in France.

But the full paradox of the highly centralized regional administration of Britain is that it serves the interests of national politics without relieving regional tensions. The Labour government did not take a suicidal stance in 1976 once its survival seemed to depend on Scotland. If the Scottish Nationalists have been no less determined than the Ulster Unionists, they have not supported violence nor have they flagrantly rejected the law of the land. Both major parties were impressed in the late 1960s by growing Scottish Nationalist strength in national and local elections. By the 1970 elections both had promised some form of regional assembly.[176] In the second 1974 election, the Scottish Nationalists placed eleven nationalists in the Commons, and Wilson had no choice but to fulfill his promises of the 1960s. His handling of the issue, and the subsequent policy of Callaghan, provides a dramatic comparison with French territorial strategies.

Crossman himself notes the 'tremendous inhibition in the Party against home rule and against constitutional innovation of any kind',[177] though like his cabinet colleagues he was seldom reluctant to use major regional projects to the advantage of the party. The decision to appoint the Royal Commission on the Constitution in 1969 was a curious result of the refusal by the Head of the Civil Service to consider regional devolution until the Redcliffe-Maud report was completed, anxiety about threats from the left wing of the Labour Party, and relief that appointing the Commission would enable the Cabinet to postpone consideration of reform of the House of Lords.[178] Labour's position was not a happy one. Earlier compromises to placate regional sentiments resulted in overrepresenting Scotland and Wales in the House of Commons. Genuine regional government would no doubt entail equal parliamentary representation and Labour might lose as many as fifteen seats were equal representation restored.[179] The grim specter arose that Labour might become the party of the celtic fringe, as the Liberals had in their decline in the 1920s, leaving the Conservatives as the champions of England and in control of Parliament. As the surveys of the Royal Commission show, nationalist feeling was as strong in the north of England as in Scotland, and a good deal stronger than in Wales.[180] Genuine regional government was, therefore, a threat to the Labour Party.

The Royal Commission served the immediate interests of both Conservatives and Labour, for both were excused from doing anything about regionalism for nearly five years, and meanwhile could tell the voters they were hard at work. The Commission outlived two of its members, and the editor of *Public Administration* greeted its report in 1973 by recalling Hume's remark on his *Treatise in Human Nature* that it fell 'dead-born from the press'.[181] The Commission's conclusions can be summarized in various ways, but there are at least seven different proposals, none of which would strike directly at the accumulated power of Westminster and Whitehall.[182] Wales and Scotland would be given directly elected regional assemblies, but England would have reinforced regional planning bodies elected indirectly by the local authorities. The Scottish and Welsh bodies would hopefully have some spending powers, but the services assigned to them would be specified later. Financial decisions would be reviewed by a regional exchequer committee with Treasury representation. Block grants would in all likelihood still be needed and voted by Parliament.

The dissent by Crowther-Hunt and Peacock is in many ways a more coherent document, although politically even less acceptable.[183] They begin with a much more trenchant assessment of the power of Parliament and the incompatibilities within and between the existing regional organizations. They recommend seven directly elected regional governments (one Scottish, one Welsh and five English) with a clear statutory connection between local government and the regions, and a statutory policymaking role for the regional assemblies. The parliamentary implications of a defined territorial base to British politics are also spelled out in an ingenious scheme to partially convert the House of Lords into a forum for regional policy discussions, and to align some House of Commons committees more clearly with regional interests. The implication is that Parliament would accommodate territorial politics and policy, rather than manipulate national policies to suit electoral advantage. The dissent deals incisively with central government resistance by simply pointing out that Britain already has an elaborate administrative system of intermediary governments, which evade local control and which allow little or no room for regional or popular representation.

The debate on the Kilbrandon report was swamped by the oil crisis, the renewed threat of war in the Middle East, and growing evidence that a floundering Heath government would soon have to go to the country. With a barely workable majority after the first 1974 election, the Wilson government needed Scottish votes to survive, and quickly got its devolution proposals for Scotland and Wales into print. A year later Wilson proposed legislation.[184] Parliamentary distrust of territorial politics and the refusal to compromise national policies were clearly conveyed in the bland assertion by the White Paper that 'It would plainly be wrong to devolve to the Scottish and Welsh Assemblies powers over activities which substantially affect people elsewhere, or the well being of the United Kingdom generally.' Indeed, the implementation of this maxim was proposed in such a way that the new assemblies would be effectively hamstrung. For Scotland, the assembly was to fall under *ultra vires* rules; there would be no independent civil service; finances were limited to the block grant voted by Parliament and a surcharge levied on the local governments; local government procedures, health, social security and higher education were specifically reserved; the legislation hedged on housing, transportation and planning; and the industrial functions of the Scottish Development Agency kept under central control. The Welsh restrictions were more strict, though in the final version of the Bill the proposed assembly was permitted to alter the structure of local government. Clearly the Labour view was that regional government should have not a voice but a whisper in making policy.

Callaghan's hopes of action in the spring of 1977 were dashed when the Liberals refused to support such weak proposals. Like the Left in France, the Liberals see their hope for survival in stronger regions, and two Labour papers in 1976 tried to meet their demands. Those who criticize French manipulation of parliamentary procedures should note that MPs were given the Christmas recess of 1976 to study 166 pages of detailed legislation. The delay delighted the Conservatives, who were mainly interested in Labour's discomfort in trying to keep its own left wing disciplined.[185] The first modifications relieved the local governments from contributing to the expenses of regions, restored control of the Scottish and Welsh development agencies to the regional assemblies, and gave the Scottish assembly power to appoint its own executives and to legislate in the field of civil law.[186] The second paper was largely concerned with reasons why nothing would be done to change the regional organization of England.[187] In this way, the most important territorial legislation that may confront Britain in this century was rewritten from day to day, hoping that a formula might be found to meet parliamentary necessities.

In a dramatic parliamentary session that alternated between slack attendance and rebellious attacks from all quarters, the Scottish Act passed the Commons in early 1978.[188] The Lords then proceeded with what many considered a more careful debate, only to have their most important amendment, proportional representation for the regional elections, swept aside by both major parties in the Commons. Whatever the 'positive Socialist answer to the phenomenon of nationalism'[189] might be, it never appeared in the parliamentary debates. With somewhat greater confusion and even less devolution of powers, the Welsh Bill also became law. Although the Kilbrandon report, as Rose notes, was an 'unintentional demonstration' of Britain's constitutional flexibility,[190] the episode also demonstrates the turmoil which territorial issues have regularly created in the British political system, and casts real doubt on the efficacy of Parliament as a policymaking body. Whatever the weaknesses of the French parliamentary process, the presumably stronger and more purposeful British Parliament spent two years in violent debate that accomplished almost nothing. Once the Scottish Nationalists lost their voting power in the 1979 elections, and the Conservatives returned to power, regional reform was forgotten.

But compared to France, British national government and administration enjoys an almost unqualified power to subordinate intergovernmental agencies to central policies and to Whitehall's preferred pattern of organization. The issue was most clearly drawn by Crowther-Hunt and Peacock, who also documented the remarkable growth of *ad hoc* agencies under direct central supervision.[191] In the 1969 Royal Commission, Derek Senior had also argued that Britain had reversed the desirable order of making territorial decisions. But national laws meticulously protect London's right to regulate local government and repeatedly underscore that the diverse regional agencies of the functional organization of services are not to be compromised. Even the political executives of the Scottish and Welsh regions are in an ambiguous position, for the Secretaries of State for Wales and Scotland remain Cabinet appointments, a kind of central watchdog for the unruly provinces. Every proposal over the last decade that might qualify national preferences for the functional organization of government has been rejected.

The effortless opportunism that has dominated the political debate about regions would be more understandable were it also the case that ministers have tried to use the formidable powers of Whitehall to bring some order into the chaos of central departments' regional structure. Although the Treasury tried from the early 1950s to persuade departments to accept standard regions, regional administration remains one of the most vivid illustrations of governmental '*ad hocery*', and, in turn, presents a virtually unintelligible array of jurisdictions to local government. Lacking political access to regional administration, local government is poorly placed either to extract assistance from the dozen or more differently drawn regional organizations or to use them as a means of coordinating policies involving larger areas. Despite the bitter fights over rationalizing regional government in France, they now provide a standard framework. The irony is even greater if we note, as Hogwood and Lindley have, that 'local authorities are being encouraged to become more "corporate" in their activities while central government is unable to organize itself in this way at the regional level'.[192]

ORGANIZATIONAL COMPLEXITY AS AN ADMINISTRATIVE CONTROL

Even though French parties and leaders are more sharply divided than are the British, a decade of administrative development suggests that France is more able and in many ways more willing, to use the administrative system to help reconcile local and national objectives. As much as administrative intervention is detested by French reformers, neither national nor local political leaders seem determined to dismantle a system which moderates political differences and helps distribute political rewards. The network helps convert the weaknesses of the French administration into strengths that serve the political interests of many levels of government and of parties on both the Left and Right.

Given the importance of the bureaucracy in the welfare state, controlling its decisions is obviously of great importance. The well-developed political sensitivities of French civil servants and their diverse roles in alleviating territorial conflicts gives them an integrative function in policymaking that is denied British civil servants. Suleiman has pointed out that the boundaries between politics and administration are vague at the national level.[193] Much the same could be said of the subnational system. In contrast, the British administrative system exercises extraordinary vigilance in guarding central administration against inroads by lower level officials. Local government policies and the reorganization itself were planned and executed by central officials whose consultations with their clients are subordinated to ministerial objectives. In a world of complex policy decisions, this structure not only insulates administration from local councils and regional conflicts, but may have adverse effects on policymaking at many levels of government. In any event, even at the height of de Gaulle's power few French ministers enjoyed the degree of unqualified control over central–local policies and administration that is routinely provided in the British political system. Combined with parliamentary customs that restrain the British MP from intervening on broad matters of policy, the effect is to concentrate more power in the British administrative system than in the French. The effect is that in Britain it is difficult to use the local government system 'as a balancing factor in the total scheme of administration'.[194]

Because the administration system has both causes and effects on the political system, there are no simple explanations of the two patterns of development. British leaders have been served well by civil servants in both national and local government. The difference is that the British administrative system, which sharply demarcates national and local responsibilities and compartmentalizes the functions of government at both levels, cannot as easily be put to work to solve policy conflicts and to devise policy options. As we have seen, there is very little evidence that either national or local leaders expect this to happen, and they often reinforce these lines of demarcation. The effect is to place national and local civil servants in a defensive position. Each seems to be asking the other to do the impossible, when the reality is that they are pursuing similar goals in relation to national policies.

In many respects the French are more aware of the weaknesses of their administrative system, at least insofar as it relates to central–local relations, than are the British. Few questions are asked about the design of the entire administrative system, and the few strong critics to be heard are uniformly ignored. The French, in contrast, have chosen to move more slowly but along multiple paths. The paradoxical effect has been to gradually reduce the power of civil servants, while at the same time encouraging them to adapt to new conditions and new objectives. Local reform was a greater threat to bureaucratic power in France than it was in Britain, but the slowly accumulating reforms went forward with more consideration of organizational and administrative problems than in Britain. All too often, the contradictions and inadequacies of British local reform have simply been left to local government to work out however they can.

The greatest irony of administrative links in the British subnational system is that local government has been expected to devise new methods and more comprehensive plans while national-level government has persistently rejected change. After a decade of national administrative reform the key relationships of top civil servants to ministers, and many of the internal weaknesses of Whitehall that were identified by the Fulton Committee in 1968, remain impervious to change. As already suggested, the careful isolation of national administration from local problems has served both to preserve Whitehall's policymaking powers and to insulate national administration against the complexities of the welfare state which have often and so effortlessly been superimposed on local government. The French administrative system could not evade these responsibilities, and in many ways the plight of the commune and the intricacy of inter-governmental relations was a stimulus for administrative change and reform itself.

But both systems have also labored under the expanded burden of government, and, as we have seen, more than a few of the changes in central–local relations in France were designed to curb excessive administrative powers. To many French reformers, creating a more varied organization at lower levels of government was a way of both displacing inefficient civil servants and creating incentives for local reorganization after the debacles of the early Gaullist years. A more direct approach to local administrative reform in Britain did not manage to eliminate the diversity of local problems, nor did it even eliminate local administrative inadequacies. As the struggle unfolded in each country, national policy slowly gravitated toward new ways of coping with central–local relationships. The spending and investment policies of local government were, and remain, vital to the success of the welfare state and it is to these changes we turn next.

NOTES: CHAPTER 5

1 Perhaps the strongest statement is by Henry Jacoby, *The Bureaucratization of the World* (trans. Eveline L. Kanes) (Berkeley, Calif.: University of California Press, 1973). This chapter will not intentionally follow any of the several schools of thought about administrative theory, though network analysis comes closest to dealing with intergovernmental problems and has influenced both British and French organizational analysis. For general background, see Herbert A. Simon, *Administrative Behavior*, 2nd edn (New York: Macmillan, 1957) which laid to rest the Weberian ideal; and also Victor A. Thompson, *Modern Organization* (New York: Knopf, 1961).

2 Figures kindly provided by the Direction de la Fonction Publique, Prime Minister's Office, Paris, 1976. The internal–external distinction does not determine where the civil servants are located. The figure excludes 235,000 temporary civil servants and about 173,000 in the separately organized social security system.

3 For details see the de Tinguy report on the 1979 law, *Rapport*, Senate, 1978–79 session, no. 307, tome II, pp. 79–97. For the past five years local personnel have been making rather spectacular increases of about 20 percent per year, especially in middle-sized towns and cities. Only about a fourth of the total personnel are relatively skilled so they are not yet a challenge to the unitary administrative system.

4 National figure taken from *Civil Service Statistics 1979* (London: HMSO, 1979), p. 10. Local figures are from Local Authorities' Conditions of Service Advisory Board (LACSAB) and exclude about 900,000 temporary employees. About a third of the total are teachers. For that historical background see Henry Maddick, 'The local government civil service', *Political Quarterly*, vol. 37 (1966), pp. 192–205.

5 See the graph on the emergence of ministries in Alain Darbel and Dominique Schnapper, *Le Système Administratif*, vol. 2 (Paris: Mouton, 1972), pp. 64ff. We are promised an updated history of the Ministry under a special project of the Prefectoral Corps and CNRS. See Roger Bellion, 'Pour une histoire du corps préfectoral', *Administration*, no. 89 (December 1977), pp. 38–42.

6 See Sir Ernest Barker, 'The Home Civil Service', in W. A. Robson, ed., *The British Civil Servant* (London: Allen & Unwin, 1937), pp. 29–45. On the early history of the Home Office, see A. P. Donajgrodzki. 'New roles for old: the Northcote-Trevelyan Report and the clerks of the Home Office 1822–48', in G. Sutherland, op. cit., pp. 82–109.

7 On postwar developments see Roger Farcat, 'L'Administration centrale du Ministère de l'Interieur: l'évolution des structures depuis la seconde guerre', *Administration*, no. 94 (December 1976), pp. 24–31. The best general study of the development of French administration between the wars is Walter Rice Sharp, *The French Civil Service: Bureaucracy in Transition* (New York: Macmillan, 1931).

8 It is appropriate to repeat here that the French system of administrative law also provided an important advantage in enabling the administration to deal with modern organizational complexity. See J. D. B. Mitchell, 'Administrative law and policy effectiveness', in J. A. G. Griffith (ed.), *From Policy to Administration* (London: Allen & Unwin, 1976), pp. 174–99.

9 The Committee on the Management of Local Government, *Report* (London: HMSO, 1967), vol. 1, p. 84, hopes that 'it may be found possible to appoint a single minister who would be responsible for co-ordinating the policy of the central government in so far as it bears on the functions of local government'. See also, Central Policy Review Staff, *Relations between Central Government and Local Authorities* (London: HMSO, 1977), op. cit., p. 36; and Eleventh Report from the Expenditure Committee, *The Civil Service*, Vol. 1 (London: HMSO, 1977), p. lxii. The changes in this direction will be discussed below.

10   *Planification concertée* is linked to ideas of the Crozier group and even the earlier ideas of Bloch-Lainé concerning ways to decentralize French decisionmaking. Pisani undertook conversion of the Ministry of Agriculture in the early 1960s, and was appointed the first minister of the consolidated Ministry of Infrastructure in 1967. Their reformist ideas led to a major struggle with the *grands corps*. See Bernard Gournay, 'Un groupe dirigeant de la société française: Les grands fonctionnaires'. *Revue Française de Science Politique*, vol. 14 (1964), pp. 215–42. Popular as the attack on the *grands corps* became, this prong of the attack faltered because the administrative elite, as in most countries, was quite capable of working out ways to run the new agencies. Suleiman describes this in detail.

11   On relations between Pompidou and Chaban-Delmas, see Roger-Gérard Schwartzberg, 'Les Impasses de la Ve bis', *Projet*, vol. 53 (1970), pp. 925–40, and Jean Charlot, 'Du parti dominant', ibid., pp. 941–52. For Chaban-Delmas' own account, see *L'Ardeur* (Paris: Stock, 1975).

12   The main objectives, which the Gaullists found easier to accept than local initiatives, were to free industry of governmental controls and to place nationalized industry on a more self-reliant foundation. The main architects were Francois Bloch-Lainé and Simon Nora. See the former's *Pour une Réforme de l'Enterprise* (Paris: Editions du Seuil, 1963), and the latter's *Rapport sur les Enterprises Publiques* (Paris: Documentation Français, 1968). A good account of the activities generated in the private sector is Pierre Dubois, *Mort de l'État-Patron* (Paris: Editions Ouvrières, 1974).

13   *The Civil Service: Report of the Committee 1966–68*, Cmnd 3638 (London: HMSO, 1968). The report was a severe attack on the elitist character of the higher civil service, and led to the creation of a Civil Service Department separate from the Treasury.

14   The British term for the relationship is revealing. The two levels of government are supposed to be 'partners', conveying a rather archaic notion of how business is done and a nostalgia for the simple world of service provision divorced from complex policy objectives. More important, it suggests how the common interests and incentives of each level are assumed to be self-evident.

15   Royal Commission on Local Government, Cmd 4040 (London: HMSO, 1969), pp. 30–2. The Commission's suggestion, a single local government association, is consistent with the view, outlined in Chapter 4, that political leaders are somehow ineffective as vehicles to express local interests. It turns out that the local government system still has the same variety of local government associations that it had before reorganization, and they still fight among themselves in much the same way. See below.

16   The Seebohm Committee on Local Authority and Allied Personal Social Services, *Report*, Cmd 3703 (London: HMSO, 1968), recommends an integration of these services at the local level which was accomplished before the reorganization. The Bains Report was assembled during the reorganization to give local government a model of integrated decisionmaking.

17   The clearest presentation of this in terms of the local government system is by Thoenig, 'French bureaucracy and collective decision making at the local level', paper prepared for CNRS, February 1975. Most of these ideas are carried over in his analysis of local government in 'La relation entre le centre et la périphérie . . .', op. cit.

18   In this respect, the attack on technocracy in French administration, most persuasively made by Michel Crozier, *The Bureaucratic Phenomenon* (Chicago: University of Chicago Press, 1964), needs revision if one is speaking of policy formation, especially in a comparative study. The technocrats fight among themselves and must bargain with both Paris and localities to achieve their aims. Furthermore, there are interesting technocratic traditions in British politics, in particular the immense influence of the physical planners since the turn of the century. See W. Ashworth, *The Genesis of Modern British Town Planning* (London: Routledge & Kegan Paul, 1954), on how a technical corps was set in motion outside government, and to that extent was even less inhibited by policy and political constraints than the *ponts et chaussées*.

19   *Vie Publique*, no. 42 (November 1975).

20   D. E. Regan, *Local Government and Education* (London: Allen & Unwin, 1977), pp. 127–9.

21   The most accomplished presentation is probably Lucien Sfez, *L'Administration prospective* (Paris: Colin, 1970). See particularly his introduction on the

intellectual origins of the group, ibid., pp. 27–46. Though it places more emphasis on cybernetics, the closest thing in English is probably Karl Deutsch, *The Nerves of Government* (Glencoe, Ill.: The Free Press, 1963).

22 Of more than passing interest is the extent to which the reorganizers of British local government continue to observe French local government with a mixture of envy and skepticism. See F. F. Ridley, *The French Prefectoral Sytem: An Example of Integrated Decentralization*, Research Paper 4, Commission on the Constitution (London: HMSO, 1973). Oddly, in the two areas where France has been an innovator, organization and finance, neither the Royal Commission on Local Government nor the Committee on Local Government Finance took much interest.

23 Figures kindly provided by Bernard Gournay and extracted from the 1974 *loi de finances*. These figures include the Conseil D'État, the Cour des Comptes, the *inspecteurs des finances*, the *corps préfectoral*, the *corps des ingénieurs de ponts et chaussées*, and the *corps diplomatique*. There are 1200 such bodies in the administration, but these six are generally placed at the top.

24 Estimate from *The Economist*, 24 January 1976, based on figures from Top Salaries Review Body. For additional detail by ministry, sex, grade, etc., see *Civil Service Statistics*, annual report.

25 *Civil Service Statistics 1979*, pp. 9–10. I have left out the Department of Health and Social Security because most of its services are run on a national basis. However, the DHSS Secretary of State did have an important voice in the reorganization of local personal and health services in the late 1960s.

26 INSEE, *Rencensement de la Fonction Publique* (Paris: Documentation Française, 1976). To help make the figures comparable I have left out the grant to the Ministry of National Education with over 800,000 employees, including all teachers. Teachers are local employees in Britain.

27 The respective figures for Britain and France are 111,000 and 155,000. However, most of these persons are in subordinate national services such as customs, tax collection, etc. The fiscal and financial problems of local government in the two countries will be discussed in Chapters 6 and 7.

28 Disputes between ministers and permanent secretaries seldom become public. One that was openly aired was Richard Crossman's disagreement with and suspicion of his inherited permanent secretary in the Ministry of Housing and Local Government, Dame Evelyn Sharp, who had been a key official since the war. See Crossman's *Diaries*, Vol. 1, pp. 23–6. Her book, *The Ministry of Housing and Local Government* (London: Allen & Unwin, 1969), provides a rare look at the internal workings of a major ministry. For a summary of these relations, see Maurice Wright, 'Ministers and civil servants: relations and responsibilities', *Parliamentary Affairs*, vol. 30 (1977), pp. 293–313.

29 Eleventh Report from the Expenditure Committee, *The Civil Service* (London: HMSO HC 535-I session 1976–7, 1977), p. 1, xvii.

30 The most frequent explanation is that civil servants are bound by the Official Secrets Act; ministers meanwhile refuse to inform Parliament, saying they are bound by Cabinet confidentiality. The British Cabinet does not even make a formal press release about its meetings.

31 Layfield Committee, *Report on Local Government Finance*, Cmnd 6453 (London: HMSO, 1976), p. 35. The historical study done for the Committee by Gerald Rhodes, 'Local government finance 1918–1966', ibid., Appendix 6, pp. 102–73, suggests that it has never been much different.

32 Ibid., p. 38. The House of Commons' Expenditure Committee has also reached these conclusions; op. cit., pp. xxxviii–xliv.

33 See Birnbaum, *Les Sommets de l'État* (Paris: Seuil, 1977), pp. 91–114; Debbasch's *L'Administration au pouvoir*; Ella Searls, 'The fragmented French Executive: ministerial *Cabinets* in the Fifth Republic', *West European Politics*, vol. 1 (1978), pp. 161–76 ; and A. Dutheillet de Lamothe, 'Ministerial Cabinets in France', *Public Administration* (UK), vol. 43 (1965), pp. 365–81.

34 Suleiman, *Politics, Power and Bureaucracy* (Princeton, NJ: Princeton University Press, 1974), p. 212. See his chapter 8 for a detailed analysis of Cabinets and also Jeanne Siwek-Pouydesseau, *Le Personnel de Direction des Ministères* (Paris: Colin, 1969).

35 Lucien Nizard, 'Le Plan', in Langrod (ed.), *La Consultation dans l'Administration Contemporaine* (Paris: Cujas, 1972), p. 419.

36 For an excellent outline of the argument raised here see Vincent Wright, 'Politics

and administration under the French Fifth Republic', *Political Studies*, vol. 22 (1972), pp. 44–65. A more realistic position is that administrators, like everyone else in government, have difficulty defining their own self-interest as well as the public interest, and policies are affected by both.

37   This section depends heavily on J. A. G. Griffith's classic, *Central Departments and Local Authorities*. On the Royal Commission's treatment of central–local relations see Owen A. Hartley, 'The relationship between central and local authorities', *Public Administration* (UK); vol. 49 (1971), pp. 439–56. The contrast with France is that there is no presumption that the relationship should be either vertical or horizontal, and that in practice it is both.

38   D. N. Chester, *Central and Local Government* (London: Macmillan, 1951), pp. 4–5.

39   Dame Evelyn Sharp, op. cit., p. 40. The basic legal guide is Sir William O. Hart's *Introduction to the Law of Local Government and Administration*, 8th edn (London: Butterworth, 1968).

40   Royal Commission, *Written Evidence of County Councils* (London: HMSO, 1967), pp. 192–7. The Local Government Act of 1972 is 449 pages long.

41   P. W. Jackson, *Local Government* (London: Butterworth, 1976), p. 287. In the next section of this chapter attention will be given to the way that the increasing unionization and professionalization of the British local civil service makes it in effect a 'nationalized' body not unlike the unified administrative system of France. However, these trends do not directly affect the policy process.

42   Griffith, op. cit., p. 503. A good summary of the types of control is by K. P. Poole, 'England and Wales', *Studies in Comparative Local Government*, vol. 4 (1970), pp. 7–19.

43   A rather technical but none the less hotly disputed control is the audit of local accounts. The complication is that under Anglo-Saxon law the individual authorizing illegal expenditures is responsible. The prison sentences imposed on George Lansbury (a prominent Labour leader in the 1920's) in the Poplar case became a *cause celèbre*. The Local Government Act of 1972 confines the audit to the strict conditions of the law. There are few such disputes today, although the Clay Cross incident involved auditing controls. See R. Minns, 'The significance of Clay Cross; a look at the district audit', *Policy and Politics*, vol. 2 (1974), pp. 309–29, and Richard Minns, 'The district audit', *New Society*, 10 July 1975, pp. 73–4. For the bitter fight between Poplar and the Conservative government in the 1920s, see B. Keith-Lucas and P. Richards, *A History of Local Government in the Twentieth Century* (London: Allen & Unwin, 1978), pp. 64–91.

44   There is an extensive literature on the individual services which is noted in the Appendix. For a general discussion of central departmental control see Jackson, op. cit., pp. 180–241.

45   Central Policy Review Staff, op. cit., pp. 12, 38.

46   There has recently been a study dealing with one facet of this problem by R. Harris and P. J. Shipp, *Communications between Central and Local Government in the Management of Local Authority Expenditure* (London: Institute of Operational Research, 1977).

47   Lord Redcliffe Maud and Bruce Wood, *English Local Government Reformed* (London: Oxford University Press, 1974), p. 133.

48   For early accounts of the relationship, see T. J. O. Hickey, 'Enemies within and without the gates?', *Political Quarterly*, vol. 37 (1966), pp. 159–67, and Sir Francis Hill, 'The partnership in theory and practice', ibid., pp. 169–79. Of course, the excesses of central control are a constant theme in the writing of W. A. Robson, starting with the *Development of Local Government* (London: Allen & Unwin, 1931, through *Local Government in Crisis*, 2nd edn (London: Allen & Unwin, 1968). A valuable and frank source of information on the variety of views that central departments represent in their relations with local government is *Evidence Given by Government Departments*, Layfield Report (London: HMSO, 1976), App. 1, and the Treasury evidence in *Relationship Between Central and Local Government*, op. cit., App. 6, pp. 14–47.

49   John Stewart, *Municipal Review*, vol. 43, no. 512 (August 1972), p. 216.

50   The restriction emerged from the Government White Paper, *The Attack on Inflation*, Cmd 6151 (London: HMSO, 1975). The orders to local governments were contained in Department of the Environment, *The Attack on Inflation – Remuneration Changes and Grants – Implications for Local Authorities*, Circular 79/75 (London: HMSO, 21 August 1975). This control was extended in

1978 when local governments were held responsible for excessive wage increases in work being done by contract. See *The Times* (London), 8 March 1978.

51 Department of the Environment, *Local Authority Expenditure*, Circular 51/75 (London: HMSO, 1975). See also the Consultative Paper circulated by the Department, 'Consultative council on local finance', CCLG(75)4, 8 May 1975. The description and evaluation is based on interviews with the Association of Municipal Authorities in August 1976 and November 1977, and with the Association of County Councils in November 1977.

52 Interviews with Under Secretary for Local Finance, Department of the Environment, November 1977. The local interest in expenditure had always been partially accommodated by consultation between the department and the local government associations. See also the comments in the *Municipal Review*, vol. 46 (November 1975), p. 236, and the editorial, 'Opening up the system', ibid., vol. 46 (March 1976), pp. ii–329. The Department of the Environment kindly made available the minutes of the 1977 meetings.

53 These statements appear in Layfield Committee, *The Relationship between Central and Local Government: Evidence and Commissioned Work* (London: HMSO, 1976), App. 6, p. 9. Also in *Municipal Review*, vol. 46 (May 1976), p. 48. The general problem of grants and investment negotiations and conditions will be more fully analyzed in Chapters 7 and 8.

54 The certainty with which most critics felt that the problem, and therefore the solution, was to be found in the central administration is testimony to the French administrative tradition. Important books at this time were Michel Crozier, *La Société Bloquée* (Paris: Editions du Seuil, 1970); Jean-Jacques Servan-Schreiber, *Le Pouvoir Régional* (Paris: Grasset, 1971); Club Jean Moulin, *Les Citoyens au Pouvoir* (Paris: Seuil, 1968). Direct attacks were Jean Meynaud, *La Technocratie: Mythe ou Réalité* (Paris: Payot, 1964); Jacques Mandrin, *L'Enarchie ou les Mandarins de la Société Bourgeoise* (Paris: La Table Ronde du Combat, 1967); and Philippe Bernard, *La France au Singulier* (Paris: Calmann-Lévy, 1968).

55 Quoted in Robert Ludwig, 'Le contrôle local des engagements de dépenses en France', *Revue de Science Financière*, vol. 63 (1971), p. 508.

56 The Socialist cities in particular resented being forced to pay fees to administrators for preparing their plans. BERU (Bureau d'Etudes et de Réalisations Urbaines) was started by Lille. See Jean-Pierre Lebreton, 'Les agences d'urbanisme', *Revue Administrative*, vol. 27 (1974), pp. 436–7.

57 These changes will be further analyzed in Chapter 7. The best single evaluation is by Max Auffret and Yves Mény, 'La déconcentration des investissements publics', *Administration*, no. 72 (1972), pp. 99–119.

58 The idea of contractual relationships had in fact also been introduced in the urban communities in 1970. The assortment of zones in French administration and planning is confusing. A good general review of the change is Yves Aubert, 'Stratégie et limites de l'initiative privée', *Projet*, vol. 54 (1971), pp. 405–13; and Francois d'Arcy, 'Le contrôle de l'urbanisation échappe aux autorités publiques', ibid., pp. 393–404.

59 Neither political extreme was happy with the various reforms of the early 1970s. The Gaullists under Chirac and Juillet eventually undermined Chaban-Delmas, and Pompidou's support weakened as the Gaullist 'barons' grew skeptical. On the Left, the tactic was unacceptable because of the shift of power to the private sector. See the neo-Marxist critique of Sylvie Biarez, 'De la planification à un système politique local', *Bulletin de l'Institut International d'Administration Publique*, vol. 37 (1976), pp. 45–84.

60 On regionalization of the plan see B. Pouyet and P. de Montbrison-Fouchère, 'La régionalisation dans le IV Plan: l'expérience des tranches opératoires', in *Administration Traditionelle et Planification Régionale* (Paris: Colin, 1964), pp. 145–232.

61 On the Fifth Plan see J.-J. Bonnaud, *Le Ve Plan, une Stratégie de l'Expansion* (Paris: Editions de l'Épargne, 1967); the book by the CGP's Director, P. Massé, *Le Plan ou l'Anti-Hasard* (Paris: Gallimard, 1965); and C. Gruson, *Renaissance du Plan* (Paris: Editions du Seuil, 1971). This was undoubtedly the pinnacle of DATAR's power. In 1967 the CGP had acquired some of the powers and funds of the old Ministry of Reconstruction, and the new Ministry of Infrastructure had not yet had time to undercut DATAR with its regional and departmental officials.

62 The main Crozier group proposals are contained in *Citoyens au pouvoir*. The more detailed research on lower-level government will be discussed below. On the

group's general views see Michel Crozier, 'Pour une analyse sociologique de la planification française', *Revue Française de Sociologie*, vol. 6 (1965), pp. 147–63; and his earlier thoughts in Club Jean Moulin, 'L'Exécution du Plan', *Cahiers de la République*, vol. 7 (1962), pp. 51–69. Pierre Grémion, 'La Théorie de l'apprentissage institutional et la régionalisation de Cinquième Plan', *Revue Française de Science Politique*, vol. 23 (1973), pp. 305–20.

63 On the Sixth Plan, see Sylvie Biarez, 'De la planification à systeme politique local: programmes et planifications locales dans la VIème Plan', *Bulletin de l'Institut International de l'Administration Publique*, no. 37 (1976), pp. 45–84; and Pierre Pascallon, *La Planification de l'économie française* (Paris: Masson, 1974). Consultation was much improved over earlier plans, and included submission to the *conseils généraux* as well as the now better-organized regional organizations. On their role see the article by the main architect, Michel Rousselot, 'La Régionalisation du VIe Plan', *Aménagement du Territoire et Développement Régional*, vol. 6 (Grenoble: Institut d'Études Politiques, 1973), pp. 39–96.

64 On the relation to the Budget Director see Diana M. Green, 'Economic and financial decision-making in the Fifth French Republic: the budgetary process 1968–1974', University of London, doctoral thesis, 1976, pp. 204–9. Green notes that by this time ceilings for investment credits were being set by the planning machinery for the plan period, and the release of these funds was then given to the Budget Directorate. Thus, each interested minister in practice has a justification to appeal any changes that were not made as a result of Cabinet decisions on larger economic issues.

65 The various devices will be further evaluated in Chapters 6 and 7. For a general assessment see Dominique Flecher-Bourjol, 'Essai de typologie fonctionelle des contrats passés entre l'État et les collectivités locales et établissements publics territoriaux', *Bulletin de l'Institut International de l'Administration Publique*, no. 38 (1976), pp. 57–90. The member of the CGP closely associated with this effort was J.-P. Duport. See his account, 'L'experience des contrats du plan', *Bulletin de l'Institut International de l'Administration Publique*, no. 37 (1973), pp. 161–75.

66 Soon after taking office the new President met with the national planning council and made his views clear. See *Moniteur*, 12 October 1974. About a year later his reservations about regionalization were clarified. See 'Halte à la région', *L'Express*, 29 September–5 October 1975; and his Dijon speech, *Le Monde*, 28 November 1975.

67 A decree moved DATAR from the Ministry of Infrastructure to the Ministry of the Interior in 1974, though DATAR's main office remained at the CGP offices. Indicative of DATAR's more specific new mission were projects on Languedoc-Roussillon, the Acquitania coast and Corsican development. For a recent assessment see André Chadeau, 'Les nouvelles priorités de l'aménagement du territoire', *Le Monde*, 21 July 1978, and Francois Grosrichard, 'Un rapport unédit de la DATAR: des villes entrepreneurs; jusqu'on ne pas aller trôp loin', *Le Monde*, 9 December 1978.

68 Interview, Commissariat Général du Plan, July 1976 and November 1977. On difficulties of the planning devices, see Yves Prat, 'L'articulation des niveaux de planification en France au cours du VI plan', *Bulletin de l'Institut International de l'Administration Publique*, no. 25 (1973), pp. 125–37; and Diana M. Green, 'The Seventh Plan – the demise of French planning', *Western European Politics*, vol. 1 (1978), pp. 60–76.

69 Jacques Fauvet, *Le Monde*, 27 March 1973.

70 See Lucien Nizard, 'Les stratégies du Ministère des Finances: les enseignements de sa participation au processus de planification', *Bulletin de l'Institut International de l'Administration Publique*, no. 37 (1976), pp. 21–44. Additional material on the competition and conflict among the field services of the ministries will be presented later in this chapter.

71 This is another respect in which the United States is much closer to the French than the British system. Over the past decade there has been a steady growth in regionally-organized federal services in health, manpower planning, retraining labor and housing. See Martha Derthick, *Between State and Nation: Regional Organizations in the United States* (Washington, D.C.: Brookings Institution, 1974); Samuel H. Beer, 'The modernization of American Federalism', *Publius*, vol. 3 (1973), pp. 49–96; and Tom Anton, 'Federal assistance programs: the politics of system transformation', in D. Ashford (ed.), *The Politics of Urban Resources* (New York: Methuen, 1980).

72 Department of the Environment, *Local Government Act 1972, Sections 101 and 110. Arrangements for the Discharge of Functions ('Agency Arrangements')*, Circular 131/72 (London: HMSO, 1972).

73 Bruce Wood, *Process of Local Government Reform* (London: Allen & Unwin, 1976), p. 171.

74 Richards, *The 'Reformed' Local Government System* (London: Allen & Unwin, 1973), p. 71.

75 See Tim Mason, 'Area management – the progress of an idea in local government organization', *Local Government Studies* (New Series), vol. 4 (1978), pp. 3–21. For additional details on efforts to introduce area management structures, see C. J. Horn *et al., Area Management: Objectives and Structures* (Birmingham: Joint Centre for Regional, Urban and Local Government Studies, 1977).

76 Robin Hambleton, 'Policies for areas', *Local Government Studies* (New Series), vol. 3 (1977), p. 23. See also Trevor Roberts, 'The organization of general improvement areas', *Local Government Studies* (New Series), vol. 1 (1975), pp. 1–16.

77 See Chapter 6 for more details on informal control through professional associations and unions.

78 Committee on the Management of Local Government, *Report*, op. cit., p. 23.

79 Louis Moss and Stanley R. Parker's 'Local government councillor', in *Management of Local Government*, Vol. 2 (London: HMSO, 1967), p. 97. Detailed information is given in Chapter 3 of their study, pp. 89–136.

80 Margaret Harrison and Alan Norton's 'Local government administration', in *Management of Local Government*, op. cit., Vol. 5, p. 196. See especially Chapter 8 of their study, pp. 191–264.

81 See, for example, 'The Basildon experiment', *Public Administration* (UK), vol. 44 (1966), pp. 213–26. John Stewart's survey of thirty-four country boroughs in 1970 showed that where management methods had been introduced the number of committees was roughly halved; *Management in Local Government: A Viewpoint* (London: Charles Knight, 1971), p. 164. See also Royston Greenwood *et al.*, 'Recent changes in the internal organisation of county boroughs: part I, committees', *Public Administration* (UK), vol. 47 (1969), pp. 151–68.

82 Royal Commission on Local Government, *Report*, op. cit., pp. 123–9.

83 Richards, *'Reformed' Local Government System*, op. cit., p. 141.

84 Study Group on Local Authority Management Structures, *The New Local Authorities: Management and Structure* (London: HMSO, 1972). Another useful document prepared at the time to assist the transition was Joyce Long and Alan Norton, *Setting up the New Authorities* (Birmingham: Institute of Local Government Studies, 1972). A similar study was prepared for Scotland, the Patterson Report. See Arthur F. Midwinter, 'The implementation of the Patterson Report in Scottish local government, 1975–77', *Local Government Studies* (New Series), vol. 4 (1978), pp. 23–38.

85 See Royston Greenwood *et al.*, 'Contingency theory and the organization of local authorities: part 1. Differentiation and integration', *Public Administration Review* (UK), vol. 53 (1975), pp. 1–23; and C. R. Hinings *et al.*, 'Contingency theory and organization of local authorities: part II. Contingencies and structure', ibid. pp. 163–90. Tables comparing 1964, 1970 and 1974 can be found in *Local Government Trends 1975* (London: CIPFA), pp. 302–6.

86 Like the efforts to extend program budgeting to lower levels in France, there were numerous efforts to institute performance budgeting techniques in Britain both before and following the reorganization. McKinsey and colleagues were called in to prepare such plans for Liverpool, Greenwich and Hull. See their report, Department of the Environment, *The Sunderland Study: Tackling Urban Problems*, 2 vols (London: HMSO, 1973); R. B. Butt, 'A feasibility study of PPBS in Gloucestershire', *Local Government Studies*, no. 2 (1972), pp. 37–52; additional studies cited in the Appendix to this volume.

87 Royston Greenwood *et al., The Organisation of Local Authorities in England and Wales: 1967–75* (Birmingham: Institute of Local Government Studies, 1975), pp. 49, 36.

88 See the evaluation by R. Greenwood, C. R. Hinings, and S. Ranson, 'The politics of the budgetary process in English local government', *Political Studies*, vol. 25 (1977), pp. 25–47; and the critique by James N. Danziger, 'A comment on "The politics of the budgetary process in English Local Government"', *Political Studies*, vol. 26 (1978), pp. 109–15. The more general question is also raised by

Douglas A. Hart, 'Ordering change and changing orders: a study of urban policy development', *Policy and Politics*, vol. 2 (1973), pp. 27–41. For the complete data from the Greenwood and Hinings project, see their *In Pursuit of Corporate Rationality: Organisational Developments in the Post-Reorganisation Period* (Birmingham: Institute of Local Government Studies, 1977).

89 *New Society*, 4 December 1975.
90 Margaret Lomer, 'The chief executive in local government 1974–76', *Local Government Studies* (New Series), vol. 3 (1977), p. 39.
91 See R. J. Haynes, 'The rejection of corporate management in Birmingham in theoretical perspective', *Local Government Studies* (New Series), vol. 4 (1978), pp. 25–38; and J. P. W. B. McAuslan and R. G. Bevans, 'The influence of officers and councillors on procedures in planning – a case study', ibid., vol. 3 (1977), pp. 7–21. The Birmingham decision does not appear to be highly political. Another strongly Conservative local authority, Cheshire, seems to thrive on the new organization. See Cristina Howick, 'Budgeting and corporate planning in Cheshire', *CES Review*, no. 3 (1978), pp. 45–62.
92 See Siwek-Pouydesseau's *Le Corps Préfectoral sous la IIIe et la IVe Républiques* (Paris: Colin, 1969), pp. 85–108. The term has at least three meanings: the departmental and regional prefects, who number at any one time about 120 persons; the entire membership of the *corps*, about 780 persons; and the administrative club of several thousands associated with territorial administration. The flexible membership and multiple contacts, of course, all help the prefectoral corps to sustain its network throughout government.
93 See Paxton's *Vichy France* (New York: Knopf, 1972), pp. 335–52. He estimates that by 1947 about half of the Vichy prefects had drifted back into the administration.
94 Until the 1970s the 'Enarques' were not attracted to the prefectoral corps. Machin's *Prefects of the Fifth Republic*, op. cit., p. 307, finds only ten ENA graduates in the prefectoral corps. Of course, a number of ENA graduates who became general administrators are assigned to prefects and in the 1960s tours of duty were used to give them practical experience. On ENA relations with the prefectoral corps, see Philippe de Quinsac, 'Des préfets, mais quels préfets?', *Revue Politique et Parlementaire*, vol. 73 (1971), pp. 33–46. See also *Vie Publique* (October 1975), for figures on Enarques in subprefectures.
95 Suleiman's *Politics, Power . . .*, op. cit., p. 203, finds twenty-eight members of the prefectoral corps in ministerial cabinets, the largest number of any of the grands corps. For a general outline of the development of the corps see Pierre Aubert and Maurice Lambert, 'Le Corps préfectoral de 1946 à 1976', *Administration*, no. 94 (December 1976), pp. 38–69.
96 Longpierre's *Les Conseillers Généraux* (Paris: Cujas, 1971), p. 109. A good memoire by an ex-prefect is Marcel Savneux, *Le Préfect: Homme à Tout Faire de la République* (Paris: Editions Alain Lefevre, 1977).
97 Quoted in Jack Hayward, *One and Indivisible Republic* (London: Weidenfeld & Nicolson, 1973), p. 53.
98 Chenot in Yves Weber, *L'Administration Consultative* (Paris: Librairie Générale de Droit et de Jurisprudence, 1968), p. 3, notes that there are over 15,000 national consultative groups. In Georges Langrod (ed.), op. cit., part II, pp. 283–634, there are discussions of each functional activity of government.
99 On the current staffing of departments see Michel Bertrand, *Revue Administrative* (April 1977), p. 276; and for a description of their role today, Jean-Emile Vié, 'Le metier de préfet', *Le Monde*, 12 September 1978.
100 Jean-Pierre Worms, *Une Préfecture Comme Organisation* (Paris: CNRS, 1968), p. 148. For a study of the internal organization at an earlier time, see Jean Blondel, 'Local government and the local officers of the ministries in a French Department', *Public Administration* (UK), vol. 37 (1959), pp. 65–74. An outline of a prefect's day can be found in Machin, 'The French prefects and local administration', *Parliamentary Affairs*, vol. 27 (1974), pp. 238–40. See also F. R. Ridley, 'The French prefectoral system revived', *Administration and Society*, vol. 6 (1974), pp. 48–72.
101 On the current distribution of elite civil service groups at the prefectoral level see Michel-Jean Bertrand, 'Les préfectures: une fonction administrative dans l'espace français', *Revue Française d'Administration Publique*, no. 2 (1977), pp. 249–93. For a discussion of current changes see the collection of articles, 'L'Administration Préfectorale: éléments pour un dossier', *Administration*, no. 98 (December 1977), pp. 19–65.

102 Siwek-Pouydesseau, op. cit., p. 150.
103 Machin, op. cit., pp. 293–4. He also notes that in areas where a prefect works smoothly with the political leadership, he or she may remain in his or her post for many years. Chaban-Delmas had a friend in the Gironde prefecture who stayed there from 1958 to 1969. Giscard d'Estaing is known to be closely associated with the Prefect of Paris, Lanier, who provides him with some restraints over the mayor, Chirac.
104 *Vie Publique*, no. 59 (May 1977), p. 14, reports eighteen departmental changes and five regional changes. André Passeron, 'Des mutations trop fréquents', *Le Monde*, 21 April 1977, reports forty-one in all. Part of the change is because new Ministers of the Interior (in this case Bonnet), want to have people they know in important departments. Poniatowski replaced twenty-four prefects when he took office in 1974. One of the prefects moved in 1977 had not been able to stifle a rather rude demonstration when the President visited Lille in late 1976. On the changes see *Le Monde*, 28 April 1978. This report estimates that nearly one hundred changes were made between 1974 and 1978.
105 The issue of the subprefects has festered ever since their abuse of power in the 1789 Revolution. The question is investigated further in a special issue of *Administration*, no. 74 (1972). See particularly Pierre Avril, 'L'Arrondissement et la réforme administrative', pp. 56–62.
106 Machin, 'The Prefects of the Fifth Republic', thesis, University of London, 1974, p. 230. Catherine Grémion's 'Décision ou indécision', thesis, Institut d'Études Politiques, 1977, p. 248, feels that political influence is more widely used and felt. There are interesting relapses. For example, the organizer of the Clubs Perspectives et Réalités, which are the loosely organized local discussion groups of the Republican Party, was made a prefect in 1977.
107 See, for example, the issue of *Administration*, no. 84–85 (June–September 1974), devoted to 'Le préfet et l'économie'. See also, Georges Dupuis, 'L'inadaption des structures administratives à leurs objectives: esquisse d'une pathologie administrative', *Administration*, no. 86 (December 1974), pp. 69–72.
108 These were not all highly significant changes. For example, the prefect no longer needed to have approval from Paris to award decorations to firemen. See Jean-Emile Vié, 'Pour une véritable déconcentration', *Administration*, no. 66 (1969), pp. 33–40.
109 Catherine Grémion, op. cit., pp. 49–53. The general question will be examined further in Chapters 6 and 7. For a review of their financial powers, see Paul Minniot, 'Le préfet et la déconcentration des investissements', *Administration*, no. 85–86 (1974), pp. 72–85.
110 J.-C. Thoenig's *L'Ère des technocrates* (Paris: Editions d'Organisation, 1973), pp. 53–72.
111 For example, when Chalandon, a minister with distinctly liberal ideas, took on the ministry in 1969, he began, like Ministers of the Interior, to appoint DDE directors of his choosing; Thoenig, op. cit., p. 120.
112 A number of central agencies have been organized to provide services and improve management. They include the Local Authorities Conditions of Service Advisory Board (LACSAB), the Local Authorities Management Services Advisory Committee (LAMSAC), to help with computers and information systems, and the Local Government Training Board (LGTB).
113 An important illustration of the mixing of indiscriminately partisan politics with administrative neutrality is Heseltine's decision to bar council members with connections to the school system from voting on local school budgets. Because many Labour councillors are teachers and educational officials, they were effectively barred, giving the remaining Conservative members a better chance of cutting school spending. After a rumpus in Parliament, the rules were rescinded. *The Times* (London), 16 January 1980.
114 The Committee was asked to submit a preliminary report on councillors' pay, which can be found in the *Report*, Appendix D, pp. 167–74. They did not favor salaries, but wanted to permit local councils to establish their own allowance rates. See 'Do councillors deserve their expenses?', *Sunday Times*, 6 July 1975, for more details.
115 *Remuneration of Councillors*, Vol. II (London: HMSO, 1977) shows that in 1974 the average councillor spent seventy-nine hours a month on local government duties compared with fifty-two hours in 1964. Full-time salaries were rejected as 'a threat to the long established voluntary principle that plays such an important

part in British public life'. To avoid having too much monetary incentive to work for local government, councillors with dual memberships would only be permitted allowances from a single authority. See reactions of the cities in *Municipal Review* (January 1978); and the counties in *County Councils Gazette* (January 1968). In 1976 about ten million pounds were paid in allowances.

116 The local elections of 1977 brought the issue to the surface and all parties made proposals. See 'Pour un vrai statut des élus locaux', *Vie Publique*, no. 64 (November 1977), pp. 23–8. The assistant mayors, whose number is also determined by law, are eligible for roughly half the mayor's allowance. The maximum amounts, as in Britain, are set by central government.

117 The Commission published an annual report for each region. See the report, *Your Local Ombudsman*, London, Local Government Commission for England, 1977 and 1978. For reactions of local government see comments in *Municipal Review* (September 1975), p. 175; and ibid. (November 1977), p. 259. Like the national-level parliamentary commissions, complaints are supposed to be submitted through members, not directly.

118 Norman Lewis and Bernard Gateshill, *The Commission for Local Administration* (London: Royal Institute of Public Administration, 1978). They feel localities respond voluntarily, but other reports do not agree. See *The Times* (London), 7 September 1977. See also Neil Collins, 'The Commissioner for Local Administration in England – notes on a seminar', *Local Government Studies* (New Series), vol. 4 (1978), pp. 15–24.

119 The wide variety of semipublic arrangements in France make the temptation even greater, as have the soaring land values of the past decade. Gabriel Aranda has written his own defense in a fascinating study of how administration and politics work at their worst, *L'Etat Piège* (Paris: Stork, 1972).

120 See Paddy French and Will Ellsworth-Jones, 'How greed ate its way into Labour's heartland', *Sunday Times*, 4 December 1977.

121 Committee on Local Government Rule of Conduct: Conduct in Local Government, *Report*, Cmd 5636 (London: HMSO, 1974). The citation is from p. 36.

122 Department of the Environment, *The National Code of Local Government Conduct*, Circular 94/75 (London: HMSO, 1975). This is a remarkably vague document.

123 Royal Commission on Standards of Conduct in Public Life (Salmon Commission), *Report*, Cmd 6524 (London: HMSO, 1976).

124 See in particular the early history of Cheshire in J. M. Lee's *Social Leaders and Public Persons* (Oxford: Clarendon Press, 1973), pp. 122–56; and A. H. Birch, *Small-Town Politics* (London: Oxford University Press, 1959).

125 For useful earlier studies see T. J. O. Hickey, 'Enemies within and without the gates', *Political Quarterly*, vol. 37 (1966), pp. 159–67; Bryan Keith-Lucas, 'Who are the policy makers? councillor or chief officer, I: councillor', *Public Administration* (UK), vol. 43 (1965), pp. 269–81; H. Hugh Heclo, 'The councillor's job', *Public Administration* (UK), vol. 47 (1969), pp. 185–202.

126 The model for Labour control comes from Morrison's long service with London local government. See G. W. Jones, 'Political leadership in local government: how Herbert Morrison governed London, 1934–1940', *Local Government Studies*, vol. 5 (1973), pp. 1–11. A good study of a modern Labour Party boss is J. Elliott, 'T. Dan Smith in Newcastle-upon-Tyne', *Local Government Studies* (New Series), vol. 1 (1975), pp. 33–43. The basis for 'winner-take-all' in the Labour Party is the Model Standing Orders; see *Local Government Handbook: England and Wales* (London: The Labour Party, 1977), Appendix 2, pp. 373–7. The Orders make caucus the standard procedure, although the party recommended in 1973 that more freedom be given to local backbenchers and more flexibility be exercised in permitting Labour members to speak in council meetings and vote freely on non-party matters; ibid., pp. 350–1.

127 Howard Elcock, 'English local government reformed: the politics of Humberside', *Public Administration* (UK), vol. 53 (1975), pp. 159–66. This should not be taken to imply that political bosses only exist in the Labour Party.

128 Stuart Haywood, 'Decision-making in local government – the case of an 'Independent' council', *Local Government Studies* (New Series), vol. 3 (1977), pp. 41–55. Another study of a less partisan council is Roger V. Clements, *Local Notables and the City Council* (London: Macmillan, 1969). A recent essay on the mayor of Manchester described how mayors are politically neutralized; Dame Kathleen Ollerenshaw, *First Citizen* (London: Hart-Davis, MacGibbon, 1977).

129 In the research of the Committee on Local Government by Moss and Parker, op. cit., p. 204, most councillors (75 percent) felt that parties did not affect the council's work. Even in the most politicized boroughs, only 48 percent saw an influence. There is a full-length study of the strong non-partisan forces within British local government, Wyn Grant, *Independent Local Politics in England and Wales* (London: Saxon House, 1977).

130 J. D. Stewart, *The Responsive Local Authority* (London: Charles Knight, 1974), p. 137. See also his 'Developments in corporate planning in British local government', *Local Government Studies*, vol. 5 (1973), pp. 13–29.

131 For example, the Plowden Report, *Children and their Primary Schools* (London: HMSO, 1967), asked that schools be more sensitive to social and environmental effects on education; the *Report of the Committee on Local Authority and Allied Personal Services*, Cmd 3703 (London: HMSO, 1968) asked for integration of social services; the Buchanan Report, *Traffic in Towns* (London: HMSO, 1963), pointed toward the environmental costs of transportation; see also the Skeffington Report, *People and Planning* (London: HMSO, 1969).

132 See John Miller, 'A personal view of the background of the report of the Bains Committee', *Local Government Studies*, vol. 4 (1972), pp. 3–23. He notes that the Home Office provided no suggestions whatever; a few suggestions came from the DES and the DHSS; the DoE was helpful but could do nothing, of course, to change other ministerial views.

133 See J. W. Glendinning and R. E. H. Bullock, *Management by Objectives in Local Government* (London: Charles Knight, 1973), p. 137.

134 See J. D. Stewart, 'The government of cities and the politics of opportunity', *Local Government Studies* (New Series), vol. 1 (1975), pp. 3–20; and his 'Corporate control can only go so far', *Municipal Review*, no. 543, pp. 356–7. As the problems of the policy committee became clearer, many of the advocates turned to buttressing local resources as an alternative. See Chapter 6.

135 David Green, 'A backbencher's right to information', *Municipal Review*, no. 570 (June 1977), pp. 70–1. See 'Readers reply to Cllr Dave Green's contention in the June MR that the backbencher councillor is virtually powerless', *Municipal Review*, no. 571 (July 1977), pp. 122–42; 'Letters', ibid., no. 572 (August 1977), p. 160; and Green's reply, 'Power to the councillor', ibid., no. 573 (September 1977), p. 195.

136 See the diagrams in Thoenig's 'La Relation entre le centre et la périphérie en France', *Bulletin de l'Institut International d'Administration Publique*, vol. 36, October–November 1975, pp. 89, 92, 95. Grémion's 'L'Administration territoriale', in Crozier (ed.), *Où va l'Administration Française* (Paris: Editions d'Organisation, 1974), pp. 75–99, reaches similar conclusions. On the recent development of the *réseau*, see Marie-Francois Souchon, 'Les réseaux des relations dans le système politico-administratif: les cas des maires élus pour la première fois en mars 1971', *Bulletin de l'Institut International d'Administration Publique*, no. 32 (1974), pp. 67–91.

137 For a description of the formal organization and activity of some large cities, Rennes, Nice, Lille and Grenoble, see Institut Français des Sciences Administratives, *L'Administration des grandes villes*, pp. 29–94. See also Bruno Jobert and Michèle Sellier, 'Les grandes villes: autonomie locale et innovation politique', *Revue Française de Science Politique*, vol. 27 (1977), pp. 225–27.

138 Laurence Wylie, *Village in the Vaucluse*, 2nd edn (Cambridge, Mass.: Harvard University Press, 1964); compare with his later community study, Wylie *et al.*, *Chanzeau: A Village in Anjou* (Cambridge, Mass.: Harvard University Press, 1966). On current administrative problems of the small communes, see Jean Condou, 'Les communes rurales doivent-elles mourir?', *Cahiers du CFPC*, no. 2 (1978), pp. 8–17; and Jacques Bourdon, 'Les problèmes d'administration de la commune rurale', ibid., pp. 18–33.

139 Raymond Ledrut, 'Politique urbaine et pouvoir local', *Espaces et sociétés*, no. 20–21 (March–June 1977), p. 12.

140 P. Grémion's *Pouvoir périphérique* (Paris: Seuil, 1976), p. 213. Later on the same idea reappears in terms of the individual protection that the system provides against centralization: 'Individual protection is assured by the resistance offered the group of peers against external aggression. The isolation of groups permits each to hold in its sphere a parcel of sovereign and absolute authority' (ibid., p. 285).

141 Ibid., p. 241.

142 Ibid., p. 304. See his similar interpretation of regional politics and policy,

'Résistance au changement de l'administration territoriale: le cas des institutions régionales', *Sociologie du Travail*, vol. 3 (1969), pp. 276–96.

143 Jeanne Becquart-Leclercq, *Paradoxes du pouvoir local* (Paris: PUF, 1976), esp. pp. 122–73; also her 'Pouvoir local et pouvoir central: une articulation complexe', *Projet*, no. 116 (June 1977), pp. 728–46. Additional studies are cited in the Appendix.

144 See the contrasting responses about elections and running the council in Becquart-Leclercq, op. cit., p. 117. Also the results of the SOFRES poll in 1971 in Lancelot's 'Les élections municipales', *Projet*, no. 56, 1971, pp. 646–9; and the 1977 polling data given in *Vie Publique* (April 1977), pp. 27–30.

145 Interview with Local Government Officer, Communist Party Headquarters, Paris, October 1977. See Becquart-Leclercq, op. cit., p. 43; also Sidney Tarrow, *Between Center and Periphery: Grassroots Politicians in Italy and France* (New Haven, Conn.: Yale University Press, 1977), p. 167; Denis Lacorne, 'On the fringe of the French political system: the beliefs of Communist municipal elites', *Comparative Politics*, vol. 9 (1977), pp. 421–42; and Chantal Balley, 'Les Comportements des maires face au développement urbain', *L'Espace Géographique*, no. 2 (1976), pp. 99–106.

146 Kesselman's *The Ambiguous Consequences* (New York: Knopf, 1967), pp. 136–49.

147 To pursue the style of mayors see any of the many volumes on their experience: Michel Laurent, *A l'Écoute des Villes de France* (Paris: Mengès, 1976); Jacques Kryn, *Lettres d'un Maire de Village* (Paris: Éditions du Seuil, 1971); Jacques Gales and Jacky Bena, *Les Nouveaux Maires Communistes* (Paris: Éditions Sociales, 1978).

148 A good example of the difficulties of arbitrary central intervention is Poniatowski's decision to move the prefecture in the department of Var. See *Vie Publique*, no. 31 (November 1974). The decision was fought for two years in the courts and eventually went to the Conseil d'Etat. *Le Monde* frequently reports on such cases; for example, 12 October 1977, when a commune in the department of Loire-Atlantique fought a budget charge forced on them by the prefect.

149 In 1972 a law established a program on training communal personnel and has been supported by Chirac and Giscard d'Estaing. In addition to the Centre de Formation in Paris, there are now three universities (Angers, Orléans and Tours) offering advanced diplomas in local administration. In 1975 the budget for training was seven milliards and some 20,000 employees participated (interview, Ministry of the Interior, July 1976).

150 Under the tradition of the *grands corps* each elite group can charge for their services even though they are, in turn, the officials who approve and defend applications. The actual amounts collected are carefully hidden, but it appears that agents of *travaux publics* collected 163 million francs in 1973, *Le Monde*, 24 November 1977. See also Michèle Champenois, 'Les ingénieurs de l'État, mercenaires des communes', *Le Monde*, 16 and 17 April 1977. Claude Sales, 'Ce que gagnent vraiment les fonctionnaires', *Le Point*, 16 May 1977, reports that departmental TPGs can receive as much as 50,000 francs a month in fees, and that high officials in the Ministry of Interior receive nearly a third of their salary in the form of special allowances. Even local employees have ways of multiplying their benefits; see *Vie Publique* (December 1974), on the manipulation of pension funds.

151 Lewis Corina, 'Elected representatives in a party system: a typology', *Policy and Politics*, vol. 3 (1974), p. 83. Similar implications can be drawn from G. W. Jones, 'The function and organization of councillors', *Public Administration* (UK), vol. 51 (1973), pp. 135–45; though he would like to see more competitive policymaking.

152 The entire issue was both provoked and complicated to a great extent by the debate over devolution which will be discussed in Chapter 7. The Royal Commission on the Constitution had reported in October 1973 and the Labour Party was also pledged to provide some form of devolution on its return to power in 1974. At the same time the National Executive Committee of the party, now more strongly influenced by the left wing, was calling for changes. See *Bringing Power Back to the People* (London: National Executive Committee, 1974); and *Devolution and Regional Government* (London: National Executive Committee, 1975).

153 Peter Shore, Secretary of State for the Environment, 'Reform of local

government', Harrogate speech, 27 January 1977, p. 22; kindly provided by the Department of the Environment.

154 The partisan character of decisions is suggested by the report in the *Sunday Times*, 21 August 1977, that when Conservative councillors in Nottingham, Leicester and other large districts indicated that they favored the redistribution of functions, they were told by the Conservative Shadow Secretary for the Environment, Michael Heseltine, to keep quiet. The Tory local government conference came out strongly against Shore's suggestions. See *Municipal Review* (April 1977), p. 26, and *The Times* (London), 6 February 1978. Southampton, one of the cities scheduled for 'organic' change, came out against the idea too. See the article by Norman Best, leader of the Southampton council, in *Centre Forward; Local Government Reorganization*, no. 2 (1978).

155 *Regional Authorities and Local Government Reform*, Consultative Document (London: The Labour Party, July 1977). The cities concerned are Bristol, Leicester, Nottingham, Hull, Plymouth, Stoke-on-Trent, Southampton, Derby and Portsmouth. Cardiff is sometimes mistakenly included, but change there awaited the outcome of the devolution debate.

156 Shore appears to have succeeded in persuading the Association of District Councils to change its stand. In *The Times* (London), 16 September 1977, the leader of the ADC protests, but on 14 February 1978, he comes out in favor. In between he had been knighted. For the ministries' opposition see *The Times* (London), 7 September 1977, for the DHSS.

157 See *Local Government Reform in England* (London: National Executive Committee, October 1978).

158 Christopher Warman, 'The Shore way for a county face-lift', *The Times* (London), 18 August 1978. By this time the position of the local government associations was more clearly aligned with the Conservatives. The ACC came out strongly against the proposals, as one would expect. See the *County Council Gazette* (October 1978), on Mr. Shore's 'hotchpotch'. Over the summer, control of the Association of Metropolitan Counties had shifted back to the Conservatives, and its journal kept a discreet silence.

159 John Boynton, 'A case for leaving local government alone for the moment', *The Times* (London), 26 September 1978. Boynton, Chief Executive of Cheshire County Council and past president of the union for top local officials, the Society of Local Authority Chief Executives (SOLACE), pointed out that the present district boundaries, closely following the old borough boundaries when the non-metropolitan counties were formed, still made little sense in many cases; that county councillors not representing major districts often do not participate in votes on large districts; and that there are some positive effects of having an intermediate level (the county) review what might be very political district educational decisions.

160 J. D. Stewart *et al.*, *A Report on Constitutional, Management and Financial Problems*, University of Birmingham Institute of Local Government Studies for the Association of County Councils, November 1978.

161 The financial and fiscal reforms will be discussed further in Chapters 6 and 7, but they also have considerable similarity. The Republican proposals are taken from *Le Projet Républicain* (Paris: Flammarion, 1978), the Party's election manifesto for the legislative elections. See also Antoine Rufenacht, 'Agir pour les communes', *L'Élu local*, no. 70 (March 1977), pp. 9–13, and the party's *Charte Municipal* from the local elections. The Gaullists are the most reluctant to change the administrative system and probably would not support many of these changes without pressure from the President. Their *Manifeste Communal* for the 1977 elections said little about departments or regions. Unless otherwise noted, the Left's proposals are based on *Le Programme Commun de Gouvernement de la Gauche: Propositions Socialistes pour l'Actualisation* (Paris: Flammarion, 1978), the Union de la Gauche election manifesto; and their early statement, *Programme Commun de Gouvernement* (Paris: Flammarion, 1973).

162 *Citoyen dans sa Commune; Propositions municipales Socialistes* (Paris: Flammarion, 1977), p. 154.

163 Statement by Marcel Rosette, the Communists' local government advisor, at a meeting of the party's local government association. *Le Monde*, 25 October 1977.

164 Guichard Report, *Vivre Ensemble* (Paris: Documentation Française, 1978), pp. 104, 70.

165 *La Réponse des Maires* (Paris: Documentation Française, 1979), pp. 52–4.

166 Maurice Bourjol, 'L'État et les collectivités territoriales: administration "à niveau" ou administration "bipolaire"', *Journée D'Études du Val-de-Loire*, 13–14 May 1977.

167 Guichard Report, *Vivre Ensemble*, op. cit., p. 39. Additional recommendations barring accumulation of offices for those sitting on the proposed new 'urban communities' are to be found on p. 226.

168 Consultations began with a government seminar at Rambouillet under the President; *Le Monde*, 29 July and 1 August 1978. See also the evaluation by Marcel Champeix, the Socialist Senate spokesman, 'Les Nouveau convertis', *Le Monde*, 27 July 1978. The Socialists later revealed their own plans, *Le Monde*, 10 October 1978, but were internally divided between strengthening the region or the department.

169 The Minister of the Interior, Bonnet, outlined the proposals before the Senate in June. See *Le Monde*, 22 June 1978; but he said nothing about *cumul des mandats*.

170 For the details on negotiations for increased local responsibilities, see the de Tinguy Report, *Rapport*, annexe au procès-verbal de la séance du 3 mai 1978, no. 307, 1978–1979 session (Paris: Imprimerie Nationale, 1978), pp. 99–119.

171 The levels of interaction could easily be given an international dimension, particularly in Western Europe where the Common Market and European Community play an increasingly important role. For an overview of this dramatic change see R. A. W. Rhodes, 'Into Europe – a guide for British local government', *Local Government Studies*, no. 3 (1972), pp. 57–62. On the international financial implications, see Commission of the European Communities, *Report of the Study Group on the Role of Public Finance in European Integration* (Brussels: The Commission, 1977).

172 See Pierre Grémion, 'Réforme régionale et démocratie locale', *Projet* (1970), pp. 411–29. On the immediate movement of the Left into multiple local-level office after the 1977 elections, see François Grosrichard, 'Des contrecoups sensibles dans plusieurs conseils régionaux', *Le Monde*, 16 March 1977.

173 See Felix Damette, 'Régions: un terrain de luttes à l'heure du XXIIe Congrès, *Économie et Politique*, nos. 264–265 (July–August 1976), pp. 4–12. On the strength of the Socialist regional governments for the Marseille and Lille regions, see *Le Monde*, 29 November 1979; and on Giscard's trip to the southwest, *Le Monde*, 25–26 November 1979.

174 An exception might be Scotland, where the Act of Union did permit the Scots to keep a different educational, legal and local government structure. The most careful study is David N. King, *Financial and Economic Aspects of Regionalism and Separatism*, Royal Commission on the Constitution, Research Paper 10 (London: HMSO, 1973). On the quasi-federal system of Northern Ireland, see Paul Arthur, 'Devolution as administrative convenience: a case study of Northern Ireland', *Parliamentary Affairs*, vol. 30 (Winter 1977), pp. 97–106. Additional materials on Scotland and Ireland are given in the Appendix.

175 See Anthony H. Birch, *Political Integration and Disintegration in the British Isles* (London: Allen & Unwin, 1977), p. 144.

176 Birch, op. cit., provides a table on the growth of the SNP, p. 123. Heath came out in favor of a Scottish Assembly in 1968, but had a hard time bringing his party around. In 1970 Heath just sneaked in under the wire, when a Scottish Constitutional Committee under the ex-Prime Minister, Sir Alec Douglas-Home, reported favorably only three months before the 1970 election. Though the left wing of the Conservative Party still supports the report, Mrs Thatcher is much less comfortable with Scottish devolution.

177 Crossman, *Diaries*, op. cit., Vol. III, p. 69. After a year and a half of urging from Crossman, who favored regional parliaments, the decision to appoint a Commission was discussed in late 1968. In addition to civil service resistance, there was outrage from the Department of Economic Affairs and the Ministry of Housing, neither of which had been consulted. Nor had Wheatley, who was then considering Scottish local government reform. Largely for electoral reasons, the two most cautious devolutionists, Wilson and Callaghan, pushed it through the Cabinet knowing that the Commission would enable them to skirt the issue in the next election. Another irony of two-party rule is that the report ended up on their desks six years later. In Wilson's book on the 1964–1970 government there are no references to the Royal Commission, but it is interesting to note that there are more entries for the Scilly Isles than for Scotland.

178 Crossman, *Diaries*, op. cit., Vol. III, p. 243.

179 See the estimate of John P. MacKintosh, 'The Report of the Royal Commission on the Constitution, 1969–1973', *Political Quarterly*, vol. 45 (1974), pp. 115–23. Scotland, Wales and Northern Ireland have, respectively, 71, 36 and 12 MPs. Were seats distributed based on the population they would have 57, 31, and 17 respectively. The reduction in Ulster seats was part of a compromise in 1922 giving them a degree of financial autonomy.

180 Another case of popular feelings being far removed from structural decisions. A good survey was done by Social and Community Planning Research, *Devolution and Other Aspects of Government: An Attitudes Survey*, Royal Commission on the Constitution, Research Paper 7 (London: HMSO, 1973).

181 Nevil Johnson, 'Royal Commission on the Constitution', (Editorial), *Public Administration* (UK), vol. 52 (1974), pp. 1–12.

182 Royal Commission on the Constitution (Kilbrandon Report), *Report*, Cmd 5460 (London: HMSO, 1973), summarizes its conclusions pp. 469–89. See also Jeffrey Stanyer, 'Nationalism, regionalism and the British system of government', *Social and Economic Administration*, vol. 8 (1974), pp. 136–57, which stresses the inconsistencies between the report and the local government system.

183 Royal Commission on the Constitution, *Memorandum of Dissent*, Cmd 5460-I (London: HMSO, 1973). They find that there are twenty different regional organizations of the Whitehall departments, of which only two coincide geographically.

184 *Our Changing Democracy: Devolution to Scotland and Wales*, Cmd 6348 (London: HMSO, 1975). The discussion paper following the first 1974 election is *Devolution within the United Kingdom* (London: HMSO, 1974). The pre-election paper was *Democracy and Devolution*, Cmd 5732 (London: HMSO, 1974).

185 Mrs Thatcher also saw thirty-four Tories defy her own three-line whip to defeat the Bill, reopened her nagging differences with Heath, and lost one member of her Shadow Cabinet. See *The Economist*, 11 December 1976. About thirty Labour MPs, particularly those from the north, were constantly opposed to concessions and formed their own unofficial group. See *The Times* (London), 2 August 1976. There was similar disarray over how to elect representatives to the European Parliament.

186 *Devolution to Scotland and Wales: Supplementary Statement*, Cmd 6585 (London: HMSO, 1976).

187 *Devolution: The English Dimension* (Consultative Document) (London: HMSO, 1976).

188 On the early votes to use the guillotine, nine Labour MPs still broke the whip, the *Economist*, 19 November 1977. In the debate on the second reading, neither party sounded very enthusiastic; *The Times* (London), 23 February 1978. It appears that fifty-three clauses were not debated. The rebellion was a joint effort by Conservative and Labour critics and requires that the referendum, which is not binding but nonetheless cannot be ignored, must have approval of 40 percent of the eligible voters.

189 Eric Heffer, one of the leaders of the left-wing resistance to the bill, in *The Times* (London), 29 August 1977. See also the position of the Conservative spokesman on the bill, Francis Pym, *The Times* (London), 23 August 1977. He particularly resents that there is no reduction of regional MPs to achieve parity with England, which would certainly reduce Labour representation in the Commons.

190 Richard Rose, 'The options for constitutional unity in Great Britain today', in *Conference Papers*, Rowntree Devolution Conference, May 1976 (London: Rowntree Trust, 1976), p. 25. The report also contains succinct papers on the position of all the major and minor political actors.

191 See in particular their careful analysis of the multiplication of intergovernmental agencies, Lord Crowther-Hunt and A. T. Peacock, *Memorandum of Dissent for the Royal Commission on the Constitution*, Cmd 5460-II (London: HMSO, 1973), Ch. V, pp. 61–83.

192 Brian W. Hogwood and Peter Lindley, 'Which English regions? An analysis of regional boundaries used by government departments and other public bodies', PSA Conference on UK Politics, August 1979, ms., p. 45. See also the analysis of Michael Keating and Malcolm Rhodes, 'Is there a regional level of government in England?', ms. presented at the same conference, and the earlier analysis of Brian C. Smith, *Regionalism in England: Regional Institutions: A Guide* (London: Acton Society Trust, 1964).

193 Suleiman, op. cit., pp. 285–302. See particularly his discussion of the British need

for a counter-bureaucracy, which has been an issue for the past twenty years. The French, by contrast, create a counter-bureaucracy within the administration.

194   Peter Self, 'Rational decentralisation', in Crick *et al*., op. cit., p. 90.

―――――――

Chapter 6

FISCAL POLICY AND LOCAL SPENDING: THE DOUBLE SQUEEZE

> It is open to question whether there is a system for local govern-
> ment finance and, if there is, who purports to control that part of
> the system that lies in the hands of the government. There are few
> signs of either a system or a coherent set of related arrangements
> so far as Whitehall is concerned. – Layfield Report.

> In a country where political battles are violent and spirits
> unscrupulous, direct taxes run the risk of being instruments of
> oppression. – Pierre Leroy-Beaulieu.

As the welfare state increased in scope and complexity, the
subnational systems of Britain and France, and most highly industrial
countries, were caught in a strange dilemma. On the one hand, local
government assumed a more important role in delivering the goods
and services provided by the state. In effect, the political system
became more dependent on local organization and execution of both
nationally and locally determined policies. At the same time, national
government, not too surprisingly, looked for new ways to be sure that
local government was adhering to national objectives. The growing
complexity of the interrelationships within the subnational system led
the state to seek new controls, many of which date from the nineteenth
century.

Modern government could not successfully impose the detailed
controls needed to supervise local spending on a service-by-service
basis, although, as we saw in Chapter 5, Britain preserved a more
diverse, and therefore, in many ways, a more demanding set of
controls over localities than did France. British moves toward more
control over local spending can easily be traced to late Victorian
England, and it is the fact that British local finance is so deeply
imbedded in national compromises about national and local taxation
that the system of huge local subsidies was devised. The result was that
British local government was, and remains, more deeply involved with
redistributive efforts of the welfare state. With the full development
of the welfare state after the Second World War, there was effectively
no turning back the policy of subsidies that both subordinated local
government to national finances, and narrowed the issue to how the
transfer would be organized and calculated. Thus, the curious effect
of more responsible local government in Britain was to make it more
dependent on national government. An even more damaging effect

was that concentrating on the expenditure side of local finance meant that local government virtually lost its influence over determining the size and nature of local resources.

Both economic and political reasons combined to preserve the bargaining role of French local government. Because they did not spend as high a proportion of national income as did British localities, they were a less visible target for economies, and, as we saw in Chapter 4, the communes were so intimately connected with national politics throughout the Third and Fourth Republics that changes in either their spending responsibilities or their taxation almost immediately became a national political issue. For all the efforts of de Gaulle to more effectively subordinate communes, the pattern does not change substantially in the Fifth Republic. While the dislocations and destruction of the two world wars, and the Depression, helped justify tighter administrative controls from roughly 1918,[1] the political linkage between locality and Paris remained strong and unlike Britain there were no major fiscal and financial reforms affecting local government between the wars.

As we shall see, the so-called 'fiscal crisis' of the cities is by no means a product of the economic problems of the 1970s. Both British and French leaders were acutely aware of the growing needs of cities from the turn of the century. There has been more than a little ideological bias in recent interpretations which serve both Conservative champions of local autonomy and Socialist believers in irreconcilable conflict. From a policymaking perspective, it becomes clearer that the pattern of fiscal and financial interdependence was both understood and vitally important for many years. Neither level of government could exist without the other. The policy problem was how to construct a new framework within which to carry on the bargaining over local resources and spending that is deeply rooted in the nineteenth century. As such, the compromises of the past few decades are built on national tax and investment policies, and reflect national economic priorities that were well known to policymakers at both levels of government. If we are more aware of the possible conflicts, it is not necessarily because national leaders intentionally set out to exploit cities, but because the importance of local government itself requires that a new framework be constructed.

Although we shall unavoidably be concerned with the economic implications of the two patterns of central–local fiscal and financial relationships,[2] the main concern of this chapter is to show how fiscal interdependence in the French system, consistent with the arguments put forth concerning political and administrative relationships in the two previous chapters, provides more opportunities for local influence over national policymaking than does the British. The explanation is not a simple one, but emerges from historical, political and administrative constraints on local actors in the two systems. In fact, a purely economic explanation is insufficient because the overall importance of the two subnational systems in relation to the national economy is actually about the same. Had the presumably more authoritarian French national government the power over the communes that the British system provides Whitehall, the tortured and intricate political process of local tax and spending reform in France would never have taken place. In contrast, British national policies toward local spending, investment (see Chapter 7) and taxation appear to be extraordinarily arbitrary, and the center has been able to impose its policies with relatively little effective resistance.

Although the spending of French local government is only about a fourth of national spending when measured by the formal accounts of each level of government, most agree that the additional funds directed to departments, regions and communes bring the total proportion of spending at the local level to roughly the British proportion of a third of public spending in local hands. Since 1966 British local government has received nearly 40 percent of its funds directly from central government in the form of the Rate Support Grant and a few remaining, but small, specific grants. By 1974 the grant amounted to two-thirds of local spending and has since been reduced to about 60 percent. Again, the formal accounts of the French local government system show that slightly less than a fourth of local receipts are from government subsidies. The main transfer is *versement représentatif de la taxe sur les salaires* or VRTS (27.8 billion francs in 1978), but if one adds to this the various other grants to local government, the total transfer becomes 53.2 billion francs or about a third of local spending.[3] In relation to current local taxes, the British local governments raise slightly more than a fourth of their revenues by local taxation, and the French local governments about 40 percent.

Although the differences in these macrofigures are not negligible, the important policy effect is that in neither country can national leaders easily ignore the fiscal and financial behavior of local government. There is no more persuasive evidence of the mutual dependence of national and local government. But the differences are considerable and more directly affect central–local policymaking in the two countries. First, the French subsidy to local government is dispersed through a variety of transfers and therefore more vulnerable to central–local politics. In this respect, the French system of subsidizing local government more closely resembles that of the United States than that of Britain.[4] There are distinct patterns of bargaining affecting both current capital and expenditure. Second, Westminster has steadfastly refused to give British local government a share of indirect taxes, and all local taxation is from a local property tax (rates). The twofold tax base of French local government introduces another dimension into central–local negotiations, which, as we shall see, has by no means uniformly worked to the advantage of central government. Third, tax bargaining in France gives the local governments a leverage over national government that tends to reproduce at the national level many of the basic political conflicts in French society. The effect in terms of central–local policymaking is congruent with the more general political and administrative relationships discussed above.

The dispersion of political power through these fiscal and financial relationships is, of course, reinforced by the territorial complexity of the system itself. Few realize, for example, that of the total spending within the French local government system, only half takes place in the communes. Though the British local councils show few propensities to collectively resist central spending and subsidy decisions, their consolidation acts as a detriment to effective bargaining for resources. The huge local budgets of British local councils plus the highly inelastic nature of the property tax relative to personal income generate understandable anxieties within each council, and the entire structure we have already described leads them into a simplified form of bargaining that basically reflects the town versus country distinction, and, in turn, fits the needs of national politics very well. French mayors have not only tax and budget negotiations, but in addition the array of investment agencies and plans (see Chapter 7), their voice in social assistance committees and public housing corporations, and the intricate bargaining over public works to enhance their influence and to provide access at the national level.

As might be expected, the French pattern of central–local finance supports and benefits from the *complicité* of central–local politics, while the simplified British system works to provide much greater powers in the hands of national policymakers. As we shall see, the concentration of fiscal and financial power over local government in Britain has, nonetheless, often been used to meet national political aims, thereby imposing erratic and abrupt changes on local finance. The point is not that British central–local finances are more stable or even more generous than those of France, but that British local politicians only indirectly influence national financial decisions affecting local government, but French mayors take a direct part in these negotiations. The overall effect is to perpetuate confrontations between national and local government, while many of the underlying policy problems are simply ignored. British local government, for example, has been pleading for an indirect tax since the turn of the century.[5] The Labour government (1974–79) steadily amended the subsidies to help their urban supporters. In a way that would be unimaginable in France, the Conservative Secretary of State for the Environment, Heseltine, proposed in 1979 simply to abolish the Rate Support Grant machinery. It is not that such abrupt and partisan intervention is unexpected, but that it can so readily manipulate the system without more attention to expressed local needs while simultaneously doing so little to devise new policies. The result is that neither national nor local policy aims have been well served.

The gradual shift of central–local relationships to fiscal and financial problems can be detected well before the more recent economic crises of each country, and, as noted above, was a function of the growing importance of local government in the life of both countries. From 1963 to 1973 local current expenditure in Britain was increasing at an annual rate of nearly 13 percent, which was 3 percent faster than the growth of national expenditure.[6] In France from 1959 to 1973 local expenditure also increased at nearly 13 percent per year or about 3 percent more than the rate of growth of national spending.[7] From a national perspective, the pressures on leaders of both countries were the same. Because the total share of public spending in relation to national income was already higher in Britain, the urgency for reform was perhaps greater in Britain.

Both countries began to look seriously on the shortcomings of central–local financial relationships in the mid-1960s, but the British did not break out of the heavy constraints imposed by the Rate Support Grant, nor did they even choose to use this control effectively until the national economic crisis became severe in the mid-1970s. Much as in the nineteenth century, the solution remained increased subsidies to forestall more fundamental reform. Although rebuffed and harassed by local political forces, the French undertook the reform of local taxation in 1966. If this intensely controversial process only drew to a close in 1979, it must also be acknowledged that the process has been the product of both national and local politics, and that in many ways it provides a more active role for local government in the allocation of national resources than does the British system. In trying to align local spending and investment with national economic objectives, the French government can, of course, call on a more elaborate administrative apparatus linked to national government.

The French Ministry of Finance has not one, but numerous networks which reach into the subnational system. The kingpin is surely the Trésorier et Payeur Général (TPG), who supervises state expenditure at all levels, but there are also the regional offices of the Direction des Impôts (the tax office) and of the Caisse des Dépôts and Consignations (CDC) which provides credit for local investment and public works. Unlike the British Treasury, the Ministry of Finance has built into its structure territorial cross-pressures and objectives that moderate its effective powers.[8] If it is possibly the most powerful agency affecting local government in France today, it is less because the *inspecteurs de finances* scheme to control communes than because the growing complexity of local tasks can only be aggregated by fiscal and financial measures.

The British Treasury does not have the field services of the French Ministry of Finance and is therefore more vulnerable should local government overspend, waste money or simply make poor forecasts, as so often happens during rapid inflation.[9] The effect is a very curious one, for the Treasury must find a way to anticipate local spending and at the same time provide local resources with almost no local defenses. The result is that the Treasury, perhaps understandably, takes its centralized controls very seriously,[10] exercises more arbitrary control over total local spending than the French Ministry can, and for more than a century has successfully confined local government to a very limited resource base. Despite the fact that Britain has one of the most heavily burdened local government systems in the world, the British fiscal system provides less flexibility and fewer alternatives at the local level than any other major country.

From the local level the fiscal and financial state of local government always appears miserable. The very different institutional structures notwithstanding, Britain and France both claim that localities have the freedom to spend whatever they wish. The 1970 reforms of the French communes provide that communes over 9,000 inhabitants do not need to have their budgets formally approved by the prefect if they are in balance. The British counties and districts have always been at liberty to increase property taxes indefinitely and their budget forecasts are not individually subject to central review. One of the few things that the central departments were able to agree on when testifying before the Layfield Committee was that the British system is 'open-ended'.[11] Of course, nothing could be more misleading than the formalities of budgetary control. Local mayors and party leaders know all too well that they cannot increase local taxes indefinitely, and national tax systems in both countries limit choice on where the burden will fall. The important difference in the two local government systems is the immense importance of local services in the British system, which has made it a natural target for equalization of benefits and resources. British local governments are by virtue of their functional importance an instrument of national policymaking in a way that is much less relevant to the French system.

The dogmatic character of the British local government system is nowhere more apparent than in the wish to provide substantial local services while simultaneously defining what services should be provided and what resources are available. Unhappily, the best of both worlds can only be enjoyed when economic growth permits the national government to freely redistribute national income. In doing so over the 1960s, the transfer from national to local government (Rate Support Grant or RSG) grew by leaps and bounds to eventually amount to approximately half the income of counties and districts.[12] Intent on equalizing services through local government, little attention was paid to increasing local resources; nor was the Treasury − more vulnerable to tax changes than to spending changes − particularly eager to make the cost of growth apparent to local government. The overall effect was to make the final accounting of spending and resources almost totally a Treasury function. In trying to obtain control over aggregate spending, it traded control of specific services. To keep control of the tax structure, which implied confining local government to the rates, it only needed to keep quiet.

The paradox is that what appears to be no control in a period of growth becomes a harsh control in a period of decline or stagnation. Put more simply, the interaction of national and local governments to adjust their spending and resources as economic constraints change is cumbersome. In fact, until 1975, the machinery did not exist, nor were ministers eager to have such devices as the Consultative Council until the near disasters of the mid-1970s.[13] In assessing the national response to local economic dilemmas, it is important to note that much the same erratic behavior can be observed in British national economic policy.[14] At the local level, the sudden shifts and reversals were most often manifested in the rapid changes in spending for public housing. Once the ineffectiveness of the Treasury's controls on total local spending had become intolerable by 1975, there was, as with national spending itself, no machinery policymaking available to restrict spending, and the extremely drastic device of cash limit budgeting was imposed from above.[15]

The network of influence that reinforces the French local government system gives local, departmental and regional political leaders a voice in many financial decisions where they in fact have only a marginal financial responsibility. Influence is apportioned more or less in proportion to fiscal and financial interest across the spectrum of governmental functions. Like British mayors, and mayors throughout the world, French mayors want to spend more without increasing the local tax burden, and they have also been relatively successful in using their political leverage to delay and amend tax reforms. Unlike Britain, France set out nearly a decade ago to revise an archaic local tax structure, and to link local taxes to the national economy through indirect taxation. While these efforts have not been entirely successful, the mayors have a stake in the economy that the property tax base has never given the British mayors. Painful as it may be to levy indirect taxes at the local level, the French system has been gradually converted to a more modern system of calculating and collecting local taxes, and the local tax structure thus interlocks with the national tax structure. Weighing the advantages and disadvantages of the two approaches is difficult. But the debate of the past decade suggests that limiting the local resource base to the property tax simply eliminates bargaining for resources, and focuses attention on bargaining over needs.

The French system of intergovernmental fiscal and financial relationships provides access to national decisions without raising global problems, while the British system separates national and local tax decisions to preserve global control. Had local government spending reached the proportions of the British system, it is unlikely that the Ministry of Finance or the mayors would have undertaken the risk of reform. Paradoxically, it is by accepting responsibilities that British local government has sacrificed leverage over its own resources. The capacity of the French local government system to adjust to fiscal realities may be underestimated, while the limited capacity of the British system may produce national economic catastrophe. To understand both structures one must look briefly at the historical development of central–local fiscal relationships in each country.

HISTORICAL BASES OF RESOURCE ALLOCATION: MONEY AND POLITICS RUN DEEP

Although tax conflicts are a more revealing indication of political strength than many more laboriously devised indices, they have, on the whole, been neglected by political science. Their importance to understanding central–local finance in the two countries cannot be underestimated, and stems from very early decisions on the just and proper way to pay for the services of the state. Though we now tend to see these controversies in terms of contemporary conflicts between national and local government, they were in fact major national controversies, and involved the major political forces of each period.[16] While we cannot do full justice to the bitter historical conflicts over how tax burdens should be shared, such national issues became the limiting conditions for increasing local resources and revenues.

If local reliance on the rates seems perplexing in the British system, it should be noted that it dates from the sixteenth century, when the Tudor monarchs brought the justices of the peace under control. The earliest procedure was to impose charges as services grew, such as a users' tax for bridges and highways; and later a rudimentary local income tax was imposed to fund the Poor Laws of 1601. Rating as now practiced was established in 1840. The principle was to distinguish between needs that were considered government general expenses, and therefore to be equally shared, and individual benefits, which the more fortunate were obliged to provide. The former became national taxes and contributions went to the monarch, while individual benefits were considered local and were paid for through property rates to the counties and parishes. Obviously, the system became extraordinarily intricate over the years, and by the late seventeenth century there were over forty different rates to which local governments were entitled, each attached to an individual service.[17]

The reform of the Poor Laws in 1834 launched a controversy about the incidence of local taxation that continued throughout the century. The effect of the debate was to distract attention from the underlying problem of the resource base allocated to the counties and boroughs. As Parliament added new local services over the century, additional rates were authorized to support the proliferation of boards, commissions and committees, making careful calculation of the burden of local taxation, its incidence and its effectiveness almost impossible to calculate.[18] The dual procedure became that local governments first calculated their estimated expenses and anticipated income from local taxes, while also adjusting to central subsidies and grants. The confusion within the local government system itself made a more explicit national debate over the division of resources and tax capabilities impossible. Unlike in France, there was simply no framework and little motivation to discuss the overall fiscal structure. This divorce between resources and needs in the calculation of local taxes in Britain has never been amended.

There were three ways in which the nineteenth century liberal state could relieve the fiscal pressures at the local level. First, it could simply exempt certain classes of local property from rates. This was first done in 1846 as a concession, when Peel made the repeal of the Corn Laws acceptable to landowners in Parliament by drawing on the Contingency Fund to relieve local rates.[19] The major beneficiaries of parliamentary pressure remain farmers, who have not had their land taxed since the Local Government Act of 1929 completely derated it. Secondly, the government could provide specific grants to local governments for services that it deemed appropriate. This was done, for example, with voluntary schools in 1833. Thirdly, the government could, in effect, placate local government by agreeing to pay part of the costs of a service. This was done with the courts, prisons and the police in the 1830s when the center acknowledged that the maintenance of law and order was a shared responsibility. The effect of these reliefs was a dramatic increase in financial transfers from national to local government. In 1830 the grant was a mere 100,000 pounds 'for trivial odds and ends',[20] but by 1870 the grant had reached a million and a quarter pounds. Over the same period of time, local rates increased from eight to sixteen million pounds – only doubling, while the center's contribution multiplied ten times. Thus, what was and remains the most arbitrary control on local spending, the conditional grant, developed very early in British practice and was further defined by public health legislation from 1848 onward.

By mid-century the political controversy over taxation centered on relief of the ratepayer (local property tax) as weighed against the 'taxpayer' (national income tax). Gladstone strongly preferred helping the latter, advocating abolition of the income tax and brushing aside a proposal in 1871 from his able advisor, Goschen, that particular revenues should be assigned to local government to relieve urban ratepayers. When Disraeli came to office, the tactic was reversed and a surplus of over a million pounds was given over to rate relief for various services. As Redlich and Hirst point out, this was a basic turning point in the relation between central and local finance, and 'Later grants assume more and more the character of mere doles to relieve some favoured class out of the purse of the general taxpayer'.[21] Although Goschen made a second attempt to make assigned revenues the basis for local government finance in the 1888 Act, the funds proved insufficient by the turn of the century.[22]

But the struggle to increase local resources in late Victorian England was not a conflict between politically aggressive local governments and national government. Until the turn of the century Parliament was in the hands of landowners, and the real fight was to achieve national reform of death duties and inheritance taxes. Just as Peel acquiesced against his better judgment in 1846 to use national funds to relieve landowners should the price effects of Corn Law repeal increase local taxes, so also the 1888 Act provided about two million pounds of local tax relief to landowners in order to get agreement on national tax reform. The inequities this imposed on local government did not seem to bother Parliament any more in 1888 than now. Even the creation of districts in 1894 was at the cost of derating land of half its value because landowners feared more local taxation. There was no doubt about the cumulative transfer of the local tax burden to the new towns and cities. In 1817 land was providing two-thirds of the rate revenues, but by 1891 only 15 percent.[23] Although Goschen insisted on the dogma that local and 'Imperial' taxes be kept distinct, he also suggested in 1868 that income tax be shared with localities. But a Parliament of landed aristocracy not only consistently refused to increase land taxes, but extracted enormous local tax exemptions in exchange for relatively minor, if urgent, national tax reform in the 1890s.

With the rapid expansion of local services following the Education Act of 1902, the system reverted to the use of conditional grants linked to national objectives. The incoherence of the grant system led Cannan, the local financial expert of the period, to lament that it would be 'difficult to devise a more atrocious jumble of finance'.[24] Grice, no friend of central government intervention, wrote, 'The National Government in the past three quarters of a century has successively "bought" the rights of inspection, audit, supervision, initiative, criticism and control in respect of one local government service after another . . .'.[25] The curious effect of the central initiative in expanding and financing local services was to force localities to politicize as a protection against the rate increases necessitated by conditional grants. Hennock persuasively argues that 'The system of local government finance tended therefore to push a section of the inhabitants, often a predominantly lower-middle-class section, into municipal politics.'[26] Though the structure elicited considerable financial ingenuity from more able local politicians,[27] like Joseph Chamberlain in Birmingham, it also established an adversary relationship between local and national interests wherein the central government, and above all the Treasury, realized that it must not lose the upper hand. At the turn of the century the central government was providing roughly one-fourth of local government revenues, and the trend was not reversed until 1977.

The foundations for the modern system of bargaining for grants were set by the Local Government Act of 1929. The nineteenth century system was clearly not working well in many ways. The percentage-based conditional grants favored richer local authorities and expenses soon exceeded the resources provided by the assigned revenues; the variety and restrictions on conditional grants were bewildering and at the local level it was clear that the rating system, still managed by local government, had serious inequities. The debate within the Cabinet went on throughout the 1920s, finally to be resolved by the determined efforts of Neville Chamberlain.[28] The 1929 legislation established the Block Grant, which in various guises continued until 1979 to be the 'unconditional' grant provided by central government out of general taxation, and distributed by the center according to an evolving set of criteria. In 1930 the grant represented about a third of all government transfers to localities. It was partly distributed by a weighted population formula and partly (the education transfer) using a crude means test. The rating system as such was not significantly changed, but the tactic was to adjust its inequities by 'objective' standards imposed by the center.

Chamberlain's experience in reforming local finance indicates how resource and spending decisions are institutionally separated in the British local government system, almost the opposite of the intricate interdependence of both national and local taxation in France. Although Chamberlain wanted a standard system of evaluation for the rates, the Conservatives refused and the outcome was a compromise that perpetuated the divorce between local and national resource calculations. This decision tended to foreclose any possibility of later introducing some common base for calculating national and local taxes; this in turn might have made a more complex system of fiscal interdependence possible. Likewise, the timing of his legislation put rating reform ahead of grant reform.

The Rating and Evaluation Act of 1925 was of higher immediate priority because of the inherited anachronisms of the Poor Law rates. Though not a major consideration at the time, this meant that when the grant system was reexamined four years later, grants were not directly linked to local needs or fiscal performance. In effect, taxation decisions emerged from the Chamberlain reforms even more firmly separated at different levels of government than they had been in the old system. Of course, when setting local rates, local councillors are not unaware of the national implications and the grant system, but unlike in France there are no explicit relationships nor direct negotiations to link decisionmaking at the two levels of government. This relationship maximizes local uncertainties, and may provoke fiscal irresponsibility. As we have seen so often, the local government associations only 'wanted more Exchequer money, but they wanted it without detailed control and inspection'.[29] In these ways, the central–local fiscal relationship became, as it has tended to remain, an adversary relationship in which the upper hand inevitably goes to the Treasury.

By the end of the Second World War, the anomalies of the Block Grant were apparent to all and had indeed been compounded by population shifts, industrial development and wartime destruction. Labour came to power determined to eliminate the inequities of the 1929 Act. Bevan, the forceful Minister of Health, was not particularly interested in reorganizing local government, but he was indignant that local evaluation of property meant that 'the local authorities (could) themselves determine the size of the spoon with which they will scoop up Exchequer money'.[30] The Local Government Act of 1948 ushered in the Exchequer Equalisation Grant to replace the Block Grant system. But the intent was not so much to find a better way of co-ordinating national and local finances, as to remove the inequities of the rating system. The rate burden was no longer to be determined by the imputed rent and assessed by the Local Authority, but in relation to average rents throughout the country and by a standardized property evaluation of the Board of Inland Revenue.[31]

Two important distinctions were introduced, the first of which did not appear as a control until much later. The Treasury was to determine 'relevant expenditure', that is, the expenses that would be allowed in arriving at the total grant. Of course, the local authorities influence the Treasury estimates of grants through their own forecasts of future spending, and by bargaining about the relevant portions of each service that will be included in calculating the total transfer. But these interventions only permit indirect bargaining on sharing public resources and cannot question the premises of the overall tax structure which affect central–local relations. As we shall see in examining the Rate Support Grant in more detail, this became an arbitrary control because 'relevance' is determined by the various central departments and the Treasury's national considerations before the local situation is examined. Unlike the more complex, and admittedly much more contentious, French system, the local authorities only enter into the decision process after many crucial policy decisions have already been made. Structuring intergovernmental fiscal negotiations in this way protects the center against local pressures, and provides the appearance of orderly central decisionmaking until the system breaks down, as it did in 1975.

The second change was to incorporate within the grant two basically incompatible objectives,[32] and, thereby, encourage national political manipulation of local fiscal decisions. The unintended effect was to encourage Parliament to neglect reform until the 1970s crisis, because the political process was distracted from any consideration of the underlying problems of the entire system. Furthermore, making the grant procedure part of a national partisan debate meant that local political interests were effectively excluded. Essentially, the new grant was to equalize the resources of local authorities by compensating for inadequate tax bases. These two aims became the 'resources' (equalizing) element and the 'needs' (tax burden) element of the grant calculation. In effect, the British designed a transfer process that was suited to a highly centralized political system, and each party could find within the procedure something that would fit its partisan objectives. Unfortunately, the political requirements did not extend to closing the open-ended system of arriving at the grant itself. For thirty years Conservatives would advocate relief for the local taxpayer (the 'needs' element) and Labour would argue for more equalization (the 'resources' element). By 1950 local governments were so dependent on the grant, and so isolated from national decisions, that they neither had nor were disposed to acquire the political leverage to make a new departure. The grant system was locked into a procedure that suited the two-party system, but at the cost of creating immense uncertainties for local governments. That the system made almost no financial sense was quite secondary.

Because the major parties and the basic considerations entering the grant system are not directly interdependent, it is not only very easy to tamper with particular parts, but it is also very easy to find grievances and inequities. The ratepayer is, of course, perpetually grieved, but the complaint over the abrupt increase of property tax when revaluation does take place cannot be totally ignored.[33]

The local governments have little national incentive to restrict spending, nor at the national level does the system help restrain ministerial demands for additional spending. Coupled with industrial relocation, the long-delayed reorganization of local government meant an increase in the variation in property values. Even at the pre-1974 scale, any mechanism for equalization short of the circuitous route devised for central intervention caused on outcry from counties and boroughs. In short, the system had no self-equilibriating qualities and a number of vulnerabilities, many of which could be exploited for short-term political advantage. Well before the 1948 system was fully implemented, Labour and Conservative spokesmen were admitting their disappointment and a new round of studies was launched.[34] In 1957 the Conservative government published a White Paper[35] and the following year a new Local Government Act transformed the grant system.

The White Paper led to a fierce debate not about the nature of the grant system but about the threat to local education departments. Under the General Grant procedure, most percentage grants were terminated and the government was to determine itself the permissible level of support rather than working from past expenditure levels. In practice, this apparently arbitrary decision could not be divorced from what local government was spending. The debate was both misdirected and futile. Under the new procedure, the Treasury and the

Table 6.1 *The Transformation of the British Grant from 1929 to 1980[a]*

Main Acts	Rationale	Distribution	Elements		
			Needs	Resources	Domestic
(Rating and Valuation Act 1925)					
Block Grants (1929)	Replace income lost by derating	Weighted population[b]	None	None	None
Exchequer Equalisation Grants (1948)	Equalize rate income[c]	National averages of rateable values	None	Resource only	None
(Rating and Valuation Act of 1957)					
General Grants (1958)	Consolidate specific grants	Dual formula	General Grant	Rate Deficiency Grant	None
(Rating Relief Act 1964)					
(Allen Committee 1965)					
Rate Support Grants (1966)	Reduce local tax burden	Complex formulas	Mainly demo-graphic factors	Standard rateable values	Rate relief factors[d]
Rate Support Grants	Increase flexibility	Regression formula	Same	Same	Flat rate
			London adjust-ments from 1975	National standard values (1975)	Fixed and variable portions (1975)
			'Safety Net' (1979)		England-Wales parts (1976)
Block Grant[e] (1980)	Create disincentives to spend	Directly calculated by DoE	National estimate 'standard expendi-ture	National estimate 'standard rate poundage'	Rate relief un-changed

[a]All these changes are incorporated in Local Government Acts of the noted years except for the Rating Act of 1966.

[b]To shift to the formula base over fifteen years similar to the VRTS transition planned in France.

[c]Coupled with a system of standard national assessment to be completed in 1956 and implemented by ministerial order.

[d]Coupled with individual rate rebates under the Rating Act of 1966 plus additional rent subsidies administered under welfare programs.

[e]The Bill plans to introduce new controls in 1980–81 and take full effect in 1981–82. Changes linked to ceilings on local rates and penalties for overspending.

Ministry of Housing and Local Government prepared a two-year forecast. Though the formulation of the grant was essentially unchanged, the proposal made the conflict in aims more distinct. The equalization component became the Rate Deficiency Grant, which would not be paid to local governments above certain levels of rate revenues. The General Grant became in essence the 'needs' component to be paid to all authorities on the basis of population, dispersion and a variety of factors which contributed to local expenses. When the first estimates of future grants were negotiated in 1958, the local governments were assured they would not be impoverished. Nonetheless, the Labour Party was furious at witnessing the restructuring of their equalization scheme, and their anger only increased with the reorganization of London government in 1963.

By now local finance figured in the platforms of both major parties, though neither had a very clear idea about what they wanted to do. As Rhodes notes, 'It was not so much . . . what was changed in 1958 as what was left unchanged that quickly brought the subject of local government finance into prominence again.'[36] Although the rates were supposed to be the means by which local government could exercise some initiative over local services, the inflexibility of the property tax and the statutory controls left the localities little choice. In 1960 the government again increased taxation on industrial property and tried to reduce taxes on homeowners, the ultimate step toward establishing central control.[37]

When Labour came to power in 1964 it was determined to undo the Conservative measures. Oddly enough, the Conservatives had actually shown their opponents how easily the system could be manipulated. What Crossman described with his usual enthusiasm as the greatest reform in rating for a hundred years, in fact did little to change the basic design of the system or the grant level.[38] What it did do was provide another way by which parties might manipulate the grant to their own designs. The 1966 Local Government Act offered no new sources of income, rejected the idea that central government might simply absorb some local expenses, and added a new component to future calculations of the grant, the 'domestic' element. The new component was basically a rent subsidy for homeowners which, as we shall see, became a political football while doing nothing to alter the grant system as a whole. Renamed the Rate Support Grant, the new system concentrated on Labour's long-standing interest that the transfer should have a redistributive effect. But, in a system with no built-in checks, this could ultimately only increase local dependence on the transfer.[39]

With regard to central–local relations, two characteristics of the transformation of the British grant system stand out. First, the dialogue about rates and other independent sources of local income was increasingly divorced from the discussion of the grant system itself. The local government associations were divided among themselves. They tended to be on the defensive where local authorities had substantial rateable values (mainly the counties), and sought more grants where they did not (mainly the boroughs). The central government was in an ideal position to play the historic game of town versus country, and as it did so the localities were paralyzed. Indeed they never even seemed concerned that the entire fiscal relationship worked to their disadvantage. Although changes in 1948, 1958 and 1966 caused furious partisan outcries, the initiative in the resource debate stayed with the center, and the localities' dependence on the center grew with the growth of transfers.

Though rates were still determined at the local level, the application of the system to different types of property (agricultural land, industrial and commercial buildings, dwellings) remained a national decision, and reconsideration of the rating system was increasingly separated from the grant structure as a whole.[40] As shown in Table 6.1, the last year when grant reforms were directly linked to local concerns was 1929, when loss of rate revenues was balanced against Chamberlain's consolidation of local taxes. In 1948 the issue was clearly one of forcing localities to take taxation and equity more seriously by linking the grant to rateable values; and in 1958 the process culminated when central government took over the definition of 'relevant expenditure', with no direct consideration of local problems. By 1966, Crossman was 'caught between his desire to break out of the dilemma by some bold radical move – abolish rates, give local authorities a better local tax – and the need, in the face of departmental skepticism about the practicality of any fundamental change, to keep the system going'. Sympathetic as he was to local democracy, the 1966 reform put central government 'in a position not only to determine in advance the total of Exchequer support to local authorities, but in effect, to control the total level of expenditure by local authorities'.[41]

But determining the nationally approved level of local expenditure is very different from actually being able to enforce it. Because the grant is based on local estimates of future expenditure which Whitehall is incapable of evaluating, Treasury controls must focus on the grant system, which further confuses the central–local debate on fiscal issues. Until the fiscal year 1977–78 the 'relevant expenditure' component constantly increased, although the increases in current spending after the imposition of cash limits in 1976 were fairly small. The disequilibrium with which national policymakers had to deal is displayed in Table 6.2. The trends of local government spending were still in relative harmony with changes in national spending and in GNP through most of the 1950s. But in the 1960s local government spending began to surge ahead of both national spending and economic capacity. Some of the largest increases came under the Conservative government of 1970–74, although the rate of increase of local expenditure was roughly twice that of GNP in the late 1960s under Labour. As we shall see, it took the disastrous economic dislocations of the 1973 oil crisis and 1974 borrowing to bring these rates of change back into line with national capacities. But perhaps the most lamentable weakness of central–local fiscal and financial relationships over the past two decades has been that despite these huge concessions to local needs, the political system has never built a more workable system of negotiation and compromise.

Table 6.2   *Rates of Growth of Local Government Expenditure, Local Grants, National Expenditure and GNP from 1890 to 1978[a]*

	Local Expenditure	Local Grants	National Expenditure	GNP
1890–00	97	91	115	32
1900–10	32	59	– 3	10
1910–20	144	115	485	183
1920–28	26	56	– 31	– 25
1928–38	33	52	45	17
1938–50	99	108	186	120
1950–55	45	62	35	44
1955–60	70	52	25	35
1960–65	72	61	56	38
1965–70	61	96	73	40
1970–72	26	31	26	26
1972–75	102	131	96	69
1975–76	13	20	13	18
1976–77	1	– .001	6	12
1977–78	6	.01	16	13

[a]Figures through 1955 taken from Peacock and Wiseman, *The Growth of Public Expenditure* (London: Allen & Unwin, 1967, rev. edn). Subsequent years from *Local Government Statistics*, Annual Report (London: HMSO), and *National Income and Expenditure* (London: HMSO, 1979), p. 63. Note that the time periods are shorter for more recent years and so the rates of growth are not always directly comparable. (Current prices.)

In contrast to the British system of local finance, the French system has never acquired the open-ended character of the British grant. For a number of reasons national leaders, even if they had a more stable party structure, would probably never have intervened in local fiscal and financial policy to the degree found in Britain. The various regimes since the Revolution did not depend on local government to provide services of a magnitude similar to that in Britain, and as local benefits grew from the Third Republic onward they were often organized outside the local government system. Lacking the harmony of political interest between levels of government found in Britain from the eighteenth century until the present, the communes and provinces were in many respects equal competitors of the state for national resources.

All this is not to deny that there were strong centralizing forces in French financial history, but they never enjoyed the almost unchallenged success of the British Treasury. As noted in Chapter 2, the financial organization of the Bourbon monarchs was diverse and unreliable. The 'tax farms' organized by Colbert in the seventeenth century were creditors of the monarch, and commercial and banking privileges were rooted in provincial organizations. The modern influence of the *grands corps* stems in part from Necker's desperate attempts to bring some order out of the fiscal chaos just before the Revolution, by using the embryo elite administrators to overcome an incoherent array of treasuries, special funds and tax collectors. 'In 1788 the Treasury received and paid scarcely more than half of the funds in the total budget of the state.'[42]

Nor did the Revolution relieve financial chaos. The Constituent Assembly despised the taxes on tobacco and salt, which were first abolished and then restored in the First Empire, and there was no reliable land register. The basic principles of the French tax system were selected for the very practical reason that fixed property was the only available way in which to assess wealth. The French tax system of 1791 had no choice but to adopt the principles of the *ancien régime* for taxing property. Today's despised system grew from historic necessity and not from any malevolent designs on the part of the administration, which, in fact, had nothing besides property taxes with which to launch the new Republic. Napoleon tried to introduce a fairer tax system, but it was rejected at the Restoration. In many respects, the struggle for tax reform has been going on for nearly 200 years, but, unlike in Britain, local notables and councillors were never fully excluded from the debate.

The national setting for the development of the local fiscal and financial system was, therefore, very different from Britain's. From Napoleonic times onward, local spending was kept under control and historically displays the same close and fairly constant relationship to macroeconomic change that can be observed over the past fifty years.[43] In part, this is simply the deeply-rooted mentality of the *rentier*, who believes that a return should be assured when an investment takes place regardless of the fortunes of the marketplace and growth. But there are also more concrete historical reasons. The Napoleonic wars were paid for with plunder and heavy penalties extracted from the victims, but the 'Hundred Days' left huge debts and to these the Allies added huge Occupation costs.[44] Out of these events came the Caisse des Dépôts (CDC), which was to become the major financial agent both for local government and for many additional state activities. Created in 1816 and intentionally organized outside the Treasury, its objectives were to protect savings from 'the cupidity and unfaithfulness of certain depositors' and 'the vicissitudes of the Treasury'.[45] Thus, the constrained nature of local spending and finance in nineteenth century France should not be interpreted solely as evidence of state oppression, but, on the contrary, as an effort to evade the uncertainties of state finance and to establish a self-reliant fiscal system.

From Poor Law reform onward Britain was adding functions to local government, whereas the French were trying to simplify the roles of local as well as national government. They insisted, as they do today, that each component of the local government system be financially distinct and fully accountable. Although the communes were heavily dependent on direct taxes, French tax principles extended levies to a variety of commercial activities (*octroi*) and thereby provided a more elastic tax base. Indeed, a nineteenth century tax expert found it 'bizarre' that British localities should place so few burdens on those who benefited most from the state.[46] Nor were the French unaware of the inequities built into the British tax system, and their political significance. Leroy-Beaulieu, the leading financial expert at the turn of the century, wrote, 'In a country where political battles are violent and spirits unscrupulous, direct taxes run the risk of being instruments of oppression.'[47] As Goschen had pointed out in his 1870 report, British direct local taxes had doubled since 1841, while national taxes had remained constant and even diminished for much of the century.

Like Britain, the Third and Fourth Republics experienced a series of crises in local finance and produced a number of reports.[48] But unlike in Britain, French problems were not the result of the continual erosion of local resources, but were part of a continued conflict between levels of government. The more balanced budgetary and financial relationship enhanced local claims. The communes and departments wanted to manage services that were in the hands of the state, but they also had to demonstrate how they were going to pay for them. The French communes remained financially self-supporting until the turn of the century, and the French system of more clearly delimiting national and local responsibilities made the use of state subsidies less controversial. Unlike Britain, the financial deterioration was not simply a question of hardpressed towns against protected counties, but the product of debt and spending commitments that French cities and rural communes incurred as communes tried individually to work out their own future.[49] In 1896 the Caillaux Commission was appointed to study local financial problems, and also recommended a local income tax, but political divisions within the Third Republic forestalled reform.

The severe damage to the north of France in the First World War helped establish subsidies as an instrument of administrative control. For example, in 1920 a third of Lille's budget was provided by the state.[50] Although the Blocquet Commission of 1920 again reviewed local financial problems and some small tax concessions were made, subsidies became more common and essential. Between 1921 and 1925 communal budgets increased by 10 percent, and between 1926 and 1929 by 18 percent. The early national reforms to help the aged and to support families, children and mothers added new subsidies for national services. Developing later than Britain, there was also a range of subsidies for road construction. As the depression deepened, the state was under new pressures to increase subsidies which gradually increased from about 6 percent of local budgets in the late 1920s to 10 percent by 1932 and 17 percent by 1938.

There were four more major studies over the next twenty years, but tax reform was no more popular in France than in Britain.[51] The most important was the Bourrel Report of 1965. Pointing to the rapid growth of local budgets in the early 1960s, the report claimed that 'since 1959 local governments have definitely renounced their Malthusian attitudes which prompted in certain municipalities the desire not to increase the fiscal charge on their taxpayers'.[52] The

Bourrel Report was followed by the Intergroup on Local Finance formed to review local problems for the Sixth Plan.[53] Renewed concern with local finance was a function of Gaullist plans to rebuild France, which inescapably gave the communes and departments a role in the new planning exercises and the formulation of national policies that far exceeded the part given to British councils. The full irony of these plans, as we have seen in Chapter 5, is that the administrative controls that the Gaullists hoped would accompany increased reliance on local government were never fully implemented, while the communes showed remarkable ingenuity in evading the financial reforms that they suggested to central government.

Quite the reverse of frequent interpretations of the all-powerful state, the administrative system itself enabled the communes to penetrate national plans, and the emphasis on *équipements collectifs* or public works needed to modernize French industry and society made the communes partners of national government. In contrast, as we shall see in more detail in Chapter 7, the British councils were (and are) confined to investments of a local nature. The major national investment plans for industrial and commercial development are in the hands of central departments. In a curious way, the French officials were caught in their own trap for they could not expand the infrastructure for national economic growth without extracting cooperation from communes.

However arbitrary the French state may seem, it was also the planners and their colleagues who, unlike the British, set fiscal reform in motion in advance of the growing local burden. Among the first acts of the Fifth Republic was the 1959 *ordonnance* requiring a reorganization of the national and local accounting system and anticipating the need to reorganize the local tax system.[54] More important, the motor force behind the reform was not abrupt or capricious, but a comprehensive and economically balanced view of how to move state investment funds to the local level. The suggestion here is not that Britain should have tried to reverse what was by 1960 a probably irreversible characteristic of the subnational system, nor is it that the French primary concern with local investments was immune to political manipulation. The point is rather that the French central government saw local fiscal reform as a long-term problem closely linked to national development. Unlike their British counterparts, French leaders foresaw that the growth of urban infrastructure was also going to multiply the operating costs of cities with no fiscal relief in sight.[55]

Like British local government, French communal and departmental spending increased at a higher rate than national spending throughout the 1960s. Achieving national objectives made local fiscal and financial reform more important in France than in Britain. Until recently, French local budgets were still calculated and financed around principles established during the Revolution. The four direct tax bases (*quatre vieilles*) date from 1791, and are nothing more than four direct property taxes devised in the chaos and uncertainty of the Revolution.[56] To understand the French local fiscal system, which can appear much more complex in detail than it is in principle, two underlying ideas must be kept in mind. Like British councils, the communes were to determine their own level of direct taxation (see Table 6.3) but until 1980 the state decided how the taxes were to be divided among the four kinds of property. The tax base and the division of tax revenues were determined by an intricate system of indexing. The communes once voted a percentage increase (*centimes additionels*) in the total local tax burden after arriving at the budget.

Until the 1973 reforms, division of the tax among its components had been determined by the archaic and now fictive principles (*principaux fictifs*) used for the direct taxes. Since 1973 the commune knows how the real values of the four property tax bases and the rate of taxation on each kind of property are arrived at, but the division of the total direct tax among the four property taxes remains indexed in an obscure way because the National Assembly could not agree in 1975 or 1978 on a new formula using the real base and incidence of each tax. The allegedly overpowering French executive repeatedly asked the legislature to decentralize decisions about direct local taxes, but it refused to do so. By far the most controversial direct tax has been the *patente* converted into the *taxe professionelle* in 1975 after long and tedious negotiations with the communes. As the Tinguy Report points out,[57] until the reforms of 1979 the entire local tax structure was 'provisional' because each change was accompanied by reservations so that the National Assembly could reconsider any changes once its effects were known.

The major indirect tax, the *taxe locale*, was introduced in 1941 when the Vichy was at a loss for means to support local government, and in 1948 was continued as a local sales tax. Had this not been done, the French local tax structure would be as hamstrung as the British. And of possibly greater significance to the politics of policymaking, the French mayors would have been deprived of effective leverage over reform of the local system. The reform of indirect local taxes has been intensely controversial because mayors do not want to create disincentives for private investment in their communes. The modifications made in 1966 resulted from the reform of national indirect taxes (VAT) and were expected to be temporary and based the tax on local payrolls. Because firms already pay very high social security taxes in France (about half the wage bill is paid to the state as social security taxes), the new tax was equally resisted by industry and commerce. The combined resistance of the communes and business led to the conversion of the tax relief in the form of the VRTS in 1968. Since that time central government has actually provided most of the funds that are still considered indirect taxes. But this does not prevent the communes from using the highly variable revenues from the tax as a bargaining instrument against Paris. Most of these changes are hard to follow because they are usually contained within annexes of the annual *loi de finances*.

The administration of taxes rests entirely with national government but administrative control and supervision is not nearly as important in central–local tax negotiations as organizational complexity. Paradoxically it was because the system was so centralized that the state could not avoid its financial responsibility and was forced to

Table 6.3 The Transformation of the French Local Tax Structure from 1966 to 1979[a]

	1966	1968	1973	1975	1979
Direct Taxes:					
Propriété bâtie (Buildings)	→	⎫	taxe foncière	⎫	phased transition to local control of tax rates
Propriété non-bâtie (Land)	→	⎬ fictional bases	taxe foncière	⎬ real base	
Mobilière (Dwellings)	→	⎭	taxe d'habitation	⎭	
Patente (Employees, buildings and equipment)[b]	→			taxe professionelle →	reduce base
Indirect Taxes:					
Taxe locale (Sales)	→	taxe locale sur les salaires[c]	VRTS		dotation globale[d] de fonctionnement
New Taxes			taxe d'équipement (1971) →	(national wage-level base)	

[a] The reorganization of direct taxes began with the 1959 *ordonnance*, but required legislation for implementation. Parliamentary approval is found in a variety of laws: in 1966 as part of the law introducing the value-added tax; in 1973 in land-zoning legislation; in 1975 with separate legislation; and in 1979 the law on direct taxation. (For details and other minor legislation, see the Voisin Report, op. cit., pp. 27–36.)

[b] Under French tax law all the possessions of a business are considered part of the direct tax system, including the payroll.

[c] For reasons explained in the text, the local salary tax existed for only six months.

[d] The DGF replaces the VRTS and is calculated provisionally on the old tax base.

reconsider the allocation of resources within the context of the local fiscal system. Although Lalumière is perfectly correct in observing that 'The state has never agreed to respect a procedure for the division of taxes which, imposed *a priori*, would disfavour it',[58] this hardly distinguishes France from most other industrial countries. The limits imposed on the British local government system are in many ways even harsher because local government has no access to indirect taxes and in 1980 the national government even extended its powers over direct local taxes. After three decades of reform designed to equalize the local tax base, the councils can now be penalized if they tax too much.

The struggle to reform French local taxes began with the 1959 *ordonnance* which set in motion the process of reconciling national and local accounting methods and began the long overdue revaluation of French property. Like the British effort, the gigantic task of assessing 1,800,000 commercial properties, 20 million homes, and 200,000 factories took nearly a decade, and was not officially enacted until 1968. The intensity of the struggle is suggested by the fact that after this enormous task was completed, national government was forced to wait until 1973 for the more accurate evaluations to be used. One of the great difficulties of understanding French central–local finance, much like central–local politics itself, is that the decisions at the two levels of government are not as distinct as they are in Britain. To add to the confusion, in 1966 the value-added tax (TVA) became part of national tax reform and is paid by communes, departments and regions on all construction as well as by all other public agencies. The political issue was that localities felt they were unjustly taxed, while Paris considered the TVA to be a key part of French economic stabilization. Thus, the central–local fight is often about an issue that formally is not even part of the local tax system. As we shall see, French mayors used this grievance to great advantage.

The real values of local property were established by the *loi foncière* of 1973, but even then the local political forces working through the National Assembly and the Senate refused to have them applied at the local level. But communes no longer voted an entirely mythical figure (*centimes additionels*), but an actual sum of money which was then divided by the fictional rules they refused to change. Even so, a compromise was made in 1973 to give special consideration to the problems of artisans and small merchants. The more accurately assessed *taxe d'habitation* (replacing the *taxe mobilière*) was accepted under strong protest.[59] The fourth element in direct local taxation, the *patente*, was not modernized until 1975, but it, too, was strongly resisted and major exemptions were made for small shopkeepers, artisans and the professions. The 1976 *loi de finances* placed a ceiling on the detested *taxe professionelle* which, in turn, cost the French state several billion francs.[60] Again in 1977 and 1978, the National Assembly refused to reform the tax. In a rejection of government designs that would be unimaginable in Britain, an energetic *rapporteur* of the 1980 reforms, Voisin, simply reversed the official design for a new base for *taxe professionelle* and persuaded the National Assembly to base it on communal-level added values.[61] The compromise was that the state would run experiments with nine departments until 1983, when the issue will again be considered. There may be areas where the French state can impose its will, but on the critical issue of local taxation the communes successfully resisted taking responsibility for five years, and, as we shall see, the 1979 reform of local taxation was accompanied by numerous reservations and severely amended.

The transformation of the main indirect tax, the *taxe locale*, has been tortuous and heated to an extent that might justify British reluctance to accept the risk of local fiscal reform. Until 1966 French indirect local tax was a small percentage of final sales (since 1955 the *taxe locale sur le chiffre des affaires*), and was disliked both by the communes and by the government because it discouraged commerce in growing areas and did little to help disadvantaged areas.[62] Under the Common Market, local sales taxes were prohibited, and in any event the financial reforms planned by Giscard d'Estaing in 1966 anticipated the introduction of a new national sales tax, the TVA.[63] In what now appears to have been a rather hasty and ill-considered decision, the communes were given a share of a salary tax (*taxe locale sur les salaires*) levied on businesses and industries as a substitute for the discontinued local sales tax. The outcry from the private sector was so intense that this tax was discontinued in a few months and a transfer, equivalent to what the communes would have received under the salary tax, was provided (*versement représentatif de la taxe sur les salaires* or VRTS).

Although replaced by the DGF in 1980, the VRTS was the most controversial element of central–local financial relationships. In 1976, the total VRTS was over twenty-two billion francs of which nearly seventeen billion went to the communes.[64] The percentage of the total VRTS going to communes barely changed since 1968, staying within a percentage point or so of 70 percent. Likewise, the percentage of total communal operating expense paid by the VRTS barely changed, and has been a third of total local revenues since 1968. What has changed over time is the percentage of indirect local taxation of communes provided by the VRTS which diminished from 87 percent in 1968 to 71 percent in 1976. Thus, in relation to taxes, there is some justification for the communes' complaints, but in relation to VRTS paid to other components of the local government system (departments, syndicats, Paris, etc.) or in relation to the total operating costs of communes, there is very little justification.

As shown in Table 6.4 indirect taxation (meaning the VRTS) was increasing more rapidly than direct taxation throughout most of the 1970s. The total indirect tax revenues of communes alone multiplied four times between 1968 and 1976, while total operating expenses multiplied three times. Both mayors and local businesses detest local taxes which may be why Britain never tried them. The curious result, however, is that the more conservative French Government is willing to subsidize local government at roughly the same level as does Britain. Even after restricting the *taxe professionelle* and paying the VRTS, during the 1980 reforms the communes could force the government to agree not to increase the rate more than the average rate of increase of the other three direct local taxes.

Table 6.4 *Rates of Increase of Direct and Indirect Local Taxes for Communes Only from 1966 to 1976 (rounded to nearest percent)[a]*

	1975–76	1974–75	1973–74	1972–73	1971–72	1970–71	1969–70	1968–69	1967–68	1966–67
Direct Taxes	13	17	21	16	15	15	15	15	10	8
Indirect Taxes	16	24	16	15	19	10	8	14	14	15

[a]Taken from the tables on percentage increases given in *Le Secteur Public Local* (Paris: Ministry of Finance), annual reports. Where earlier figures have been corrected in later reports, the most recent calculation is used.

Although the state had no alternative but to provide the missing local revenues from the national budget, the mayors thought they were being unfairly deprived of the value-added tax paid by their communes. Their resentment was, and remains, fueled by the value-added tax paid by both public and private sectors in France.[65] In fact, there is no direct connection between the TVA and the reorganization of local indirect taxes other than the commonly found aversion of local governments in every country to levying and collecting taxes. The main difference compared with the British system is that French mayors could use their tax leverage in order to take a direct role in reforming the fiscal system, even though they did not approve of the local taxes on the more wealthy and influential members of the communes.[66]

Unlike in Britain, fiscal pressures increased at both levels of government as inflation and rising costs created local-level financial distress. There were, of course, large increases in British local rates, but the tax structure and the grant operate so that neither party has an incentive (and locally there is no opportunity) to negotiate tax settlements. Like British mayors, the French mayors frequently complain about the rapid increases in local taxes, and as Table 6.5 shows their complaints are not entirely unfounded. Nevertheless, it is also the case that indirect taxes, relieved by the VRTS of central government, were rising more rapidly. Pressures on both levels of government exist because the communes can claim an indirect tax, which, in turn, makes Paris sensitive to local tax problems in ways that elude the simpler British local tax system. French indirect local taxes first exceeded direct taxes in 1962. To add to national pressures for reform, since 1973 national direct taxes have also increased more than local direct taxes.

The general trends of national and local expenditure are given in Table 6.5. Compared to Britain, the complexity of central–local tax negotiation contributes to the rough equilibrium maintained between national and local spending increases. The pattern changed in 1972 when local expenditure began to surge ahead more rapidly, and local grants also surged ahead. Indeed, after 1974 the problems of local spending in France were similar to Britain's problem insofar as it was easier for the French to reduce national rather than local spending. As the table also clearly shows, the consequent shortfalls were taken up by huge increases in local grants, though rarely at rates of growth as those ineluctably superimposed on the RSG until 1976.

The comparison between Britain and France in the relationship of the growth of local expenditure to the growth of national economic capacity is even more dramatic. Although the calculations for comparing the two national economies are not the same, it can be seen in Table 6.2 that British local spending was increasing much faster than the GNP from the early 1960s. Except for the surge in French local spending after the 1968 uprisings, France did not experience similar disequilibrium until the early 1970s; especially after the 1973 oil crisis and with the inflation of the mid-1970s. Though it is not necessarily a defense of the obscurities of French central–local finance (and even less of French economic conservatism), the rates of change demonstrate the advantages of a tax structure, reinforced by central–local political interdependence, which helps minimize local excesses.

Although Tables 6.2 and 6.5 are in current prices, and therefore not directly comparable, it should be noted that the shift of spending to central government in Britain is greater in relation to the growth of local spending, and in relation to the trends in France. Over the period 1965 to 1977, British central spending increased roughly 30 percent more than GNP, while local spending increased about 20 percent more than GNP even with the large increases in the rate of local spending. In France, national spending increased less than the rate of growth of GDP, while local spending was roughly 25 percent more than the growth of GDP in the same time period. Thus, Britain's fiscal trends were toward further centralizing spending powers, while France was actually decentralizing fiscal influences, although this is partly due to the conservative economic policies of national government.

Unlike the British council leaders, who have never been able to make a coordinated attack on the national tax structure, the French mayors have for the past decade been in a state of constant warfare over tax grievances, some real and some imagined. Much of this highly exploitable confusion arises from the problems inherent in modernizing both the tax base and the tax procedures at the same time. As in the case of the direct taxes, the VRTS was necessarily distributed on a fictional base, the income that communes would have had under the detested salary tax. The facts that the communes receive more money than they would have had under the old sales tax, and that the VRTS has increased at a considerably faster rate than inflation, make little difference.[67] The ultimate irony is that finding an agreement for local determination of the distribution of direct local taxation was purchased at so high a price by national government.

The distribution of the VRTS was based on a ten-year sliding scale, starting from 1968 when the entire amount was distributed according to the ratios of the earlier salary tax, and replaced by gradually applying an index of local fiscal effort derived from the various taxes paid by households.[68] The purpose of the formula is to remove the inequities of salary-based distribution and gradually to substitute a resource-based formula, the local tax effort. The change is similar to the reform of the British system in 1948, but even this modest change could not be forced on the communes and in 1977 the transition to the tax effort was stopped by the National Assembly. The VRTS includes a modest redistributive component, the *Fonds d'Action Locale* (FAL), which receives an increasing percentage of the total transfer, which was supposed to reach 5 percent in 1978.[69] The fund is administered by a committee of central and local officials, not unlike the British Consultative Council on Local Finance. A rather complex procedure establishes a per capita minimum revenue figure each year for the distribution of the FAL money.[70]

The fight for tax reform over 1978–79 centered on three main financial issues (plus the reform affecting mayors and commune personnel discussed in Chapter 5): the *dotation globale de fonctionnement* (DGF) to replace the VRTS; the *dotation globale*

Table 6.5 *Rates of Growth of Local and National Expenditure, Local Grants and GDP in France from 1967 to 1976 (rounded to nearest percent)*

	1975–76	1974–75	1973–74	1972–73	1971–72	1970–71	1969–70	1968–69	1967–68
Local Expenditure[a]	18	22	21	17	10	9	10	19	10
Local Grants[b]	34	24	20	18	2	11	9	18	8
National Expenditure[c]	11	19	21	11	9	4	9	9	11
GDP[d]	15	13	15	14	12	11	12	14	9

[a]Local expenditure includes both operating and capital expenditure and is taken from *Le secteur public local*, Paris, Ministry of Finance, annual reports. British local budgets do not include capital spending because separate capital funds are kept locally. See Chapter 7.

[b]Local grants from same source and contain both operating and capital subsidies. For details of capital expenditure subsidies see Chapter 7. Operating subsidies may be overestimated because national statistics group subsidies and reimbursement for services.

[c]National budget figures taken from *Tableaux de l'Economie Française* (Paris: INSEE, 1978), p. 147.

[d]Note that French customarily use GDP (gross domestic product) to measure economic growth. Calculated from *Annuaire des Statistiques de la France*, France, 1978, pp. 780–81. (Current prices.)

d'équipement (DGE) to simplify investment subsidies (see Chapter 7); and finally agreement that the communes would themselves decide how direct taxes were to be divided among the four property taxes. Indicative of the power of the mayors, and their allies in the National Assembly and the Senate, the DGF was considered first. True to its history as the defender of the communes, the Senate at one point voted to abolish the four property taxes and create a single property tax.[71] Only the pleadings of the Minister of the Interior, Bonnet, avoided this catastrophe. In both legislatures, the DGF plan was severely amended.

The total DGF was fixed at 16.45 percent of the TVA, and was divided in two parts: a minimum operating subsidy to all communes under 2,000 (about 27,000 communes) of 180 francs per inhabitant; and a much smaller equalization portion to be distributed on the basis of 'fiscal effort'.[72] To please the Socialists a special provision was made to compensate communes at the center of large urban areas. To please the Gaullists (once the enemies of small communes) amendments were accepted to enlarge the new administrative body, the Committee on Local Finance, to fifteen members (from eleven), and to include three mayors of small (under 2,000 persons) communes. To please the Communists, it was agreed that full details on the use of the equalization portion of the DGF would be published. After two months of stormy debate, the DGF law was passed in early 1979.[73]

Although the 1979 tax reforms were subject to a variety of exemptions and reservations, the larger significance of French reform should not be missed. As the subnational system becomes increasingly responsible for vital services and benefits of the welfare state, and, in turn, accounts for a large portion of public spending, a way must be found to link local expenditure to economic cycles. The United States has done this by giving increased importance to local sales and income taxes; the Germans by linking local taxation to a national fund from income tax; and the Canadians by a no less intricate compromise between provincial and national interests.[74] Essentially, the rigid limitation of British local taxation to the inelastic property tax provides no way to relate local spending to national economic conditions other than the strict controls introduced after 1975. In France, the hook on which the communes hung their argument was the TVA, even though this is a national tax. The 1979 reform of the professional tax was linked to the added-values (initially a ceiling of 9 percent but to be adjusted), and the new *dotation globale de fonctionnement* was directly tied to the TVA. In a circuitous way, France has made the compromise that nearly every welfare state has made, namely, giving localities more discretion over taxation in return for their acceptance that spending must be linked to changes in the national economy.

In effect, the British local government system is excluded from such a debate. The alternative of creating minimum standards, in order to restore local discretion and to give resource allocation an explicit foundation, is unwieldy and extraordinarily complex.[75] However ironical the French debate about local finance might be, the communal and departmental councils were able to engage Paris in a debate affecting not only their own taxes, but the national system of transfer payments and taxation. Of course, British local governments and the local government associations *were* consulted as the system transformed over the past thirty years, but always in terms of either rating changes or transfer problems. Resource allocation was never discussed in its totality. Under the pressure of the welfare state, at least as it has evolved in Britain, local service burdens are so great and the aversion to property taxes so strong that there was no way for local councils to exercise leverage on national fiscal decisions. Paradoxically, these same local councils were not given serious national consideration until it was necessary to restrain the rate of growth of local services in the mid-1970s. Their enormous spending gave them political power, but only in a game where external economic forces dictated the result. Even then, the downward adjustments, if negotiated at all, were still negotiated around the objectives and plans of central departments.

The possibility that British local government might engage the center in a debate on resource allocation was probably foreclosed in 1966, when rate relief was combined with the transfer,[76] which made the effects of the grant system ambiguous. No matter how one wishes to calculate it and no matter whether the funds come from direct or indirect taxes, superimposing local exemptions on the already ambiguously calculated RSG left local councils virtually incapable of bargaining with Whitehall. So long as the General Grant was providing either spending support (needs element) or income support (resource element), the income and spending effects of grants could still be calculated at each level of government. Introducing the domestic element in 1966 was not only an extremely 'political' act,[77] it encouraged political manipulation by the national government. Within a year, Labour made this portion of the grant into a flat-rate transfer, which disadvantaged the less populated rural areas. Not too surprisingly, the portion of the Rate Support Grant determined by the domestic element rose steadily until 1977, while the portion allocated according to needs declined.[78] Policies that simultaneously affect both spending and income constitute, in terms of the politics of finance, the most severe of all possible central controls, because as a result it becomes virtually impossible for local authorities to detect their effects.

Although the British RSG is often admired in France because of its alleged redistributive effects, the large grant has also become the lever for central controls that far exceed anything proposed by French officials. The point is not that redistribution is undesirable, but that in relation to central–local policymaking it is as easily used for political as for social reasons. Perhaps this is a price worth paying, but Heseltine's 1979 proposals show how redistributive aims and local autonomy conflict. The new Block Grant would return to the 1948 concept that the subsidy be simply calculated in relation to local tax resources, but the proposed law also gives the Secretary of State arbitrary powers to introduce a 'multiplier'; to increase or decrease the amounts given to each authority; to change the amounts if in his opinion a local government cannot provide adequate justification of its expenditure (including *post hoc* adjustments); to adjust the grant if any tax decreases occur after the announcement; and to disallow any local expenditures above agreed total levels.[79] There are few French *inspecteurs de finances* who have even dreamt of such powerful controls.

BUDGET STRUGGLES IN THE 1970S: LEARNING TO LIVE WITH LESS

In the 1970s, the terms and conditions of transfers were the focal point of new political controversies. As the state relies more heavily on lower-level government, it must also engage in more direct, if technically somewhat more obscure, bargaining with its local agents. There are two national strategies for controlling local spending, limiting spending or limiting resources. The historical development of the grant system meant that Britain was virtually confined to the first of these strategies.[80] The grant was shifted to resources by a Labour government in 1948 in the hope that resource equalization would also equalize services. Although it might seem in conflict with their values the Conservatives made the important shift to a needs-based grant when they introduced a complex needs formula with only a small resource element in 1958.

When Labour introduced the Rate Support Grant in 1966, they were essentially only taking the Conservative reform to its logical conclusion, and adding rate relief to equalize even further. Whitehall achieved its redistributive aims, but in doing so the RSG became unintelligible and offered new incentives for political manipulation. National government had made councils heavily dependent on the grant, but so long as Whitehall provided an ever increasing transfer local government had no complaint, and redistribution was relatively painless. In fact, as Table 6.2 shows, local expenditure increased twice as fast as GNP from 1955 to 1970, and 10 to 30 percent faster than national expenditure. It was a system built on acquiescence, not bargaining, and for this reason was completely inappropriate for the difficult economic conditions to arise over the 1970s. By 1970 the size of the transfer meant that local councils had very few ways in which they could independently affect their income or their expenditure.

The French problem is more complex. First, because fewer responsibilities were placed on the communes, there was less pressure to think only in spending terms. In this sense, the territorial and organizational complexity of French government paid distinct dividends for local government. Secondly, even though communes bear little of indirect tax burdens, mostly because the mayors dislike the salary tax, a portion of local income was indirectly linked to an elastic tax base (the rejected salary tax under the VRTS and value-added amounts under the DGF). The overall effect was that with inflation France was under less pressure to take draconian measures to reduce local spending, and could rely to some extent on the built-in constraints of the indirect tax base to achieve this end. The choice is never a happy one, but at least the French system provided distinct alternatives. Put somewhat differently, even if Britain were to adopt the organizational means that would permit more local choice about spending, it would probably be of little avail because local councils have very little choice about their resources.

Although the national budget struggles of the 1970s were of a fundamentally different character in the two countries, this is not entirely due to the greater magnitude of local spending in Britain. The explanation lies much more in the increasing importance of public sector spending itself, perhaps most dramatically visible, oddly enough, during the latter years of the Conservative Heath government. After keeping both national and local spending in line with GNP from 1970 to 1972, the system broke down seriously in 1972 to 1975. The reason is that the simplicity of central–local finance (an open-ended subsidy for spending and an inelastic local tax) is so vulnerable to inflation that neither level of government can exercise much control on the other during financial and economic crises. In this sense, it is perhaps best to think of British central–local finance as virtually unguided during the crisis, at least until drastic budgetary controls were introduced in 1976. Two decades of reform and reorganization had not built a self-adjusting mechanism because, on the one hand, Parliament would not give localities an elastic tax base, and, on the other hand, local government was accustomed to an ever increasing grant.

Local government has only two ways to improve finances: to increase local charges for services, which naturally both Labour and Conservative local councils are reluctant to do, or to ask for a larger grant.[81] The other major activity is public housing, with rents supporting about two-thirds of expenditure. Raising rents, selling public housing, and providing a variety of public housing relief and subsidies are perhaps the most sensitive political issues in local government,[82] but for present purposes it may suffice to note that there are few, if any, ways in which growing general costs might be relieved by surpluses in the housing account. Although the Layfield Committee considered various alternatives for simply relieving local government of major burdens, most particularly that of education, it concluded that 'transfer of expenditure would lead to loss of local discretion, distortion in local planning and limitations on the future development of services without any compensating advantages in the form of greater efficiency, greater control over costs or better distribution of grant'.[83] Functional responsibilities tend to be irreversible while also making local government more vulnerable to economic cycles.

Unable to agree on a major reallocation of functions, the result was that national government had little choice but to constantly increase the amount of local spending judged appropriate for subsidy ('relevant expenditure') and the percentage of such expenditure under the RSG until 1976. Relevant expenditure went up about half a billion pounds a year from 1970 onward, and the percentage to be paid as Rate Support Grant from 57 percent in 1970–71 to 67 percent in 1975–76. Though inflation made the increases dramatic, it should be noted that in only five of the fifteen time periods in Table 6.2 has the rate of increase of local expenditures been in equilibrium with the rate of growth of the GNP. Possibly of even greater topical interest, considering the alleged excesses of local government, is that the rate of increase of local expenditure has generally lagged *behind* national expenditure increases except in the Conservative period of 1955 to 1965. Thus, the most curious dilemma of British central–local finance is that the administrative and political links between levels of government neither permit local government to make its strongest case nor permit national government to alter local spending short of draconian measures.

Having decided that local expenditure could not be altered, the Layfield Committee was left with no alternative but to suggest more income, namely, the local income tax.[84] As with the report of the Royal Commission in 1969, a debate of significant proportions never took place.[85] The reason for this is twofold. By defending the system as it existed, proponents of structural change were unable to use the substantial services that local government provide as leverage in negotiating with central government. Were the localities to agree, for example, that one or more local services should simply be returned to central government, Whitehall would be struck at its most vulnerable point, namely, that the central government in Britain, unlike France, cannot provide vital services and implement its own policies without the cooperation of local government. Of course, the traditions of a century as well as the schisms both between the various local government associations and between rural and urban authorities made this most unlikely. In effect, the local government system was disarmed of its most powerful weapon against central government, namely, its enormous importance in the life of every citizen.

Neither major political party saw the Layfield debate as particularly important to their primary national objective,[86] winning national elections, because, as has been pointed out in Chapter 4, local political forces are effectively neutralized in order to meet the needs of national politics. This does not mean that the political complexion of local councils is unrelated to spending decisions at the local level,[87] but that in confrontation with national politics the local government system has no collective impact. In a period of double-digit inflation, a rancorous debate over Scotland and the daily perils of negotiating wage policy, the Layfield proposals, even if accompanied with political clout, had little chance of being seriously considered. From 1973 onward, the local government shared public spending cuts decided by the Treasury with little or no consultation, but the grant still grew uncontrollably.[88] As national finances deteriorated, the Treasury also had no choice but to provide supplementary Rate Support Grants as demanded by wage agreements and inflation.[89]

Perhaps the most intriguing aspect of the carefully constructed stand-off between national and local government in Britain is that what would appear to be drastic control in the French system had very little effect on spending in Britain. Monitoring rates began in 1973, and the Manpower Watch on local personnel was organized in 1974.[90] In 1976 cash limits were imposed on both local and national spending, and the next year the local authorities were told not to expect relief if they exceeded cash limitations even where the excesses were due to inflation.[91] When the government and unions agreed on wage policy, the localities were told they would have to absorb any excesses of local pay bargains and later that they were also responsible for any excesses that might be passed on by local government contractors. In the topsy turvy world of financial uncertainty, the local governments were criticized one year for overspending, only to be chastized the next for underspending.[92] Though the ratepayers' share of local government costs was declining, it was politically impossible to impose rate increases proportionate to inflation.[93]

One of the contrasts between the spending problems of France and Britain is that, while communes have been trying to increase the personnel hired by communes in order to reduce dependence on the central administration, the British system was trying to reduce local government personnel. The heavy service responsibilities of the British councils require them to employ over 11 percent of the working population; and total local government employment doubled between 1952 and 1974.[94] Because much of this labor force is organized in strong national unions, local government can only obtain fiscal relief by threatening the salaries of local civil servants. The response to the fiscal problems after 1975 was complicated not only because local government is a key element in the success of national wage policy, but also because wage bargaining is now largely outside the hands of the localities themselves. The Manpower Watch therefore depended on the success of national economic policy which rests, in turn, on the intricate structure of public sector wage bargaining.[95] The local governments now arrive at wage settlements through twenty-two national negotiating committees, organized according to the major functions of local government, which involve eighty-five trades union. The complex organization for negotiation is coordinated and monitored by the Local Authorities Conditions of Service and Advisory Boards (LACSAB).[96] There was no effective constraint until the cash limit budget, and the first reduction ever recorded in local government employment was in 1976. About 25,000 jobs were eliminated, and in 1977 a further 15,000 jobs.[97]

A secondary effect of nationwide financial uncertainty was to accentuate, rather than moderate, political manipulation from the center. Each party wanted to favor the regions, services or types of local government most relevant to its traditional voters. Much like the situation in 1958, the invitation to grant manipulation came from the Conservatives who in 1974 introduced a variable formula for calculating the domestic element of the Rate Support Grant which tended to favor non-metropolitan districts. When Labour returned to office later in 1974 the legislation was amended to retain the use of a flat-rate calculation that favors the metropolitan districts. Rate relief became the 'most political' of the grant components, and the Labour Party decided to make a substantial shift in the apportioning of the entire Rate Support Grant in favor of the domestic element.[98] Beginning with the 1974 negotiations, special provisions were made for London, which was not only suffering from soaring costs but had also turned Conservative. The 1975 negotiations brought new modifications of the domestic element which favored Wales and in 1976 a three-stage 'dampening' of the needs formula was adopted, which made the entire process even more unintelligible. There was also the temptation for any government to revive specific grants in order to achieve its objectives, in part because of the unpredictable effects of the grant at the local level and in part because resources were generally scarce for any new program.[99]

With the return of a Conservative government in 1979, the manipulation of the transfer went full circle and for the first time in six years adjustments in the grant formula began to favor the counties rather than the more urban areas.[100] But the real impact of the manipulation is not that it fails to serve the national objectives, but that its built-in obscurities exclude local bargaining except in the most general terms. As Lynch has pointed out,[101] each element of the RSG (needs, resources, domestic) varies in its relevance to each type of local authority so that minor adjustments can have diverse and unequal effects on the grant for any one type of authority, depending on which part of the total RSG central government decides to change. Put simply, even with a grant that aimed at redistribution, there were still political problems of how to equalize. Even with new central controls, it proved difficult to reduce the grant in 1979–80 and, despite Treasury objections, the grant for 1980–81 was set at 61 percent of 'relevant expenditure', the same as the previous year.[102]

What might be regarded as the final insult to local autonomy was the decision to impose stricter limits on local tax increases. For all the elaborate procedures involved in calculating the RSG, Heseltine found that it was only possible to detect overspending in relation to the needs element of the grant. The open-ended nature of the RSG means that whatever increase in spending an authority achieves by increasing taxes in one year unavoidably becomes part of an increase in subsidy in the following year. Thus, when spending is being arbitrarily held constant, high-spending councils can increase their share of the RSG at the expense of low-spending councils simply by increasing rates. For this reason, Heseltine also sought special powers in the 1980 Bill to penalize local governments *either* for overspending *or* 'over-taxing' once national limits were set. In a display of extraordinary *post hoc* administrative power, the fines are to be designated *after* local governments set the rates so that in effect the Secretary of State for the Environment is selecting which individual authorities will be penalized.[103]

From a policy perspective it is doubtful, or at best unclear, whether growing standards of services cause local fiscal distress. Doing more costs more, but this truism tells us little about how the grant machinery and local services have actually grown. A dissenting member of the Layfield Committee points out that causation may run 'from political aims and policies to financial mechanisms, rather than in the opposite direction from financial mechanisms to political aims and policies'.[104] The examination of the use of the grant by politicians over the past fifty years gives some credence to his view. Again, the point is not that parties should not pursue their political self-interests, but whether instruments of financial policy should so effectively exclude the local level of government. The generous grant to British local government is no less political than French local government subsidies, but also gives central government in Britain the ability to dictate successive transformations of the grant system as may meet immediate political objectives.

After leaving the issue of local resources dormant for a year, the Callaghan government published a Green Paper on the Layfield Report rejecting the local income tax.[105] Labour proposed to consider what the Conservative government achieved in a few months: a 'unitary grant' merging the needs and resources elements of the old grant into one single transfer. Oddly enough, this financial halfway house attracted both major parties and assures that the debate will continue to be intense and, in all likelihood, futile for years to come. The needs element was introduced in 1958 to provide relief to less populated areas which are, of course, often Conservative, as well as to more heavily populated areas with higher costs. Contrary to the hopes of the Layfield Committee, the unitary grant contains the germs of even more central control. As outlined by both the Labour and Conservative governments, the new grant system will both set the taxation level needed in each locality, to provide roughly the same level of services, and also give clearer indications of permissible levels of expenditure for separate services.[106] Both devices provide the central government with new screws to tighten on both local taxation and on standards of service. Followed to its logical conclusion, the grant system would be totally converted to central calculations and, in effect, become a giant specific grant in the clothing of a general grant.[107]

The unified fiscal and financial structure of French government has made the debate over fiscal reform very different from the British debate. Although the French mayors are by no means happy with the outcome of the last decade's fight against the government, one should not lose sight of this basic difference. French mayors have ways of fighting for resources that are denied British mayors, and, thanks to an accident of history, have an indirect claim on a flexible resource that British localities have been persistently denied. Since the war the French municipalities, like British local government, have lost fiscal and political influence with the nationalization of utilities, the growth of the social security system and other reorganizations of justice, education and tourism.[108] But in a curious way, their assured position within the national fiscal system provided a claim on national taxes, and gave them access to the debate on national fiscal reorganization under the Gaullists, and later under Giscard d'Estaing. The unified system, of course, carries some real disadvantages, such as the obligation to deposit all funds and surpluses in the national Treasury.[109] At the local level mayors must deal with an arbitrary and often frustrating administration, including the TPG who approves spending, the *receveur* who actually releases money and the departmental tax officials who allocate budget increases.[110] On the other hand, they have the national political influence, described in Chapter 4, are immersed in administrative decisionmaking at many levels of the system, and have a legal claim on resources that exceeds that of British localities.

The parallel in the way national and local politics interlock and the interdependence of national and local fiscal policy is striking. National representative bodies in France, like those in Britain, do not have the resources, information or parliamentary time to scrutinize budgetary and tax legislation.[111] As the fiscal importance of local government has grown in both countries, British local politicians find themselves admitted to national policy decisions only with great reluctance, but the French mayors have a long experience in dealing with financial and administrative hurdles that higher-level officials may put in their way. Moreover, territorial diversity provides a check on central decisionmaking which grows in importance as resources diminish.

The French local government system is inescapably imbedded in the overall conduct of national fiscal and financial policy. Indeed, the fiscal reforms that have been discussed above were not designed as a search for local resources disconnected from national objectives, but were set in motion as part of the national reorganization of the tax system.[112] Such a reorganization could not take place without involving the mayors. In such curious ways does local government in France sustain its voice in national policymaking, even though there are undoubtedly both politicians and administrators at the center who would like to see the mayors excluded.

The mayors' ability to intervene is reflected in the structure of local budgets themselves. The unified budget system makes the relation between national and local spending clearer than do the compartmentalized funds of British local budgets. Elected officials at the departmental and regional levels, as well as in the various special purpose syndicates and in the public establishments, enter decisionmaking. French national officials share fiscal and financial decisionmaking with communes, because they cannot change the territorial organization of the state. When all the territorial organizations included in local budgets are aggregated, their fiscal importance in the national system is equivalent to that in the British system, roughly one-third of total public expenditure. However misconceived the 1972 territorial reorganization may have been, its greatest political cost to localities was that territorial consolidation combined with central financial controls to leave them politically impotent. If the acquiescence of British local government in its own demise seems strange, it is important to recall that these trends can be traced back historically at least to Victorian times.

If the financial crisis of the 1970s was less severe for France than in Britain, it was no less crippling for local government – the communes and departments. The French national government has, of course, exercised stricter and more conservative control over the country's economy than the British. At the very beginning of the inflationary spirals of the 1970s, France imposed stiff deflationary measures, and these had significant repercussions through the indexed spending control.[113] There was little doubt that conservative national economic policy, combined with inflation and local controls, was pushing the communes to the limit of their resources. The mayors' protest was vehement during the 1973 debate on reorganizing direct taxes, and continued in meetings of the Association of French Mayors. In 1974 a nonpartisan organization of mayors of large cities was formed to demand relief.[114] Neither the controversy nor the concessions have the apparent tidiness of the British system because the fight over spending interlocks with the issue of resource allocation, an inescapable conflict once local government has a flexible tax base that can be diminished by inflation and unemployment. As in Britain, tempers flared, and the outspoken Minister of the Interior, Poniatowski, did little to calm the debate by accusing the Socialist mayor of Vienne, which had a deficit of 2.5 million francs, of flagrant overspending. Financial distress is not confined to communes of the Left, and in 1979 Amboise, whose mayor is the Gaullist leader, Debré, was also placed under administrative supervision because of its persistent deficits and huge debt.[115]

In the more complex fiscal system of French local government, it is difficult to estimate how much relief was actually forthcoming. The state had agreed in the early 1970s to absorb the costs of secondary schools and state forests. In 1972 an additional grant was established for local roads. But, unlike in Britain, bargaining over the sharing of expenditures is not directly linked to the sharing of resources. To the extent that spending and revenue bargaining take place independently, the mayors have additional leverage over their resources, and the bargaining machinery becomes more complex. Admittedly, mayors acquire this political advantage by accepting the risk that external economic pressures will adversely affect revenues they receive through the indirect tax base. In fact, with the wage increases of the late 1960s and early 1970s, the VRTS increased at a faster rate than anticipated by the government, and it was difficult to restrict as inflation-based wage increases continue.[116] Thus inflation made national government *more* dependent on local governments even though local governments were, of course, also more desperate to find new resources. In an almost exact reverse of the interaction in Britain, financial distress in France made both levels of government more aware of the necessity to compromise their aims, and led to the long-delayed reforms of direct local taxes in 1979 and 1980. Lest one assume that the delay in reform was simply a subterfuge of national officials, it should be noted that the old tax system, which included a ceiling on the permissible level of the *taxe professionelle*, cost the French Treasury a billion francs in 1978.[117]

At the root of the VRTS controversy was the inability of the state and the communes to agree on the calculation and division of the transfer, as the system still rests on the indices compiled for the discarded salary tax. The mayors argued that the increases in the VRTS did not keep pace with their increased expenditures, and that in most cases expenditure was obligatory and could not be reduced. The argument has no wholly satisfactory solution, because any indirect tax has to vary with economic conditions. Thus with prosperity or with decline the apportionment of the increase or decrease becomes an issue of national policy. The communes claimed they were more severely hit by inflation, had to have privileged treatment and in any event were only claiming their own tax.[118] It is, of course, precisely this trial of strength that the British system has successfully avoided by leaving the grant system open-ended.

In the course of these various adjustments, some of which were in direct response to the mayors' demands, the VRTS formula became increasingly obscure and eventually drew criticism from the Cour des Comptes.[119] The impasse was a difficult one, for the central government had in fact no way of adjusting the tax to a fairer formula until the tax had a meaningful base. Even when the base was modernized, the equalization was questionable because property remained outside the formula.[120] The risk to national government was that the VRTS would become an open-ended grant, but it had no alternative solution for its division without tax reform. At the national level, the Ministry of the Interior was pushing the Ministry of Finance to accept a revision to the old *patente*, which became the *taxe professionelle* in 1975.[121]

The compromise worked out over 1979 was that the base for the *taxe professionelle* would be reduced if communes would accept the political risks of themselves allocating how direct taxes would be distributed among the four direct local taxes. This compromise rested, in turn, on the compromise on indirect local taxes or the DGF, described above. Essentially, what the state gained was acceptance by communes to share the risks of inflation. If the process seems complex, it is well to remember that the ostensibly simpler British system provides no mechanism for such compromises and only seems to generate increasingly rigid central controls without addressing the underlying national economic issue of inflation. The French reforms were designed to share economic risks between levels of government, while under economic strain Britain seemed to have no alternative but to resort to even more draconian national control.

Before either the national or local governments could sensibly debate the indirect tax, the *patente* had to be modernized. The evolution of the tax over nearly 200 years had resulted in hundreds of exemptions, and the index completely lost its meaning.[122] The tax was of course still being collected, representing over half the direct income of the local governments and applicable to about 2.2 million persons. The *patente* was disliked by all and has been correctly described as a 'winded, exhausted, complicated and a generally condemned tax'.[123] Its reform, planned for 1974, was postponed by Pompidou's death and placed high on the agenda for 1975 by Giscard d'Estaing, who had launched the entire fiscal reform in 1968. The burden of the reformed *patente* falls essentially on two groups, the liberal professions and businessmen. In the debate over the law in 1975 sizable exemptions were introduced for small businesses and artisans, and large increases were shifted to the wages paid by larger industrialists. The reform was fought by conservative industrial interests, who saw it as another tax on corporate income, and by the Left, who demanded that the base must not be changed until agreement had been reached on the division.[124] It is unfortunately most difficult to discuss how to divide a local tax until one knows where and how much it might yield. The result was that the Parliament approved the new tax, but insisted that it be provisionally divided according to the old *principaux fictifs*. Paradoxical as this may sound, it was a compromise between the necessity to modernize the base of the tax and the need to assure communes that their incomes would not be abruptly altered. Britain has had this same difficulty, but the rigidity of the tax system provides no options to either level of government.

The local disadvantages of a flexible tax became apparent within a year. Privileged groups, above all the professions, managed to get themselves largely exempted, and the tax fell on large industry, which was estimated to be carrying over 90 percent of the burden in 1976.[125] Parliament was faced with the unhappy choice of either increasing the amounts derived from the direct taxes or expanding the professional tax base. For the third time running, the Assembly and the Senate could not agree on the new formula and the central government, at least temporarily, was faced with making up the tax's low yield by providing 2.7 billion francs from national funds.[126] The difference between this and the British local fiscal system should not be missed. British local government receives indirect taxes, but only indirectly and by virtue of central decisions about the transfer. The French, however, have devised a system whereby the uncertainties of both types of taxes are shared between both levels of government.

Because the communes have a claim on flexible resources, the Guichard Report was able to devise a compromise that is effectively excluded in the more centralized British system of transfers. Recommending that the national activities imposed on communes (census, elections, police, etc.) simply be paid for by the state, the Guichard suggestion was that the 'absurdity' of the VRTS division be replaced by annual negotiations of the formula similar to the British transfer. But the safety mechanism retained by the communes, however politically painful it may be to impose local taxes on industry and the middle class, is the *taxe professionelle*. To relieve inequities in its calculation and distribution, Guichard recommended that it be distributed among the new 'communities' of communes, leaving direct taxes to the old communes.[127] The solution was ingenious in that it recognized that equalizing wealth (resources) and services (needs) are distinct activities. If there is to be some degree of local government choice, the local government system should have some voice in adjustments on both sides of this equation.

As a result the Presidential program to reform local government introduced new laws to reorganize the direct and indirect components of local taxation. To induce localities to take on the responsibility of distributing the four direct taxes, the government proposed to lighten the burden of the *taxe professionelle* and the *taxe d'habitation*. In the area of indirect taxation, the aim was to persuade the communes to accept more equalization in the distribution of the transfer (decreasing the *dotation forfaitaire* or fixed *per capita* payment) in return for linking the transfer more directly to the value-added tax. Thus, the transfer would be linked more closely to national economic indicators and the VRTS would become the *dotation globale de fonctionnement*.[128] As Barre commented to a special delegation from the Chamber of Commerce, who feared additional taxes on local business, 'It is a devilish business.'[129] But it is also a debate that will almost surely never take place in Britain.

The growth of transfers to local government is no doubt an unavoidable corollary of the emergence of the welfare state. Even if localities could have retained their grasp of the past century on national resources during the industrialization and population movements of the past thirty years, there would still be pressure to equalize services. My argument has not been that this pressure is ill-advised, but that the bargaining process, and to some extent the very direction of change, is determined by the ways in which local governments and their agents may enter the national debate on resource allocation. The outcome is a function of the organization of the transfer and how central–local political relationships structure possibilities for aggregating and organizing local influence. For a century or more the British government has been prepared to make larger grants in order to encourage local reforms that national government could not execute. From the national perspective more equalization in benefits and services served national political aims so the battle between levels of government was never really joined. Confrontation is partly avoided because the four kinds of local authorities are organized into different associations,[130] each of which represents one major component of the local government system. In some ways the competing local government associations made Whitehall's neglect of fiscal reform less apparent though this was certainly not the intent of the associations.

Whether the local government associations have been co-opted by Whitehall or are effective as local agents is difficult to estimate. From the turn of the century until the postwar period, they were essentially lobbying associations for boroughs whose purpose was to get Private Bills (non-partisan, specific legislation) passed for individual local councils. For example, the Association of Municipal Councils (now the Association of Metropolitan Authorities) from the time of its foundation in 1872 until 1944 was the instrument of two men, father and son, who were masters in getting Private Bills introduced and passed in Parliament. As Keith-Lucas and Richards state, the secretaries of the major local authority associations were 'almost part of the constitution, with an accepted right to be consulted on both policy and detail of proposed legislation and in almost daily contact with senior civil servants, or with ministers themselves'.[131] Thus until the 1920s, the local government associations were not in any collective sense a pressure group for local interests, but rather a service to circumvent, simplify or amend the awesome powers of *ultra vires* control from the center. It was, of course, essential that such a lobbying body should try to remain politically neutral, collecting its diffused strength from sympathetic MPs rather than from political parties.

With the development of the grant and its subsequent transformation into an instrument for the redistribution of funds, this naturally became increasingly difficult to accomplish. The associations were regularly consulted about the grant, and have almost certainly been able to exercise direct influence on Whitehall decisions.[132] The difference from French local influence on national decisions is twofold. First, conditions and terms of bargaining, as outlined above, are basically determined by the central government through procedures that are carefully sheltered from local influence. Secondly, the associations themselves follow the ground rules of parliamentary behavior and tend simply to reproduce national partisan politics. Their role is not to mobilize local political interests and pressure, but to provide central government with a convenient and useful sounding board for Rate Support Grant estimates and, since 1975, for spending estimates. Their effectiveness as bargainers on issues where national and local interests conflict is limited by their own partisan organization. In this way they are confined by the same structural and constitutional constraints that neutralize the British parties as potential advocates of local interests and demands, described in Chapter 4.

With the nationalization of local politics each association drifted toward a caucus system of decisionmaking. Labour and Conservative caucuses now control the organizations and their committees. The party caucuses meet regularly in advance of most association meetings to determine how their votes will be cast and operate under the same parliamentary rules that govern Westminster.[133]

The French Association of Mayors

For these reasons, the local government associations conform to the adversary structure of national politics. They are consulted on a number of problems, sit on hundreds of advisory groups and have an important place on the Consultative Council. But as their committee organization reflects, they are structured around services and restrained by the confidentiality that surrounds any discussion of future parliamentary decisions. As might be predicted from the complexity of the French local government system, the Association of French Mayors has difficulty in mobilizing political support, and even more difficulty in being seriously consulted by government. But the changes of the past decade have, if anything, increased its influence. The government needs cooperation in working out the regrouping of communes and in legislating tax reform. The smallness of many municipalities, in turn, makes a sympathetic advisor in Paris valuable. A determined effort by the Minister of the Interior to undercut the mayors' influence in the early 1960s failed,[134] and the Association's close links with the Senate have been reinforced by Poher, President of the Senate.

The more direct relationship between mayors and decisionmaking at higher levels of government works to make the French Mayors Association a more vocal, if not more effective, group than its British counterparts, but the strength of the administrative system also means that it has less access to government. The organization is outspokenly political in ways that would embarrass British pressure groups. At its 1975 Congress, Chirac bravely sat through a series of speeches condemning the government's neglect of communal finance and in 1976 the government was not even invited to attend.[135] The election of the group's president brings into play all the political divisions within France.[136] In 1974 the mayors of forty large cities formed their own association (Association des Maires des Grands Villes), also working from their Senate bastion. Once again French mayors ignored party differences in order to carry on their struggle against Paris. Had their association opposed tax reform in 1979 and 1980, it most likely would never have survived in the Senate.

The main argument of this chapter has been that fiscal relationships between levels of government have an important effect on the method of bargaining over resource allocation. Political analysis has sometimes tended to oversimplify this issue by presuming that only spending is politically relevant. On the contrary, the British case shows that freedom to spend without the power to claim more resources is vulnerable and politically less advantageous from a local perspective. Economic fluctuations are indeed an important limiting condition, but they do not determine the political responses between levels of government, nor do they define the institutional limits on resource bargaining. Some of these constraints are more or less immutable. National and local budget cycles inevitably overlap and calculations must be adjusted later to allow both for inflation and for new burdens imposed by central government.[137] The disaggregation of national economic objectives in programs and their distribution among local governments cannot be accomplished instantly, much less the specific local functions to be affected.

In comparing Britain and France, our general conclusion is that in relation to these continuing conflicts of intergovernmental fiscal relations, it is more desirable to be involved continually, as the French mayors are, than passively to await the national crisis which compels central government to reconsider local spending.

The more important political aspect of fiscal interdependence is how central–local relations are structured by fiscal policy itself. Like the more complex administrative and political intergovernmental relationships in France, the communes' claim on an elastic resource creates more complex bargaining for resources. True, French mayors did not enjoy sharing fiscal responsibility with Paris, but their discontent also stimulated them to mobilize their political resources. Depriving local government of new sources of income, as is the British practice, is a primitive form of centralized control and under economic duress provides no option but rigid limitation of local spending. But to permit local government to enter into the central process of making decisions on resource allocation would both hamper national redistributive policies and compromise Westminster's influence. As we have seen, British towns and cities were satisfied for many years by the simple and costly expedient of an open-ended grant. The Consultative Council is an improvement, but actually only provides limited access to national fiscal policies.[138]

In this respect, central–local financial relationships in Britain have changed little since the turn of the century when Barnstable wrote, 'Local finance is concerned with the steady or only slowly changing conditions of ordinary life.'[139] Such complacency would be more understandable if it contributed to solutions of either national or local fiscal and financial problems. As we have seen, the more rigid relationship in Britain seems to do neither. Central controls on spending do not appear to have achieved equalization of services or equalization of resources.[140] On the contrary, central political manipulation of the grant, plus the diverse and changing demands of Whitehall departments, mean that these two objectives are thoroughly confused. As Sir Laurence Boyle observed some years ago,[141] the tax system itself makes meaningful equalization impossible. There is perhaps no less confusion in French central—local finance, but there at least it is partly the product of local political preferences.

Although France is often charged with having the most arbitrary of governments, the British government has itself assembled an extraordinary array of controls over the local fiscal system even before the new controls of the Thatcher government. The Treasury, with the ministries, defines 'relevant expenditure'; it sets the percentage of this expenditure that can be approved under the Rate Support Grant, and it determines what additional relief, if any, should be forthcoming. More recently, local governments have been made responsible for wage guidelines over which they have no influence, and even for violations of price and wage guidelines in contracts with third parties. Though the rates are the preserve of the counties and districts, the assessment level for taxing types of property is defined by Parliament; national laws determine how the burden of rates will fall; and the rate itself is increasingly becoming a residual function of the grant. Until 1980 the grant itself was manipulated by central decisions on how the total should be apportioned among its three elements, on the factors entering into the several formulas, and in recent years by the decisions to subdivide the elements regionally, to introduce new specific grants, and to make special concessions to London.

Among the more curious contradictions of the French central—local finance is the claim communes make on both the value-added tax they pay and the VRTS made available from national taxes. The fact that Paris is compelled to treat such economic contradictions as political realities suggests the importance of French legal and administrative formalities, at least for the local government system. For present purposes, the contradiction of compensating communes twice for the same reason is not as important as the knowledge that intergovernmental fiscal dependence provides alternative policy solutions and gives local governments access to central decisions. In fact, the Minister of Finance made concessions on locally paid value-added tax in 1974, but also picked up the giant shortfall in the *taxe professionelle* several years later.[142] Preoccupation with the obviously oppressive characteristics of French administration may have blinded us to the vulnerabilities of a system which does indeed like to think that it can manage everything. The communes did not do all that badly, receiving over a billion francs of tax refund in 1974 and later having nearly three billion francs taken from the national budget to meet the shortfall in local indirect taxes.

There are two basic questions to be asked in evaluating intergovernmental fiscal relationships in the two countries. In the light of increasingly difficult problems of controlling the economy, and the longer trend of increasing public expenditure, which pattern offers more alternatives to central and local policymakers? The British system places immense power to make abrupt changes in the hands of the Treasury, often with unforeseen and troubling consequences for local government. At the same time, the Treasury has little direct leverage over local spending, not simply because of administrative formalities, but also because the Chancellor is himself vulnerable on all sides to ministerial demands and Cabinet politics. Even the ruthless economies of the Thatcher government were modified to meet the undeniable needs of local government. To extract more funds, the localities have either to make the difficult political choice to raise the rates or to follow the circuitous route which leads from their own compartmentalized structure to central departments and again eventually the Treasury.[143]

The French Ministry of Finance is not incapable of arbitrary decisionmaking, but it is forced to deal more directly both with other ministers and with local government. As we have seen, there are a multitude of possible adjustments because decisions on both expenditure and resources are jointly made. In the British system, the localities have no choice if their spending exceeds national limits, and no choice about their resource base. As the Ministry of Finance seems to have hoped might be the outcome in 1979 (though did not entirely achieve), the reform of the French local taxation shares the impact of macroeconomic adjustments between levels of government. This is not to say that British counties and cities have not had their share of economic shocks, but they are invariably in the position of *reacting* to new national requirements, rather than *helping* to define policy objectives.

A second and more difficult question involves the relations between bargaining for resources and central–local politics in the two countries. Fiscal and financial relationships between national and local government are not the simple product of economic necessity, even though government, like any element of society, must adjust to economic cycles. The fiscal relationships found in France and Britain bear a remarkable resemblance to the political complexities of each system. In the complex reciprocal causation of French policymaking, it is difficult to determine whether the *complicité* of central–local politics sustains bargaining for national resources or simply uses it in its own self-interest. It is clear that the Ministry of Finance, much as it wanted reform of local taxation, was reluctant to give the communes an unlimited claim on a flexible resource. But here the similarity with Britain ends, for the allegedly more arbitrary powers of the French Ministry were not able to prevent the making of a compromise with local government, while the British Treasury only conceded a slight elaboration of consultation to impose rigid limits. Neither Labour nor the Conservatives wanted to see the concentrated powers of Cabinet and Parliament compromised by a more complex arrangement of resource allocation. Thus, both Labour in 1978 and the Conservatives in 1979 proposed virtually identical new controls over the transfer despite the differences in their partisan political interests.

Put somewhat differently, if the political weight of local government, not to mention its immense economic importance, could be brought to bear on national decisions in Britain, would it expect the same outcome as in France? The structural relationships between levels of government restrain the potential collective influence of the British local government over Whitehall. That councillors can be effectively subdued by higher civil servants who have less capacity than French *fonctionnaires* to perform the tasks of local government only adds to the paradox. The price of compartmentalization of national and local fiscal problems is not negligible. By excluding local government from many larger economic calculations, Britain loses one means of adjusting public spending to national economic policy and thus must rely more heavily on arbitrary and often more erratic controls than the French. The British also forego the possibility of redefining the needs of the local government system through political competition. At very little political cost, both national parties can seize and exploit the short-term advantages which fiscal subordination provides. One does not need to be French to marvel at a Labour government contriving ways to introduce 'organic change' one year and a Conservative government choosing to abolish the transfer system in the next year.

The more numerous ways to influence intergovernmental fiscal relationships in France are consistent with the needs of a multiparty system and a way of compensating for a relatively weak Parliament. It is almost as if the French mayors are fulfilling their historic role by making political institutions work better despite the shortcomings of democratic government in France. The power of national policy-makers is to this extent reduced, as it further is by the more direct political impact that mayors have on the political system as a whole. There is a remarkable degree of consensus across the wide spectrum of parties in France about fiscal and financial reform. To be sure, many of their policies simply involve increasing local incomes in whatever way possible, but conflict about resource allocation also stimulates a lively debate between levels of government about institutional change itself. Like most policy discussions it would not be taking place if both national and local politicians did not realize that a certain degree of cooperation was essential to the success of both. The debate did not stop after the 1978 legislative elections, nor is it likely to stop after the 1979–80 reforms.

With the development of the welfare state, the fiscal interdependence of national and local government has acquired crucial importance, but the primary claim of the state in the making of economic policy is not in question. Choices arise in determining how the various levels of government are to become involved. The refusal of the British system to yield even marginal control over the allocation of resources is evidence both of the political subordination of local government and of the reluctance of local politicians to mobilize their political potential. The more rigid stance of British government is thus a function of both national and local institutional constraints. There is little to suggest that even a left-wing French government would be able simply to ignore the political and administrative complexities of the subnational system. Much the same conclusion might be drawn for the exercise of controls on capital spending, to be discussed in the next chapter.

NOTES: CHAPTER 6

1 On the superimposition of state controls following the First World War, see Jean-Claude Thoenig, 'Subsidies and state centralization under the Third Republic', in D. Ashford (ed.), *Financing Cities in the Welfare State* (London: Croom Helm, 1980); and R. Ludwig, 'Le contrôle local des engagements de dépenses en France; de l'histoire d'un chec (1936) à l'éspoir d'une réussite (1970)', *Revue de Science Financière*, vol. 63 (July–September 1971), pp. 505–594.

2 In France there is an annual accounting, *Le Secteur Public Local* (Paris: Ministry of Finance), published since the early 1960s. Further figures can be gleaned from the annual *Loi de finances* though it is difficult to decipher; and the aggregate final accounts are published as *Rapports sur les Comptes de la Nation* (Paris: INSEE), annually. Probably the best single volume on the French local fiscal system for localities is Dominique Flecher and Henri Fort, *Les Finances Locales* (Paris: Masson, 1977); dated, but with more institutional material, is P. Guerrier and L. Bauchard, *Économie Financière des Collectivités Locales* (Paris: Colin, 1972). For current figures on British local spending see *Local Government Financial Statistics* (London: HMSO), annually; tables in *Local Government Trends* (London: CIPFA), since 1974; and the *Rate Support Grant*, published since 1968 by the Association of County Councils. The best general account from the local perspective is N. P. Hepworth, *The Finance of Local Government*, 2nd edn (London: Allen & Unwin, 1979). More managerial is A. H. Marshall, *Financial Management in Local Government* (London: Allen & Unwin, 1974).

3 On recent developments and conflicts see Yves Fréville, 'VRTS et équité', *Les Cahiers du CFPC*, no. 2 (1978), pp. 34–67; and for a general account, G. Finkel, 'Le versement répresentatif de la taxe sur les salaires (VRTS)', *Revue de Science Financière*, vol. 69 (July–September 1977), pp. 797–831.

4 On the transformation of the American system of transfers, see Tom Anton, 'Federal assistance programs: the politics of system transformation', in D. Ashford (ed.), *The Politics of Urban Resources* (London: Croom Helm and New York: Methuen, 1980); and Martha Derthick, *Uncontrollable Spending for Social Service Grants* (Washington, DC: Brookings Institution, 1975).

5 See D. Ashford, 'A Victorian drama: growth of the transfer in nineteenth century Britain', in D. Ashford (ed.), *Financing Cities . . .*, op. cit.; and Sir Gwilym Gibbon, 'The expenditure and revenue of local authorities', *Journal of the Royal Statistical Society*, vol. 99 (1936), pp. 457–515.

6 See the testimony of the Department of the Environment to the Layfield Committee, 'Evidence by government departments' in *Relationship Between Central and Local Government* (London: HMSO, 1976), App. I, pp. 40–7. Current figures.

7 From 1959 to 1973 local expenses increased at 12.5 percent a year, while the gross national product increased at 10.7 percent and the national budget at 9.8 percent; Pierre Lalumière, *Les Finances Publiques*, 2nd edn (Paris: Colin, 1976), p. 109.

8 There is unfortunately no good political study of the French Ministry of Finance. The best study of how it works is Pierre Lalumière, op. cit. See also his earlier study *L'Inspection des Finances* (Paris: PUF, 1959).

9 For example, an ambitious attempt was made to anticipate economic changes by Beckerman *et al.*, *The British Economy in 1975* (Cambridge: Cambridge University Press, 1965). The assumption at the time was that gross national product would rise by 56 percent between 1963 and 1975; in fact, the rise was 31 percent.

10 Probably the best study on the Treasury's internal decisionmaking methods, if not the content, is Hugh Heclo and Aaron Wildavsky, *The Private Government of Public Money* (Berkeley: University of California Press, 1974). On political implications see Samuel H. Beer, *Treasury Control* (London: Oxford University Press, 1957). A fine history is Henry Roseveare, *The Evolution of a British Institution: The Treasury* (New York: Columbia University Press, 1969).

11 See the testimony of the DES and the DoE in 'Evidence by government departments', Layfield Report, op. cit., pp. 18–55; and especially the oral evidence from the Treasury, pp. 295–319.

12 Though a fine point, the way one arrives at the importance of the grant makes a great deal of difference in fiscal calculations. The figure given here is the grant in relation to all spending by local government, that is, including municipal corporations and housing. Using the Treasury's terms, the grant amounted to

two-thirds of local spending in 1976 and has gradually diminished since then. See A. Crispin, 'Local government finance: assessing the central government's contribution', *Public Administration* (UK), vol. 50 (1976), pp. 45–61.

13 The underlying reason, as the studies of the Treasury cited above make clear, is the political importance of the Exchequer in the Cabinet and the parliamentary process. The ritual of the Chancellor's red box and the secrecy about the Budget has, of course, become more a ritual than a reality with the numerous mini-budgets needed to adjust throughout the budgetary year to inflation, and with the development of more sophisticated forecasting models. Preserving the political role of the Treasury was a major problem in the modernization of British public expenditure.

14 There are now a number of studies of the erratic effects of British public spending controls. See, for example, T. S. Ward and R. R. Neild, *The Measurement and Reform of Budgetary Policy* (London: Heinemann, 1978).

15 Cash limits do not apply to all local government spending, but only to that portion under national supervision, that is, relevant expenditure or roughly 60 percent of local current spending. See Chancellor of the Exchequer, *Cash Limits 1978–79*, Cmd 7681 (London: HMSO, 1978).

16 An understanding of national taxation is essential to assessing local taxation. See Robert Schnerb, *Deux Siècles de Fiscalité Française XIXe-XXe siècle* (Paris and The Hague: Mouton, 1973); and J. M. Kay and M. A. King, *The British Tax System* (Oxford: Oxford University Press, 1978). For details on France, see Ludwig, op. cit., and Jacques Wolff, 'Fiscalité et développement en France entre 1919 et 1939', *Revue de Science Financière*, vol. 62 (1970), pp. 705–727.

17 J. Redlich and F. W. Hirst, *Local Government in England* (London: Macmillan, 1903), vol. I, p. 156. For a full account of the development of the rating system from 1601, see Edwin Cannan, *The History of Local Rates in England,* 2nd edn (London: P. S. King, 1912). There is a major historical controversy over pauperism and rates. See Daniel A. Baugh, 'The cost of poor relief in South-East England, 1790–1834', *Economic History Review*, vol. 28 (1975), pp. 50–68.

18 The most complete early report on the state of local finances, and the difficulties of calculating local finances, is George J. Goschen's 'Local taxation report of 1871', to be found in Goschen, *Reports and Speeches on Local Taxation* (London: Macmillan, 1872), pp. 2–51, with numerous financial tables. For a more detailed account, see D. Ashford, 'A Victorian drama: . . ., op. cit.

19 Redlich and Hirst, op. cit., vol. 1, pp. 158–9. Oddly enough Peel was forced to make this concession against his better judgment, and insisted that additional grants needed to obtain passage of the law be conditional.

20 Smellie, *A History of Local Government* (London: Allen & Unwin, 1968, 4th edn), p. 148. At this time one of the first modern inquiries into the rating system by a House of Commons Select Committee was held. Concessions were made largely in response to its recommendations. A full account of how the grants grew in Victorian England can be found in J. Watson Grice, *National and Local Finance* (London: P. S. King, 1910), pp. 31–117.

21 See Redlich and Hirst, op. cit., vol. 1, p. 161.

22 It rapidly became apparent that the Treasury was simply refusing to transfer the assigned revenues to local accounts. See *The Economist*, vol. 48, 11 October 1890, pp. 1268–78; and vol. 46, 24 March 1888, pp. 371–3. A second major report on local taxation, following the lines of Goschen's report of 1871, was made in 1893 by Henry Fowler, president of the Local Government Board. It can be found in *House of Commons Papers*, vol. 127 (1893), pp. i–iii. By this time the argument centered almost entirely on how the burden of local taxation was shared between landowners and urban dwellers. See also Charles Henry Sargant, *Urban Rating: Being an Inquiry into the Incidence of Local Taxation in Towns* (London: Longman Green, 1890).

23 H. Fowler, 'Report of the local government Board', *House of Commons Papers*, vol. 58 (1893), p. xi. His report continues from the 1870 analysis of Sir George Goschen, reprinted in his *Reports and Speeches on Local Taxation* (London: Macmillan, 1872).

24 Cannan, op. cit., p. 149.

25 Grice, op. cit., p. ix. At the turn of the century eleven reports were prepared by the Royal Commission on Local Taxation. Their work is summarized in the final *Report*, Cmd 638 (London: HMSO, 1901); but the Conservative government decided to make no changes with a political fight looming with the Liberal Party.

On the general situation at the turn of the century, see Percy Ashley, 'The financial control of local authorities', *Economic Journal*, vol. 12 (1902), pp. 182–91.

26   E. P. Hennock, 'Finance and politics in urban local government in England, 1835–1900', *The Historical Journal*, vol. 6 (1963), p. 216. His study, *Fit and Proper Persons* (London: Arnold, 1973), is an analysis of, among other things, how local politics and budgetary manipulation interacted.

27   Ingenuity was doubly important after the Borough Funds Act of 1872 forbade boroughs to use the rates in order to promote municipal gas or water companies. See Redlich and Hirst, op. cit., vol. 1, pp. 364–7.

28   The best account of the 1920s debate is the essay by Gerald Rhodes, 'Local government finance 1918–1966', in Layfield Committee (London: HMSO, 1976), *Relationship between Central and Local Government*, App. 6, pp. 102–73. The debate is notable for bringing formidable opponents into action; Winston Churchill, who had rejoined the Conservative party, was Chancellor of the Exchequer at the time.

29   Rhodes, op. cit., p. 133.

30   Quoted in Smellie, op. cit., p. 133. Still one of the best expositions on the various kinds of grants and their early history after the war is D. N. Chester, *Central and Local Authorities* (London: Macmillan, 1951).

31   The initial aim was to revalue all property by 1952, later postponed to 1956. There have since been additional revaluations in 1963 and 1973. Though the technical aspects of local taxation virtually escape public consideration, they can be of considerable political interest. Imposing new values was again delayed by the Conservatives in 1961 and 1980. Another unworkable feature of the old rating system was that rent restrictions after the war further distorted imputed rents. See Rhodes, op. cit., pp. 118–24. A detailed discussion can be found in the Layfield Committee, *Report*, op. cit., pp. 143–82.

32   The clearest statement of this conflict and its effects on the grant is by Francis Cripps and Wynne Godley, *Local Government Finance and its Reform: A Critique of the Layfield Committee's Report* (University of Cambridge; Department of Applied Economics, 1976). Actually this is not so much a critique of Layfield as of the incoherent development of the grant system since 1929.

33   See David N. King, 'Why do local authority rate poundages differ?', *Public Administration* (UK), vol. 51 (1973), pp. 165–73. The Layfield Committee's *Report*, op. cit., pp. 158–65, produced good evidence that the rating system is regressive, though the regression is wiped out by income tax. The more acute problem is that property evaluations lag behind during inflation. Although rates have increased in relation to income, they have not increased in relation to the value of property. In 1960 rates were 2 percent of disposable income and in 1975 only 2.4 percent. See 'Evidence by local authority associations', Layfield Report, op. cit., App. 2, p. 43. Even these figures are, however, open to some errors, for they do not include rent rebates (introduced in 1966) and a variety of additional rate relief payments under the Supplementary Benefits or welfare system. It is the inability to find out what the rate does, in addition to how it combines with many additional programs and policies affecting property, that makes it a less and less suitable tax base.

34   See Rhodes, op. cit., pp. 124–30. The main conclusion of the study by the Royal Institute of Public Administration, *New Sources of Local Revenue* (London: Allen & Unwin, 1956), was that 'derating' or exemptions from rates should be abolished, and supplementary income be found. After the 1958 Act agricultural property was still totally exempt, and industrial property taxed at 50 percent, an increase from 25 percent.

35   *Local Government Finance (England and Wales)*, Cmd 209 (London: HMSO, 1957). The report was fashioned entirely within Whitehall and caught the local authority associations unprepared for its recommendations. Its aims were similar to those outlined in the *First Report of the Local Government Manpower Committee*, Cmd 7870 (London: HMSO, 1950), which advised that local authorities be delegated additional responsibilities and freed from excessive central control. See the evaluation of B. Keith-Lucas, 'Three White Papers on local government', *Political Quarterly*, vol. 28 (1957), pp. 328–38.

36   Rhodes, op. cit., p. 136.

37   Partly as a preparation for the coming elections, the Conservative Party conducted yet another inquiry into the rate system. See Committee of Inquiry into

the Impact of Rates on Households (Allen Committee), *Report*, Cmnd 2582 (London: HMSO, 1963). There were also new studies by the County Councils Association and the Association of Municipal Councils.

38 Rhodes, op. cit., p. 143. The White Paper, *Local Government Finance England and Wales*, Cmnd 2923 (London: HMSO, 1966), was published just as the Royal Commission on Local Government was taking shape. This provided, as further commissions and inquiries often do, another reason to delay serious action. The percentage of expenditure from grants barely changed (about 43 to 44 percent) between 1957 and 1969. See the evaluation of D. N. Chester, 'Local finance', *Political Quarterly*, vol. 37 (1966), pp. 180–91.

39 Like the Conservatives previously, Labour postponed the revaluation of property in 1968. Labour also introduced rate rebates to relieve directly rate pressure on low-income families. This affected 2.5 million households. Another two million had rates paid in full under Supplementary Benefits; Layfield Report, op. cit., p. 161. All this made the rating system an even greater anomaly and the very incidence of rates more difficult to assess. The decision was also made at this time to deduct specific grants from 'relevant expenditure' before distributing the Rate Support Grant. This in effect favored those localities getting more specific grants and encouraged politicians to rely more heavily on specific grants in order to redistribute resources.

40 The successive reorganizations of the rating system are noted in parentheses in Table 6.1. In the mid-1950s the Conservatives, threatened by a tax revolt, appointed the Allen Committee to study the incidence of rates. See Allen Committee Report, op. cit. See also N. P. Hepworth, op. cit., pp. 76–91. Like the Layfield Committee a decade later, the Allen Committee found the rating system regressive. This became the natural target for the party debate, while the real issue, the declining importance of rates as a source of local income, was neglected by both parties.

41 Both quotations from Rhodes, op. cit., pp. 144, 151, respectively.

42 Bosher, 'French administration and public finance in their European setting', in *Cambridge New Modern History*, Vol. 8 (Cambridge: Cambridge University Press, 1965), p. 587. I have relied heavily on his essay for this paragraph.

43 See Christine André *et al.*, op. cit. Also Louis Fontvielle, 'Dépenses publiques et problematique de la dévalorisation du capital', unpublished manuscript, which provides an excellent historical analysis of debt and growth.

44 Even so, the British debt from the Napoleonic wars was much greater than the French debt. For additional details see Roger Priouret, *La Caisse des Dépôts* (Paris: PUF, 1966), pp. 6–56. In a curious repetition of history, new funds were organized throughout the nineteenth century, such as the Caisse d'Epargne and the Caisse de Retraits, and they were attached to the CDC, not to the government. The efforts of the Gaullist modernizers might from this perspective be seen as trying to undo the rigidities of a previous century.

45 Joseph Duplouy, *Le Crédit aux collectivités locales* (Paris: Berger Levrault, 1967), p. 74. The role of the CDC will be further elaborated in Chapter 8.

46 Marc Himbourg, *Droit Français des Finances Communales* (Paris: Gilard, 1891), p. 354.

47 Paul Leroy-Beaulieu, *Traité de la Science des Finances*, Vol. 1, 5th edn (Paris: Guillamin, 1892), p. 251.

48 There is a good English account of the situation under the Third Republic in Grice, op. cit., pp. 119–72. See also Jacques Wolff, 'Fiscalité et développement en France entre 1919 et 1939', *Revue de Science Financière*, vol. 62, no. 4 (October–December 1970), pp. 705–27. The classic French work of the period is L. Paul-Dobois, *Essai sur les finances communales* (Paris: Perrin, 1898). The French local taxation system under the Second Empire and the early Third Republic was no model of administrative efficiency. See the intriguing account of Le Comte de Franqueville, 'Local government finance', in J. W. Probyn (ed.), *Government and Taxation* (London: Cassell, Petter and Galpin, 1875), pp. 283–308.

49 Himbourg, op. cit., pp. 130–1.

50 From Thoenig, in Ashford (ed.), *Financing Cities in the Welfare State*, op. cit.

51 The Aubaud Commission was appointed by the Blum government in 1936 but its efforts to relieve the pressure of direct taxes were cut short by the war. The Provisional Government appointed the Barrau Commission in 1945 which recommended a new state fund to relieve fiscal pressure. Another report was

made by Masteau in 1962. The Bourrel Commission was in part a product of the Fifth Plan, when it was decided to make a huge increase in urban investment.

52 *Rapport de la Commission d'Étude des Finances Locales à Monsieur le Premier Ministre* (Paris: Office of the Prime Minister, 1965), p. 28.

53 *Rapport de l'Intergroupe d'Étude des Finances Locales* (Paris: Documentation Française (Commissariat Générale du Plan), 1971).

54 Lest one think this too enlightened a view, it should be noted that the 1959 *ordonnance* did not go into effect until 1968, although the fiscal reform began in 1966. By the mid-1960s the local budgets no longer appeared in simple cash-flow terms and they appear now, unlike British local budgets which are aggregated from three funds (Revenue, Housing and Services), in an integrated report. Though the technical problems should not detain us, working out a computerized modern accounting system for 36,000 units of local government is clearly no simple task.

55 This seems to me perhaps the most important reason why French admiration of British local government is misplaced, though this is not to say that there are not things to admire about the British counties and cities. But the fiscal crisis of France was the product of capital spending, and there was never any desire or intention by mayors or Paris to enlarge the role of local government to include what was already being done by other government agencies.

56 In fact, the *principaux fictifs* have lost their meaning with revaluation by re-calculating their bases. It is easy to be overawed by the various fictional aspects of French local taxes. The apparently more concrete procedure of Britain does not escape this problem, nor do most tax systems. See, for example, Layfield Report, op. cit., p. 169, which concludes that the rate has now no empirical basis because there is no free market for rentals. Combined with all the housing measures and relief from rates, the British 'rate' is thus no less fictional than the French. The Rate Support Grant, a wholly arbitrary figure, derives from macroeconomic estimates.

57 Commission Spéciale Chargée d'Examiner le Projet de Loi (no. 689) (Voisin Report), *Rapport*, Paris, Assemblée Nationale, no. 1043, Annexe au procès verbal de la séance du 9 mai 1979, p. 36. Voisin's meticulous study of the inequities of the burden and distribution of the *taxe professionelle* led to overturning the government proposals.

58 Lalumière, op. cit., p. 116.

59 No less bitterly resisted than the reform of the direct taxes, the *taxe locale d'équipement* of 1967 gave communes (over 10,000) the right to tax new construction. Obviously, no mayor wishes to discourage growth in his community so it has not been successful in producing new income. In 1975 this tax was converted to an indemnity to be paid for exceeding specified levels of population density in new construction and linked to the *loi foncière*.

60 Voisin Report, op. cit., p. 132. See also G. Finkel, op. cit.

61 Because of the initial base on payrolls, the *taxe professionelle* falls more heavily on labor-intensive firms and, in turn, discourages job formation. It also appears that many capital-intensive firms which tend to be more profitable pay less. See the Voisin Report, op. cit., Part Three, pp. 47–80, for a detailed exposition.

62 In 1966 three-fourths of the communes collected only the guaranteed minimum of 43 francs per inhabitant, while many large cities collected 200 francs or more per person: Lalumière, op. cit., p. 125. Lourdes reached 422 francs per person; Mény, *Centralisation et Décentralisation dans le Débat Politique Français* (Paris: Librairie Générale de Droit et de Jurisprudence, 1974), p. 273.

63 For additional details see J. Bourdon and J. M. Pontier, 'Les collectivités locales et la TVA', *Revue de Science Financière*, vol. 65, no. 3 (1973), pp. 509–52. Though it involves a slight exaggeration, the requirements of a unified Europe, so suspect in de Gaulle's eyes, may be said to have dislodged the problem of local finance in France.

64 From *Le Secteur Public Local* (1976), op. cit.

65 In 1970, for example, the communes paid 3.2 billion francs for the TVA and received 8.2 billion francs in subsidies. See Guerrier and Bauchard, op. cit., p. 311.

66 A comparison with the increases in income and corporate taxes as well as the four direct local taxes since 1970 will be found in the Voisin Report, op. cit., p. 32.

67 See the table in Flecher and Bourjol, op. cit., p. 147.

68 For details of the index, see Flecher and Bourjol, op. cit., pp. 148–9.

69 The FAL began with 1 percent of the salary tax and is to gradually increase, reaching 4.7 percent of the imputed salary tax in 1977. For the VRTS a dual system of distribution was devised. In 1968 all the funds were distributed according to the *attribution de garantie*, or precisely as the salary tax would have allocated them – in 5 percent intervals through 1988, this to be converted to the *attribution de répartition*, or fiscal effort based on a combined index of other local taxes. See Flecher and Fort, op. cit., pp. 148–9.

70 See Fréville, 'VRTS et équité', *Les Cahiers du C.F.P.C.*, no. 2, June 1978, pp. 34–66.

71 On the debate over the *taxe professionelle* reform in the National Assembly which overturned the government's plan, see Alain Vernholes, 'Des idées pour plus tard', *Le Monde*, 13 October 1979.

72 The Senate debate on the DGF in late 1978 momentarily threatened the government with a defeat similar to that in the National Assembly. At one point, the Senate voted to simply abolish the system of direct taxes in favor of a single property tax, which presumably would fall on homeowners and exempt business. See *Le Monde*, 11 and 16 November 1978.

73 The debates on the reforms in the fall of 1979 suffered from the growing tensions between the President and the Gaullists on national issues, although they also clearly differed on efforts to strengthen departmental government. In 1978 relations were so bad that on one occasion the Gaullist group in the Senate refused to support the government. See *Le Monde*, 17 November 1978.

74 On reforms in the USA, see James A. Maxwell and J. Richard Aronson, *Financing State and Local Governments* (Washington, D.C.: The Brookings Institution, 1977). On Germany, see B. Reissert, 'The politics of federal and state transfers', in D. Ashford (ed.), *National Resources and Urban Policy*; and J. H. Knott, 'Stabilization policy, grants-in-aid, and the federal system in Western Germany', in W. E. Oates (ed.), *The Political Economy of Fiscal Federalism* (Lexington, Mass.: Heath, 1977), pp. 75–92. On Canada, see Thomas J. Courchene, *Refinancing the Canadian Federation: the 1977 Fiscal Arrangements Act* (Montreal: C. D. Howe Research Institute, 1977).

75 Calculating minimal standards is virtually impossible because of the diversity of costs. The possibility was considered and rejected by the Layfield Committee, *Report*, op. cit., pp. 59–62, and App. 12, pp. 403–6. Alan Day dissented, ibid., pp. 305–14, arguing that a cost–benefit analysis would enable the center to determine the level of income where local discretion might better be exercised.

76 On the failure to reconsider the grant during the British reorganization, see David Peschk, 'The reorganisation story: the reform that never was', *Municipal Review* (July 1976), p. 74. This should be compared with the extended preparation and consultation in France which is helpfully summarized by Raymond Muzellac, 'Sur la consultation des Maires de France (30 Juin 1977)', *Revue du Droit Public*, vol. 94 (September–October 1978), pp. 1401–15.

77 See *Local Government Trends 1974* (London: CIPFA), p. 75; and *Rate Support Grant, Sixth Period*, pp. 6, 12; later divided into fixed and variable portions. On the unpredictable effects of changing the various elements of the RSG, see Anthony Harris and Stewart Lansley, 'Rate increases 1979', *CFS Review*, no. 7 (September 1979), pp. 17–31; and Anthony Harris *et al.*, 'Needs grant: which way now?', *CFS Review*, no. 6 (May 1979), pp. 18–31.

78 In 1968 the domestic element was only 1.8 percent of the total Rate Support Grant; by 1975 it was 14.5 percent. In the same period, the needs element declined from 81.9 percent to 62 percent (calculated from the *Rate Support Group Reports*).

79 The new controls are found in the *Local Government Planning and Land Bill* (London: HMSO, 29 November 1979), pp. 36–46. Originally introduced in the House of Lords to facilitate debate, the protest from the Opposition over introducing a key piece of legislation in the Lords forced the government to withdraw it and await a Commons debate. The complexity of the Bill (246 clauses and 288 pages) also forced the government to remove some parts in a revised Bill, but the spending controls were not materially changed.

80 For a recent suggestion that British rates should be tied to income, see Della Adam Nevitt, 'The "burden" of domestic rates', *Policy and Politics*, vol. 2 (1973), pp. 1–25. This might relieve local problems, but it would effectively convert rates into an income tax without giving local councils leverage on national tax policy.

81 Layfield Committee, *Report*, op. cit., pp. 132–42. These ideas are explored by

Roland Freeman, 'Layfield: science of the logical or art of the possible?', *Municipal Review*, no. 559 (1976), pp. 96–7; and Arthur Seldon, 'Layfield: why not charge for services?', ibid., pp. 98–9. See also Alan K. Maynard and David N. King, *Rates or Prices? A Study of the Economics of Local Government and its Replacement by the Market* (London: Institute of Economic Affairs, 1975). However, the local governments have taken seriously ways of making modest economies and bolstering service income. See Association of Metropolitan Authorities, *Value for Money: Local Authorities and Cost-Effectiveness* (London: AMA, 1978). Income from these sources has in fact grown since 1950, when it was 32 percent of total income; in 1974 it was nearly 36 percent. Over the same period, rate income fell from 34 percent of income to 25 percent. The difference has been assumed by grants.

82   The most heated dispute has been over the Conservatives' 1972 Housing Finance Act which tried to restore something approaching market-determined rents by issuing a 'fair rent' device. Labour immediately repealed this legislation on coming to office in 1974. Housing policy has suffered from the 'stop-and-go' that has characterized economic policy generally.

83   Layfield Committee, op. cit., p. 108.

84   See Layfield Report, op. cit., pp. 165–301. The most important technical problem the Committee explored is that over 80 percent of income tax is deducted from payrolls, and there is no simple way to attach income tax to areas. Local income tax has been raised in the Conservative discussion paper, *The Future Shape of Local Government Finance*, Cmd 4741 (London: HMSO, 1971), but no stand was taken at that time. The Conservatives also received two reports from their Grants Working Group. The 1972 report could not be squeezed into the parliamentary schedule and the 1974 report appeared after the party's defeat at the General Election.

85   *See Municipal Review*, no. 559 (July 1976), p. 116. There were valiant efforts by the Chairman and several members, particularly two academics, George Jones and John Stewart. For the latter two see respectively, 'Layfield: this is no time to avoid the issue of local control', *Municipal Review*, no. 566 (February 1977), pp. 309, 335, and 'Time to take the uneasy road of local control?', *Municipal Review*, no. 558 (June 1976), p. ii, in the Special Issue on the Layfield Report. See also the special issue of *Public Administration* (UK), vol. 55 (Spring 1977), on the Layfield Report.

86   See 'Evidence by political parties', Layfield Report, op. cit., App. 3. The Conservatives boycotted the Committee and sent a three-page memo. Labour supported the income tax on the condition that it would have to be sharply progressive. Perhaps Labour's most revealing comment (ibid., p. 30) was to recognize a dual tax objective to redistribute the burden both within and among local governments. Such a system could only be managed from the center, as the party admitted. The same conclusion is reached by the local finance expert, N. P. Hepworth, 'The real issues facing Layfield and their implications', *Local Government Studies* (New Series), vol. 2 (1976), pp. 1–14. The Conservatives have considered radical reform of rating. See Roland Freeman, *The Rates Riddle* (London: The Bow Group, 1978).

87   The micro-studies of local spending are summarized in Ken Newton and L. J. Sharpe, 'Local outputs research: some reflections and proposals', *Policy and Politics*, vol. 5 (1977), pp. 61–82. The most complete study of political influences in boroughs is Noel Boaden, *Urban Policy-Making* (Cambridge: Cambridge University Press, 1971).

88   These began with cuts of 192 million pounds in 1973 and are recorded in *Rate Support Grant* annual reports of the Association to County Councils. I have not found any study of the net effect of the public spending cuts and the rate support increases required by inflation and wage increases. See Christopher Forster, 'Price of local freedom', *Municipal Review*, no. 553 (January 1976), pp. 276–7, and also R. R. Nield and T. S. Ward, 'The forecasts and financing of local government expenditure', Layfield Report, op. cit., App. 6, pp. 81–97.

89   There are generally two Rate Support Grant Increase Orders each year. They have usually been tied to major pay awards for teachers, police, etc., or to new inflation statistics. They are also recorded in appendices to the *Rate Support Grant* publications.

90   On the effectiveness of the Manpower Watch, see Cristina Howick, 'Manpower in local authorities: the joint Manpower Watch', *CES Review*, no. 1 (July 1977),

pp. 11–18, who concludes that the initial improvement was achieved by reducing the numbers of temporary employees and teachers and therefore had little long-term effect on expenditure reduction. When the Watch Committee's work began, 22 percent of the local authorities failed to return the local employment questionnaire; *Local Government Trends 1973*, p. 289.

91 As shown in Table 6.2, the rate of increase of local expenditure did decrease dramatically from 1976. However, Labour's last PESC paper forecast modest increases in local spending, and much of the clamor over Heseltine's reductions in 1980 is actually about lowering the forecast to levels that Labour had itself imposed in earlier years. For this reason, the attack on the Heseltine cuts by the Opposition Shadow Secretary of State for the DoE, Hattersley, was rather feeble. See *Guardian*, 25 October 1979.

92 1976 was nicknamed the 'Year of Circular 45' because of a DoE circular in mid-year insisting that local governments hold to PESC estimates of local expenditure.

93 The increases in rates helped justify the special treatment of London, described below. For more background, see Jane Morton, 'The future of the rates', *New Society*, 18 July 1974, pp. 144–6; and Gavin Weightman, 'The politics of the rates', *New Society*, 1 January 1976, pp. 15–16.

94 Layfield Report, op. cit., pp. 21, 381. For trends by local departments see *Local Government Trends 1974* (London: CIPFA), p. 96. Health service employment increased by 170 percent. These trends are not unique to Britain. From 1955 to 1974 in the United States, state and local employees increased in number by 125 percent compared to the federal increase of 19 percent. See *Significant Features of Fiscal Federalism* (Washington D.C.: Advisory Committee on Intergovernmental Relations, 1976).

95 The major agreements are on teachers' pay, under the Burnham arrangements with the National Union of Teachers; the police; the firemen; manual workers (concentrated in the National Union of Public Employees); and administrative, technical and clerical staff (concentrated in NALGO and NUPE). Previous to LACSAB there had been a regional organization where local authorities were directly represented. For details see A. W. J. Thomson and P. B. Beaumont, *Public Sector Bargaining: A Study of Relative Gain* (London: Saxon House, 1978).

96 While this effort was taking place, local governments were also being asked to hire *more* persons under the Job Creation Programme and in 1976, for example, actually added nearly 7000 persons for this reason. See *Local Government Trends 1976*, p. 256. Much to the distaste of the local governments, all pay agreements had to be submitted to the DoE, and two weeks' prior notice was required. See *The Times* (London), 5 December 1977. For additional information on the organization and conditions of service of local government employees, see K. P. Poole, *Local Government Service in England and Wales* (London: Allen & Unwin, 1978).

97 See the description in the *Report* (Layfield Committee), op. cit., Annex 13, pp. 406–7. Also *Rate Support Grant (Fifth Period)*, pp. 13–14. On Labour's revenge, *Rate Support Grant (Sixth Period)*, pp. 12, 52.

98 *Local Government Trends 1974*, p. 75. The domestic element was nearly doubled from 6.1 to 10.3 percent of the total grant: it then increased to 10.7 percent and has stayed about there since.

99 The Association of Municipal Authorities saw this trend coming and gave warning in an editorial in *Municipal Review*, no. 568 (March 1977), p. ii. A first step in this direction, under the guise of reducing local burdens, was the Transportation Grant introduced in 1975. In mid-1977 the DES made it known that it, too, would like more specific grants; *Municipal Review*, no. 571 (July 1977), p. 114. These changes could only succeed by reducing the General Grant and would potentially be doubly political in both reducing general support and tempting ministers to divert General Grant funds toward their favorite projects and policies.

100 Under the Thatcher government both fiddling with the RSG formula and control of rates worked to the advantage of the counties. See Tony Travers, 'Buckinghamshire is destined to suffer, Manchester could do well, while Solihull looks a poor bet', *Guardian*, 13 November 1979. Even so, expected rate increases ran counter to the Thatcher government's austerity goals and were expected to be between 20 and 30 percent in 1980. A further innovation was for the Treasury to hold back a billion pounds of the grant to pay for expected increases in local

government wages, rather than supplementing the grant after awards were made.

101   Barry Lynch, 'Grant deficiency: how much do local authorities rely on central government support?', *CES Review*, no. 6 (November 1979), pp. 64–9. It is almost impossible to show any clear relationship statistical between spending and grant; see Ashford, 'The effects of central finance', *British Journal of Political Sciences*, vol. 7 (July 1970), pp. 305–22.

102   *The Times* (London), 13 November 1979. The 61 percent rate of relevant expenditure was a relief to some authorities who feared a reduction of 4 percent. The second control, the cash limit, was set at 14 percent.

103   Given the multiplicity of controls, central government still does not have accurate information on the effects of its own decisions; nor is there room for bargaining as in France. Thus arbitrary decisions are virtually forced on central government. It was well known, for example, which local authorities would suffer from *post hoc* penalties, many of them high-spending, Labour-held London boroughs, but no way of estimating what the effects would be.

104   'Note of reservation' by Professor Alan Day, Layfield Report, op. cit., pp. 307–17. See also support for Day in Bleddyn Davies, 'Layfield's split vision', *New Society*, 26 May 1976.

105   See *Local Government Finance*, Cmd 6813 (London: HMSO, 1977). The arrangements for Scotland are different because the Scottish Office already acts as the filter for Scottish grants, even though they, too, come under the same statutory controls. See *Local Government Finance: Finance in Scotland*, Cmd 6811 (London: HMSO, 1977). See also John D. Stewart, 'The Green Paper on local government finance – a viewpoint', *Local Government Studies* (New Series), vol. 3 (1977), pp. 9–15; and *The Economist*, 18 May 1977. A year later Shore, after supporting property evaluation in real terms rather than in rental terms, withdrew the proposal; see *The Times* (London), 11 May 1978. He postponed new evaluation to 1982.

106   There is a certain irony in Shore's decision about what to publish and what not to publish. The conditional form of this publication would inevitably become political and bring pressure on local governments that underspent. In contrast, during the crisis he refused to publish which authorities overspent, more likely to be Labour-controlled. See *Rate Support Grant (Eighth Order)*, p. 93.

107   The alternative is to define minimum standards; though this, of course, does not solve the cost differential problem among authorities. The idea was rejected by the Layfield Committee, *Report*, op. cit., p. 73, for this reason, but supported by Day, ibid., pp. 303–5. It would provide choice to exceed given levels with local resources. This is unacceptable to Labour, though it would provide, in Day's words, a 'middle way' to bring resource calculations back into the calculation of the grant. The use of 'middle-way' in the Green Paper is different, suggesting only, as before, that the grant remain entirely open-ended. Another minor but significant partisan concern was to terminate 'precepting', or transfers from first to second tiers of the grant, which rankled the metropolitan districts, usually Labour, in the new counties, usually Conservative.

108   See Jean-Marie Pontier, 'La Répartition des competences entre l'État et les collectivités locales: bilan et perspectives', in Debbasch (ed.), op. cit., pp. 117–22.

109   The communes have approximately 25 billion francs in the national Treasury. Were this deposited in commercial banks, interest earnings might reach about 2 billion a year. See *Vie Publique* (December 1974), p. 43. The actual transfer of funds to communes takes place through a monthly deposit from the Treasury to their credit, based on estimated direct taxes. For details, see Guichard Report, op. cit., pp. 375–84.

110   See Robert Ludwig, 'Le contrôle local des engagements de dépenses en France', *Revue de Science Financière*, vol. 63 (1971), pp. 503–94.

111   See J. Caritey, 'Le Contrôle parlementaire en matière financière', *Revue de Droit Public et des Sciences Politiques*, vol. 90 (1974), pp. 1451–73.

112   A good brief account is by Jean-Peirre Fourcade, 'Quelle réforme fiscale?', *Le Monde*, 16 February 1978. See the response by a mayor, Pierre Girault, 'Comment réformer la fiscalité locale?', *Le Monde*, 28 March 1978. The prime mover was Giscard d'Estaing, Minister of Finance in 1969, who was determined to reduce the value-added tax from 50 to 47 percent of state taxes. Fourcade was Giscard's Minister of Finance until 1976 and is now a Senator-mayor. See also Loic Philip, 'Les finances locales et l'impératif de décentralisation: bilan et perspectives', in Debbasch (ed.), op. cit., pp. 157–66; and Pierre Gaudez, 'La

modernisation de la gestion municipale', *Bulletin de l'Institut International Administration Publique*, no. 24 (1973), pp. 711–24.

113   Despite all the anomalies and fictions described above, the statistics used in calculating local expenses and needs are indexed and therefore more readily adjusted to economic changes. See *Méthode d'analyse financière des budgets communaux par les rations et les indices*, 7th edn (Paris: Ministry of the Interior, March 1975); also *Guide des Ratios des Communes de Plus de 10,000 Habitants*, 2nd edn (Paris: Ministry of the Interior, October 1976). See the explanation in Guerrier and Bauchard, op. cit., pp. 206–26.

114   The mayors of the large cities were closely associated with the Senator–mayors and for a time worked from the Senate offices. Their important contribution to the debate was a carefully prepared study of the inflationary effects of the previous five years. See *Les grandes villes devant l'avenir: Livre Blanc sur les finances locales* (Paris: Association des Maires de Grandes Villes de France (1975). As in Britain, large cities were suffering double the inflationary effects experienced by smaller towns and rural communes.

115   See Etienne Dumont, 'Reglements et comtes . . . administratifs à Vienne', *Vie Publique*, no. 38 (June 1975), pp. 62–7. On placing Amboise under prefectoral supervision, see *Le Monde*, 7 December 1979.

116   The VRTS decisions are carefully reproduced in *Moniteur*. See, for example, 'Le versement représentatif de la taxe sur les salaires revenant aux collectivités locales de 1975', *Moniteur*, 4 January 1975, pp. 23–4; 'Des Resources nouvelles pour les collectivités locales en 1976', *Moniteur*, 14 February 1976, pp. 21–2.

117   Voisin Report, op. cit., p. 132.

118   See the complaints of André Morice, mayor of Nantes and a leading figure among the mayors of large cities, *Vie Publique*, no. 42 (November 1975), pp. 8–9. Given the complexity of the calculations, the competing claims are most difficult to unravel. If the percentage of indirect tax received from the VRTS is calculated since 1968, it has declined from 88 percent to 82 percent in 1974. However, the loss has been made up by increasing other indirect taxes, because the percentage of the total tax revenue from direct taxes has also decreased from 57 percent in 1968 to 53 percent in 1974. Calculated from *Le Secteur Public*.

119   See *Rapport au Président de la République* (Paris: Cour des Comptes, 1977), pp. 20–2. There is a good diagram of how the division works in the Guichard Report, *Vivre Ensemble*, Annex (Paris: Documentation Français, 1978), pp. 61–9. Even now there is no way to disaggregate the burden to the level of the communes, and the division still operates on departmental level indices.

120   The changes in the formula are discussed in *Vivre Ensemble*, pp. 330–2, and the divergence from the initial formula displayed in the Annex, p. 62.

121   The overall tax revision for local government had been accepted in 1968 and reaffirmed in the 1973 legislation. However, the Ministry of Finance saw the modernization of the salary tax as a threat to its power. See *Vie Publique*, no. 24 (March 1974). Early in 1975 the Ministry of the Interior announced a new tax 'package' for communes. See 'Les relations État-collectivités locales', *Moniteur*, 19 April 1975, pp. 25–6.

122   The old law on the *patente* ran to 140 pages, and had over 1600 different conditions under which it was assessed and levied. See Delorme, op. cit., pp. 20–1. Also 'Le Remplacement de la patente par une taxe professionelle', *Moniteur*, 7 June 1975.

123   *Le Monde*, 12 June 1975.

124   The Socialists wanted an experimental year; this was rejected. The Right wanted more resources allocated from the state. In 1977 the final compromise was that a 'platform', or ceiling, of 70 percent was put on the total to be raised, and the state promised to pay the difference if the ceiling was exceeded. In an interesting reversal of the intent of the Constitution, the Socialists challenged the law under Art. 40 which prohibits the parliament from voting expenses without providing funds. See *Le Monde*, 8 July 1975. It was also agreed that a small portion would be given to the department to assist poor communes and to provide an incentive for regrouping communes.

125   See Alain Verboles, 'Haro sur la patente', *Le Monde*, 11 November 1976.

126   See Thierry Moulonguet, 'Taxe professionelle: ce qu'il faut changer', *Vie Publique*, no. 56 (February 1977), pp. 41–3; also *Le Monde*, 12 May 1977. The not unfamiliar decision was to conduct more research, and another survey of 40,000 firms will also be conducted. The government was forced to pay part of the

professional tax because a ceiling was placed on the industrialists' contribution by the Assembly.

127 See the discussion of the VRTS in *Vivre Ensemble*, pp. 329–47. Although the report refers to the British grant system and provides a rough version of the needs element formula of the Rate Support Grant (ibid., p. 336), it should be noted that the overall negotiation is in a political sense very differently structured. The report also raises the issues of norms of service (ibid., pp. 103–7), but does not indicate how, if at all, these should be linked to the VRTS.

128 See *Le Monde*, 25 October 1978. The priority given to the reform was suggested by a special Cabinet meeting held by the President just prior to the Senate debate; *Le Monde*, 1 November 1978. The official version of the fiscal reforms is described in a new circular from the Direction des Collectivités Locales, Ministry of the Interior. See the first two issues of *Démocratie Locale*, September and October 1978.

129 *Le Monde*, 16 November 1978.

130 The four associations are: Association of County Councils (formerly the County Councils Association); Association of Metropolitan Authorities (formerly Association of Municipal Corporations); Association of District Councils; and the London Borough Association. London is now a member of the AMA, but can also exert considerable direct pressure on the government. With reorganization in 1972, the AMA underwent the most thorough change because many old boroughs were abolished and many new district councils were created. Many hoped, as did the Royal Commission on Local Government (see *Report*, vol. 1, p. 32), that continuing the diverse organizations would be a 'disaster'.

131 Keith-Lucas and Richards, op. cit., p. 185; for additional details see their entire chapter on the associations, pp. 180–98. See also the analysis of how organization in four associations has consistently paralyzed their attempts to make major policy recommendations, in Jack Brand, *Local Government Reform in England* (London: Croom Helm, 1974), pp. 88–130. See also K. Isaac-Henry, 'Local authority associations and local government reform', *Local Government Studies* (New Series), vol. 1 (1975), pp. 1–12.

132 Their role is shrouded by rules governing confidentiality so in fact it is virtually impossible to decide how well they have represented local interests. However, they have been privy to most major decisions. Interviews, AMA, July 1976 and November 1977; and CCA, June 1978.

133 On the whole, the parties have followed the practice of 'winner take all' on committee appointments, etc., though there are exceptions. The associations' effectiveness, even as partisan spokesmen is, of course, diminished by the fact that local elections can put an association out of phase with national party strength. For example, after the Labour defeats in local elections during 1977, the AMA Chairman, Jack Smart, resigned and advised all Labour AMA committee chairmen to do the same, *Municipal Review* (June 1978), p. 63. With the renewed controversy about reorganization in 1977 and 1978 the associations were further divided internally.

134 The Minister, Frey, was heckled at the 1963 Congress of the Association over rumors of a compulsory regrouping of communes, and a campaign continued to attract the mayors' compliance. See M. Kesselman, *Ambiguous Consensus* (New York: Knopf, 1967), pp. 104–11.

135 See 'Les difficultés financières des collectivités locales', *Montieur*, 31 May 1975. The way that multiple roles require versatility was neatly displayed a year later when Chirac, as mayor of Paris, regularly criticized the government's unfair treatment of his city. See for example his very reasonable complaint about excessive police charges, *Le Monde*, 29 April 1978. Also Interview, Secretary General of AMF, Paris, August 1976.

136 After the 1977 municipal elections an early indication of the strain between the Socialists and the Communists was their separate nominations of candidates for the AMF presidency. The left then united to try to make the AMF more representative. See *Le Monde*, 18 November 1977, and 19 November 1977. As noted in Chapter 5, each party also has its own association for communes, but these are rarely consulted by government.

137 See, for example, D. A. Hallows (ed.), *Developments in Budgetary Procedures in British Local Government* (Birmingham: Institute of Local Government Studies, 1974). Especially during high inflation, the mechanics of the transfer are extremely important. In Britain, when inflation was at its worst a local govern-

ment could lose 10 percent of the value of the grant in six months.

138 Under the financial pressures of the mid-1970s the government did decide to ask CIPFA to make better estimates of local expenditure, but these are still not linked to the initial stages of departmental decisions. See Department of the Environment, *Local Authority Current Expenditure 1976/77*, Circular 45/76 (London: HMSO, 22 May. 1976). A year earlier the department had told local authorities that the PESC estimates were not to be relied on in estimating needs for the future years. See Department of the Environment, *Local Authority Expenditure in 1976/77 – Forward Planning*, Circular 88/75 (London: HMSO, 5 September 1975).

139 'The distribution of revenue between the central government and local authorities', *Economic Journal*, vol. 9 (1899), p. 549. Of course, the economic complexity of the advanced welfare state makes this assumption totally false.

140 See the example of the Housing Finance Act of 1972 which came into force in two weeks after being ratified by Parliament and placed new requirements on localities. Layfield Report, p. 43. Even de Gaulle had difficulty getting his laws passed this quickly, especially when they affected communes.

141 Even with strong controls over local spending, the variations among local authorities remain great. Neither national nor local government appears to achieve its objectives. An important reason is that costs vary immensely throughout the country, and the fiscal controls have no cost basis. An unpublished report of the ACC showed as high as 50 percent variations; see *Guardian*, 25 September 1979.

142 In 1974 Fourcade agreed to refund 800 million francs in value-added tax on the transactions of *régies*, or local trading, and 340 million francs paid on school construction. The additional concession was an investment fund receiving local value-added tax payments, to be described in Chapter 7. See the interview, 'La situation de certaines communes n'est pas uniquement imputable à l'État', *Vie Publique*, no. 41 (October 1975), pp. 66–9. Nearly three billion francs were picked up in 1977 when the Assembly refused to change the *taxe professionelle*.

143 One of the major new spending impositions was the cost of reorganization itself, for which local government was never reimbursed. This would be unimaginable in France. Cheshire estimated the cost at 200 million pounds, according to *Costs of Reform* (Cheshire County Council, 1970).

Chapter 7

CONTROLLING THE FUTURE: CAPITAL SPENDING AND LAND USE

> We have in England an apparently invincible prejudice not only that our English local government is the best in the world, but also that no other country has anything to teach us on the subject.
> – Sidney Webb

> Listen to all the complaints which are brought to you about inequalities in allocation of the rolls of the *tailles*, and do everything which you consider appropriate to stamp out inequities and to make the allocation as fair as possible. Examine with the same thoroughness the expenses which are incurred, both by the receivers in relation to the collectors and by the collectors in relation to the taxpayers. – Colbert to the intendents, 1680

Few policies better reveal the growing interdependence of national and local policies than decisions affecting capital spending and land use. Over the past decade, both Britain and France have been forced to reconsider how these policies affect urban development and, more specifically, have had to review and amend land-use procedures. For reasons which differ slightly between the two countries, these decisions have entered directly into local political calculations. For popular support and prestige, the French mayor depends on his ability to equip his municipality. While the mayors of large cities can effectively evade the direct controls set by national government, mayors in moderate sized and small communes are still obliged to operate within the intricate network of state loans, subsidies and construction controls.

The British local councillor is less dependent on public works for his popularity, partly because nationalization since the war has taken much construction out of the control of local government and partly because intervention is more difficult in such investment decisions. Even so, a good part of British local government history revolves around land disputes between different types of local authorities.[1] Although British local authorities compete for industries and employment, they are not as closely linked to industrial development as French communes, nor does the central government encourage them to take part in national economic programs.

THE NATIONAL INTEREST IN CAPITAL INVESTMENT

As in the case of current spending, the aggregate figures on capital spending provide a rough indication of the focus of the policymaking process. The more conservative orientation of the French government results in less dependence on the public sector to make capital spending decisions. Only about a tenth of gross capital accumulation is accounted for by the French government, compared with roughly a quarter of all capital accumulation in Britain.[2] Perhaps more immediately pertinent is the relation of capital spending to the two levels of government in each country. The French local government system accounts for approximately 60 percent of public sector capital spending, while the British localities account for about 40 percent of public capital spending.[3] Although the capital spending of French central government appears to provide less leverage in global terms, there is a closer relationship between business, banking and government in France than in Britain.[4]

The French central government, if it is to influence local capital spending, depends more heavily on influencing local decisions. Working with the financial machinery of the state, the French government and administration do indeed have a greater capacity to intervene at the local level. This is not, as we shall see, necessarily to say that the British government does not exercise more rigid controls on total local capital expenditure. As might be expected from these general figures, capital spending plays a larger part in the local budgets of the communes, about 40 percent of their annual spending, than in the local budgets of the British councils, where it is about 30 percent of annual spending. This also suggests why French mayors have on the whole been more interested than British local councillors in influencing investment decisions, and more interested in industrial and economic policies.

All national governments have several special concerns about local investment that tend to require more careful control of capital spending than of current spending. In terms of national economic policy, the way in which local governments borrow can affect interest rates and national debt management.[5] Capital spending is also a favorite object of short-term economic policy. As Britain found in the 1970s, current spending cannot be abruptly terminated, but capital spending projects can be delayed, prolonged and even cancelled. The most commonly affected activity is public housing, although there are serious doubts whether even in housing a 'stop and go' policy has a substantial effect on the major national objective – the control of aggregate demand.[6] In terms of national policymaking, the French have been less favorably placed than the British over the past decade, because rapid increase in local investment was essential to industrial modernization and rapid urbanization over the past two decades. From 1964 to 1969, capital spending of communes increased at the rate of 13 percent a year. In the early 1970s, the rate increased to about 20 percent, with some towns, such as Orléans, Besançon and Reims, making huge annual increases of 40 percent. The problem was one of searching for a formula to influence local decisions in the direction of national plans and needs, and improving the cumbersome procedures for transferring capital funds from the center to the locality. The complexity of procedures had been under fire constantly from the early 1960s from both mayors and national planners, though as might be expected, each had different interests in the control of local investment.

The general pattern of local capital expenditure for all French local governments and for the communes alone is given for the past decade in Table 7.1. Possibly the most important aspect of French local capital expenditure is the rather complex and diverse procedures for determining local capital subsidies (*subventions*) which is the main central policy instrument for controlling local capital spending. A major complaint of the mayors is that the state has not increased subventions as rapidly as local government has increased expenditure, which is borne out by the first two columns of the table. In the first years of the Chaban–Delmas government (1970–72), subsidies dropped dramatically, perhaps to force communes into accepting the new contractual policies. In the first full year of Giscard's presidency (1975), there was a huge increase in subsidies, possibly to promote his centrist political strategy at the local level.

By comparing the rates of increase for the whole local government system with those for the communes alone, it is apparent that increased capital expenditure and subsidies were being shifted to the intermediate levels of the system (*departments, syndicats* and *établissements publiques*). The central–local financial struggle, however, was not entirely one-sided. In most years, communes did increase loans more rapidly than total capital spending. The massive increase in loans in 1972 actually spread panic in the national credit agencies such as the CDC because mayors were finding more favorable borrowing terms on the short-term capital market. However burdened French mayors may be with technical and administrative investment requirements, they generally get favorable interest rates from government.

Consistent with the more general political and administrative relationships discussed in previous chapters, the main difference between Britain and France with regard to capital spending is that the former can make national policy about local investment with little or no consultation with localities, while in France for a number of reasons much closer attention is paid to local concerns and difficulties. The statutory subordination of British local government forces each local authority to obtain from the central government, most often the functional ministry interested in the project and in consultation with the Treasury, a 'sanction' for each investment, which is essentially permission to borrow money on the open market.

In a manner similar to the problems of aligning the national PESC spending estimates with local expenditure, described in Chapter 6, the central government does not have the capacity to design an overall investment plan for the country. Individual ministries compete for investment allocations in annual estimates, and these allocations are aligned in turn with national economic needs and estimates by the Treasury with little or no local consultation.[7] The overall effect is that,

Table 7.1   *Rates of Increase of Total Local and Communal Capital
Expenditure and Subsidies in France from 1967 to 1976[a]*

| | All Collectivities | | Communes Only | | |
	Total	Subsidies	Total	Subsidies	Loans
1968–67	12	11	6	0	2
1969–68	21	17	12	4	6
1970–69	9	6	6	4	9
1971–70	4	−4	4	0	10
1972–71	12	6	35	4	58
1973–72	20	21	10	4	3
1974–73	21	12	5	3	2
1975–74	22	31	32	43	40
1976–75	17	12	5	6	6

[a]Compiled from *Le Secteur Public Local*, op. cit., appropriate years.

no matter what the quality of the local investment plan, 'its works programme is dismembered on arrival in Whitehall, the functional components are considered in isolation one from another, and any necessary scaling down . . . is likely to upset the balance of development in the local authority's area'.[8] The aims are to establish the aggregate of lending and investment that the government can bear, and to make certain that these estimates are not exceeded. Decision-making is in this sense centralized, and nearly all British authorities agree that capital spending is tightly controlled.[9]

Whether intentional or not, Table 7.2 makes the erratic pattern of local capital expenditure unmistakable. As shown in the column for national capital spending, the national changes are no less abrupt and dramatic. The pattern confirms the numerous accusations concerning 'stop and go' economic policymaking in Britain, and must have severe repercussions on credit institutions and the construction industry, not to mention the immense uncertainties created for local councils in trying to anticipate their capital investment programs. As can be seen, there were huge increases during Heath's expansionary economic policies of the early 1970s, followed by brutal reductions under the Callaghan government at both levels of government. As in France, once a loan sanction has been obtained, government loans are obtained under more favorable terms. But Britain provides very little capital subsidization (about 200 million pounds per year), and it is not a major control on local capital spending decisions.

Control by sanctions is suited to Treasury needs and effective in the aggregate, but not in terms of any comprehensive planning of local infrastructure and development. Much to the dismay of the French mayors, national government exercises more detailed control over local investment, but at the cost of maintaining both a more elaborate system of consultation over long-term plans, and a labyrinth of specific project controls. The policy objectives are more ambitious

Table 7.2   *Rates of Increase of Local and National Capital Expenditure and Local Government Loans from 1967 to 1978*[a]

	National	Local	Local Government Loans
1968–67	3	5	48
1969–68	−1	1	−6
1970–69	10	11	29
1971–70	18	8	2
1972–71	−3	13	19
1973–72	3	42	16
1974–73	27	23	26
1975–74	35	7	−7
1976–75	−17	−5	−57
1977–76	−20	−13	175
1978–77	20	−10	−74

[a]Calculated from *National Income and Expenditure 1979* (London: HMSO, 1979); and *National Income and Expenditure 1967–77* (London: HMSO, 1977).

than in Britain. With varying degrees of success, the French have tried to fuse industrial and regional planning with the territorial jurisdictions of the local government system.[10] Under the Fifth and Sixth Plans, elaborate schemes were set in motion to devise investment plans for regions (Programmes régionaux de développement économique or PRDE) and for urban planning areas or *agglomérations* (Programmes de modernisation et d'équipement or PME).[11] While in some cases these plans became little more than shopping lists, the objective was to integrate public investment, industrial development and regional planning. A further aim was to improve vertical coordination of capital spending between the various levels of the local government system, a capacity which has never been very highly developed in the British regional structure.[12] If the effort to bring local investment into harmony with national investment and development placed heavy burdens on the communes, departments and regions, it also gave French local politicians a voice in the various elected and consultative bodies which British locally elected officials never enjoy in the centrally-run regional development programs and ministerial investment plans.

While using the regions for large-scale investment planning, the government in the mid-1960s also embarked on an ambitious program of urban investment. The urban dimension was, as in most countries, closely related to problems of land use and also provided the springboard for the multiplication of contractual relationships both between levels of government and between public and private interests. Essential to the workings of these new procedures was the inter-ministerial fund, which ministers could use to subsidize local investments. The most important of the many funds affecting urban development is FNAFU (Fonds nationales d'aménagement foncier et d'urbanisation).[13] The directing committee for FNAFU is an influential agency within the Ministry of Infrastructure, the Direction d'Aménagement Foncier et d'Urbanisme (DAFU). Taking hold of the urban investment programs was a crucial step in rebuilding the influence of the *grands corps* of the *ponts et chaussées*, although their decisions are reviewed by the Groupe Interministeriel Foncier, which includes the Ministries of the Interior and Finance, the Planning Commissariat, DATAR, a Paris representative, and the CDC. Much of this central reorganization took place in 1965 and 1966, the same time as the departmental and regional extension of the Ministry of Infrastructure. The influence of this national policymaking group was, of course, immense, and in 1964 alone about 9 billion francs were invested under their supervision.[14]

Whether this vast organizational network among national ministries and local planning groups is a liability or an asset in the development of French cities is a hotly debated and complex judgment. On the one hand, it is extremely doubtful if the communes and departments could have independently invested such huge sums of money in the mid-1960s. It would have been not only uncharacteristic of French administration to expect less complex links, but also probably unwise to spend such large sums without some sort of planning controls. On the other hand, a decade later the local government system found it had inherited a set of supervisory controls that were in many ways redundant and excessive since the major task had been accomplished. As we shall see, the major finding of nearly every investigation of local investment programs and planning for the next decade condemns the rigidity and inefficiencies of the capital spending controls. These controls have also become a major grievance of the mayors.

From a comparative perspective, however, it should also be noted that the simplified and compartmentalized British intergovernmental structures are incapable of operating such an intricate network of decisionmaking, and in its absence much investment that might have been directed through local government has tended to be parceled out according to the priorities of the central departments. The British system is not incapable of devising obscure procedures, as we have seen in the Rate Support Grant reformulations, but it tends to locate them within the corridors of Whitehall, where the curiosities of modern government are more difficult to observe.

The intricate structure involved in local capital spending decisions could not have been built without the financial superstructure of the French state. As noted in Chapter 6, the key national institution is the Caisse des Dépôts et Consignations, which, until 1860, was the sole lending agency of the government. As new credit facilities were developed in the late nineteenth century, such as the Crédit Foncier, and as new national deposit funds were created, such as the Caisse d'Épargne, they were all linked to this 'state within the state'.[15] The second stage in the proliferation of financial agencies was the formation within the CDC of a series of semipublic corporations charged with different aspects of urban and local development lending.[16] The most important of these in the funding of local projects became the Société Centrale pour l'Équipement du Territoire (SCET),[17] labeled by one mayor as 'the triumph of technocracy'.

Accompanied by the growing financial and technical services of the CDC that were developed by Bloch-Lainé, an institutional nucleus took shape in order to join public and private capital in rebuilding and expanding French cities. The instrument of this nucleus became the *société d'économie mixte*, a joint venture of local government and private interests usually formed to undertake a specific local development project. There were 700 of these groups involved in urban development by 1967. In a way analogous to the more complex structure of local taxation and spending, the French constructed an instrument for local-level investment that hinged on private developmental interests and that tapped private investment funds.

Just as the French local government system excels in penetrating the institutional fabric of France, so also does the system devise extraordinary ways of knitting it all together. Perhaps the two most important devices affecting local investment have been the *subvention* and the land-use zone, which will be examined below. Though the use of capital subsidies has been particularly pernicious for the communes, it is sometimes forgotten that subsidies are a commonly used policy instrument in France for *all* sectors of the economy, and for all kinds of public agencies. In 1969, for example, the government provided over forty billion francs in operating and capital subsidies, about three-fourths of this amount going to firms and to government to cover operating losses. Of the slightly more than 11 billion francs used for capital investment, more than half went to industry and only about 3.5 billion to government.[18] In 1977 the national budget carried a total of twenty-one billion francs in subsidies for local government, not including the VRTS, of which nearly seven billion were to subsidize equipment, land purchase, and construction.[19] The investment subsidies are attached to the budgets of the various ministries who must then convert them into projects based on local proposals, under the financial supervision of the CDC and the Ministry of Finance, and with the cooperation of the various local and departmental offices of the field services. Whether the subsidy has become the cement which holds the system together or the oppressive instrument of an overcentralized government is perhaps the most intense controversy presently affecting French local government.

From the local perspective, the oppressive feature of the subsidy device is that a commune or department has very little chance of obtaining a low interest loan from the state without a subsidy. A project must be approved, and often also designed, by administrative officials who, under the 1980 reforms, were in effect paid twice for the same task, through the fee they extract from the locality and through their salary from the government. Though not part of the array of reforms over 1979 and 1980, the Minister for Infrastructure (changed to Environment in 1978) was asked to devise a new system to reimburse national civil servants, mostly from the *ponts et chaussées* and *génie rural*, for their local services. In 1978 the former received 258 million francs in fees, representing roughly a 40 percent supplement to their income. Because small communes rely more heavily on state agents, communes with less than 2,000 persons will contribute 2.5 francs per inhabitant to a central fund, and large communes will pay a standard fee based on the complexity of the investment project. (Only about half the projects of large cities are planned by state agents.) The agents, in turn, will be paid from these contributions plus a national contribution according to their rank and the difficulty of the project.[20]

The paperwork of the subvention system is immense because a project is in most cases approved twice: once to get the subsidy and again to get the loan. In the meantime, particularly in a period of inflation, costs increase rapidly and loan approvals arriving two or three years after the application often no longer cover the cost of the investment. Examples abound of the absurd results: to build a secondary school a commune must obtain twenty-four permissions across four ministries and four levels of government; the construction of one small hospital required a hundred authorizations and took eight years to emerge from the administrative labyrinth.[21] There are often a number of different scales for determining the size of the subsidy for the same kind of project, and the scale eventually used depends on which ministry is most directly concerned, on the type of local authority involved, and on the current priorities of the central government. The study group on local finance for the Sixth Plan found the subsidies scattered in over a hundred places in the national budget, and governed by about two hundred different laws.[22]

Like many burdensome administrative practices, it is much easier to find fault with the subsidy than to figure out what should replace it. In the 1960s, the device made fairly good sense. It could be adjusted to types of communal grouping, and became an incentive to overcome the fragmentation of the communes. It enabled ministries to design large programs to construct schools, cultural centers, sports facilities, etc., using the administrative machinery, however cumbersome, that existed and that will take decades to reform. Nor is France unique among the modern democracies in using capital transfers to communicate national priorities to the local level. For all its inadequacies, it is difficult to imagine how the urban infrastructure of contemporary France could otherwise have been constructed in a single decade. In fact, steps were taken from the very early stages of the urban expansion to soften the rigidities of public works subsidies. Regions were given more general loans from 1964, and global loans (*prêts globaux*) to cities were tried in 1965. Steps were also taken to increase local access to the private capital market, and a new banking facility was formed, the Caisse d'aide à l'équipement des collectivités locales (CAECL), where for the first time municipalities could deposit their money and receive modest interest.[23] By 1970 the government itself had recognized that the system, if not chaotic, was at least incomprehensible to mayors, and quite possibly to the central government.

In their relation to national policymaking, the systems of control of local investment in Britain and France could hardly be more different. The two political systems have quite different objectives. The British Treasury is most concerned about the control of aggregate demand and finding effective ways to make adjustments in national economic policy. Because the local government system accounts for so much public spending, and in particular because local capital spending is vulnerable to fairly abrupt change, the Treasury focuses on controlling the total amount of investment and borrowing. The ministries, as in the case of current spending, are left more or less to themselves in designing future investment programs for each service of local government. Though the local administrators are no doubt consulted as these plans evolve, there is relatively little pressure for comprehensive planning of local capital expenditure at either level of government. Only in more recent years have the overlapping problems of inner city decay, racial unrest, industrial decline and land development begun to push the British government system toward a more integrated concept of local investment planning.

Because of the immense pressure on French towns and cities over the past two decades, France approached the problem of controlling local investment very differently. A more articulated local government system made planning more important, and a unified administrative system made it possible. But the tradition of more carefully regulating the *équipement collectif* is also an old one in France, and the rudiments of the present system can be found in earlier Republics. The subsidy and the land-use plan, much as they were disliked by the mayors, provided the central government with powerful devices to intervene in local policies and decisions. Initially, the region appeared as the natural unit to coordinate capital spending, but moves in this direction were quickly overcome by the pressing needs of the major cities. Unlike Britain, since Napoleonic times France has had an interlocking array of financial institutions that reach to the grassroots, and the energetic planners of the 1960s were quick to see, in turn, how the administrative system could more effectively guide the communes and departments into the future.

PLANNING CAPITAL EXPENDITURES: WHO IS CONTROLLING WHOM?

Capital spending decisions are viewed very differently in the two political systems. There are two critical issues for local government: how much latitude they will be given in deciding what projects to undertake, and how they will be limited in finding the money. The British central–local relationship, as it relates to investment, concentrates on the latter question; and this is consistent with more general interpretations of economic policymaking in Britain, the influence of Keynesian thinking generally, and the tendency to insulate central government against local government rather than consult it on national decisions. In France, the emphasis has been the reverse: how to guide local investment toward specific objectives within a more elaborate set of public financial institutions that simply do not exist in the British system. Beneath these trends are deeper distinctions still persisting in British finance that tend to separate the private and public financial worlds more sharply than France.

But Britain also insists that many local projects receive central departmental approval and, if anything, specific project controls have been increased over the past decade. In this curious way the British local government system seems to have the worst of both worlds: it is more directly subject to national economic policy while having less access to national decisions, and it is also legally bound by an arbitrary procedure for sanctions that carries few reciprocal benefits in terms of lower interest rates or sharing the cost of investment planning itself. Whether one prefers to be coerced from afar, as in Britain, or more directly, as in France, is not a happy choice, but it does mean that capital spending decisions in France enter directly into local politics while in Britain they tend to be treated as a residual aspect of providing services.

Unlike current spending budgets, capital budgets often conceal more than they reveal. For example, the British councils appear to be contributing a fairly small amount of their current revenues to local investment, but in terms of the surplus put in various local funds and then transferred to local projects, their contribution is quite large, possibly twice as much (in percentage terms) as the surpluses that French communes contribute to local development.[24] That the British local governments make such a substantial contribution and yet are still deprived of a general voice in local capital spending is another demonstration of how the British local government system is isolated from national policy, and how it effectively loses its potential bargaining power with central government. The ease and frequency of central intervention in capital spending is all the more surprising because, unlike the French communes, British local councils maintain their own capital funds. A local authority, for example, cannot build a primary school without permission from the DES. Total housing investment is under strict central control, although local authorities have some choice over the type of housing investments they make.[25] There is, of course, an array of specific construction requirements from each ministry for each service facility that approximates the French technical supervision exercised in the field.

The British central government provides very few direct subsidies to capital spending, and these are nearly always for specific purposes. In contrast to France, borrowing operations are carried on locally through a fund accounting system, which, in turn, makes British local councils more dependent on the private capital market than French communes. In effect, the Treasury cannot predict when local councils will enter the capital market and only controls the total volume of borrowing through the system of sanctions. More specific controls enter through the capital spending controls imposed by ministries.

While the compartmentalization of capital spending decisions may preserve the local councils' sense of autonomy, it also means that local government may threaten national financial policy, especially in periods of inflation, and makes the large spending ministries concerned with local government heavily dependent on the specific, sometimes heavy-handed, controls over how the money is spent. Local choice is itself more apparent than real because, since 1971, local capital spending has been divided by the central government into 'key' and 'locally determined' sectors.[26] There are minor exceptions to this determination for land acquisition and housing, but the effect is to superimpose on local investment planning a set of constraints that are only softened by consultation with the local government associations.

The Conservatives claimed these would increase local choice over capital spending, but approximately five-sixths of local capital expenditure has been designated 'key sector', including most of education, housing and transportation.[27]

The Public Works Loan Board (PWLB), dating from 1875, monitors local government loans. But its powers are very limited, because the Treasury sets interest rates and the national budget authorizes lending levels. The history of the PWLB suggests that the simplification of local capital spending, much like the simplification of current spending, does not serve either national or local interests very well.

In 1945, Labour wanted local authorities to borrow entirely from the PWLB, but the Conservatives eased these restrictions in 1952. In the early 1960s, the Conservatives again turned to the financing problem, reviving access to the PWLB, but trying to reduce the attractiveness of its loans. When Labour returned to power, the party again tried to encourage borrowing from the public agency, and raised the limits that local governments might take from the PWLB. After the capital planning measures imposed by the Conservatives in 1971, Labour once again returned to erase earlier rulings.[28] While all these changes make useful ammunition for the two-party system, there has been, in fact, no fundamental change in the principle that localities should finance their loans on the private capital market. In this respect, the policy has been a remarkably nonpartisan one, with both major parties subscribing to the view that localities should be allowed to take relatively little initiative in investment planning.

Loan sanctions provide a central control on borrowing, but they do not determine when capital spending will take place nor do they limit local spending from reserves. As the issues of inflation and public sector borrowing loomed larger in British national economic policy, local investment controls were inadequate. Part of Heseltine's 1980 reform was to impose capital spending controls that most local councils thought even more oppressive than the new grant and taxation controls. In effect, national government would directly limit the amounts to be invested each year. Even the Conservative-dominated local councils vehemently protested, another indication of the dislocation of national and local partisan politics. As local pressures mounted, Heseltine agreed that although the new controls would be administered in five general categories of local investment (housing, education, transportation, social services and others), the councils could transfer funds from one category to another.[29]

The French local budgets for capital spending show the relatively greater importance of subsidies, roughly one-fourth of local capital income for 1975, and the direct way in which the French system links annual spending surpluses to the capital budget. Because the communes account for more than half of capital spending in the local government system, the French system, however oppressive, has to accommodate itself to the territorial complexity of the system, and, in turn, has diverse territorial units to which to direct funds in order to achieve national aims. Neither of these choices is of substantial importance in the British system, both because the local government units are consolidated and because intermediate-level agencies are usually organized around a single function. Although the French mayors have numerous and justifiable grievances about the complex system of controls on capital spending, the system provides numerous points of access to higher-level decisions and is consistent with the political needs of the multiparty structure. Indeed, were the French system as completely in the hands of central government as the British system, procedural complaints by the French mayors would very likely have even more bitter objections. In a way, the main virtue of the French capital spending system is that it accommodates itself to both local and national politics.

Because statistics on French local spending are published with considerable breakdown by size of commune and level of government, it is possible to follow how much capital allocations have indeed changed over the past decade. Direct investment is largely the acquisition of fixed capital and its distribution according to size of commune changed only slightly between 1964 to 1974. One might expect that cities over 100,000 would be expending a much larger proportion of the total direct investment over the decade, but actually it increased by only 2 percent.[30] Given the severe needs of the larger cities, the new agencies for urban development take on more importance. Essentially, what has happened is a redistribution of the subsidies. In 1967 the communes received 61 percent of all investment subsidies, but in 1974 only 48 percent. The subsidies have been moved toward syndicates of communes, which received only 20 percent of subsidies in 1967, but had increased their share to 30 percent by 1974.[31] The overall effect is fairly clear. The small communes have been forced to finance their capital improvements out of operating surpluses, while the larger units have been given incentives to increase infrastructure. At least in terms of choices among elements of the local government system, complexity has not been entirely self-defeating; it has responded to the need to improve facilities in highly urban communes, and has helped to overcome the weaknesses of the overarticulated territorial structure.

A crucial feature of the French local reforms over 1979 and 1980 was to simplify the cumbersome system of subventions, and it is significant that the *dotation globale d'équipement* (DGE) was proposed and accepted in advance of the more controversial changes in local taxation and local responsibilities. Like all public corporations and state agencies, the communes and departments pay value-added tax on construction and materials. The amount for 1979 was 3.2 billion francs, estimated at 9.4 percent of local investments.[32] Although taxing public agencies seems strange within the Anglo-Saxon legal tradition, it is not a new practice under continental law. Nonetheless, right across the political spectrum, the tax on local construction was a major grievance of mayors, and a refund was no doubt a prerequisite to the whole battery of reform legislation in 1979 and 1980. The debate also permitted the mayors to extract concessions on the payment of fees for technical assistance, and the same protection was extended to private firms working for communes.

In many respects, the DGE is more properly considered an internal struggle of national government because the globalization of subsidies required ministerial agreements on the use of the tax refunds as the new DGE. Coupled with relief from fees for technical services from state agencies, the DGE represents a major step toward decentralization of administrative control, as well as a financial concession to the communes. In 1980, about half the total amount of subsidies (1.9 billion francs) will be transferred directly to communes, eliminating the costly and lengthy procedures for preliminary central approval. About half this sum is for local roads and water supplies. In 1981, the DGE could reach 3.5 billion francs when large sewerage, urban transport and public housing loan subsidies are to be added. There are still important battles to be fought as the rules for the division of the DGE are to be worked out by the Conseil d'État. To encourage inter-communal cooperation there are provisions allowing communes to transfer their share of the DGE to intercommunal agencies, and assuring consolidated communes that they will be given some privileged access.

REGIONAL POLICY AND LOCAL INVESTMENT: INTERGOVERNMENTAL LINKAGES

The effect of inertia that the local government system has on national policy can be seen through its relationship to capital spending as well as to current spending. The growing complexity of the social and economic supports of the welfare state means that local government can no longer be left to itself in the allocation of public investment. (It is questionable that it ever was, even in the market economies of the nineteenth century.) But by the same token, central government cannot make the thousands of individual decisions about land use, industrial location and local infrastructure. While both France and Britain have used regions primarily for industrial development, the comparison rests more on how local government is or is not involved in regional-level decisions. Like many of the more general political and administrative characteristics of the two subnational systems, the separation of regional and local decisionmaking is more pronounced in Britain than in France.[33] Scottish and possibly Welsh nationalism made regional government a delicate issue in Britain, but most regional agencies remained appendages of central government ministries. Until the Town and Country Planning Act of 1968, British local councils had no statutory role in British regional planning. The higher degree of politicization of French local government, in contrast, has had visible effects on the development of regional policy, and the communes and departments are directly involved in investment planning at the regional level.

Aligning national objectives with the preferences and capabilities of regions and local governments is no simple task. France has by no means enjoyed unqualified success with some regional policies, particularly with such massive problems as the declining steel industry and the Fos steel complex. On the other hand, British efforts to revive declining industries, such as the shipbuilding yards of the Tyne and Clyde, have not been uniformly successful. My purpose here is to underscore the more basic institutional and organizational differences, particularly the British tendency to exclude local government from decisions about regions compared with the inability of the French policymakers to keep local politicians out of regional decisions. Although both countries have primarily used the regions to implement industrial policy, the results are no more easily compared than the institutions themselves. The important difference is that France set out to design regional programs and policies that would involve both the private and public sectors at lower levels of government, which would, in turn, link these programs to the investment decisions of communes and departments. Although the French government initially planned to make the regions an instrument of central administration, the political and the administrative complexities of the local government system forced a modification after 1964. In contrast, British regional plans have never had explicit local objectives and, with the exception of several of the northern regions, where there are deeper suspicions of London's aims,[34] relationships between levels of government have rarely been a problem because Whitehall avoided joint decisionmaking.

The missing link between local and national policy is one of the most curious characteristics of the British subnational system, and like many structural properties of modern government has important historical origins. Regional policy in Britain grew from efforts in the 1930s to provide employment in depressed areas,[35] and, after the Second World War, from the town planning program.[36] Neither of these activities was directly dependent on local government, and both were organized as the instruments of central government. The result a generation later is that 'Instead of a regional political authority, or a regional *ad hoc* body with independence of action, or even locally co-ordinated and partially controlled regional administration, there is merely a proliferation of separate London controlled bureaucratic empires.'[37] Until the devolution debate of the 1970s, neither national politicians nor central administrators thought of regional policy as a matter requiring local coordination, much less did they wish to cultivate the degree of local intervention found in French regions. Underlying this trend is the divorce between private and public sector policy which is deeply rooted in British institutions, and which went unchallenged even by Labour after the Second World War.

As in the case of the current spending estimates and forecasts discussed in Chapter 6, it is doubtful whether Whitehall either has or wants the capacity to engage in locally-disaggregated investment planning. To do so would make the higher civil service more vulnerable to national and local politicians. Thus the Treasury was strongly opposed to Wilson's experiment with a Department of Economic Affairs in 1964, and its regional plans never went beyond the industrial development strategy of the earlier Macmillan government.[38] Although the Regional Economic Planning Councils and Boards survived, they are staffed with central government officials, have only hortatory powers over local government, and no direct control over investment.[39] When Mrs Thatcher abolished the Regional Councils in 1979, there was no effective local resistance. As

Wright and Young point out, 'The attempt to predict and alter future events is a novel departure for British government.'[40] The central department officers working at the regional level lack the organization, the resources and the incentives that might generate the horizontal coordination essential to comprehensive regional planning. They do not have the statutory or the financial responsibilities given their French counterparts in order to influence local decisions. 'Among those central departments power was functionally diffused: a confusion of departments and agencies whose objectives rarely coincided, whose policies often conflicted, and who competed with each other for a larger share of national resources.'[41] The overall effect has been that decisions are made in Whitehall and for the most part compartmentalized by departmental responsibilities in the same way we have already noted in local services and spending.

The relatively weak links between regional and local government in Britain would be less surprising were the scale of regional programs and regionally administered funds smaller. In the early 1970s, nearly half the British population lived in areas receiving special assistance (development, special development, intermediate and land clearance areas).[42] MacCallum estimates that, in the financial year ending 1974, regional agencies and programs spent approximately 400 million pounds.[43] The system is relatively susceptible to short-term manipulation by national politicians, and offers tempting possibilities to increase assistance for electoral purposes. Industrial legislation in 1950 (Distribution of Industries Act), in 1966 (Industrial Development Act) and again in 1970 (Local Government Employment Act) are notable examples of preelection regional legislation. MacCallum points out the close correspondence between the assisted areas and Labour's voting strength, and shows how the swing to the Conservatives in 1971 came almost entirely from nonassisted areas.[44] Given the geography of industrial decline in Britain, this division is not surprising. What it does, however, is to discourage national politicians from allocating regional decisions to lower levels of government. Regional assistance, much like the local government itself, conforms to the needs of national-level politics and the two-party structure.

Very similar organizational discontinuities exist in the planning machinery which links local and central government, and help preserve a degree of ministerial and departmental intervention in local decisions that would be difficult to construct within the French subnational system. Local plans and projects, for example, come under the General Development Order, which states twenty-three kinds of construction that localities cannot govern.[45] Though central government departments must consult local government on most projects, the way this is done and the recourses open to a reluctant local authority are poorly defined, particularly in the case of industrial development. National rivalries have no doubt made it difficult to construct an economic strategy that would give localities the more active role in industrial and developmental programs such as found in France. When Sir Geoffrey Howe, Mrs Thatcher's Chancellor of the Exchequer, announced plans for new local industrial development corporations, it appeared that the local councils had not even been consulted on the plans.[46] Likewise, the Secretary of State for the Environment, Michael Heseltine, included in his Omnibus Bill proposals for large public corporations to develop the Port of London and the Clyde which are to be directly dependent on central government.[47] Both the vertical compartmentalization of the local government system and the dispositions of ambitious ministers mean that an important potential resource for economic development goes unused. What the French practice to excess, the British appear to ignore.

The divorce between national and local politics, and the consequent weaknesses of intergovernmental policymaking, can impose very high costs on government. At the national level, the tendency has been to perpetuate the old system without critical evaluation. When the Labour government was criticized by the House of Commons Public Accounts Committee for the lax administration of industrial assistance in 1977, the Committee's advice was simply rejected.[48] Both major parties prefer to be disengaged from regional policy, which also leaves many crucial decisions to Whitehall departments.[49]

There are no reasons, of course, why ministers should dismantle their empires, even though it is generally conceded that the one regional agency with a more comprehensive policy role, the Scottish Development Office, which reviews all planning decisions, is the most effective one. The British government has no way, short of Cabinet orders, to force the diverse regional organization of central departments into a similar and single territorial mould.[50] Regional territorial diversity has itself further complicated policy coordination at lower levels of government.[51] There is an apparently irresistible tendency in each aspiring department of government to generate its own regional structure, a tendency seen in the creation of two northern regional boards by the National Enterprise Board.[52] Such decisions are, of course, not unrelated to the aspirations of ambitious ministers. But the sectoral investment plans of the major departments for housing, roads, ports, etc., are directly translated into local projects by Whitehall, and seldom appear in regional terms.[53] While Whitehall plays its game of departmental dominoes, each department in effect guards ministerial programs and reinforces the functional compartmentalization that also characterizes local-level policymaking.

Public spending, a third of which rests with local authorities, has no clear link to the regional agencies nor to regional industrial development programs. Nor can the regions themselves act very effectively, as Donnison has suggested, to relate such complex local needs as welfare and community development to regional assistance. As functions such as transportation, health and water are taken from the local level, another array of functionally differentiated agencies is organized. Although local councillors are represented on these bodies, they are so burdened with the heavy responsibilities of local government, that they have a difficult time influencing regional decisions, even in this disconnected structure. The administration of regional policy therefore follows that of local government, by providing for the needs of ministers and the higher civil service while sheltering them from the consequences of their decisions.

Although the French regions have been labeled 'the triumph of the Jacobin state',[54] it is doubtful that the Gaullists achieved the administrative centralization they had hoped would emerge from the early regional experiment of the 1960s. Nor does this urge to centralize square easily with the efforts to get elected representatives on regional bodies, to provide numerous regional breakdowns of the national budget, and to coordinate the capital spending plans of the various ministries within the regional programs. Compared to Britain, the French concern with regional policies and decisions seems a populist outburst.[55] The interlocking nature of French regional and local government differs from the British approach in part because the French regions *preceded* local reorganization and were from the beginning thought of as policy instruments, however devious Parisian motives might have been.[56]

For these reasons, regional investment and its local implications differ dramatically in the two countries. What the French have done perhaps poorly and with considerable local discomfort, the British, except for the consultative role of councillors on regional bodies for specific purposes, have not done at all. The French regional planning apparatus dates from 1964, and over the past decade a special effort has been made to make this machinery work smoothly, especially in the area of capital spending and credit. Though Pompidou and Chaban-Delmas did not see eye to eye on the role of the regions, they did agree that regional decisions, above all on the subsidies for capital spending, needed to be more closely linked to regional and local plans.[57] A decree of November 1970 established the *globalisation des investissements*, dividing investment decisions into four categories: national, regional, departmental and local.[58] In principle, the administrative and political officials at each level were to make their own investment decisions, based on the classification of all public investment for infrastructure. As Lefebvre pointed out, the proposal was a curious mixture of administrative *déconcentration* and timid decentralization.[59] Given the elaborate technical and financial controls over public investments, it clearly would not work without the full cooperation of the ministries and their field services. Above all, it presupposed a relaxation of the numerous checks exercised by the Ministry of Finance, at the time under Giscard d'Estaing.

An interministerial committee under Jean Iehle was formed to oversee the reform, and his reports provide ample testimony to the difficulties in changing French administration.[60] In 1972, for example, the total capital expenditure of the government was nearly twenty-eight billion francs, of which slightly less than eight billion actually entered into the globalization scheme. The major ministries found numerous reasons why their special projects should not be included. The Ministry of Education reserved decisions about secondary schools. The Ministry of Infrastructure moved some of its industrial development grants to Paris to evade the classification. The Ministry of Agriculture, one of the least cooperative, argued that its rural development projects did not correspond to the local administrative structure.[61] The Ministry of Youth and Sports was much too politically sensitive to see its choice projects devolve to lower levels.

About half the investment decisions that were relaxed went to the regions, where ministries could still intervene, and the fourth category, communal decisions, received a derisory 100 million francs for the entire country. The Ministry of Finance refused to relax its numerous prior controls on investment decisions, which meant that the new scheme once implemented added yet another step in the laborious process of getting approval for capital spending.

Nor were the technical complications negligible. The nomenclature of the Planning Commissariat and the Ministry of Finance did not match, and, despite a simplification of the national budget, the investment items were scattered in a hundred different places. Much like the problems of relating the British PESC forecasts to local spending, the compression of national, regional and departmental budget decisions into a single program proved difficult. By 1972, it had become apparent that the early local investment plans (PRDE and PME) were not well linked to national objectives, and that they caused endless grievances and inconveniences to mayors. The steps to lighten the *tutelle* in early 1971 had been largely negated by the technical and financial supervision exercised over project applications and transfers. While the variations among regional producers and politics that had been uncovered in the early studies of the Crozier group continue, the complexities of regional decisionmaking also became apparent in the intervening years.

The most detailed study, preparatory to the 1972 regional reorganization, was of Limousin. Contrary to fears of a new form of centralization, the real problem appeared to lie in the administrative and political differences between Limousin and Paris. The operating staff of the region (*mission régionale*) were unable to work without higher departmental authority. At the regional and departmental levels the regional prefect was constantly checked by his dependence on other lower-level departmental officials. While the system of consultation seemed to work quite well and the investment plans were reviewed by several thousand local leaders, the fatal weakness of the region was its lack of resources with which to bargain independently in the intricate system of local decisionmaking. Thus, efforts to globalize local investment form another chapter in the internecine warfare and political *complicité* of French administration. The curious result was not to increase the power of Paris, but to force policymakers to look to lower levels of government to break the *impasse*.

The second attempt to simplify central controls over local investment was to globalize the subsidies. Linked to Chaban-Delmas' efforts to strengthen regional government, the 1972 reform began the transition to more dispersed investment controls. For all their difficulties, the old regional governments had begun to produce regional investment plans that were integrated into the Sixth Plan, and progress was made in preparing comprehensive investment programs for the *villes nouvelles* and the urban communities. Even before the regional reorganization of July 1972,[62] the Prime Minister had endorsed circulars designed to strengthen the regional prefects. The new strategy was to globalize subsidies in order to overcome the resistance to globalized investments.[63] This decision was consistent with the shift to contracts for local projects, and revealed the growing influence of the CDC and its affiliates. The subsidies were, of course, part of the financial control exercised by the state, but they were also closely linked to the approval of loans and projects outside the administration. An unintended consequence of the subsidies is to provide a foundation for financial machinery which circumvents cumbersome administrative control. The underlying concept had been developed and used for many years in the private sector and, once Giscard d'Estaing became President, was applied more energetically to public investment planning and implementation.

The checks that these reforms encountered reveal the power of the central administration, but they also display how France redirects administrative energies by redefining public policy. Such experiments have rarely been tried in Britain. Although Chaban-Delmas later blamed the Ministry of Finance for obstructing his efforts to globalize investments and subsidies,[64] administrative conflict can itself create new priorities and emphases within an administrative system. But the reforms also increased the powers of the regional and departmental TPG, and the Ministry of Finance again made it clear that it would not forego *a priori* review of local projects and plans.[65]

One must also ask whether more could be expected. The budgets of the regional councils and agencies are very small. In 1977 their current spending was just under two billion francs and their loans slightly more than half a billion francs – a small portion of the total financial resources flowing through the local government system.[66] Most investment credits went to build local facilities and were located at the level of departments, communes and the various public establishments, which accounted for more than one billion francs of globalized investment operations in 1976.[67] These sums do not take into account the additional investment organized through housing programs, the social security system and the national road network, to name only a few. Thus, it is easy to exaggerate the importance of the public sector and how much any single component of the administrative machinery can in fact dominate diverse sources of local investments and credits. To some extent, the administration is only a useful foil in larger political conflicts where it may become the victim rather than the conspirator. Indeed, the next step in reorganizing local capital spending and investment did just this by allocating more decisions to joint agreements between the private and public sectors, based on the ubiquitous public establishment device.

The *privatisation* of local investment decisions in France has no precise parallel in the British local government system, although this is not to say that British localities have been unaware of the importance of their roads, industrial sites, and water services to the private sector. The political calculations are probably no less shrewd than those made in France, but they take place mainly within the Cabinet. The move to contractual relationships for local investment projects displays both the weaknesses and the strengths of the intricate network linking mayors to Paris. A key element in the Chaban-Delmas design was finding a device to ease the administrative complexity in the approval of local projects, the transfer of funds to lower levels and the preparation of specific projects. The globalization of subsidies in March 1972 can be linked to the strategy of the concerted economy espoused by Bloch-Lainé, and others who felt that France must have more flexible decisionmaking machinery.[68] This meant linking local investment decisions more closely to market conditions and providing incentives for private investors. But paradoxically, it also meant reducing the influence of the administration over urban and local investment, lightening the *tutelle*, and challenging the power of the Ministry of Finance. While the challenge to local development in the 1960s came mainly from the prefect, in the 1970s the administrative struggle gradually shifted to the Ministry of Finance.

Within the existing administrative framework of the local government system, contracts had already been used with the urban communities[69] and the *villes nouvelles*. The important departure under Chaban-Delmas was to extend the contractualization scheme to the *villes moyennes*, or middle-sized cities. The decrees of December 1970 extended contracts to cities between 20,000 and 100,000 persons, and brought more than two-thirds of the French population and practically the entire urban structure of France under the new device. Recommended in the Sixth Plan[70] and endorsed by the Economic and Social Council,[71] the administration moved quickly to organize experimental contracts for two declining cities, Rodez and Angoulème, and, not too surprisingly, Chaban-Delmas' home region of Acquitania.[72] The proposals presented the Ministry of Infrastructure with new opportunities to expand, because it developed the contracts through its department GEP and was given special responsibilities for the Interministerial Group on *Villes Moyennes* (GIVM). The new program also brought about the relocation of DATAR within the Ministry of Infrastructure in 1973, which, under the energetic Guichard, became the driving force for the new policy. By the end of 1976, thirty contracts had been signed and another fifty were under active consideration.[73]

Under Giscard d'Estaing and Chirac the contractualization schemes underwent a minor explosion which also tended to reduce their value as a policy instrument and to make them more political. There were at least two important political elements in this redirection. The new President was extremely skeptical about the regionalization efforts, in part a heritage of rivalries during his years at the Ministry of Finance and in part the early signs of tension between the Gaullists and the Giscardians. The President's second interest in expanding the contractual device was his own long-standing doubts about the efficacy of national planning. The economic dislocations of the early 1970s had already derailed the Sixth Plan, and he was less than enthusiastic as the Seventh Plan began to take shape in the early years of his presidency. His distaste for the planners goes back to the rivalry between his Stabilization Plan and the Gaullist planners in the early 1960s.

Emphasis on contracts contributed to the decline of the region as a policy instrument. In his speech to the Rhine–Rhone Interregional Assembly, the President made it clear that he regarded the commune and the department as the main vehicles of regional policy.[74] He wanted additional powers delegated to regional and departmental prefects, and investments for school equipment, local roads and sports facilities were soon delegated to the regional level.[75] Associated with these efforts are the gradual erosion of the contract as a planning device of the center, and the proliferation of smaller contracts to be arranged by lower-level officials. The major addition was the *contrat du pays* or rural contracts, of which more than a dozen had been fashioned by the end of 1976 with another 40 during 1977.[76] This new instrument was followed with contractual agreements for cultural programs, green space, immigrant housing and eventually *petites villes* or cities under 20,000. The shift in emphasis was consistent with the President's desire to fashion a more humane image of government and responded to the growing concern in France, as elsewhere, with the quality of life and conservation of the countryside.

While there is little doubt that in Britain national and local politicians take regional projects and investments seriously, local leaders are most often consulted through the party machinery, and therefore we have little evidence of their preferences or influence. But consultation and even concealed patronage is very different from the entrepreneurial quality of French mayors. One case study of the Picardy region portrays the richness of political life at the regional level.[77] There are nine political parties represented on the Regional Council, including four Socialists and four Communists. The major decision of the year is the allocation of the investment credits from Paris, supplemented by the modest tax revenues of the region. Although the members from the Left hotly dispute most decisions, the actual process of dividing the investment credit works smoothly, and major controversies with the regional prefect are rare. The regional attitude toward Paris is rather like that of the communes, for it concentrates on how to engage the national government and to exploit the administrative machinery. Regional Council Presidents are nearly all national politicians. In 1978, fourteen of the twenty-two were either Senators or deputies, and twelve were presidents or members of departmental councils.[78] Thus the fears that regional government would be captured by the state must be weighed against the same *complicité* at the regional level as found at the communal and departmental levels. The various efforts to reorganize local investment credits have, if anything, played into the hands of local politicians and have made central control more difficult.

Despite their relatively modest financial role, the regions have been the object of political controversy because of the actual and potential influence they can exercise over local investments. The mayors have regularly demanded that more investments be classified in the communal and departmental categories, and following his 1975 speech on regions, the President made some concessions in this direction.[79] One of the distinguishing features of the centrist coalition that Giscard d'Estaing has built is that both Gaullist 'barons' on the Right and Communist leaders on the Left want more regional autonomy, the latter even at the expense of the departments.[80] Hence the paradox of five Gaullist deputies who are also Regional Council Presidents aligning themselves with Republican deputies in 1977 to defeat regional budget cuts proposed by their own government[81] – a kind of territorial politics that would be unimaginable in Britain. Political interest in local investments also makes it possible to use the subsidies as an incentive for local reorganization. One of the more daring recommendations of the Guichard Commission was to convert roughly 40 percent of the local investment subsidies (2.9 billion francs in 1974) into a grant to be divided and administered by the new 'communities of communes'.[82] Thus, instead of regional policies being the instrument of central departments, as they tend to be in Britain, they become in France part of the decisionmaking network which links policy and politics at lower levels of government.

In terms of the administrative connection, the contrast lies in the way in which regionalized investment and the contractualization projects become embedded in the administrative system, rather than as in Britain being parceled out to particular ministries. Each of the proliferating contractual schemes produced another fund, and thereby another lever for interministerial bargaining and exchange.[83] Even the fiscal reforms are linked to investment. The creation of the value-added tax in 1968 spawned the Fonds d'Action Locale (FAL), administered by a joint committee of elected and administrative officials. Part of the legislative compromise for the 1975 tax reform was to create the Fonds d'Équipement des Collectivités Locales (FECL), also administered by the FAL committee but linked to the Ministry of the Interior.[84] The competition among ministries over the use of such funds becomes a constraint on arbitrary administrative decisions, while the increasing dispersion of investment decisions to the lower levels of government makes it more difficult to exercise control from Paris. The mayors of all political colorations work to see that they have a direct voice in the reconstruction and improvement of their communes.

INVESTMENT AND LAND: THE CRUCIAL MIX

From Ricardo onward, modern economists have been perplexed by the relation of land to economic growth and industrial production.[85] Without attempting to summarize a debate that has already lasted almost two centuries, the use of this physically limited resource and the strange ways in which it accrues in value strike close to the heart of complexities linking levels of government. The issue has become even more acute with the growth of the welfare state, the acceptance that unearned and windfall profits are in some sense 'social' rather than individual earnings, and the fact that the gradual disappearance of a free land market determines fair prices and controls supplies of this vital commodity and creates new public responsibility. From the turn of the century in Britain, and since the Second World War in France, government has freely intervened in the land market to meet urban needs.[86] My concern in this section is particularly with the attempts of the two countries to combine land-use policy with the investment support and developmental needs of local government. The major policy instrument designed to reconcile public needs with private ownership has been planning. How the two countries have managed to reconcile planning aspirations with land use in order to enable cities to grow, to build housing, and to attract industry provides one of the most revealing comparisons of national and local policymaking in Britain and France.

British land policy since 1945 provides a microlevel illustration of what is in many ways the general argument of this study. The Town and Country Planning Act of 1947 opted for a global solution to local land-use problems and planning, and a generation of experimentation and political struggle followed to iron out how land would in fact be priced, allocated and, most important, linked to local needs. In 1947 the assumption was that private development of land 'would not be very important anyway',[87] with the result that Britain has since experienced a pattern of periods of soaring land prices and severe shortages followed by erratic and politically inspired efforts to redress the problem. The 1947 Act went beyond what was thought to be the very advanced proposal of the 1942 Uthwatt Commission,[88] to nationalize development rights, to the much larger claim that the government should manage the development of all land and thus should claim all development values. For wholly central policies such as new town construction, the concept was workable; but as a device to involve local and national planners in the shared problem of how to reconstruct cities and industries it was, if not a disaster, at least unable to respond to the structural complexity of the problem. By making land policy a gigantic clash of values, the effect seems to have been the same as having no policy at all.[89]

The illusion was, and to a remarkable extent remains, the assumption that social values, even if commonly held, are readily translated into the policies and easily accommodated to the political pressures found at various levels of government. While British towns and cities bitterly fought the counties to obtain land for public housing, national politics became a rhetorical battleground where Labour and Conservative leaders could successively undo each other's proposals. The main beneficiaries of the debate were precisely those whom Labour had hoped to restrain – the land speculators and landowners. Under the 1947 legislation a weak Land Board had been able to purchase only thirty-five plots of land for public use, and even a stronger Land Commission established by the Land Commission Act of 1967 only bought 2,800 acres.[90] The accompanying Town and Country Planning Act of 1968 is particularly interesting from the perspective of integrating central and local needs, for it was based on a land-use planning system which itself proved most difficult to implement. Essentially, there were to be two levels of land-use planning, a general and long-term design called the 'structural plan' and a specific and localized operational land-use plan called the 'action area plan'.[91] The compulsory purchase powers of the new legislation depended on the ability of the old local government system to work out their needs in these plans, and in their absence the Land Commission had great difficulty purchasing land in advance of demonstrated need. Like large landowners, the counties only needed to do nothing in order to block land acquisition while the cities were dependent on the rather whimsical determinations of the central government in order to obtain additional land for housing, industry, etc.

The powers retained by British ministers in this process are no less onerous than those of the most exalted French minister, and in Britain can be used with less local consultation. In addition, the British administrative system provides none of the protection of administrative law that always stands as the last recourse of an incensed commune.[92] The British minister can insist on publicity for a plan; a public inquiry on objections must be headed by a person who has ministerial approval; and where necessary the minister can simply force a local authority to submit a plan under the old laws or, in default, produce his or her own plan.[93] Thus it is misleading to think that only French administrators have arbitrary powers, but even more misleading to think that officials in either country can use such powers capriciously. The serious obstacles were the divorce of British land policy from planning procedures, and, in turn, the inability of the locality to influence land acquisition. This remained a centrally-controlled procedure geared to the needs of national parties rather than to local needs. There is little doubt among British planners, hard as they have worked and, some would say, prospered[94] under this legislation, that the highly abstract form of the structure plan has itself contributed to the confusion; indeed, many local authorities have simply ignored the long-term strategy, as has national government where specific decisions had to be made. McLoughlin is particularly outspoken and, consistent with the general structure of local government services, sees planning bogged down by 'the strong vertical *department*, dominated by one or two *professions* and with a continuous chain of command and communication between policy and implementation *with respect to one service at a time*'.[95]

On the whole, the French make more plans but take them less seriously than the British. But the important difference is that the investment and subsidy machinery provides a working link between general planning objectives, often even vaguer than British structure plans,[96] and the operational needs of the communes. Of the seventy-four structure plans needed to chart Britain's communities into the next century, seven had been submitted to the DoE, as required by law, by the end of 1974. The DoE review of these four took roughly two years for each plan.[97] The unforeseen pitfalls of imposing nationally uniform procedures became more visible with the 1972 Local Government Act. The new local government structure increased local planning authorities from 177 to 458 (not including Scotland), and, of course, where major boundary changes took place plans in process needed major revision.

While the structure plans move slowly toward completion and eventual revision, the central departments continue to generate their own plans of strategic importance to housing, transportation, urban renewal, growth areas, education and water.[98] The curious aspect of these efforts is not so much that the pious hope survives that their objectives will be harmonious, but that the local councils, even after the significant consolidation of 1972, had relatively little leeway in reconciling nationally determined objectives for housing, schools and industrial development to land-use planning. On the other hand, national policies relating to land use have no bearing on the elaborate land-use plans. Conservatives want to preserve the privately owned land market, while Labour imposes unwieldy and costly proposals to recover increased land values. The locality is caught in the middle of this adversarial tug-of-war. One of the costly, unintended effects is that local councils, public corporations and even national departments tend to hoard land which both drives up land prices and immobilizes local government assets. One of the most welcome changes in Heseltine's omnibus reform proposals of 1980 was to simplify land planning procedures and to virtually eliminate national approvals on urban land use.

The impossibly divergent objectives of land-use planning as viewed from the center for partisan purposes and as required by the locality become even more apparent when one examines the plight of the local council. The first problem is how more conservative counties will relate their structure plans to the local plans now existing for cities under Labour control. The entire local machinery for land-use planning could become entangled in partisan intransigence, particularly because local policies on controversial problems are so often set down by national party leaders. A more immediate and potentially paralyzing problem has been the handling of land-use appeals when individuals and groups conflict with the local plan.[99] In 1973, appeals to the DoE reached the astronomic level of 19,000. The Dobry Report was commissioned to try to stem the flow which had caused a backlog of 13,500 undecided cases.[100] Though in part a procedural and legal problem, appeals may also be exacerbated by the rigid division between local land-use planning and the larger issue of how land is allocated, priced and used in relation to national policy. As several British planners have noted, the British system of dual control paradoxically produces strategic plans so loose and discretionary that they prove locally ineffective and thus leave individual decisions to Whitehall. On the other hand, local land-use policies become so rigid that local choice tends to be swamped in paperwork.[101] Local governments are placed in the position of enforcing and regulating land-use policies without enjoying the more positive instruments of joint development schemes and public–private sector agreements that are common among French communes.

While it may be true, as Newton has pointed out, that centrally designed plans were accepted in Britain long before Labour came to power,[102] this does not explain why a country with so much expertise and success in some facets of land-use planning should continue to follow such divergent policies at the national and local levels. When Labour returned to power in 1974 the old controversy about land nationalization was revived, and in 1975 the Community Land Act again tried to combine a radical national land policy with the problems of local government land use.[103] The new law was to take effect in two stages: first, a period of continued land purchase by the local governments with a development tax divided between national and local government, followed eventually by the compulsory purchase of all land designated for development in the structure plan. With the local government system largely in the hands of Conservatives, and the severe shortage of funds for land purchase, the Act became an exercise in symbolic politics and, of course, was immediately denounced by the Conservative Party. By the end of 1977, only 1,571 acres had been purchased at a cost of slightly over twelve million pounds.[104] The interim measure, a development land tax, discouraged both private and public landowners[105] from putting their land on the market, and by 1978 there was renewed concern that cities would simply have no new supply of land.[106] Finally, in 1980 the Thatcher government simply repealed the Community Land Act.

The unhappy experience with the Community Land Act suggests some of the difficulties in trying to solve intricate intergovernmental problems using partisan politics, and underscores in a more detailed way weaknesses of intergovernmental policy coordination in the British local government system. Land nationalization was proposed to placate the left wing of the Labour Party in the House of Commons, not as a solution to local land problems. In fact, everyone knew when it was passed that there was little chance of implementing it. The effect was simply to pass down to the local level an intractable issue without helping local councils meet their land needs. Unfortunately, political excess almost always produces intransigence, especially with local government problems, and the local councils simply refused to buy land under these terms. Without rejecting the larger objective of the Labour Party, political differences have been a less important obstacle to French land-use schemes. Indeed, a leading Socialist mayor has found the French system readily adapted to his aims,[107] while the British relationship only produced more wrist-slapping of localities by a frustrated central government.[108] The difference is fundamental in comparing the two subnational systems: France puts partisan politics to work, Britain allows it to obstruct decisionmaking and to complicate local government.

Combining land policies with local investment plans is a complex problem because it involves several levels of government as well as representing conflicting economic and social values. There are immense organizational and territorial problems inherent in an ill-conceived or idealized approach. In examining the planning problems of southeast Lancashire, for example, Green finds that decisions involved seventeen central departments, seventy-six local authorities and the even more numerous committees in each of them, and six public corporations.[109] By early 1977 the 22,000 persons employed in planning for England and Wales had made 509 local plans which will no doubt become the effective instrument in local land-use and investment decisions.[110] Obtaining decisions is itself a worthy policy objective under such difficult conditions. But national land policies seldom recognized the organizational complexity of the local government system,[111] nor did they learn from local experience.

In all mixed economies, and in state-managed economies as well, there must be some device for aligning local land-use and development needs with the larger aims of the national government. While the formulation of land-use plans in France has not been any more rapid or simple than the British effort, the French have been prepared to rely heavily on the market to supply land to communes, while at the same time erecting an array of programs and incentives to bring development in line with local needs. As in the intricate general relationship between center and locality, outlined in Chapters 4 and 5, the approach is twofold: to bring local developers into the fold of locally and nationally approved projects, while simultaneously using the national land-use planning prerogatives in a differentiated way to respond to needs for housing, roads, industrial development, etc. In part, the more diffused control has worked because politics is not as easily polarized around planning objectives at the local level, and in part because planning legislation in France has generally included, and often been tied to, the allocation of land. The steady evolution of French land-use policy over the past decade suggests that they may be less doctrinaire policymakers than the British.

The transformation of the central–local links for local investment decisions proceeded in relatively clear stages, but was not fully developed until the Presidency of Giscard d'Estaing. Whether one finds the changes of the past decade significant depends on one's interpretation of the evolution of the contractualization schemes and the policy processes for allocating capital to the local-level influences. In terms of the decision process of the 1960s, which revolved around direct intervention and aimed at increased administrative control, the change is evidently extremely significant, and it tells us a great deal about the nature of French policymaking. Linked to the investment planning procedures are a number of localized contractual schemes designed to bring land acquisition and land values within reach of urban projects. The simple methods of centralized investment control failed because the administrative system could not handle such detailed decisions handed down from Paris. Although the French local government system puts mayors and administrative officials in much closer proximity than does the British, there have still been difficulties even in France linking local and national objectives.[112] A new policy can be dated from the *loi foncière* of 1967, which began to build links between local plans and land use. The major cities were, among other things, required to have an *agence d'urbanisme* to help produce more and better urban plans. By the end of 1975 there were twenty-four planning agencies at work for cities of over 150,000 persons, and proposals to add about twenty more.[113] Not too surprisingly, the effort to give cities some independent leverage over decisionmaking was opposed by nearly all the ministries.

The 1967 law also established the framework for urban planning, the Schémas Directeurs d'Aménagement et d'Urbanisme (SDAU),[114] comparable to the British structure plans, and the *plans d'occupation des sols* (POS), comparable to the British local plans. Launching the new urban plans was the responsibility of the Ministry of Infrastructure, and rested mainly on the influential planning department within the ministry, the Direction de l'Aménagement Foncier et de l'Urbanisme (DAFU). At the local level the planning effort brought about increased powers for the DDE and, in particular, the GEP. The effort was immense. In 1961 France spent only 11 million francs on urban planning, but in 1975 more than 125 million francs.[115] Unlike in

Britain, the cost of preparing these plans is shared by the state, while communes and departments bear the costs of project preparation and design. Although the SDAU are conceived as strategic plans, they are of a smaller scale than the British structure plans and, therefore, more likely to relate in meaningful terms to project designs. A total of 392 are planned for the country, to include about a quarter of French territory and 70 percent of the population. By the end of 1975, seventy-five schematic plans had been approved and 114 were under consideration, covering roughly half the targeted number and population.[116]

The second element in the law, the provision for the POS, envisaged the production of approximately 5,000 local plans by 1971. More important reasons than the mere technical complexity of this task intervened to slow their preparation. Shortly after the 1967 law was passed, the new Minister of Infrastructure, Chalandon, took office and made no secret of his distaste for the interventionist methods of the French state.[117] In his first major speech in the fall of 1968, he condemned France's 'terribly restrictive urban policy of heavy and incoherent procedures, and of complex and archaic techniques'.[118] He was in no hurry to put more regulation in the path of local development, and, more than any recent French minister, had unabashed confidence in the ability of the private marketplace to solve public problems. But the preparation of detailed local plans takes time and skill. Two years elapsed before details for their preparation were made known by decree and only by 1976 were they beginning to appear in large numbers. By mid-1977, 2,188 had been completed and 812 had been fully approved, affecting seventeen million persons.[118] But the new land planning exercises moved too slowly to meet the needs of rapid urbanization and Zone d'Aménagement Concertée or ZAC was invented both to mobilize land resources and to circumvent the administration.

To understand the importance and use of the ZAC, a brief look at earlier French zoning arrangements is necessary. ZACs are not the typical land use plans familiar in Britain and the United States, but detailed contractual statements of how public and private interests may combine within the framework of administrative law in order to use land. The progenitor of the ZAC was the Zone à Urbaniser par Priorité (ZUP), established by decree in 1958 and blessed by law in 1959.[120] In 1962 a supporting zonal agreement, the Zone d'Aménagement Différé (ZAD), was established. The ZUP and its amended form ZAD were used to organize a land reserve for public housing, new towns, etc., on the outskirts of cities. In the early 1970s, when they began to be phased out, there were 155 ZUPs controlling slightly over 16,000 hectares of land.[121] Essentially, they were financing agreements drawn up between landowners and the local government or state, usually accompanied by an agreement from the CDC to extend credit as land was purchased, and supervised by the CDC affiliate, the Société Centrale pour l'Équipement du Territoire (SCET).[122] At the local level these proposals were approved by the department and region, including the prefects, the TPG and the DDE. Neither type of zonal agreement was particularly popular with administrators, who found them too limited in their application, or with landowners, who found the financial incentives too small.

The ZAC represents an advance over the earlier zonal agreements in several respects. First, there had been no provision for shared ownership in the earlier land agreements, and officials, particularly those in banking and the CDC, wanted to tap private funding in order to relieve the burden on the government. The ZAC could be organized either under a local government with a private investor or as a ZAC *privée*, a privately operated project with partial public financing. Secondly, the old zonal arrangements did not respond to new planning needs. The ZAC was initially offered to the localities on the condition that they complete a SDAU or a POS. Thirdly, the old ZUPs had resulted in the construction of tower blocks and urban jungles on the outskirts of cities, and clearly were not encouraging the development of integrated cities. The resultant political backlash became apparent in the local elections of 1971 and 1977, when major cities found themselves surrounded by Socialist and Communist suburbs. The ZAC also denotes the first awareness of the need for a participatory element in urban development. For the first time plans were required to be publicized, although this provision was not properly enforced until the mid-1970s.[123]

Although the ZAC is sometimes attributed to Chalandon's eagerness to 'privatize' urban development, the amendment adding the ZAC to the 1967 law came from the Senate and had been accepted by Parliament before he became Minister of Infrastructure. The more likely history is that the scheme was worked out by the Ministry so that localities and private investors could evade the planning requirements. After 1969 a Plan d'Aménagement de Zone (PAZ) could be substituted for the POS, thereby avoiding the necessity of a local plan which might well restrict projects and land use. In any event, the ZAC is clearly traceable to the growing interest, in the late 1960s, to extend contractual relationships from the private to the public sector, and the concept of an *économie concertée* finds a parallel in *aménagement concerté*.[124] By mid-1977, 1,568 ZACs had been organized, affecting more than 81,000 hectares of land. About three hundred were organized in Paris, two hundred in the major provincial cities, and over a thousand through administratively designated *agglomérations* and other groupings of local government.[125]

The general direction of French urban development has, of course, never been a secret. If anything, the attempt to inject liberal notions into French local plans was simultaneously a repudiation of the administrative system and, however much oriented to the private sector, a way of getting local projects and preferences more directly involved in capital spending. Most important perhaps, it provided a groundwork for urban growth that compromised the power of central administration and enabled France to link public lending and finance to urban development. With the change of Presidents only a few years later it became possible to make major adjustments in this system and to enlarge the framework for local involvement in urban growth.

By the early 1970s, the manipulation of land-use requirements was creating embarrassment for the Pompidou government and popular resistance to indiscriminate building was growing.[126] More important, perhaps, it was increasingly apparent to the political leaders of the Right that the cumulative effects of their urban plans might prove disastrous. Shortly after Guichard replaced Chalandon in July 1972, steps were taken to encourage the preparation of the POS and the 1967 law was substantially revised. Guichard's 'new strategy' for urban development emphasized both the development of contractual relationships and the social costs of France's rapid urbanization.[127] The 1973 *loi foncière* turned attention to inner city problems, much like similar changes in Britain at the time. At this time the proliferation of contractual schemes took place and the new system of direct taxes outlined in Chapter 6 was introduced. In 1974 a decree closed the major planning loophole in the 1967 law, oddly enough only to generate new complaints from the communes that they could not handle the planning requirements.[128] The general objective of the new urban policy appears to have been to restore powers to the commune and department, and to diminish regional influence even further.

The effort to coordinate land, resources and spending reached its full development under the new President, no doubt stimulated by the fiscal and financial problems that the communes experienced in the mid-1970s and the approaching elections of 1977 and 1978. Like Pompidou, Giscard d'Estaing had made it clear that he distrusted further augmentation of regional government and that he was discontented with the more free-wheeling liberalism of the early 1970s. Though what 'an urban policy' might be is difficult to describe, France in recent years has constructed an entirely new set of laws to govern central–local policymaking. A first step was the *loi Galley* of 1975, named after the new President's Minister of Infrastructure. Under new legislation another zonal arrangement was introduced, the Zone d'Intervention Foncière (ZIF) which automatically protected local land claims once a POS was established. Another important development was to provide a scheme whereby land developers compensate the communes in relation to the benefits they derive from a project (*plafond légal de densité*).[129] Over the next two years, laws followed to protect the environment against developers, to try to raise architectural standards, and to simplify the procedures for obtaining building permits. The 1980 communal reform met all of the most cherished desires of French mayors by giving them control of construction permits. Out of the confusing jumble of urban legislation came a reasonably coherent set of guidelines for the future development of the French cities and towns. The President's 'urbanisme à la française'[130] owed much to the past, but it was also the product of an attack sustained over several years on urban issues that would be difficult to achieve in Britain.

INVESTMENT POLICIES AND PAYING FOR MISTAKES

There is accumulating evidence that central–local relationships will increasingly be mediated through the fiscal and financial links between levels of government. This is in part due to the very complexity of urban problems which, contrary to our expectations, requires more rather than less policy coordination at lower levels of government for the successful implementation of policy. It is also due to the inability of higher decisionmaking agencies of government to monitor, guide and adjust policies as the role of the state expands. Even the more unified administrative system of France has been hard pressed to keep pace with the requirements of a more complex world, and its internal crises have in no small measure been due to increasing pressures to delegate decisionmaking to lower levels. One of the contradictions, if not weaknesses, of the British local government system is that in a period when local needs require more localized coordination, it formed *larger* units and territories, but did not provide new local powers to influence crucial aspects of urban development. The private sector was suspect and the central government guarded its old controls.

The general argument in the last two chapters has been that the redistributive concerns of the British central government gave localities heavy service responsibilities, but left their councils with a minor role in investment and resource decisions. The central government exercised more rigid control over local capital spending than did France. The benefits from rebuilding cities eventually accrue to the society at large, but they must be calculated and planned in smaller units. Without minimizing the cumbersome nature of the French compromise, it has enabled mayors of all political colors to pursue investment funds, and has given mayors a tangible stake in the economic development of their cities and towns. The ability of the French local government system to do this is, of course, a function both of its less heavy service obligations, as well as of the more articulated territorial structure of the communes. Despite their outspoken criticism and complaints about Parisian influence, the French mayors when polled show a remarkable agreement about the objectives of French urban policy and find that the efforts to lighten the supervisory powers of the administration have had some effect.[131] Unlike Britain, the French system was able to adjust both the territorial and administrative constraints on urban development.

Although it did not quell the mayors' complaints about urban finance, the *globalisation des prêts* of the mid-1970s illustrates the continued search for new policy solutions. Globalizing subsidies simplified financial procedures, but loans were still provided in instalments and were difficult to adjust to more complex urban projects. Globalizing loans also marks the growing influence of the CDC and its affiliate SCET in the finance of urban infrastructure. In 1975 there were 125 urban *sociétés d'économie mixte*, of which about eighty were constituted to build urban projects. Their importance is suggested by the sum of their operations, reaching 3.6 billion francs in 1977. The negotiation of these loans is totally in the hands of the thirteen regional offices of SCET. By the end of 1977, over 300 cities had converted their lending to the new system.[132]

Britain has on the whole found it more difficult both to redirect its resources to new urban problems and to cross over departmental lines in order to provide adequate support. One revealing illustration is the

Inner City Programme, which DoE officials once hoped would provide a billion pounds to reconstruct British cities and towns. The inner cities program emerged as the most important in a confusing and sometimes contradictory series of attempts to prevent urban decay.[133] The local authorities, though sensitive to the need, were presented with a single formula, and, of course, were dependent on additional grants from the center. Like many issues that become overly politicized in British politics, the decision was actually shaped by both major parties. The inner city proposals were launched by the Heath government and implemented by the Callaghan government.

The early inquiries of 1972 were made by Peter Walker, the Conservative Secretary of State for the DoE, under a Cabinet committee which, as one observer noted, 'is somewhat ironic given the demonstrated need for Government departments to work in unison especially in relation to inner city areas'.[134] When the Labour White Paper emerged five years later, it acknowledged the recurrent difficulties of building an integrated approach to British local government. 'The activities of central government have themselves at times been over-compartmentalized. The Government intend to develop a more integrated approach to urban problems.' Given the ways Whitehall guards industrial policy and regional assistance, there is perhaps more irony in the recognition that 'Local authorities with inner area problems will need to be entrepreneurial in the attraction of industry and commerce.'[135] The difficult questions were, of course, why local authorities had not been encouraged to be more entrepreneurial in the past, and how resources were to be allocated under the new program in order to create a more competitive spirit.

The depletion and depopulation of the major cities is associated with a noteworthy change in the language of central government, which from 1976 began to talk more about its 'partnership' with local government. Whether such a partnership could begin to relieve the problems described in the pilot studies[136] remains to be seen, but the initial appropriations of thirty million pounds in 1977 and 125 million in 1978 will not go far. The more interesting evidence concerns the problem of organizing central government to make a concentrated attack; for the program involves land clearance under the Ministry for Industry, the easing of planning and housing restrictions under the aegis of the DoE, and eventually services within the DES and DHSS. By early 1978, forty-three local authorities with fifteen million persons had been declared eligible for 'inner areas assistance' by the DoE.[137] At least in these early stages, the inner city program bears a remarkable resemblance to the reallocation of local responsibilities proposed by the Secretary of State in early 1977, and the policy issue is not unconnected. With a minimal policymaking role assigned to local government, and little interest at the center in allocating the new appropriations on a competitive basis, the new funds may become another political football.[138] But at a time when Labour was suffering severe defeats in local elections, it had obvious attractions. Devising a partnership to link local officials to national inner city policymaking is, nonetheless, an important innovation from standard administrative practice in Britain. The compartmentalized functional organization of local government coincides with departmental boundaries in Whitehall to make comprehensive attacks on policy problems, such as energy, environment and housing, awkward and sometimes contradictory. Even though Mrs Thatcher disliked the inherited commitment to inner cities, there was little she could do to recover such funds.

All local government systems are vulnerable to local inertia. The important question is how to align local decisions with national policy objectives and involve localities in national programs and planning. As outlined in this and the preceding chapter, France does this by allocating an elastic source of income to communes even though this provokes a constant battle, and by moving toward a system of resource allocation that places important investment decisions at the local level. If it is a system which labors under a top-heavy administration, it is also a system that has devised ways to adapt, and at times to circumvent, administrative decisionmaking to meet local needs and preferences. In contrast to the British system, French policymakers have devised one with substantial local involvement in investment decisions. National objectives have shifted from the uncompromising attitude of the early years of the Fifth Republic to the gradual redress of relationships under Pompidou, and eventually began to adjust to increased dispersion of urban programs and planning under Giscard d'Estaing. Policy aims, of course, also require new policy instruments, and in this respect France has been an innovator. In contrast, the partisan changes of planning and land policies in Britain have created immense uncertainties for local government, while leaving both major parties dissatisfied with urban plans and programs.

So long as the welfare state exists in a mixed economy, a fundamental choice will be whether to involve private interests in public decisions, no doubt at a price, or to try to organize the public sector independently of private interests, which (it is sometimes forgotten) can also impose costs on society. For reasons that are both historical and political, Britain has had difficulty dealing with the intersectoral and intergovernmental complexities of local government. Only in the past few years has British government begun to break down the well-guarded borders between administration and politics, the public and private sectors, and central and local government. From the perspective of local government, there are decided advantages to the French array of intersectoral and interterritorial development agencies. As the British discovered so painfully in 1975 and 1976, a local government system burdened with relatively fixed responsibilities has great difficulties adjusting to economic changes.

Less concerned than the British that every policy instrument should have a clear link to the center, the French *société d'économie mixte* was able to serve mayors of all political persuasions and, in periods of economic dislocation, even protected them from bearing all the costs of overambitious plans. There is more than a little irony in Deferre's repudiation of a seven million franc deficit from the new city of Berre, built on the outskirts of Marseilles, because he has been one of the most entrepreneurial of French mayors.[139] Likewise, when the large housing societies which build around Paris are approaching bankruptcy, the communes of Yvelines and Val-d'Oise meet to decide whether they wish to help rescue what now appear to be overly elaborate designs of central administrators and local developers.[140] The point is not that one government has made more errors than the other, for error like success has to be calculated in terms appropriate to the system. Britain, too, has had to reduce excessive commitments such as new towns.[141] More important is how well the agencies involved in the increasingly complex pattern of intergovernmental relationships can cushion the financial shocks that affect local government. A financial partnership with Paris may not be any more comfortable than a partnership with London, but the French mayor is better protected against central government errors.

In comparing policymaking for local government, it is crucial to see how policymaking both supports and constrains the two different systems of government. Underlying detailed questions of how well modern democracies can devise policy instruments, and how decisions may or may not be shared between levels of government, is the more fundamental question of how these two countries, and the local government systems of all the welfare states, may or may not redefine our notion of local democracy itself. The general argument has been that success and failure in this larger political objective depends increasingly on the policymaking links among and between levels of government, and less and less on the autonomy of the locality considered in isolation. The comparison of Britain and France shows that within each country, local government has been transformed by central government's wishes to provide more benefits and services to citizens. Neither French communes nor British councils were ever actually asked if they thought this was a good idea. For the most fundamental political question of our generation, the traditional defense of local inertia has been of no use whatsoever. The state has changed, and with that change the issue has become how local democratic forces, if they survive, will mesh with national politics and policymaking in the future.

NOTES: CHAPTER 7

1 See, for example, the long-standing dispute between Cheshire County Council and Manchester described in J. M. Lee, *Social Leaders and Public Persons* (Oxford: Clarendon Press, 1963), pp. 83–122.

2 The difference between the two economies in terms of capital formation is not, as one might have guessed, private corporations; these provide about half in both systems. It is that French households account for about a third of capital formation, compared with roughly a fifth in Britain. See *National Accounts Yearbook* (New York: United Nations, 1975), pp. 373, 662.

3 The difference is even greater if one also takes into account that about a quarter of British local government capital spending is for housing, which is not a local function in France. For recent times for Britain, see Layfield Committee, *Relationship between Central and Local Government* (London: HMSO, 1976), pp. 27–8. For France, Guichard Report, *Vivre Ensemble*, Annex, (Paris: Documentation Français, 1978), p. 81.

4 It should be remembered that the contractual relationship was first developed for industry. See Yves Madiot, *Aux frontières du contract et de l'acte administratif unilatéral: recherches sur la notion d'acte mixte en droit public français* (Paris: Librairie Générale de Droit et de Jurisprudence, 1971).

5 The most important issue in relation to national finance is the possibility of a short-term credit squeeze if local governments launch too many loans at the same

time and thereby affect the capital market for industry. See the alarm expressed by the Treasury in the early 1960s, *The Economist*, 17 November 1962; ibid., 4 April 1964. In France, this alternative leaves national banking institutions with excess credit on their hands. A rapid decrease in local borrowing from state institutions in 1972 produced a special report by the CDC, *Enquête sur les disponibilités des collectivités locales*, Paris, 23 January 1974.

6 See the thesis by Ian Ball, 'Local authority capital expenditure in the United Kingdom 1950–1973', University of Birmingham, 1976. His major findings appear as 'Urban investment controls in Britain', in D. Ashford (ed.), *National Resources and Urban Policy* (London: Croom Helm, 1980).

7 Each ministry has its own methods for calculating and forecasting investment needs in the various functional sectors. See N. P. Hepworth, *The Finance of Local Government* (London: Allen & Unwin, 1979, 5th edn). Part of the aim of improved local budgeting, discussed in Chapter 5, was to provide better local investment programs, and to anticipate more carefully the operating costs of capital spending.

8 From Senior's dissent to the Royal Commission on Local Government, Report, vol. 2, p. 153.

9 See Dame Evelyn Sharp, *The Ministry of Housing and Local Government* (London: Allen & Unwin, 1969), pp. 29–31; Griffith, *Central Departments and Local Authorities* (London: Allen & Unwin, 1966), pp. 88–9. The Layfield Report, op. cit., pp. 117–31, is largely concerned with indebtedness and capital finance, not investment decisions.

10 See Prud'homme, in N. Hansen (ed.), *Public Policy and Regional Development* (Cambridge, Mass.: Ballinger Press) for an economist's evaluation. Also Guy Isaac and Joël Molinier, 'L'exercice par les nouvelles institutions régionales de leurs pouvoirs financiers', *Bulletin de l'Institut International de l'Administration Publique*, no. 34 (April–June 1975), pp. 341–408. Since the late 1960s a regional version of investment plans has appeared, with the annual *loi de finances* (yellow version). See *Régionalisation de Budget d'Équipement et Aménagement du Territoire* (Paris: Imprimérie Nationale, annually).

11 On the procedures and relationships to the plans, see Guerrier and I. Bauchard, *Économie Finacière des Collectivités Locales* (Paris: Colin, 1972), pp. 256–63; also d'Arcy, *Structures Administratives et Urbanisation: le SCET* (Paris: Berger Levrault, 1968), pp. 241–76.

12 See Gordon C. Cameron, 'Regional economic policy in the United Kingdom', in Hansen (ed.), op. cit., pp. 65–102.

13 For a list of the many funds working in various ministries, see Douglas E. Ashford, 'British idealism and French pragmatism', *Comparative Political Studies*, vol. 11 (July 1978), pp. 231–54.

14 Duplouy, *Le Crédit aux Collectivités Locales* (Paris: Berger Levrault, 1967), p. 19. For more details on the institutional machinery see ibid., pp. 132–9. FNAFU was created in 1963 from the older fund, Fonds nationales d'aménagement du territoire, or FNAT, originally organized in 1950 to assist urban reconstruction.

15 On the history of the CDC see Prirouet, *La Caisse des Dépôts* (Paris: PUF, 1966); and Duplouy, op. cit., Ch. 4. In the current debate about the influence of the CDC in French public finance, it is often forgotten that the CDC was a remarkably conservative lending agency until the Fourth Republic, and often had to be prodded by the Minister of Finance or the Bank of France to undertake new investments in the public sector. The critical stage in the modernization of the CDC is quite recent and actually came in the closing years of the Fourth Republic.

16 There were four public corporations organized under the CDC umbrella: the Société centrale immobilière de la caisse (SCIC), the Société centrale d'aide au développement des collectivités (SCDC), the Société d'études pour le développement économique et social (SEDES) and SCET.

17 An early and less critical study of SCET's work is J. Fabre *et al.*, *Les Sociétés Locales d'Économie Mixte et Leur Contrôle* (Paris: Berger-Levrault, 1964); and a more critical study is François d'Arcy, *Structures Administratives et Urbanisation: SCET* (Paris: Berger-Levrault, 1968).

18 *Les Comptes de la Nation 1969*, Paris, Notes et Études Documentaires, no. 3725–3726, 7 October 1970, p. 45.

19 'État récapitulatif des concours de l'État aux collectivités locales', *Projet de Loi de Finances pour 1978* (Paris: Ministry of Finance 1978), p. 177.

20 *Le Monde*, 16 October 1979.

21 See Octave Gélinier, 'Vers de nouveaux concepts pour organiser l'administration', in Peyrefitte (ed.), *Décentraliser les Responsabilités* (Paris: Documentation Français, 1974), pp. 39–56.

22 Commission Générale du Plan, *Rapport de l'Intergroupe d'Étude des Finances Locales* (Paris: Documentation Français, 1971), p. 67. One of the most important reasons why simply condemning administrators does not make sense is that this report, probably the most severe critique of local finance in France, was written by the Director General of the CDC himself, with top officials from DATAR, the Plan and INSEE. See also the Bourrel Report, *Rapport de la Commission d'Étude des Finances Locales* (Paris: Office of the Prime Minister, 1965), pp. 66–76.

23 The best account of these reforms is René Barberye, 'Les interventions financières de la Caisse des Dépôts dans le domaine de l'équipement local et du logement social', *Bulletin Economique et Financière* (1973), pp. 139–68.

24 This is a somewhat technical point, but nonetheless indicative of the very different relationships between center and locality in the two countries. The Treasury testified (based on annual accounting figures) before the Layfield Committee, *Report*, op. cit., App. 6, p. 17, that the local contribution to capital expenditure is 'insignificant'. But in terms of financing of total investment in the country, local surpluses provide close to 30 percent. See R. R. Neild and T. S. Ward, 'The financing and forecasts of local government expenditure', in *Layfield Report*, Appendix 6, op. cit., p. 90. The closest comparison with the French system is the figure for *autofinancement disponible* in *Le Secteur Public* reports. In percentage terms, self-financing for communes only declined from 15 percent of investment income in 1967 to 7 percent in 1974.

25 See testimony to Layfield Committee, *Report*, op. cit., App. 1, pp. 32–3. Not much has been written about how the sanctions affect specific services. See Ken Judge, 'Territorial justice and local autonomy: loan sanctions in the personal social services', *Politics and Policy*, vol. 3 (1975), pp. 43–70. Also R. J. Nicholson and N. Topham, 'Investment decisions and the size of local authorities', *Policy and Politics*, vol. 1 (1975), pp. 23–45.

26 The details of these arrangements are given in Hepworth, *Financing Local Government*, op. cit., pp. 330–4. See also I. A. Corden and J. M. Curley, 'Control over the capital investment of local authorities', *Public Finance and Accountancy*, vol. 1 (1974), pp. 231–3.

27 Calculated from the PESC reports, *Public Expenditure to 1978–79*, Cmnd 5879 (London: HMSO, 1975), pp. 156–7; and *The Government's Expenditure Plans*, Cmnd 6721–II (London: HMSO, 1977), pp. 130–1.

28 See Hepworth, op. cit., pp. 138–44. On the debate in the 1960s, see 'An alternative to the PWLB', *The Economist*, 26 October 1962; and 'A new look at local finance', *The Economist*, 26 October 1963.

29 All the early 1970 measures are revoked in Department of the Environment, *Capital Programmes*, Circular 86/74 (London: HMSO, 17 June 1974). *The Times* (London), 23 January 1980. Note also the Layfield Committee, *Report*, op. cit., pp. 129–130, on the sparse information on local capital holdings.

30 Calculated from *Les Finances du Secteur public* records, for the appropriate years. Over this period the total amount nearly tripled to seventeen billion francs for the entire local system in 1974.

31 Also from *Les Finances du Secteur public*. There is also a slight decline in subventions to departments (from 11 to 8 percent). The total amount only begins to appear in 1967.

32 *Le Monde*, 28 October 1977.

33 See J. L. Quermonne, 'Vers un regionalisme fonctionnel', *Revue Française de Science Politique*, vol. 13 (1963), pp. 849–76.

34 The most 'political' of the British regions was the northeast where a political boss, Dan Smith, not the local councils, intervened. He was associated with the Labour Party and chaired the Regional Council for many years. See Joanna Mack, 'The north: or T. Dan Smith land revisited', *New Society*, 18 November 1976.

35 For historical background see J. C. Banks, *Federal Britain?* (London: Harrap, 1971), pp. 142–60; Gavin McCrone, *Regional Policy in Britain* (London: Allen & Unwin, 1969); G. Manners *et al.*, *Regional Development in Britain* (London: Wiley, 1972).

36 There are numerous case studies of town planning decisions. See P. H. Levin, *Government and Planning Process* (London: Allen & Unwin, 1976), on Central

Lancashire; and Michael Harloe, *Swindon: A Town in Transition* (London: Heinemann, 1975).

37   J. D. MacCallum in Cameron and Wingo (eds), *Cities, Regions, and Public Policy* (Edinburgh: Edinburgh University Press, 1973), p. 296.

38   One revealing account is by the DEA minister himself, Lord George Brown, *In My Way* (London: Gollancz, 1971). See also the reflections of another Labour minister of the period, Edmund Dell, *Political Responsibility and Industry* (London: Allen & Unwin, 1973).

39   On regional economic policy, see John Vaizey (ed.), *Economic Sovereignty and Regional Policy* (London: Halsted Press, 1975); B. E. Coates and E. W. Rawstrom, *Regional Variations in Britain* (London: Batsford, 1971); William Thornhill, *The Case for Regional Reform* (London: Nelson, 1972).

40   Maurice Wright and Stephen Young, 'Regional planning in Britain', in J. Hayward and M. Watson (eds), *Planning, Politics and Public Policy* (Cambridge: Cambridge University Press, 1975), p. 252.

41   Ibid., p. 260.

42   Special development areas date from 1934; and the development areas from 1945 and 1950. Intermediate areas were introduced in 1970 after the Hunt Report, *The Intermediate Areas: Report of a Committee of Inquiry, under the Chairmanship of Sir Joseph Hunt*, Cmd 3998 (London: HMSO, 1969), conducted to study assistance for parts of the country excluded from the older development areas. The fact that these areas have been most often manipulated by the Labour Party is not particularly significant, because most of their voters are in depressed regions. What it does mean, however, is that social and economic polarization makes reconsideration of these policies very difficult, and the Conservatives, too, found them useful when preparing for the 1974 elections.

43   MacCallum, op. cit., p. 292. For current details see *Local Government Trends: 1978* (London: CIPFA, 1978), p. 68. In 1977 regional industrial development grants alone totaled 400 million pounds.

44   MacCallum, op. cit., p. 283, fn. 11.

45   For a longer account of these relationships and how they neutralize local planning efforts, see J. B. McLoughlin, *Control and Urban Planning* (London: Faber, 1973), pp. 36–59.

46   *The Times* (London), 27 August 1979.

47   *Guardian*, 5 December 1979. Heseltine's proposals also gave the DoE authority to set up more urban development corporations in any part of the country, but he said that no more were anticipated.

48   *The Times* (London), 2 March 1978.

49   The major Conservative regional statements are Department of Trade and Industry, *Investment Incentives*, Cmnd 4516 (London: HMSO, 1970), which espoused moving incentives back to the tax system rather than making direct payments; and *Industrial and Regional Development*, Cmd 4942 (London: HMSO, 1972) which tended to move back to the old system as Conservative economic policy began to disintegrate.

50   *The Times* (London), 3 November 1977; and 17 December 1977.

51   On the complexities of regional administrative organization, see Michael Keating and Malcolm Rhodes, 'Is there a regional level of government in England?', unpublished manuscript, UK Politics Workgroup Conference, August, 1979; and Brian W. Hogwood and Peter Lindley, 'Which English regions?', unpublished manuscript, same conference.

52   *The Times* (London), 9 November 1977.

53   Under pressure from the short-lived Department of Economic Affairs, the Central Statistical Office began an *Abstract of Regional Statistics* in 1967.

54   Edgar Pisani, *La Région – Pour Quoi Faire? Ou le Triomphe des Jacobins* (Paris: Calman Levy, 1969). A similar critique came from the Club Jean Moulin, *Quelle Reforme? Quelle Régions?* (Paris: Seuil, 1969).

55   The regional budgets are seized upon by the locally oriented agencies of government and the communes, particularly in regard to the decisions of the Interministerial Committee on Infrastructure (CIAT) when DATAR programs are announced. See, for example, *Moniteur*, 19 April 1975, and 26 February 1976.

56   The regions have actually been debated in French politics since the time of the Revolution, as noted in Chapter 2. See M. Bourjol, *Les Institutions Régionales de 1789 à Nos Jours* (Paris: Berger-Levrault, 1969; Christian Gras and Georges Livet, *Régions et Régionalism en France* (Paris: PUF, 1978); Ilan Greilsammer,

'The ideological basis of French regionalism', *Publius*, vol. 5 (1975), pp. 83–100; and P. Barral, 'Idéologie et pratique du régionalisme dans le régime de Vichy', *Revue Française de Science Politique*, vol. 34 (1974), pp. 911–40.

57 See the outline of the President's regional ideas by Jacques Fauvet, 'Le régime des notables', *Le Monde*, 5 November 1970.

58 Published in *Moniteur*, 21 November 1970. On the application, see *Moniteur*, 2 January 1971. The classification of investments naturally became a new source of friction between local leaders and the government, especially the division between regional and departmental funds. For a revised classification by ministries, see *Moniteur*, 3 January 1975.

59 François Lefebvre, 'La déconcentration des décisions de l'État en matière d'équipements publics', *Moniteur*, 2 January 1971.

60 Unless otherwise noted, the information for this paragraph comes from the series of reports by the Iehle Committee for the Ministry of Administrative Reform. They are: 'Déconcentration en matière d'investissements publics', 26 April 1973; 'Bilan des six premières années d'application des mesures de concentration un matière d'investissements publics', 30 May 1973; and 'Organisation des services de l'État aux niveau régionales', 13 July 1973. Iehle provides a good overview of his evaluation in Institut Français des Sciences Administratives, *La Gestion Déconcentrée des Finances de l'État* (Paris: Cujas, 1973), pp. 10–20.

61 A complete classification of the Ministry of Agriculture's investment budget was not completed until 1976. See *Moniteur*, 14 February 1976.

62 The creation of Regional Councils, and Regional Economic and Social Committees, in order to give indirect representation to the regional agencies, will not be discussed in detail. See Vincent Wright and Howard Machin, 'The French regional reforms of July 1972: a case of disguised centralisation?', *Policy and Politics*, vol. 3 (1975), pp. 3–27.

63 See J. Hourticq, 'La réforme du régime des subventions d'investissement de l'État aux collectivités locales', *Revue Administrative*, vol. 26 (January–March 1974), pp. 65–8. On the relationship to regional budgets, see Jacques Lefebvre and Christian Charlet, 'Régionalisation du budget et budget régional', *Moniteur*, 26 January 1974, pp. 17–26; and 'Collectifs et la décentralization', in C. Debbasch (ed.), *La Décentralisation*, op. cit., pp. 207–18.

64 *Le Monde*, 30 April 1974.

65 Top French administrators are not afraid to come to their own defense in public. See, for example, the revealing account by a TPG in the colloquium *La Gestion Déconcentrée*, pp. 46–54. The easy way to undermine the subsidies is simply not to revise the allowances as inflation continues. See *Vie Publique* (December 1974), p. 42, for an account of this tactic.

66 From a report, 'Situation financière des régions', kindly provided by the Ministry of the Interior. On lending, see also the report in *Colloques*, no. 15 (April 1978), p. 16. The ministry report did show substantial rates of increase based on partial reports for 1978: a 62 percent increase in operating budgets and a 30 percent increase in lending. The main resource is a per capita tax levied by the Regional Council and adjusted annually in the *loi de finances*. For 1977, regions could tax up to thirty-five francs per person; for 1978, forty-five francs.

67 *Moniteur*, 28 February 1976, p. 43. On the shortcomings of the early globalization and overall credits, see also Christian Charlet, 'L'évolution de la régionalisation', *Moniteur*, 15 February 1975, pp. 10–20.

68 As noted above, contracts with industry had been used throughout the 1960s, and at this time were also becoming a common device in organizing state agencies: state radio (ORTF) 1972, Electricité de France 1970, the railroads (SNCF) 1971 and the Paris commuter trains (RATP) 1972. They were proposed for nationalized industries in the Nora Report of 1967. Even the idea of grouping commune subsidies was not new and was possible, if unexploited, under the 1964 reforms. See Flecher–Bourjol, 'Essai de typologie fonctionelle des contrats passés entre l'état et les collectivités locales et établissements publics territoriaux', *Bulletin de l'Institut International d'Administration Publique*, vol. 38 (April–June 1976), pp. 57–90; also Michel Nault, 'L'État et les collectivités locales: un nouveau style de relations?', *Revue Politique et Parlementaire*, vol. 78 (1976), pp. 44–53; Yves Pimont, 'Les contrats de plan', *Revue de Science Financière*, vol. 63 (1971), pp. 697–746; and J.-P. Duport, 'L'expérience des contrats du plan', *Bulletin de l'Institut International d'Administration Publique*, no. 25 (January–March 1973), pp. 161–75.

69 See J.-P. Duport, 'De nouvelles relations financières entre l'État et les communautés urbaines: l'expérience des contrats de plan', *Moniteur*, 20 February 1971. A list of contracts is given in Flecher-Bourjol, op. cit., p. 78.

70 See both the *Rapport de la Commission des Villes sur les Orientations Souhaitables de la Politique Urbaine au Cours de VIe Plan* (Paris: Documentation Française, 1970); and *Rapport Générale de la Commission des Villes* (Paris: Documentation Française, 1971).

71 Known as the Lajugie Report, the account appears in the *Rapports du Conseil Economique et Social, Journal Officiel*, no. 13 (7 August 1973), pp. 553–604.

72 The most complete account is Philippe Leruste, *Le Contrat d'aménagement de villes moyennes*, Paris, Notes et Études Documentaires, no. 4234–4236, 17 November 1975, especially the revealing chronology on p. 74. See also Claude Buron, 'Les contrats d'aménagement conclus entre l'État et les villes moyennes', *Actualité Juridique et Droit Administratif* (October 1976), pp. 510–18. The contracts do not appear to have been distributed in a highly partisan way. Among the first twelve there were two mayors aligned with the Republican Independents, one UDR, four favorable to the coalition, and five with only local identities. The deputies from the towns were Socialist in three cases, UDR in two, RI in two, and five were various shades of reformist, probably supporting the coalition.

73 Interview, Commissariat du Plan, July 1977. Full accounts of the contracts appear in *Moniteur* as they are completed, and they are listed in the announcements of the Interministerial Committee on Aménagement du Territoire (CIAT); *Moniteur*, 19 April 1975, 3 July 1976, and 14 March 1977.

74 See reports in *Le Monde*, 25 November 1975, and Raymond Barrillon, 'Un décentralisateur jacobin', *Le Monde*, 26 November 1975. Also 'Halte à la région', *L'Exprès*, 29 September–5 October 1975. With the growing power of the Left at this time, the coalition parties were under renewed attack from Mitterrand and Marchais to elect the regional councils. The older Gaullists were also toying with ways to strengthen regions, and Chaban-Delmas had come out in favor of elected regional councils in September 1975.

75 *Moniteur*, 14 February 1976, p. 12. The President took a personal interest in the progress of the rural communes, and himself inaugurated the Plömerel contract. See *Moniteur*, 29 January 1977.

76 Michael Prouzet, 'Les contrats du pays', *Moniteur*, 17 July 1967, pp. 9–13; and *Le Monde*, 25 November 1977.

77 Jacques Chevallier and Danièle Loschak, *Les Nouvelles Institutions Régionales en Picardie 1973–75; Bilan d'une Recherche* (Amiens: Centre Universitaire de Recherche Administrative et Politique, 1976).

78 Calculations based on the list of Regional Council Presidents in *Colloques*, no. 15 (April 1978), p. 17.

79 See the requests outlined in *Vie Publique*, no. 36 (April 1975). The mayors want consultation on category I, and full powers over categories II and III. After his November 1975 speech, the President had some investments moved from category II to III.

80 Chirac and Debré are much less enthusiastic about stronger regions than the five Gaullists heading Regional Councils: E. Faure (Franche-Comté), Chaban-Delmas (Acquitania), Guichard (Loire), Sudreau (Centre) and Giraud (Ile-de-France). On the Left's views, see A. Jourlin, 'L'Aménagement du territoire sous le pouvoir des monopoles', *Cahiers du Communisme*, no. 5 (1964); the work of the CERES leader, Yves Durrieu, *Régionaliser la France* (Paris: Editions Flammarion, 1972); and Mény in Debbasch (ed.), op. cit., pp. 71–85.

81 *Le Monde*, 17 November 1977, and *Le Point*, 28 November 1977. As relations between the Gaullists and the President deteriorated, Guichard came out publicly to accuse him of being hostile to regions. See *Le Monde*, 14 February 1978.

82 *Vivre Ensemble*, pp. 354–64.

83 For cultural programs there are the Fonds d'Intervention Culturale, *Moniteur*, 8 May 1976; for environmental projects, the Fonds d'Intervention et Aménagement de Nature et d'Environment, *Moniteur*, 25 January 1975; and for inner city rehabilitation, the Fonds d'Aménagement Urbain, *Vie Publique*, no. 51 (September 1976).

84 FELC was from its inception an investment fund and the subject of severe criticism from the Ministry of Finance, which did not want to share power with the Ministry of the Interior. Its funds come from both land charges and the value-added tax, and it was a partial response to the mayors' complaints about tax

injustices. In 1976 it received a billion francs, and in 1977 a billion and a half, so its importance is considerable. See D. Flecher and H. Fort, *Les Finances Locales*, (Paris: Masson, 1977), pp. 161–3 and *Moniteur*, 14 February 1976, on its creation.

85   A good introduction to the economic perplexities is John Ratcliffe, *Land Policy: An Exploration of the Nature of Land and Society* (London: Hutchinson, 1976), pp. 9–27, which outlines the classical positions. Political science has tended to leave the issue to the economists or to deal only with the conflict surrounding supply. See the British and French chapters in Hayward and Watson (eds), op. cit., pp. 295–357 and 378–89.

86   Though Britain clearly pioneered modern land-use planning through such men as Patrick Geddes, Ebenezer Howard and Sir Patrick Abercrombie, it is noteworthy that the early legislation of 1909 was partly inspired by the beauty and order of French cities. See McLoughlin, op. cit., p. 115. A good history of land planning is Peter Hall, 'The origins: urban growth in England 1801–1939', in Hall *et al.* (eds), *The Containment of Urban England* (London: Allen & Unwin, 1973), pp. 59–90; also his *Urban and Regional Planning* (Harmondsworth: Penguin, 1974).

87   Harry Gracey and Peter Hall, 'The origins: evolution of planning from social movement to social policy', in Hall *et al.* (eds), op. cit., Vol. 1, p. 111.

88   A. Uthwatt, *Final Report of the Expert Committee on Compensation and Betterment*, Cmd 6386 (London: HMSO, 1942). Though it does not enter as directly into central–local issues, the other major report concerning land was the Barlow Report, *Report of the Royal Commission on the Distribution of the Industrial Population*, Cmd 6153 (London: HMSO, 1940). In neither case was there extensive local consultation. See also the critique of early land policy by Christopher C. Hood, *The Limits of Administration* (London: Wiley, 1976), pp. 94–114.

89   The main conclusion reached by Peter Hall *et al.*, 'The 1947 planning system: objectives', in Hall *et al.* (eds), op. cit., pp. 33–71. Much the same criticism is made by McLoughlin, op. cit., pp. 161–81.

90   These figures and much of the material in this paragraph come from Roy Drewett, 'Land values and the suburban land market', in Hall *et al.* (eds), op. cit., Vol. II, pp. 197–245.

91   The proposals actually stem from the Planning Advisory Group (PAG) organized by the Conservative Minister of Housing, Sir Keith Joseph; see *The Future of Development Plans* (London: HMSO, 1965). Labour adopted the two-tiered planning process with few changes. See their White Paper, *Town and Country Planning*, Cmd 3333 (London: HMSO, 1967).

92   See, for example, how the local land-use plan was annulled by the Conseil d'État on appeal from a local environmentalist group, *Le Monde*, 10 January 1978.

93   McLoughlin, op. cit., p. 127; and J. B. Cullingworth, *Housing and Local Government* (London: Allen & Unwin, 1969), pp. 156–7. The latter also points out that under certain conditions either central or local government can acquire land with no right of public inquiry, and with no disclosure of the purpose of the acquisition.

94   Like French administrators, British planners are constantly engaged in a devastating self-critique which belies the too-easy interpretation that their misdeeds have autocratic motives. See, for example, David Eversley, *The Planner in Society: The Changing Role of a Profession* (London: Faber, 1973), p. 82, where he considers British planners to be a century too late in their ideas; or McLoughlin's critique of local planning departments, op. cit., pp. 60–71.

95   McLoughlin, op. cit., p. 265, his emphases.

96   The French government, for example, has been happy to support for a number of years a futurist study of France under DATAR auspices. See *Une image de la France en l'an 2000, Scenario de l'inacceptable* (Paris: Documentation Française, 1971); and the sequel *Le Scenario de l'inacceptable septs ans après* (Paris: Documentation Française, 1977). These and a number of additional 'think-papers' appear in the series *Travaux et Recherches de Prospective* and have been, to the best of my knowledge, uniformly ignored by the government at all levels.

97   George Dobry, *Review of the Development Control System: Final Report* (London: HMSO, 1975), pp. 30–1. On the implementation see Department of the Environment, 'Review of the development control system: final report by Mr George Dobry, QC', Circular 113/75, 13 November 1975. By the end of 1976 there were twenty-four submitted to the DoE, of which six were approved; *Local Government Trends: 1976*, p. 251.

98   See Ratcliffe, op. cit., p. 85. These plans do not include additional major projects such as a third London airport, the proposed Channel tunnel, major port and dock developments, etc., nor the regional agencies noted above that can effectively wipe out a structure plan. For an account of how the problems noted here can affect city planning, see Gordon E. Cherry (ed.), *Urban Planning Problems* (London: Leonard Hill, 1974). Peter Hall *et al.* (eds), op. cit., p. 417, gives a fine example of how compartmentalized policies may conflict. In 1959 local authorities were required to pay market value for land for public housing, so the central government then had to increase subsidies and provide additional housing credits to cover increased costs.

99   See the section in Cullingworth, op. cit., pp. 50–4, explaining why the absence of an administrative law tradition places this burden on government, effectively giving the DoE important quasi-judicial powers.

100   Dobry Report, op. cit., p. 53. For some reason Dobry's estimate is much higher than the published figures. For 1973 the figure is 11,393; *Local Government Trends: 1976*, p. 246. For the year ending 1975 the published number is 13,159. Even with the decline in appeals after 1973, the tables show that nearly one in ten development and building application permits was appealed to the DoE.

101   McLoughlin, op. cit., p. 57. Peter Hall *et al.* (eds), op. cit., Vol. II, p. 424, point out that the reason the 'new towns' policy worked well was that the development corporations were exempt from paying increased land values.

102   Ken Newton, 'Community decision makers and community decision-making in England and the United States', in T. Clark (ed.), *Comparative Community Politics* (New York: Wiley (Halsted), 1974), p. 70.

103   The proposal was put forward in the White Paper, *Land*, Cmd 5730 (London: HMSO, 1974). The implementation is outlined in Department of the Environment, 'Community land – circular 1, general introduction and priorities', Circular 121/75, 3 December 1975. Actually, the implementation waited for subsequent legislation on the development land tax (four months later). On problems of implementation see Alan Norton and Joyce Long, *The Community Land Legislation and Its Implementation* (Birmingham: INLOGOV, 1975).

104   See 'Community land – a skeptical view', *Local Government Chronicle*, 6 February 1976; Michael Eyers, 'The Land Bill – a recipe for its own repeal?', *New Society*, 17 October 1975; Gavin Weightman, 'A Land Bill for Wigan?', *New Society*, 21 August 1975; and 'Community Land Act: floperoo', *The Economist*, 20 November 1976. The competing views are summarized by David E. Regan, 'The pathology of British land use planning', *Local Government Studies* (New Series), vol. 4 (1978), pp. 3–24.

105   Explained in 'Land tax: good grief', *The Economist*, 27 March 1976. In 1976–77 local governments saved about five million pounds from the tax and an estimated twenty million in 1977–78. See *Municipal Review* (August 1977), p. 157. The irony of the entire effort was that it appeared that public landholders, like the large nationalized industries, were holding huge amounts of land in the inner cities and probably causing more developmental problems than private landholders.

106   *The Times* (London), 20 June 1978.

107   See the account of urban planning and development in Grenoble by Anne Simeont and Jena-Michel Leger, *De la Coopération Intercommunale au Regroupement de Communes* (Paris: Comité de Sociologie Économique et Politique, 1975).

108   *The Times* (London), 20 June 1978.

109   L. P. Green, *Provincial Metropolis: The Future of Local Government in South East Lancashire* (London: Allen & Unwin, 1959), p. 219. See also Jon Gower Davies, *The Evangelistic Bureaucrat: A Study of a Planning Exercise in Newcastle-upon-Tyne* (London: Tavistock, 1972).

110   Response to a parliamentary question quoted in *Municipal Review* (February 1977), p. 331.

111   For a sensitive discussion of the organizational issues, see John Friend, 'Planners, politics and organizational boundaries: some recent developments in Britain', *Policy and Politics*, vol. 5 (1976), pp. 25–46.

112   On the basic planning framework see René Magnan *et al.*, *Conception et Instruments de la Planification Urbaine*, 2nd edn (Paris: Centre de Recherche d'Urbanisme, 1975). The best work linking the financial structure to urban problems is Claude Pottier, *La Logique de Financement Public de l'Urbanisation* (Paris: Mouton, 1975).

113   The clearest exposition of the law and its relations to the various land-use plans is

Pierre Veltz, *Les Plans d'Occupation des sols* (Paris: BETURE, 1975). See in particular his careful analysis of how the law was changed by parliament and affected by the implementing decrees, pp. 83–93. As in the *loi Marcellin*, the Deputies and Senators were able to make substantial changes. For a shorter treatment, see M. Arrou-Vignod *et al.*, 'La loi d'orientation foncière', *Revue Politique et Parlementaire*, vol. 74 (1972), pp. 1–18. There follows a discussion, pp. 19–31, on how the *villes nouvelles* relate to the new legislation.

114 See *SADU: Notes et reflexions; légende et instructions* (Paris: Documentation Française, April 1976), pp. 78–86 for details on their preparation and relevant articles of the 1967 law. A good general critique is François d'Arcy, 'Les différents outils de planification urbaine (SDAU, POS . . .), leur articulation et leur pouvoir contraignant', *Aménagement du Territoire et Développement Régionale*, Vol. 3 (Grenoble: IEP, 1970), pp. 33–61.

115 *Études d'Urbanisme* (Paris: Documentation Français, 1975), p. 55.

116 *Recueils d'Informations Statistiques sur l'Urbanisme* (Paris: Direction de l'Aménagement Foncier et de l'Urbanisme, September 1976), pp. 32–7, including listing by departments.

117 Abin Chalandon was Minister of Infrastructure from July 1968 to July 1972, under two Prime Ministers: Couve de Murville and Chaban-Delmas. Lest one consider his brand of unfettered liberalism typical of the Gaullists, it is important to note that he was removed by the conventional Gaullists in 1973.

118 *Moniteur*, 21 September 1968, p. 35.

119 *Moniteur*, 18 July 1977. Forty-four cities over 50,000 composed the most important gaps. In one year the number of POS had nearly doubled. See *Recueil d'Informations*, pp. 36–7. The deadline has been regularly postponed for seven years, most recently to January 1978. See *Vie Publique*, no. 74 (February 1975).

120 See Sylvie Biarez, 'Les zones à urbanizer en priorité logique et contradictions', *Bulletin de l'Institut International d'Administration Publique*, no. 24 (October–November 1972), pp. 753–74. Though somewhat dated, the most complete study is J. Jamois, *Les ZUP (Zones à Urbaniser par Priorité)* (Paris: Berger-Levrault, 1968).

121 *Les ZUP (Zones à Urbaniser en Priorité): Situation au 31 Décembre 1973* (Paris: Ministry of Infrastructure, DAFU, n.d.), p. 2. The report gives a departmental and communal breakdown.

122 The complexity of the financing and ZUP's penetration of the various ministerial funds is beautifully illustrated in Pottier's table, op. cit., p. 152. Roughly one-third of all assistance was going to Paris. The total financing for ZUPs, industrial zones, urban renewal, etc., for land acquisition and urban investment in 1967 was nearly three billion francs.

123 Much of the information in this and the following paragraphs on the ZAC comes from interviews with the Director of Finance, SCET, October 1977, and with CDC officials in 1976 and 1977. For a summary account see Christian Hortas, 'Les zones d'aménagement concerté', *Bulletin de l'Institut International de l'Administration Publique*, no. 24 (October–December 1972), pp. 725–51.

124 See R. Gray, 'L'Aménagement Concerté', in Parfait (ed.), *La Planification Urbaine* (Paris: Eyrolles, 1973), pp. 163–86. For an economic assessment, see Pottier, op. cit., pp. 155–90.

125 Figures kindly provided by the Ministry of Infrastructure. For figures up to the early 1970s see *Les Zones d'Aménagement Concerté (1969–1973)* (Paris: Ministry of Infrastructure, DAFU, n.d.). There were 900 ZACs in 1973.

126 The year 1972 was filled with land scandals. See, for example, 'Le conseil général met en cause l'aménagement de la ville nouvelle de Saint Quentin-en-Yvelines', *Le Monde*, 9 June 1972; 'Le gouvernement accepte de remettre en cause le schéma d'urbanisme du "Grand-Fos"', *Le Monde*, 17 November 1972.

127 See O. Guichard, 'Une nouvelle stratégie', *Le Monde*, 9 January 1974. Earlier statements are found in *Moniteur*, 26 May 1973, and 7 July 1973. At this time DATAR was brought within the Ministry of Infrastructure and its activity subordinated to the new contractual schemes.

128 *Moniteur*, 9 February 1974. On local reactions see Claire Mossolin, 'L'Heure de vérité, *Vie Publique*, no. 28 (1974), pp. 327–42; Daniel Valot, 'Ou trouver l'argent?', *Vie Publique*, no. 26 (1974), pp. 84–90.

129 See Antoine Laporte, 'Une profonde réforme des règles d'urbanisme', *Vie Publique*, no. 40 (September 1975), pp. 35–40; and no. 41 (October 1975), pp. 40–8. Also 'La réforme de l'urbanisme', *Moniteur*, 7 February 1977.

130	The array of laws are described in *Moniteur*, 18 July 1977; and by the Director of DAFU, P. Mayet, 'La réforme de l'urbanisme', *Moniteur*, 26 September 1977, pp. 13–16.

131	See the poll reported by Armand Vaillié, 'L'Urbanisme que veulent les maires', and the IFOP poll reported by Guy Sorman, 'Les maires et leur ville', *Vie Publique*, no. 31 (1974), pp. 85–91.

132	Figures provided by the Director of Finance, SCET, Interview, November 1977.

133	Since 1968 there have been six programs under way, each the pet project of a specific ministry and most proposed with no local consultation. They are: the Urban and Education Priority Areas of the DES, the Community Development Project and Comprehensive Community Programmes of the Home Office, the Central Improvement Areas and the Housing Action Areas spawned by the DoE, and the studies noted here. One excellent evaluation is by Richard Batley and John Edwards, *The Politics of Positive Discrimination: An Evaluation of the Urban Programme 1967–1975* (London: Methuen, 1978).

134	Kenneth Spencer, 'How the inner area studies point the way forward', *Municipal Review*, no. 575 (November 1977), pp. 238–9.

135	*Policy for the Inner Cities*, Cmd 6845 (London: HMSO, 1977), p. 8. For an acerbic but revealing Conservative response, see Anthony Steen, 'Good neighbours are what our cities really need', *The Times* (London), 26 October 1977.

136	The pilot studies are *Unequal City: Final Report of the Birmingham Inner Area Study*, by Llewelyn-Davies Weeks *et al.*; *Inner London: Politics for Dispersal and Balance; Final Report of the Lambeth Inner Area Study*, by Graeme Shankerland *et al.*; and *Change or Decay: Final Report of the Liverpool Inner Areas Study*, by Hugh Wilson *et al.*, all published by the DoE in 1977.

137	See the statement of Peter Shore, Secretary of State for the DoE, on the Inner City Bill in the House of Commons, *The Times* (London), 20 May 1978; and statements in the Lords, *The Times* (London), 10 February 1978. An interesting disclosure was that the London boroughs had no specific powers to assist industry; also that the new program might be administered under a corporate arrangement similar to the French system, but using the much stronger powers of the old New Towns Act.

138	See the criticism of excessive bureaucracy by the newly elected Conservative leader of the AMA, *The Times* (London), 28 July 1978; and the Labour and Conservative estimates of the program in the *Municipal Review*, no. 585 (September–October 1978), pp. 124–5.

139	*Le Monde*, 16 November 1977. As might be expected, the *sociétés* also have their own national organization. For an account of the 1976 meeting, when these problems were first appearing, see *Moniteur*, 20 March 1976, pp. 21–3; for 1977 see *Le Monde*, 29 September 1977.

140	The total deficit of the development agreements around Paris is estimated to be around 500 million francs; *Le Monde*, 28 September 1977. On the two councils' decisions, see *Le Monde*, 5–6 February 1978.

141	See, for example, Roger Smith, 'Stonehouse – an obituary for a new town', *Local Government Studies* (New Series), vol. 4 (1978), pp. 57–64.

Chapter 8

CONCLUSION: CENTRAL–LOCAL POLITICS IN THE WELFARE STATE: INDULGENCE OR NECESSITY?

Local self-government was a product of the nineteenth century liberal democratic state. Nor surprisingly, it was designed to mesh with the prevailing *laissez-faire* values that also prevailed in the society and the economy more generally. But from the late nineteenth century onward, national government decided to provide many more social benefits and to intervene directly in the national economy. In a period of Tocquevillian self-reliance, the active community was expected to look after its own needs which, in turn, meant that relative to the range and scope of national policymaking, the local governments effectively designed and implemented policies that we would now associate with national government. Local government could effectively design policies of national significance because national governments made so few of them. The rise of the welfare state has irreversibly altered the political conditions and the institutional relationships which made possible this division of policymaking responsibilities.

My intention is not to castigate the welfare state, for few of us would wish to return to Booth's London or even Haussmann's Paris.[1] The point is simply that local self-sufficiency no longer provides the support once associated with local autonomy, and once considered a precondition of democratic government. Although deeply rooted in history, the efforts to reorganize and redirect local government over the past three decades reveal many of the dilemmas that every advanced industrial nation faces in trying to reconcile democratic values with the expanded role of national government. Because the reorganization of local government was so often an institutional after-thought,[2] it has often been relegated to secondary importance in political studies, and widely regarded as too legalistic and too technical a subject to fit into more general theories of politics and society. But local government and local politics can also be analyzed as I have tried to do, as a policy area where political habits and political oversight are readily observed. As such, local government and local politics provide us with an important insight into the diversity of the institutional compromises of various democratic systems as national governments grew in order to meet rising expectations and to enlarge the economic role of the state.

Thus, the argument of the book has been that the complexity of the welfare state has caused many of the problems that plague local government, and explains the gradual drift toward fiscal and financial measures to guide the subnational system. Each country must devise its own strategy in constructing new relationships between the expanded powers of national government and the transformation of local government. The political bargaining that takes place during this metamorphosis is an unparelleled opportunity to observe the policy process of the welfare state and the way in which institutionalized authority is applied in making some critical choices. In this respect, the book deals more with national politics than local politics, and focuses on the policy process as a way of exposing how power is used in the two political systems. As we have seen, local government and politics is a veritable minefield of 'non-decisions',[3] and those who ignore (or simply disapprove) of the potent political forces of procrastination and inertia are not likely to uncover the national significance of the transformation of central–local relationships over the past generation.

STRUCTURAL ANALYSIS AND THE SUBNATIONAL SYSTEM

Structural analysis of politics is a way of dealing with the historical and institutional diversity of political systems. Because more quantitative and behavioral analysis has prevailed in political science for nearly half a century, the discipline has lost touch with a powerful analytical tool, and has dismissed a vast reservoir of information that does not easily fit more rigorous empirical explanations of behavior. Structural analysis begins by rejecting the notions that human activity can be reliably observed by means of continuous variables, which, in turn, permit us to build quantitative models; and that those conditions that do not readily lend themselves to such quantification can be safely treated as 'constants'. More rigorous empirical analysis can be of great value in understanding political and social change within fairly restricted limits and over short periods of time, but it is not likely to come to grips with the full complexity of such problems as the transformation of intergovernmental relationships over long periods of time, or, as the Marxists have stressed, the changing relationship of social classes and economic power over time.

The great difficulty in applying structural analysis is that causal relationships are specified rather than deduced as in more conventional, empirical analysis. This is obviously most clear in the case of Marxist interpretations of social class as it relates to both social and political change, but there are also less dramatic illustrations, such as the economists' distinction between primary, secondary and tertiary industrial sectors. The structural problem with which this comparison has been concerned is the relationship between territorial democracy, which is rooted in local government, and national democratic government, now complicated by the large tasks imposed at the national level by the emergence of the welfare state. More abstract socioeconomic theories would likely focus on why the state has indeed taken on these additional tasks and how the expanded activity of government relates to an underlying historical interpretation of society. There is now, for example, a growing body of studies of local government and politics that try to assimilate central–local relationships into a more general Marxist theory of society.[4] In fact, there are a variety of interpretations ranging from the locality as simply a way of reproducing the social structure of capitalist society generally to more detailed analyses which see local government and politics as ways of reinforcing the economic power of the privileged classes and essentially repressing class conflict that might otherwise lead to more dramatic social change.

The Marxist structural analysis applied to local problems has done much to enrich and to enliven our debates about local government and politics, but it is important to remember that it is only one form of structural analysis, and one which operates, like all structural analyses, from particular assumptions about the crucial dynamics of social and political change. There is no doubt that broadly conceived social and economic variables can 'explain away' much that happens at the local level. Oddly enough, this was precisely the findings of much early quantitative investigation into state and local politics in the United States.[5] My hesitation over more freely applying Marxist structural assumptions to central–local politics and policymaking is that it may be too abstract a theory to deal with the intricacies of central–local relationships. There is no doubt that local government is in many ways intimately linked to a particular way of organizing society, but is this the structural issue of paramount importance? Indeed, is it surprising that liberal democratic values have permeated local government as they have the organization of work, leisure and rewards more generally?

By focusing more heavily on the relative influence of national and local politics in the policymaking process, I have tried to show that structural analysis can be used in other ways, and can help us understand other problems of the modern welfare state. The growth of the welfare state not only poses certain contradictions for Marxist interpretations of the future, but also raises important questions about the relation of existing democratic values to political systems. At the individual level, the dilemma arises over the extent to which collective decisions at lower levels of government will indeed be able to influence national choices. Nineteenth century government was not as clearly faced with this choice, although the Victorian debates over improved sanitation and health show how early this issue arose in the most advanced industrial nation of the period. Though in many ways less awe-inspiring than the transformation of society, there remain important questions whether citizens can use their local government, or other voluntary associations working through local government, to express concern about major issues such as the environment, the organization of social services, and the range of educational opportunities. Another important question, with which I have been particularly concerned, is how the politics of local government interacts with national decisionmaking and national democratic institutions in order to sustain the effectiveness and vitality of modern democratic institutions.

My concern with how democratic values can be articulated by subunits of government can, of course, be subsumed within a more general social theory, but how the complexity of national government affects territorial democracy is a separate problem from a more general social theory. Even if social opportunities and rewards are not as fully equalized as some may feel necessary, there is, for example, little doubt that the redistribution of real incomes and the specialized individual care that has been organized would not have been possible without the assistance of local government. Viewed within the framework of democratic government as we know it, there is nothing necessarily trivial in a community preferring park benches to nursery schools. Democratic politics is the sum of individual choices and must take place in both the larger territory of the nation as well as in the smaller territories of local government. While it may be argued with some persuasiveness that decisions at both levels tend to reproduce existing social relationships, they also have an independent political meaning in permitting citizens to make adjustments and choices that may be contrary to the announced aims of national government. Were this not the case, then many would feel that democratic values as we have evolved them for several centuries no longer exist.

But there is also a second meaning to structural analysis as used in this study which takes us into the problems of comparative analysis and institutional change. As democratic values have been institutionalized over several centuries, each country has constructed somewhat different procedures to translate collective authority into effective decisions. Although the institutionalization of power has received attention from neo-Marxists,[6] it is perhaps fair to say that from a neo-Marxist perspective, any form of institutionalization within a society that tolerates inequality and relies on capitalist forms of production is unsatisfactory. Institutional analysis of democracies thus only reveals the symptoms of oppression, rather than showing how political bargaining and compromises are made. In this sense, the internal dynamics of policy choices are in many ways of secondary concern to a more general structural theory of society. But if we take the conflicts and dilemmas of democratic political systems as intrinsically important, then an understanding of institutional constraints and processes can be related to relations between levels of government, as well as to numerous other problems confronting the welfare state.

The neglect of institutional analysis in political science stems from many of the same reasons that explain disinterest in structural analysis. Differentiating 'institutions' from the political system is not a simple task and prone to falling into the trap of using such legalistic and formalized definitions that earlier aversions to dealing with institutional complexities may seem justified. But nonetheless, institutionalized relationships within the political system are an identifiable problem, and in many ways institutions are the empirically observable manifestation of those characteristics of political exchange and bargaining that the society agrees to be of primary importance.

Political institutions deal with a wide variety of problems that elude theories of society, at least when such theories are directly imposed on political systems. Democratic institutions are concerned with redistribution and equality, but are also concerned with individual rights and expression, with mediating the internal conflicts and choices of government itself, and with the effectiveness of decisions and policies.

As I have repeatedly argued in this analysis, the evolution of the welfare state has multiplied these additional problems, of which local government is a critically important component. Inertia may have served the immediate interests of local government in an age of simpler government, but procrastination is no longer a defense against institutional change (or social change) and the difficult organizational problems of modern political institutions mean that local government has the difficult choice of either recognizing mutual dependence with national government or being eroded as a significant institutional element of modern government.

For a number of reasons, policy analysis has played an important role in enabling us to see more clearly what are the structural requirements and contradictions of institutionalized power in the welfare state. Indeed, more difficult institutional choices would seem a natural consequence of enlarging the scope and range of government activity at both the national and local levels. The welfare state means that more conflicts arise among entrenched groups and interests within government, and that the process of converting objectives into accomplishments is more extended in time and distance, involves more actors, and presupposes more skillful coordination of political institutions of many kinds. In short, policy formation and implementation is a way of observing institutional change and for this reason the interaction of national and local government in the policy process is one important way of assessing how various political systems undergo institutional change. In this respect, the structural analysis of institutions in relation to political systems is not analytically different from the structural analysis of political systems using social theories, but seeks to disaggregate the analysis another step by making more explicit the essential requirements or institutionalized assumptions of structuring government in different ways.

The comparison of Britain and France as they seek to reorganize local government is, of course, only one such issue that is subject to institutional structural analysis. But hypothetically speaking, if for any one country the identification of the critically important structural features in institutionalized power is correct, one would find similar structural features in a number of policy areas.[7] One illustration is not enough, any more than one revolution is enough to persuade us that more radical theories of society adequately allow for the resilience of political systems and their institutions. Thus, the study in itself is not a complete structural analysis of the institutions of either country, but points toward fundamental political relationships that influence institutions, their organization and their objectives.

Britain places an enormously high value on adversarial politics at the national level. Britain first developed democratic political institutions, and the critical importance of adversarial politics is rooted in seventeenth and eighteenth century struggles with the monarchy. It was essential to British democracy that statutory law be the supreme law of the land and that discretionary authority be kept to an absolute minimum. The institutional solution was to assert the power of the Cabinet and Parliament over all other forms of authority, and in many respects this remains the underlying institutional constraint on British local government, as on many other political institutions in Britain. This historic compromise has provided Britain with a degree of political stability and continuity that no other democracy has enjoyed, but it has also meant that local government was excluded in principle and in practice from having an effective policymaking role at the national level. Put somewhat differently, were British local councils to assume the political importance of French municipal councils, the constitutional and institutional assumptions of British democracy would be sorely strained.

As mass democracy evolved over the nineteenth century, British institutions showed a remarkable ability to subsume new political and social demands to the requirement of parliamentary supremacy, and to adapt to new conditions the adversarial behavior that focuses attention on Parliament and provides the keystone to British democracy. For most of the century, the aristocratic consensus that upheld parliamentary democracy and implied the political subservience of local government to national politics remained intact. Likewise, the administrative needs of an increasingly complex government were subordinated to national political leaders by the formation of a carefully insulated higher civil service, while the local governments acquired the vast bulk of the new officials needed to construct the welfare state. In doing so, national political leaders were assured that they would not be as troubled with the details of policy implementation and administrative infighting as are most other democracies, including France. The greatest irony of local government in Britain may be that it did so much to relieve national government of the growing complexity of modern government, but had so little to say about the institutional response to complexity. Its unrecognized consequence of immense importance in preserving British democracy was that it left national politics and national administration to concentrate on those issues that best suited adversarial combat, and thereby helped preserve social and political consensus at a time when many other democracies were more severely divided over social conflicts and local resistance to the growth of government.[8]

France did not enjoy the acquiescence of local government as democracy developed. From the debates of the Constituent Assembly of 1791 until the controversies of the 1960s over regional and local reform, French national institutions and politics have had a very different relationship to local government, but the compromise is no less rooted in the democratic vision that inspires French democracy. From the Revolution onward, France aspired to create a society in which citizens would be politically equal, and the commune became a partner in this enterprise. Territorial democracy was, and remains, a more difficult problem for French institutions than for British. The acknowledgment that the communes are 'small republics' was only the first in a long series of political compromises that have kept local politics and communal demands at the forefront of French politics.

The basic institutional relationship between national and local government, therefore, was founded on very different principles, and permeates French political institutions. The preoccupation was not so much to construct a system that would forever exclude monarchial excess, but to find institutions that would effectively aggregate power so that a democratic national government could exist. True, the relapses of the successive monarchies and empires of the nineteenth century made limiting the power of national government a problem, but the solution of the Third Republic, and in many respects the Fourth and Fifth Republics, has been to give the communes a strong voice in the national policies that affect them directly, and, possibly in unintended ways, to enable them to extend their influence at the national level in many policy areas where British local councils are excluded by Westminster and Whitehall. The turbulence of the historical development of French democracy meant, too, that the administration became an essential component of both national and local political institutions.[9] As we have seen, there is also evidence that having been cast in an integrative role, the administration became more adaptive. An important adaptation was to divide its interests in order to respond to territorial demands in ways that were not developed in Britain in either national or local administration. As Hoffman observes, 'When the watchdog became a greyhound, those who had been holding the leash had to learn to run.'[10]

Thus, the structural principles or assumptions underlying central–local relations in the two countries respond to the requirements of each democratic tradition. Whether one laments or cherishes the particular institutional solutions that Britain and France devised, the subnational system evolved under very different institutional conditions and it is not surprising that citizens as well as governments are slow to change such fundamental institutional relationships. France had to become a politically integrated nation under more difficult conditions than Britain, and the communes were assigned a critically important role in aggregating local views and local political influence so that democracy could survive. As government became more complex, they even had an important role in curbing administrative excesses, and they continue to exercise sufficient influence over national policies and policymaking to defeat no less a political hero than de Gaulle. Exasperated as ministers and elite administrators may be with the French communes, they would not be likely to exclaim, as Lord Salisbury did, 'I wish there was no such thing as Local Government.'[11] As the French parties of both the Right and the Left confess, localized power and influence are essential to French democracy.

POLICYMAKING AND COMPARATIVE POLITICS

There are many possible uses of policy analysis, and no claim is made here that its application to comparative politics either exhausts or surpasses its application for other reasons.[12] But if one sees the institutionalized structure of government as a distinguishable and important question for political analysis, as outlined in the previous section, then we clearly need new methods and concepts to link institutions to the demands and performance of government. The existing general theories of political systems are not particularly helpful. On the one hand, there is the equilibrium concept of Eastonian analysis that essentially views political systems as ways of finding an acceptable balance between political demands and performance. One of the important reasons to exercise caution in applying an equilibrium model is that several leading economists, who often espouse equilibrium in analyzing economic behavior, have themselves expressed profound doubts over its applicability to the complexities of institutionalized behavior.[13]

On the other hand, we are left with several neo-Marxist evaluations of the performance of democratic government where the common thread seems to be that government is most often preoccupied with dampening class conflict. If these objections have not been more persuasive, it is at least in part because the alternative ways to formulate and to implement policies under a Marxist-inspired regime remain rather cloudy. Lest this criticism be misinterpreted, it is not intended to deprecate in any way the social ideals of a potentially more equalitarian social system, but only to point out that unless one can specify more clearly how these goals will be achieved in actual practice, socialists are not likely to draw support from voters or even to provide workable solutions for social democratic governments. In this respect, understanding the relationship of institutionalized behavior to policymaking is as important to the radical Left as to the radical Right, and both appear to have great difficulty in defining and implementing their policies.

The development of more useful concepts to link the performance of the modern welfare state to the study of politics remains one of the major tasks of political science. The approach used in this study, namely, examining decisions in order to extract the salient political conditions that appear to influence decisions in a broad area of policy-making, is only one of many, and would not necessarily be suitable for other kinds of policy analysis.[14] The concern has been with differentiating what is distinctly 'political', that is, investigating how political institutions produce what appear to be lasting constraints or pre-conditions on important policy choices. As in other forms of structural analysis, it is the consistencies of the policy process that reveal the underlying assumptions of the political system. Thus, one is not studying policymaking in order to discover whether policies are efficiently, and even effectively, implemented as much as to uncover those regularities of policymaking that represent essential features of the political system.

Such an approach not only puts more emphasis on 'non-decisions' than do other more narrowly conceived forms of policy analysis, but also directs our attention to political circumstances that might not enter into a policy study with more specific purposes. For this reason, I have often spoken of the 'strategy' of local government reform, meaning how major political actors evaluated the problem well before change was initiated, and how the major institutions of the political system did or did not play a part in formulating the issue. As explained in the Introduction, if one defines local government purely in the legalistic and administrative terms used in each system, then policy analysis of this kind, though very likely valuable to the particular policymaker or government concerned, will not encompass a sufficiently broad range of decisions to assure us that we are indeed observing how political and institutional constraints operate in that political system. For this reason, I devised the concept of the subnational system, and sketched out the network of relationships that encompass a wide variety of decisions affecting central–local relationships. Much the same could be done for major policy areas.[15] Reform of the existing local government system is, of course, the central concern of analyzing how this network is influenced and changed, but, as I hope later chapters of the study have illustrated, by no means my sole concern.

The advantage of conceiving policy problems more broadly is, of course, that we can observe diverse forms of political intervention in the policy process. The general conclusions concerning politics of policymaking in the British system are that policies concerning the subnational system tend to isolate interdependent choices, to fix on rather narrow goals, and to arrive at relatively singular strategies for change. This is not to claim that in the more concrete sense of policy choice within local government local councils do not differ in their interpretation of national policy objectives. One would not expect anything else in so complex a network of decisionmaking. In fact the costs, preferences and services of British councils vary immensely.[16] But the continued wide internal variations in performance further demonstrate the dogmatism that characterized British efforts to reform local government. As Sharpe and others have argued,[17] the high level of services of British local government is one of its hallmarks, but this strength has not been converted into policymaking influence at higher levels of government. The most frequent complaint of local councils is that they are subject to new, sometimes contradictory, demands, forced on them by Parliament in a relatively incoherent way. My concern, then, has been policy *about* the subnational system, not policy *within* local government.

In this broader context, the dogmatism of British policymaking becomes clearer. Although the 1972 Local Government Act was about many problems besides boundaries, the parliamentary debate and the most salient political issue soon became 'town versus country'. The issue was inescapable once Labour embarked on a substantial consolidation of local government areas, which may have been their most serious error. But the political and institutional constraints on central–local relationships left them, and later the Conservatives, with very little choice. British parliamentary democracy could not accept the elaborate process of bargaining and aggregation of preferences found in the French central–local network. There are few reasons why ministers or MPs would wish to risk a century or more of relative political stability, enshrined in Cabinet government, in the hopes that local politicians might refashion their role or that MPs would more forcefully intervene in national policies affecting local government. Were the already overburdened local council members able to free themselves in order to enter into more direct bargaining with Whitehall and Westminster, the status of ministers and departments would be endangered. Were MPs to intervene actively, Cabinet government itself would be challenged. Moreover, Britain has evolved a horizontally structured division of labor between national and local administration that is now almost impossible to change.

Thus, the emphasis on boundaries and consolidation was a natural response to the need for reform because it was consistent with the institutional and political constraints of British democracy. In many ways, the strategy of change was safe for Parliament because local politicians were so heavily encumbered with local duties, while simultaneously the strategy was consistent with adversarial habits at the national level because MPs could promise redistribution of services, more efficient organization and more resources. The irony is, of course, that in the absence of a closer relationship between national and local politics, the political costs of failing to meet these promises never falls on either MPs or on local councils. Everyone appears dissatisfied with the results of a generation of reform effort, but no one takes responsibility. Both the formulation of the issue and performance are very loosely related to political success and failure. The subsequent patchwork attempted by Shore under Labour and Heseltine under the Conservatives was no less a simplification of the real complexities of central–local relations than earlier reform efforts.

Although reform has become a more lively issue than it was in 1888, when one critic described local government as 'the peculiar preserve of parliamentary dullards',[18] the mobilization of local political interests and influence is relatively weak compared with most other democratic systems. The national and local electoral systems, the relationship of national and local parties, and very different orientations of national and local party leaders, serve to attenuate local issues and to isolate local politics from higher level decisions. While we know much less about political bargaining between national and local administrators, the fact that each local service operates under a different set of national departmental priorities and traditions in itself means that the administrative system as a whole is difficult to change. The specialization of the vast local services makes them less open to political change, and there are few political incentives for ministers to see their departmental patterns of control and influence amended. In fact, confidentiality means that many key policy decisions in Whitehall and Westminster cannot even be scrutinized by Parliament, much less by MPs and local politicians.

The politics of policymaking concerning the French subnational system presents a very different picture. National policies affecting the communes more often have multiple objectives, have been gradually implemented as compromises (adjustments are made during implementation), and have depended much more heavily on the careful mobilization of local political support for reform. National political leaders cannot extract law from the National Assembly with the ease of British Prime Ministers. The reason is not the strength of the Assembly, but the internal divisions of the major parties, the close association of local and national elections, and the dispersed and localized structure of party organizations (except for the Communists). As we have seen, the reforms of 1964 and 1971 and the entire process of financial reform since 1966 have been plagued by local resistance and local compromises. As Grémion noted, and contrary to the conventional interpretation of French policymaking,'the state has lost its privileged position' in France.[19] Underlying this change is the necessity of aggregating power in order to make major decisions and the continuing importance of local politicians in French politics.

Another structural feature of French political institutions requiring a more complex strategy for local reform is the unified administration. The functional importance of British local government in the subnational system, and to the effective operation of government as a whole, means that departments guard their boundaries carefully, and, as we have seen, interdepartmental coordination is difficult. The strength of the French *grands corps* and the politicization of policy-making in France mean that ministers and their higher civil servants are not as insulated from the consequences of their decisions. As Suleiman notes, 'There is scarcely a question that can be settled within a single *direction* or in a single ministry; jurisdiction is widely distributed and often without the least concession to rationality.'[20] The interpenetration of politics and administration, in turn, leads to *complicité* and the balancing of national and local interests by the major departments of national government. By virtue of being more visible and unified, the administration becomes a focus of local politics and is, in turn, curbed by the communes.

The clearest illustration has been the complex process of reforming local taxation in France. Both politicians and administrators have been hardpressed to provide incentives for reform, and in the prolonged struggle have devised a series of policy devices to meet mayors' demands for more public works, more local investment and more loans. The *loi Bonnet* of 1979–80 was only the most recent in a long series of struggles between national and local political forces, and would be almost unimaginable in Britain. Preliminary bargaining and compromise is the prerequisite to French policymaking, and there is no sharper contrast than the hastily assembled and abrupt changes proposed in Britain by Heseltine in 1979. Less obvious are the confusions and delay incurred in Britain over more complex central–local problems such as racial discrimination, public housing, pollution, inner city rehabilitation and land-use planning. French policymakers do not have the indulgence of considering a single issue at a time nor can they demand changes in local government without also providing incentives for change. Although the presidentialism of the Fifth Republic may be at odds with French democratic traditions,[21] a strong executive has been forced to recognize local political leadership and its repercussions throughout the policy process through the *cumul des mandats*.

From a comparative perspective, the aim of the study has been to show how policymaking is imbedded in the institutional and political fabric of the two countries. British dogmatism appears in the difficulties of redefining policy objectives, linking aims to implementation and performance, and learning from earlier policy experiences. But the rigidities of the British policymaking process are not simply those of intransigent leaders and wilful neglect. On the contrary, actors in the process have worked extremely hard to change the nature of British central–local relations. The dogmatic quality of British policymaking appears more in the inability to adapt institutions to new problems and to experiment with organizational innovations.[22] The organizational and institutional requirements of policymaking under conditions of great complexity, largely the result of an expanding welfare state, seem to elude British policymakers. In the subnational system, these characteristics are revealed in both the weak vertical links between political leaders at various levels of government and in the horizontal compartmentalization of the administrative system. The new organizations and intergovernmental agencies that might cut across such self-imposed insulation of national policymaking are also more clearly subordinated to ministerial and departmental control than in most modern democracies. The multiplication of centrally nominated bodies for regional planning, arts, sports, water development, tourism, health and transportation were labeled by Keith-Lucas as 'monuments to the lack of faith on the part of central government in local democracy'.[23]

Contrary to the often expressed image of France as a highly centralized state, policies affecting communes, and a fairly wide range of related policies, are open to local political influence. Nor is it as clear as Crozier and others have argued that administrative resistance in itself explains the more incremental policymaking approach of the French. The technical and administrative elite have made numerous blunders and have been frequently repulsed in their attempts to impose new policies. The 'honeycomb' of central–local relationships, as described by Thoenig,[24] may produce more durable, more acceptable and more effective policy changes. Initiating change presupposes more careful efforts to aggregate support which, in turn, means that information and compromises are more likely to be considered in advance of reform. The more complex setting also means that incentives and bargaining commit both lower-level politicians and administrators to new policy objectives and to their implementation. The price, of course, is that France cannot engage in massive structural change of the subnational system. On the other hand, British efforts to make more ambitious reforms without fully involving lower levels of government and divorced from the administrative system as a whole have fallen short of their announced aims.

LOCAL DEMOCRACY: DISPERSING POWER IN THE WELFARE STATE

The fundamental issue of local democracy in the welfare state is whether local political initiatives can any longer influence national policies. In Britain this issue has been clouded by frequent insistence that local autonomy in itself is the only acceptable evidence of local democracy, an argument that was perhaps most forcefully made in the Layfield Report. But the complex decisions and policies of the welfare state no longer permit such a clear separation of decisions and areas of responsibility. Were local government only about activities that could be readily separated from national interests and from social and economic changes affecting the society as a whole, one might realistically consider specific functions or specific choices that might be reserved to local councils. Even the financial support that the

Layfield Committee hoped would be given local government would not be likely to detach localities from the burdens of changing interest rates, lending controls, unemployment levels, industrial relocation, etc., that affect the context of local decisions and inescapably bring national government into policy areas affecting localities. The wide variations in services and spending among British local authorities suggests that there are already considerable differences in their behavior and policies. The point is not that autonomy is not a desirable quality of local government, but that governmental complexity and changing policy problems require a supple, adaptable relationship between local and national government.

Modern democratic government is faced with not just one problem, local democracy, but also how national democratic institutions will adjust to an expanded state. Democratic government, at all levels, depends on how partisan demands can enter into policymaking choices. Quite conceivably, one could have a highly democratic national politics with very little effective policy responsibility at the local level. The countries often described as consociational democracies appear to have tendencies in this direction although it is significant that even in these cases there is evidence that many national policies depend heavily on local support for implementation. Britain opted for a form of democracy that placed enormous importance on adversarial behavior at the national level. As Johnson wrote, 'Few countries' systems of government can have institutionalized the role of Mephistopheles as the British.'[25]

But the close examination of local reform policies, and very possibly other policy areas as well, suggests that adversarial politics can only endure while it exercises severe self-restraint. As happened with the 1972 Local Government Act, the polarized contenders for power can only live with each other by promising that they will not habitually undo the other's work. Were parliamentary majorities, reinforced by strong Cabinet government, to unleash their full constitutional powers to reverse and disassemble their competitors' policies, British policymaking would be incoherent and the British welfare state reduced to a shambles.

Thus, the British problem about the future of local democracy is imbedded in the political system of which it is a part. While the effort to enlarge the area of independent choice of local government is no doubt a worthy objective, it is likely to falter in Britain, as in any democratic system, when local reform presupposes changes at the national level which the system cannot accept. In this sense, there are political restraints to policymaking. The point was well made by Norton in commenting on a recent inquiry about the Greater London Council, and his observations suggest how national adversarial politics so easily overrides local government. The report, he writes, follows 'the tradition of official reports by making no reference to the political system' and he continues to ask '. . . does not our system of local democracy depend on offering strategic alternatives at all levels of government and does this not imply conflict?'[26] Though one can easily find specific decisions that have been mediated by ministers to favor local authorities aligned with their party, Norton seems to be underscoring a more basic characteristic of partisan policymaking in British national politics. Favors are one thing, but it is the ease with which locally expressed partisan differences can be ignored that differentiates Britain from France, and from most modern democracies.

If the effect of partisan decisions on policymaking is taken as one indicator of the strength of democratic politics, British politics is in some respects almost self-consciously bipartisan. Put in policy terms, partisan decisionmaking enters into problems only when they have been considerably simplified and often produces, not surprisingly, rather narrowly conceived solutions. In part, this is because of the enormous concentration of power in Parliament and the great risks to British democracy were this power misused. It is also because over the past century, British politics, as Beer has so admirably shown, has been preoccupied with the transformation of parties, ideological threats to political consensus, and the preservation of parliamentary stability. But these achievements have been purchased by narrowing the scope, and very likely the effectiveness, of partisan politics in the policy process. As the issue of local reform has demonstrated, Parliament rarely considers the interlocking problems of national and local government and Cabinets regularly conduct local inquiries and reports in ways that exclude consideration of national policymaking. In the later stages of policy implementation and evaluation, ministers and even MPs (compared to most democratic systems) are remarkably vulnerable to the shortcomings and weaknesses of their own choices. Were they not, as has been pointed out, strong Cabinet government and parliamentary supremacy would be at risk.[27]

In contrast, the French seem to thrive on institutional and organizational tension, not only among the various levels of government but also within the administrative system. As Suleiman notes, within the administration 'authority is challenged incessantly'.[28] The form of 'institutionalized blackmail' that Hayward sees within the British political system,[29] and that is concentrated in Westminster and Whitehall, simply does not work in France. The system is much more complex than simplistic models of pluralist politics would suggest, and is probably best observed by tracing partisan effects on major policy choices such as local reform. Partisan influence over policies is not the reserve of central government, but is dispersed among the major actors and interests for nearly any major issue confronting the country. To some extent this is because of the instability of French government itself and, more recently, the challenge to the governing majority (itself a changing composite of parties) by the Left. But as we have seen, elections permeate the entire structure of government and parties depend on regional, departmental and local office to assemble their political forces. The result is that it has been much more difficult to nationalize French politics than British politics, and, in turn, to exclude local politics from national decisions.

Of course, within the context of French politics, local democracy also pays a price, but it does not seem as high as that extracted in order to subordinate British local councils to national policies. First, national government has been regularly defeated in trying to impose reform arbitrarily. Second, it has not been possible to divorce local spending and investment decisions from national taxation and investment plans. Third, the local politicians, reinforced by their cohorts in the Senate and the National Assembly, infiltrate the administration. Even ideologically, partisan forces are subdued. Communists and Socialists are the equal of any Gaullist or Republican mayor in extracting benefits from Paris. In fact, the subnational system is able to play an important integrative role in French politics because its policymaking role is important. In simpler terms, the entire subnational system is politicized and the activity of politicians at many levels of government is essential in framing questions as well as implementing decisions.

Within the communes there also appears to be a wider range of choice for democratic government. In the small communes, it pays to have a national figure as mayor. Pinay, for example, was mayor of Saint Chaumond for nearly forty years and limited his activity in local elections to a single poster, 'recalling to my citizens that I am always a candidate'.[30] But a Socialist mayor of Marseille, Deferre, has also organized a formidable party machine, and a leading Socialist of the north, Mauroy, is mayor of Lille, president of the regional council and an influential deputy. As we have seen, the Gaullists did not have strong local roots in 1958, and they learned to qualify their *dirigiste* style of national decisionmaking under the pressures of local politics and the threat of electoral defeat in many parts of France. Thus, local democracy can have a larger part in French politics because French politics and institutions have never been as completely nationalized as British politics and institutions.

Given the immense variation in the size and resources of French communes, the French have been less prone than the British to see the commune as an instrument of national redistributive policies, an almost inescapable consequence of the heavy service burden of British local councils. The result has been that communes have had a voice in national decisions while also being less obligated to fulfil national policy objectives. Favored by the rapid urbanization of France over the past twenty years, cooperation from the communes was essential to meet national economic and industrial aims, and the large communes in particular were able to extract numerous fiscal and investment benefits from Paris. There were, then, incentives to maintain the vitality and initiative of local politics which, despite the more global reform in Britain, never arose in the British subnational system. What British central government wished to extract from local councils could be accomplished at very low political costs, most visible perhaps in the fiscal constraints on local spending.

In so far as national and local democracy are any longer separable issues in the age of the welfare state, it has almost inevitably become a function of the ability of local government to enter into national decisions. Community politics may have influence within limited areas of choice and voluntary groups still have an important role in making local needs and preferences known, but the complexity of policy choices produces mutual dependence between levels of government. Indeed, the more important economic issues such as levels of spending, investment and taxation become, the greater the interdependence of national and local decisions. The politics of policymaking in the welfare state eludes reliable and durable disaggregation in territorial units. The irony is that the inability of French national government to make sense of 36,000 communes forced Paris to recognize local politics as an important force in the national decisions, while the relative ease of territorial consolidation in Britain helped preserve an insular notion of local democracy that probably cannot endure in an age of highly intricate and interdependent decisions.

From this perspective, the threat to local democracy is no different than the threat to national democracy. By virtue of expanding the role of the state, redistributing income and enlarging opportunities, Britain, France and most advanced industrial states have seen the public sector grow rapidly. The issue becomes one of whether both locally and nationally elected officials can enter into the policy process. As this study has argued, there are numerous features of British national and local institutions that compartmentalize decisions, isolate levels of government from each other, and insulate national leaders from local politics. Much of this behavior can be observed by studying 'non-decisions'. Many policy options might have brought national and local policymaking into closer proximity, but were foregone, most often to protect Cabinet government and Parliament. British local reform has been geared toward increasing the efficiency of local government and toward improving its service capabilities, but political interaction within the subnational system has changed very little since the rise of the Labour Party.

The consolidation of local authority areas, the multiplication of the intergovernmental and regional agencies of Whitehall, the reshuffling of functions, and most spectacularly of all, devolution, have all demonstrated that Parliament, and very likely the higher civil service, does not want to be engaged in continuous and laborious bargaining and compromises with local government. In short, if there is no structure that continually and effectively links local options and decisions to national policies at many stages of the policy process, then local democracy is eroded by default for there are few incentives and little evidence that local political activity is a force to contend with. This is not to deny that many local services fail to generate strong partisan feelings, but even policies toward public housing, transport and services are inextricably dependent on national decisions concerning the future of the public sector, national fiscal and monetary policy, and how national departments and agencies also concerned with these policies establish priorities. All too often the only political choice left to the local authority is direct confrontation with national government which serves neither national nor local interests.

There are numerous reasons why the French subnational system has never been as easily divorced from national policymaking. The mayors have a direct claim on political legitimacy, the administrative system is often divided or uncertain, the weaker multiple party system enhances local leaders, and the territorial complexity of the communes requires patience and planning by national officials in order to achieve national objectives. Neither national nor local politicians can disregard their interdependence, and both have learned to use mutual dependence as a political weapon. Because the communes have always been considered 'small republics' in French political rhetoric, one might think that local democracy would be a more burning issue in France than Britain. In reality, it is virtually the reverse. The communes are a political base from which to infiltrate and permeate the entire policy process. Knowing that the intervention of local political leaders has real policy consequences, French voters turn out in great numbers for local elections and are enthusiastic participants in the struggle against 'l'État'. The fact that the state is in many ways no more coherent than the locality deters few in constructing the intricate networks of political influence that mediate national and local political interests.

If the future of local democracy is inextricably tied to the effectiveness of national democracy, the risk to both is that the intricacy and interdependence of policymaking in the welfare state will make local political actors obsolete. If this seems a grim possibility, it should also be remembered that the accomplishments of the welfare state would not have been achieved without effective local actors. There are few reasons to think that their importance in implementing and evaluating public policies will diminish. The more difficult political problem is whether national policymakers will acknowledge their dependence on local actors and will have the ingenuity to construct ways to express the reciprocal interests of national and local government. In the case of Britain, what is surprising is that Westminster and Whitehall could be so dependent on local councils and their work without constructing more explicit ways of considering their mutual interests, while in the case of France the risk for the future is more that the system of *complicité* will become a damaging burden in devising new options and establishing new national priorities. What may be lacking in Britain may be practiced to excess in France.

Our conclusion, then, is that central–local relations, viewed through the multidimensional components of the subnational system, are paradoxically more formal and rigid in Britain, a country often admired for its pragmatic politics. In France, the subnational system is more important to the political system and the formalities of administrative and political behavior can easily cloak the more flexible and diverse ways that political actors have devised to influence each other. But it should be remembered that the more dogmatic British view of central–local relations, and of local government reform more generally, is imbedded in a democratic system that places unique and extraordinary powers in national government, while the suppleness and ingenuity of French central–local relations is the product of a more fragile democracy. British politics, if not British government, would be little changed were local councils to disappear. Without the commune, however, French politics would be unimaginable.

NOTES: CHAPTER 8

1 Charles Booth conducted an immense study of poverty in London at the turn of the century, *Life and Labour of the People in London*, 17 Vols (London: Macmillan,

1903). Haussmann was commissioned by Napoleon III to rebuild Paris. For a lively account of this early bulldozing operation see Brian Chapman, 'Baron Haussmann and the planning of Paris', *Town Planning Review* (October 1953), pp. 177–92.

2   The pressures for restructuring central–local relations have almost uniformly been the product of new national initiatives and needs. See, for example, Martha Derthick, *Between State and Nation* (Washington, D.C.: Brookings Institution, 1974); Donald Smiley, *Canada in Question: Federalism in the Seventies* (New York: McGraw-Hill, 1972); and the materials on West Germany, Holland and Sweden in Kenneth Hanpf and Fritz W. Scharpf (eds), *Interorganizational Policy Making* (Beverly Hills, Calif.: Sage Publications, 1978).

3   Though not focused on policy studies as such, the important work raising the issue was Peter Bachrach, *The Theory of Democratic Elitism* (Boston: Little Brown, 1967).

4   There are now a variety of Marxist approaches to central–local and urban problems. A more standard Marxist version which concentrates on class politics is Manuel Castells, *City, Class and Power* (trans. by Elizabeth Lebas) (London: Macmillan, 1978). More structural Marxist interpretations see the locality as an instrument of a capitalist-inspired state, such as Cynthia Cockburn, *The Local State* (London: Pluto Press, 1978); and James O'Connor, *The Fiscal Crisis of the State* (New York: St Martin's, 1973).

5   See Thomas R. Dye, *Politics, Economics and the Public: Policy Outcomes in American States* (Chicago: Rand McNally, 1967).

6   Local institutions pose a difficult choice for Marxists. On the one hand, local problems may be seen as a manifestation of working class protest and, therefore, advancing their particular interpretation of history. On the other hand, they may be interpreted as a buffer for a capitalist state and a way of dividing social classes. Perhaps the most interesting evidence of this problem, in many ways very similar to those preferring a more political interpretation, is the divergence within and between Socialist and Communist Parties over local government policy and strategy.

7   For a structural analysis stressing the political requirements of British politics and how they affect other policy areas, see Douglas E. Ashford, *Politics and Policy in Britain: The Limits of Consensus* (Oxford: Blackwell, and Philadelphia, Pa.: Temple University Press, 1981).

8   The classic study is Samuel H. Beer, *British Politics in the Collectivist Age* (New York: Knopf, 1967). Although the reconciliation which he discusses does not bear directly on local politics, it was of course essential to the British consensual compromise that divisive local politics and ideological splinter groups be excluded.

9   On the interwar period see Stéphane Rials, *Administration et Organisation 1910–1930* (Paris: Editions Beauchesne, 1977); on the postwar period, Ezra Suleiman, *Elites in French Society: The Politics of Survival* (Princeton, NJ: Princeton University Press, 1978).

10 Stanley Hoffman, *Decline or Renewal? France Since the 1930s* (New York: Viking Press, 1974), p. 450.

11 Quoted in J. P. D. Dunabin, 'V. The politics of the establishment of county councils', *The Historical Journal*, vol. 6 (1963), p. 226. Even the growth of local government functions was viewed with alarm. See, for example, M. Foster, 'The growth of the local government board', *Nineteenth Century*, vol. 53 (1903), pp. 107–12.

12 There are reasons to think that comparative analysis of political authority is well suited to institutional analysis. See Douglas E. Ashford, 'The structural analyses of policy or institutions really do matter', in Ashford (ed.), *Comparing Public Policies* (Beverly Hills, Calif.: Sage Publications, 1978), pp. 81–98. A similar view at the level of political systems is Harry Eckstein, 'Authority patterns: a structural basis for political inquiry', *American Political Science Review*, vol. 67 (December 1973), pp. 1142–61.

13 For example, see Fred Hirsch, *Social Limits to Growth* (Cambridge, Mass.: Harvard University Press, 1976); and Albert Breton, *An Economic Theory of Representative Government* (New York: Beresford Book Service, 1974).

14 Essentially, the task is to see how much variance in a system can be accounted for by distinctly political factors. The most ambitious attempt to explicate the problem is Adam Prezaorski and Henry Teune, *The Logic of Comparative Analysis* (New York: Wiley, 1970). For application of this kind of analysis to local government, see Douglas E. Ashford, 'Theories of local government: some comparative

considerations', *Comparative Political Studies*, vol. 8 (April 1975), pp. 90–107.

15 For example, see Hugh Heclo, *Modern Social Politics in Britain and Sweden* (New Haven, Conn.: Yale University Press, 1974).

16 For microstudies of the relationship between spending, resources and party politics, see the Appendix. Oddly enough, the variation is used by both major parties to justify new controls. See the recent study of Ian Coutts, 'Cuts and costs', *County Councils Gazette*, vol. 72 (September 1979), pp. 180–1.

17 L. J. Sharpe, 'Theories and values of local government', *Political Studies*, vol. 18 (June 1970), pp. 153–74.

18 No author, 'What the Local Government Bill should be', *Westminster Review*, vol. 12 (1888), p. 277. The writer estimates that there were about 32,000 local authorities and boards at the time.

19 Pierre Grémion, 'L'Administration territoriale', in M. Crozier (ed.), *Ou va l'administration française?* (Paris: Éditions d'Organisation, 1974), p. 84.

20 Ezra Suleiman, *Power, Politics and Bureaucracy* (Princeton, NJ: Princeton University Press, 1974), p. 213.

21 The most sober evaluation of this raging controversy is by Pierre Massot, *Le Chef du Gouvernement en France* (Paris: Documentation Française, 1979).

22 This problem appears most dramatically in organizational studies of British decisionmaking. See Les Metcalfe, 'Policy making in a turbulent environment', in Hanpf and Scharpf (eds), op. cit., pp. 37–55.

23 Bryan Keith-Lucas, 'What price local democracy?', *New Society*, 12 August 1976, p. 340. For a full account of the nineteenth century see Henry Parris, *Constitutional Bureaucracy* (London: Allen & Unwin, 1969).

24 For his exposition of the 'honey-comb', see J.-C. Thoenig, 'State bureaucracies and local government in France', in Hanpf and Scharpf (eds), op. cit., pp. 167–97.

25 Nevil Johnson, *In Search of the British Constitution* (Oxford: Pergamon, 1977), p. 69.

26 Alan Norton, 'Editorial – Local government reorganization in the 1980s?', *Local Government Studies* (New Series), vol. 4 (1978), p. 5.

27 Recent dramatic evidence is the dispute within the Labour Party over reselection of MPs. There are few modern democracies where the modest proposals of the Labour Left would be considered very radical or even very new.

28 Ezra Suleiman, *Politics, Power and Bureaucracy*, op. cit., p. 30.

29 Jack Hayward, 'Institutional inertia and political impetus in France and Britain', *European Journal of Political Research*, vol. 4, 1976, p. 350.

30 *Le Monde*, 5 March 1965.

Appendix

BIBLIOGRAPHIC ESSAY AND RESEARCH
GUIDANCE

GENERAL

The works cited in this volume are listed by author in the index.
Rather than list them once again, I decided that it would be more
useful to provide those interested in pursuing research on
central–local relations with my own estimate of various sources in the
two countries, many of them yet to be fully explored and analyzed. In
citing works in this Appendix, I provide only the date if the full
citation is located in the end-of-chapter notes. There is somewhat less
notation concerning national studies, though these I believe to be
essential if one is to place the local government system in context. To
some extent, this essay reflects my own experience in interviewing
officials, using libraries and sharing scholarly opinions in the two
countries. As such, I hope it will be both an encouragement and an aid
for those who pursue research on this or related topics.

The 1970s witnessed a renewal of interest in central–local relations
for reasons which form the theme of this study. Until recently, then,
the two countries have usually been treated separately or in wholly
institutional or legal terms. These characteristics make Brian
Chapman's studies of local government (1953) and prefects (1955) no
less valuable and they remain useful starting points in studying French
local government. The reorientation of American political science in
the 1960s tended to neglect intergovernmental relations and central–
local relations in particular. For this reason Mark Kesselman's study
(1967) is in many ways a landmark, and his essay on over-institutionalization in France (1970) an important analytical departure from
mainstream research of that period. The long-standing interest of
British scholars in France was kept alive in the 1960s by Phillip
Williams (1958, 1964) whose national studies often pinpoint the local
roots of French politics. The work of Jack Hayward and Michael
Watson (eds) (1975) on regional government and planning deals with
many questions on central–local relations. Hayward's strong interest
in local and regional politics is well documented in his textbook on
France (1973) which looks at the French system from a policy perspective, as does V. Wright's textbook (1978). There is also a useful set of
essays, edited by V. Wright and L. Lagroye, *Local Government and*

*A number of persons read the early version of this bibliography and made helpful
notes and additions: Michèle Breuillard (Lille), Peter Gourevitch (San Diego), David
McKay (Essex), Yves Mény (Rennes), Peter Richards (Southampton), Gail Russell
(Swarthmore), R. A. W. Rhodes (Essex), Jerry Webman (Princeton) and Bruce Wood
(Manchester).*

Administration in Britain and France (London: Allen & Unwin, 1978).

Given the nature of the French local government system, there is no separate book on all aspects of the system. Jacques Moreau's guide to local government law (1976, 3rd edn) is indispensable and contains a great deal of helpful information. The relationship between levels of government is perhaps best conveyed in the earlier studies of the Crozier group, particularly Grémion and Worms (1968) and Grémion (1969). Jean-Claude Thoenig's study of the formation of the Ministry of Infrastructure (1973) is excellent in order to understand central–local interaction.

For the beginning student there are numerous basic books on Britain. On the basic structure there is Peter Richards (1978, 3rd edn); P. W. Jackson (1976); Redcliffe-Maud and Wood (1974); and Brand (1974). The latter places the British system in a more distinctly political setting, but the case study of passing the law (Wood, 1976) is a rich political chronicle. American students wishing to grasp the British perspective on their system can still read Sharpe's article (1970) with profit. Newton has also written several pieces contrasting the American and British urban politics: *Political Studies*, vol. 17 (1969), pp. 208–18 and in Terry Clark (ed.), *Comparative Community Politics* (New York: Halstead, 1974), pp. 55–86. A brief version of the ideas for this study is contained in my contribution to S. Tarrow *et al.* (eds) (1978), pp. 245–289. For someone who has not thought much about central–local issues Chapter 9 of Gordon Smith's book, *Politics in Western Europe* (New York: Holmes & Meier, 1973), is a good overview.

There were so many critical articles on the Royal Commission on Local Government that it is difficult to select the most important. Those raising more theoretical questions are Rhodes (1974), Ashford (1974), Bristow (1972) and Hartley (1971). In addition to the accounts of the Commission in the local government texts, see B. Rose (ed.), *England Looks at Maud* (London: 1970); Jane Morton, *The Best Laid Schemes* (London: 1970); and Bryan Keith-Lucas and Michael Steed, *The Maud Report* (London: 1970). There is a good account of its organization and members by Wiseman in the book he edited, *Policy Making and Royal Commissions*, pp. 96–144. More recently, the Commission's Research Director, L. J. Sharpe, has provided an insider's account, in M. Bulmer (ed.), *Social Research and Royal Commissions* (London: Macmillan, 1980), pp. 18–33. A no less critical assessment in French is Jack Hayward's, 'Société bloquée et collectivités locales en Angleterre: La réforme rétrograde en 1972', *Bulletin de l'Institut International d'Administration Publique*, vol. 39 (1975), pp. 453–71.

Although the British and French have been observing each other closely (and often with apprehension) for centuries, there has been remarkably little comparison of the two systems. There is beginning to be a more substantial introductory literature in English on French central–local relations. Peter Gourevitch contributed a good analysis of French regional politics and policy to Tarrow *et al.* (eds) (1978), pp. 28–63, and has an article on recent changes in *Comparative Politics*, vol. 10 (1978), pp. 69–88. Another account of recent policies is provided by Machin in *West European Politics*, vol. 1 (1978), pp. 133–50. The relation to national policymaking is taken up in a review article I did for *Comparative Politics*, vol. 9 (1977), pp. 483–99. On the divisions among local elites see the essay of Suzanne Berger *et al.*, *Political Quarterly*, vol. 40 (1969), pp. 436–60. Keeping track of the centralization debate in France is a formidable task, but the volumes (formerly theses) of Yves Mény (1974), Henry Roussillon (1972) and Georges Dawson (1969) provide excellent material. The studies of Yves Madiot (1973) and Paul Bernard (1969) are good overall presentations of how the system works and the need for reform. On the complexities of urban policymaking see Milch's study of Montpellier and Toulouse, *British Journal of Political Science*, vol. 4 (1974), pp. 139–62. Jerry Webman's thesis (1977) has been noted and is an excellent comparison of policymaking in Lyon and Birmingham. On the recent local elections there are summary articles that include good material on the nature of local party conflicts: Hayward and Wright (1971) and (1977). Hayward's study (1969) of the 1969 plebiscite also tells a lot about national and local party interaction.

French local government has never been divorced from national politics. There is important information in the administrative histories, of which Pierre Legendre (1969) is typical and well documented. Jacques Lagroye's study of the rise of Chaban-Delmas (1973), Jean-Marie Denquin's account of Chirac in Corrèze (1976) and the edited volume of Albert Mabileau (1971) are important reading. Though organized in a curious way, Maurice Bourjol's study of municipal reform (1975) is packed with information and provoking questions. Most books on national politics consider the problems of local government: the study of de Gaulle's regime by his collaborators G. Pilleul (ed.), '*L'Entourage' et de Gaulle* (Paris: Plon, 1979) and on territorial administration in particular by Jacques Aubert, 'L'administration du territoire', in B. Tricot *et al.*, *De Gaulle et le Service de l'Etat* (Paris: Plon, 1977), pp. 281–323, the Crozier group's collective work on administration (1974), the early volume of Charles Debbasch on administrative power (1969) and his more recently edited work (1976); and the critical study of the French elite by Birnbaum (1977). Among basic books on the communal system the works of Madiot (1973), Bernard (1969) and de Savigny (1971) are all useful. There is a good history study of Breton nationalism by Jack E. Reece, *The Bretons Against France* (Chapel Hill, N.C.: University of North Carolina, 1977), as well as Jack Hayward's analyses (1969, 1977).

Perhaps nothing portrays how levels of government are separated in Britain more closely than the more traditional studies of British local government. There is a longer tradition of local government history than in France, starting from the enormous historical studies of the Webbs and the invaluable study of Redlich and Hirst (1901, 2 Vols). Until the 1960s political writing on British local government was overshadowed by William A. Robson who made the London School of Economics a leader in local government scholarship. He saw the reluctance of central government to restructure local government (1931) and after the war became a vocal and persuasive advocate of reform (1966). Dame Evelyn Sharp's long tenure as Permanent Secretary of the old Ministry of Housing and Local Government makes her memoire (1969) extremely valuable. Another valuable study of how central and local policy relate was made by Sir Norman Chester (1951). Combined with what remains the most complete administrative study of central–local relations, Griffith's study (1966) suggests that many scholars saw the dilemmas of the British system. The Crossman *Diaries* (Vol. 1, 1975) covering his tenure at the ministry are a lively account of how ministerial influence is actually used.

There are a number of good, basic books on the British local government system, though most of the early works reflect the structural separation of the system itself and deal relatively little with central–local relations. Perhaps the best standard text is P. W. Jackson (1976, 3rd edn), though the early editions of J. H. Warren's *The English Local Government System* (London: Allen & Unwin, 1965, 8th edn) and P. G. Richards' *The English Local Government System* (London: Allen & Unwin, 1978, 3rd edn) are useful to follow the evolution of the system. The volume by Lord Redcliffe-Maud and Bruce Wood (1974) provides a straightforward account, as does Peter Richards' *'Reformed' Local Government System* (London: Allen & Unwin, 1973). By far the richest source is The New Local Government Series of Allen and Unwin, edited by Peter Richards. In that series, his own book on the implementation of the Local Government Act of 1972 (1975) and Bruce Wood's study of making the law (1976) are essential reading. In the series there are also books on education by David Reagan (1977), on housing by J. B. Cullingworth (1966), on finance by N. P. Hepworth (1977, 3rd edn), on participation by Dilys Hill (1974) and thirteen additional titles. The recent publication in the series of a twentieth century history by Bryan Keith-Lucas and Peter Richards (1978) is especially welcome. Jack Brand's study of the system (1978) has both historical perspective and a strong policy emphasis.

There are several useful bibliographies, but more could be done to assemble records of the growing volume of local government studies. The ECPR Workshop on Local Government and Politics published a twenty-nine page list on France in its *Newsletter*, no. 4 (September 1976) (part I) and no. 8 (September 1978) (part II) by Lise Chazel. Another on Britain appeared in the *Newsletter*, no. 1 (April 1975). A selected bibliography for Britain and France appears in Ashford, Pempel and Katzenstein, *Comparative Public Policy: A Bibliography* (Beverly Hills, Calif.: Sage, 1978). See also *Bibliography of British and Irish Municipal History* by G. H. Martin and S. McIntyre (Leicester University Press, 1972); and an earlier version on Britain only by C. Cross (1966). The HMSO publishes sectional lists from time to time, listing important publications of the DoE and other ministries. The DoE continues to publish a guide to research they are sponsoring. Perhaps the most widely available bibliography of all official documents is the HMSO listing which appears monthly and in an annual volume. It is especially helpful in picking one's way through committee hearings, White Papers and annual reports.

Publications of Documentation Française can be confusing, but a careful reading of the *Répertoire des Publications Periodiques et de Serie de l'Administration Française* is helpful. Although it lists mostly administrative documents and books, the *Bulletin Signaletique de Science Administrative*, Centre de Documentation en Sciences Humains, CNRS, contains a great deal on local problems. Now dated, but still useful, is a volume by Wilfred H. Snape, *How to Find Out about Local Government* (Oxford: Pergamon, 1969). A more recent listing of all local authorities with office locations, chief executives and phones is *Godwin's Concise Guide to Local Authorities in England and Wales* (London: Godwin, 1974). Another standard British source with a variety of information is the *Municipal Yearbook*, and the ever-handy *Whittaker's Almanac* has a short section on local government. Mention should also be made of the regional newspapers which can be consulted in the Periodicals Library of the British Museum at Colindale. Papers such as the *Birmingham Post* and old *Manchester Guardian* provided detailed information on local elections, local voluntary associations and even listings of local notables from time to time.

A number of statistical publications have been noted in the book. The data is now quite good and improving steadily for both Britain and France. Under the title *Les Finances du Secteur Public Local* since 1975, and *Le Secteur Public Local* from the early 1960s, the Direction de la Comptabilité Publique, Ministry of the Economy and Finance (now Ministry of the Budget) publishes local income and spending accounts. From 1972 there are three volumes: *Communes, Départements et Établissements Publics, Les Hopitaux Publics, les Organismes d'HLM, les Sociétés d'Économie Mixte* and *Les Communes de Moins de 10,000 Habitants*. From 1968 these statistics are much more complete than in earlier years, and from 1972 the breakdown by size of commune is extremely useful. Since 1962, as part of the *loi de finances*, there is an annual publication *Statistiques et Indicateurs des Régions Françaises*, with a variety of social, financial, economic and demographic information. Since 1975 DAFU has annually published *Recueil d'Informations Statistiques sur l'Urbanisme*, which provides basic information on progress of urban plans, zoning permissions, etc., as does *Études d'Urbanisme* published by Documentation Française.

The Chartered Institute of Public Finance and Accountancy (CIPFA, formerly the Institute of Municipal Treasurers and Accountants or IMTA) publishes detailed annual accounts on each spending category of all local authorities, covering the Rate Fund itself, education, housing, amenities, and all other local services. Details on the Rate Support Grant are traditionally published annually by the Association of County Councils on behalf of all the local government associations. *Local Government Trends* (CIPFA, annual since 1973) also provides a full account of Rate Support Grant negotiations and changes from year to year. For many years the HMSO has published *Local Government Financial Statistics: England and Wales*, with comparable figures for Scotland published by the Scottish Office. Because local election statistics, even in the aggregate, have been hard to find, the HMSO annual *Local Government Election Statistics*, begun in 1972, is very welcome though not broken down by authority. For earlier periods one must either rely on the partial information in the excellent accounts in *The Economist* or compile them from fairly complete accounts to be found in *The Times* and the regional newspapers. For more detailed voting results one is dependent on the local and regional newspapers.

THEORIES

Students often ask why there is not more theoretical work on local politics and government. The answer is that there are indeed a number of relevant theories, and the problem is more one of picking one's way among various interpretations. Nineteenth century political thought is replete with debates about decentralization from the classics of Tocqueville onward. The philosophical links are sketched by Wickwar (1970), and for France by Hoffman (in Maas (ed.), 1959) and Nelson (1975). As this book argues, historical circumstances seem to explain why there is less explicitly philosophical discussion for Britain, but J. S. Mill has much to say on the importance of local government. A promising departure into more general theories of democracy is by Paul Cousins, 'Theories of democracy and local government', *Public Administration Bulletin*, no. 23 (April 1977), pp. 40–53.

Perhaps the first contemporary effort to assess local government theories in Britain was MacKenzie (1961). Because territorial and regional conflicts have been renewed in Britain, the studies of Maas (1959) and the work of Fesler (1949, 1965) deserve attention. The entire American debate over fiscal federalism, introduced in the work of Oates (ed.) (1977), now seems relevant to the resource debates in Britain and France. There is also a lively debate about local autonomy in the United States of which the articles of Kirkpatrick (1970) and Stephens (1974) are good introductions.

There are probably five distinct theoretical debates. The first stems from the community power debate in the United States which dominated much theoretical discussion in the 1960s and is too extensive for citation. Clark's work probably best assembles the various viewpoints, (1974) and the (1972) article. The theoretical debate never took hold in British local research, but was related to France by Roig (1966). British disinterest may be a function of ease of subordination of local politics, and is to some extent reflected in the earlier writing of Sharpe (1970).

As noted in my Introduction and Conclusion, spatial and territorial concerns are not easily integrated into more general social and economic theories, so local government research has tended to neglect a second area of work by geographers. Possibly the best introductory work is by Cox (ed.) (1974, 1978), though one should also read Harvey's Marxist critique based on his own background in geography (1974). There are also good introductions to other aspects of spatial planning and social policy by Massam (1975), and by J. T. Coppock and W. R. D. Sewell (eds), *Spatial Dimensions of Public Policy* (London: Pergamon, 1976). The challenging theoretical issue is how to resolve these ideas with inequities in territorial representation itself. Important basic materials can be found in R. W. Johnston, *Political, Electoral and Spatial Systems* (Oxford: Oxford University Press, 1979).

A third distinguishable body of theoretical writing concerns policy formation and intergovernmental bargaining which raises difficult problems of distinguishing how political variance and policy outcomes can be conceived and measured between levels of government. Perhaps the most ambitious work is by Lundquist (1972) but there are less explicit concerns in Hood's study, *The Limits of Administration* (London: Wiley, 1976). My essays, (1974) and (1979), raise some of the comparative issues, and also an earlier Sage Professional Paper on Comparative Politics (1976), where I discuss some of the problems linking policies with the study of local politics. The Sage Paper of Kesselman and Rosenthal (1976) also has a distinct intergovernmental interest. On developments in Britain, see the essay of Andrew Gray, 'The study of public policy in local government: some reflections for British political science', *Public Administration Bulletin* (UK), vol. 18 (1975), pp. 13–23. Intergovernmental politics tends to spill over into group politics, which is well researched by Dearlove (1973 and 1979).

A fourth stream of theoretical writing, as yet not well integrated into central–local comparisons, concerns bureaucracy and administrative theory. For obvious reasons, the French instinctively associate administrative reform with territorial politics, as the work of Crozier (1964, 1974) and his students (Grémion, 1974; Thoenig, 1973; Grémion and Worms, 1969) so amply illustrated. Possibly the most exciting departure in French administrative writing is the effort of Sfez to link the juridical tradition to administrative theory in his *Décision et Pouvoir* (Paris: Union Générale d'Éditions, 1973) and in his colloque, *L'Objet Local* (Paris: Union Générale d'Editions, 1977) where one will find a fascinating diversity of views. Again, it is striking how the overall effects of the administrative system elude British writers, though the work of Self (1977, 2nd edn) is sensitive to the interaction of central and dispersed decisionmaking. Given the functional emphasis of British local government, it is not surprising that the most original work involves social administration for which the work of P. Hall, *Change, Choice and Conflict in Social Policy* (London: Heineman, 1975), is a good introduction. There are numerous specialized writings on the organization of health, personal social services, transportation, regional assistance and land-use planning.

More recent work on administration has branched into the sociology of organizations, most well represented by the work of Greenwood and Hinings (1973, 1974, 1977). They summarize their ideas in 'The study of local government: towards an organizational analysis', *Public Administration Bulletin*, no. 23 (April 1977), pp. 2–15; and more ideas for new inquiries are presented by M. J. Goldsmith and R. A. W. Rhodes (eds), 'New trends in local government research', an entire issue of *Public Administration Bulletin*, no. 28 (December 1978).

The fifth, and probably the most controversial, debate is between the neo-Marxist and neo-liberal writers. The first see central–local relations and localized influence as an extension of capitalist suppression; and the second express almost the opposite view in looking to restructured government and dispersed decisionmaking to articulate the external or social costs of government. Among the important neo-Marxist French writers are Castells (1974, 1978) and Lojkine (1972, 1973); and for Britain, Cockburn (1978) and parts of Dearlove (1979). There is also a good introductory book by Paul Saunders, *Urban Politics* (Harmondsworth: Penguin, 1979), which draws heavily on this tradition. The differences among French neo-Marxists have been well outlined by C. Pickvance, 'Marxist approaches to the study of urban politics', *International Journal of Urban and Regional Research*, vol. 1 (1977), pp. 218–55. See also the essays of Castells and Lojkine in M. Harloe (ed.), *Captive Cities* (New York: Wiley, 1977). The public choice group are interested in virtually the opposite problem: how best to disaggregate decisions, resource allocation and public spending. The broad concerns are found in Mancur Olson, 'The principle of "financial equivalence"; the division of responsibility among different levels of government', *American Economic Review*, vol. 59 (May 1969), pp. 479–87; and extended to local and state government by Gregg, 'Limits and levels of analysis', *Publius*, vol. 4 (1974), pp. 59–85. Both schools of thought are highly abstract, and might be profitably read against the critique of Harry W. Richardson in *Urban Studies*, vol. 9 (February 1972), pp. 29–48.

HISTORY

Many of the standard national histories are cited in relevant sections of this book. For France, the numerous regimes of the past two centuries have made it difficult to write a single historical account from a local perspective. Although meant as a bibliography of quantitative sources on French history, the volume edited by Val Lorwin and Jacob M. Price, *The Dimensions of the Past* (New Haven, Conn.: Yale University Press, 1972), provides a large number of local history sources. Recent work on the prefects of each regime suggests that the continuities may be greater than once recognized and that the prefect's integrative role in the development of the communes and departments may be underestimated, a position argued in particular by Guy Thuillier and Vincent Wright (1975). There is now a full account of the origins of the *intendants* in Richard Bonney, *Political Change in France under Richelieu and Mazarin 1624–1661* (Oxford: Oxford University Press, 1978). The work of Pierre Henri (1950) is rather formal, but traces their role from Napoleon to the Third Republic. There are now good studies in more depth for most periods. The Consulate and First Empire by Regnier (1907); the Restoration by Richardson (1966); the Second Empire by Le Clère and Wright (1973); the Third and Fourth Republics by Jeanne Siwek-Pouydessau (1969); and the early Fifth Republic by Howard Machin (1977).

The persisting regional identities in France mean that the superb regional studies tend to concentrate on more local problems and less on interaction with the center. See Dupeux (1962), and Phillipe Vigier,

La Second République dans la Région Alpine, 2 Vols (Paris: PUF, 1961); Paul Leuilliot, *L'Alsace au Début du XIXe Siècle: Essai d'Histoire Politique, Économique et Religieuse 1815–1830* (Paris: SEVPEN, 1960); Paul Bois, *Les Paysans de l'Ouest; des Structures Économiques et Sociales aux Options Politiques Depuis l'Époque Révolutionnaire dans la Sarthe* (Le Mans: Vilaire, 1960); Pierre Barral, *Le Département de l'Isère sous la Troisième République* (Paris: Colin, 1962); and André Armengaud, *Les Populations de l'Est Aquitain, au Début de l'Époque Contemporaine* (Paris: Imprimérie Nationale, 1961). To grasp the influence of rural France on national and local politics one should read Susanne Berger's *Peasants Against Politics* (Cambridge, Mass.: Harvard University Press, 1972). There are numerous histories of Paris, but an ambitious project to provide a complete administrative and political history has begun. The first volume, Jean Tulard, *Paris et son administration* (Paris: Fayard, 1976), covers 1800 to 1830.

An extremely useful book in understanding the continuing debate on decentralization in France is Odilon Barrot's *De la Décentralisation et des ses Éfforts* (Paris: Didier, 1871 – actually written in 1860). There is also a good monograph by B. Basdevant-Gaudement (1973) on the Decentralization Commission of Napoleon III. Local government in France has never been too distant from central finance and the study of L. Paul-Dubois, *Essai sur les Finances Communales* (Paris: Librairies-Editeurs, 1898) conveys the tenor and the details of this relationship at the turn of the century. There is also the fine history of the Caisse de Dépôts by Priouret (1966). Central–local relations also figure heavily in the writing of the turn of the century administrative reformers, Chardon (1911) and Leroy-Beaulieu (1871). On the departmental councils in the nineteenth century, see L. Girard *et al., Les Conseilleurs Généraux en 1870* (Paris: PUF, 1967).

Urban history in France tends to follow the pattern of provincial history, being mostly confined to local developments. Although rather elaborate books, the urban series published by Privat (Paris) is a good source for the general reader. The existing volumes are Jean Meyer (ed.), *Histoire de Rennes* (1971); Louis Trenard, *Histoire d'une Métropole: Lille-Roubaix-Tourcoing* (1977); Michel Mollat (ed.), *Histoire de l'Isle-de-France* (1971); and André Latreille, *Histoire de Lyons et du Lyonnais* (1975). French nineteenth century history is almost too controversial to hazard suggested reading. Nonetheless, Zeldin's monumental study (1972) portrays local life and the notables in rich detail. On the rebellious nature of the French countryside from the Revolution, Charles Tilly's *The Vendée* (Cambridge, Mass.: Harvard University Press, 1976), provides the groundwork and additional sources in a good bibliography. Another insightful study of rural development and local politics is E. W. Fox's *History in Geographic Perspective* (New York: Norton, 1971). John Merriman's *The Agony of the Republic* (New Haven, Conn.: Yale University Press, 1978) is sensitive to local affairs and documents a critical turning point of the century.

Thanks to André Siegfried and Georges Goguel there are numerous local studies of electoral geography. They reflect the national importance attributed to local elections in the French system. In addition to Barral (1962) see Serge Bernstein, 'La Vie du Parti radical: la fédération des Saone-et-Loire de 1919 à 1939', *Revue Français de Science Politique*, vol. 20 (1970), pp. 1136–80; Jean-Pierre Florin, 'Le radical-socialisme dans le département du Nord, (1911–1936)', *Revue Française de Politique*, vol. 24 (1974), pp. 236–76; Cristiane Marie, *L'Evolution du Comportement Politique dans une Ville en Expansion: Grenoble, 1871–1965* (Paris: Colin, 1966); Joseph Franchesi, *Un Demi-Siècle de Consultations Nationales dans la Circonscription de Charenton* (Paris: Les Editions de l'An 2000, 1972); Jean Quellion, *Les Élections dans la Manche: Étude de Sociologie Électorale 1919–1969* (Coutances: OECP, 1973); A. Olivesi and M. Roncayolo, *Geographie Electorale des Bouches-des-Rhône sous la Quatrième République* (Paris: Colin, 1961).

On the nineteenth century history of British local government, Redlich and Hirst (1901) remain the fullest account. However, there is a succinct and readable shorter history by K. B. Smellie (1968, 4th edn) in the Allen and Unwin Series. Keith-Lucas' book (1952) on the growth of the local government franchise conveys how British local politics was subordinated to national trends. Asa Briggs has written a good deal on Victorian cities and his book (1963) of the same name is most readable. The collection of writings by C. Lambert and D. Weir (1973) is also a good overview. More recently the University of Leicester Press has undertaken an urban history series of which the comparative urban study of Derek Frazer (1976) is excellent and the study of conservative domination of London by Ken Young (1975) is essential to understanding Labour's jubilation of 1934. Under the editorship of H. J. Dyos, Leicester began a biannual *Urban History Newsletter* and from 1974 an *Urban History Yearbook*. Raymond Williams's *The Country and the City* (London: Chatto & Windus, 1973) is highly readable and explains British rural romanticism.

Because the growth of services in Britain depended so heavily on local government, the basic histories of welfare record important changes at the local level, especially the books of Frazer (1973) and Bruce (1961) which explain much about the service orientation of British local government. The nineteenth century British debate on central–local relations was in many ways no less financial than in France and there is a fine history by Edwin Cannan (1912). To capture the richness of the debate one should also read George J. Goschen's reports and speeches (1872) and E. P. Hennock's excellent essay (1963) on urban finance in the nineteenth century. Another useful book, including several chapters on France and directly related to central–local relations, is J. Watson Grice, *National and Local Finance* (London: King, 1910).

By far the most complete history of the early development of British local government is the monumental series of eleven volumes published over a thirty-year period by Sidney and Beatrice Webb which trace its development from the early parish to the Municipal Corporation Act of 1835. To understand the early Victorian period, Sir Edwin Chadwick is a pivotal personality and his biography by S. Finer (1957) is also fun to read. Royston Lambert's biography of Sir

John Simon (1963) also reveals how the services orientation was imbedded in British local government. Though the Webbs' perspective is limited by their concentration on the statutory basis for local government, the first four volumes remain an unparalleled historical work: *The Parish and the County* (1906), *The Manor and the Borough* (1908, 2 Vols); and *Statutory Authorities for Special Purposes* (1922), all published by Longman, and now reprinted from the original plates by Archon Books.

The diverse internal politics of British cities is captured by Françoise Vigier in *Change and Apathy: Liverpool and Manchester during the Industrial Revolution* (Cambridge, Mass.: MIT Press, 1970). Although British county politics seldom influenced national affairs as directly as provincial relationships in France, there are some useful county histories like Sir Francis Hill on Lincoln (1974); J. D. Marshall (ed.), on Lancashire (1977). There are excellent studies on Leicester by Patterson (1954), on Bristol by Bush (1976), and by Hennock on several northern cities (1973). The most ambitious local history project is the Victorian History of the Counties of England, now nearly twenty volumes. Another excellent local history is Keith-Lucas' *The Unreformed System* (London: Croom Helm, 1980).

LIBRARIES AND MINISTRIES

Learning one's way around a foreign government can be frustrating. An indispensable document for France is the *Répertoire Administratif* published annually, listing top-level officials, addresses, phones and outlining ministerial organization. The comparable publication for Britain is the *Civil Service Yearbook* (London: HMSO, annually). My experience has been that officials are generally willing to spend an hour or more with serious questions from outsiders, though they sometimes want a week or two notice for appointments. Their free time can vary with parliamentary calendars and budget cycles when they are harder pressed. In France, it helps to have an introduction, though on the whole French officials have always seemed more accessible than British. French officials and secretaries making appointments are more relaxed when one conforms to the French habit of presenting a well-documented calling card. Do not be discouraged if you are sent to an assistant of a high official for he or she may have more time both to converse and to think about the work of the agency. Never fail to ask who else might be helpful or to mention other agencies where you might wish to meet someone. The most hospitable officials will often phone directly to their friends in the network and make an appointment for you.

My general impression is that government libraries are under-exploited by scholars interested in current problems. Remember, they exist to meet current needs of officials, though French ministerial libraries, in particular, have large collections from earlier periods. Knowing the organizational history of a ministry helps because collections have been shifted about with reorganizations over the years. Like most librarians, those working in ministerial libraries are usually helpful. Government libraries tend to be understaffed so one needs patience and tact. On the whole, American scholars of contemporary affairs tend to neglect the Public Records Office and parliamentary papers. On the recent effort to make public records more accessible, see M. Roper, 'Public records and the policy process in the twentieth century', *Public Administration* (UK), vol. 55 (1977). Any library collecting the British Parliamentary Papers will have the annual reports of the Local Government Boards from 1871 to 1929 which are included in the series – along with the major Royal Commission reports.

French librarians like you to know exactly what you want. Reasonably accessible libraries with all government documents are the Documentation Français, the Bibliothèque Nationale and the Fondation Nationale de Science Politique. There are good libraries for the Ministry of Infrastructure, Ministry of Finance and the Ministry of the Interior, though they prefer an introduction. In Britain, the old Ministry of Housing Library is the basic collection of the Department of the Environment. In all these libraries, there are quite good catalogs to the collections. Remember that administrative officials normally work with at most a six-month time frame so you can save time by reading earlier reports before interviewing them; and generally officials do not keep anything handy that is more than a year old.

The library of the École Nationale d'Administration is not open to the public, but one should try to be introduced there. It is well staffed, the librarians know both government and social science publications and the periodical collection is very good. Many of the French regional universities also have good collections, often with amazingly detailed catalogs of articles and clippings. The local government collection at the Universities of Bordeaux, Grenoble and Rennes are especially good. In Britain the only comparable collection is at the Institute for Local Government (INLOGOV) at the University of Birmingham, which is especially good in keeping track of DoE circulars, consultative papers, etc. Many British university libraries collect local government literature because of its importance as an employer. The library of the Royal Institute of Public Administration also has a good collection on local government and administration.

Although they have been used mainly by historians, part of the official responsibility of the department and the commune is to maintain records. For the larger cities these collections are extremely good. Because their librarians are not as heavily taxed as those in Paris, one is often more welcome and gets more help. A special note should be made of the French custom of keeping newspaper clipping files. These range all the way from the voluminous dossiers of *Le Monde* to those found at the Science Po library. Clipping files are a standard French library service and will be found in most provincial and departmental libraries as well. There are a number of excellent libraries maintained in Paris by the major pressure groups such as the Chambres de Commerce and the Conseil National du Patronat that are very well managed and have been extremely helpful to foreign scholars. Given the strong regional and local ties of these groups they collect a large amount of local documentation as well as most official information on local policy.

CENTERS

The major centers for local government research in Britain are INLOGOV at the University of Birmingham, the Urban Studies Unit at the University of Kent and the more recently established School of Advanced Urban Studies at the University of Bristol. In London the Centre for Environmental Studies does more quantitative research on urban planning but also conducts a variety of research on urban problems. More closely linked to regional and town planning are the planning units under Peter Hall at Reading University and George Cameron at Glasgow University. But nearly every university has one or more scholars with strong local government interests. Some years ago, the British SSRC sponsored a number of community studies, most of which are cited in this volume. In 1978 another series of studies was begun by the SSRC under George Jones.

Provincial France is still apparent in the vigorous and well-supported local government centers at many regional universities. Among the more prominent are the Centre d'Étude et Recherche sur la Vie Locale (CERVL) of the Institut d'Études Politiques, University of Bordeaux; the Centre d'Études et de Recherche sur l'Administration Économique et l'Aménagement du Territoire (CERAT), Institut d'Études Politiques, University of Grenoble; and the Centre de Recherches Administrative, Politiques et Sociales (CRAPS), University of Lille II. Central–local relations also figure heavily in the work of the Centre de Recherche et d'Études sur la Décision Administrative et Politique (CREDAP) under Sfez, and at the Centre Universitaire de Recherches Administratives et Politique de Picardie (CURAPP), whose director, J. Chevallier, and his colleagues wrote *Centre, Périphérie, Territoire* (Paris: PUF, 1979). The French publish an intermittent list of all urban studies centers, *Fiches Analytiques de le Recherche Urbaine en France*, edited by the Centre de Documentation sur l'Urbanisme, DAFU, Ministry of Infrastructure.

In the late 1960s the French government decided to invest heavily in local studies of many kinds. The funds came from the Centre National de la Recherche Scientifique (CNRS), often coordinated with ministerial proposals and plans. Of the latter, the most influential group has been the Centre de Recherche Urbaine under the Direction de l'Aménagement Foncier et de l'Urbanisme (DAFU), Ministry of Infrastructure (now renamed Ministry of the Environment and Quality of Life). Quantitative analysis of local spending has been done by Buinot (1976) and Fréville (1971, 1978) at the University of Rennes. There is also an urban research group associated with the Institut d'Économie des Transports, École des Mines. With the growing importance of the Caisse des Dépôts et Consignations, it now also follows local research more carefully. Over the 1960s, the expansion of DATAR meant that it, too, became a major sponsor of research, most of which can be found in its library. Because their quarters are cramped an introduction to DATAR is important. In 1978 CNRS undertook better coordination of its many sponsored projects by forming a Groupe de Recherche Coordonnées sur l'Administration Locale (GRAL) under Georges Dupois and Jean Buinot.

Paris seems to house a local research group for every taste. Comparable to American urban planning groups is the Institut d'Urbanisme de Paris at Créteil. There are two neo-Marxist groups, one led by Lojkine and the other by Castells. The Centre de Sociologie Urbaine in Paris has done many studies on the inequalities of urban services. The École des Hautes Études de Sciences Sociales also has an urban group. Though not primarily engaged in local government, the Institut Français des Sciences Administratives has undertaken an historical series on French administration under Guy Braibant, Michel Fleury and Jean Tulard which will add much to our knowledge of central–local relations. An official history of the *corps préfectorale* has begun at the Ministry of the Interior under Pierre Aubert (*Administration*, no. 98, December 1977).

PARTIES AND PRESSURE GROUPS

Not too surprisingly, the French parties are more active publishers and propagandists on local government and politics than the British, but the parties do not have substantial Parisian offices except for the Communists. Marcel Rosette (1977) is in charge of local government policy for the PCF which publishes numerous model programs and proposals. A number of general articles on regional and local politics appear in the *Cahier du Communisme*, the official intellectual review, and current news in *Communes et Départements Aujourd'hui*, an irregularly appearing monthly. The PCF also has its own local pressure group, the Association des Élus Communistes et Républicains. The Socialists also publish a monthly, *Communes et Régions de France*, and have their own local pressure group of Socialist mayors and councillors, the Fédération Nationale des Élus Socialistes et Républicains. The Gaullist local organization, the Mouvement National des Élus Locaux (MNEL) publishes a great deal of material, including the monthly *L'élu Local*. The MNEL is linked to a similarly conservative group defending rural areas, the Centre d'Information des Communes Rurales. As might be expected, the radicals also have an Association Nationale des Élus de la Gauche Radicale et Républicaine. On the Left is also found the Association pour la Démocratie et d'Education Locale et Sociale (ADELS) loosely linked to the PSU. ADELS publishes a monthly, *Correspondances Municipales*.

Obtaining general information from party headquarters varies a great deal with the structure and electoral requirements placed on the parties in each country. In general, party headquarters in Paris are rather closely guarded offices but their documents are widely available. In Britain there is a striking difference between the Labour Party which maintains only a skeletal staff and generally leaves electoral concerns to their constituency organizations, and the Conservative Party which seems to take local political organization more seriously. The Conservatives have a small staff working only on local government and publish very complete materials on local elections, at least until the reorganization made it harder to make sense of local voting data. The Labour Party has two local government officials who write circulars and news sheets, but their main task is to explain general party policy and to update the *Local Government Handbook* which provides overall direction for their local councillors.

Amid the various parties, there are several less overtly political groups. The Association des Maires de France (AMF) is the largest. Its monthly, *Département et Communes*, has been published since 1952, and contains a great deal of technical information for mayors. In the late 1960s there appeared an informal, but nonetheless influential group, the Association des Maires des Grandes Villes. The group thrived during the period of strong, independent mayors, and has recently been reorganized to represent major cities outside Paris. Since 1954 there has been an Assemblée des Presidents des Conseils Généraux. Another less influential group for departments is the Union Amicale des Conseillers Généraux de France. The Fédération Nationale des Maires de France – Communes Rurales is obviously conservative and publishes a bimonthly bulletin. Not to be outdone in segmenting the mayors, there is also an Association des Jeunes Élus with information published irregularly. Municipal councillors have the Fédération Nationale des Élus Républicains Municipaux et Cantonaux, and a monthly, *Communes de France*. A group which is less known, but considered influential in government circles is the Société des Secrétaires Généraux, the executive officers of large cities and towns. There is also a national committee of Presidents of Regional Councils. Although the Group d'Action Municipale (GAM) has lost strength they still hold an annual congress as do nearly all the party and pressure group organizations listed above.

Although political control of the British local government associations changes from time to time, they are quite objective reporters of current information, official decisions, committee proceedings, etc. (The Association of County Councils does speak of 'Socialists' rather frequently.) The ACC has published a monthly, the *County Councils Gazette*, for over seventy years and the AMA (formerly AMC or Association of Municipal Councils) publishes the *Municipal Review* and a more general periodical, *The Councillor*. CIPFA began publishing *Local Government Trends* in 1973, which included fairly lengthy accounts of all the major services until taking on a more skimpy format in 1977. CIPFA also publishes *Public Finance and Accountancy* (formerly *Local Government Finance*) which has some good general articles as well as details on financial, accounting and auditing changes. Perhaps the best French monthly on the day-to-day problems of the communes is *Vie Publique*, though it has less political news since changing ownership in 1974. The former editor, Guy Sorman, now publishes *La Lettre du Maire* which has a good deal of current news, *Correspondance Hebdomadaire* (a weekly) and *La J. O. du Maire* (a monthly with more technical information).

Although they are not strictly political writing, accounts of regional nationalism in France are used by parties, especially by the Socialists. The works of Lafont (1968, 1971, 1976) are typical of this literature. Perhaps more instructive is the book by the Breton leader who became a Socialist, Michel Philipponneau, *Débout Bretagne?* (Saint-Brieuc: Presses Universitaires de Bretagne, 1970); and Renaud Dulong, *La Question Bretonne* (Paris: Presses de la Fondation Nationale des Sciences Politiques, 1975). Regionalism is of course one of the forces which parties as well as government struggle with in France. An assessment of the internal colonialism interpretation is found in Eugene Weber's *Peasants into Frenchmen: the Modernization of Rural France, 1870–1914* (Stanford, Calif.: Stanford University Press, 1976), chapter 29. A more contemporary evaluation is provided by Jack Hayward, 'Dissentient France: the Counter Political Culture', *West European Politics*, vol. 1 (1978), pp. 53–67.

Like most questions, British regionalist sympathies have been readily subsumed, if not muffled, by national parties, though there are books, such as J. Osmond on Wales, *Creative Conflict* (London: Routledge Kegan Paul, 1978), and T. Nairn, *Devolution: The End of Britain?* (London: Jonathan Cape, 1977), showing that nationalism can be intense. For a sociological analysis, see Michael Hecter, 'The persistence of regionalism in the British Isles, 1885–1966', *American Journal of Sociology*, vol. 79 (September 1973), pp. 319–42, which should be read alongside Edward Page's critique, 'Michael Hecter's internal colonialism thesis: some theoretical and methodological problems', *European Journal of Political Research*, vol. 6 (1978), pp. 295–318. However, there are a number of standard studies of regional differences in Britain, such as Birch (1977), McCrone (1973), Holland (1976) and Bognador (1979) that deal more with the political problems.

As I note in this study, the reasons why the French see regional tensions as a common national problem, while the British tend to differentiate each regional protest, bears more investigation. In addition to the book of R. Rose on Northern Ireland (1971), the article of Paul Arthur in *Parliamentary Affairs*, vol. 30 (Winter 1977), pp. 97–106, provides a good account of long-standing conflict. On Scotland, L. J. Sharpe has written a provoking analysis in 'British politics and the two regionalisms', in W. D. Wright and D. H. Stewart (eds), *The Exploding City* (Edinburgh: Edinburgh University Press, 1972). The relative success of Scottish compared to the English local reorganization has been noted by J. D. Stewart in *Municipal Journal*, vol. 19 (January 1977), and there are longer articles on Scottish central–local relations by E. Page and on policyplanning by A. Midwinter in *Public Administration Bulletin*, no. 28 (Winter 1978).

The political and territorial diversity of the communes means that the French do less on the background and behavior of municipal councillors, although the Ministry of the Interior publishes their occupational background after local elections, and there is a good sociological study by J. Verdès-Leroux in the *Revue Français de Science Politique*, vol. 20 (1970), pp. 974–90. In contrast, there is a great deal done on British councillors: L. J. Sharpe, 'Elected representatives in local government', *British Journal of Sociology*, vol. 13 (1962), pp. 189–209; G. Jones on their functions and organization, *Public Administration* (UK), vol. 51 (1973), pp. 135–41; Stanyer on their managerial dispositions, same journal, vol. 49 (1971), pp. 73–97; J. Brand on their party organization and recruitment, *British Journal of Political Science*, vol. 3 (1973), pp. 473–86; Rhodes on proximity and urban influences on their behavior, same journal, vol. 1 (1971), pp. 123–8; a volume by I. Budge, *Political Stratification and Democracy* (Toronto University Press, 1972); an essay by Paul Spencer in A. Richards and A. Kuper (eds), *Councils in Action* (Cambridge University Press, 1971), pp. 171–201.

In addition to the basic studies of party politics of Bulpitt (1967) and Gyford (1976), there is one on *Independent Local Politics in England and Wales* by W. Grant (London: Saxon House, 1977). The most careful study of political consequences of reorganization on party politics is 'Local politics after reorganisation: the homogenisation of local government in England and Wales', by S. Bristow, *Public Administration Bulletin*, no. 28 (December 1978), pp. 4–16. One should not forget the research study by Moss and Parker, 'The local councillor', for the Committee on Local Government Management (1968) and the ample data provided by the Robinson Committee (Cmnd 7010, 1977). Dearlove's book (1979) also reviews the entire argument about councillors and their influence.

Policymaking and party politics figure more heavily in A. Rees and T. Smith, *Town Councillors: A Study of Barking* (Action Society Trust, 1964); H. Wiseman, 'The working of local government in Leeds', *Public Administration* (UK), vol. 41 (1963), pp. 51–69; N. Thomas and B. Stoten on health service differences in K. Jones (ed.), *Yearbook of Social Policy: 1973* (London: Routledge & Kegan Paul, 1974), pp. 48–70; Kantor on elite politics in London, *British Journal of Political Science*, vol. 6 (1976), pp. 311–34; I. Henry in the *South Western Review of Public Administration*, vol. 11 (1972), pp. 29–37; P. Peterson on interest group politics in three cities in *Comparative Politics*, vol. 3 (1971), pp. 381–402. Though titled *Local Government Reorganisation*, E. Wistrich's study of Camden (Borough Council of Camden, 1972) is really more about political relationships and the conduct of the council business. French local politics and policy appear more in electoral combat, for example, the legislative elections of 1973 described for Lille by M. Wolf in the *Revue Française de Science Politique*, vol. 25 (1975), pp. 159–90; and for Marseille by D. Bell, *Political Studies*, vol. 21 (1973), pp. 243–74.

OFFICIAL DOCUMENTS

An indispensable source of articles by influential civil servants and of current decisions is the *Moniteur de Travaux Publics*, a monthly from the Ministère d'Équipement with regular supplements giving the texts of new laws, decrees, etc. For those wishing to follow financial decisions, *Colloques*, a monthly from the CDC, is very useful. There is also the *Cahiers de l'Expansion Régionale* published by the Conseil National des Économies Régionales et de la Productivité. A very good review, *Cahiers du CFPC*, was started in 1978 by the Centre de Formation des Personnel Communaux. As Giscard began his push to reform local government, the Ministry of the Interior began publishing *Démocratie Locale*, clearly aimed at persuading mayors to support the legislation but nonetheless with useful information. The

Ministry has published a more technical monthly, *Études et Problèmes Municipaux*, for many years. Under the umbrella of the Ministry, the prefectoral corps publishes *Administration* which has some revealing articles by prefects and reflects current pressures on and within departmental administration. Anyone starting out on local politics and administration today has an invaluable account in the Guichard Report, *Vivre Ensemble* (1976), which examines the communes from many aspects and has very useful appendices.

British official publications reflect the calmer atmosphere of Whitehall where ministries less often undertake propaganda against each other, and where nearly all official reporting comes from HMSO or from groups like the local government associations who have undertaken these responsibilities. Nonetheless, there are immense amounts of information in the succession of official reports, local audits, inquiries, departmental annual reports, etc., published by HMSO. In many respects the Herbert Report or the Royal Commission on Local Government in Greater London (Cmd 1164, 1960) marks the kick-off for the central–local debate that continues through subsequent commissions. The testimony of the old London boroughs alone filled 2,500 pages in four volumes.

The proliferation of planning documents over the past twenty years makes any complete listing virtually impossible. They are excellent sources to learn the ins and outs of local decisionmaking and how national influence is brought to bear at the local level. In Britain plans are both regional, of which Peter Hall's monumental study (1973) provides ample general information, and for towns, which are well outlined by P. H. Levin (1976). On urban planning J. Brian McLoughlin (1973) and the edited volume of Gordon E. Cherry, *Urban Planning Problems* (London: Leonard Hill, 1974) provide good overviews. As this book argues, the British have tended to keep spatial and regional planning apart from local and social planning so there are really two separate literatures to follow. Eversley's study, *The Planner in Society* (1973) reflects on these and other problems of British planning. A short paperback by Francis Gladstone, *The Politics of Planning* (London: Temple Smith, 1976), directly addresses the political complications of urban planning. Simmie's book *Citizens in Conflict* (1974) deals with the sociological implications of planning and Hill (1974) with participatory aspects of local planning.

As more policy analysis is done on local problems the plans will become a valuable resource as well as a fascinating record of changing government priorities. Despite the vogue that French national planning has enjoyed, the British have been the most enthusiastic local planners by far. The *Town Planning Review* has been published since 1910 and *Town and Country Planning* since 1932. The Town and Country Planning Association issued its seventy-ninth report in 1978. The Town Planning Institute publishes a yearbook and, since 1965, the *Town Planning Quarterly*. To my knowledge there are no similar journals for France, but *Metropolis* is the leading urban planning and development journal and DATAR publishes copious quantities of regional studies and documents. Unlike British local planning, which has been largely spatial and physical, French local plans often contain a good deal of financial and more general information.

In both countries, a number of scholars work closely with officials and the planning literature is immense. For France, see A. Lefebvre, *Villes et Planification* (1973); Claude Jannoud and Marie-Hélène Pinel, *La Prémière Ville Nouvelle* (1974); Yves Brissy, *Les Villes Nouvelles: le Role de l'État et des Collectivités Locales* (1974); F. Parfait *et al.*, *La Planification Urbaine* (1978), for comprehensive studies of official efforts to rebuild cities. As I have outlined, Britain enters less directly into urban development plans and efforts have been dispersed among new towns, inner city assistance and development plans. An intriguing critique of the town planning effort is M. L. Harrison, 'British town planning ideology and the welfare state', *Journal of Social Policy*, vol. 4 (1975), pp. 259–74. On development planning, see an assessment by David L. Smith in *Local Government Studies*, vol. 9 (1974), pp. 21–34, as well as other planning books cited in the text. The jointly written books of D. McKay and A. Cox (1979) and also of J. Edwards and R. Batley (1978) happily bring together informed assessment of programs to assist cities. The British regional development plans are published along with the extensive hearings and inquiries that they have provoked, and a useful jumping off point is Peter Self's 'Regional planning in Britain: analysis and evaluation', *Regional Studies*, vol. 1 (1967), pp. 3–10. An array of policies affecting cities is discussed in M. Loney and M. Allen (eds), *The Crisis of the Inner City* (London: Macmillan, 1979).

Although the OREAM (Organisations d'études d'aménagement des aires métropolitaines) plans from the mid-1960s are now largely obsolete as a policy instrument they live on like most administrative documents. There are ten for the major development areas and they contain a great deal of information. The list can be found in the *Recueil d'Informations* (1976), p. 28. The 392 SDAU plans discussed in the book cover nearly 10,000 communes and there are 1,207 POS plans in 1976. These are largely physical and spatial plans but are often linked to local industrial development schemes. Of a more distinctly economic nature, there are the plans for the various zonal arrangements and the contractural plans for *nouvelles villes* and the successor contracts of other kinds discussed in the book. All these documents are public and can be found in departmental libraries and in the libraries of larger communes. The interdependence and organization of this huge local planning apparatus is discussed in Parfait (1973), Pottier (1975), and A. Lefebvre (1973) and in more partisan terms by Granet (1975).

Although they are individually cited in the book, mention should also be made of the important budgetary documents relating to local politics and policy. For both the Fifth and Sixth Plans special attention was given to urban problems, particularly by the Intergroup on Local Finance (1971) and the special commission on cities (1971). Though they appear infrequently, the reports of the Conseil Économique et Social such as the Grossman Report (1973) are exhaustive and informed. Local budgets receive less attention in the French debates on the national budget than they do in Britain because there is no direct attachment between the two. Starting in the early 1970s the British gave more attention to local spending. The key guideline to what the Treasury will allow each year appears in the Public Expenditure Plans or PESC reports, even though local budgets are not formally part of the British national budget.

ADMINISTRATIVE STUDIES

In contrast to British administrative studies, most French studies have a section devoted to local government. The standard work in English is Ridley and Blondel (1964), now accompanied by the excellent study of internal administrative politics of Suleiman (1974). There are numerous French works such as Gérard Belorgey, *Le Gouvernement et l'Administration de la France* (Paris: Colin, 1967); Francis de Baecque, *l'Administration Centrale de la France* (Paris: Colin, 1973); Charles Debbasch, *Institutions Administratives*, 2nd edn (Libraire Général de Droit et de Jurisprudence, 1972); and Pierre Soudet, *l'Administration par les Siens . . . et par d'Autres*, 2nd edn (Paris: Berger-Levrault, 1972). A valuable study of the territorial distribution of the French civil service is Luc-Alexandre Ménard, *Administration Centrale et l'Aménagement du Territoire* (Paris: Documentation Française, 1973).

As had been noted several times in the book, the French write numerous polemical and heavily critical books about the state. Among the more serious are Crozier (1970), Crozier *et al.* (1974), Servan-Schreiber (1971), Meynaud (1964), Debbasch (1969), Mandrin (1967) and Bernard (1967). More recently the collective works by officials close to de Gaulle, *De Gaulle et le Service de l'État* (Paris: Plon, 1977) and *'L'Entourage' et de Gaulle* (Paris: Plon, 1979), as well as a short book of Francis de Baecque, *Qui Gouverne la France?* (Paris: PUF, 1976), outline important changes under the Fifth Republic.

British administrative studies tend to be more sharply divided between central and local government. On central administration Brian Smith's study, *Policy Making in British Government* (London: Martin Robertson, 1976) is a good overview as is R. G. S. Brown's *The Administrative Process in Britain* (London: Methuen, 1970). Decentralization is specifically considered in Jeffrey Stanyer and Brian Smith *Administering Britain* (London: Fontana, 1976 and reprinted, Oxford: Martin Robertson, 1980), Frank Stacey's *British Government 1966–1975* (London: Oxford University Press, 1975), and W. J. Stankiewicz's *British Government in an Era of Reform* (London: Collier Macmillan, 1976). Though now somewhat dated, Griffith's study (1966) is still the most complete work dealing with central–local administrative relations.

Both countries had their flirtation with advanced budgeting forms in the 1960s and its application often reveals a good deal about central–local relations. There is a good basic study by two of its French advocates, P. Huet and J. Bravo (1973). For France see Jean-Claude Ducros, 'La Rationalisation des choix budgétaires et l'organisation de l'Administration', *Revue de Science Financière*, vol.

51 (1969), pp. 617–63; Jacques Bravo, 'L'Experience française des budgets de programmes', *Revue Economique*, vol. 24 (1973), pp. 1–65; and his essay 'La RCB et le management de l'Etat', *Revue de Science Financière*, vol. 54 (1972), pp. 289–350. On the local effects of RCB see Claude Bozon, 'L'Administration à l'heure du "management"', *Moniteur*, 21 July 1973, pp. 17–22. On the political relevance of these reforms, see Jeanne Siwek-Pouydesseau, 'La Critique idéologique du management en France', *Revue Française de Science Politique*, vol. 24 (1974), pp. 966–93.

On Britain see A. W. Petersen, 'Planning, programming and budgeting in the GLC: what and why?', *Public Administration* (UK), vol. 50 (1972), pp. 119–28; Ralph James, 'Is there a case for local authority policy planning?', *Public Administration* (UK), vol. 51 (1973), pp. 147–64; J. K. Friend and W. N. Jessop, *Local Government and Strategic Choice: An Operational Research Approach to the Processes of Public Planning* (London: Tavistock, 1969); J. W. Glendinning and R. E. H. Bullock, *Management by Objectives in Local Government* (London: Charles Knight, 1973); Local Government Chronicle, *Corporate Management in Action* (London: Brown, Knight & Truscott, 1974); Royston Greenwood and J. D. Stewart, *Corporate Planning in English Local Government* (London: Charles Knight, 1974). Since 1977 the *Corporate Planning Journal*, edited by the Centre for Regional, Urban and Local Government Studies, University of Birmingham, has provided a steady stream of articles and analysis, in addition to numerous articles in *Local Government Studies*.

Because of the heavy service obligations of British local government there are extensive materials on most of the major local activities. On health and social policy see R. G. S. Brown, *The Management of Welfare* (London: Fontana, 1975): Phoebe Hall *et al., Change, Choice and Conflict in Social Policy* (London: Heinemann, 1975), esp. pp. 55–85. On planning the best general book in a highly developed literature is J. B. Cullingworth, *Town and Country Planning*, 4th edn (London: Allen & Unwin, 1972), pp. 47–70. Though sometimes polemical, a controversial account of housing controls is given by Fred Berry, *Housing: The Great British Failure* (London: Charles Knight, 1975); other good studies are A. Murie, *Housing Policy and the Housing System* (London: Allen & Unwin, 1976), and Roger H. Duclaud-Williams, *The Politics of Housing in Britain and France* (London: Heinemann, 1978), which is especially good in portraying how the French use a mixture of private and public intervention. The relationship to education is extremely complex, but good introductions are Gerald Fowler *et al., Decision Making in British Education* (London: Heinemann, 1973); Maurice Kogan, *The Politics of Educational Change* (London: Fontana, 1978); and R. E. Jennings, *Education and Politics: Policymaking in Local Education Authorities* (London: Batsford, 1977).

ECONOMIC STUDIES

Because the French local budgets are so numerous and, relative to

Britain, a smaller percentage of public spending, there has been less economic analysis of the communes. The most complete analysis of large cities has been done by Fréville (1973) and more recently his work on the transfer (1978). Fréville also has an article on urban finances of large cities in the *Aménagement du Territoire et Développement Régional*, vol. 3 (1970), pp. 93–132. Kopielski has a thesis (1974) on political influences on local expenditure. Buinot (1976) has also done some advanced statistical analysis of economic, social and regional variations in local spending and investment. There are many examples of the inequities of French local budgets and finance in the de Tinguy (1979) and Voisin (1979) Reports for the *loi Bonnet*, and for investment problems see the Grossman Report (1973). One published official study is *Inégalités des finances municipales sur la processus de croissance urbaine*, Notes et Études Documentaires, no. 3543 (Paris: Documentation Française, 9 December 1968). The Guichard Report (1976) is full of budgetary, tax and investment information, and there is a critique in the *Cahier de l'Institut Française des Sciences Administratives*, no. 15 (1977).

To understand local budgeting, the book of Flecher and Fort (1978) is good, but others prefer F. Gicquel, *La Commune, son Budget, ses Comptes* (Paris: Éditions Techniques, 1970). There are a few regionally defined studies of local budgets. Michel Laget, 'Données financières de la gestion communale', *Revue de l'Économie Méridionale*, no. 73 (1971), pp. 1–15, writes on the southeast. On the efforts to reformulate the budget procedures there is the work of Pierre Guilliot, 'Réflexions sur la fiscalité locale', *Administration*, vol. 61 (1968), pp. 41–9; and Patrice Cahart, 'La Nouvelle fiscalité locale française', *Problèmes Économiques*, no. 1455 (January 1976), pp. 3–12; and Lalumière, op. cit., pp. 109–58. There is also a complete outline of the procedures in Lalumière (1976), pp. 109–58 and Guerrier and Bauchard (1971), pp. 142–205, as well as the official publication by Alain Delorme, *La Modernisation de la Fiscalité Directe Locale (1959–1975)*, Notes et Études Documentaires, no. 4277–8 (Paris: Documentation Française, 5 April 1976). A carefully done study of regional resource inequities is R. Prud'homme, 'La répartition spatiale des fonds budgétaires', *Revue d'Économie Politique*, vol. 65 (1975), pp. 38–59.

The quantitative analysis of British local budgets received an early start with Claus A. Moser and W. Scott's, *British Towns, A Statistical Study of Their Social and Economic Differences* (London: Oliver and Boyd, 1961). There are now more current studies of Boaden (1971) and Danziger (1978). For additional studies of the determinants of local spending see James E. Alt, 'Some social and political correlates of county borough expenditure', *British Journal of Political Science*, vol. 1 (1971), pp. 49–62; P. R. Oliver and J. Stanyer, 'Some aspects of the financial behaviour of county boroughs', *Public Administration* (UK), vol. 47 (1969), pp. 169–84; Douglas E. Ashford, 'Resources, spending and party politics in British local government', *Administration and Society*, vol. 7 (1975), pp. 286–311; Noel T. Boaden and Robert T. Alford, 'Sources of diversity in English local government', *Political Studies*, vol. 19 (1971), pp. 416–29; and James

N. Danziger, 'Twenty-six outputs in search of a taxonomy', *Policy and Politics*, vol. 5 (1976), pp. 201–12; Johnathon F. Brown, 'Some social and political correlates of county borough expenditures – a comment' and James E. Alt, 'Rejoinder', *British Journal of Political Science*, vol. 2 (1972), pp. 131–2; R. Greenwood, C. R. Hinings and Stewart Ranson, 'The politics of the budgetary process', *Political Studies*, vol. 25 (1977), pp. 25–47; and J. N. Danziger, 'Assessing incrementalism in British municipal budgeting', *British Journal of Political Science*, vol. 6 (1976), pp. 335–50; and J. N. Danziger, 'A comment on the politics of the budgetary process in English local government', *Political Studies*, vol. 26 (1977), pp. 109–15.

There have also been some careful studies of the relations between need and spending. See Bleddyn P. Davies, *Social Needs and Resources: Local Services* (London: Joseph, 1968): Davies *et al.*, *Variations in Services for the Aged* (London: Bell, 1971); and Davies *et al.*, *Variations in Children Services among British Local Authorities* (London: Bell, 1972); D. J. Storey, 'Statistical analysis of education expenditure in county councils', *Local Government Studies* (New Series), vol. 1 (1975) and Jerry Miner, 'British local expenditure analysis: an American evaluation', *Policy and Politics*, vol. 1 (1973), pp. 357–61.

On microeconomic study of localities, see Julian Le Grand, 'Fiscal equity and central government grants to local authorities', *The Economic Journal*, vol. 85 (1975), pp. 531–47; and J. Le Grand and D. Winter, 'Towards an economic model of local government behaviour', *Policy and Politics*, vol. 5 (1977), pp. 23–41; and Berne, Ashford and Schramm (1976). As I argue in the book, the basic fiscal dilemma of British central–local exchange has not changed for many years, and the most lucid explication of this impasse remains Sir Laurence Boyle's *Equalisation and the Future of Local Government Finance* (Edinburgh: Oliver and Boyd, 1966). The Layfield Report (1978) and its studies are invaluable. For a critical analysis of the Consultative Council on Local Finance, see J. Taylor in *Local Government Studies* (New Series), vol. 5 (May–June 1979), pp. 7–36.

COMMUNITY STUDIES

This study has made use of the numerous micro-level studies of local politics and society that have appeared over the past two decades. Local political studies have a longer history in Britain than in France, starting with A. H. Birch on Glossop (1959). Since then there have been books on Newcastle-under-Lyme by F. Bealey *et al.* (1965); on Sheffield by W. Hampton (1970); on Birmingham by K. Newton (1976); on Cheshire county government in earlier times by J. M. Lee (1963) and more recently by Lee and B. Wood (1974); on Wolverhampton by G. W. Jones (1969); on the London borough of Camden by E. Wistrich (1972); on Bristol local leaders by R. V. Clements (1969); on local and social leaders in Glasgow by Ian Budge *et al.* (1972); on the London boroughs of Kensington and Chelsea by J. Dearlove (1973); on rural Wales by P. J. Madgewick *et al.* (1974); and on voting in eleven cities, edited by L. J. Sharpe (1967). Though a biography, D. V. Donoughue and G. W. Jones, *Professional Politicians: the Life of Herbert Morrison 1888–1965* (London: Weidenfeld & Nicolson, 1973) is fascinating reading on one of the few leaders who took local government and politics seriously once he gained national recognition.

Community studies in France got their early push from the Institut d'Études Politiques at Grenoble where P. Kukawa, C. Mingasson and C. Roig (*Recherche sur la Structure du Pouvoir Local en Milieu Urbain*, 1969) encouraged local level research. There were two studies by another Grenoble scholar, M.-F. Souchon, *Le Maire, Élu Local dans une Société en Changement* (Paris: Cujas, 1968); and *La Compagnie Nationale d'Aménagement de la Région du Bas-Rhône-Languedoc* (Paris: Cujas, 1968). In a more anthropological vein, Wylie's study (1957) of the rural commune of Peyrane has become a classic, followed by his work (1966) on the Anjou village of Chanzeau. There is less of this kind of research done in Britain although R. Blythe's study of Akenfield (1969) is absorbing. Also anthropological in concept is L. Bernot and R. Blanchard, *Nouville, un Village Française* (Paris: Institut d'Ethnologie, 1953).

More recent community studies in France take on a more distinctly political character, such as Edgar Morin's study of Plodément (1967) now translated by A. M. Sheridan, *The Red and the White* (New York: Pantheon, 1970), and Sylvie Biarez's study *Institution Communale et Pouvoir Politique: le Cas de Roanne* (Paris: Mouton, 1973). Perhaps the most ambitious effort to aggregate the meaning of local society and politics for the French national political system is by P. Grémion (1976), which I have found extremely rewarding. The notion of the network of *réseau* is also developed in articles by M.-F. Souchon (1974) and J.-C. Thoenig (1975). Longepierre's study of departmental general councils (1971) also sheds considerable light on the network and how it escalates. Jeanne Becquart-Leclercq's study of eighty-two communes around Lille (1976) deals with the network but adds information about electoral practices and campaigns. Tarrow's study (1977) describes the brokerage role of mayors and how they are valued for their administrative ingenuity. Three additional community studies with considerable policy content are Sylvie Biarez *et al.*, *Les Élus Locaux de l'Aménagement Urbain dans l'Agglomeration Grenobloise* (Grenoble: Institut d'Études Politiques, 1970); Beaunez and A. Rousseau, *L'Expérience de Grenoble: Possibilités et Limites de l'Action Municipale* (Paris: Éditions Ouvrières, 1971); and J.-P. Hoss, *Communes en Banlieu: Argenteuil et Bezons* (Paris: Colin, 1969). For a list of community studies done as *Mémoires* of graduate students, see C. Leleu, *Géographie des Élections Françaises Depuis 1936* (Paris: Colin, 1971), pp. 201–8.

Though they are not properly speaking community studies, there has also been a rash of studies of urban problems stimulated by the various Marxist groups in Paris which deal more heavily with policy issues than more traditional community studies. In addition to Manuel Castells's general study of urbanism (1977, new edn), there is the study of Dunkerque (1974). From a different Marxist perspective, Jean Lojkine, *La Politique Urbaine dans la Région Lyonnaise* (Paris:

Écoles Practiques des Hautes Études, 1973) and his *La Politique Urbaine dans la Région Parisienne 1945–72* (Paris: Mouton, 1972) both contain detailed information on social structure and social change. Anne Simonet and Jean-Michel Leger have written a fine policy study of the Lyon and Dunkerque urban communities, *De la Coopération Intercommunale au Regroupement de Communes* (Paris: Comité de Sociologie Économique et Politique, 1975). Somewhat more loosely written are two studies of regrouping by J. O. Retal (1973, 1974). There is a useful summary on French urban sociology by Jean-René Tréanton, 'Quelque travaux récents d'histoire et de sociologie urbaines', *Revue Française de Sociologie*, vol. 9 (1971), pp. 589–96. The most complete study which shows how Communist mayors can live comfortably in the system is Denis Lacorne, *Les Notables Rouges* (Paris: Presses de la Fondation Nationale des Sciences Politiques, 1980).

An intriguing sequel to, and a possible consequence of, the difficulties of massive reorganization of subnational systems in the 1960s has been the wave of publications in the 1970s on community politics and local and national politics. For Britain there is a shift in emphasis of Sharpe's writing, revealed in his essays in his edited volume, *Decentralist Trends in Western Democracies* (London: Sage Publications, 1980), pp. 9–70; and in his contribution, 'Reforming the grassroots', in D. Butler and A. H. Halsey (eds), *Politics and Policy* (London: Macmillan, 1978). There is an excellent bibliography on participation by A. Barker (1979) which gives numerous sources on grassroots politics. In France, where the electoral system and weak parties enhance small movements, and controversies over pollution and nuclear energy have mobilized community politics, there is now a large literature on the *écologistes* and the *mouvement vert*.

AUTHOR INDEX

This index includes the names of authors cited in the text and the appendix (but not chapter notes).

GENERAL INDEX

administration: 9, 70, 186, 207–8; in
    Britain, 3–4, 10, 12–13, 39, 46–8,
    187–8, 189–90, 193, 194, 233–5,
    284, 331; in France, 3, 8, 10, 11, 12,
    57–8, 187–90, 192, 193–4, 214, 233,
    234, 331 *see also* Field Admini-
    stration
Agences d'urbanisme 23, 334
Agglomération 102
Alderman 55, 63
Amboise 287
Aménagement du territoire 92 *see also*
    Regional Policy
Ancien Régime 8, 34–7, 267
Arrondissements 7, 44, 132
Assemblée des Présidents de Conseils
    Généraux 384
Association des Élus Communistes 383
Association des Maires des Grandes Villes
    291, 384
Association du Corps Préfectoral 88
Association of County Councils 223
Association of French Mayors 111, 146,
    287, 291–2, 384
Association of Metropolitan Authorities
    (AMA) 290, 384
Association of Municipal Councils
    (AMC) 105, 160, 384 *see also*
    Association of Metropolitan
    Authorities (AMA) and Local
    Government Associations
Aubert Report *see* Bécam Report
autogestion 162

Bains Report 209, 210
Barre, Edmond 144, 160, 216, 289
Barrot, Odilon 56, 59
Bécam Report 225
Benthamites 40, 41, 45, 46
Bevan, Aneurin 89, 261
Birmingham 158, 210, 260
Block Grants 91, table 6.1 *see also*
    Intergovernmental Transfers
Blum, Léon 88
Board of Health 47
Bonnet, Christian 278 *see also* Loi Bonnet
Bordeaux 142, 189
Bourrel Report (1965) 268
Bourges 142
Boundary Commission (1945) 88, 89–90
Boundary Commission (1958) 95, 96

Bristol 147
Britain: Administration 8, 14, 39, 47–8,
    56, 61, 114–15, 127, 188, 219;
    Aristocracy 14, 35, 38–40, 48, 55;
    Local Councils 6, 10, 17, 40; Local
    Government History 2, 4, 12, 13, 14,
    15, 45–8, 55, 60–1, 88–90, 114, 131;
    Ministerial Power 10, 18, 50, 69, 126,
    188, 196–7, 316, 317; National Powers
    3, 12, 50–1, 72; Revolution (1688) 14,
    34
Brittany 93
Broglie, Duc de 66
Brooke, Norman 96
budgetary control 56

Caillaux Commission (1896) 268
Caisse d'aide à l'équipement des
    collectivités locales (CAECL) 315
Caisse des Dépôts (CDD) 12, 255, 267,
    313–4, 324, 335, 338, 386
Callaghan, James 108, 223, 231
Canada 278
capital spending *see* local investment
Centimes additionels 270, 272
Central Policy Review Staff (CPRS) 5,
    197, 200
Centralization: 15–16, 19; Britain and
    France 12, 17–18, 310, 322, 325,
    361–2; Debate in France 58; in
    Britain 7, 8, 50; in France, 9, 51, 57,
    Theories of 9, 16–17
Centre de Formation des Personnel Com-
    munaux 386
Chaban-Delmas, Jacques 129–30, 142,
    191, 220, 310, 324, 325, 326, 327
Chadwick, *Sir* Edwin 45, 46, 47, 72–3
Chamberlain, Joseph 62, 71, 134, 165,
    260
Chamberlain, Neville 260
Chalandon, Abin 335, 336
Chartered Institute of Public Finance and
    Accountancy 374, 384
Cheshire 135, 158
Chirac, Jacques 97, 144, 153, 327; Mayor
    of Paris 154
circonscriptions 7
Claudius-Petit, E. 92
Collectivités Locales 3 *see also* Com-
    munes; France
Clay Cross 16